M000307107

AN ESSAY CONCERNING TOLERATION AND OTHER WRITINGS ON LAW AND POLITICS, 1667–1683

This volume contains the first critical edition of John Locke's *Essay concerning Toleration* and a number of his other writings on law and politics composed between his joining Lord Ashley's household in 1667 and his departure from England in 1683. Although he never published any of them himself these works are of very great interest to students of his intellectual development in that they are markedly unlike the ones he had written while at Oxford and show him working out ideas that were to appear in his mature political writings, the *Two Treatises of Government* and the *Epistola de Tolerantia*.

Although the *Essay concerning Toleration* has been in print since the nineteenth century, this volume contains the first edition based on a full collation of all the extant manuscripts, together with accounts of contemporary debates on comprehension and toleration, and of Locke's arguments for toleration. Also included are a number of shorter writings on church and state, including a set of queries (not previously published) on Scottish church government (1668), Locke's notes on Samuel Parker's *Discourse of Ecclesiastical Politie* (1669), a short tract on excommunication (1674), and the entries on political and related topics in Locke's commonplace books.

The other two main works published here are rather different in character. One is a recently discovered tract on jury selection written by Locke at the time of the Earl of Shaftesbury's imprisonment in 1681. The other is *A Letter from a Person of Quality*, a political pamphlet written in 1675 as part of Shaftesbury's campaign against the Earl of Danby. Published anonymously, this was first attributed to Locke in 1720 and since then has occupied an uncertain place in the Locke canon. This volume contains the first critical edition based on contemporary printed editions and manuscripts, and it includes a detailed account of the *Letter's* composition, authorship, and subsequent publication history.

J. R. Milton is a Professor of the History of Philosophy at King's College London

Philip Milton is a Lecturer in Law at the University of Leicester

THE CLARENDON EDITION OF THE
WORKS OF JOHN LOCKE

GENERAL EDITOR: M. A. STEWART

EDITORIAL BOARD

M. R. Ayers · Jonquil Bevan · John Dunn · Mark Goldie ·
J. R. Milton · G. A. J. Rogers · M. A. Stewart · James Tully

JOHN LOCKE

AN ESSAY CONCERNING TOLERATION

AND OTHER WRITINGS ON LAW AND POLITICS 1667–1683

Edited with an Introduction, Critical Apparatus, Notes, and Transcription of Ancillary Manuscripts by

J. R. Milton

and

Philip Milton

CLARENDON PRESS · OXFORD

OXFORD

UNIVERSITY PRESS

Great Clarendon Street, Oxford OX2 6DP

Oxford University Press is a department of the University of Oxford.
It furthers the University's objective of excellence in research, scholarship,
and education by publishing worldwide in

Oxford New York

Auckland Cape Town Dar es Salaam Hong Kong Karachi
Kuala Lumpur Madrid Melbourne Mexico City Nairobi
New Delhi Shanghai Taipei Toronto

With offices in

Argentina Austria Brazil Chile Czech Republic France Greece
Guatemala Hungary Italy Japan Poland Portugal Singapore
South Korea Switzerland Thailand Turkey Ukraine Vietnam

Oxford is a registered trade mark of Oxford University Press
in the UK and in certain other countries

Published in the United States
by Oxford University Press Inc., New York

British Library Cataloguing in Publication Data

Data available

Library of Congress Cataloging in Publication Data
Locke, John, 1632–1704.
[Epistola de tolerantia. English. 2006.]
John Locke : an essay concerning toleration and other writings on law and politics,
1667–1683 / edited with an introduction, critical apparatus, notes,
and transcription of ancillary manuscripts by J. R. Milton and Philip Milton.
p. cm.
1. Religious tolerance–History–17th century. 2. Locke, John, 1632–1704.
Epistola de tolerantia. I. Title: Essay concerning toleration and other
writings on law and politics, 1667–1683. II. Milton, J. R. (John R.)
III. Milton, Philip. IV. Title.
BR1610.L823 2006 261.7′2–dc22 2005029405

Typeset by SPI Publisher Services, Pondicherry, India
Printed in Great Britain
on acid-free paper by
CPI Antony Rowe

ISBN 978–0–19–823721–1 (Hbk)
978–0–19–957573–2 (Pbk)

1 3 5 7 9 10 8 6 4 2

PREFACE

THIS volume contains all Locke's known writings on religious toleration, law, and politics for the years 1667 to 1683, except for the *Fundamental Constitutions of Carolina*, the *Two Treatises of Government*, and the Critical Notes on Stillingfleet, all of which will be appearing elsewhere in the Clarendon Edition.

With the exception of *A Letter from a Person of Quality*, all the works included in the main part of the book are unquestionably by Locke. The *Letter* was first publicly attributed to Locke in 1720, and since then it has occupied a rather uncertain place in the Locke canon. It was undoubtedly written for Locke's patron, the Earl of Shaftesbury, and there are good reasons for thinking that Locke played an important part in its composition. Whether it should count as one of Locke's works is a nice question. Substantial parts of it were assembled from pre-existing materials, some of which have survived and are printed as Appendices to this volume, and it is quite likely that other material was used that has since been lost. For this reason little would be gained by using stylometric evidence to try to establish authorship, and we have not attempted to do this. It is also clear that the *Letter* should not be used as evidence of Locke's own views: if it reflects anyone's outlook it is Shaftesbury's.

Two works that survive in manuscript among Locke's own papers, *Philanthropy* and the *Queries on Catholic Infallibility*, have been placed in the Appendices. Their inclusion in this volume does not indicate that the editors believe that they are by Locke. Locke owned and kept copies of them, and he may have been involved in their composition: in the absence of further evidence there is little more that can be said.

It is possible—indeed very likely—that other manuscripts exist that would provide further information about the events we have described, especially in relation to the writing of the *Letter from a Person of Quality*. One of the two manuscript copies of this, British Library Add. MS 74273, was purchased by the British Library in 1999, and only came to our notice when our work on the text of the *Letter* was quite well advanced. We also began work on the *Reasons against the Bill for the Test* with a knowledge of only one manuscript, the copy in the Shaftesbury papers; further research has unearthed another five, and it would seem extremely likely that further copies exist.

A work of this kind creates many debts. We would like to thank Michael Ayers, John Dunn, Mark Goldie, John Rogers, Sandy Stewart, and James Tully, all of whom read the first version of the book and made valuable suggestions and comments. We would also like to thank David Armitage for sending us a photocopy of the relevant part of the Harvard microfilm of Adversaria 1661, Kimimasa Inoue for providing a copy of his edition of the *Essay concerning Toleration*, Robin Robbins for reading a draft of the section of the Textual Introduction concerned with the *Letter from a Person of Quality*, and John Spurr for advice about the Compton Census.

Most of the research was carried out in the Bodleian Library, the British Library, Cambridge University Library, and the National Archives, and we would like to thank the staff of these institutions and of the other libraries and record offices we used for their help and assistance. Particular thanks are due to Mary Robertson and her colleagues at the Huntington Library, who did so much to make our visit there an enjoyable one. We would also like to thank the staff at Oxford University Press, and in particular Peter Momtchiloff and Laurien Berkeley.

We are grateful to the Bodleian Library, the Huntington Library, the Hampshire Record Office, the National Archives, and M. Henri Schiller for permission to publish the texts of manuscripts in their possession, and to Cambridge University Library, the Huntington Library, and the National Archives for permission to reproduce photographs of some of these manuscripts and of several pages from the two 1675 editions of the *Letter from a Person of Quality*.

Finally, we would both like to thank Julia Milton, who, as wife to one editor and sister-in-law to the other, had to live with the project almost as closely as they did. We are both immensely grateful to her for reading and commenting on the two Introductions, and for her advice, encouragement, and forbearance.

J. R. Milton
Philip Milton

7 July 2005

PREFACE TO THE PAPERBACK EDITION

The reissue of this book in paperback has provided an opportunity to correct a number of misprints and other minor errors which had appeared in the first edition; we are grateful to Roger Woolhouse and Timothy Stanton for drawing some of these to our attention. The indexes have also been corrected and expanded, and some other small changes have been made, but no attempt has been made to revise the work in the light of more recent publications on any of the matters with which it deals.

JRM
PM

10 July 2009

CONTENTS

Contents

LIST OF PLATES

ABBREVIATIONS

The following abbreviations are used in the notes:

Barrell, *Shaftesbury*	*Anthony Ashley Cooper Earl of Shaftesbury (1671–1713) and 'Le Refuge Français'-Correspondence*, ed. Rex A. Barrell (Lewiston, NY, 1989)
BL	British Library, London
Bodl.	Bodleian Library, Oxford
Bulstrode Papers	*The Collection of Autograph Letters and Historical Documents formed by Alfred Morrison, The Bulstrode Papers*, i: *1667–1675* (n.p., 1897)
Burnet	*Burnet's History of My Own Time*, ed. Osmund Airy, 2 vols. (Oxford, 1897–1900)
Christie	W. D. Christie, *A Life of Anthony Ashley Cooper, First Earl of Shaftesbury, 1621–1683*, 2 vols. (London, 1871)
CJ	*Journals of the House of Commons*
Correspondence	*The Correspondence of John Locke*, ed. E. S. de Beer, 9 vols. (Oxford, 1976–)
Cranston	Maurice Cranston, *John Locke: A Biography* (London, 1957)
CSPD	*Calendar of State Papers, Domestic*
CSPV	*Calendar of State Papers, Venetian*
CUL	Cambridge University Library
Drafts, i	John Locke, *Drafts for the 'Essay concerning Human Understanding' and Other Philosophical Writings*, i, ed. Peter H. Nidditch and G. A. J. Rogers (Oxford, 1990)
DWL	Dr Williams's Library, London
Essex Papers, i	*Essex Papers*, ed. Osmund Airy, Camden Society, 2nd ser., 47 (London, 1890).
Essex Papers, ii	*Selections form the Correspondence of Arthur Capel Earl of Essex 1675–1677*, ed. C. E. Pike, Camden Society, 3rd ser., 24 (London, 1913).
Fox Bourne	H. R. Fox Bourne, *The Life of John Locke*, 2 vols. (London, 1876)
Goldie	John Locke, *Political Essays*, ed. Mark Goldie (Cambridge, 1997)
Haley	K. H. D. Haley, *The First Earl of Shaftesbury* (Oxford, 1968)

Heawood	E. Heawood, *Watermarks Mainly of the 17th and 18th Centuries (Hilversum, 1950)*
Henning	*The House of Commons 1660–1690*, ed. Basil Duke Henning, 3 vols. (London, 1983)
HLRO	House of Lords Record Office
HMC	Historical Manuscripts Commission
King	Peter King, *The Life of John Locke* (London, 1829; 2nd edn., 2 vols., London, 1830)
LJ	*Journals of the House of Lords*
LL	John Harrison and Peter Laslett, *The Library of John Locke*, 2nd edn. (Oxford, 1971)
LPQ	*A Letter from a Person of Quality, to His Friend in the Country* ([London], 1675)
Luttrell	Narcissus Luttrell, *A Brief Historical Relation of State Affairs*, 6 vols. (Oxford, 1857)
Milward	*The Diary of John Milward, Esq., Member of Parliament for Derbyshire, September 1666 to May 1668*, ed. Caroline Robbins (Cambridge, 1938)
MS Locke	Bodleian Library, MS Locke
NA	National Archives, Kew
NS	new series
ODNB	*Oxford Dictionary of National Biography*
OED	*Oxford English Dictionary*
Pepys	*The Diary of Samuel Pepys*, ed. Robert Latham and William Matthews, 11 vols. (London, 1970–83)
PRO 30/24	The National Archives, Kew, Shaftesbury papers
Rand, *Shaftesbury*	*The Life, Unpublished Letters, and Philosophical Regimen of Anthony, Earl of Shaftesbury, Author of the 'Characteristics'*, ed. Benjamin Rand (London, 1900)
RO	Record Office
SR	*Statutes of the Realm*, 11 vols. (London, 1810–28)
Summary Catalogue	P. Long, *A Summary Catalogue of the Lovelace Collection of the Papers of John Locke in the Bodleian Library* (Oxford, 1959)
Term Catalogue	*The Term Catalogues 1668–1709 A.D.*, ed. Edward Arber, 3 vols. (London, 1903–6)
Wing	*Short-Title Catalogue of Books Printed in England, Scotland, Ireland, Wales, and British America and of English Books Printed in Other Countries*, comp. Donald Wing, 2nd edn., 4 vols. (New York, 1972–98)

GENERAL INTRODUCTION

WITH a few minor exceptions of uncertain date, all the writings printed
in this volume were written between April 1667, when Locke left Oxford
to join the household of Lord Ashley in London, and January 1683, when
Ashley, by now the Earl of Shaftesbury, died in exile in Amsterdam.[1] All
Locke's known writings on religious toleration, law, and politics from
this period have been included except for the *Two Treatises of Government*
and the attack on Stillingfleet's *The Mischief of Separation* and *The
Unreasonableness of Separation* (MS Locke c. 34), which will appear in
separate volumes.

LOCKE AND THE EARL OF SHAFTESBURY

Locke met his future patron entirely by chance in the summer of 1666.[2]
Ashley was visiting Oxford in order to see his son, then a boy of fourteen
and an undergraduate at Trinity. He was forty-four years old, and had
been the Chancellor of the Exchequer since 1661. Locke was thirty-three,
and had been a Student of Christ Church ever since his arrival in Oxford
in 1652.[3] He had held a series of teaching posts within the college and was
still the tutor of a small group of undergraduate pupils, but he had
published nothing apart from some contributions to volumes of con-
gratulatory poems published by the university.[4] Studentships at Christ

---

[1] Shaftesbury began life in 1621 as Anthony Ashley Cooper, becoming successively Sir
Anthony on his father's death in March 1631, Lord Ashley in April 1661, and first Earl of
Shaftesbury in March 1672.

[2] There are two slightly divergent accounts of their meeting, one from Lady Masham and
one from the third Earl of Shaftesbury. The former has been reprinted in Masham, 'Lady
Masham's Account of Locke', 174–5. The latter is in the third Earl's letter to Jean Le Clerc,
8 Feb. 1705; there are copies in the third Earl's letter book, PRO 30/24/22/2, fos. 39–40,
and in PRO 30/24/22/5, fo. 377. It has been printed in *Notes and Queries*, 1st ser., 3 (1851),
97–9; Rand, *Shaftesbury*, 329–31; Barrell, *Shaftesbury*, 84–9 (with an incorrect date); and
Yolton, *A Locke Miscellany*, 27–33.

[3] A Studentship at Christ Church was approximately the equivalent of a fellowship at
one of the other Oxford colleges, the main differences being that Students were elected
before graduation and had no part in the government of the college, which was in the hands
of the Dean and Chapter. An account of Locke's years at Christ Church is given in Milton,
'Locke at Oxford'.

[4] On Locke's activities as a tutor, see Milton, 'Locke's Pupils'. The poems are printed in
Goldie, 201–4, 209–11.

Church could be held for life provided that their holder never married and took holy orders when of sufficient seniority to do so;[1] despite various sentimental friendships Locke seems never to have been in serious danger of losing his studentship for the former reason, but by the mid-1660s at least he was strongly averse to ordination and his place at Christ Church was far from secure.[2] In the winter of 1665–6 he had paid a visit to Cleves as a member of a diplomatic mission, but though his letters home suggest that he enjoyed the experience, he seems not to have been attracted to diplomacy as a career.[3] In the autumn of 1666 he made a short trip to London to stay with Ashley, through whose influence he was able to procure a royal order allowing him to retain his studentship without taking orders.[4] Having secured his position at Oxford, he could now safely absent himself: he moved to London and became a member of Ashley's household in the late spring of the following year.[5]

From May 1667 to November 1675 Locke spent most of his time at Exeter House, a large sixteenth-century building in the Strand which Ashley had leased from the Earl of Exeter; it was demolished in 1676, while Locke was away in France. Apart from his earliest years at Oxford, this is the part of Locke's adult life that is least well documented. Only twenty-three letters by him from this period are known to exist—just under three per year—and there are quite long periods, especially in the late 1660s, from which little or nothing survives.[6] Even a basic narrative of his life is difficult to construct: he had not yet begun keeping

---

[1] A detailed account of the workings of Christ Church can be found in Bill, *Education at Christ Church*, 91–165. The four (later five) Faculty Studentships in law or medicine exempted their holders from the requirement of being in orders, but they were infrequently vacated and Locke did not obtain one until 1675.

[2] On the insecurity of Locke's place at Christ Church, see Milton, 'Locke at Oxford', 30–2. His attitude towards ordination is set out in letters from John Strachey, 18 Nov. 1663, and to John Parry, *c.*15 Dec. 1666, *Correspondence*, i. 214–16, 303–4.

[3] His letters from Cleves are in *Correspondence*, i. 227–59. The offer of the post of secretary to the envoy to Sweden is mentioned in Charles Perrot to Locke, 21 Aug. 1666, ibid. 289–90.

[4] NA, SP 44/14, p. 103, dated 14 Nov. 1666. There is a copy in Locke's hand in MS Locke c. 25, fo. 11, and one by an amanuensis in PRO 30/24/47/22, fo. 9.

[5] Locke had left Oxford at the beginning of April and spent the next few weeks in Somerset seeing old friends and dealing with business relating to his land; at the end of the month he set off for London, making a detour via Salisbury to stay with David Thomas, Bodl., MS Film 79, pp. 12–32. He probably arrived at Exeter House around the middle of May: a note (ibid. 7) records that he received books sent from Oxford on 24 and 30 May.

[6] Apart from the draft of a report sent to a French physician after Ashley's operation (*Correspondence*, i. 316–17), there is nothing either to or from Locke between the end of November 1667 and April 1669.

a journal and it is often impossible to say where he was at any given time, or to give a detailed account of his movements.[1] He made several journeys to Somerset to see old friends and look after his property there,[2] and a few more to Dorset when Ashley was visiting his estate at Wimborne St Giles.[3] In the summer of 1669 he was asked by Ashley to go to Belvoir Castle in Leicestershire to oversee the negotiations that preceded the marriage of his son to Lady Dorothy Manners.[4] In the autumn of 1672 he paid a short visit to Paris, his first trip abroad since the mission to Cleves.[5] He is known to have gone back to Oxford only twice, once in the late summer of 1671 to see his cousin Peter, an undergraduate at Christ Church, and once in February 1675 to take his bachelor of medicine.[6] Other short journeys may have left no record, but it seems safe to say that he spent by far the greatest part of his time in London.

The precise position that Locke occupied on his arrival in Ashley's household is not entirely certain. According to the third Earl of Shaftesbury, he acted as tutor to Ashley's son, who had left Oxford shortly before Locke.[7] Nothing in the second Earl's later career suggests that he would have been a rewarding pupil, and it is not unlikely that such activity as Locke undertook in this area soon came to an end. He certainly had time within a year of his arrival to write the *Essay concerning Toleration*, discussed below. In the following year he drafted a paper on rates of interest,[8] which after much alteration and augmentation was to form part of *Some Considerations of the Consequences of the Lowering of Interest, and Raising the Value of Money*, published in 1692.

---

[1] Apart from Locke's correspondence, the main sources are the surviving members of the series of pocket memorandum books that he used: for 1667 (Bodl., MS Film 79), 1669 (BL, Add. MS 46470), 1672 (MS Locke f. 48), and 1674 (MS Locke f. 13). From 1671 onwards there are entries in the ledger MS Locke c. 1, and there is further information in the weather register at the end of MS Locke d. 9, in the account book MS Locke f. 12, and in the medical case notes BL, Add. MS 5714.

[2] In April 1668, October/November 1671, about August 1673, August 1674, and possibly also in April/May 1670, *Correspondence*, i. 360–3, 388; MSS Locke f. 12, p. 16; f. 13, pp. 25–7; c. 26, fo. 65^r.

[3] In June/July 1671 and July/September 1675, *Correspondence*, i. 356–7, 359, 428–9; below, p. 98.   [4] *Correspondence*, i. 321–3.

[5] Ibid. i. 366–72.

[6] On 6 February 1675, MS Locke b. 5, item 10. Information about Locke's visits to Oxford is provided by the Disbursement Books at Christ Church. The Students' stipends were paid quarterly, and had to be signed for. Normally one of Locke's friends did this, but Locke signed for the third quarter of 1671 and the first quarter of 1675.

[7] Shaftesbury to Le Clerc, 8 Feb. 1705, PRO 30/24/22/2, fo. 40^r. This is unconfirmed but not contradicted by contemporary evidence.   [8] *Locke on Money*, 167–92.

Locke also had enough leisure to pursue his other interests, notably medicine.[1] Soon after arriving in London he met Thomas Sydenham, with whom he worked closely for the next four years, visiting patients together and collaborating on several medical treatises.[2] Their most important patient was Ashley himself. He had suffered for years from a hydatid cyst of the liver, and by the early summer of 1668 his health had deteriorated so badly that he was prepared to undergo an immensely risky operation to drain the abscess. This took place on 12 June, and during the months that followed Ashley slowly recovered his health.[3]

According to the third Earl of Shaftesbury, the success of the operation greatly raised Locke's standing in the household:

After this Cure Mr Lock grew so much in Esteem with my Grandfather that as great a man as he had experienc'd him in Physick he look'd upon this but as his least part. he encourag'd him to turn his Thoughts another way nor wou'd he suffer him to practice Physick except in his own Family and as a kindness to some particular Friends. he putt him upon the Study of the Religiouse and Civill affairs of the Nation with whattsoever related to the buissness of a Minister of State in which he was so successfull that my Grandfather began soon to use him as a Friend and consult with him on all occasions of that kind. he was not only with him in his Library and Clossett but in Company with the great Men of those times the Duke of Buckingham, Lord Hallifax, & others...[4]

There is nothing implausible about this—if Locke's own testimony is to be trusted, Ashley himself believed that the operation had saved his life.[5] Nevertheless, the third Earl was not himself a witness of the events he described: he had not even been born at the time of the operation, and was relying on his memory of what others had once told him. Locke did

---

[1] In 1667–75 at least three-quarters of the entries in Locke's surviving commonplace books are on medical topics (mostly in MS Locke d. 9, also in MSS Locke f. 19 and d. 11); there are also other medical notebooks, MSS Locke f. 21 and f. 22, and two volumes of medical papers, MS Locke c. 29 and PRO 30/24/47/2. The main source of information about non-medical reading is the commonplace book Adversaria 1661, in use from *c.*1670; there are also extracts from books read in MS Locke d. 11 and Locke's interleaved Bible, *LL* 309 (Bodl., Locke 16.25).

[2] BL, Add. MS 5714; PRO 30/24/47/2, fos. 31–8, 47–57, 60–9. Dewhurst, *John Locke*, 38–43.

[3] The main file of papers relating to the case is PRO 30/24/47/2, fos. 1–30, 81–2; a substantial part of this is printed in Osler, 'John Locke as a Physician', 98–114. See also Locke to de Briolay de Beaupreau, undated [late 1668?], and 20 Jan. 1671, *Correspondence*, i. 316–17, 347–9.

[4] Shaftesbury to Le Clerc, 8 Feb. 1705, PRO 30/24/22/2, fo. 39ᵛ, some punctuation supplied. On the delivery of letters to Buckingham and others, see Ashley to Locke, 29 Aug. 1670, *Correspondence*, i. 343.

[5] The most direct evidence for Shaftesbury's gratitude comes from Locke's letter to Pembroke, 28 Nov. 1684, *Correspondence*, ii. 662.

not perform the operation himself, and the file of papers relating to both preparations and the nursing care that followed do not suggest that he was in overall charge—Ashley could, and did, call on the services of far more experienced physicians.[1]

Both Locke's and Shaftesbury's biographers have denied that Locke was paid for his services. According to Cranston, 'Locke did not get much material reward for the work he did for Ashley,' while Haley states that 'Locke was not an employee of Ashley's, to be rewarded for services rendered; he was a friend, with other sources of income, who had been invited to live in Ashley's household.'[2] Locke did have other sources of income, though quite modest ones,[3] but during his first years at Exeter House these were augmented by payments from his patron. From Michaelmas 1668, and perhaps earlier, he received £20 every quarter, which brought his total average annual income to a little under £200.[4] These payments ceased in the autumn of 1670, when he was made a registrar of the excise, with an annual salary of £175, out of which he had to find £60 to pay a clerk.[5]

During his first two years at Exeter House, Locke seems to have performed little if any secretarial work for his new patron.[6] None of the drafts or copies of letters sent by Ashley during this period is in Locke's hand, and none of them was docketed and filed by him.[7] By the second half of 1669, however, Locke was doing a considerable amount of administrative work.[8] Nearly all of this concerned the colony of Carolina,

---

[1] Including Sydenham, Francis Glisson, and Sir George Ent: PRO 30/24/47/2, fos. 3, 10–11, 81–2. [2] Cranston, 114; Haley, 206.

[3] He drew an annual income of around £70 from his land in Somerset, augmented by a variable sum of about £25 to £30 payable to him as a Student of Christ Church; for much of the time he also obtained £10 or £11 per annum from letting his rooms in the college. The accounts including these payments are in MS Locke f. 12, pp. 227–43; one example is quoted *in extenso* by Cranston, 114–15.

[4] In the accounts in MS Locke f. 12, pp. 235, 237, 239, 241, 243, Ashley's payments are marked 'L'; his identity is given by BL, Add. MS 46470, fos. 27ʳ, 28ʳ.

[5] MSS Locke c. 1, pp. 19, 61, 71, 77; f. 48, p. 15.

[6] Robert Blayney is described as Ashley's secretary in John Skelton to Williamson, 23 Apr. 1667, NA, SP 29/198/20, in Pepys, ix. 152 (6 Apr. 1668), and in Joseph West to Ashley, 21 Mar. 1671, PRO 30/24/48/65.

[7] Among the Shaftesbury papers there are drafts or copies of nine letters dated between August 1668 and October 1670, of which four are to Locke (PRO 30/24/4/175–7, 191). None of the others is in his hand or bears his endorsement: PRO 30/24/4/171 is in Ashley's hand; PRO 30/24/4/178 contains two letters from this period, both later copies; PRO 30/24/4/181, 196 were both written by Stringer. Ashley's letter of 9 August 1669 to the Duke of Richmond is in his own hand, BL, Add. MS 21947, fo. 247.

[8] The first surviving letter to Ashley that was endorsed by Locke was from William Sayle, 25 June 1669, PRO 30/24/48/24.

of which Ashley was one of the Lords Proprietors: Locke was involved in the drafting of the *Fundamental Constitutions of Carolina*,[1] and he handled much of the routine business of the new colony, drafting and receiving letters, and taking minutes at the meetings of the Lords Proprietors.[2]

Locke's secretarial work left him with enough time and energy to pursue other interests. In 1671 he began pursuing the epistemological enquiries that would eventually lead to the *Essay concerning Human Understanding*. Two incomplete drafts dated 1671 survive,[3] and it is likely that their composition occupied a large part of the second half of 1671, and possibly part of 1672 as well. Despite considerable turmoil in the world outside—on 15 March 1672 Charles II issued his Declaration of Indulgence—he is not known to have written anything on politics or religious toleration during this period.[4]

On 17 November 1672 Shaftesbury was appointed Lord Chancellor. One of the many responsibilities of his new office was to exercise patronage over the less valuable ecclesiastical benefices controlled by the Crown. The management of this was given to Locke, and a considerable body of surviving papers testifies to the care with which he carried out his duties.[5] When Shaftesbury was dismissed on 9 November 1673, Locke also lost his post. This was quite normal: he was not a civil servant in the modern sense, and Shaftesbury's successor[6] would have had his own followers to reward.

---

[1] The copy in the Shaftesbury papers, PRO 30/24/47/3, is dated 21 July 1669. Only a small part of the manuscript is in Locke's hand: on problems of authorship, see Milton, 'John Locke and the Fundamental Constitutions of Carolina', 111–33. A full account of the *Fundamental Constitutions* will be given by David Armitage in a forthcoming volume in the Clarendon Edition; some of his preliminary findings are in 'John Locke, Carolina, and the *Two Treatises of Government*', 607–15.

[2] NA, CO 5/286, fos. 30ᵛ–31ʳ, 39ʳ–42ʳ; MS Locke c. 30, fos. 1–11. Only a small fraction of the hundreds of letters and papers on colonial matters in PRO 30/24/48 and PRO 30/24/49 are in Locke's hand, but many more were corrected or annotated by him, or bear his endorsement: see Milton, 'Locke Manuscripts among the Shaftesbury Papers', 128–30.

[3] Adversaria 1661, pp. 56–89, 94–5 (Draft A), MS Locke f. 26 (Draft B); printed in *Drafts*, i. 1–83, 101–270.

[4] On the authorship of PRO 30/24/6B/427, 429, and 430, see below, pp. 148–52. The copy of the *Essay concerning Toleration* in Adversaria 1661 was made early in 1672 or thereabouts; the additions to the same work in MS Locke c. 28 are of unknown date and may possibly date from about this time.

[5] The main file is PRO 30/24/42/59; also MS Locke c. 44, pp. 1–23, PRO 30/24/5/257, Victoria and Albert Museum, MS Forster 48. G. 3/20, 21.

[6] Heneage Finch (1621–82), subsequently Earl of Nottingham, was initially made Lord Keeper, and later Lord Chancellor (Dec. 1675). Burnet (ii. 43) commented on the care he took over ecclesiastical patronage.

A glimpse of Locke's place in Shaftesbury's household is provided by a document listing 'My Lord Chancellors Family' as it existed at Christmas in 1672.[1] Locke did not dine at Shaftesbury's own table, but at the second table, presided over by Shaftesbury's steward, Thomas Stringer; his position was given as 'Secretary for the Clergie'. His companions were two other secretaries, for the petitioners and for the defendants, the seal bearer, the clerk for the justices, the gentlemen usher, and the gentleman for the horses; on occasion they might be joined by the chaplain, Locke's friend Nathaniel Hodges, and by the serjeant-at-arms, who both normally dined at Shaftesbury's own table. How Locke's position would have been described either before or after Shaftesbury's time as Lord Chancellor is uncertain; in the only surviving list of the household made outside this period—in July 1675 when Shaftesbury was at St Giles—Locke's name is absent, presumably because he was elsewhere or because he was dining at Shaftesbury's own table, the occupants of which were not listed.[2]

After his dismissal from the post of Lord Chancellor, Shaftesbury was given no further office until he was made Lord President of the Council in April 1679. He moved rapidly into opposition to the policies of the King's new chief minister, the Earl of Danby, and on 9 May 1674 was removed from the Privy Council.[3] While still Lord Chancellor he had arranged for Locke to be appointed as secretary to the Council for Trade and Plantations, and Locke soon also became the treasurer.[4] For much of 1674 Locke was busy with his new responsibilities, but the Council was dissolved in December and his posts disappeared with it.[5] In the spring of 1675 he lost his place in the excise;[6] he was not to secure any further government employment until after the Revolution. In financial terms, however, he was still reasonably secure, having recently purchased an annuity of £100 from Shaftesbury.[7] Given that Locke lived for another

---

[1] PRO 30/24/4/236; there is a similar list dating from November 1672 in PRO 30/24/5/264/2.

[2] PRO 30/24/5/286. For a further discussion of this document see below, p. 98.

[3] 'His Majestie this day in Counsill Declaring his displeasure against the Earle of Shaftesbury Commanded the Clerk of the Councill That his name be henceforth left out of the number of Privy Councellors', NA, PC 2/64, p. 227.

[4] He was appointed on 14 October 1673 and sworn in as secretary on 15 October, *Officials of the Boards of Trade, 1660–1870*, 23; *Correspondence*, i. 354; Henry Ball to Joseph Williamson, 17 Oct. 1673, *Letters to Williamson*, ii. 47.

[5] 21 Dec. 1674, *Officials of the Boards of Trade, 1660–1870*, 2.

[6] The last payment was on 1 April 1675, MS Locke c. 1, p. 76.

[7] For the annuity, which cost £700, see MSS Locke b. 5, items 6, 7; c. 19, fo. 114ᵛ; Shaftesbury to Locke, 23 Nov. 1674, *Correspondence*, i. 420. It was paid twice-yearly, Locke receiving his first payment on 24 June 1675, MS Locke c. 1, p. 82.

thirty years it was a bargain, and one that subsequently caused considerable resentment among other members of Shaftesbury's family.[1]

During the summer and early autumn of 1675 Locke was with Shaftesbury at St Giles, or nearby, and was probably involved in the composition of the *Letter from a Person of Quality*. On 12 November, two days after the *Letter* was publicly burned by order of the House of Lords, he left London, and two days later he sailed for France, where he remained until the end of April 1679.[2] Most of his time was spent in Montpellier or Paris; his movements are recorded in detail in the journal that he began keeping on leaving England.[3] He kept in touch with events in Shaftesbury's household through a regular correspondence with Stringer; there is only one short letter from Shaftesbury, asking Locke to look after Caleb, the young son of Sir John Banks.[4] There is no reason to suppose that Locke did any political work for his patron. Shaftesbury's main concerns seem to have been horticultural; Locke sent cuttings back to England and amassed a large quantity of notes on fruits of all kinds— grapes, peaches, olives, and figs.[5]

Locke seems to have taken few if any of his manuscripts with him to France, and notes on his reading were made either in his journal or on loose sheets of paper.[6] Apart from some entries in the commonplace book

---

[1] Locke to Clarke, 11 Mar. 1692, *Correspondence*, iv. 411; Locke to Ashley, 11 Mar. 1692, ibid. 412–13; Ashley to Locke, 26 Mar. 1692, ibid. iv. 423–4; Wheelock to Locke, 10 May 1692, ibid. iv. 451–2; Locke to Clarke, 16 May 1692, ibid. iv. 455; Wheelock to Locke, 31 May 1692, ibid. iv. 456–7; Locke to Ashley, 5 Aug. 1699, ibid. vi. 665; Shaftesbury to Locke, 23 May 1702, ibid. vii. 617–18; Locke to Shaftesbury, 12 Mar. 1703, Shaftesbury to Locke, 15 Mar. 1703, Olin Library, Washington University, St Louis, Bixby papers, 15/104, 15/132; Voitle, *The Third Earl of Shaftesbury*, 61–4.

[2] MS Locke f. 1, p. 1, *Locke's Travels in France*, 1. On the furore that followed the publication of the letter, see below, pp. 94–7.

[3] The volumes of the journal are MSS Locke f. 1–f. 3 and BL, Add. MS 15642; most of these are printed in *Locke's Travels in France*; the many medical entries omitted by Lough are in Dewhurst, *John Locke, Physician and Philosopher*, 62–151. Philosophical entries (1676–82) are in *An Early Draft of Locke's Essay*, 77–125, and some shorthand entries from 1676 in *Essays on the Law of Nature*, 254–81. [4] 23 Feb. 1677, *Correspondence*, i. 464.

[5] MSS Locke c. 31, fos. 160–6; f. 15, pp. 26, 42; plants sent by Locke from France are mentioned in Shaftesbury's Book of Memorandums on the gardens at St Giles, PRO 30/24/5/293; *Correspondence*, i. 434–5, 437, 444. Locke also sent Shaftesbury maps and books, *Locke's Travels in France*, 174, 181, 188; *Correspondence*, i. 511–12, 516, 517, 566.

[6] The reading notes are in MS Locke c. 33, fos. 1–16. The only commonplace book that appears to have been started while Locke was in France is MS Locke d. 1, discussed below. There are several entries on toleration in his journal, the most important being 'The Obligation of Penal Laws' and 'Lex Humana', 25 Feb. 1676, MS Locke f. 1, pp. 123–6; 'Toleration', 23 Aug. 1676, ibid. 412–15; and 'Toleration', 19 Apr. 1678, MS Locke f. 3, p. 107; all are printed in Goldie, 235–7, 246–8.

MS Locke d. 1 and two short notes in MS Locke c. 33, none of the writings printed in this volume was written during this period.

From May 1679 until August 1683 Locke was back in England, but though he was provided with accommodation at Shaftesbury's new London residence, Thanet House in Aldersgate Street, he did not resume his former secretarial duties. His greatly reduced role in the business of the household can be seen in the Shaftesbury papers. For the period 1667–75 there are hundreds of items that have some visible connection with him, either by being wholly or partly in his hand, or by bearing his endorsement—indeed between 1672 and 1675 most of the administrative work of the household seems to have been performed either by Locke or by Stringer. For the period 1679–83 the most frequently identifiable hands are those of Stringer and Shaftesbury's new secretary, Samuel Wilson. There are only five documents in Locke's hand: a fair copy of his *Observations upon the Growth and Culture of Vines and Olives*, dated 1 February 1679[/80] and presented to Shaftesbury himself; two lists of French books; the 1681 tract on the selection of juries, printed below; and a copy, also dating from 1681, of a deposition made by Brian Haynes, one of the Irish witnesses against Shaftesbury.[1] This change cannot be put down to the seizure or destruction of potentially incriminating material at the time of Shaftesbury's arrest in 1681 or subsequently: it is the absence of *routine* business in Locke's hand that is so striking.

It is very hard to say how far Locke was involved in Shaftesbury's most secret political activities during the time that he spent at Thanet House. Some years later he told Pembroke that he had 'made litle acquaintance, and kept litle company in an house where soe much came, and for that litle my choyse was of bookish not busy men',[2] and though this was written to clear his name it may well be the truth. What is certain is that he was often away from London. Only half of his time was spent there—twenty-seven months out of the fifty-two between his return to England and his departure for Holland at the end of August 1683. A large and increasing part of the remainder was spent either at Christ Church or with his friend James Tyrrell at Oakley in Buckinghamshire—ten weeks in 1680, five months in 1681, six months in 1682.[3]

---

[1] PRO 30/24/47/35; PRO 30/24/6A/312; PRO 30/24/47/30, fos. 48–9, 32–5; PRO 30/24/43/63, fo. 171.

[2] Locke to Pembroke, 28 Nov./8 Dec. 1684, *Correspondence*, ii. 663.

[3] These figures are taken from his journal (MSS Locke f. 4–f. 7) which gives a detailed account of his whereabouts up until the end of June 1683.

Locke might therefore be called a semi-detached member of Shaftesbury's household—someone who was often absent, but could be summoned when help was needed. In July 1680 he accompanied Shaftesbury to St Giles, and after returning to London sent him a letter full of political news.[1] In February 1681 he was busy arranging Shaftesbury's accommodation for the Oxford parliament, and was also entrusted with the delicate task of trying to persuade two Whig candidates to stand down.[2] Later that year, when Shaftesbury was in the Tower charged with treason, Locke played an important part in preparations for his defence and wrote the short tract on the selection of juries; his part in these events is described in more detail in a later section of this Introduction.[3]

Much of 1682 was taken up with a struggle for control of the City of London, a contest the government decisively won. Defeat left Shaftesbury with only two options: to go into exile while he was still able or to try to mount some kind of *coup d'état*. Plans for an insurrection were discussed with Monmouth and others, but nothing came of them and towards the end of November Shaftesbury slipped away to Holland where he died two months later. Locke may well have known something of his plans for an insurrection, but an examination of his movements does not suggest any readiness to participate in them.[4] He did not accompany Shaftesbury into exile, though he did travel down to St Giles for his funeral and subsequently composed a sonorous Latin epitaph.[5] He was not mentioned in Shaftesbury's will.[6] Six months later he too went into exile in Holland, where he remained until after the Revolution.

One consequence of Locke's residence in Shaftesbury's household is that his papers came to be divided, with some of the manuscripts of his writings—and other documents he collected—surviving among Shaftesbury's papers, and some among his own. The division of material seems often to have been a matter of chance. The Shaftesbury papers contain numerous documents connected with Locke that cannot possibly have been of any interest to Shaftesbury himself: personal letters, a Latin

---

[1] Locke to Shaftesbury, 5 Aug. 1680, *Correspondence*, ii. 225–7. He was at St Giles from 23 to 31 July, MS Locke f. 4, pp. 143, 145.

[2] Locke to Shaftesbury, 6, 19 Feb. 1681, *Correspondence*, ii. 360–6, 378; cf. Haley, 625.

[3] Below, pp. 131–6.

[4] For a full account, see Milton, 'John Locke and the Rye House Plot'.

[5] MS Locke f. 7, p. 19 (26 Feb. 1683). The epitaph is in *Posthumous Works*, 307; there is an English version that diverges in several respects from the Latin in PRO 30/24/6A/385.

[6] Christie, ii. 458–9.

disputation on respiration, a note on the ages of members of Locke's family, even some accounts with his pupils at Christ Church.[1] Conversely there are documents among Locke's papers that were docketed and filed by him, but which are much more relevant to Shaftesbury's affairs.[2] In the absence of other considerations, the fact that a document has come to rest in one collection rather than the other is of little significance; certainly one cannot use it to draw any conclusions about whether it was or was not written at Shaftesbury's request, or in order to be read by him.

It is also important to bear in mind that the designation of one section of the Shaftesbury papers as 'Locke's Letters and Papers' (now PRO 30/24/47) reflects decisions made—often entirely without warrant—by the nineteenth-century cataloguer of those papers, W. Noel Sainsbury, and not any pre-existing division within the archive. Many of the papers in this section are demonstrably not by Locke, and one of them was manifestly written at least fifteen years after his death.[3]

AN ESSAY CONCERNING TOLERATION

The *Essay concerning Toleration* was the first work Locke wrote while at Exeter House. It can be seen in a succession of widening contexts: Locke's own intellectual development, his relations with Ashley, the comprehension and toleration proposals of 1667–8, and settlement of the church at the Restoration.

The Restoration Settlement of the Church

At the time of the Restoration there was a widespread belief, which the events of the previous twenty years had done little to dispel, that civil order and tranquillity required religious uniformity. There was less agreement about what form this should take, and for a time there seemed to be a possibility that a compromise would be reached, as had happened

[1] PRO 30/24/47/2, fos. 71–4; PRO 30/24/47/30, fos. 6–9; PRO 30/24/47/31.
[2] MS Locke b. 4, fos. 27–33 (on precedents for Shaftesbury's actions in issuing writs for by-elections, 1673), 36–7 (on *Crispe* v *Dalmahoy*, 1675).
[3] PRO 30/24/47/4, 30/24/47/6, 30/24/47/29, 30/24/47/32, the last of these a poem on events that occurred in 1719; all were described by Sainsbury as being in Locke's hand. For further comments, see Milton, 'Lockean Political Apocrypha', 259–66.

in civil affairs. Instead, the settlement that emerged in 1661–2 was a decisive victory for the episcopalian clergy and gentry, especially the latter.[1] It was not an accommodating settlement, and its makers did not intend it to be. Most people either approved of it or at least felt that they could live with it, and as in all the religious upheavals since the 1530s the great majority of the parish clergy stayed put. There was, however, a significant minority among them who were not prepared to conform, and between 1660 and 1663 about 1,880 clergy in England and Wales left their livings, though about a tenth of them later conformed.[2] Many of the laity shared their objections, and though no precise figure can be given, it would appear that at least 5 per cent of the population obstinately refused to attend Anglican services, and a great many more were reluctant or only occasional conformists.[3] Something like a fifth of the MPs and lay peers were dissenters or had dissenting sympathies.[4]

The expulsion of the non-conforming clergy was accomplished remarkably smoothly, but any hopes that dissent would simply disappear were not borne out by events. This left three possible courses of action. One, which had the support of almost all of the Anglican hierarchy and most MPs, was to enforce existing laws and if necessary pass new ones. The Act of Uniformity of 1662 was followed by a succession of statutes intended to reduce and ultimately eliminate dissent. The Conventicles Act of 1664 forbade unauthorized religious meetings and laid down a graduated series of penalties culminating in transportation for seven years for persistent offenders; household worship was not affected. Its title, 'An

---

[1] Green, *The Re-establishment of the Church of England*; Seaward, *Cavalier Parliament*, ch. 7; Hutton, *The Restoration*, 166–80; Miller, *After the Civil Wars*, 174–81.

[2] Spurr, *The Restoration Church of England*, 43. For a slightly lower figure, see *Calamy Revised*, pp. xii–xiii.

[3] In the ecclesiastical survey of 1676, commonly known as the Compton Census, the returns for the province of Canterbury (those for York are incomplete) indicated 2,123,362 conformists, 93,154 nonconformists (4.18%), and 11,870 papists (0.53%); for a breakdown by diocese, see *The Compton Census of 1676*, 2. These figures were dependent on the honesty and diligence of those who provided them, but there is no evidence of deliberate distortion and the number of nonconformists is probably fairly accurate provided it is realized that it did not include partial and occasional conformists. There were wide local and regional variations, and in London dissenters may have amounted to 15–20 per cent of the population, perhaps even more: Harris, *London Crowds in the Reign of Charles II*, 66. These figures may be compared with a survey, commonly known as the Evans list, carried out by the main dissenting denominations between 1715 and 1718, which came up with a figure of 355,890 dissenters out of a total population for England and Wales of 5,751,420, a proportion of 6.2%: Watts, *The Dissenters*, 267–89, 491–510.

[4] Henning, i. 52; Davis, 'The "Presbyterian" Opposition and the Emergence of Party in the House of Lords in the Reign of Charles II', 6–7; Lacey, *Dissent and Parliamentary Politics*, App. ii.

Act to prevent and supresse seditious Conventicles', and the reference in the preamble to 'the growing and dangerous Practises of Seditious Sectaryes and other disloyall persons who under pretence of Tender Consciences doe at their Meetings contrive Insurrections' indicate quite clearly that it was aimed at sedition, not heterodoxy.[1] Similar motives underlay the Five Mile Act of 1665, which forbade the clergy ejected in 1662 from coming within five miles of any corporate town or any parish where they had once been ministers unless they would swear not to take up arms against the King or attempt to alter the government in church or state. The enforcement of these statutes was irregular and intermittent, and caused considerable suffering to the nonconformists without noticeably reducing their numbers.[2]

The other two possibilities were comprehension and toleration (or as contemporaries usually called it, indulgence). Many years later Locke explained the distinction to Limborch:

> The question of Toleration has been taken up in Parliament under a twofold title, namely *Comprehension* and *Indulgence*. The former signifies extension of the boundaries of the Church, with a view to including greater numbers by a removal of part of the ceremonies. The latter signifies toleration of those who are either unwilling or unable to unite themselves to the Church of England on the terms offered to them.[3]

Neither policy was without its difficulties.[4] Comprehension was only of interest to moderate Presbyterians, and even here it was difficult if not impossible to devise terms that both sides would be prepared to accept. Minor changes would have achieved very little, while substantial ones would have raised the spectre of a schism within the church, something which for many Anglicans—both clergy and laity—was even less acceptable than indulgence. In principle indulgence was simpler, since it left intact the doctrine, discipline, and ceremonies of the Church of England. In reality it too was beset with problems, the most troublesome being whether it was to extend to Catholics and whether it could be granted by the royal prerogative. These two issues were inextricably intertwined,

---

[1] 16 Car. II, c. 4, *SR* v. 516.

[2] See Fletcher, 'The Enforcement of the Conventicle Acts'; Cragg, *Puritanism*, chs. 1–4.

[3] Locke to Limborch, 12 Mar. 1689, *Correspondence*, iii. 583–4; translation slightly modified.

[4] There are several excellent accounts, including Sykes, *From Sheldon to Secker*, ch. 2; Thomas, 'Comprehension and Indulgence'; Spurr, 'The Church of England, Comprehension and the Toleration Act of 1689'; Horwitz, 'Protestant Reconciliation in the Exclusion Crisis'.

since Charles II was uninterested in any indulgence that did not include Catholics, while Parliament was not prepared to enact any that did.

The Comprehension and Toleration proposals of 1667–1668

In 1662–3 various attempts were made to amend the Act of Uniformity, but these foundered on the obdurate hostility of the House of Commons.[1] For the next few years the issue remained dormant, but it revived in the summer of 1667 in the aftermath of the Medway disaster. This had revealed a woeful catalogue of incompetence, mismanagement, and corruption, and the government found itself dangerously short of both money and popular support. Even before Clarendon's dismissal at the end of August there were many who thought it would be necessary to come to terms with the dissenters.[2] At the beginning of September a newsletter reported the preparation of a bill dispensing with the Act of Uniformity; later that month another letter mentioned 'much discourse of an Act of Comprehension'.[3] At the beginning of October Henry Oldenburg wrote to Robert Boyle, who was then in Oxford, informing him that 'Most people here look for an Act of Comprehension; but how farr it shall extend, and whether it shall take the subjects of this favour into the Church, and to Church-livings, or onely tolerate them in the free exercise of their way, is yet uncertain.'[4]

One person in Oxford who did know more was Thomas Barlow, Provost of Queen's College.[5] A Calvinist by persuasion, Barlow does not appear to have looked upon these proposals with any more favour than did most of his Anglican colleagues, and there is no evidence that he was personally involved.[6] Locke seems to have known him, or at least to have moved in the same circles.[7]

[1] Abernathy, 'Clarendon and the Declaration of Indulgence'; Seaward, *Cavalier Parliament*, 179–85, 188–9; Spurr, 'The Church of England, Comprehension and the Toleration Act of 1689', 931–3; Miller, *Popery and Politics*, 100–2; Haley, 163–6.

[2] Pepys, viii. 275, 305 (17, 29 June 1667).

[3] NA, SP 29/216/19; John Nicholas to Sir Edward Nicholas, 20 Sept. 1667, BL, Egerton MS 2539, fo. 119ʳ.

[4] 1 Oct. 1667, *Correspondence of Robert Boyle*, iii. 346. Locke wrote to Boyle six weeks later, but his letter (*Correspondence*, i. 314–15) contains nothing on these matters.

[5] See Bodl., B 14.15 Linc., a bound volume of pamphlets from Barlow's library that includes a manuscript account of the comprehension proposals of 1667–8 and notes on the publication dates of many of the pamphlets.

[6] Tyacke, *Seventeenth-Century Oxford*, 605–6.

[7] On 22 September 1666 William Glanville wrote from London telling Locke that 'I have sent Mr Provost of Queens by this post, a paper of the most Creditable Newes I can pick upp, and lett mee tell you, Newes is now a Commodity hard to come by; I have intreated

In the autumn of 1667 Barlow obtained a copy of a comprehension bill which had been drafted by Sir Robert Atkyns, MP for East Looe.[1] It would have recognized Presbyterian ordinations made 'in the late times'; the surplice, the use of the cross in baptism, and kneeling at communion would have become optional; the oath abjuring the Covenant would have been laid aside, and ministers would not have been required to subscribe to those of the Thirty-Nine Articles that concerned church government.[2] These changes would have given moderate Presbyterians what they were looking for but stood no realistic chance of getting through Parliament. Barlow noted that the bill was never 'brought into the House though Col: Birch intended it, and once faintly offerd it, but (despaireinge of successe) sate downe'.[3] According to Barlow, the bill was 'disliked by the Contrivers'—by which he probably meant the now dominant faction headed by the Duke of Buckingham.[4] Atkyns and Birch were supporters of Clarendon, which would not have endeared them to Buckingham and his friends.[5] There is no indication that the King or any of his ministers were involved in their plans.

There was, however, another scheme for comprehension that did have the backing of at least some members of the government.[6] In November the Lord Keeper, Sir Orlando Bridgeman, sent for Thomas Manton, one of the moderate Presbyterian ministers who had resigned his living in

Mr Provost, that he will communicate my paper to mr [David] Thomas and then you will see It . . . pray present my affectionate Respects to Mr Thomas, and tell him Doctor Barloe will shew him my paper . . .', *Correspondence*, i. 294. There is no extant correspondence between Locke and Barlow, but years later Locke possessed a manuscript treatise by Barlow on excommunication, Tyrrell to Locke, 13 Feb. 1692, *Correspondence*, iv. 386.

[1] Atkyns was Solicitor-General to the Queen, not a post likely to have been occupied by an opponent of the Court, and seems to have been a moderate Anglican; he was made Chief Baron of the Exchequer in 1689. Shaftesbury described him as 'most able' and consulted him when facing charges of treason in 1681, Hampshire RO, 9M73/G220.

[2] Bodl., B 14.15 Linc., p. 5. The bill is discussed in Sykes, *Sheldon to Secker*, 71–2; Thomas, 'Comprehension and Indulgence', 197–200; Spurr, 'The Church of England, Comprehension and the Toleration Act of 1689', 933.

[3] Bodl., B 14.15 Linc., p. 5. Colonel John Birch, MP for Penryn, had fought for Parliament in the Civil War and was an outspoken Presbyterian: see Lacey, *Dissent and Parliamentary Politics*, 379–80. Burnet (ii. 90) described him as 'the roughest and boldest speaker in the house'. On a later speech for the dissenters, see Milward, 248.

[4] Bodl., B 14.15 Linc., p. 8. On 21 December Pepys (viii. 584–5) was told by Sir William Coventry, who was currently out of favour, that 'the Caball at present' consisted of Buckingham, Bridgeman, Albemarle, and Robartes. Albemarle and Robartes had Presbyterian sympathies, and though Buckingham was hardly an exemplar of the puritan virtues he was no friend of the bishops. [5] Henning, i. 566, 655; Milward, 80, 118, 120.

[6] For further details, see Sykes, *Sheldon to Secker*, 72–5; Thomas, 'Comprehension and Indulgence', 198–200; Lacey, *Dissent and Parliamentary Politics*, 56–8; Spurr, 'The Church of England, Comprehension and the Toleration Act of 1689', 933–4; Burnet, i. 465–8.

1662.[1] In January Richard Baxter received a letter from Manton informing him that Bridgeman wished to speak with him about comprehension and toleration. When Baxter came to London, Sir John Baber, a Presbyterian physician who frequently acted as intermediary in such matters, told him that 'he had certain proposals to offer us; and that many great Courtiers were our friends in the business, but that to speak plainly, if we would carry it, we must make use of such as were for a Toleration of the *Papists* also'.[2] Discussions proceeded on this basis, the Presbyterians being represented by Manton, Baxter, and William Bates, the Anglicans by John Wilkins and Hezekiah Burton, Bridgeman's chaplain.[3] Wilkins was the key figure: Baxter described him as 'the Author of the Proposals, and of the whole business'.[4] An Interregnum conformist and brother-in-law of Cromwell, Wilkins was well qualified to build bridges between Anglicans and Presbyterians, and was for that reason distrusted by many of his Anglican colleagues. In 1667–8 he was Dean of Ripon, and in September 1668 became Bishop of Chester. Six months later Pepys noted a rumour that he would be translated to Winchester, and described him as 'a mighty rising man, as being a Latitudinarian—and the Duke of Buckingham his great friend'.[5]

'After some days of conference,' Baxter wrote, 'we were come to agreement in all things, as to the necessary terms', and a bill was drafted by Sir Matthew Hale, Chief Baron of the Exchequer and a friend of Bridgeman, Wilkins, and Baxter.[6] As regards the vexed question of ordination, it was agreed after some discussion that those in Presbyterian orders should be admitted to the exercise of their ministerial function by episcopal imposition of hands using the formula 'Take thou a Legall Authority to preach the word of God & to administer the Holy Sacraments in any Congregation of the Church of England, where thou shalt

---

[1] See Manton's memorandum, DWL, Baxter Treatises, V, fo. 214.

[2] *Reliquiae Baxterianae*, pt. III, § 62. See also Baxter, *Additional Notes on the Life and Death of Sir Matthew Hale*, 20.

[3] According to Burnet (i. 466) John Tillotson and Edward Stillingfleet were also involved; this is not impossible, though neither was mentioned by Baxter. Both were involved in the abortive comprehension proposals of February 1674, for which, see Sykes, *Sheldon to Secker*, 79–81; Spurr, 'The Church of England, Comprehension and the Toleration Act of 1689', 935–6.   [4] *Reliquiae Baxterianae*, pt. III, § 64.

[5] Pepys, ix. 485 (16 Mar. 1669).

[6] Baxter, *Additional Notes on the Life and Death of Sir Matthew Hale*, 20; for Hale's part in these events, see Cromartie, *Sir Matthew Hale 1609–76*, 187–90. The provisions in the bill are listed in Bodl., B 14.15 Linc., pp. 9–13; there are other copies in Bodl., MS Tanner 290, fo. 242^{r-v}, and BL, Lansdowne MS 1039, fo. 135, with a slightly different version in *Reliquiae Baxterianae*, pt. III, § 76, and a summary in BL, Add. MS 19526, fo. 157^{v}.

be lawfully appoynted thereunto'.[1] Other contentious matters—the surplice, the sign of the cross, and so on—were to be left optional, and a number of minor liturgical changes were proposed. The bill containing these proposals was secretly drafted, as Baxter recorded:

> And thus it was agreed, That the papers should be all delivered to the Lord Chief Baron [Hale], to draw them up into an Act. And because I lived near him, he was pleased to shew me the Copy of his Draught, which was done according to all our Sense; but secretly, lest the noise of a prepared Act should be displeasing to the Parliament.[2]

A separate bill was drawn up granting 'such Protestants, as cannot be comprehended' the liberty to exercise their own religion, but at the cost of being disabled from holding public office.[3]

News of these proposals soon leaked out and became, in Burnet's words, 'a common subject of discourse'.[4] On 20 January Pepys recorded that there was a 'great presumption that there will be a Toleration granted'.[5] On 31 January Birch told him that 'the King is for Toleration', adding that he was worried that 'some will stand for the tolerating of papists with the rest' and that he thought that 'the sober party will be without it rather then have it upon those terms'.[6] On 5 February Pepys was informed (by Sandwich's lawyer) that 'an Act of Comprehension is likely to pass this Parliament, for admitting of all persuasions in religion to the public observation of their perticular worship'.[7] Others thought the same: one of Williamson's correspondents reported from Yarmouth that 'the people here are generally very confident that a bill of Comprehension as they call it will pass this Sessions of parliament which makes them very brisk'.[8] The Commons, however, had different ideas. As Barlow noted, they had received many complaints about the 'boldness and Insolence both of Papists, Presbyterians, and fanatiques', and were not minded to change the law.[9] On 6 February they voted not to receive any new business until the whole house had assembled; this, as Milward commented, was 'to prevent the bringing in the bill of comprehension, which will be brought in and countenanced by very great persons'.[10] According to one contemporary newsletter,

---

[1] Bodl., B 14.15 Linc., p. 9.   [2] *Reliquiae Baxterianae*, pt. III, § 76.

[3] Bodl., B 14.15 Linc., p. 13; Bodl., MS Tanner 290, fos. 242ᵛ–243ʳ; BL, Lansdowne MS 1039, fo. 136.   [4] Burnet, i. 466.

[5] Pepys, ix. 31.   [6] Ibid. 45–6.   [7] Ibid. 51.

[8] Richard Bower to Joseph Williamson, 7 Feb. 1668, NA, SP 29/234/100.

[9] Bodl., B 14.15 Linc., p. 266.

[10] Milward, 179. Milward was MP for Derbyshire.

as soone as they mett on monday [10 February] they tooke notice of the rumor about towne of a Comprehensive bill, and liberty of Conscience, and before the King made his speech, though Sir Tho: Littleton and others earnestly desired they would forbeare the question till they had heard what the King would say to them, they would not agree to it, but voted That the house do speedily desire the King that he would forthwith publish his proclamation for the effectuall execution of the Lawes for Conformity and suppressing seditious Conventicles ... [1]

Pepys gave a similar account:

But before the King's coming, the House of Commons met; and upon information given them of a Bill intended to be brought in, as common report said, for Comprehension, they did mightily and generally inveigh against it, and did vote that the King should be desired by the House, and the message delivered by the Privy-counsellors of the House, that the laws against breakers of the Act of Uniformity should be put in execution. And it was moved in the House that if any people had a mind to bring any new laws into the House about religion, they might come as a proposer of new laws did in Athens, with ropes about their necks. [2]

In his opening speech the King told Parliament that he hoped they 'would seriously think of some course to beget a better Union and Composure in the Minds of My Protestant Subjects in Matters of Religion; whereby they may be induced not only to submit quietly to the Government, but also chearfully give their Assistance to the Support of it'. [3] The Commons, however, were in no mood to comply:

The Commons coming to their House, it was moved that the vote passed this morning might be suspended, because of the King's speech, till the House was full and called over two days hence; but it was denied, so furious they are against this Bill; and thereby a great blow either given to the King and presbyters; or, which is the rather of the two, to the House itself, by denying a thing desired by the King and so much desired by much the greater part of the nation. Whatever the consequence be, if the King be a man of any stomach and heat, all do believe that he will resent this vote. [4]

Very likely he did, but his overriding need for money meant that he had to back down: on 10 March a royal proclamation was issued for enforcing the laws against conventicles. [5] On 11 March the Commons debated the

[1] [John Starkey?] to Sir Willoughby Aston, 11 Feb. 1668, BL, Add. MS 36916, fo. 66ʳ. See also Guicciardini Ayloff to Roger Kenyon, 11 Feb. 1668, HMC Kenyon, 81; Milward, 180; *Bulstrode Papers*, i. 24.   [2] Pepys, ix. 60 (10 Feb. 1668).
[3] *LJ* xii. 181.   [4] Pepys, ix. 60–1.
[5] *A Proclamation for Inforcing the Laws against Conventicles, and for preservation of the Publick Peace, against Unlawful Assemblies of Papists and Non-conformists*; Steele, *Bibliography of the Royal Proclamations*, i. 424.

King's speech.[1] Some of those who spoke were clearly in favour of toleration:

Sir William Thompson moved for a toleration and liberty of conscience, because those that desired it were true worshippers of God, and that a restraint would prove destructive to trade, by driving many of them into foreign countries, and so take the trade with them, and experience (saith he) shows that where a restraint hath been put upon tender consciences those countries have decayed and become low . . . [2]

Others saw things very differently. Sir John Birkenhead, one of the most intransigent royalists, was not prepared to make any concessions at all:

If (saith he) we look upon the covenant, how they [the puritans] took it with hands lifted up to heaven to extirpate prelacy and the government established in the Church of England, and that they would not admit any into the ministry or to spiritual living, nor so much as to teach a school, although it were but in a private family, unless he would first take the covenant. . . . When we remember the villainies that those men committed under pretence of conscience, the younger sort of them unlearned and ignorant, and that no oath (of which they had taken many) would bind or hold the older, we may well be cautious that we be not again cheated and destroyed by indulging their conscience into a new rebellion.[3]

Evidently the wounds of the Civil War were still very raw. Lord Fanshawe—an Irish peer who sat as MP for Hertford—spoke to similar effect.[4] There were, however, some supporters of the Church of England who were willing to consider granting indulgence without comprehension. One such was Edward Seymour, Speaker in the Danby era and one of the first Tories to go over to William of Orange:

Mr. Seymour was against the bill of comprehension, for (saith he) three Presbyterians did endeavour to be three bishops; he was also against referring this debate to the Convocation, nor was he for rending a seamless coat by schism, but he would have every man to wear his coat after his own fancy; if one would wear a plain coat let him so wear it, and if another will wear a fringed coat let him please himself, without any restraint put upon him; but because this strict government of the Church hath not wrought the peaceable effect that was intended, therefore he moved that we should try a more easy way, by taking the restraint off tender consciences and using lenity and giving them some indulgence; for acts of severity

---

[1] Milward, 214–22; *Debates*, ed. Grey, i. 110–15.
[2] Milward, 216. Thompson was MP for London and a Presbyterian; he should not be confused with the barrister William Thomson, whose advice Shaftesbury and Locke obtained in 1681.   [3] Milward, 220.
[4] Ibid. 221.

never gain love, and where there is not love to a government it will never be truly and cordially obeyed.[1]

Throughout these debates the members' arguments were concerned with this world, not the next. Some argued, as Locke once had, that ceremonies were an indifferent matter which the civil authority had power to determine and enforce. Others placed emphasis on liberty of conscience. Several argued that toleration would be good for trade. Some blamed the puritan clergy for having fomented the Civil War by factious and intemperate preaching, a view Locke himself had shared in 1660–1.[2] Others said that penal measures should be abandoned because experience showed they had not worked. No one proposed coercing dissenters to secure their eternal salvation.

The Commons returned to the question on 8 April, but after three or four hours' debate a motion to refer the issue back to the King was defeated by 176 votes to 70.[3] Parliament was adjourned on 9 May and did not meet again until the autumn of 1669.

This was a setback for those advocating comprehension, but on the face of it the King remained committed to their cause. In September he met a group of Presbyterian ministers in Lord Arlington's house, and assured them that he would 'doe his utmost to get us comprehended within the Publicke Establishment', though he warned them that 'this was a worke of difficulty and time' and that they should therefore be patient.[4] It would appear, however, that the Presbyterians were being strung along. Soon afterwards Manton wrote to Baxter telling him that he had heard that

the comprehension thought of by some and endeavoured by our friends in Court was frustrated by Dr. Owens proposal of a toleration which was intertained and carried on by other persons and those opposite to them who had of their owne inclination interested themselves in the buisinesse of comprehension for our sakes...[5]

When Owen heard of these accusations he went round to see Manton and bluntly told him that 'Comprehension would neither doe the Kings buisinesse nor ours'.[6] Owen did not welcome comprehension because it

---

[1] Milward, 221. See also Sir John Holland's speech, ibid. 325–6.

[2] *Two Tracts*, 160–1. For examples of what Locke had in mind, see Trevor-Roper, 'The Fast Sermons of the Long Parliament', 302–3, 307–8.

[3] Milward, 248–50; *Debates*, ed. Grey, i. 126–32; *CJ* ix. 77.

[4] Manton to Baxter, *c.*Sept. 1668, *Baxter Correspondence*, ii. 63; *Reliquiae Baxterianae*, pt. III, § 85.   [5] Manton to Baxter, 26 Sept. 1668, *Baxter Correspondence*, ii. 65.

[6] Ibid.

would have left him and his fellow Independents isolated and vulnerable. The King's objection was that it would be of no benefit to Catholics and would if anything make toleration of them less likely. This was not a motive that could openly be acknowledged, but there were those who realized what was going on. The comprehension proposals, Burnet wrote, were opposed not only by the bishops and their supporters in the Commons (who were quite open about it) but also by those who

designed to shelter the *Papists* from the Execution of the Law, and saw clearly that nothing could bring in *Popery* so well as a *Toleration*. But to tolerate *Popery* bare-faced, would have startled the Nation too much; so it was necessary to hinder all the Propositions for Union, since the keeping up the differences was the best Colour they could find, for getting the Tolleration to pass only as a slackning the Laws against Dissenters, whose Numbers and Wealth made it adviseable to have some regard to them; and under this pretence *Popery* might have crept in more covered, and less regarded: So these Councils being more acceptable to some *concealed Papists* then in great Power, as has since appeared but too Evidently, the whole Project for *Comprehension* was let fall . . . [1]

This was published in 1682, and Burnet prudently did not name these concealed papists. In his *History* he could afford to be less reticent:

The king had such a command of himself, that when his interest led him to serve any end, or court any sort of men, he did it so dexterously, and with such an air of sincerity, that till men were well practised with him, he was apt to impose on them. He seemed now to go into moderation and comprehension with so much heartiness, that both Bridgeman and Wilkins believed he was in earnest in it: though there was nothing that the popish counsels were more fixed in, than to oppose all motions of that kind. [2]

As an analysis of Charles's motives this is probably not far from the mark. Duplicity and dissimulation came easily to him, and by 1668 he had had plenty of practice. His conduct in foreign affairs shows how ready he was to sabotage the efforts of his ministers by pursuing contrary policies behind their backs. Neither tolerant nor intolerant as a matter of principle, he adopted those policies he considered best calculated to further his own interests, and when circumstances changed, his policies changed with them. At the Restoration he had favoured a broad settlement, but after 1662 there is little if any sign of a genuine commitment to comprehension and in his later years he lost interest in it entirely.

---

[1] Burnet, *The Life and Death of Sir Matthew Hale*, 72–3.
[2] Burnet, i. 455; cf. 317–18.

The Pamphlet Debate

The advocates of comprehension and indulgence were well aware of the need to obtain public support. 'The Presbyterians', Barlow wrote, 'havinge some intelligence and hopes (by their freinds at Court) that his Majesty when the Parliament mett (which was to be Oct: 10. 1667) would be willinge to grant them some indulgence and a Toleration, to make way for it, caused a *little booke* to be writt and printed, call'd *A Proposition for the safety and happiness of the King and Kingdome* &c'.[1] The full title of the little book was *A Proposition for the Safety & Happiness of the King and Kingdom both in Church and State, and prevention of the Common Enemy; by way of Accommodation and Indulgence in matters of Religion. Tendered to the Consideration of his Majesty and the Parliament against their next Session. By a lover of Sincerity & Peace.* Its author was John Humfrey, a Presbyterian minister who had taken episcopal orders in 1661 but had subsequently renounced them.[2] The common enemy was, of course, popery. The book seems to have been written during the summer: there is a reference on pages 5–6 to the 'late calamity . . . upon our Ships'—the Medway disaster of 12 June—and a date of 18 June 1667 is given on the final page; according to Barlow it was published around the beginning of August, and reprinted in October.[3]

Humfrey's book was primarily a plea for comprehension, though he also proposed toleration for those Protestants who were not prepared to be re-admitted to the Church of England however the terms of subscription might be relaxed. The same position can be found in a work published anonymously by another Presbyterian minister, John Corbet, whose *Discourse of the Religion of England. Asserting, That Reformed Christianity Setled in its Due Latitude is the Stability and Advancement of this Kingdom* probably came out in September, a month or so after Humfrey's book. The line taken by Corbet is indicated by his title: the welfare of the kingdom would be best secured by a broadly based state church, with as few Protestants outside it as possible.

Humfrey's and Corbet's books were answered by Thomas Tomkins, one of Archbishop Sheldon's chaplains, in *The Inconveniences of Toleration*, published on 10 October. Sheldon's other chaplain, Samuel Parker, appears on this occasion to have remained uncharacteristically silent. The conformist position was also defended anonymously by Richard

---

[1] Bodl., B 14.15 Linc., p. 4. Unfortunately Barlow did not identify these friends at court.
[2] Sykes, *Old Priest and New Presbyter*, 123–4; Nuttall, 'The First Nonconformists', 180–2.
[3] Bodl., B 14.15 Linc., p. 18.

Perrinchief in *A Discourse of Toleration*, published at some time in the autumn, and by John Pearson in *Promiscuous Ordinations are Destructive to the Honour & Safety of the Church of England*, a reply to Humfrey published on 3 November. The validity or invalidity of non-episcopal ordination was a matter of intense concern to the clergy; it is one of the few issues raised in the debate about which Locke was wholly silent.

The viewpoint of the Independents was expressed in another anonymous tract, *Bentivolyo, or Good Will to all that are Called Unconformists*, which was published on 13 November. On the next day John Owen entered the debate with *A Peace-Offering in an Apology and humble Plea for Indulgence and Liberty of Conscience*. Humfrey and Corbet both made replies to their critics, and Corbet and Owen were in turn attacked again by Perrinchief.[1] Other tracts followed, of which a high proportion were carefully collected—though unfortunately seldom dated—by Barlow.[2] Whether Locke read any of them is not known; none was recorded in his library catalogue or mentioned in any of his commonplace books.[3]

The main argument used by the opponents of toleration was political: that the stability, prosperity, and even survival of the state required uniformity in religion. Perrinchief made the point as succinctly as anyone: 'It is for the Interest of *England* as much as for any other State, to have no *Factions*, nor to permit any thing that may either form or nourish them.'[4] In Restoration England the most likely source of faction was religion: '*Faction* in the *State* being thus interwoven with *Dissentions* in *Religion*, the Toleration of one sort is the permission of another.'[5] Comprehension was no answer, because it would bring into the church men whose aim was to destroy it:

If men that are perswaded in their Consciences, that our Ceremonies are *Idolatrous*, and *Superstitious*, and at best but trifles, our Liturgy and Government *Popish and Antichristian*, be joyned with men far otherwise perswaded in their Consciences; what a vanity is it to think we shall have peace?[6]

This was entirely unfair, at least as far as men like Humfrey and Corbet were concerned. The moderate Presbyterians who were seeking

---

[1] [Humfrey], *A Defence of the Proposition*; [Corbet], *A Second Discourse of the Religion of England*; [Perrinchief], *Indulgence not Justified*.

[2] For a full list, see Note A, below.

[3] The fact that none of them appears in his library catalogue is not conclusive: Locke read with great care a number of works not listed there, including Parker's *Discourse of Ecclesiastical Politie*, and Stillingfleet's *Unreasonableness of Separation* and *Mischief of Separation*. Some evidence that he had read Humfrey's *Proposition for the Safety & Happiness of the King and Kingdom* is discussed in Note B, below.   [4] *A Discourse of Toleration*, 25.

[5] Ibid. 26.   [6] Ibid. 47.

comprehension certainly did not regard the Book of Common Prayer as idolatrous and anti-Christian—indeed in many cases they continued to attend and take communion at their parish churches.[1] Their opponents, however, were not inclined to be conciliatory, and some of them suspected that the advocates for liberty of conscience were not always what they claimed to be, and that they were acting 'under a vizard, persuading themselves, that if they can get in the Presbyterian Needle, the long thred of Sectaries must necessarily follow after'.[2] The sects contained many quite open enemies of the established church, but in the eyes of their more intransigent opponents the moderate Presbyterians were no better: 'the Nation well enough perceives, that *you the wiser sort of Dissenters*, are as readie now for War in your minds, as you were 28 Years ago, when it was first begun'.[3] The events of the Civil War and Interregnum were still fresh in everyone's minds, and memories of what both the Presbyterians and the Independents had done when in power did not dispose the now triumphant Anglicans—either clerical or lay—to exercise restraint.

Presbyterian advocates of comprehension like Humfrey and Corbet did not fundamentally disagree with Perrinchief's claim that political stability required—or at least would be greatly assisted by—religious uniformity: they merely differed from him in supposing that it was a goal that would best be achieved by a broadly based church, with a limited toleration for the (it was hoped) relatively few Protestants who would choose to remain outside it. A quite different approach was taken by Independents like John Owen, who had no desire to become members of such a church. The main argument for toleration used by Owen was that no one had the right to compel anyone to worship contrary to their own conscience:

The *sole Question* is, Whether God hath Authorized, and doth warrant any man, of what sort soever, to compell others to Worship and serve him, contrary to the way and manner that they are in their Consciences perswaded that he doth accept and approve.[4]

Men vary greatly in their understanding of spiritual things, and this diversity of apprehensions make it very unlikely that there will ever be

---

[1] As Humfrey made clear in *A Defence of the Proposition: Or, Some Reasons rendred why the Nonconformist-Minister who comes to his Parish-Church and Common-Prayer, cannot yet yeeld to other things that are enjoyned, without some Moderation ...* , published early in 1668. On those nonconformists who did regard the Prayer Book—and indeed any set form of worship—as idolatrous, see Nuttall, 'The First Nonconformists', 166–70.

[2] Abraham Philotheus [Abraham Wright], *Anarchie Reviving*, 12.

[3] *Dolus an Virtus?*, 15.   [4] *Indulgence and Toleration Considered*, 16.

any ecclesiastical organization to whose doctrines and practices everyone can give unfeigned assent, at least in a country with the religious history of England in the reign of Charles II:

> All the World knows, how full at this day it is of various Opinions and Practises in things concerning Religion; and how unsuccessful the Attempts of all sorts have been for their Extinguishment. It is no less known ... how unavoidable unto Men, considering the various *Alotments* of their Condition in Divine Providence, their different Apprehensions and Perswasions about these things are. He therefore that will build the Interest of a Nation, on an Uniformity of *Sentiment* and Practises in these things, had need well fix this *floating Delos*, if he intend not to have his Government continually tossed up and down.[1]

In this respect Owen's argument was quite different from those of the Presbyterian advocates of comprehension like Humfrey and Corbet: for Owen the stability and welfare of the kingdom could only be secured by general toleration of Protestant dissenters, including the Independent congregations. A single state church was neither practicable nor desirable, and he had no interest in any proposals for comprehension.[2]

Of all the participants in the debate, the one who probably came closest to Locke in his general outlook was Sir Charles Wolseley. He was a layman and, like Locke, an advocate of rational religion, the future author of *The Unreasonableness of Atheism* (1669) and *The Reasonableness of Scripture-Belief* (1672).[3] He was also a defender of toleration, though like Locke he was not prepared to extend it to Catholics.[4] Sometimes his arguments were exactly the same as Locke's:

> He that would have the Magistrate force all men to his Religion, will himself be burnt by his own Principles, when he comes into a Countrey, where the State-Religion differs from him: To say, He is in the right, and the state that does it in the wrong, is a miserable begging the Question. If one Magistrate be to do it, all are to do it, and there can be no other rule of Truth and Error in that case, but what they think so.[5]

---

[1] Ibid. 18–19.

[2] Owen did not propose any dismantling of the Church of England: 'It is also granted that all outward Priviledges, Incouragements, Advantages, Promotions, Preferments, Dignities, Publick Conveniencies, Legal Maintainance, are still to be confined unto the Church, and its *Conformists*; as also that those who desire the benefit of *Indulgence*, must together with an Exemption from all these, pay all Dues required by the Law to them...', ibid. 26–7.

[3] For a discussion of his views, see Worden, 'Toleration and the Cromwellian Protectorate', 229–33.

[4] His reasons were the same, namely that no Catholic can ever be 'a true and hearty Subject to a Protestant Prince', *Liberty of Conscience, the Magistrates Interest*, 14.

[5] Ibid. 19.

However, Wolseley quite explicitly rejected the view, which was to play a central part in Locke's argument, that 'The Magistrate hath nothing at all to do in Religious concerns, that he is a meer Civil-Officer, to take care of mens Civil-Interests, and hath nothing to do with things of a Spiritual nature.'[1] For him, as for so many of his predecessors, the magistrate was 'Gods chief Officer in the World, directed by the Light of Nature, as well as otherwise, to see that which God reveals to be his Will, put in execution'.[2] This was the principle that Locke came entirely to reject.

Locke and the Essay concerning Toleration

The comprehension and toleration proposals of 1667–8 form part of the background to Locke's *Essay concerning Toleration*, but it is very difficult to say what effect they had on his deliberations. Although the *Essay* begins with a reference to 'the Question of liberty of conscience, which has for some years beene soe much bandied among us', there is no mention of these proposals, or the accompanying pamphlet debate, or indeed any contemporary events at all. Locke's own papers are equally unhelpful: nothing in his correspondence or in any of his other manuscripts throws any light on the date of the *Essay* or the circumstances of its composition.

In the early 1660s Locke had written at length in defence of the magistrate's power to impose the use of indifferent things in religious worship, but these writings were not concerned with the general issue of toleration.[3] After 1662 he turned his attention to other matters. His visit to Cleves may well have opened his eyes to the possibility of religious pluralism,[4] but if it led to any theoretical reflections on toleration no trace of them has survived among his papers. After his return to England he had spent much of his time working on chemistry and medicine, and there is no sign in his commonplace books, or anywhere else, that he was doing any reading on toleration, or on political matters of any kind.[5]

---

[1] *Liberty of Conscience Upon its true and proper Grounds, Asserted & Vindicated*, 17, italics suppressed.

[2] Ibid. 26. Compare Corbet's statement that the 'most proper Work of the Magistrate, who is Gods Minister and Vicegerent, [is] to be *custos & vindex utriusque Tabulae*', *A Second Discourse of the Religion of England*, 27.

[3] For evidence that Locke was not unsympathetic to toleration, see his draft letter to Henry Stubbe, Sept. 1659, *Correspondence*, i. 109–12.

[4] See Locke to Boyle, 12/22 Dec. 1665, *Correspondence*, i. 228; Locke to Strachey, 14/24 Dec. 1665, 26 Dec. 1665/5 Jan. 1666, *Correspondence*, i. 235–7, 244–50.

[5] The main sources for Locke's activities at this time are the commonplace books MSS Locke f. 19 and d. 9, and the chemical notebook, MS Locke f. 25; on the dating of the last of

There can be little doubt that Locke began writing the *Essay* after he joined Ashley's household in May 1667. The intellectual atmosphere he encountered there would have been very unlike the one he had known at Christ Church. Although outwardly a conforming Anglican, Ashley's private opinions seem to have been far from orthodox. According to Burnet, 'he was a deist, and seemed to believe nothing of Christianity, but only that it contained good morals; he was against bringing in religion to the state or imposing it on any'.[1] He was certainly a supporter of toleration for dissenting Protestants, and perhaps even for Catholics,[2] though there does not appear to be any evidence linking him with the comprehension and toleration proposals of 1667–8; his health was poor at the time and such energy as he had was probably taken up with his duties as Chancellor of the Exchequer and as a member of the newly formed Treasury Commission. It is not easy to say what part if any he had in the genesis of the *Essay*. He may have suggested to Locke that he should write something on the subject of toleration, but in the absence of further evidence this is not something about which it is possible to be certain.

The earliest surviving version of the *Essay*, the First Draft, is a short paper of just over 1,600 words in length. Locke began by stating that he supposed that there were only two things that have a right to toleration: speculative opinions and religious worship. He did not define what he meant by speculative opinions, but gave such examples as 'beleife of a trinity, fall, antipodes atoms &c'. These should be tolerated because they have no reference at all to society and 'cannot either disturb the state or inconvenience my neigbour'. The same is true of religious worship, which for Locke is a matter between the individual believer and the deity he worships and is of no concern to the magistrate or to anyone else. The magistrate therefore has no right to dictate anyone's religious worship: he is merely an umpire whose task is confined to the adjudication of disputes about the things of this world.[3]

these, see Walmsley and Milton, 'Locke's Notebook "Adversaria 4" and his Early Training in Chemistry'. See also Locke to Boyle, 24 Feb., 24 Mar. 1667, *Correspondence*, i. 307–11.

[1] Burnet, *Supplement*, 58. The published version (Burnet, i. 172) described him as 'a deist at best'.

[2] In the *Letter from a Person of Quality* (p. 5, italics reversed; below, p. 343), the author described how Shaftesbury 'confest to me, that it was his opinion, and always had been, that the *Papists* ought to have no other pressure laid upon them, but to be made uncapable of Office, Court, or Armes, and to pay so much as might bring them at least to a ballance with the Protestants, for those chargable Offices they are lyable unto . . .'.

[3] Below, pp. 303–4.

Locke did not propose any kind of doctrinal test for toleration—indeed it would have been wholly inconsistent with his argument to have done so. He did, however, admit two exceptions to the general rule that speculative opinions and religious worship should be tolerated. One was where those professing a religion trespassed on the magistrate's jurisdiction by maintaining that they were entitled to convert others by force or to break faith with heretics; those who held such views—and Locke evidently had Catholics in mind—were not to be tolerated further than the magistrate thought convenient. The other was where 'the professors of any worship shall grow soe numerous & unquiet as manifestly to threaten disturbance to the state'. A mere threat was enough: anything that might give men 'an oportunity to number their forces know their strength be confident of one an other, & upon any occasion readily unite' should be watched and if necessary dealt with by the magistrate. This was not because the magistrate had the right to enforce orthodox belief or any particular mode of worship: Locke made it clear that such people 'are not restraind because of this or that opinion but because such a number of opinion what soever that dissented would be dangerous'. The Quakers were singled out as an example of such a potentially dangerous sect.[1]

At the end of the First Draft Locke set down four numbered conclusions, all concerned with the papists. He acknowledged that they were entitled to toleration so far as their speculative opinions and religious worship were concerned, but he added that since they had 'adopted into their religion as fundamental truths, severall opinions that are oposite & destructive to any government but the popes' they had 'no title to toleration'. He therefore concluded that they were 'to be tolerated & suppressed proportionably as either of these usages may serve to lessen their number & weaken their party'. He seems initially to have thought that the same should apply to Protestant dissenters, because he then added 'And these perhaps may be rules for other partys as well as Papist'. He must, however, have had second thoughts about this—or perhaps someone he showed it to raised objections—because he then deleted it and added a fifth and final point concerning Protestant dissenters. He indicated that the appropriate policy would depend on the number of dissenters and the variety of their opinions, but in all cases he recommended that they should receive a toleration. He did not mention comprehension and made no proposals for any changes to the doctrine, discipline, or worship of the Church of England.

---

[1] Below, p. 306.

It is not known whether Locke showed the First Draft to anyone or what response he received, but some time after finishing it—it is not possible to say how long—he began work on a new and very much longer version. The survival of his foul papers, the Rough Draft, shows that he began, as he had in the First Draft, with speculative opinions. His main argument, as before, was that such opinions should be tolerated because they 'cannot by any means either disturb the state or inconvenience my neigbour', but he also maintained that they should be tolerated because beliefs were essentially involuntary: 'a man can not command his owne understanding, or positively determine to day what opinion he will be of to morrow'.[1] Coercion is not merely wrong: it is also futile, at least if it is intended to produce inward belief as well as outward conformity.

Locke did not change his views on this, but he must subsequently have decided that it was not the best place to start. He therefore made a fresh beginning, indicating the purpose of the work as a whole:

In the question of liberty of conscience which has for some years beene soe much bandied among us One thing that hath cheifly perplexed the question kept up the dispute & increasd the animosity hath been I conceive this, That both partys have with equall zeale, & mistake too much enlargd their pretensions, whilst one side preach up absolute obedience, & the other claime universall liberty in matters of conscience, without assigneing the matter which has a title to liberty or shewing the boundarys of imposition & obedience.[2]

This setting of boundaries is very characteristic of Locke.[3] In his earlier writings the key criterion was indifferency, and he argued that the civil magistrate must necessarily have absolute power over indifferent things.[4] In the *Essay concerning Toleration* he produced an entirely different argument. He began by laying down what he called a 'sure & unmoveable foundation':

That the whole trust power & authority of the magistrate is vested in him for noe other purpose but to be made use of for the good preservation & peace of that society over which he is set, & therefor this alone is & ought to be the standard & measure according to which he ought to square & proportion his laws, model & frame his government For if men could live quietly & peacably togeather without growing into a common wealth, there would be noe need at all of magistrates or polities, which were only made to preserve men in this world from the fraud & violence of one another.[5]

[1] Below, pp. 399, 400.   [2] Below, p. 398.
[3] Cf. *Essay concerning Human Understanding*, I. i. 7; IV. xviii. 1, 11.
[4] *Two Tracts*, 123, 129, 232.   [5] Below, p. 398.

This is an amplification of Locke's earlier principle that the magistrate is 'but umpire between man & man'. The word 'umpire' is not entirely happy because it may suggest that he thought that the fundamental institutions of the state are judicial ones. He did of course think that the first job of the state is to settle disputes, but in all of his political writings he either stated or simply assumed that the fundamental power in the state is legislative—the power to make and to enforce laws.[1] In the *Two Treatises of Government* it is the legislative that exercises umpirage, and it is the taking away of this power that dissolves government.[2]

Another problem is with the term 'magistrate', which Locke used throughout the *Essay* but did not define. In the English Tract on Government of 1660–1 he had given a definition: 'By the magistrate I understand the supreme legislative power of any society not considering the form of government or number of persons wherein it is placed.'[3] In England this meant that the magistrate was the King in Parliament, not the King acting alone. It may be that Locke meant the same in the *Essay concerning Toleration*, but there are some passages that point to a different interpretation. For example, he described how the magistrate 'shall hereafter be accountable to god for his actions as a man', and in one of the later additions to the *Essay* which Locke made in Adversaria 1661 there is a reference to the magistrate commanding things 'within that church whereof he him self is a member'.[4] In both of these examples the magistrate is the King. Similar remarks may be found in the *Epistola de Tolerantia*.[5] In both works Locke used the term 'magistrate' to refer sometimes to the legislative, sometimes to the monarch, and sometimes simply to the civil power.[6] In some ways this did not greatly matter, since his aim was to show that the civil power in any form lacked the authority to impose religious uniformity, but it did lead to a certain fuzziness when applied to the contemporary situation in England where the King and Parliament were pursuing divergent policies.

Locke's account of the *nature* of the state is quite conventional; much more important and more original is his account of its *functions*. One of

---

[1] *Two Tracts*, 212–13; *Essay on Infallibility*, Goldie, 205; *Two Treatises*, II. 3, 150.
[2] *Two Treatises*, II. 212, 227.   [3] *Two Tracts*, 125.   [4] Below, p. 311.
[5] *Epistola de Tolerantia*, 81.
[6] The *Two Treatises of Government* contains a very different account. Locke distinguished between the supreme magistrate and inferior magistrates, but made it clear that the former is no more than the '*Supream Executor* of the Law' (II. 151) and that his power is limited by the terms of his commission (II. 202). The difference between the supreme magistrate and inferior magistrates is therefore one of degree, not kind, and the supreme body in the state is the legislative, not the magistracy (II. 134).

his underlying assumptions, both in the *Essay concerning Toleration* and in his later political writings, was that the goods we pursue are not intrinsically civil in that they do not logically depend on civil society and could therefore in principle be enjoyed outside it. Perhaps the clearest statement of this can be found in the *Third Letter for Toleration*, written in 1692:

The End of a Commonwealth constituted can be supposed no other, than what Men in the Constitution of, and entring into it propos'd; and that could be nothing but Protection from such Injuries from other Men, which they desiring to avoid, nothing but Force could prevent or remedy: all things but this being as well attainable by Men living in Neighbourhood without the Bonds of a Commonwealth, they could propose to themselves no other thing but this in quitting their Natural Liberty, and putting themselves under the Umpirage of a *Civil Soveraign*, who therefore had the Force of all the Members of the Commonwealth put into his Hands . . . [1]

For Locke the basic function of the state is to protect people from violence: 'were there noe feare of violence, there would be noe government in the world, nor any need of it'.[2] On this his views were much the same as Hobbes's; where they differed was in the kind of powers they believed necessary to secure this limited aim. Hobbes, who was obsessed with fears of civil disorder and violent death, believed that absolute power was required and that nothing less would suffice. Locke too was concerned with civil disorder, though never to the quite same extent as Hobbes, but by 1667 he had come to a radically different conclusion about the best way to prevent it. In the early 1660s he had argued that the civil magistrate should have unlimited jurisdiction in indifferent things, including the power to impose forms of religious worship, but by the time he came to write the *Essay concerning Toleration* he had changed his mind. He was now concerned to limit the magistrate to 'secureing the civill peace & proprietys of his subjects', which meant that laws should be made 'only for the security of the government & protection of the people in their lives, estates, & libertys'.[3] Exactly the same doctrine can be found in both the *Two Treatises of Government* and the *Essay concerning Human Understanding*.[4]

These views should not be construed too narrowly. It would be surprising if Locke, living in London only two years after the Great Plague, would have denied the state the right to take measures to secure public

---

[1] *A Third Letter for Toleration*, 60.
[2] Below, p. 287. [3] Below, pp. 270–1, 278–9.
[4] *Two Treatises*, II. 94, 123–4; *Essay concerning Human Understanding*, II. xxviii. 9.

health and prevent the spread of disease. In the *Epistola de Tolerantia* he held that the function of the state was solely to secure civil goods, namely 'life, liberty, bodily health and freedom from pain, and the possession of outward things'.[1] The essential thing for his argument is that these are goods which are to be enjoyed in this world, not in the next.

Locke also held that even in matters of this world the magistrate has no right to 'injoyne men the care of their private civill concernments, or force them to a prosecution of their owne private interests'.[2] This distinction between the private and the public is quite different from the distinction between this world and the next, though the two are perfectly compatible. Locke clearly assumed that religious worship is essentially a private matter, since its sole purpose is individual salvation. It follows that for Locke there cannot be any public worship as Hobbes conceived it, namely 'the Worship that a Common-wealth performeth, as one Person'.[3] On this point at least a Lockean commonwealth is more secular than a Hobbesian one.

Locke's account of the state is only one part of his argument, the other being his account of religion. Both parts are essential, and the cutting effect of Locke's argument, like that of a pair of scissors, lies in their combination. Like his account of the state, his account of religion is deeply individualistic; it is also profoundly other-worldly. His starting point, the foundation on which everything rests, was that everyone has two destinies, one in this world and the other in the next. Of these the latter is by far the more important, since it promises 'infinite happinesse or infinite misery'.[4] The primary purpose of religion is to secure the one and avoid the other, and religious considerations must take priority over secular ones.

Locke was not, however, trying to demarcate the boundaries between church and state, conceived of as two separate institutions seeking some kind of *modus vivendi*. His starting point was not the church as an institution but the individual believer seeking salvation in the world to come. This means that the essential relationship is between each believer and the deity he worships, not between one believer and another:

Religious worship being that homage which I pay to that god I adore in a way I judg acceptable to him, & soe being an action or commerce passeing only between

---

[1] 'Bona civilia voco vitam, libertatem, corporis integritatem et indolentiam, et rerum externarum possessiones', *Epistola de Tolerantia*, 66. [2] Below, p. 272.
[3] *Leviathan*, 189. [4] Below, p. 274.

god & my self, hath in its owne nature noe reference at all to my governor or to my neigbour, & soe necessarily produces noe action which disturbs the community.[1]

On this Locke's views were the same as Luther's:

every man runs his own risk in believing as he does, and he must see to it himself that he believes rightly. As nobody else can go to heaven or hell for me, so nobody else can believe or disbelieve for me; as nobody else can open or close heaven or hell to me, so nobody else can drive me to belief or unbelief. How he believes or disbelieves is a matter for the conscience of each individual, and since this takes nothing away from the temporal authority the latter should be content to attend to its own affairs and let men believe this or that as they are able and willing, and constrain no one by force.[2]

Very few of Locke's contemporaries would have accepted so restricted an account of the role of the state in religious affairs. Some held that the church had an inherent power to punish heresy and schism and that it was the duty of the civil magistrate to support this with temporal sanctions. Some believed that God has given the magistrate authority to enforce the true religion, or at least to prohibit false and idolatrous ones. Others adopted the more *politique* view that civil order requires religious uniformity, and that the proliferation of sects leads first to civil disturbance and ultimately to civil war.[3]

Locke never seems to have been attracted by the first or second of these views, though in the early 1660s he had adopted something very much like the third.[4] He did not discuss the first view anywhere in the *Essay concerning Toleration*, though there can be no doubt that he utterly rejected it. He had rather more to say about the second. Although he scornfully dismissed *jure divino* monarchy, he did not deny that the civil magistrate has divine authority. He did, however, deny that this authority extends to matters of religion:

God hath appointed the magistrate his vice gerent in this world, with power to command; but tis but like other deputys, to command only in the affairs of that place where he is vice gerent. who ever medle in the concernments of the other world, have noe other power, but to intreate, & perswade. The magistrate hath noe thing to doe with the good of mens soules or their concernments in an other

---

[1] Below, p. 274. For similar views, see MS Locke c. 34, pp. 76–7, Locke, *Writings on Religion*, 74–5. [2] *On Temporal Authority* (1523), *Luther's Works*, xxxxv. 108.
[3] For general accounts, see Goldie, 'The Theory of Religious Intolerance in Restoration England'; Coffey, *Persecution and Toleration in Protestant England*, ch. 2.
[4] *Two Tracts*, 120–1, 210–12.

life but is ordeind, & intrusted with his power, only for the quiet & comfortable liveing of men in society one with an other . . .[1]

This raises an obvious question: why should God have limited the magistrate's authority in this fashion and not given him the authority to enforce the true religion? Locke's answer was that the identity of the true religion was itself a matter of dispute and that magistrates have 'noe more certain or more infallible knowledg of the way to attain it then I my self, where we are both equally inquirers both equally subjects'.[2] He had little more to add on this in the *Essay concerning Toleration*, but in the controversies with Jonas Proast that followed the publication of the *Letter concerning Toleration* he repeatedly insisted that the magistrate can only enforce the religion he *believes* to be true. In the *Fourth Letter for Toleration*, written only a few months before his death, he told Proast that the magistrate

haveing no certain demonstrative knowledg of the true religion all that was left him to determin him in the application of force (which you make the proper instrument of promoteing the true religion) for the promoteing the true religion, was onely his perswasion beleif or assurance of the true religion which was always his owne, & so in this state the religion which by force the magistrates of the world must of necessity promote must be either their owne or none at all.[3]

The result in either case is that 'much more Harm than Good would be done towards the propagation of true Religion in the World'.[4]

There was, Locke believed, a further reason why the civil magistrate would not have been given any power to enforce the true religion even if he had been fortunate enough to discover what this was. Any attempt to impose it by force would be inconsistent with the true ends of religion:

But if god (which is the point in question) would have men forcd to heaven, it must not be by the outward violence of the magistrate on mens bodys, but the inward constraints of his owne spirit on their minds, which are not to be wrought on by any humane compulsion, The way to salvation not being any forced exterior performance, but the voluntary & secret choise of the minde, & it cannot be supposd that god would make use of any means, which could not reach but would rather crosse the attainment of the end.[5]

This indicates a change in Locke's views about the use of force in securing outward conformity. In 1660 he had acknowledged that it would

[1] Below, pp. 281–2.   [2] Below, p. 273.
[3] *A Fourth Letter for Toleration*, MS Locke d. 4, fo. 12ʳ.
[4] *A Third Letter for Toleration*, 61.   [5] Below, p. 273.

be wholly vain for a magistrate to try to compel his subjects to give internal assent to any religious doctrines, but he held that such considerations did not apply to external and indifferent actions, such as kneeling at communion or wearing a surplice. Although we cannot choose what to believe, we can choose whether or not to perform actions of this kind, and Locke held that this gave the magistrate jurisdiction over them. He therefore concluded that 'rigour which cannot work an internal persuasion may notwithstanding [make] an outward conformity, all that is here required, and may be as necessary in the one as useless in the other'.[1] Nothing to this effect can be found in the *Essay concerning Toleration* or in Locke's later writings. His earlier argument had depended on keeping a sharp distinction between religious belief and religious practice, at least where indifferent things were concerned, but in later years he came increasingly to the view that belief and practice are so inseparably interwoven that in religious worship nothing can be truly indifferent.

Locke then turned his attention to the other main account of the origins of the magistrate's powers, that they were derived from the grant and consent of the people. In the early 1660s he had been prepared to entertain this view but he had insisted that political power 'can never be established unless each and every one surrenders the whole of this natural liberty of his, however great it may be, to a legislator'.[2] This was of course Hobbes's view. By 1667 Locke had changed his mind, and he now argued that any powers granted would always be limited, since people would not be prepared to 'give any one or more of their fellow men an authority over them for any other purpose then their owne preservation, or extend the limits of their jurisdiction beyond the limits of this life'.[3] There are two possible reasons for this. The first is that people lack the capacity to grant the magistrate any authority over religious belief or worship, just as in Locke's later political theory they lack the capacity to submit themselves to an absolute monarch or to sell themselves into slavery.[4] Locke did not consider this in the *Essay concerning Toleration*, but it is wholly consistent with his fundamental belief that everyone is responsible before God for his own spiritual destiny and he cannot abdicate this responsibility to anyone else. This was a matter on which he came to feel very strongly, as can be seen in a remark in the preface to *A Paraphrase and Notes on the Epistles of St Paul*:

[1] *Two Tracts*, 128; cf. *Leviathan*, 309.
[2] *Two Tracts*, 231, translation slightly altered.   [3] Below, p. 270.
[4] *Two Treatises*, II. 23.

35

If I must believe for my self, it is unavoidable that I must understand for my self. For if I blindly and with an Implicit Faith take the Pope's Interpretation of the Sacred Scripture, without examining whether it be Christ's Meaning, 'tis the Pope I believe in, and not in Christ . . . 'Tis the same thing when I set up any other Man in Christ's place, and make him the Authentique Interpreter of Sacred Scripture to my self. He may possibly understand the Sacred Scripture as right as any Man, but I shall do well to examin my self, whether that which I do not know, nay (which in the way I take) I can never know, can justifie me in making my self his Disciple, instead of Jesus Christ's, who of Right is alone and ought to be my only Lord and Master . . . [1]

The second reason is that even if people did possess the capacity to hand over their eternal fate to the magistrate, no one in his right mind would do so. Locke clearly thought this, as can be seen from a passage taken almost word for word from the First Draft:

Nor can it be thought that men should give the magistrate a power to choose for them their way to salvation which is too great to give away, if not impossible to part with, since whatever the magistrate injoynd in the worship of god, men must in this necessarily follow what they them selves thought best, since noe consideration could be sufficient to force a man from or to that, which he was fully perswaded, was the way to infinite happinesse or infinite misery.[2]

It is not clear from this whether Locke meant that it is psychologically impossible for men to transfer their power of choosing to the magistrate, or that it would be wholly irrational for them to do so. Subsequent remarks suggest the latter. Anyone doing so would be blindly gambling with his eternal destiny, and the odds would not in Locke's view be at all favourable. In the *Fourth Letter for Toleration* he remarked that out of 500 magistrates 499 would pursue false religion and only one the true.[3] Such figures should not be taken too literally, but it is clear that no one genuinely concerned with his eternal salvation would willingly entrust it to a prince who was no more knowledgeable about these matters than he was himself. Locke made the point forcefully in his critique of Stillingfleet:

The question in short is whether it be best, that men should be compelld blindly to submit to, or publickly owne the doctrines & worship that others impose, right

---

[1] *A Paraphrase and Notes*, i. 115. Compare the remark in 'Pacific Christians', written in 1688: 'Noe man or society of men [has] any authority to impose their opinions or interpretations on any other the meanest Christian. Since in matters of Religion every one must know & believe, & give an account for himself', MS Locke c. 27, fo. 80ar.

[2] Below, pp. 273–4.

[3] MS Locke d. 4, fo. 21r; cf. MS Locke c. 34, p. 87; *A Third Letter for Toleration*, 296.

or wrong whether he beleives them or no; or that those who are in earnest concernd for their soules should seek out the best way they could find to their Salvation: the one is to put a mans greatest concernement his eternal happynesse or misery into his care whose greatest interest it is to look after it. The other is to put it barely into the hands of Chance, or which is worse, often into the hands of those who make use of this power onely to serve the secular ends of their ambition, & greatnesse...[1]

A survey of contemporary monarchs—Charles II, Louis XIV, the imbecile Carlos II of Spain—would reinforce Locke's point.

It is noticeable that Locke's argument does not depend on explicitly Christian premisses and was intended to apply just as much to other religions as to Christianity. His argument is, however, very far from being a purely secular one, since it depends on the possibility of a future life. This is not a matter on which Locke seems to have had any personal doubts, but his argument does not require that the existence of a future life be established with certainty or even beyond reasonable doubt. Only a possibility is needed, nothing more.[2] It is indeed this very uncertainty of our future fate that for Locke creates the need for toleration: if it were transparently clear what would (or would not) happen to us after death then the whole problem would hardly arise. Locke's point was a very simple one: since I do not *know* what my fate will be after my death (and nor does anyone else) and since this fate will be *my* fate, I and I alone have the right to make the relevant decisions. No one else has any right to make them for me because no one else can compensate me for any mistakes made.

This argument does not depend on any assumption that people will necessarily or even usually make the correct decisions: the essential thing is that any decisions they make are *their* decisions. Those who are condemned can only justly be condemned for faults of their own. As he himself later wrote, "'Tis necessary for the Vindication of God's Justice and Goodness, that those who miscarry should do so by their own Fault, that their Destruction should be from themselves, and they be left inexcusable...'[3]

All of Locke's arguments were designed to secure liberty of belief and worship, not liberty of conscience. This placed him at odds with a great

---

[1] MS Locke c. 34, p. 108. The manuscript is in the hands of Locke, Brounower, and Tyrrell; this passage is in Tyrrell's hand, with one marginal correction by Locke.

[2] *Essay concerning Human Understanding*, II. xxi. 70.

[3] *A Third Letter for Toleration*, 16.

many nonconformists, who pleaded for the liberty of tender consciences.[1] John Humfrey, for example, insisted that 'in all matters that *are* against mens Consciences the Magistrate hath no authority, and cannot use his Sword; but in all matters that are *not* against their Consciences, or that are according to them, he may use it'.[2] Locke entirely disagreed. For him conscience cannot provide any kind of guide to the legislator, since there is nothing that someone may not imagine his conscience to require or forbid: conscience is simply moral belief and nothing more. In 1660 he had dismissed it as 'nothing but an opinion of the truth of any practical position',[3] and this was not a matter on which he ever changed his mind. Conscience, he later wrote, 'is nothing else, but our own Opinion or Judgment of the Moral Rectitude or Pravity of our own Actions'.[4] To give it any higher status would be to treat it as a form of innate knowledge, something to which he was and always remained implacably opposed.

When therefore Locke held that 'the conscience, or persuasion of the subject, cannot possibly be a measure by which the magistrate can, or ought to frame his laws', he was being entirely consistent with his general principles. The reason for this was that

there being noe thing soe indifferent which the consciences of some or other, doe not check at, a toleration of men in all that which they pretend out of conscience they cannot submit to, will wholy take away all the civil laws, & all the magistrates power, & soe there will be noe law, nor government . . .[5]

These considerations also apply to the magistrate, who is not entitled to punish speculative opinions or impose forms of worship on the grounds that doing so is required by his conscience. He would, Locke wrote, 'be accountable to god for his actions as a man, according as they are suited to his owne conscience & perswasion', but in his capacity as a magistrate he should act only for the 'good, preservation, & quiet of all his subjects in this world'.[6]

If the magistrate were to require his subjects to do what their consciences forbade, they would, in Locke's view, have no choice but 'quietly to submitt to the penaltys the law inflicts on such disobedience'.[7] This is the classic doctrine of passive obedience, but it only seems to have been applicable in cases where the magistrate acted within his legitimate

---

[1] For an illuminating discussion of this, see Worden, 'Toleration and the Cromwellian Protectorate', 209–10.   [2] Humfrey, *The Authority of the Magistrate*, 104.
[3] *Two Tracts*, 138.
[4] *Essay concerning Human Understanding*, I. iii. 8; cf. Draft B, § 5, *Drafts*, i. 110.
[5] Below, p. 276.   [6] Below, p. 277.   [7] Below, p. 279.

powers. What would happen if he did not was left unclear. In the *Two Treatises* Locke was prepared to countenance active disobedience when rulers had so abused their powers as to procure a dissolution of government, but he did not list religious coercion as one of the ways this might happen.[1] In the *Epistola de Tolerantia* he held, as he had in the *Essay concerning Toleration*, that if the magistrate were to command something contrary to the conscience of a private person then that person should abstain from the action and 'undergo the punishment which it is not unlawful for him to bear'. This may suggest passive obedience, but he added that 'if the law concerns things which lie outside the magistrate's province...those who disagree are not obliged by that law, because political society was instituted only to preserve for each private man his possession of the things of this life, and for no other purpose'.[2] Although he did not explicitly state that subjects had an active right of resistance, the argument clearly implies this.

Having laid down the general principles of toleration, Locke turned, as he had in the First Draft, to the exceptions. These arise because 'men usually take up their religion in grosse, & assume to them selves the opinions of their party all at once in a bundle', with the result that 'they mix with their religious worship, & speculative opinions, other doctrines absolutely destructive to the society wherein they live', such as 'that faith may be broken with hereticks, that if the magistrate doth not reforme religion the subjects may, that one is bound to broach & propagate any opinion he beleives himself & such like'. Such doctrines cannot be tolerated at all.[3]

For Locke the prime threat came from the papists, and he had two distinct though compatible reasons why they should not be tolerated. One was that they could not be loyal subjects because 'they owe a blinde obedience to an infalible pope, who has the keys of their consciences tied to his girdle'.[4] The other was that toleration should only be allowed to

---

[1] There is a reference (II. 209) to people fearing 'that their Laws, and with them their Estates, Liberties, and Lives are in danger, and perhaps their Religion too', and another (II. 210) to 'that Religion underhand favoured (though publickly proclaimed against)'. Both refer to covert royal support for popery, not to disputes between the Church of England and Protestant dissenters.　　　　[2] *Epistola de Tolerantia*, 127, 129.
[3] Below, pp. 284, 288–9. There are similar examples in *Epistola de Tolerantia*, 85, 131, 133. See also the reference in the *Essays on the Law of Nature* (p. 175) to 'those who break the great bond of humanity by their teaching that faith is not to be kept with hereticks'.
[4] Below, p. 291. For an earlier expression of this view, see Locke to Henry Stubbe, Sept. 1659, *Correspondence*, i. 111.

those who are themselves ready to practise it. Neither of these reasons had anything to do with the content of Catholic worship or theology, both of which, as Locke had indicated in the First Draft, were entitled to toleration. His refusal to tolerate popery was essentially political, and he did not share the belief—widespread among nonconformists, who were anxious to secure toleration for themselves—that Catholic worship, both public and private, should be prohibited as idolatrous.[1]

When it came to the toleration of Protestant dissenters, Locke was pulled by two different considerations. On the one hand he clearly believed that they should be allowed to worship God in whatever way they chose, but on the other he was afraid that their very act of separating themselves could pose a threat to civil order; it was of course this fear that had led him in 1660 to advocate the imposition of uniformity. By 1667 he had come to think that this was not the solution, but his fear of disorder remained. He therefore concluded that the magistrate had the power to suppress any religious group he considered dangerous, provided he did so purely for reasons of public order.[2] Locke laboured this point at considerable length and seems to have been very anxious to assure his readers—and perhaps also himself—that such coercion would not amount to religious persecution because the motives behind it were not religious.

In the first half of the *Essay* Locke had been concerned to lay down the general principles of toleration; in the second half he considered how these principles should be applied to the situation in England.

So far as papists were concerned, he was quite sure that force was justified in principle and likely to be effective in practice. He was aware that 'restraint'—his word—often evoked sympathy in bystanders who 'have compassion for sufferers & esteeme for that religion as pure, & the professors of it as sincere which can stand the test of persecution', but he thought that this would not apply to Catholics, 'who are lesse apt to be pittyed then others because they receive noe other usage then what the cruelty of their owne principles & practises are knowne to deserve'. He clearly regarded Catholicism as little more than a blend of superstition,

---

[1] For an example of this view, see 'Of True Religion, Haeresie, Schism, Toleration, And what best means may be us'd against the growth of Popery' (1672), in *Complete Prose Works of John Milton*, viii. 430. Locke did not discuss idolatry in the *Essay concerning Toleration*, but in the *Epistola de Tolerantia* (pp. 111–21) he held that the magistrate has no authority to suppress idolatrous worship and that the Old Testament laws punishing idolatry applied to the Jews and to them alone.   [2] Below, pp. 285–8.

ignorance, and priestcraft, 'brought in upon the ignorant & zealous world by the art & industry of their clergy, & kept up by the same artifice backd by power & force', and therefore 'the most likely of any religion to decay where the secular power handles them severely'.[1]

When it came to Protestant nonconformists Locke was far more sympathetic. Instead of advocating that they should be 'severely handled', he placed great emphasis on the cruelty and ineffectiveness of persecution. He asked the Anglican clergy and gentry

who in the late times soe firmly stood the ineffectuall persecution them selves & found how little it obteind on their opinions, & yet are now soe forward to trye it upon others, whether all the severity in the world could have drawne them one step nearer to a hearty & sincere imbraceing the opinions that were then uppermost...[2]

If persecution had not worked in their own case, Locke asked, what grounds had they for thinking that similar measures against nonconformists would prove any more effective? The present policy was simply futile. It would of course be possible to use more ruthless methods—Locke's examples were the St Bartholomew's Day massacres and the extermination of the Japanese Christians—but he asked whether those in power would really be prepared to countenance them.

Just before the end Locke wrote a heading, 'To give a full prospect of this subject there remaine yet these following particulars to be handled', followed by a list of five topics requiring further consideration:

1° To shew what influence Toleration is like to have upon the number & industry of your people on which depends the power & riches of the kingdom

2° That if force must compell all to an Uniformity in England to consider what party alone, or what partys are likelyest to unite to make a force able to compell the rest.

3° To shew that all that speake against toleration seeme to suppose that severity & force are the only arts of government & way to suppresse any faction, which is a mistake

4° That for the most part the matters of controversy & destinction between sects, are noe parts or very inconsiderable ones and appendixes of true religion

5° To consider how it comes to passe that Christian religion hath made more factions wars, & disturbances in civil societys then any other, & whether tolleration & Latitudinisme would prevent those evils.[3]

---

[1] Below, pp. 291–2. Locke's attitude to Catholicism was not always so harsh: see Locke to John Strachey, *c.*26 Dec. 1665, *Correspondence*, i. 246.   [2] Below, p. 294.
[3] Below, p. 301.

These do not correspond in any way to the five conclusions at the end of the First Draft. At the end of them he wrote, 'But of these when I have more leisure'. He subsequently crossed this out and added two further points. The sixth, which recommended 'makeing the termes of church communion as large as may be, i.e. that your articles in speculative opinions be few & large, & ceremonys in worship few & easy', looks like an argument for comprehension rather than toleration. The seventh attacked subscription to 'doctrines which are confesd to be incomprehensible'. The reference to 'the Doctors of your severall churches' indicates that he did not have the Church of England solely in mind.[1]

Having made these additional points Locke again wrote, 'But of these when I have more leisure', though he never in fact returned to them. Perhaps his closing remark was a mere literary device, but there were at least two major calls on his time during 1668.

The first, and more easily datable, occurred in the summer. The operation to drain the abscess on Ashley's liver took place on 12 June. Locke was not in overall charge—his role was as a secretary and coordinator—but he was the man on the spot, and it is clear that he was kept quite busy until late September, and intermittently thereafter.[2]

The other call on Locke's time came from his work on a paper entitled 'Some of the Consequences that are like to follow upon Lessening of Interest to 4 Per Cent'.[3] This was occasioned by a controversy that began with the publication early in 1668 of Josiah Child's *Brief Observations concerning Trade, and Interest of Money*. A bill to regulate rates of interest had its first reading in the Commons on 22 April, but was lost when Parliament was adjourned in May.[4] Whether Locke's paper was written around this time or later is uncertain; Patrick Kelly favours a date in the later part of the year, but there is no decisive evidence either way.[5]

The failure of the comprehension and toleration proposals provides a further reason for Locke to have put the *Essay* to one side in the spring of 1668. The theoretical case for toleration remained as good as ever, but the decisive rejection by the Commons of any proposals for comprehension or toleration had made it very clear that nothing was going to happen in the near future.

Even before Locke finished revising the *Essay* he had a copy made, now MS Locke c. 28, fos. 21–30. From this a fair copy (PRO 30/24/47/1)

---

[1] Below, p. 302.
[2] Notes on the nursing care are PRO 30/24/47/2, fos. 1–2, 19–30.
[3] *Locke on Money*, 167–92.   [4] Milward, 270–1; *CJ* ix. 79, 81.
[5] *Locke on Money*, 10.

was made, probably for Ashley himself; it is not possible to say who else may have read it. Neither copy can be dated precisely, but both were probably made in late in 1667 or early in 1668. Some years later, probably late in 1671 or early in 1672, Locke had a third scribal copy made in his notebook Adversaria 1661. All of these manuscripts are described in detail in the Textual Introduction.

The copy in Adversaria 1661 does not contain any major changes to the main part of the *Essay*, but it is followed by two additions unique to this manuscript. The first, of some 200 words, is in the same hand as the main part of the *Essay*, and was presumably copied at the same time; when Locke originally wrote it can only be surmised. The second is in Locke's hand and was written in 1674 or (more probably) in 1675.

One of the most striking features of both these additions, especially the second, is their anticlericalism. In the first addition the Anglican clergy are described as 'impudently railing' at their dissenting brethren, and accused of acting from mercenary motives: 'This makes some men suspect that tis not the feeding of the sheep but the benefit of the fleece that makes these men endeavour by such methods to enlarge theire fold'. In the second addition the target is wider and the criticism still more bitter: since Christianity became a national religion 'it hath been the cause of more disorders tumults & bloudshed then all other causes put togeather'. The cause of this lay not in the teachings of Christ himself, but in the ambitions of the clergy, who

as Christianity spread asserting dominion laid claime to a preisthood derived by succession from Christ & soe independent from the civill power, receiveing (as they pretend) by the imposition of hands & some othere ceremonys agreed on (but variously) by the preisthoods of the severall factions, an indelible character particular sanctity & a power immediately from heaven, to doe severall things which are not lawfull to be donne by other men . . . [1]

For Locke, by contrast, 'there is noe thing which a preist can doe which an other man without any such ordination . . . may not lawfully performe & doe'. In this he was merely repeating the fundamental Lutheran doctrine of the priesthood of all believers. Luther had insisted that ordination conferred no indelible power on its recipients and that the clergy were merely office-holders and no more.[2] Locke's position was the same: Christian ministers resemble 'Justices of peace & other officers who had noe ordination or laying on of hands to fit them to be Justices, & by

---

[1] Below, pp. 310–11, 312–13.
[2] *To the Christian Nobility of the German Nation* (1520), *Luther's Works*, xxxiv. 127–30.

takeing away their commissions may cease to be soe'. Once the clergy of any church come to regard themselves as priests possessing powers received directly from God then they begin (when circumstances permit) first to free themselves from civil authority and then to exercise dominion for themselves:

> Soe that ordination that begins in preisthood if it be let alone will certainly grow up to absolute empire, & though Christ declares him self to have noe Kingdom of this world, his successors have (when ever they can but grasp the power) a large commission to execute & that rigorously civil dominion.[1]

This is very similar in tone and substance to the concluding section of the *Letter from a Person of Quality*, which must have been written at about the same time.

The copy of the *Essay* in MS Locke c. 28 contains several substantial alterations: three sections of the earlier text amounting to nearly 1,100 words were deleted, and there are three additions in Locke's own hand. This new material, in total just over 700 words, is not dated, but it would seem likely that it was added some considerable time after the main text had been copied. The main reason for supposing this is that the changes reveal a considerable shift not merely of emphasis but of doctrine. In the First Draft Locke had been prepared to give the magistrate power to suppress religious dissent if there was any reason to suppose that it might pose a threat to public order. These passages from the First Draft appear with only minor changes in the full version of the *Essay* in Huntington Library HM 584, from which the original text of MS Locke c. 28 was copied, but when Locke revised MS Locke c. 28 they were deleted and replaced by material expressing a very different outlook. His previous view was mentioned only to be rejected:

> I answer if all things that may occasion disorder or conspiracy in a commonwealth must not be endurd in it All discontented & active men must be removd, & whispering must be lesse tolerated then preaching as much likelier to carry on & foment a conspiracy. & if all numbers of men joynd in an union & corporation destinct from the publique be not to be sufferd all charters of Towns espetially great ones are presently to be taken away.[2]

Religious dissent only becomes dangerous when governments attempt to suppress it: 'we have reason to imagin that noe Religion can become

---

[1] Below, p. 315. There are milder but still unfavourable comments about Christian ministers who see themselves as priests in 'Sacerdos' (1698), Adversaria 1661, p. 93, Goldie, 344–5.   [2] Below, p. 309.

suspected to the state of ill intention to it till the government first by a partiall usage of them different from the rest of the subjects declare its ill intentions to its professors, & soe make a state business of it'.[1] This looks like a general principle, but the context makes it clear that Locke saw it as applying only to Protestant dissenters; the passages in the earlier versions ruling out toleration for Catholics were not only retained but strengthened.[2]

Locke also introduced a major exception to his general principle that speculative opinions were entitled to toleration:

I must only remarke before I leave this head of speculative opinions that the beleif of a deitie is not to be recond amongst puerly speculative opinions for it being the foundation of all morality & that which influences the whole life & actions of men without which a man is to be counted noe other then one of the most dangerous sorts of wild beasts & soe uncapeable of all societie.[3]

Similar considerations would presumably apply to any other speculative opinions that undermined the foundations of morality and therefore of society. Locke refused to tolerate atheism because he believed that it destroyed the whole basis of morality. As he later wrote,

The originall & foundation of all Law is dependency. A dependent intelligent being is under the power & direction & dominion of him on whom he depends & must be for the ends appointed him by that superior being. If man were independent he could have noe law but his own will noe end but himself. He would be a god to himself, and the satisfaction of his own will the sole measure & end of all his actions.[4]

Such remarks indicate the vast gulf between Locke's outlook and more recent accounts of autonomous individuals attempting to live by moral standards that they have chosen and imposed upon themselves. Locke would have thought such a project doomed from the outset. He certainly believed that men are *politically* autonomous, in that no legitimate polity could be set up without their agreement and consent, but he was very far from thinking that they are or ever could be *morally* autonomous, or that it would be in any way desirable for them to behave as if they were. This combination of equality as regards each other and dependency on God

---

[1] Below, p. 310. [2] Below, p. 309.
[3] Below, p. 308. The same point was made even more forcefully in the *Epistola de Tolerantia*, 135.
[4] 'Ethica B', MS Locke c. 28, fo. 141ʳ. See also 'Of Ethick in General', MS Locke c. 28, fo. 152ʳ; *Essay concerning Human Understanding*, I. iii. 12, I. iv. 8; Draft B, § 5, *Drafts*, i. 109; *Essays on the Law of Nature*, 183.

lies at the heart of Locke's political thought both in his writings on toleration and in the *Two Treatises of Government*.[1]

Locke did not indicate what practical measures he thought should be taken to combat atheism. Given that he believed, at least in his later writings, that the existence of God was demonstrable, it might appear that he thought that atheism would be confined to those who were wilfully prejudiced or who had given the matter insufficient attention, though other remarks indicate that he thought it quite widespread.[2] Perhaps he would have favoured something along the lines of the *Fundamental Constitutions of Carolina*, which laid down that everyone had to acknowledge the existence of God and to be a member of a church, though not of any particular church.[3] Although neutral between the claims of particular churches, the Lockean state has a very strong interest in maintaining religion and is very far from being purely secular.

Locke also clarified his views on things indifferent. In 1660 he had written in defence of the magistrate's power to impose conformity in religious worship, arguing that 'it is impossible there should be any supreme legislative power which hath not the full and unlimited disposure of all indifferent things'.[4] These included all outward and visible manifestations of religious worship:

All that God looks for in his worship now under the gospel is the sacrifice of a broken and a contrite heart, which may be willingly and acceptably given to God in any place or posture, but he hath left it to the discretion of those who are entrusted with the care of the society to determine what shall be *order* and *decency* ...[5]

This was the standard Anglican position, but by 1667 Locke had begun to depart from it. In the First Draft he stated that

There remains then only things indifferent, *except those which are part or circumstances of my worship of god*, which however private mens consciences may approve or disallow of yet are undoubtedly under the coercive power of the magistrate otherwise there can be noe law nor government.[6]

The words italicized here are an interlinear addition. Locke had little more to say in the full version of the *Essay*, but in one of the additions in

---

[1] *Two Treatises*, II. 4, 6.

[2] *Essay concerning Human Understanding*, I. iv. 8, 16; IV. x. 6.

[3] PRO 30/24/47/3, §§ 86, 87, 91. These provisions are not in Locke's hand and do not contain any corrections or amendments by him. They correspond to §§ 95, 100, 101 in the version dated 1 Mar. 1669[/70], printed in *A Collection of Several Pieces of Mr. John Locke* and in Locke's collected works.   [4] *Two Tracts*, 129.

[5] Ibid. 146.   [6] Below, p. 304, italics added.

MS Locke c. 28 he stated explicitly that

in religious worship noething is indifferent for it being the useing of those habits gestures &c & noe other which I thinke acceptable to god in my worshiping of him, however they may be in their own nature perfectly indifferent, yet when I am worshipping my god in a way I thinke he has prescribd & will approve of I cannot alter omit or adde any circumstance in that which I thinke the true way of worship.[1]

A similar account may be found in his critique of Stillingfleet:

Many things that are of their owne nature indifferent cease to be soe when they come into the concernement of Religion. Kneeling or not Kneeling is certainly a very indifferent action in it self & yet the magistrate cannot therefor injoyn or forbid it his Christian subjects in the receiveing of the sacrament for in those that beleive transubstantiation it would be irreligious not to kneele & in those who thinke kneeling an act of worship it would be Idolatry to kneele to that which they thought but bread & wine & in others that thought it only a more reverend posture it would be neither.[2]

Locke probably agreed with the last group, as may be seen in the anecdote recounted in 'Conformitas'.[3] It is difficult to believe that he himself regarded such matters as being of great importance, but he did object very strongly to forcible imposition.

Locke not only denied the civil magistrate any power to institute religious ceremonies: he also came increasingly to restrict the powers of churches to do so. His reasons were essentially theological. In a commonplace book entry entitled 'Ecclesia', dated 1682, he argued that some ceremonies are unalterable, having been imposed by divine command, while others can be instituted by human decision, though only with the consent of the worshippers themselves:

noe body can impose any ceremonys unlesse positively & clearly by revelation injoynd, any farther then every one who joyns in the use of them is perswaded in his conscience they are acceptable to god. for if his conscience condemns any part of unrevealed worship he cannot by any sanction of men be obleiged to it.[4]

This gave churches a limited power to institute ceremonies, though only for their own members. However, in the *Epistola de Tolerantia* he adopted a more restrictive position:

Things in their own nature indifferent cannot, by human authority and decision, be made part of divine worship, and for this very reason, that they are indifferent.

---

[1] Below, p. 308.
[2] MS Locke c. 34, p. 119. This is one of the passages in Locke's hand.
[3] MS Locke d. 1, p. 5, below, pp. 386–7.   [4] MS Locke d. 10, p. 43, below, p. 392.

For since indifferent things are not naturally capable, by any virtue of their own, of propitiating the Deity, no human power or authority can confer on them so much dignity and excellence as to enable them to merit divine favour.... In divine worship things indifferent are not otherwise lawful than as they are instituted by God, and as he, by some positive command, has made them worthy of becoming part of the worship which his Divine Majesty will vouchsafe to accept at the hands of poor sinful men.[1]

It is clear that Locke felt very strongly about this. To use one of his own examples, actions such as eating fish and drinking beer are in themselves wholly indifferent, but if 'they are introduced into sacred ritual without divine authority, they are as abominable to God as the sacrifice of a dog'.[2] It is not for us to decide what God would find acceptable. All that churches—the plural should be noted—can do is to determine circumstances such as 'the time and place of worship, or the habit and posture of the worshipper',[3] and even here their power extends only to their own members: no church has any right whatever to interfere in the worship of another church.

It is by no means clear what caused Locke to begin writing the *Essay*, or what readership he had in mind. The notes on toleration in his commonplace books and his journal seem to have been made purely for his own use, but the *Essay* gives every appearance of having been written to persuade, or at least to inform, others. One obvious candidate is Locke's new patron.

Several writers on Locke have stated quite firmly that he wrote the *Essay* at Ashley's request. According to Maurice Cranston:

We have evidence of Locke's opinions in the form of a series of memoranda he prepared for Shaftesbury in 1667. It sets out in skeleton form some of the arguments for toleration that he was to expound in writings for publication in the 1680s and afterwards, but it is given a certain emphasis, imposed by the demands of Shaftesbury's campaign.[4]

A similar account was given by Peter Laslett:

on the subject of toleration [Locke's] association with the acknowledged champion of religious freedom swiftly transformed the traditionalist and authoritarian

---

[1] *Epistola de Tolerantia*, 105.   [2] Ibid. 107; the reference is to Deut. 23: 18.
[3] Ibid. 109.
[4] 'John Locke and the Case for Toleration', 80. A footnote (96) adds that 'It is possible that this memorandum has to be read as an exercise in "speech writing" done by Locke for Shaftesbury's use: and parts may even have been dictated by Shaftesbury.'

views written into the Oxford treatises. In 1667, during the first months of his residence at Exeter House, he composed an *Essay on Toleration* which turned his earlier arguments into a vigorous defence of the right of dissent, proceeding from analysis of the intellectual problem to positive recommendations about national policy. Advice of this sort was now expected of him . . . [1]

Laslett saw the *Essay* as the first of a succession of works written by Locke for his patron:

> But his important literary function was to write out for Shaftesbury's use an account of this or that political or social problem, telling him what had been thought or written about it, what arguments were likely to convince intelligent people of the correctness of a certain attitude to it. The successive drafts on toleration, economics, even perhaps on education and philosophy fit into this context . . . [2]

This is not a very accurate characterization of any of Locke's writings, and certainly not of the *Essay concerning Toleration*: far from telling the reader what had been thought or written about toleration, the *Essay* is wholly silent about the contemporary debate. One cannot rule out the possibility that Locke was asked by Ashley to prepare a summary of the works written for and against toleration in 1667–8, but if he did, no evidence whatever has survived.

The *Essay* does, however, have one stylistic peculiarity that may shed some light on Locke's intentions. This is his use of the second person. One example can be found at the end of the First Draft, and the full version of the *Essay* contains a great many more: 'As to secureing your safety & peace, there is but one way which is that your freinds at home be many & vigorous, & your enemys few & contemptible. or at least that the inequality of their number make it very dangerous & difficult for male-contents to molest you'.[3] There are other references to 'your subjects', 'your government', 'your profession', 'your people', 'your articles in speculative opinions', and 'your severall churches'.[4] On the face of it the only person who could have been addressed in this manner was the King, and it has been suggested that the *Essay* may have been written to be read by him.[5] This may at first sight seem plausible, but one can hardly suppose that anyone would have contemplated presenting Charles II with the *Essay* in anything like its present form. Monarchs expected to be approached in a suitably deferential manner, and though Charles

---

[1] Introduction to *Two Treatises of Government*, 29.　　　　[2] Ibid. 30.
[3] Below, pp. 289–90.　　　　[4] Below, pp. 290, 291, 293, 297, 302.
[5] Marshall, *John Locke*, 49, 54 n.; Baumgartner, *Naturrecht und Toleranz*, 79; Tully, 'Locke', 646.

cultivated a certain informality it would have been a gross solecism for anyone in Locke's position to have addressed him simply as 'you'.[1] One only has to compare the *Essay* with another contemporary document recommending toleration, now preserved in the Shaftesbury papers. Though only a rough draft, this was written in a much more obsequious manner, beginning with 'May it please your Majestie' and continuing with expressions like 'I shall not doubt, but your Majestie will pardon this my addresse', 'its humbly offered to your Majestie', and so on.[2]

Though it is hard to believe that anyone contemplated presenting the *Essay* to the King himself, it may be suggested that it was intended to influence government policy.[3] If this had been the aim, much of its content was ill-judged. Charles was doubtless quite willing to allow a fair degree of latitude on purely theological matters, but he valued his prerogatives and would not have relished being told that the magistrate's powers were limited to securing civil peace and the property of his subjects.

Any offence this might have caused would have been compounded by another of Locke's remarks, a later addition in the original manuscript:

Nor can there be a greater provocation to the supreme preserver of mankinde, then that the magistrate should make use of that power, which was given him only for the preservation of all his subjects, & every particular person amongst them, as far as it is practicable; should misuse it to the service of his pleasure, vanity, or passion, & imploy it to the disquieting or oppression of his fellow men, between whome & himself in respect of the King of Kings there is but a small & accidentall difference.[4]

The reference to 'the service of his pleasure, vanity, or passion' would not have gone down well, and the conclusion, reminiscent of Andrew Melville at his most forthright, might well have given Charles disagreeable memories of the ministers he had encountered in Scotland in 1650–1.

---

[1] When Locke wrote to Shaftesbury, he consistently addressed him as 'your Lordship': *Correspondence*, ii. 225–7, 360–5.

[2] PRO 30/24/49/8, printed (not entirely accurately) in Martyn and Kippis, *Shaftesbury*, i. 369–76, and Christie, vol. ii. app. I, pp. v–ix. This is an anonymous paper on the decay of trade, a state of affairs which it proposed to remedy by a variety of means, including religious toleration for Protestant dissenters. Both Martyn and Kippis and Christie ascribed it to Ashley. Cranston (pp. 130, 133) stated that in 1669 Ashley 'presented [it] to the King', who read it 'sympathetically'; no evidence is cited for this. Haley (pp. 257–8) argued that Ashley cannot have written it, and that it was 'passed on to him by the King'. The paper is undated, but a reference to 'the late Plague and Warre' suggests the late 1660s.

[3] For suggestions to this effect, see Laslett, Introduction to *Two Treatises of Government*, 29; Zagorin, *How the Idea of Religious Toleration Came to the West*, 251–2.

[4] Below, p. 279.

The King would have been similarly displeased by Locke's treatment of Catholics. Charles was outwardly a member of the Church of England, but his mother, wife, and favourite mistress (Castlemaine) were all Catholics, and he was widely—and correctly—rumoured to have leanings that way himself. His desire to extend toleration to Catholics was a matter of record:

We think it may become Us to avow to the World a due sense We have of the greatest part of Our Roman Catholick Subjects of this Kingdom, having deserved well from Our Royal Father of Blessed Memory, and from Us, and even from the Protestant Religion it self, in adhering to Us with their Lives and Fortunes for the maintenance of Our Crown in the Religion established, against those who under the name of zealous Protestants, imployed both Fire and Sword to overthrow them both. We shall with as much freedom profess unto the world, that it is not Our Intention to exclude Our Roman Catholick Subjects, who have so demeaned [i.e. conducted] themselves, from all share in the benefit of such an Act, as in pursuance of Our Promises, the wisdom of Our Parliament shall think fit to offer unto Us for the ease of tender Consciences.[1]

Locke took exactly the opposite view:

It being impossible either by indulgence or severity to make Papists whilst Papists freinds to your government being enemys to it both in their principles & interest, & therefor considering them as irreconcileable enemys of whose fidelity you can never be securd, whilst they owe a blinde obedience to an infalible pope, who has the keys of their consciences tied to his girdle, & can upon occasion dispense with all their oaths promises & the obligations they have to their prince espetially being an heritick & arme them to the disturbance of the government I think they ought not to enjoy the benefit of toleration[2]

One cannot imagine Charles being persuaded by this, or being moved by Locke's claim that 'the interest of the King of England as head of the Protestants will be much improvd by the discountenanceing of popery amongst us'.[3] This was not at all how he saw his role in international affairs, though it was only after 1672 that most of his subjects became aware of this.

This use of the second person is not unique to the *Essay concerning Toleration*: it may also be found, though not as frequently, in Locke's 1668 paper on interest:

If therefore Use be lessened and you cannot tye forainers to your termes then the ill effects fall onely on your owne Landholders and Artisans—If forainers can be

---

[1] *His Majesties Declaration to All His loving Subjects, December 26, 1662*, 10–11.
[2] Below, p. 291.   [3] Below, p. 292.

forced by your Law to lend you money onely at your owne rate or not lend at all, is it not more Likely they will rather take it home and thinck it saffer in their owne country at 4 per Cent: then abroade? Nor can their over-plus of money bring them to lend it you on your termes for when your Merchants want of Money shall have sunck the price of your Market, A Dutchman will find it more gaines to buy your commodityes himselfe. . . . But that a law cannot keepe your owne subjects much less straingers from takeing more use then you set . . . [1]

Another reference to 'your people' occurs in his 1674 'Notes on Trade', where domestic manufacture is defined as 'all labour imploid by your people in prepareing commodities for the consumption, either of your owne people . . . or of foreigners'.[2] No one has ever supposed that this was written for Charles II.

Other examples of Locke using the second person when writing purely for his own purposes can be found in his journal:

But let us suppose yet that all dissenters are in error are out of their wits. esto. but your law found them in this delirium and will you make a law that will hang all that are beside themselves. But we fear their rage and violence. If you fear them only because they are capeable of a raging fit you may as well fear all other men who are liable to the same distemper. If you fear it because you treat them ill and that produces some symptom of it you ought to change your method and not punish them for what you fear because you go the way to produce it.[3]

Locke's use of the second person in the *Essay concerning Toleration* and the 1668 paper on interest may indicate that he expected them to be read by persons in authority, but even this is far from certain. The paper on interest was certainly read outside Exeter House: there is a scribal copy of the original paper—i.e. excluding both the 1668 supplement and the further material added in 1674—among the papers of Sir William Coventry, a member of the Treasury Commission.[4] No similar evidence has come to light regarding the *Essay concerning Toleration*, but it is quite possible that the fair copy in the Shaftesbury papers was passed on to others.

It is not possible to say what works if any Locke consulted while writing the *Essay concerning Toleration*. His library catalogues list several

---

[1] *Locke on Money*, 169–70. Most of this appears virtually unchanged in *Some Considerations of the Consequences of the Lowering of Interest, and Raising the Value of Money* (ibid. 226–7) though the last sentence with its reference to 'your owne subjects' was omitted. A subsequent reference to 'your owne subjects' was changed to 'your own People', ibid. 173, 234.   [2] MS Locke c. 30, fo. 18^r, *Locke on Money*, 485.
[3] MS Locke f. 1, p. 426 (23 Aug. 1676), punctuation added.
[4] BL, Add. MS 32094, fos. 289–93.

well-known defences of toleration, including Acontius' *Stratagemata Satanae* and Castellio's *De Hereticis Gladio Coercendis*, as well as works by Coornhert and Episcopius, but it would appear from various booklists preserved among his papers that they were all purchased in Holland in the later 1680s.[1] There is no evidence of his reading any of these works in the 1660s. In 1659 he read and commented favourably upon Henry Stubbe's *An Essay in Defence of the Good Old Cause*,[2] but no evidence has yet come to light indicating that he ever read the tolerationist writings of Roger Williams, John Goodwin, or any of the Levellers.[3]

Patrick Kelly has remarked that what is striking about Locke's 1668 paper on money 'is its lack of polemical intent and the effort to go beyond appearances and analyse what was really at issue'.[4] Exactly the same can be said of the *Essay concerning Toleration*. The arguments Locke employed were his own, and it is clear from his autograph, and especially from the chaotically disorganized early pages of the Rough Draft, that he worked them out as he was writing. Above all he was determined to get down to first principles and to found his argument for toleration on a general account of the purpose of religion and the powers of the civil magistrate. It was this characteristically *philosophical* enquiry that he proposed to undertake, one that prefigures his attempt in the *Essay concerning Human Understanding* to determine the true extent of the knowledge to which mankind may properly aspire.

WRITINGS ON CHURCH AND STATE, 1668–1674

Queries on Scottish Church Government

The Scottish Reformation of 1559–60 brought into existence a church order which was not straightforwardly either presbyterian or episcopalian, as those terms came later to be understood.[5] By the late 1570s two opposing parties had formed: one, drawing inspiration from Theodore

---

[1] *LL* 7, 618, 620, 843, 844, 1060; MSS Locke b. 2, fos. 43ʳ, 86ᵛ, 87ʳ, 91ʳ, 95ʳ, 98ʳ, 99ʳ; f. 9, p. 100; f. 29, p. 74. Copies of Acontius and Castellio were sold to Ashley in 1690, MSS Locke f. 10, pp. 28, 32; c. 1, p. 192. Locke made notes from *Stratagemata Satanae* in 1696, MS Locke d. 10, p. 169.

[2] *LL* 2800ª; Locke to Stubbe, Sept 1659, *Correspondence*, i. 109–12.

[3] For the lack of Leveller influence on Locke, see Aylmer, 'Locke no Leveller'. There is also no evidence of any Leveller writings being bought for Shaftesbury's library.

[4] *Locke on Money*, 9.

[5] 'The system set up in the 1560s cannot be called presbyterian, and if it must be explained at all in later terminology, it might best be described as congregationalism tempered by episcopacy and Erastianism', Donaldson, *The Scottish Reformation*, 146–7.

Beza in Geneva and organized in Scotland by Andrew Melville, sought the removal of the remaining bishops and their replacement by a fully presbyterian system; the other, preferred by James VI, sought to revive the episcopate and establish a system broadly similar to that which existed in England and in the Lutheran states of Denmark and Sweden. The outcome that emerged by the end of James's reign was a compromise. The bishops had been restored to the thirteen pre-Reformation dioceses (a fourteenth, Edinburgh, was added in 1633), while at the same time the country was covered by a system of presbyteries, formed out of groups of parishes. The bishops lacked many of the powers exercised by their predecessors before the Reformation (and by their contemporaries in England), acting instead as chairmen of their diocesan synods and administering their dioceses in collaboration with their leading ministers. In 1638, following Charles I's ill-advised attempt to impose a new prayer book on an unappreciative population, the bishops were driven out and a purely presbyterian system was reintroduced.

Charles II's experience of Scottish presbyterianism in 1650–1 gave him a profound aversion to the system and its more zealous advocates which he never thereafter lost.[1] During the first months that followed the Restoration he kept his intentions obscure, but in August 1661 the restoration of episcopal government was announced. Only one of the former bishops, Thomas Sydserf of Galloway, was still alive, and in December four new bishops were consecrated in Westminster Abbey by the Bishop of London and three of his colleagues. Later consecrations were performed in Scotland, but the restored episcopate was seen by many Scots as an alien importation from England.[2]

In Scotland there was no equivalent to the English Act of Uniformity, and the return of the bishops was not accompanied by the reissue of the service book. Ministers were not required to use the Book of Common Prayer, let alone give their unfeigned assent and consent to it. There were no altars or surplices, no kneeling at communion or use of the cross in baptism, indeed no formal liturgy of any kind.[3] As contemporaries themselves noticed, the forms of service hardly differed from those used by the Presbyterians in England.[4] This meant that disputes about

---

[1] It was not, he told Lauderdale, 'a religion for gentlemen', Burnet, i. 195.

[2] The fullest accounts are Buckroyd, *Church and State in Scotland*, chs. 3–4; Davies and Hardacre, 'The Restoration of the Scottish Episcopacy'. There are briefer accounts in Donaldson, *James V–James VII*, 360–8; Hutton, *Charles II*, 149–50, 160–2, 178–80.

[3] Donaldson, *James V–James VII*, 364; Foster, *Bishop and Presbytery*, 125–6.

[4] Foster, *Bishop and Presbytery*, 125–7; Mathieson, *Politics and Religion*, ii. 258.

worship and ritual, the issues that had concerned Locke and Bagshaw in 1660, were not of great importance in Scotland. The really divisive issue was church government, above all episcopacy.

The Restoration reintroduced the hybrid episcopalian–presbyterian system that had existed before 1638. This was very unlike anything to be found in England, where the system of ecclesiastical government had been taken over largely unchanged from the pre-Reformation church. The government of the Scottish church was through a hierarchy of courts. At the lowest level were the parochial or kirk sessions, which were responsible for the affairs of each parish; they met weekly and were attended by the minister and by the elders and deacons of the parish. Parishes were grouped together into presbyteries, whose meetings were attended by the ministers of the parishes and any other licensed preachers in the area. These bodies met monthly and performed much of the work of inspection and discipline within the church. Diocesan synods normally met twice yearly, in the spring and autumn, and were attended by all members of the presbyteries in the diocese; the bishop acted as moderator and had the power of veto. An Act of Parliament in 1663[1] set up a National Synod, corresponding to the previous General Assembly, but despite periodic agitation it was never allowed to meet. The Archbishop of St Andrews would have been the president; the other members would have been the Archbishop of Glasgow and the remaining bishops, all the deans and archdeacons, and two representative ministers from each presbytery.[2]

Though the Scottish Restoration settlement made many more concessions to the Presbyterians than did the English, it proved much more divisive.[3] Episcopacy had shallower roots and the Presbyterians were more numerous and far more militant. They also showed no signs of disappearing. After the Pentland Rising of November 1666 there was a widespread feeling that coercion alone would not succeed and that some form of conciliation would be needed.[4] The first steps seem to have been taken in the autumn of 1667. In September the Archbishop of Glasgow, an opponent of conciliation in any form, complained of 'new propositions

---

[1] *Acts of the Parliaments of Scotland*, vii. 465.

[2] The account below is based on Foster, *Bishop and Presbytery*, ch. 4.

[3] About 270 ministers were deprived, about a quarter of the total and a higher proportion than in England. Most of these were in the south-west: for details, see Mathieson, *Politics and Religion*, ii. 193 n.

[4] Buckroyd, *Church and State in Scotland*, ch. 6; Cowan, *The Scottish Covenanters*, ch. 5.

made for securing the peace of the state, which (they say) will in due tyme settle and secure the Church'.[1]

Two quite separate schemes were put forward. Robert Leighton, Bishop of Dunblane, was prevailed upon to go to London where he had two audiences with Charles II. He proposed a scheme of comprehension (in Scotland called accommodation) which went far beyond anything put forward in the contemporary English comprehension proposals, and which would, as even Burnet admitted, have 'left little more than the name of a bishop'.[2] Nothing came of it: Leighton did not have the backing of his fellow bishops or of the secular rulers of Scotland, above all the Duke of Lauderdale.

Lauderdale was not a committed episcopalian. As Clarendon had once observed, he 'would acquiesce in whatever the King determines about the Church if he thought the Kingdom to be of that mind; conscience for the peace prevails more with him than conscience for the purity of religion'.[3] His policy was to divide the Presbyterians by allowing moderate and peaceable ministers to be appointed to vacant livings while suppressing unlawful and seditious conventicles.[4] On 7 June 1669 the King sent the Scottish Privy Council a letter of indulgence which can in many ways be seen as a precursor of the English Declaration of Indulgence of 1672, though it differed in that it indulged nonconforming ministers inside the church rather than outside it.[5] This was purely an act of the prerogative and of dubious legality, but it was followed in November by a statute asserting the royal supremacy in all ecclesiastical causes, a measure that indicated very clearly where the government's priorities lay.[6] As Lauderdale was able to report to the King, 'Never was king so absolute as you in poor old Scotland.'[7]

Locke's queries coincide in time with these moves to revise the Scottish settlement, but their connection with them, if there was one, remains obscure. They were concerned with technical detail, not high policy or

---

[1] Alexander Burnet to Sheldon, 23 Sept. 1667, *Lauderdale Papers*, vol. ii. app., pp. xlix–li. See also Lauderdale to Sharp, 2 Oct. 1667, *Lauderdale Correspondence, 1660–77*, 261–3.

[2] Burnet, i. 443, 497–9; Alexander Burnet to Sheldon, 9 Aug. 1667, *Lauderdale Papers*, vol. ii. app., pp. xlviii–xlix. For Leighton's earlier proposals, see Butler, *Robert Leighton*, 403–13, 422–32.

[3] Hyde to Middleton, 26 Mar. 1661, *Calendar of the Clarendon State Papers*, v. 88.

[4] Charles II to Lauderdale, undated, *Lauderdale Papers*, ii. 185–6.

[5] *The Register of the Privy Council of Scotland*, 3rd ser., iii. 38–40; Burnet, i. 507.

[6] *Acts of the Parliaments of Scotland*, vii. 554; Burnet, i. 511–13.

[7] Lauderdale to Charles II, 16 Nov. 1669, *Lauderdale Papers*, ii. 163–4.

general principle, and manifest some knowledge of the organization of the Scottish church. The source of his information has not been identified, but his use of the distinctive (and to many Englishmen wholly unfamiliar) vocabulary which its members employed—'exercises', 'common heads', and the like—together with an evident uncertainty about their precise significance, suggests that he was drawing on a written, perhaps printed, source in which these terms were used without being adequately explained. Whether Locke began these enquiries on his own initiative or was given the task by Ashley is unknown, but it is not unlikely that someone in Ashley's circle thought it worth investigating whether Scotland might provide an example for a revised and more comprehensive settlement of the Church of England. Just how many of the English Presbyterians would have conformed to a church remodelled in this way can only be conjectured, but by the time Locke was drawing up his queries it had become only too clear that many of their Scottish counterparts had chosen not to, and that the bitterness of religious divisions in Scotland was greater even than in England. There was no possibility whatever that Archbishop Sheldon and his colleagues would voluntarily have relinquished a significant part of their powers in order to accommodate the Presbyterians, and though the King and Parliament could, if they had been of one mind, have imposed such a settlement on them, neither had any such intention.

Notes on Samuel Parker's Discourse of Ecclesiastical Politie

Towards the end of 1669[1] an anonymous work was published in London, with the title *A Discourse of Ecclesiastical Politie: Wherein The Authority of the Civil Magistrate Over the Consciences of Subjects in Matters of Religion is Asserted; The Mischiefs and Inconveniences of Toleration are Represented, And All Pretenses Pleaded in Behalf of Liberty of Conscience are Fully Answered.*[2] Its author was Samuel Parker, a rising young Anglican divine with an unusual background. He had been born into a strongly parliamentarian family and appears to have had a strict puritan upbringing.

---

[1] It bore a date of 1670 on the title-page, but was entered into the Stationers' Company register (ii. 405) on 23 September 1669 and listed in the Term Catalogue for 22 November (i. 21).

[2] There are two editions with 1670 on the title-page, both published by John Martyn. In the second the title was amended to read '... *Matters of External Religion* ...', the text was reset, and the irregular signatures and pagination were corrected; for details, see Black, 'The Unrecorded Second Edition of Samuel Parker's *A Discourse of Ecclesiastical Politie* (1670)'. A third edition with the same title as the second was published in 1671.

In 1656 he was sent to Wadham College, Oxford, where, according to Anthony Wood,

he did, according to his former breeding, lead a strict and religious life, fasted, prayed with other Students weekly together, and for their refection feeding on thin broth, made of Oatmeal and water only, they were commonly called *Grewellers*. He and they did also usually go every week, or oftner, to an house in the Parish of *Halywell* near their College, possessed by *Bess Hampton* an old and crooked Maid that drove the trade of Laundrey; who being from her youth very much given to the Presbyterian Religion had frequent meetings for the *Godly party* . . . [1]

After the Restoration Parker turned violently against his upbringing and became a bitter opponent of the nonconformists. He was ordained in 1664, and in 1667 was made one of Sheldon's chaplains. He does not appear to have participated in the pamphlet debate over the comprehension and toleration proposals of 1667–8, but his *Discourse of Ecclesiastical Politie* may be seen as a belated contribution. The title recalls Hooker's great work, and Parker may have envisaged himself in a similar role. He made, however, no attempt to imitate Hooker's measured and urbane prose: the most striking thing about the book is its intemperate and abusive style, with frequent references to 'Wild and Fanatique Rabble', 'Wild and Fanatick Consciences', 'Hot-headed and Brain-sick people', 'Religious lunacies', 'Madmen', 'vermin', 'Wild and Giddy People', 'Wild and extravagant Pretenses', 'giddy and distemper'd Zealots', and so on.[2] Parker appears to have been a very bad judge of his own character, assuring his readers that he was 'a Person of such a tame and soft humour, and so cold a Complexion, that he thinks himself scarce capable of hot and passionate Impressions'.[3] This is not how his readers saw him.

Parker's *Discourse* caused dismay and anger among those he had vilified, and responses were quick to appear. The most considerable was by John Owen: *Truth and Innocence Vindicated: In a Survey of a Discourse Concerning Ecclesiastical Polity; And the Authority of the Civil Magistrate over the Consciences of Subjects in Matters of Religion*. Owen was less

---

[1] Wood, *Athenae Oxonienses*, ii. 616. Marvell gave a similar account in *The Rehearsal Transpros'd: The Second Part*, 181.

[2] *A Discourse of Ecclesiastical Politie*, pp. iv, xl, l, 21, 58, 118, 139, 197; cited below as *Ecclesiastical Politie*.

[3] Ibid., p. iii. Parker persisted in this delusion: 'My humour is neither Fierce nor Abusive; I love not to treat an Adversary with rough Language and unkind Words', *A Defence and Continuation of the Ecclesiastical Politie*, Preface, sig. A4^r.

vituperative than Parker, but hardly less severe, describing Parker's version of Christianity as 'the rudest, most imperfect, and weakest *Scheme of Christian Religion* that ever yet I saw'.[1]

In 1670, perhaps as a reward for his efforts, Parker was appointed Archdeacon of Canterbury. Later that year he responded to his critics with *A Defence and Continuation of the Ecclesiastical Politie*.[2] In 1672 he wrote *A Preface Shewing what grounds there are of Fears and Jealousies of Popery*, which was prefixed to Bishop John Bramhall's *Vindication of himself and the Episcopal Clergy from the Presbyterian Charge of Popery*. Despite its title Parker's preface was largely an attack on nonconformity; according to one of Baxter's correspondents it was 'generally very much disgusted by moderate & wise men of all parties as the most feirce & intemperate language that hath been committed to press this many yeares'.[3] It provoked Andrew Marvell into writing *The Rehearsal Transpros'd* (1672), the aim of which was to make Parker a figure of ridicule.[4] Parker responded with *A Reproof to the Rehearsal Transpros'd* (1673), which Marvell described as 'the rudest book, one or other, that ever was publisht (I may say), since the first invention of printing'.[5] Marvell countered with *The Rehearsal Transpros'd: The Second Part* (1673), which heaped further scorn on Parker. Parker did not reply, and it was generally acknowledged, even by those who had some sympathies with him, that he had the worse of the encounter.[6]

This was not the only embarrassment he suffered during those years. One of his duties as Archbishop's chaplain was licensing books on religion, and in 1673 he unwisely licensed a short pamphlet entitled *Mr. Baxter Baptiz'd in Bloud; or, A Sad History of the unparallel'd cruelty of the Anabaptists in New England. Faithfully Relating the Cruel, Barbarous and Bloudy Murther of Mr. Baxter an Orthodox Minister, who was kill'd by the Anabaptists, and his Skin most cruelly flead off from his Body*. This was

[1] Owen, *Truth and Innocence*, 198.

[2] It bore a date of 1671 on the title-page but was entered into the Stationers' Company register (ii. 417) on 24 October 1670. According to Baxter, 'Parker contriv'd to have his Answer ready against the Sessions of the Parliament (in Octob. 1670.)', *Reliquiae Baxterianae*, pt. III, §95.

[3] Robert Middleton to Baxter, 26 Feb. 1673, *Baxter Correspondence*, ii. 143. See also Humfrey, *The Authority of the Magistrate*, 4.

[4] Locke possessed two copies of the first part (*LL* 1931, 1932) and one of the second (*LL* 1933), as well as a copy of Parker's reply (*LL* 2199). For a suggestion that Marvell may have made use of Locke's library, see Patterson and Dzelzainis, 'Marvell and the Earl of Anglesey', 720–2.

[5] Marvell to Sir Edward Harley, 3 May 1673, in *Poems and Letters*, ii. 328.

[6] Wood, *Athenae Oxonienses*, ii. 619.

supposedly written by one Benjamin Baxter, the victim's brother, though Marvell thought that Parker wrote it himself.[1] The story was investigated by the Privy Council and found to be entirely false, and Parker had to make a shamefaced apology.[2] The whole affair was described with relish in a pamphlet, *Forgery Detected and Innocency Vindicated*, published by John Darby, Marvell's publisher.

These misfortunes did nothing to mellow Parker, and he retained his violent antipathy not only to nonconformists but to anyone who might be thought to sympathize with them. Burnet described one characteristic incident:

When the *Prince* and *Princess* of *Orange* were Married [1677], he was perhaps the only Man in *England* that expressed his uneasiness at that happy Conjunction, in so clownish a manner, that when their *highnesses* past thro *Canterbury* he would not go with the rest of that Body, to which he was so long a Blemish, to pay his Duty to them, and when he was Asked the Reason, he said, *He could have no regard to a Calvinist Prince*.[3]

Parker's prospects suffered a further setback when his patron, Archbishop Sheldon, died in 1676. He was on bad terms with William Sancroft, Sheldon's successor,[4] and his career was only rescued from the doldrums by James II, who after his break with the Tories needed suitably compliant clergy to forward his ecclesiastical policies. Parker was an ideal choice, and in August 1686 was nominated to the see of Oxford in succession to John Fell.[5] It was not an appointment greatly welcomed: Burnet thought that he had been 'picked out of the body of the English clergy to betray and destroy it'.[6]

Parker did his best to please his royal master. In his earlier writings he had insisted that religious uniformity was essential for the maintenance of civil society, but now he backed James's campaign for the repeal of the Test Acts, and in 1688 he published a pamphlet entitled *Reasons for Abrogating the Test, Imposed upon All Members of Parliament*. This change of line did not go unnoticed, and he was promptly answered by a pamphlet entitled *Sam. Ld. Bp. of Oxon, His Celebrated Reasons for Abrogating the Test, and notion of Idolatry, Answered by Samuel, Arch-Deacon of*

---

[1] *The Rehearsal Transpros'd*, 196.

[2] NA, PC 2/64, p. 30; SP 29/335/235; Bodl., MS Tanner 290, fo. 202; *Reliquiae Baxterianae*, pt. III, §236; Henry Ball to Joseph Williamson, 9 June 1673, *Letters to Williamson*, i. 28.

[3] *An Enquiry into the Reasons for Abrogating the Test*, 8. Locke owned a copy, *LL* 2200.

[4] Spurr, *The Restoration Church of England*, 89, 157.   [5] NA, SP 44/57, p. 130.

[6] Burnet, *Supplement*, 216.

Canterbury, which quoted back to him his earlier arguments in the *Discourse of Ecclesiastical Politie*.[1]

Parker's last appointment, and the one that did most to destroy his reputation, was as President of Magdalen College, Oxford. In August 1687 the King ordered the fellows of Magdalen to admit him as President, against their wishes and contrary to the college statutes.[2] His time there was not a happy one. Careerist though he was, Parker retained some loyalty to the Church of England and resented being required to admit a succession of Catholic fellows. One of his servants described his last days:

> I am sure I never saw him in such a passion in the sixteen years I lived with him. He walked up and down the room, and smote his breast and said, 'There is no trust in man: there is no trust in Princes. Is this the kindness the King promised me? To set me here to make me his tool and his prop? To place me with a company of men, which he knows I hate the conversation of!' So he sat down in his chair, and fell into a convulsive fit, and never went down stairs more till he was carried down.[3]

He died on 20 March 1688.[4] Perhaps he was fortunate to die when he did, though previous form suggests he would have found some way of coming to terms with the Revolution.

Parker was an ambitious ecclesiastical careerist with deplorable controversial manners, and it is very easy to form an unfavourable opinion of him. Many of his contemporaries did. Burnet, who clearly detested him, described him as 'a man that has no regard either to religion or virtue, but will accomodate himself to everything that may gratify either his covetousness or his ambition'.[5] Later historians have echoed such views.[6] Parker was, however, very far from being a fool, and his opponents had good reason to take him seriously.

---

[1] Locke appears to have read this with Benjamin Furly: see Furly to Locke, 25 Nov./5 Dec. 1690, *Correspondence*, iv. 172.

[2] NA, SP 44/57, p. 177. Parker's admission is described in Tyrrell to Locke, 2 Nov. 1687, *Correspondence*, iii. 287–9.

[3] Mary Harding to Samuel Parker, undated, in *Magdalen College and King James II*, 240.

[4] Wood, *Athenae Oxonienses*, ii. 621; Evelyn, *Diary*, iv. 574 (23 Mar. 1688).

[5] Burnet, *Supplement*, 215–16. This was written while Parker was still alive, but Burnet's later verdict was not much kinder: 'Parker . . . was full of satirical vivacity, and was considerably learned; but was a man of no judgment, and of as little virtue, and as to religion he seemed rather to have become quite impious', Burnet, i. 467.

[6] Macaulay described him as 'a parasite, whose religion, if he had any religion, was that of Rome, and who called himself a Protestant only because he was encumbered with a wife', *History of England*, ii. 740.

There is no evidence that Locke and Parker ever met, and one can be quite sure that neither would have found the other's company or opinions congenial.[1] Nevertheless, they had more in common than one might initially suppose. In philosophical matters Parker was a modern, with little time for old opinions. In 1666 he published *A Free and Impartial Censure of the Platonick Philosophie*, which included a defence of the new philosophy:

The cheif reason therefore, why I prefer the Mechanical and Experimental Philosophie before the *Aristotelean*, is not so much because of its so much greater certainty, but because it puts inquisitive men into a method to attain it, whereas the other serves only to obstruct their industry by amusing them with empty and insignificant Notions. And therefore we may rationally expect a greater Improvement of Natural Philosophie from the *Royal Society*, (if they pursue their design) then it has had in all former ages . . .[2]

Parker was himself elected a Fellow of the Royal Society in June 1666—two years before Locke—having been proposed by John Wilkins.[3]

Opposition to Aristotelianism was only one of several areas where Parker's views were close to Locke's—*A Free and Impartial Censure* also contained a short but forceful attack on the doctrine of innate ideas.[4] Both men also saw religion primarily in moral terms:

And this is the substance and main Design of all the Laws of Religion, to oblige Mankind to behave themselves in all their actions as becomes Creatures endued with Reason and Understanding, and in ways sutable to Rational Beings, to prepare and qualifie themselves for the state of Glory and Immortality. And as this is the proper End of all Religion, That Mankind might live happily here, and happily hereafter; so to this end nothing contributes more than the Practice of all Moral Vertues . . .[5]

---

[1] There is a reference to 'our old Friend Dr: P. Bishop of oxford' in Tyrrell to Locke, 29 Aug. 1687, *Correspondence*, iii. 257, but this is presumably sarcastic.

[2] *A Free and Impartial Censure*, 45. Parker was quite prepared to use the concepts of the mechanical philosophy to give a reductive account of religious experience as the 'meer results of a natural and mechanical Enthusiasm', *A Defence and Continuation of the Ecclesiastical Politie*, 342.

[3] Hunter, *The Royal Society and its Fellows*, 198. Locke was elected in November 1668, ibid. 206.

[4] *A Free and Impartial Censure*, 55–7; Yolton, *John Locke and the Way of Ideas*, 44–5.

[5] *Ecclesiastical Politie*, 68. Compare 'Pacific Christians' (1688): 'Since the Christian religion we profess is not a notional science to furnish speculation to the brain or discourse to the tongue, but a rule of righteousness to influence our lives . . . We profess the only businesse of our publique assemblys to be to exhort thereunto, & laying aside all controversye & speculative questions instruct & incourage one another in the dutys of a good life, which is acknowledged to be the great businesse of true religion', MS Locke c. 27, fo. 80^{ar-v}, Goldie, 305.

In adopting such a view of religion Parker was (characteristically) moving with an increasingly fashionable tide.[1] His fundamentally moralistic conception of Christianity had much in common with that of moderate churchmen such as Wilkins and Tillotson, both deeply distrusted by the High Church party: what distinguished him from them was his intemperate language and his total unwillingness to make even the smallest concessions to Protestant dissenters. Parker cannot properly be described as a High Churchman; it is perhaps best to see him occupying the extreme anti-tolerationist end of the latitudinarian position.

For Parker the only alternative to moralistic religion was the enthusiasm of the sects: 'all Religion must of necessity be resolv'd into Enthusiasm or Morality. The former is meer Imposture, and therefore all that is true must be reduced to the latter ... '.[2] Apart from the abusive language, it was this aspect of Parker's book that his nonconformist critics most disliked.[3] They were dismayed at what they saw as the transformation of Christianity from a religion of divine grace to one centred around the cultivation of moral virtue. Parker did not discard the traditional language of grace, but his account of what it was might have surprised St Paul:

all that the Scripture intends by the Graces of the Spirit, are only Vertuous Qualities of the Soul, that are therefore styled Graces, because they were derived purely from Gods free Grace and Goodness, in that in the first Ages of Christianity he was pleased, out of his infinite concern for its Propagation, in a miraculous Manner to inspire its Converts with all sorts of Vertue.[4]

Owen was appalled, and in response set out a detailed account of how grace differs from virtue; his arguments were repeated a few years later at even greater length by Robert Ferguson.[5]

---

[1] Exemplified by *The Whole Duty of Man* (1658), which was even recommended by Hobbes, *Behemoth*, 47. A general account of the changing outlook is given in Rivers, *Reason, Grace and Sentiment*, i. 77–88.   [2] *Ecclesiastical Politie*, 76–7.

[3] *Insolence and Impudence triumphant*, 12; R[obert] F[erguson], *A Sober Enquiry into the Nature, Measure, and Principle of Moral Virtue, in Distinction from Gospel-Holiness*, 3; *The Rehearsal Transpros'd*, 48, 53–4.

[4] *Ecclesiastical Politie*, 72. 'My plain design was to represent Grace and Vertue as the same thing', *A Defence and Continuation of the Ecclesiastical Politie*, 329.

[5] Owen, *Truth and Innocence*, 213–27; R.F., *A Sober Enquiry*. Locke was quite prepared to import the notion of virtue into the New Testament, where (as Owen and Ferguson rightly remarked) it is scarcely to be found. In the *Essay concerning Human Understanding* (I. i. 5) he quoted the Greek text of 2 Pet. 1: 3, πάντα πρὸς ζωὴν καὶ εὐσέβειαν. The Authorized Version translates this quite literally as 'all things that pertain unto life and Godliness'; Locke paraphrased it as 'Whatsoever is necessary for the Conveniences of Life, and Information of Vertue'.

However unsatisfactory it may have seemed to Owen, Parker's viewpoint was in no sense secular. Religion is about the rational pursuit of happiness in this world and the next.[1] On this issue Locke's views were much closer to Parker's than they were to Owen's, and Owen's comment on Parker, that 'the *Scheme* he hath given us of Religion, or Religious duties, wherein there is mention neither of Sin, nor a Redeemer, without which no man can entertain any one true notion of *Christian Religion*, would rather bespeak him a Philosopher, than a Christian',[2] prefigures similar objections made by John Edwards and others to the *Reasonableness of Christianity*.

Parker also agreed with Locke in denying the magistrate any power over purely speculative beliefs:

Hence it is that the Divine Providence is so highly solicitous not to have it farther restrained than needs must; and therefore in all Matters of pure Speculation it leaves the Mind of Man entirely free to judge of the Truth and Falshood of things, and will not suffer it to be usurp't upon by any Authority whatsoever: And whatsoever Opinion any man entertains of things of this Nature, he injures no man by it, and therefore no man can have any reason to commence any Quarrel with him for it; Every man here judges for himself and not for others, and Matters of meer Opinion having no reference to the Publick, there is no need of any Publick Judgment to determine them.[3]

This might seem to open the door to a general religious toleration, but in Parker's eyes it did not. The problem with the fanatics—a term that he (unlike Locke) had no qualms about applying to the entire body of nonconformists—was that their beliefs extended to matters that were in no sense purely speculative:

There are some Sects whose Principles, and some Persons whose Tempers will not suffer them to live peaceably in any Common-wealth. For what if some men believe, That if Princes refuse to reform Religion themselves, 'tis lawful for their Godly Subjects to do it, and that by Violence and force of Arms? What if they believe, That Princes are but Executioners of the Decrees of the Presbytery; and that in case of Disobedience to their Spiritual Governors, they may be Excommunicated, and by consequence Deposed? What if they believe, That Dominion is founded in Grace; and therefore that all wicked Kings forfeit their

---

[1] 'Man is sent into the World to live happily here, and prepare himself for Happiness hereafter; this is attain'd by the practise of Moral Vertues and Pious Devotions,' *Ecclesiastical Politie*, 80. On the pursuit of happiness, see Rivers, 'Grace, Holiness and the Pursuit of Happiness', 53–5, 57–9.　　　　[2] Owen, *Truth and Innocence*, 10.
[3] *Ecclesiastical Politie*, 93.

Crowns, and that it is in the Power of the People of God to bestow them where they please?[1]

Locke would have agreed with this—he had used similar examples in the *Essay concerning Toleration* and would use them again in the *Epistola de Tolerantia*.[2] The difference between them is that by 1667 at least Locke saw most Protestant nonconformists as sober and peaceable men who desired only to worship God in a manner acceptable to their own consciences. Parker did not: he had a very low opinion of the rationality and good sense of 'the Common Herd',[3] as he called them, and was obsessed with the dangers their folly in religious matters presented to civil order. This was a threat that was always liable to reappear whenever discipline was relaxed:

There is no Observation in the world establish'd upon a more certain and universal Experience, than that the generality of mankind are not so obnoxious to any sort of Follies and Vices, as to wild and unreasonable conceits of Religion; and that, when their heads are possess'd with them, there are no principles so pregnant with mischief and disturbance as they. And if Princes would but consider, how liable mankind are to abuse themselves with serious and conscientious Villanies, they would quickly see it to be absolutely necessary to the Peace and Happiness of their Kingdoms, that there be set up a more severe Government over mens Consciences and Religious perswasions, than over their Vices and Immoralities.[4]

This last point went down very badly with Parker's nonconformist critics, for whom Charles II's government was far too ready to punish religious dissent and far too lax in suppressing vice and immorality. Locke shared their view. In the *Essay concerning Toleration* he had recommended 'makeing & executeing strict laws concerning vertue & vice, but makeing the termes of church communion as large as may be',[5] and the Critical Notes on Stillingfleet contain a complaint that

a known drunken or debaucht person if he does but bow at his [Jesus's] name, & conforme zealously to other outward imposd ceremonyes shall be a good Member of the Church & scape all ecclesiastical censure when a sober, & devout Christian endeavouring with a sincere obedience to observe all the rules of the Gospel shall passe for a phanatick because he cannot bow at the name of Jesus.[6]

---

[1] Ibid. 147–8.

[2] *An Essay concerning Toleration*, below, pp. 288–9; *Epistola de Tolerantia*, 85, 131–3.

[3] *Ecclesiastical Politie*, 153.   [4] Ibid., pp. lii–liii.   [5] Below, p. 302.

[6] MS Locke c. 34, p. 144, in Tyrrell's hand with corrections by Locke. In Locke's proposals for the reform of the poor law (1697), he complained of the 'relaxation of Discipline and Corruption of Manners', proposing that the debauchery of the poor should be restrained by 'a strict execution of the Laws provided against it', NA, CO 388/5, fos. 232[r], 232[v], Goldie, 184.

Locke and Parker also disagreed fundamentally on the nature of political authority. Parker was a thoroughgoing absolutist and, like Filmer, a patriarchalist:

And hence the Wisdom of Providence . . . so ordered Affairs, that no man could be born into the World without being subject to some Superiour: every Father being by Nature Vested with a Right to govern his Children. And the first Governments in the world were establisht purely upon the natural Rights of Paternal Authority, which afterward grew up to a Kingly Power by the encrease of Posterity. . . . and hence it came to pass that in the first ages of the World, Monarchy was its only Government . . . [1]

Locke's response was exactly the same as he later used against Filmer.

Whether allowing the paternall right of government (which is asserted not proved) that paternall monarchy descended upon death of the father it descended wholy to the eldest sonne, or else all the brothers had an equall power over their respective issues? if the first then Monarchy is certainly jure naturali, but then there can be but one rightfull monarch in the whole world i.e. the right heire of Adam, if the second, all governments whether monarchicall or other is only from the consent of the people.[2]

According to Parker these early monarchs were also priests:

For as in the first Ages of the world, the Fathers of Families were vested with a Kingly Power over their own Posterity; so also were they with the Priestly Office executing all the Holy Functions of Priesthood in their own Persons. . . . And this custom of investing the Sovereign Power with the Supreme Priesthood, was (as divers Authors both Antient and Modern observe) universally practised over all Kingdoms of the world for well nigh 2500 years, without any one president [*sic*] to the contrary.[3]

In ancient Israel the kings exercised no sacerdotal functions, but the priests who did were wholly subject to their authority:

And though in the Jewish Commonwealth, the Priestly Office was upon Reasons peculiar to that State separated by a Divine positive Command from the Kingly Power; yet the Power and Jurisdiction of the Priest remained still subject to the Sovereign Prince . . . [4]

The coming of Christ made remarkably little difference. Parker was quite emphatic that the magistrate's ecclesiastical jurisdiction was not derived 'from any grant of our Saviours, but from an antecedent right wherewith

---

[1] *Ecclesiastical Politie*, 29. [2] Below, p. 325; cf. *Two Treatises*, I. 111, 121, 124, 142.
[3] *Ecclesiastical Politie*, 31. [4] Ibid. 32.

all Sovereign Power was indued before ever he was born into the world'.[1]
Christ was himself born a subject and preached obedience to earthly
rulers, and nothing in his teaching deprives them of any power:

> yet no where he takes upon him to settle, much less to limit the Prerogatives of
> Princes; and therefore the Government of Religion being vested in them by an
> antecedent and natural Right, must without all Controversie belong to them, till it
> is derogated from them by some Superior Authority: so that unless our Saviour
> had expressly disrobed the Royal Power of its Ecclesiastical Jurisdiction, nothing
> else can alienate it from their Prerogative.[2]

Parker did not say whether Christ could have removed power over
religious matters from civil magistrates, but was quite clear that he did
not: 'Our Saviour never took any part of the Civil Power upon himself,
and upon that score could not make penal and coercive Laws'.[3]

Throughout his life Locke shared this view. In the Latin tract of the
early 1660s he observed that

> the New Testament nowhere makes any mention of the controlling or limiting of
> the magistrate's authority since no precept appointed for the civil magistrate
> appears either in the Gospel or in the Epistles. In truth it is for the most part
> silent as to government and civil power, or rather Christ himself, often lighting on
> occasions of discussing this matter, seems to refuse deliberately to involve himself
> in civil affairs and, not owning any kingdom but the divine spiritual one as his
> own, he let the civil government of the commonwealth go by unchanged.[4]

In the *Epistola de Tolerantia* he made it equally clear that the coming of
Christianity did not alter the powers of the civil magistrate:

> But there is absolutely no such thing under the Gospel as a Christian common-
> wealth. I admit that there are many kingdoms and cities which have been con-
> verted to the Christian faith, but they have retained and preserved their ancient
> form of government, on which Christ enjoined nothing in his law. He taught the
> faith and conduct by which individuals might obtain eternal life, but he instituted
> no commonwealth, he introduced no new form of government, peculiar to his
> own people . . . [5]

Locke and Parker were therefore wholly in agreement that any coercive
powers a Christian magistrate might have in religious affairs were not
derived from Christ himself but were part of the general powers possessed by all magistrates, Christian and non-Christian. They also agreed

---

[1] Ibid. 40.   [2] Ibid. 34.
[3] Ibid. 42. '[Christ] himself was not invested with any secular Power, and so could not
use those methods of Government, that are proper to its Jurisdiction', ibid. 42–3.
[4] *Two Tracts*, 233.   [5] *Epistola de Tolerantia*, 117; cf. MS Locke c. 34, p. 49.

General Introduction

that the Apostles and their successors had no coercive powers. Parker, however, saw the absence of these powers in the early church as a temporary deficiency, to be rectified by God's immediate providence in the form of miraculous intervention, 'so necessary is a coercive Jurisdiction to the due Government and Discipline of the Church, that God himself was fain to bestow it on the Apostles in a miraculous manner'.[1] It is characteristic of Parker that he supposed that miraculous powers were given to the Apostles primarily to cause diseases rather than to cure them. Apostolic denunciation was indeed so regularly followed by illness or death that 'Criminals must have [had] as much reason to dread the Rod of the Apostles, as the Sword of the Civil Magistrate'.[2]

The conversion of Constantine and the subsequent institution of Christianity as the state religion of the Roman empire were seen by many Protestant nonconformists as having corrupted the church. For Parker it was a restitution of the natural state of affairs:

But when Christianity had once prevail'd and triumphed over all the oppositions of Pagan Superstition, and had gain'd the Empire of the world into its own possession, and was become the Imperial Religion, then began its Government to re-settle where nature had placed it, and the Ecclesiastical Jurisdiction was annexed to the Civil Power . . .[3]

It followed that any coercive authority the clergy might possess derives not by succession from Christ and the Apostles but from the civil power. For Parker the civil magistrate is supreme and could himself exercise any priestly (and presumably episcopal) powers should he so wish: 'he alone having Authority to assign to every Subject his proper Function, and among others this of the Priesthood; the exercise whereof as he has power to transfer to another, so may he, if he please, reserve it to himself'.[4]

Hobbes had indeed said much the same, and it is therefore hardly surprising that a good many of Parker's critics saw him as an ecclesiastical Hobbist.[5] He would not have accepted this and inveighed in his usual intemperate fashion against those who 'swallow down the Principles of the *Malmsbury Philosophy*, without any chewing, or consideration'.[6] He had, however, swallowed rather more of it than he was perhaps aware: there is something distinctly Hobbesian about such remarks as 'all the Magistrates Power of instituting Significant Ceremonies amounts to no

[1] *Ecclesiastical Politie*, 48. [2] Ibid. 45. [3] Ibid. 48. [4] Ibid. 32.
[5] *Leviathan*, 295–7; *The Rehearsal Transpros'd*, 214–15; Humfrey, *The Authority of the Magistrate*, 67–71. See also Locke's comments, below, p. 326.
[6] *Ecclesiastical Politie*, p. xxv; the allusion is to *Leviathan*, 256.

68

more than a Power of Determining what shall or shall not be Visible Signs of Honour'.[1] The same can be said of his claim that 'to avoid these and all other Inconveniences that would naturally follow upon a state of War, it was necessary there should be one Supreme and Publick Judgment, to whose Determinations the private Judgment of every single Person should be obliged to submit it self'.[2]

In some ways Parker's *Discourse of Ecclesiastical Politie* reads like an extreme and intemperate version of the arguments Locke had himself put forward in the early 1660s. There were obvious similarities, above all the pervasive fear of civil disorder and of what Locke called 'the *tyranny* of a *religious rage*',[3] but there were also important differences. Locke had insisted that the civil magistrate must necessarily have an absolute and arbitrary power over all indifferent actions, but he never argued that this power should extend to all matters of religious worship or doctrine. Parker did:

'tis absolutely necessary to the Peace and Tranquillity of the Commonwealth, which, though it be the prime and most important end of Government, can never be sufficiently secured, unless Religion be subject to the Authority of the supreme Power, in that it has the strongest influence upon humane affairs; and therefore if the Sovereign Power cannot order and manage it, it would be but a very incompetent Instrument of publique happiness, would want the better half of it self, and be utterly weak and ineffectual for the ends of Government.[4]

There is no limitation here to indifferent things. Indeed, one of the most striking features of Parker's account is that the magistrate's right to impose religious uniformity is entirely independent of the content of the doctrines imposed. As Marvell noted:

'Tis true, the Author sometimes for fashion-sake speaks in that Book of Religion and a of Deity, but his Principles do necessarily, if not in terms, make the Princes Power *Paramount* to both those, and if he may by his uncontroulable and unlimited universal Authority introduce what Religion, he may of consequence what Deity also he pleases.[5]

Locke also noted that Parker 'does not suppose the magistrates power to proceed from his being in the right'.[6] Indeed Parker himself made it quite clear that 'Princes [must] have Power to bind their subjects to that Religion that they apprehend most advantageous to publique Peace and

[1] *Ecclesiastical Politie*, 108.   [2] Ibid. 28–9; cf. *Leviathan*, 168–9.
[3] *Two Tracts*, 120.   [4] *Ecclesiastical Politie*, 11–12.
[5] *The Rehearsal Transpros'd*, 65.   [6] Below, p. 324.

Tranquillity, and restrain those Religious mistakes that tend to its sub-version'.[1] Locke saw the consequence of this:

> Whether by *binde the subject to his religion*, he means that whether the magistrates opinion be right or wrong he has power to force the subject to renownce his owne opinions however quiet & peaceable & declare assent & consent to those of the magistrate? & if soe why Christ & the Apostles directed not their discourses, & addressed their miracles to the princes & magistrates of the world to perswade them, whereas by preaching to & converting the people they according to this doctrine ⟨were⟩ under a necessity of being either Seditious or Martyrs.[2]

The natural implication of Parker's argument—though for obvious reasons not one he himself was prepared to draw—was that emperors such as Decius and Diocletian had been fully entitled to persecute their Christian subjects as propagators of subversion and disorder. The same could be said of the systematic extermination of the Japanese Christians described by Locke in the *Essay concerning Toleration*.[3]

Locke bought a copy of Parker's *Discourse* very soon after its publication in the autumn of 1669;[4] it was apparently purchased for Ashley, and no copy is listed in any of Locke's own library catalogues. His notes appear to have been made during the winter of 1669–70,[5] but his reasons for making them can only be conjectured. The notes on fo. 7 relate to pages 11–29 of Parker's book, and those on fo. 9 to pages 144–53. There is no obvious reason why Locke should have confined his comments to these particular parts of Parker's book, and it would seem likely that these two sheets are stray survivors from a considerably fuller body of notes that have since been lost. It may well be that Locke contemplated writing a detailed critique of Parker's book, but if he did the project would seem to have been abandoned.

Excommunication

In the first quarter of 1674 Locke made a draft of a short untitled paper setting out what he saw to be the fundamental contrast between civil and religious society. It contains an exposition of general principles rather than an attempt to apply them to any particular situation, and is wholly

---

[1] *Ecclesiastical Politie*, 12.   [2] Below, p. 324.   [3] Below, pp. 300–1.
[4] BL, Add. MS 46470, fo. 40ʳ.
[5] MS Locke c. 39, fos. 5–10; fo. 8ᵛ is endorsed 'Qs On S.Ps discourse of toleration. 69'.

devoid of references to other writers or to contemporary events. Were it not for the date supplied by Locke's endorsement, 'Excommunication $7\frac{3}{4}$' it would have been very difficult indeed to date it with any precision: on internal grounds alone all that could confidently be said is that it must have been written after he had completed the original version of the *Essay concerning Toleration*, but before he started the *Epistola de Tolerantia* nearly twenty years later. In the absence of a title supplied by Locke the name he used to file the paper has been adopted as the title of the whole work.

The first part of *Excommunication* is in double-column format, with the two columns headed 'Civill Society or the State' and 'Religious Society or the Church'. These two distinct societies exist because men have a '2 fold concernment...to attaine a 2 fold happinesse, viz: That of this world and that of the other'. The contrast between the two interests in this world and the next had been clearly stated in the *Essay concerning Toleration*; the emphasis on happiness is not entirely new, but it became an increasingly marked feature of Locke's thought from the 1670s onwards. When he came to write the *Essay concerning Human Understanding*, he was firmly of the view that happiness alone can move desire and that we pursue goods only in so far as we take them to be conducive to our own happiness.[1] Indeed we are not alone in this: 'God Almighty himself is under the necessity of being happy'.[2] But Locke did not think that the state was under a duty to procure the happiness of its members, still less to procure their greatest happiness. Its aims were more limited: 'The End of Civill Society is Civill Peace and prosperity or the preservation of the Society and every Member theereof in a free and peaceable enjoyment of all the good things of this life that belong to each of them...'.[3] This does not differ in any important respect from the views put forward in the *Essay concerning Toleration*, where the magistrate's duty had been described as being 'the preservation as much as is possible of the propriety quiet & life of every individuall'.[4] Indeed the account of the state in *Excommunication* is little more than a summary of the views put forward in the earlier work.

Where Locke broke new ground was in his account of the nature of a church and of the kind of authority it can legitimately exercise over its members. These were topics that had hardly been touched on in the *Essay concerning Toleration*, which had been concerned primarily with

---

[1] II. xxi. 41, 43, 71.   [2] Ibid. II. xxi. 50.   [3] Below, p. 327.
[4] Below, p. 287.

establishing limits to the power of the state in religious matters. For Locke religion is essentially other-worldly: its purpose is to obtain happiness in the world to come, and worship and other religious observances are ways of trying to achieve this. The state and the church are parallel institutions pursuing quite different goals, and Locke's aim was to keep them as far apart as possible. The chief problem he faced—one he was well aware of—was that although religious societies have their goals in the next world, they operate in this one, and must therefore exercise some kind of authority over their own proceedings and members. Locke readily accepted this, but he made it quite clear that while the state has authority to administer coercive punishments, religious societies do not. One reason for this is that in religious matters coercion is ineffective:

> punishment is never sufficient to keepe men to the obedience of any law, where the evil it brings is not certainly greater, then the good which is obtained or expected from the disobedience. And therefor noe temporal worldly punishment can be sufficient to perswade a man to that or from that way which he beleives leads to everlasting happynesse or misery.[1]

This is true in some cases but not all. Most people lack the fortitude to become martyrs, and though coercion may be ineffective in producing sincere belief, it will in most cases secure outward compliance.

Another reason is that coercion is unjust because 'my faith or religious worship hurts not an other man in any concernment of his': 'in Civil Society one mans good is involved & complicated with an other, but in religious Societys every mans concerns are seperate, & one mans transgression hurts not an other any farther then he imitates him, & if he erre he errs at his owne private cost'.[2] In other words, religious goods are essentially non-competitive: someone who gains salvation does not do so at the expense of anyone else. There is, therefore, no need for an umpire to settle disputes between different religious bodies offering rival ways to salvation.

The conclusion Locke drew from this is that 'Church membership is perfectly voluntary & may end when ever any one pleases, without any prejudice to him . . .'.[3] This conception of a church as a purely voluntary society suggests that Locke had already arrived at the account set out in the *Epistola de Tolerantia*, where a church is described as 'a free society of men, joining together of their own accord for the public worship of God in such manner as they believe will be acceptable to the Deity for the

---

[1] Below, p. 330.   [2] Ibid. 330–1.   [3] Ibid. 331.

salvation of their souls'.[1] It should, however, be noted that in *Excommunication* he always referred to *the* church, not to *a* church or to churches. Perhaps his double-column format was to blame: it made for convenient exposition but was potentially misleading since it suggests that he was attempting to determine the boundaries of the church and the state, conceived as two institutions with separate and distinct spheres of competence. On his own argument there was no such thing as *the* church, merely particular churches.

Locke fully accepted that any religious society had to be able to exclude disruptive or disobedient members, but he was insistent that no further punishment should be inflicted. He was also well aware that in most parts of Europe this was not the case, and that a variety of civil penalties or disabilities were imposed on those who had been excommunicated. In England excommunication was a censure imposed by the ecclesiastical courts, but at common law persons who had been excommunicated suffered from a number of civil disabilities, including the inability to bring real or personal actions and to sit on juries, and were liable to imprisonment under the writ *de excommunicato capiendo*.[2] In Scotland the consequences of greater excommunication were even more severe.

In the second part of *Excommunication* Locke abandoned the double-column format he had hitherto used, and set out to give a general account of when sentences of excommunication might be given. He began by stating that 'religious societys are of two sorts, wherein their circumstances very much differ', but the distinction he had in mind was left unexplained. The part of the work that he did complete contains an analysis of four different ways in which church and state were related, with examples from various parts of Europe:

1. Where 'Civil & Religious Societys are coextended, i.e. Both the Magistrate, & every subject of the same common wealth is also member of the same church'. The example given is Muscovy. Here there is no need for excommunication for immorality, since the magistrate can deal with this. The church can, however, expel members on religious grounds:

> But if any one differ from the Church in fide aut Cultu [in faith or worship] I thinke first the civil Magistrate may punish him for it, where he is fully perswaded that it is likely to disturbe the civil peace, otherwise not. But the religious

---

[1] 'Ecclesia mihi videtur societas libera hominum sponte sua coeuntium, ut Deum publice colant eo modo quem credunt numini acceptum fore ad salutem animarum', *Epistola de Tolerantia*, 70; cf. MS Locke c. 34, p. 145. [2] Blackstone, *Commentaries*, iii. 101–3.

society may certainly excommunicate him, the peace whereof may by this means be preserved, but noe other evil ought to follow him upon that excommunication as such, but only upon the consideration of the publique peace, for if he will silently conceale his opinion or carry away his opinion or differing worship out of the Verge of that Government I know not by what right he can be hindered.

Dissenters appear to have a right to emigrate or to stay quiet without being harassed, but there is no indication that they have any right to engage in public, or even private, worship.

2. In other places 'the Commonwealth though all of one religion is but a part of the church, or religious Society which acts & is acknowledged to be one entire society, & soe is it in Spaine & all the principalitys of Italy'. There is religious uniformity, but the church that exists in each state is part of a wider organization. Here too 'the Church may excommunicate for faults in faith & worship, but not those faults in manners which the Magistrate hath annexed penaltys to for the preservation of Civil Society & happynesse'. In this case Locke says nothing at all about dissenters.

3. 'In some places the Religion of the Commonwealth i.e. the publique establishd religion is not received by all the subjects of the Common wealth.' Examples include England, Brandenburg, and Sweden. Here the same rule applies as in the second case.

4. 'In some places the Religion of part of the people is different from the Governing part of the civil Society, & Thus the presbiterian Inde-pendent Anabaptist quaker, Papist & Jewish in England, the Lutheran & Popish in Cleve &c.' Here Locke thought that a different rule applies:

I thinke the church hath power to Excommunicate for matters of faith, Worship or manners, though the Magistrate punish the same immoralitys with his sword, because the church cannot otherwise remove the Scandal which is necessary for its preservation & the propagation of its doctrine.

This is followed by a later addition:

And this power of being judges who are fit to be of their Society the magistrate cannot deny to any Religious Society, which is permitted within his dominions. This was the state of the church til Constantine.

Locke's view seems therefore to have been that established churches do not have the right to excommunicate immoral members, but that dis-senting congregations do. At the beginning of the discussion he had said that there are two sorts of religious societies with different powers, and these are perhaps the two kinds of church distinguished here. The dis-cussion is clearly unfinished, and it is likely that Locke was still getting his thoughts in order.

A LETTER FROM A PERSON OF QUALITY, TO
HIS FRIEND IN THE COUNTRY

The *Letter from a Person of Quality* differs from the other works included in this volume in that it was published during Locke's lifetime, in the autumn of 1675. Although it appeared anonymously, no one has ever doubted that it was written by someone in Shaftesbury's circle and for Shaftesbury's purposes; it is attributed to him both in the British Library catalogue and in Wing. Contemporaries also ascribed it to him,[1] and the government reply, published the following year, was pointedly entitled *A Pacquet of Advices and Animadversions, Sent from London To the Men of Shaftsbury*. It is, however, rather less clear who actually wrote it. Locke never laid claim to it, and while he was alive no one appears to have attributed it to him. So far as is known, the first person to have done so was Pierre Des Maizeaux, a Huguenot exile, journalist, and man of letters, who in 1720 included it in *A Collection of Several Pieces of Mr. John Locke, Never before printed, or not extant in his Works*. It was included in the fifth edition of *The Works of John Locke* (1751) and in all subsequent editions until the twelfth (1824). Since then it has occupied an uncertain place in the Locke canon. John Attig included it among Locke's works, though he thought that it was 'most likely...written largely by Shaftesbury himself, with the assistance of various colleagues and political advisors, possibly including Locke'.[2] Jean Yolton placed it, along with the *Fundamental Constitutions of Carolina*, among the doubtful and spurious works.[3]

Danby's Test Bill

The *Letter* was occasioned by the unsuccessful attempt made in the spring of 1675 to enact a bill that would impose a non-resistance test on peers, MPs, and other office-holders.[4] The bill—entitled 'An Act to prevent the Dangers which may arise from Persons disaffected to the Government', but commonly known as the Test Bill or the Bill for

---

[1] On the title-page of his own copy, Bodl., B 2.1(1) Linc., Thomas Barlow wrote, 'By the E of Shaftesbury as is generally beleived'. It was also attributed to Shaftesbury in Wood, *Athenae Oxonienses*, vol. ii, col. 545; Wood, *Life and Times*, ii. 330.

[2] Attig, *The Works of John Locke*, 7.

[3] Yolton, *John Locke: A Descriptive Bibliography*, 434–5.

[4] Copies of the bill are in Bodl., MS Rawl. A 162, fos. 54^r–55^r, and BL, Add. MS 41656, fos. 79^r–80^r. It is printed in Appendix VI, below.

the Test—aroused considerable disquiet, and was presented by its opponents, among whom Shaftesbury was one of the most prominent, as part of a long-standing conspiracy to secure absolute monarchy, divine right episcopacy, and government by a standing army. Its chief promoter was the Lord Treasurer, the Earl of Danby.

Danby had been appointed primarily to manage the royal finances, but he was someone with very definite aims of his own, the chief of which were the maintenance of the Anglican interest at home and the further-ance of the Protestant interest abroad.[1] Many of his troubles stemmed from the fact that neither the King nor his brother truly shared these aims. Charles was a Francophile, and though he was careful never to make any open breach with the Church of England, his commitment to it was at best lukewarm; James, the heir presumptive, was openly a Catholic. Danby was neither, and he was very well aware that his usefulness—and therefore his tenure of office—rested largely on his ability to manage Parliament. This was no easy matter. The existing Parliament had been elected in 1661 at the high tide of Anglican and Cavalier fortunes, but it had in recent years become increasingly fractious and troublesome. Partly this was due to changing membership—by the mid-1670s something like half the original membership had been replaced—but much of the blame lay with the policies the King had pursued in recent years, especially the Stop of the Exchequer, the Declaration of Indulgence, and the Third Dutch War. Even more damaging was his brother's conversion to Catholicism. Nothing much could be done about James, who stuck to his new faith with the obstinacy of a convert, but Danby was able to impress on Charles the need to change direction and take steps to restore confidence.

Parliament had been prorogued in February 1674 and was not scheduled to meet again until April 1675, which gave Danby ample time to make preparations. In October 1674 he went to Farnham Castle—the residence of George Morley, Bishop of Winchester—and, according to one contemporary letter, 'in his Majestyes name told the Bishops of a Consultation which would be necessary among the fathers of the Church, and with some of the Privy Councill, how to propose some things that might unite and best pacify the minds of People against the next session of Parlyament'.[2] The bishops duly conferred, and on 26 January 1675

---

[1] Danby's aims can be most clearly seen in the series of memoranda written between 1673 and 1677, printed in Browning, *Danby*, ii. 63–71. See also Lindsey to Danby, 25 Aug. 1675, HMC, 14th Report, Appendix, Part IX (Lindsey MSS), 377.

[2] Sir Robert Southwell to Ormonde, 24 Oct. 1674, Bodl., MS Carte 72, fo. 229^{r-v}.

eight of them—the Archbishop of Canterbury and the Bishops of Durham, Winchester, Salisbury, Peterborough, Rochester, Chichester, and Chester—submitted to the King a representation which told of their concern not only at the growth of atheism and profaneness, but also at the frequent defections to either the 'superstitious and idolatrous practices and usurpations of Rome' or the 'pernicious and destructive novelties of the various Sects'. The bishops concluded that 'nothing is more necessary than the suppression of Atheism, profaneness and open and professed wickedness', adding that it was their unanimous opinion that the existing laws against popery and dissent were sufficient if properly enforced.[1]

On the same day there was a meeting at Lambeth House, attended by six of the eight bishops—Durham and Peterborough were absent—and by five of the King's ministers. Danby was there, as were the Lord Keeper, Lord Finch, and the two Secretaries of State, Sir Joseph Williamson and Henry Coventry. All were solid Anglicans. Also present, though it is not clear in what capacity, was the Commissioner for Scotland, the Duke of Lauderdale. Six recommendations were agreed on: that the conviction of Roman Catholics be 'encouraged, quickened and made effectual'; that 'no Masse be celebrated in any part of this kingdome, the Queen's Majesty's Chappels and the chappels of foreign Ministers only excepted'; that all English priests should be banished; that English subjects being educated abroad at 'Popish Colleges or Seminaries' should be recalled; that 'Papists or reputed Papists' at Court should receive 'some publique mark' of the King's displeasure; and that 'his Majesty be pleased to take effectual care for the suppressing of Conventicles'.[2] Of these six proposals, five were concerned with the suppression of popery and only one with Protestant dissent. No new legislation was proposed.

The writer of the *Letter from a Person of Quality* knew something of these meetings, and in a passage of remarkable bitterness did his best to portray Danby, Finch, and Lauderdale as subservient tools of the clergy:

the Bishops had found a *Scotch* Lord, and two new Ministers, or rather Great Officers of *England*, who were desperate and rash enough, to put their Masters business upon so narrow and weak a bottom; And that *old Covenanter Lauderdale*, is become the *Patron of the Church*, and has his Coach and table fil'd with Bishops. The Keeper and the Treasurer are of a just size to this affair, for it is a certain rule with the Church Men, to endure (as seldom as they can) in business, Men abler then themselves. But his Grace of *Scotland* was least to be excused of the Three,

---

[1] Leicestershire RO, DG7/Ecc. 2 (i); copy in NA, SP 29/367/131.
[2] Leicestershire RO, DG7/Ecc. 2 (ii); copy in NA, SP 29/367/132.

for having fall'n from *Presbytery*, *Protestant* Religion, and all principles of Publick good and private friendship, and become the Slave of *Clifford* to carry on the Ruine of all that he had professed to support, does now also quit even *Clifford's* generous Principles, and betake himself to a sort of Men . . . who would do the worst of things by the worst of means, enslave their country, and betray them, under the mask of Religion . . . [1]

The writer evidently had a very deep grudge against all three, Lauderdale especially,[2] but he was mistaken in supposing that the initiative came from the bishops: everything indicates that Danby was the prime mover. The clergy were themselves divided. According to the Venetian ambassador, those who planned the meeting 'had excluded such bishops as were mildly inclined, taking only three good and quiet ones, the turbulent Salisbury [Seth Ward] and his follower Winchester'. The proposals, he added, were supported by Finch, Danby, Lauderdale, Coventry, and the Bishops of Salisbury and Winchester; Williamson, the Archbishop of Canterbury, and the Bishops of Chester and Rochester gave their silent consent.[3]

Danby had some reason to feel pleased with how things were going. On 28 January he informed the Earl of Essex that

His Majesty is takeing most effectuall courses to cure the suspicions which many had received here of the incouragement or att least connivance which was given to popery, haveing requir'd the bishops to acquainte him with what they judge necessary to be done for suppressing the growth of itt, which they have done accordingly, and his Majestie is resolved to putt effectually in execution; so that when the Parliament meets next itt will take off all disguises, and shew them bare fac't who made religion a pretence to their other designes.[4]

---

[1] *LPQ* 7, below, pp. 345–6. These jibes against Lauderdale were based on fact: 'The Duke of Lauderdale continues very Zealous in his conversation among the Bishops, and is very sincere for the Church of England, his Grace went over with 3 or 4 of them to dine this day at Lambeth', Southwell to Ormonde, 6 Feb. 1675, Bodl., MS Carte 38, fo. 252^r; cf. Marvell to Sir Henry Thompson, [late Jan. 1675], *Poems and Letters*, ii. 338. Danby did not welcome Lauderdale's meddling in English affairs: see Browning, *Danby*, i. 148.

[2] In earlier years Shaftesbury had been on good terms with Lauderdale, but by the autumn of 1673 their enmity had become common knowledge: Haley, 159, 169–70, 186, 193, 340–1; Lauderdale to Charles II, 20 Nov. 1673, *Lauderdale Papers*, iii. 16. For a later hostile remark, see Shaftesbury to Locke, 20 Mar. 1680, *Correspondence*, ii. 160. Shaftesbury's aversion to Danby is suggested by a passage in Stringer's memoir, where he is described as 'a much worse man to all Intents and Purposes then Lord Clifford he being a Bold Undertaker a Brazen Lyer a Violent Prosecutor of Malice and revenge', PRO 30/24/6B/441, fo. 7^r.

[3] Alberti to the Doge and Senate, 5/15 Feb. 1675, *CSPV 1673–1675*, 357–8.

[4] BL, Stowe MS 207, fo. 106, Browning, *Danby*, ii. 55.

On 29 January the Lambeth proposals were discussed by the Privy Council.[1] There seems to have been some opposition, or at least disquiet. The Earl of Anglesey, Lord Privy Seal, noted in his diary that 'the King communicated the proceedings at Lambeth for reformation which we debated a while but desired time if our advice was expected it being I conceived a weighty affair'.[2] According to the Venetian ambassador, Lords Holles, Halifax, Carlisle, and Dorchester asked for time to examine the proposal more fully, and the Duke of York declared that 'he did not believe the measure beneficial for his majesty'.[3] Nevertheless, the majority decided to press ahead. On 2 February Henry Coventry informed the Duke of Ormonde that 'To morrow is like to bee a greate day in Councell where something will apparently bee concluded with more severity then hath of late beene expected from the Court against all sorts of recusants...'.[4] The Council ordered that the laws against recusants be executed 'with more care and Diligence then of late they have bin', the Attorney-General was asked 'whether any persons of quality who are suspected to be Popish Recusants have bin omitted to be presented', and the justices of the peace were ordered to proceed against recusants.[5] On 12 February the King issued a declaration ordering that 'the Conviction of *Popish Recusants* be every where Encouraged, Quickened, and made Effectual'; it was quite explicit that 'care be taken, that no Persons of Quality, who shall be suspected to be *Popish Recusants*, be omitted to be Presented; and that no delay be used, nor any practice suffered, which may hinder or obstruct the compleating of such convictions as are now preparing'.[6] A few days later Coventry reported that 'his Majesty seemeth very well resolved in the course hee hath begunne to take in satisfying his people in point of Religion and I

---

[1] Henry Thynne to Essex, 30 Jan. 1675, BL, Stowe MS 207, fo. 114ʳ, *Essex Papers*, i. 293–4.

[2] BL, Add. MS 40860, fo. 82ᵛ. See also Southwell to Ormonde, 30 Jan. 1675, Bodl., MS Carte 72, fos. 261–2.

[3] Alberti to the Doge and Senate, 5/15 Feb. 1675, *CSPV 1673–1675*, 357. See also Clarke, *The Life of James the Second*, i. 499–500; Miller, *James II*, 78–9.

[4] Bodl., MS Carte 243, fo. 190ᵛ; copies in BL, Add. MS 25124, fo. 14ʳ, Longleat House, Wiltshire, Coventry MS 83, fo. 72ᵛ (microfilm in the Institute of Historical Research, London, XR 60/67). [5] NA, PC 2/64, pp. 364 (3 Feb.), 368 (5 Feb.).

[6] *His Majesties Declaration for Enforcing a late Order Made in Council*, 4–5; NA, PC 2/64, p. 372 (10 Feb.). It was insinuated in the *Letter from a Person of Quality* that all this was really a sham, and the enforcement of the laws against papists 'of best quality and fortune' was being deliberately obstructed. In fact the laws were enforced with such rigour that on 23 June the Attorney-General was ordered to halt proceedings against the Penderells of Boscobel and others who had helped the King escape after the battle of Worcester, NA, PC 2/64, p. 449.

beleeve will give them farther testimonys at the meeting of the Parliament'.[1]

Shaftesbury had been at St Giles while all this was going on, but he too was making preparations for the next session of Parliament. On 3 February he wrote a letter to the Earl of Carlisle, which though not printed seems to have been very widely circulated.[2] After some opening remarks indicating his desire 'to improve any opportunitie of a good Correspondence or understanding between the Royall Family & the People', he went on to explain that the only advice he knew 'truly serviceable to the King, affectionate to the duke, or sincere unto the Country' was to summon a new Parliament. Until this was done he would remain in opposition:

> But I will assure your Lordship, there is noe Place or Condition will invite me to Court during this Parliament. Nor untill I see the King thinks frequent new Parliaments as much his Interest as they are the Peoples Right; For untill then, I can neyther serve the King as well as I would or think a great place safe enough for a second adventure. When our great men have tryed a little longer, they will be of my minde, in the mean while noe kinde of usage shall put me out of the duty & respect I owe the King & duke; but I think it would not be unwise, for the men in great office (that are at ease, and where they would be), to be ordinary Civill to a Man in my Condition; since they may be assured that all theire Places putt together shall not buy me from my Principles . . .[3]

These assurances of loyalty may seem disingenuous, especially where James was concerned, but they should not be entirely discounted. Shaftesbury may well have distrusted Charles and disliked James, but he

---

[1] Coventry to Essex, 15 Feb. 1675, BL, Stowe MS 207, fo. 169ᵛ, *Essex Papers*, i. 302.

[2] According to *A Pacquet of Advices and Animadversions, Sent from London To the Men of Shaftsbury* (p. 46), it was circulated 'not only to many Lords in and about the City, but likewise to all the most noted *Coffee-houses*'. See also Lord Aston to Williamson, Apr. 1675, NA, SP 29/370/33. There are three copies in the Shaftesbury papers: PRO 30/24/5/284; PRO 30/24/5/294, pp. 11–14; and PRO 30/24/6B/393. Other copies are in Bodl., MS Carte 38, fo. 286; MS Carte 59, fo. 543; MS Carte 81, fo. 606; MS Carte 228, fo. 125; Bodl., MS Don. b. 8, pp. 501–2; Bodl., MS Rawl. A 185, fos. 71–2; BL, Add. MS 32094, fo. 346; NA, SP 29/442/31; Yale, Osborn Shelves, fb. 155, pp. 455–6; Yale, Osborn Shelves, b. 120, unfoliated; Yale, Osborn Shelves, b. 157, unfoliated; Yale, OSB MSS 6, item 20; Downing College, Cambridge, MS Z. 4. 17/17 (cited from Scott, *England's Troubles*, 356). The letter was first printed in 1721 in Sir Richard Bulstrode, *Memoirs and Reflections*, 264–6, and subsequently in Martyn and Kippis, *Shaftesbury*, ii. 109–12; Christie, ii. 200–2; and Brown, *Shaftesbury*, 226–7.

[3] PRO 30/24/5/284. The manuscript, seriously damaged by damp, is in Stringer's hand; it appears to be a copy rather than a draft, as suggested by Louise Fargo Brown, *Shaftesbury*, 226. Some minor lacunae in the text have been filled, using the copies in Bodl., MS Carte 81, fo. 606, and MS Carte 228, fo. 125, which in other respects are closest to the text in PRO 30/24/5/284.

was still hoping to persuade the King to dismiss his ministers and change his policies, and he knew perfectly well that royal support for Danby was more a matter of convenience than conviction.

Danby knew this as well, and he too had made preparations for the new session. On 13 April the King opened it with a short speech in which he assured his audience that he had done all he could to extinguish the 'Fears and Jelousies of Popery' and that he would 'leave nothing undone that may shew the World My Zeal for the Protestant Religion as it is established in the Church of *England*, from which I will never depart'.[1] This was followed by a longer speech by the Lord Keeper which proclaimed that

His Majesty, with equal and impartial Justice, hath revived all the Laws against Dissenters and Non-conformists; but not with equal Severity; for the Laws against the Papists are edged, and the Execution of them quickened, by new Rewards proposed to the Informers; those against Disenters are left to that Strength they have already.[2]

Neither speaker made any mention of the Test Bill, which was introduced two days later into the Lords by Danby's brother-in-law, the Earl of Lindsey.[3] The bill was evidently intended to catch its opponents by surprise. At its heart lay the requirement that all office-holders, members of both Houses of Parliament, and justices of the peace should subscribe the following:

I A. B. do declare that it is not Lawful upon any pretence whatsoever, to take up Armes against the King, and that I do abhorr that Traiterous position of taking Armes by His authority, against His Person, or against those that are commission'd by Him in pursuance of such Commission, And I do swear that I will not at any time endeavor the Alteration of the Government, either in Church or State.[4]

There was nothing at all novel about this oath. Since the Restoration a series of statutes had imposed similar oaths on the Anglican and

---

[1] *LJ* xii. 653. There is a version of this speech with rather different wording in Leicestershire RO, DG7/PP 36. It is in Finch's hand throughout and was endorsed by Daniel Finch 'Speech not approved per L. Treasurer'.　　　　　　　　　　　　　　　[2] *LJ* xii. 653–4.
[3] *LJ* xii. 659.
[4] *LPQ* 9, below, p. 349. The content of the oath was of considerable interest to contemporaries: other versions differing slightly in wording but not in substance are in Bodl., MS Rawl. A 162, fo. 54ʳ; MS Rawl. D 924, fo. 300ʳ; William Ball to Francis Parry, 6 Nov. 1675, BL, Add. MS 41568, fo. 2ʳ; BL, Add. MS 41656, fo. 79ʳ; BL, Harleian MS 5277, fo. 33ᵛ; Hampshire RO, 9M73/G197, pp. 49–50; NA, SP 29/370/111; PRO 30/24/5/294, p. 11; Yale, Osborn Shelves, b. 157, unfoliated; Marvell to Hull Corporation, 22 Apr. 1675, *Poems and Letters*, ii. 148–9; HMC Portland, iii. 352–3; *Reliquiae Baxterianae*, pt. III, § 298.

nonconformist clergy, on schoolmasters and university teachers, on militia officers, and on members of vestries and corporations;[1] as a tutor at Christ Church Locke would have been required to take the oath prescribed in the Act of Uniformity. Members of Parliament were, however, readier to impose such constraints on others than on themselves, and in the thinly attended Oxford session of 1665 a bill to impose an oath of this kind on the whole nation was narrowly defeated.[2] On that occasion Danby and Lindsey had been among the bill's opponents, a fact sardonically noted in the *Letter from a Person of Quality*.[3]

By 1675 Danby had secured high office and his priorities had changed. His prime need was now to manage Parliament, and the imposition of such an oath and declaration promised to be a very effective way of doing this, since it offered the possibility of driving a great many of his opponents out of public life. Three years later the Test Act of 1678 (30 Car. II, st. 2, c. 1) showed what could be done: by imposing a declaration against transubstantiation it removed Catholics from Parliament for the next 150 years. The Test Bill of 1675 had comparable objectives, though it was aimed primarily at Protestant nonconformists and those who sympathized with them.

The *Letter from a Person of Quality* blamed the bishops for the bill, but though they gave it their approval the idea does not seem to have originated with them: the Lambeth meeting had decided that no new legislation was needed. The bill appears to have been devised by Danby himself. In June 1675, after it had failed to pass the Lords, he had a long conversation with the Earl of Orrery,[4] during which he acknowledged that 'it was fram'd at severall Meetings at his house'.[5] He also gave Orrery an account of his reasons:

My Ld T . . . protested to me, having for some Months intently Imployd his Thoughts on what might be most eligible for securing the Protestant Religion, &

---

[1] Corporation Act 1661, 13 Car. II, st. 2, c. 1 (*SR* v. 322); Militia Act 1662, 14 Car. II, c. 3 (*SR* v. 361); Act of Uniformity 1662, 14 Car. II, c. 4 (*SR* v. 366); Vestries Act 1663, 15 Car. II. c. 5 (*SR* v. 446); Five Mile Act 1665, 17 Car. II, c. 2 (*SR* v. 575); the oath in the last of these is virtually identical to that in the Test Bill. For further details, see Seaward, *Cavalier Parliament*, 142–9, 152–7, 166–75, 192–3; Hutton, *Restoration*, 158–61, 171–6; Miller, *After the Civil Wars*, 132–5, 171–81; Seaward, 'London Vestries', 65–7.

[2] Robbins, 'The Oxford Session of the Long Parliament of Charles II', 221–2.

[3] *LPQ* 3, below, pp. 339–40.

[4] Roger Boyle, first Earl of Orrery (1621–79), *ODNB*, was an elder brother of Robert Boyle. A detailed account of his conversations with Danby is contained in 'Some Memorialls of my Journey into England 1675'; the original appears to be lost, but there are two early copies, National Art Library, MS Forster 47. A. 47, and BL, Add. MS 70500.

[5] National Art Library, MS Forster 47. A. 47, p. 14; BL, Add. MS 70500, fo. 93^r.

the Crown, he was satisfyed the King could rest with safety on noe party but that of the Church: nor could the Protestant Religion in his Judgment be Saved but by setting that party uppermost. Without doeing soe, the King would be left wholly without a Party, which he esteemed the unsafest condition he could be reduced to, and therefore having layd the making of the Church Party the foundation to build upon, he had judged it adviseable to make it as strong by Law as he could; and therefore had introduced this Test and Oath. . . . He farther added, that thô he had, by the advice of severall wise and honest Men, Pitch'd on this Oath, & Test, yett he was not soe wedded to it, but if I could propose what was better, he would embrace it; for to doe what was best he only aim'd at.[1]

This is Orrery's version but it perfectly fits everything known about Danby's motives and character. Danby was a sincere Protestant and a firm supporter of the Crown, but neither his opposition in 1665 nor his conduct in 1688 indicates any deeply rooted adherence to the principles of non-resistance. The bill was designed to make Parliament easier to manage, not to abolish it.

Danby may well have had another reason which he was less ready to acknowledge. A solidly Anglican and Cavalier Parliament would indeed support the King, but (as James II was to find in 1685) only if he pursued policies it favoured. James was not the most sharp-witted of men, but even he realized that Danby's bill was not to his advantage:

The duke acquainted me [Burnet wrote] with this scheme: he disliked it much. He thought this would raise the church party too high. He looked on them as intractable in the point of popery: therefore he thought it was better to keep them under by supporting the dissenters, by which colour he could better protect the papists. He looked upon the whole project as both knavish and foolish: and upon this he spoke severely of duke Lauderdale, who he saw would do any thing to save himself.[2]

The Earl of Anglesey was another opponent.[3] On 19 April he had a private meeting with Danby and Finch at which he 'urged many arguments against the test or new oath'.[4] These arguments evidently did not prevail. This placed Anglesey in an awkward position: he knew very well that any open opposition to the bill would have cost him his job, so he prudently confined himself to reminding the bishops that they sat in the

---

[1] National Art Library, MS Forster 47. A. 47, p. 26; BL, Add. MS 70500, fo. 98[r-v].
[2] Burnet, ii. 62–3; cf. BL, Add. MS 63057B, fo. 27[r].
[3] He conformed to the Church of England but his sympathies were strongly Presbyterian: Lacey, *Dissent and Parliamentary Politics*, 459–63. Edward Bagshaw, Locke's former opponent, served as his chaplain in the 1660s.
[4] Anglesey's diary, BL, Add. MS 40860, fo. 86[r].

House by Act of Parliament and should therefore be cautious in what they said.[1] It is noticeable that he was not singled out for criticism in the *Letter from a Person of Quality*.

Danby was confident he could get the bill through the Lords, though he was less sure about the Commons. He knew he would have the support of the bishops and by far the greater part of the church and cavalier party, and he also ensured he had the public backing of the King, who indicated his support by frequently attending the debates in person. He compiled a list of forty-four lay peers whom he thought could be counted as potential supporters, though in the event five of them voted with the opposition.[2] Thirty-six peers can be identified as opponents: twenty-five signed one or more of the four protests and another eleven were mentioned in the *Letter from a Person of Quality*.[3] Many but by no means all were future Whigs.[4] Some of the strongest opposition came from those with nonconformist sympathies. The Earl of Bedford and Lords Crew, Delamere, Holles, and Wharton were Presbyterians or had leanings that way; all had backed Parliament during the Civil War and all opposed the bill. Danby cannot have been surprised by this, but he must have found it disconcerting to find the bill opposed by the Earls of Clarendon, Bridgewater, and Ailesbury, all of whose support he had counted on. Clarendon was a firm Anglican and must have seemed an obvious supporter, but he had personal reasons for disliking Danby, who had helped lead the pack against his father in 1667.[5] Bridgewater was another solid Anglican who in the 1660s had been one of the government's strongest supporters; he had chaired the Lords' committees on the Uniformity, Conventicle, and Five Mile Bills, and had been Clarendon's choice as Lord Treasurer in 1667.[6] Ailesbury had similar views.

The Catholics were divided, torn between their habitual loyalty to the monarchy and their fear that any test would set an unwelcome precedent

[1] William Denton to Ralph Verney, 24 Apr. 1675, HMC, 7th Report, 492a.
[2] The Earls of Berkshire, Bridgewater, Clarendon, and Dorset, and Lord Petre. The list is printed in Browning, *Danby*, iii. 122–4.
[3] A full list is given in Note C, below, pp. 159–61.
[4] By the time of the vote on the Exclusion Bill in November 1680, fifteen of thirty-six were dead or had been excluded as Catholics. Of the remainder, eight (Bedford, Salisbury, Shaftesbury, Stamford, Delamere, Eure, Grey of Rolleston, and Wharton) are known to have voted for Exclusion, and four (Ailesbury, Bridgewater, Clarendon, and Halifax) are known to have voted against. Six of those who had supported the Test Bill voted for Exclusion: the Duke of Monmouth and the Earls of Anglesey, Essex, Macclesfield, Northampton, and Sunderland. These figures are taken from Davis, 'The "Presbyterian" Opposition and the Emergence of Party', 17–18, 27–35.   [5] Browning, *Danby*, i. 53–5.
[6] Seaward, *Cavalier Parliament*, 66, 93–4, 97.

that would eventually lead to their exclusion from Parliament. Five supported the bill: the Earl of Powis, Viscount Stafford, and Lords Bellasis, Carrington, and Widdrington. Four were opposed: the Earls of Berkshire and Bristol, and Lords Audley and Petre. The rest (including the Duke of York) abstained or stayed away.

The lay peers were almost evenly divided—of those whose allegiance can be identified thirty-nine were in favour and thirty-six against—and it was the votes of the bishops that gave Danby a clear majority.[1] They were some of his most disciplined and reliable supporters: they attended assiduously or sent proxies, and they voted together as a coherent group, something noted with asperity in the *Letter from a Person of Quality*:

for I must acquaint you that our great Prelates were so neer an Infallibility, that they were always found in this Session of one mind in the *Lords House*; yet the Lay Lords, not understanding from how excellent a Principle this proceeded, commonly called them for that reason *the dead Weight*.[2]

The bill had its first reading on 15 April and its second reading five days later.[3] On 21 April the debate began at 9 a.m. and continued until nearly midnight, with no break for dinner—an exceptionally late sitting by the standards of the time.[4] The opponents of the bill tried to have it thrown out, claiming that it entrenched upon the privileges of the House; when this failed (by sixty-one votes to twenty-seven) twenty-three of them entered a protest in the Journal.[5] Two days later, according to one report, 'the Test Bill was retained in the Lords' House by one vote only, and if some had not been at dinner it would have been cast out with indignation'.[6] Its supporters had declined in number from sixty-one to thirty-nine, and some of the majority only gave their votes 'because the King seem'd to countenance the Bill'.[7] On 26 April the bill was sent to a

---

[1] The average attendance during the session was 75 lay peers and 14 bishops. In all 134 out of 168 eligible to sit attended at one time or another; most of those who attended only occasionally were supporters of the Court. The King was present on 43 days out of 49. On two occasions (23 and 26 April) the bishops' votes were decisive. See Swatland, *House of Lords*, 32, 35, 37, 98.

[2] *LPQ* 8, below, p. 348. When Parliament met again in the autumn, Shaftesbury made a more extended attack on the bishops: 'I have often seen in this House, that the Arguments, with strongest reason, and most convincing to the Lay Lords in General, have not had the same effect upon the bishops Bench; but that they have unanimously gone against us in matters, that many of us have thought Essential and undoubted Rights...', *Two Speeches*, 9. [3] *LJ* xii. 659, 664.

[4] *Bulstrode Papers*, i. 286; Alberti to the Doge and Senate, 23 Apr./3 May 1675, *CSPV 1673–1675*, 397; Marvell to Hull Corporation, 22 Apr. 1675, *Poems and Letters*, ii. 148.

[5] *LPQ* 9–10, below, pp. 349–50; *LJ* xii. 665; HMC, 9th Report, Appendix, Part II, 51a.

[6] William Denton to Ralph Verney, 24 Apr. 1675, HMC, 7th Report, 492a.

[7] *Bulstrode Papers*, i. 287.

committee of the whole House, and twelve peers signed a second protest; two more followed on 29 April and 4 May, signed by twenty-one and sixteen peers.[1] One of the bill's supporters reported 'great heats in the House of Lords about passing the Test, in which noething is gained but by Inches, and every Line contested till 10 a clock at night'.[2] The bill was further considered on 7, 10, 12, 14, 21, and 28 May.[3] On 31 May the Lords sat for fourteen or fifteen hours and did not rise until midnight; the King made his own support very clear by sitting with them.[4]

The opposition to the bill was led by Shaftesbury, Buckingham, Halifax, Holles, and Wharton, Shaftesbury being especially active. Many years later Mrs Stringer recalled that

I have heard Mr Stringer say he [Shaftesbury] did to a Miracle for 6 Weeks together, violently oppose King, Lords, and Commons Singly by himself, he argued with such Strength of reason till 10. 11. & sometimes till 12 a Clock at ⟨night⟩, that when he got home, he seem'd to be quite Spent, his Health being much impair'd by it. I was at that Time in the Country at our own Estate in Essex, but I had this account from Mr Stringer, both by Letter & word of Mouth often & also from Mr Hoskins, who were both Ear & Eye Witnesses to the debates, & many times as much as My Lord was able, he wou'd repeat most of the Debates to them after he got home . . .[5]

Other accounts recall Shaftesbury's prominence in these debates. Burnet was no admirer of his but he acknowledged that

Lord Shaftesbury distinguished himself more in this session than ever he had done before. He spoke once a whole hour, to shew the inconvenience of condemning all resistance upon any pretence whatsoever. He said it might be proper to lay such ties upon those who served in the militia, and in corporations, because

---

[1] *LPQ* 10–11, 11–12, 13–14, below, pp. 350–1, 351–2, 353–4; *LJ* xii. 669, 670–1, 674–5; HMC, 9th Report, Appendix, Part II, 51a–b.

[2] Conway to Essex, 4 May 1675, BL, Stowe MS 207, fo. 370ʳ, *Essex Papers*, ii. 8.

[3] *LJ* xii. 682, 684–5, 692, 702, 708; HMC, 9th Report, Appendix, Part II, 51b–52b; NA, SP 29/370/111–13, 138, 155, 227, 259–61.

[4] *Bulstrode Papers*, i. 297; Francis Godolphin to Essex, 1 June 1675, *Essex Papers*, ii. 23; Marvell to Hull Corporation, 1 June 1675, *Poems and Letters*, ii. 160.

[5] [Jane Hill, formerly Stringer] to [Lady Elizabeth Harris, née Ashley Cooper], undated, PRO 30/24/6B/417; printed in Christie, vol. ii, p. cxxvii, where it is dated to 1734. A reference to Burnet shows that it was written after the appearance of the first volume of his *History of My Own Time* (1724). It is not certain that Mrs Stringer was referring to the debates on the Test Bill—she only married Stringer on 19 June 1675 and eight months later was described by her husband as 'settled at Bexwells in Essex', Stringer to Locke, 10 Feb. 1676, *Correspondence*, i. 436. However, her account fits the Test Bill much better than it does either of the Exclusion bills, where Shaftesbury can scarcely be described as opposing the Commons 'singly by himself'.

there was still a superior power in the parliament to declare the extent of the oath. But it might be of very ill consequence to lay it on a parliament: since there might be cases, though far out of view, so that it was hard to suppose them, in which he believed no man would say it was not lawful to resist. If a king would make us a province, and tributary to France, and subdue the nation by a French army to the French or the papal authority, must we be bound in that case tamely to submit? Upon which he said many things that did cut to the quick: and yet, though his words were watched, so that it was resolved to have sent him to the Tower if any one word had fallen from him that had made him liable to such a censure, he spoke both with so much boldness and so much caution, that, though he provoked the court extremely, no advantage could be taken against him.[1]

Many of these arguments were to reappear in the *Letter from a Person of Quality*.

The opponents of the bill argued their case with great force and on some occasions reduced its supporters to silence, but Danby still possessed a majority in the Lords and would have been able to get the bill through the House had it not been for a jurisdictional dispute with the Commons.[2] This was occasioned by two cases, *Shirley* v *Fagg* and *Crispe* v *Dalmahoy*, both of which concerned the right of the Lords to hear appeals from Chancery where members of the Commons were parties to the action. The Lords were naturally in favour, but the Commons viewed it as a breach of privilege, and neither side was willing to give way. Tempers were further inflamed by the high-handed behaviour of the Speaker of the Commons, Sir Edward Seymour, and by the deliberately obstructive tactics of Shaftesbury and his allies, who saw an ideal opportunity for disruption.[3] These tactics paid off: on 4 June the Lords ordered 'That this House will proceed upon no other Business (except what shall be recommended by his Majesty), till they have received full satisfaction, and Vindicated themselves in the Breach of their Privileges'.[4] Since the Commons was not prepared to back down, the result was

---

[1] Burnet, ii. 83–4; cf. BL, Add. MS 63057B, fo. 31ʳ.

[2] What would have happened to the bill in the Commons is necessarily a matter of conjecture, but its prospects were not good: Orrery told the King that it would never have passed by the Commons, and he said the same to Danby himself, National Art Library, MS Forster 47. A. 47, pp. 3, 13; BL, Add. MS 70500, fos. 88ʳ, 92ʳ⁻ᵛ.

[3] *LJ* xii. 673–4, 679, 682, 691–2, 694, 698, 700, 711, 713–14, 715–16, 718–19, 720–2, 723; *CJ* ix. 329, 335, 336–7, 339–40, 344, 349–54; HMC, 9th Report, Appendix, Part II, 53a–54b, 56b–58a; Dering, *Diaries and Papers*, 79, 83–7, 91–4, 97–101; Marvell to Hull Corporation, 13 May to 10 June 1675, *Poems and Letters*, ii. 155–63; Burnet, ii. 84–5. There is a copy of the Lords' declaration in *Crispe* v *Dalmahoy* and the Commons' reply in MS Locke b. 4, fos. 36–7; it is not in Locke's hand but was endorsed by him and dated June 1675.

[4] *LJ* xii. 723; *CJ* ix. 354.

deadlock. With business at a halt there was little point in continuing the session, and on 9 June Parliament was prorogued until the autumn. The Test Bill, which still had to be reported from committee, lapsed; it was never reintroduced.

Two days after the prorogation a newsletter concluded that

This Parlement must be dissolved, for no good can be expected from them. It is but lost labour to try them any longer, but the tests & the Bishops beare the greater blame. The highest Cavaliers & best Protestants are now convinced that persecution & English episcopacy is too narrow a foundation for our great monarchy to be built upon, considering the excessive odds between the numbers of the orthodox Churchmen & dissenters, & therefore begin to be persuaded that a liberty of conscience so regulated as to secure the present government of Church & State is ten times more likely to succeed as to the settlement of this kingdome in peace & plenty.[1]

This was a striking analysis, and it indicates just how far public opinion had moved since 1661–2. Others took a similar view. 'The clergie', one Scottish observer wrote, 'are now verry sensible that they are outwitted and it is thought they never did any thing which hath so much weakened their interest in Ingland, and that they now heartily wish that they had never moved it'.[2] The bishops came in for especially heavy criticism. Baxter thought the debates 'did more weaken the Interest and Reputation of the Bishops with the Nobles, than any thing that ever befel them since the King came in'.[3] 'Never', Marvell gloated, 'were poor Men exposed and abused, all the Session, as the Bishops were by the *Duke of Buckingham*, upon the Test; never the like, nor so infinitely pleasant: and no Men were ever grown so odiously ridiculous.'[4]

For Danby the failure of the bill was a very serious setback, and for a time his position appeared under threat. On 14 June a newsletter reported that 'The whole discourse of the town this day is that the Treasurer & all the present Ministers are to be routed & remov'd, & the Earle of Shaftesbury & other protesting Lords to be receiv'd into favour & imployment'.[5] Five days later a confidential letter to the Earl of Essex gave a vivid picture of the intrigues taking place. It was rumoured not only that Danby had lost ground with the King, and that there was a

---

[1] *Bulstrode Papers*, i. 301.
[2] George Scott to James Scott, 17 June 1675, HMC Laing, i. 403.
[3] *Reliquiae Baxterianae*, pt. III, § 297.
[4] Marvell to William Popple, 24 July 1675, *Poems and Letters*, ii. 343. See also Marvell, *An Account of the Growth of Popery, and Arbitrary Government in England*, 60–1.
[5] *Bulstrode Papers*, i. 302.

great party at work against him, but 'that the Duke is endeavouring to bring in Shaftesbury'.[1] Danby, however, was fighting back:

this morning the Treasurer got the King into the Treasury Chamber all alone for three hours. I was all that time waiting there, the Treasurer had ordered that none should be admitted; & I watched the King at his coming out & observed great troubles in his minde which makes me think that he did not goe away well satisfied. & this night I hear from a great privado of his that he will putt off his journy to Bathe & that the Duke did refuse a conference with him yesterday; & was 2 hours alone with Shaftesbury.[2]

On this occasion Danby's arguments must have been persuasive, for a few days later Shaftesbury was told to stay away from Court.[3] He left London shortly afterwards and spent the remainder of the summer at St Giles.

The Origins and Publication of the Letter from a Person of Quality

Shaftesbury was well aware of the need to appeal to public opinion. While the Test Bill was still before Parliament, copies of a work entitled *Reasons against the Bill for the Test* had been circulated in manuscript. This was undoubtedly written by, or at least for, Shaftesbury and was based on the speech Burnet described. The original manuscript is lost, but six contemporary copies are known to survive.[4] More probably remain to be discovered, and it is likely that the number originally produced was larger still.

Shaftesbury could very easily have reached a wider readership by having the *Reasons against the Bill for the Test* printed, but he decided instead to issue the same arguments, suitably expanded and augmented, in an anonymous pamphlet purportedly written by someone else. For Shaftesbury this had a number of advantages. It enabled him to praise himself and his supporters, to pour scorn and derision on his opponents, and to offer a much-needed defence of his own conduct at the time of the Declaration of Indulgence. Above all, an anonymous pamphlet could be

---

[1] William Harbord to Essex, 19 June 1675, BL, Stowe MS 208, fo. 88ʳ, *Essex Papers*, ii. 32.
[2] Ibid.
[3] George Scott to James Scott, 26 June 1675, HMC Laing, i. 404.
[4] PRO 30/24/5/294, pp. 1–10; Bodl., MS Rawl. A 191, fos. 3ʳ–4ʳ; MS Rawl. D 924, fos. 297ʳ–300ʳ; Leicestershire RO, DG7/PP30; Surrey History Centre, LM/1331/60; Yale, Osborn Shelves, b. 157, unfoliated. An account of the manuscripts is given in the Textual Introduction, pp. 238–43, and a complete text of the work in Appendix IV, below.

far more wide-ranging and hard-hitting than anything he could have issued under his own name, and it meant that he could portray the Test Bill not as an isolated measure but as the culmination of a long-running conspiracy going back to the Restoration, and indeed to the time of Archbishop Laud.

It is clear that whoever wrote the *Letter from a Person of Quality* had a copy of the *Reasons against the Bill for the Test* in front of him. Ten passages, amounting to some 1,400 words out of 1,900, were copied, often virtually word for word. One example will indicate just how close the borrowing was:

Reasons against the Bill for the Test	*A Letter from a Person of Quality*
I mean that famous instance of Henry the 6th who being a soft and weak Prince when taken prisoner by his cousin Edward the 4th that pretended to the Crown, and that Bustling Earle of Warwicke, was carried in their Armyes gave what orders and Commissions they pleased, whilst all those that were Loyall to him, as a Man adhered to his wife and son, and fought a pitcht Battle against him in person[1] and retook him. This was directly taking up armes by Henry the 6ths Authority against his person and against those that were Commissioned by him, and yet to this day no man hath ever blamed them, or thought but that if they had done other they had betrayed their Prince	*The Famous instance of Hen.* 6. who being a soft and weak Prince, when taken Prisoner by his Cousin *Edward* 4. that pretended to the Crown, and the great Earl of *Warwick*, was carried in their Armies, gave what orders and Commissions they pleased, and yet all those that were Loyal to him adhered to his Wife and Son, fought in a pitcht battel against him in person, and retook him: This was directly taking up Armes by His Authority against his person, and against those that were Commission'd by Him, and yet to this day no Man hath ever blamed them, or thought but that, if they had done other, they had betray'd their Prince.[2]

The writer of the *Letter* also made use of a report of another of Shaftesbury's speeches. The only known manuscript was kept among his papers, but other copies seem to have been in circulation—one was certainly available to the Whig historian John Oldmixon, writing just over fifty years later.[3] Whoever wrote the *Letter from a Person of Quality*

---

[1] The words 'in person' are found in Bodl., MS Rawl. A 191, fo. 3^r, and Surrey History Centre, LM/1331/60, p. 2, but not in the other MSS.

[2] Appendix IV, below, p. 410; *LPQ* 17, below, p. 358.

[3] '1675 The Earle of Shaftesbury's Speech in the H. of L. against the Test', now among the Malmesbury papers, Hampshire RO, 9M73/G201/1; *The History of England, During the Reigns of the Royal House of Stuart*, 590.

clearly had access to one such manuscript—indeed, he copied it almost word for word, apart from changing the first person to the third and the present tense to the past:

The Earle of Shaftesbury's Speech in the H. of L. against the Test	*A Letter from a Person of Quality*
I beg so much Charity of you to believe that I know the Protestant Religion so well, & am so confirm'd in it, that I hope I shou'd burn for the Witness of it, if Providence shou'd call me to it. But I may perhaps think some things not necessary which you account Essential: Nay I may think some things not True or agreable to Scripture, which you may call Doctrines of the Church. Besides, when I am to swear *never to endeavour to alter*, it is certainly necessary to know how far the Extent of this oath is; but since you have told me that the Protestant Religion is in those five Tracts, I have still power to ask, whether you mean those whole Tracts were the Protestant Religion, or only that the Protestant Religion is contain'd in all these, but that every part of These are not the Protestant Religion?	To this the Earl of *Shaftsbury* replied, that he begg'd so much Charity of them to believe, that he knew the *Protestant* Religion so well, and was so confirmed in it, that he hoped he should *burn* for the witness of it, if Providence should call him to it: But he might perhaps think some things not *necessary*, that they accounted *Essential*, nay he might think some things *not true*, or agreeable to the Scripture, that they might call *Doctrines of the Church*: Besides when he was to swear *never to endeavor to alter*, it was certainly necessary to know *how far the just extent of this Oath was*; but since they had told him that the Protestant Religion was in those 5 *tracts*, he had still to ask, whether they meant those whole Tracts were the *Protestant* Religion, or only that the Protestant Religion was contained in all those, but that every part of those was not the Protestant Religion.[1]

The survival of these documents establishes beyond doubt that the *Letter from a Person of Quality* was put together from material supplied by Shaftesbury. The writer of the *Letter* must also have been provided with a detailed narrative of events in the House of Lords, together with the texts of the four protests and the names of those who signed them. Shaftesbury must have written or dictated parts of the *Letter* himself, notably the interview in which he defended his part in the Declaration of Indulgence and the comments made on the peers who had supported or opposed the bill. He was, however, a busy man with many other calls on his time and it would not be surprising if he left to others the task of

---

[1] Appendix V, below; *LPQ* 21, below, p. 362.

putting all this material together, of revising it where necessary, of supplying linking passages, and of writing an appropriate introduction and conclusion.

No exact date of composition for the *Letter* can be fixed, but it would seem very likely that Shaftesbury took the completed manuscript with him when he returned to London shortly before the opening of the new session of Parliament on 13 October.[1] This picked up where the previous session had left off, with the dispute in *Shirley* v *Fagg*. Shaftesbury remained determined to procure a dissolution, and this meant keeping tempers high. On 20 October he made a long speech in the House of Lords, a copy of which was taken down in shorthand.[2] Much of his speech was concerned with the particular issues raised in *Shirley* v *Fagg*, but its peroration closely resembled the final paragraph of the *Letter from a Person of Quality*:

This *Laudean* Doctrine was the root that produced the *Bill of Test* last *Session*, and some very perplexed Oaths that are of the same nature with that, and yet imposed by several *Acts of this Parliament*.

In a word, if this Doctrine be true, our *Magna Charta* is of no force, our Laws are but Rules amongst our selves during the Kings pleasure. Monarchy, if of Divine Right, cannot be bounded or limited by humane Laws, nay, whats more, cannot bind it self; and All our Claims of right by the Law, or the Constitution of

---

[1] Shaftesbury was still in Dorset in late September, Nathaniel Osborne to Williamson, 2 Oct. 1675, NA, SP 29/373/257.

[2] The speech was printed in a quarto pamphlet, *Two Speeches. I. The Earl of Shaftsbury's Speech in the House of Lords the 20th. of October, 1675. II. The D. of Buckinghams Speech in the House of Lords the 16th. of November 1675*. Two editions of this were both ostensibly published in Amsterdam in 1675, though it is likely that both were printed in London: a fuller description is given in the Textual Introduction (pp. 208–9). Copies of the speech also circulated in manuscript with the title 'Notes taken in short hand of the Earle of Shaftsburys Speech in the house of Lords upon the debates of appointing a day for the hearing Dr Shirlyes Cause 20th of October 1675': one (in an unidentified hand) was kept among Shaftesbury's own papers, and is now in the Malmesbury papers, Hampshire RO, 9M73/G201/2. Other copies are in BL, Add. MS 32094, fos. 389ʳ–93ᵛ; BL, Egerton MS 3383, fos. 69ʳ–72ᵛ; BL, Harleian MS 5277, fos. 72ʳ–78ʳ; Huntington Library, EL 8416; NA, SP 29/375/63; and Surrey History Centre, 371/14/J/1. In none of these manuscripts was the text derived from that printed in *Two Speeches*. A slightly shortened and textually corrupt version of the speech taken from one such manuscript was subsequently printed in an undated four-page folio pamphlet, *Notes taken in Short-hand of a Speech in the House of Lords on the Debates of appointing a day for Hearing Dr. Shirley's Cause, Octob. 20. 1675*. Yet another version appeared in 1680, in *Two Speeches Made in the House of Peers. The one November 20. 1675. The other in November 1678*, ostensibly published in The Hague, though this too is almost certainly a false imprint; the text is corrupt and was not derived from either edition of the *Two Speeches*. A partially modernized and rather inaccurate text, apparently derived from the earlier 1675 edition, is printed in Christie, vol. ii, Appendix, pp. lxxxiv–xciv.

the Government, All the Jurisdiction and Priviledge of this House, All the Rights and Priviledges of the House of Commons, All the Properties and Liberties of the People, are to give way, not onely to the interest, but the will and pleasure of the Crown.[1]

One passage was particularly close:

Shaftesbury's Speech of 20 October	*A Letter from a Person of Quality*
Arch-Bishop Laud was the first Author that I remember of it . . . 'Tis the first of the Cannons published by the Convocation, 1640. *That Monarchy is of Divine Right.* This Doctrine was then preached up, and maintained by *Sibthorp, Manwaring,* and others, and of later years, by a Book published by Dr. *Sanderson, Bishop of Lincoln,* under the name of *Arch-Bishop Usher;* and how much it is spread amongst our Dignified Clergy, is very easily known.	Archbishop *Laud* was the first Founder of this Device; in his Canons of 1640. you shall find an Oath very like this, and a Declaratory Canon preceding, *that Monarchy is of divine Right,* which was also affirmed in this debate by our Reverend Prelates, and is owned in Print by no less Men then A. Bishop *Usher,* and B. *Sanderson;* and I am afraid it is the avowd opinion of much the greater part of our dignified Clergie . . . [2]

It is not particularly surprising that Shaftesbury should have attacked Laud or that he should have linked him with Sibthorpe and Manwaring, whose sermons in defence of Charles I's forced loan had caused such offence in the 1620s,[3] but his references to Sanderson and Ussher require some explanation. Ussher's book was *The Power Communicated by God to the Prince, and the Obedience Required of the Subject,* posthumously published in 1661 with a preface by Sanderson and fulsome dedication to Charles II by Ussher's grandson—and Locke's friend—James Tyrrell.[4] One cannot be sure, but it would seem quite likely that Locke provided Shaftesbury with the reference.

---

[1] *Two Speeches,* 11. One minor correction has been made to the text here: the word 'the' before 'Constitution' is missing from both 1675 editions, but is present in both the later printed versions, *Notes taken in Short-hand* and *Two Speeches Made in the House of Peers,* and in all the manuscripts except NA, SP 29/375/63, where the text is corrupt.

[2] *Two Speeches,* 10; *LPQ* 34, below, p. 375.

[3] Locke made a similar point in *Two Treatises,* I. 5: 'By whom this Doctrine came at first to be broach'd, and brought in fashion amongst us, and what sad Effects it gave rise to, I leave to *Historians* to relate, or to the Memory of those who were Contemporaries with *Sibthorp* and *Manwering* to recollect.' For Sibthorpe and Manwaring, see Sommerville, *Politics and Ideology in England,* 127–31.

[4] Sanderson's preface, dated 31 Dec. 1660, appears to have been added as an after-thought: it is to be found on five gatherings, signed a–e, inserted between the preliminaries and dedication on gathering A and the main text, which begins on gathering B.

The *Letter from a Person of Quality* appears to have gone on public sale during the first week in November.[1] The response was swift. On Monday 8 November the Lords Journals recorded that

Complaint was made to the House of a dangerous Book, printed, intituled, *A Letter from a Person of Quality to his Friend in the Country*.

Which was read; and thereupon it is ORDERED, That the said Printed Book shall be burnt at *The Royall Exchange* in *London*, and in *The Old Palace Yard* at *Westminster*, by the Hand of the Common Hangman, between the Hours of Twelve and One of the Clock, on *Wednesday* the Tenth Day this Instant *November*; and that the Sheriffs of *London* and *Middlesex* do take Care that Execution be done accordingly.[2]

The Lords also appointed a committee of twenty-nine lay peers and six bishops 'to enquire out the Author, Publisher, and Printer of it'. Danby was on the committee, but Shaftesbury, who was absent that day, was not.

The following day a newsletter reported that 'The Lords have been againe very angry about the booke which they yesterday condemn'd to be burn'd, & quarrel'd the Lord Privy Seal [Anglesey], who was the Chaireman to the Committee appointed to examine it, for not being severe enough upon it'.[3] To make their disapproval clear, the House therefore declared the *Letter* to be 'a lying, scandalous, and seditious Book'.[4] On the following day it was

ORDERED, by the Lords Spiritual and Temporal in Parliament assembled, That the Lords Committees appointed to consider what Brand and Judgement by this House shall be set and given upon a Printed Book, intituled, *A Letter from a Person of Quality to his Friend in the Country*, and to enquire out the Author, Publisher, and Printer of it, have hereby Power given them, to send for Persons, Books, and Writings; and in particular Mr. *Starkey*, the Bookseller; and that their Lordships have likewise Power to require the Master and Wardens of the Company of Stationers to do their Duties enjoined by the Statute of 14° *Car'l.* 2[di], concerning searching for seditious Books.[5]

---

[1] According to Louise Fargo Brown, 'publication was so timed that the pamphlet was in the hands of members when parliament assembled on October 13', *Shaftesbury*, 233. The evidence she cited for this is Longleat, Coventry MS 83, fo. 94 (microfilm in the Institute of Historical Research, London, XR 60/67). This is a letter book of Henry Coventry, but the letters—to Leoline Jenkins (6 Sept.) and Colonel Sandys (21 Sept.)—do not mention the *Letter from a Person of Quality*.   [2] *LJ* xiii. 13.

[3] *Bulstrode Papers*, i. 323.   [4] *LJ* xiii. 14.

[5] *LJ* xiii. 17. For John Starkey, see Plomer, *A Dictionary of Printers and Booksellers 1641 to 1667*, 170–1. He is not known to have had anything to do with the *Letter from a Person of Quality*.

Meanwhile a parallel investigation was being conducted by one of the Secretaries of State, Sir Joseph Williamson. On 8 November a warrant was issued to Sir Roger L'Estrange to seize all copies of the *Letter* and to search for its author, printer, and publisher. On 9 November another warrant was issued to search the house of Katherine Knight.[1] The following day she was examined before Williamson. She told him that she had been left 150 copies on Saturday 30 October; they were in sheets and she stitched them up herself, unassisted. She did not (she said) know who had left them or where they had come from, but she had discovered them when she returned home at ten that morning. She had disposed of most of them to a woman she would not name who had been in her chamber when she was apprehended, but who had slipped away. She also said that on Monday 1 November she had sold twenty-five or fifty copies (at 18*d.* a copy) to a fat woman who kept a booksellers near the Court of Requests.[2]

The Lords' committee was also busy at work. On 9 November they questioned Mrs Anne Breach, who kept a shop at the stair foot in Westminster Hall. She said she had seen the *Letter* but had not sold it and did not know either the author or the printer. The committee then produced a Mr Patricius Roberts, who said he had bought a copy from her. She then admitted that she had sold such a book; it cost her half a crown, but she claimed not to know from whom she had bought it.[3]

On 11 November the Master and Wardens of the Stationers' Company and the King's printer were called in. They told the committee that they had found the dispersers. One Mary White had bought three dozen copies, of which six were found upon her, probably supplied by Katherine Knight, who had also sold a large number to a Mrs Jackson of Charterhouse Lane. The books, they added, were wet yesterday and were too well printed for a private press. Two days later Mary White was questioned.[4] She told the committee that she had had about three dozen at a shilling apiece, but that she did not know the woman who brought them to her. Katherine Knight said that 150 copies had been left at her house and that she had sold all except the thirty Williamson had taken.[5] On 8 December the Attorney-General was ordered to prosecute her.[6]

---

[1] NA, SP 44/334, p. 89. [2] NA, SP 29/374/261.

[3] HLRO, Minutes of Committees 1672–85, p. 115; HMC, 9th Report, Appendix, Part II, 66a. For Anne Breach, see Plomer, *A Dictionary of Printers and Booksellers 1641 to 1667*, 31.

[4] She had previously been examined for Williamson by Sir Robert Vyner, who found her 'a poore inocent weake creature, that to gett a penny knew not what shee did. Shee promisst to stay the party that brought them to her, but its like they have taken Alarm & doe not appeare', Vyner to Williamson, 12 Nov. 1675, NA, SP 29/374/281.

[5] HMC, 9th Report, Appendix, Part II, 66b. [6] NA, PC 2/65, p. 62.

On 20 December she was indicted by the Middlesex grand jury. At the ensuing sessions she was convicted, fined £26 13s. 4d., and committed to Newgate until the fine was paid; Anne Breach suffered a similar fate.[1]

All this provides a revealing account of how clandestine pamphlets were distributed, but the authorities had not yet obtained what they were really looking for: the names of the author, publisher, and printer. On 7 January a proclamation was issued, promising a reward of £20 for the discovery of any private printing press, and £50 for the names of either the authors of such pamphlets or those who had conveyed them to the press.[2] On 29 March another warrant was issued to L'Estrange to continue his searches.[3] On 15 February 1677 a new session of Parliament opened, the first since November 1675, and on the following day the Lords appointed a committee to make inquiries into the authors and printers of certain libellous pamphlets.[4] On 30 March the committee questioned Henry Bridges (or Bruges) and John Marlow, two London printers:

Hen: Bruges and Jo Marlow are called in and asked whether they printed the Two Speeches Entitled the Earl of Shaftsbury and D Bucks Speechs and for whom. They say they did print the E Shaftsburys for Tho: Sawbridge. They say they also printed part of the Booke entitled A letter from a person of Quality to his friend in the Country. They say that Wm Sawbridge told Marlow that his brother Thomas said that if he would not print his unlicensed worke he should not print his licensed work. Marlow deposed that the Stationers incourage him to print such by giving him notice when any search is to be made.[5]

On 9 April L'Estrange recommended that 'the King may be moved that Bridges and Marlow who printed the Test and who have made discoveries may be pardoned'.[6] L'Estrange did not, however, abandon his investigations, and in August 1678 he was able to report that

With much difficulty I have found out the Widow Brewsters lodging. I can prove against her, the bringing of three Libells to the presse in manuscript: viz. *The Letter about the Test; The Two Speeches of the D: of Buck: and Ld Shaftsbury*; and

---

[1] *Middlesex County Records*, iv. 66–9.
[2] *A Proclamation for the Better Discovery of Seditious Libellers*.
[3] NA, SP 44/334, p. 161.
[4] *LJ* xiii. 42; HMC, 9th Report, Appendix, Part II, 69a.
[5] HLRO, Minutes of Committees 1672–85, p. 185; cf. HMC, 9th Report, Appendix, Part II, 78a–b. For biographical details, see Plomer, *A Dictionary of Booksellers and Printers 1641 to 1667*, 32–3; *A Dictionary of Printers and Booksellers 1668 to 1725*, 197, 263.
[6] HLRO, Minutes of Committees 1672–85, p. 199; cf. HMC, 9th Report, Appendix, Part II, 79a.

Jenks his Speech, upon which Accompt, she hath so long conceald her selfe. She is in the House of a person formerly an officer under Cromwell: that writes three or foure very good Hands, and owns to have been employd in Transcribing things for a Counsellor in the Temple. From which Circumstances one may fayrly presume that all those Delicate Copyes which Brewster carryed to the Presse, were written by Brewsters Landlord, and Copyd by him, from the Authour.[1]

Ann Brewster was the widow of Thomas Brewster, who had been appointed official printer to the Council of State in 1653.[2] L'Estrange did not indicate how he obtained his information, but he may well have been correct in thinking that the manuscript she delivered to the press was a fair copy made by her landlord. If so, this adds another link to the chain—and a further opportunity for textual corruption. Those ultimately responsible for the *Letter* had certainly taken effective steps to ensure that it could not be traced back to them.

Locke and the Letter from a Person of Quality

It is not at all easy to determine whether Locke was in any way involved in the events described here. He was always prudent, cautious, and secretive, and if he had helped write the *Letter* he would have done his best to conceal the fact. This creates problems for the historian, and it must be acknowledged that there is no incontrovertible evidence connecting him with the *Letter*—no personal admissions, no drafts in his hand, no unimpeachable contemporary testimony, and no passages that could only have been written by him. Such evidence as we have is fragmentary and purely circumstantial: none of it is decisive, and not all of it points the same way.

Locke's whereabouts in 1675 are often difficult to ascertain, but there can be little doubt that he was in London for most if not all of the time the Test Bill was before Parliament. A letter to Henry Oldenburg on the subject of poisonous fish—the only surviving letter from Locke for the whole of 1675—establishes that he was at Exeter House on 20 May.[3] He was treating Shaftesbury for a sore throat early in May.[4] A series of

---

[1] L'Estrange to Williamson, 23 Aug. 1678, NA, SP 29/406/37, underlined in original. Jenks's speech and the reaction to it are described in Haley, 409–10. For Brewster's part in printing *The Long Parliament dissolved*, see HMC, 9th Report, Appendix, Part II, 70a.

[2] Plomer, *A Dictionary of Booksellers and Printers 1641 to 1667*, 32; *A Dictionary of Printers and Booksellers 1668 to 1725*, 48. [3] *Correspondence*, i. 423.

[4] MS Locke d. 9, p. 131.

minutes in his hand shows that he attended meetings of the Lords Proprietors of Carolina on 9 April and 18 June, and the Bahamas Company on 11 May.[1] There are weather reports (indicating his presence in London) for 25–8 April, 2 and 23 May, and 8–10 and 13–14 June.[2]

Locke's movements during the later part of the summer are less easy to determine. Towards the end of June Shaftesbury left London for St Giles, and the entries in Locke's ledger suggest that Locke accompanied him.[3] Locke was, however, not mentioned in a document preserved in the Shaftesbury papers listing the household at St Giles in July 1675.[4] He may have been absent when the list was drawn up, or he may have sat at Shaftesbury's own table, the occupants of which were not listed. If he was absent, it may have been because he was staying with David Thomas at Salisbury, which is only about fifteen miles from St Giles: his ledger records a payment from Thomas on 24 July.[5] Locke also had dealings at this time with Thomas Stringer, whose name was included in the list of the household: on 18 July he received £50 'by the hands of Mr Stringer' and paid him £45.[6] Apart from a letter which may indicate Locke's presence at St Giles on 1 August[7] there is no evidence at all of what he was doing in August and early September; evidence that he was still in Dorset (or nearby) in mid-September is provided by further payments from David Thomas on 12 and 20 September, and by a letter from London addressed to Locke at St Giles.[8]

---

[1] MS Locke c. 30, fos. 5, 9, 11; Shaftesbury was present at all these meetings. There is also an entry in Locke's hand with the date 9 June 1675 in the Carolina Entry Book, NA, CO 5/286, fo. 43ᵛ.   [2] MS Locke d. 9, p. 527; after these there were no more until 1680.

[3] His ledger (MS Locke c. 1) records numerous small payments and receipts up until 24 June but then very few until November; there are none at all for August. On 26 June he paid 'Mr Hix in full of all demands' the sum of £2 5s., MS Locke c. 1, p. 85; this was presumably John Hicks, the tailor whose lodgings were used by Locke as an accommodation address after 1679, *Correspondence*, i. 448 n.

[4] 'Orders for my Lord Shaftesburys House at St Giles in Dorsettshire Setled in July 1675', PRO 30/24/5/286. The text printed in Christie, ii. 211–14, is considerably longer than that in the extant manuscript, now only a single leaf, and it would seem that the last part has been lost since Christie copied it. Two references in the missing portion to 'Mr Locke's boy' suggest Locke's presence in Dorset or nearby (e.g. at Salisbury).

[5] MS Locke c. 1, p. 67.

[6] MS Locke c. 1, pp. 83, 85; Stringer's note of the payment is in MS Locke b. 1, fo. 24ʳ.

[7] The Malmesbury papers contain two letters in Locke's hand from Shaftesbury to Stringer, both sent from St Giles (Hampshire RO, 9M73/G237/8, 9); one was dated 19 July, the other 1 August, no year being given. Neither letter is easily dated on internal evidence, but a reference in the second to Shaftesbury's desire to sell the lease of Exeter House suggests a date of 1675; he sold Exeter House in March 1676 and moved out in June: Haley, 408; Stringer to Locke, 5 June, 8 July 1676, *Correspondence*, i. 447, 452.

[8] MS Locke c. 1, p. 89; W. Fanshawe to Locke, 14 Sept. 1675, *Correspondence*, i. 428–9.

It is likely that Locke returned to London with Shaftesbury early in October. He remained there for another month, but on 12 November, four days after the *Letter from a Person of Quality* was condemned and two days after it was burned, he left London. Two days later he arrived in France, where he remained for the next three and a half years. Ostensibly he went for reasons of health, but there have been some, beginning with the third Earl of Shaftesbury, who have suspected that the timing of his departure was no mere coincidence and that his poor health was simply a pretext, or at least not the whole truth.[1] The point has been put most forcefully by Richard Ashcraft:

> He [Locke] did not have time to go to Oxford to obtain permission for his absence from the chapter of the college, as courtesy dictated. Someone else in Oxford packed up his belongings and books for him. Someone made an inventory of goods he had left behind at Shaftesbury's residence. Locke did not even wait to receive his half-yearly rents that his uncle had collected for him. . . . Everything, in other words, points to a very hasty departure on Locke's part, simultaneous with the appearance in print of the *Letter*.[2]

Locke's departure was rather less hasty than this suggests, and his health was poor, though not perhaps quite as bad as he believed.[3] We do not know when he first decided to go to France, but it would appear to have been well before the *Letter* was published.[4] At the end of 1674 he lost his job as secretary and treasurer to the Council of Trade and Plantations, which removed one reason for staying in England. His annuity from Shaftesbury and the income from his land in Somerset and his studentship at Christ Church gave him more than enough to live on without having to take further employment. On 2 May 1675 he obtained a bill of exchange for £20 addressed to an English merchant at Nantes.[5]

One may wonder why, if Locke was already thinking of going to France, he did not leave that summer, when travelling conditions would have been much easier than in November. Perhaps it was because he still had outstanding business in England, including the composition of the *Letter from a Person of Quality*. There is, however, another and simpler reason: he did not travel alone. His companion was George Walls, a

---

[1] Shaftesbury to Le Clerc, 8 Feb. 1705, PRO 30/24/22/2, fo. 40^{r-v}; the letter is discussed below.   [2] Ashcraft, *Revolutionary Politics*, 122 n.–3 n.

[3] For details, see Sydenham to Locke, *c*.Nov. 1674, *Correspondence*, i. 415–16.

[4] Locke had talked of going to Montpellier as early as 1671, Locke to Mapletoft, [27?] Oct. 1671, *Correspondence*, i. 363.

[5] MS Locke c. 23, fo. 61; Stringer to Locke, 17 Feb. 1676, *Correspondence*, i. 438.

Student of Christ Church and a former pupil.[1] Walls was an entirely respectable Anglican clergyman—he eventually became a canon of St Paul's—who had no reason to make a hurried departure from England. Since Walls was to be away for nearly two years (he returned in July 1677) and Locke for considerably longer, it is unlikely that their departure was planned at the last minute. It was certainly arranged before the *Letter* was condemned: writing from Christ Church on 8 November, Humphrey Prideaux noted that 'George Wall goeth to London on monday in order to a journy into France what is his businesse there I know not unlesse it be John Locks chaplain whom he accompanyeth thither.'[2] Before leaving Oxford Walls had time to compile an inventory of Locke's goods, which were to be looked after by another Student of Christ Church, Samuel Thomas.[3]

It is clear that Locke's decision to leave must have been made by the beginning of November at the very latest. On 2 November he wrote to his uncle to tell him that he was going to France for reasons of his health.[4] He must also have written to the Dean of Christ Church at about this time, because on 8 November Fell sent him an affectionate letter telling him that he was sorry that he was having to go abroad and that there was no need for him to add to his journey by going to Oxford 'upon the score of ceremony'.[5] On 11 November Locke settled his accounts with Shaftesbury and with his bookbinder, and executed a power of attorney in favour of 'my beloved Friend Thomas Stringer'.[6] When he sailed from Dover to Calais three days later, it was apparently in the yacht provided for the English ambassador, Lord Berkeley of Stratton.[7]

There is nothing here to indicate a sudden and panicky departure, and Locke's choice of transport does not suggest a fugitive fleeing from justice. He had no reason to behave like one. Shaftesbury was widely and correctly thought to be behind the *Letter*, though no proceedings were

---

[1] Walls is incorrectly identified in *Correspondence*, i. 430 n.: Locke's companion was his future correspondent George Walls of Worcester (letters 409, 422, etc.). See Milton, 'John Locke, George Wall and George Walls'.

[2] Prideaux to John Ellis, 8 Nov. 1675, BL, Add. MS 28929, fo. 20^r, *Letters of Humphrey Prideaux*, 49.

[3] MS Locke c. 25, fos. 14, 15; Thomas to Locke, 11 Nov. 1675, *Correspondence*, i. 430–1.

[4] The letter, no longer extant, is mentioned in Peter Locke to Locke, 13 Nov. 1675, *Correspondence*, i. 433.   [5] Fell to Locke, 8 Nov. 1675, *Correspondence*, i. 430.

[6] PRO 30/24/47/30, fos. 16, 17; MS Locke c. 1, pp. 82, 83; Hampshire RO, 9M73/G242.

[7] MS Locke f. 1, p. 1, printed in *Locke's Travels in France*, 1; Stringer to Locke, 25 Nov. 1675, *Correspondence*, i. 434.

ever brought against him. No evidence has yet come to light that anyone was pointing the finger at Locke.[1]

It was not until 1720, forty-five years after the *Letter* was published and sixteen years after Locke's death, that it was first publicly attributed to him, by Pierre Des Maizeaux. Born in France in 1673, Des Maizeaux was the son of a Huguenot minister who later fled the country after the revocation of the Edict of Nantes. He was educated at Geneva and in the spring of 1699 went to Holland where he met a number of Locke's friends, including Jean Le Clerc and Benjamin Furly; he also began learning English—an unusual step for a Frenchman—and was soon described by Pierre Coste as 'déja fort avancé dans la connoissance de la Langue Angloise'.[2] In the summer of 1699 he came to England bearing a letter from Le Clerc to Locke which described him as a very respectable man and recommended him as a suitable children's tutor if any of Locke's friends were looking for one.[3] Since Des Maizeaux delivered the letter himself[4] it is quite likely that he met Locke, though there is no evidence of any subsequent contact. He did, however, become well acquainted with a number of Locke's friends, including Pierre Coste, Anthony Collins, and the third Earl of Shaftesbury. Collins became one of his closest friends.[5]

After a spell as a children's tutor, Des Maizeaux made a successful career as a journalist, editor, and translator.[6] He does not appear to have been involved in any of the earlier editions of Locke's writings, but in 1720 he published *A Collection of Several Pieces of Mr. John Locke*. This

---

[1] According to Fox Bourne (i. 482), 'It would seem that long before Locke's visit to Holland his known abilities had caused him to be credited with the authorship of the "Letter from a Person of Quality"'. No evidence was given for this.

[2] Coste to Locke, 29 June 1699, *Correspondence*, vi. 652.

[3] 'Je profite présentement de l'occasion qui s'offre de Mr. Desmaiseaux, qui est un fort honête homme, et dont mes amis de Geneve me disent toute sorte de bien. Il va en Angleterre, à dessein d'y chercher quelque emploi, car il n'y en a point pour les étrangers, dans le païs d'où il vient. Si quelcun de vos Amis avoit besoin d'un Gouverneur, pour ses enfans, je ne doute pas qu'on ne fût très-satisfait de lui', Le Clerc to Locke, 8/18 June 1699, *Correspondence*, vi. 636.

[4] 'On m'écrit de Hollande qu'un jeune homme françois, nommé Mr. Desmaiseaux est parti pour l'Angleterre et qu'il vous porte une Lettre de Mr. Le Clerc', Coste to Locke, 29 June 1699, *Correspondence*, vi. 649. Rand (*Shaftesbury*, 307 n.) stated incorrectly that Des Maizeaux travelled to England with Ashley. Ashley left Holland in late April and was in London by the beginning of May, Furly to Locke, 21 Apr./1 May 1699, *Correspondence*, vi. 604; Stringer to Ashley, 5 May 1699, PRO 30/24/44/77, fo. 9ʳ.

[5] Des Maizeaux's papers contain sixty-six letters from Collins written between 1712 and 1727, BL, Add. MS 4282, fos. 116–239; his letters to Collins appear to have been lost.

[6] There is no general biography, but a full treatment of one side of his career is given in Almagor, *Pierre Des Maizeaux*.

General Introduction

was an octavo volume of 446 pages containing a number of Locke's letters, several minor works that had not previously been printed, and two longer ones that had been printed but not under Locke's name: the *Letter from a Person of Quality* and the *Fundamental Constitutions of Carolina*. It was prefaced with a long dedicatory letter, dated 23 March 1719[/20], addressed to Hugh Wrottesley, an antiquarian and book-collector.[1] This began with Des Maizeaux's reasons for undertaking the edition:

Having met with several of Mr. LOCKE's Works, which were never printed; I thought myself obliged to impart them to the Public, together with some Pieces, of that illustrious Writer, which had indeed been published before, but without his name to them, and were grown very scarce. The value you have for every thing that was written by Mr. LOCKE, and your esteem for some of his friends concern'd in this Collection, emboldens me to offer it to you . . .[2]

Anthony Collins—who subsequently married Wrottesley's sister Elizabeth—was undoubtedly one of the friends Des Maizeaux was referring to. He was not mentioned by name in the first edition of *A Collection of Several Pieces*, but the second edition, published in 1739, a decade after his death, had on the title-page 'Publish'd by Mr. Desmaizeaux, under the Direction of Anthony Collins, Esq.'. Collins seems to have left the routine editorial work to Des Maizeaux, but he supplied material, including copies of thirty-two letters from Locke,[3] and he did what he could to find more. At the end of February 1719 he informed Des Maizeaux that he intended 'to write in a few days to Mr [Awnsham] Churchil to press my Lord Cheif Justice King for some further works of Mr Locke, and particularly for his *Discourse of Space*, and his Treatise *Of Hell Torments and the Resurrection*'.[4] Four weeks later Collins wrote again to tell Des Maizeaux that Churchill 'has been with Sir Peter King; and it is not unlikely, but that he may get the two manuscripts I wrote about'.[5] King seems not to have been as helpful as hoped, and Collins had to tell Des Maizeaux that 'I yesterday receivd a letter from Mr Churchil, by which I find Sir P. K. will not communicate the two treatises.'[6] Churchill was

---

[1] Hugh Wrottesley (d. 1725), younger son of Sir Walter Wrottesley, a Staffordshire baronet; there is a full account of the family in Wrottesley, 'A History of the Family of Wrottesley'. [2] *A Collection of Several Pieces*, sig. A2^{r–v}.
[3] BL, Add. MS 4290, fos. 1^r–2^r, 17^r–55^r.
[4] Collins to Des Maizeaux, 28 Feb. 1718[/9], BL, Add. MS 4282, fo. 159^v. The latter was presumably 'Resurrectio et quae sequuntur', MS Locke c. 27, fos. 162–73, printed in *A Paraphrase and Notes on the Epistles of St Paul*, ii. 679–84.
[5] Collins to Des Maizeaux, 23 Mar. 1718[/9], BL, Add. MS 4282, fo. 166^r.
[6] Collins to Des Maizeaux, undated, BL, Add. MS 4282, fo. 228^v. No exact date can be given for the letter, but it was sent from Baddow Hall, where Collins moved in the summer

102

even less obliging and seems to have regarded Des Maizeaux as an unwelcome interloper. In October Collins complained that Churchill 'would have no body to print any of Mr Lockes works but himself; and yet would have them for nothing. I believe he is not to be dealt with: and therefore I leave the matter to you, who may therein wholly follow your own judgment and interest.'[1] Des Maizeaux was not put off by Churchill's opposition, and by the end of the year a part at least of the edition had been sent to the printer.[2] Collins received his copy of the book at the end of March and wrote to thank Des Maizeaux, telling him that he was 'very well pleased' with the preface, and that he hoped Wrottesley would be.[3]

Des Maizeaux's dedicatory letter contains a detailed account of the works he had chosen to include and his reasons for doing so. His account of the *Letter from a Person of Quality* is of the greatest interest:

The Debates occasion'd by that Bill [the 1675 Test Bill], fail'd not to make a great noise throughout the whole Kingdom: and because there were but few persons duly apprized thereof, and every body spoke of it, as they stood affected; my Lord SHAFTSBURY, who was, as [*sic*] the Head of the Country-Party, thought it necessary to publish an exact relation of every thing that had pass'd upon that occasion; in order, not only to open the Peoples eyes upon the secret views of the Court; but to do justice to the Country-Lords, and thereby to secure to them the continuance of the affection and attachment of such as were of the same opinion with themselves, which was the most considerable part of the Nation. But tho' this Lord had all the faculties of an orator; yet, not having time to exercise himself in the art of writing, he desir'd Mr. LOCKE to draw up this relation; which he did under his Lordship's inspection, and only committed to writing, what my Lord SHAFTSBURY did in a manner dictate to him. Accordingly, you will find in it a great many strokes, which could proceed from no body, but my Lord SHAFTSBURY

of 1718, and mention of a visit from Toland indicates that it cannot be later than early 1722. There is another mention of King's unhelpfulness in a later letter: 'By my sons last to me I find that Sir P K will not part with the Papers', Collins to Des Maizeaux, 17 Apr. 1722, BL, Add. MS 4282, fo. 192ᵛ. It is unlikely that King lent the manuscript of the *Remarks upon some of Mr. Norris's Books* that is still among Locke's papers (MS Locke d. 3, pp. 89–112): Des Maizeaux was a careful editor, and there are too many differences between the two texts. It is possible that King had a further copy made for Des Maizeaux to use, but even this is unlikely. In two places where the readings in MS Locke d. 3 were altered, Des Maizeaux's text has the original readings, which suggests he was using an independent manuscript.

[1] Collins to Des Maizeaux, 25 Oct. 1719, BL, Add. MS 4282, fo. 168ʳ.
[2] 'I like very much the sheet you sent me; and suppose the impression goes on', Collins to Des Maizeaux, 27 Dec. 1719, BL, Add. MS 4282, fo. 170ʳ.
[3] Collins to Des Maizeaux, 1 Apr. 1720, BL, Add. MS 4282, fo. 172ʳ.

himself; and among others, the Characters and Elogiums of such Lords, as had signaliz'd themselves, in the cause of publick Liberty.[1]

This is clear, circumstantial, and far from implausible. It also emphasized that Locke's role was essentially a secondary one, in that he only wrote down what Shaftesbury had told him to. On this point Des Maizeaux's drafts were even more emphatic than the published version:

Mais comme ce Seigneur, qui savoit si bien parler, ne s'etoit pas beaucoup attaché d'ecrire; il pria Mr. Locke de faire cette Relation. Ainsi Mr. Locke la dressa sous ses yeux; & ne fit que coucher par écrit, ce que Mylord Shaftsbury lui disoit de bouche, & pour ainsi dire, lui dictoit.[2]

Unfortunately Des Maizeaux did not reveal how or from whom he had obtained this account of the *Letter*'s composition. It is exceedingly unlikely that he obtained it directly from Locke himself. Locke could be pathologically secretive on matters of authorship, and if he was unwilling to admit even to an old friend like Tyrrell that he had written the *Two Treatises of Government* and the *Epistola de Tolerantia*, it can hardly be supposed that he would have told a Frenchman he barely knew that he had once written a pamphlet which had been condemned by the House of Lords and burned by the public hangman.

There is a general agreement among those modern writers who have expressed views on the matter that Des Maizeaux obtained his story from one of Locke's friends, though different and incompatible accounts have been given of how this is supposed to have happened. One version, stated by Cranston and followed by Ashcraft, is that Des Maizeaux printed the *Letter* 'from manuscripts given him by Locke's cousin Peter King'.[3] Cranston gave no source for this, but he was probably relying on H. O. Christophersen's bibliography, which claimed that Des Maizeaux included the *Letter* in his edition because 'a manuscript copy of it was found among Locke's papers'. Christophersen added that 'It has probably been written by Locke after the dictation of Shaftesbury. This explains how a draught of it has been mixed up with Locke's papers.'[4] Taken strictly, this implies that two manuscripts were found in Locke's papers—a 'draught' and a 'copy'—though Christophersen was probably writing loosely. Where he got his story from one cannot say for certain, but he had no access to Locke's papers and his version of events cannot

---

[1] *A Collection of Several Pieces*, sigs. A6^v–A7^r.
[2] BL, Add. MS 4222, fo. 248^r; other drafts on fos. 230^r, 238^r do not differ in essentials.
[3] Cranston, 158; Ashcraft, *Revolutionary Politics*, 120.
[4] *A Bibliographical Introduction to the Study of John Locke*, 9, 10.

be relied on.[1] It is quite clear from Des Maizeaux's own account that the text he printed was taken from the two 1675 editions, not from manuscripts supplied by King or anyone else.[2]

A variant of this story was provided by Haley, who stated that Des Maizeaux was given the account of the *Letter*'s composition by Collins, who had obtained it from Peter King.[3] Haley did not indicate his source for this, but he may have taken it partly from Cranston and partly from Lord King, who quoted Des Maizeaux's preface at length but wrongly attributed it to Collins.[4] Des Maizeaux's drafts show that he wrote the preface himself.

Collins would doubtless have told Des Maizeaux anything he knew about the authorship of the *Letter* and the circumstances of its composition, but as he had not even been born when it was written, any information he may have had could only have come from others. He first met Locke in the spring of 1703, and though it is certainly less implausible to suppose that Locke revealed his part in the composition of the *Letter* to him than to Des Maizeaux, it is still very unlikely. Locke undoubtedly took a great liking to Collins, but there is no sign of his becoming garrulous in old age. In 1704 he asked Collins to obtain some copies of the *Epistola de Tolerantia* to send to some of his friends. Collins duly obliged, adding that 'You will pardon me if I tell you, that I believe I can read so much of the Title page as to find out the Authors name and his country.'[5] Locke did not rise to the bait: in his reply he referred to 'my Essay of H U' and 'the *Epistola de Tolerantia*', and he continued to refer to the *Epistola* by its title alone in subsequent letters.[6] If he was still unwilling to acknowledge what had long been an open secret,[7] it is very hard to believe he would have been more forthcoming about any part he may have had in writing the *Letter from a Person of Quality*.

Peter King was seven years older than Collins, but he had only been a child when the *Letter* was written and was therefore equally reliant on the testimony of others. He was, of course, Locke's cousin and executor, but

---

[1] He also stated (ibid. 10) that 'The Fundamental Constitutions of Carolina were found among Locke's papers after his death and in his handwriting'. This is equally untrue.

[2] *A Collection of Several Pieces*, sigs. A7^v–A8^v.   [3] Haley, 392.

[4] King (1830), i. 71.

[5] Collins to Locke, 21 Mar. 1704, *Correspondence*, viii. 249. Collins was referring to the cryptogram on the title-page: 'Scripta à P.A.P.O.I.L.A.'

[6] Locke to Collins, 21 Mar., 14 May, 9 June 1704, *Correspondence*, viii. 255–6, 287, 315.

[7] Within a year of its publication Locke's authorship was described as being 'publiquement connu en engleterre', Pieter Guenellon to Locke 8/18 Apr. 1690, *Correspondence*, iv. 51; see also Tyrrell to Locke, 18 Mar. 1690, *Correspondence*, iv. 36.

Locke's surviving papers contain nothing linking him with the *Letter*, and there is no reason to think they contained any more when King acquired them. Locke was not someone to retain drafts or copies of incriminating material. His correspondence with King is equally unrevealing, and though his last letter contained directions for the publication of some of his unpublished writings, it said nothing about the *Letter from a Person of Quality*.[1]

It is therefore very unlikely that Locke himself was the ultimate source of Des Maizeaux's account, and it is more likely that the story of his involvement came from within Shaftesbury's household. If this is the case, then by far the most plausible intermediary is the third Earl. He was himself only a small child at the time the *Letter* was written, but he had access both to his grandfather's papers and to members of the Shaftesbury household. Nothing in the career of the second Earl suggests that he would have been entrusted with any political secrets, but both his wife and the first Earl's widow were intelligent women who are likely to have known at least something of what was going on.

The first Earl's servants would certainly have been willing to tell his grandson things they would have withheld from strangers. One possible source was Thomas Stringer, the first Earl's steward and one of his most trusted associates. In 1675 Stringer was on excellent terms with Locke, though in later years they became estranged; he remained on good terms with the third Earl until his death in 1702.[2] Another possible source was John Wheelock, Locke's manservant during the time the *Letter* was written and subsequently the third Earl's steward. Wheelock started working for Locke in February 1674 and was at St Giles in the summer of 1675, but when Locke left for France he stayed behind at Exeter House. He became one of Shaftesbury's principal servants and in 1682 accompanied him to Holland, where Shaftesbury died in his arms. After Shaftesbury's death he continued in the household of the dowager Countess. After the third Earl succeeded to this title in 1699 Wheelock become his steward, and it is clear from the letter the third Earl wrote to him on his deathbed that they were on close and affectionate terms.[3]

---

[1] Locke to King, 4 and 25 Oct. 1704, *Correspondence*, viii. 412–17.

[2] Voitle, *The Third Earl of Shaftesbury*, 75, 77, 94–5, 203; there are twenty letters from the third Earl to Stringer in Hampshire RO, 9M73/G238/2–21, dating from 1689 to 1702.

[3] MSS Locke f. 13, p. 5; c. 1, pp. 58–9; Stringer to Locke, 10 Feb. 1676, 5 Oct. 1677, *Correspondence*, i. 436, 519; Haley, 732; MS Locke f. 10, pp. 12, 297, 309–10, 397, 587; Wheelock to Locke, 10, 31 May 1692, *Correspondence*, iv. 451–2, 455–7; Ashley to Locke, 30 Apr. 1697, 9 Apr. 1698, *Correspondence*, vi. 103, 370; Shaftesbury to Wheelock, 10 Jan. 1713, PRO 30/24/21/221, printed in Rand, *Shaftesbury*, 533–4.

The third Earl certainly knew Des Maizeaux, who had been recommended to him by Pierre Bayle.[1] In December 1700 Bayle wrote to him stating that 'je prends la liberté d'envoyer cette Lettre à un François Refugié nommé M^r D* M**,—homme de beaucoup de merite, & de beaucoup d'erudition; & certainement très digne de votre Protection'.[2] Des Maizeaux delivered the letter himself, and evidently made a good impression. Eight months later Shaftesbury wrote asking him to apologize to Bayle for 'having never once writt to him since his kind & obliging Letter I receivd by you & in which I have an additionall obligation to him by the acquaintance he has given me of one so deserving as your Self: which is a favour I shall allways own to him'. In a postscript he assured him that 'If there be any service that I can do you or that your Circumstances need my assistance I begg you would be free with me as with a Friend: for I intend you should use me so.'[3]

Shaftesbury set Des Maizeaux to work on a French translation of his *Inquiry concerning Virtue*, which had been published anonymously in 1699. Des Maizeaux's English was still imperfect and he found the task something of a struggle; despite some encouragement from Shaftesbury the translation was never completed.[4] One gets the impression that the relationship cooled after this, though in his last letter—undated, but written in 1708 or 1709—Shaftesbury assured Des Maizeaux that 'I shall be allways ready to do you any Service that lyes in my Power', adding that when he returned to Chelsea he would be glad at any time to see him there.[5] The only mention of Locke in the entire correspondence is in Des Maizeaux's last extant letter, written four months after Locke's death, in which he made some disparaging remarks about Locke's bequests and told Shaftesbury—who had not received anything—'qu'il n'avoit pas eû pour Vôtre Grandeur la reconnoissance que meritoient les Faveurs

---

[1] Shaftesbury to Halifax, 16 Dec. 1708, Rand, *Shaftesbury*, 395. There are four letters from Shaftesbury in Des Maizeaux's papers (BL, Add. MS 4288, fos. 95–103) and five from Des Maizeaux in Shaftesbury's papers (PRO 30/24/27/17, PRO 30/24/45/80, fo. 87); they are printed in Barrell, *Shaftesbury*, 218–37. There are no letters from Des Maizeaux in the Malmesbury papers.

[2] Bayle to Shaftesbury, 14 Dec. 1700, Barrell, *Shaftesbury*, 31.

[3] Shaftesbury to Des Maizeaux, 5 Aug. 1701, BL, Add. MS 4288, fo. 99^r, printed in Barrell, *Shaftesbury*, 230.

[4] Des Maizeaux to Shaftesbury, 21 July, 12 Aug., 25 Sept. 1701, PRO 30/24/27/17, fos. 2–7; Des Maizeaux to Shaftesbury, 19 Sept. 1701, PRO 30/24/45/80, fo. 87; Shaftesbury to Des Maizeaux, 5 Aug. 1701, 17 Feb. [1702], BL, Add. MS 4288, fos. 95–6, 98.

[5] BL, Add. MS 4288, fo. 102^r. The letter was sent from Beachworth [Betchworth] in Surrey, where Shaftesbury spent much of his time from the summer of 1708 until his marriage in August 1709: see Voitle, *The Third Earl of Shaftesbury*, 283, 285–6, 287–8, 302.

qu'elle repandoit sur lui tous les ans'.[1] None of the letters contains any references to the *Letter from a Person of Quality*.

The main reason for doubting whether Des Maizeaux obtained his information directly from Shaftesbury is that Shaftesbury died seven years before *A Collection of Several Pieces* was published. It is quite possible that the information passed through an intermediary, perhaps John Toland.[2] Des Maizeaux knew him well, and after his death published a two-volume collection of his writings with a biographical memoir.[3] Toland was also very well acquainted with Shaftesbury, who encouraged him to write a pamphlet against standing armies, *The Militia Reformed*, and collaborated with him in writing *The Danger of Mercenary Parliaments*, both published in 1698.[4] It is this shared opposition to standing armies that provides a possible link with the *Letter from a Person of Quality*. Toland was nothing if not inquisitive and would certainly have been curious about its authorship.

All this may seem to be little more than speculation, but there is independent evidence that Shaftesbury believed that Locke had assisted his grandfather in writing political pamphlets in or around 1675. In January 1705, three months after Locke's death, he received a letter from Le Clerc asking him to send what information he could about Locke's life, particularly the earlier part when he had been living with the first Earl.[5] He replied that he was at present in the country (he was at St Giles) recovering from a long sickness, which 'must make me longer in consulting my Relations & those old People of my Family in Town who can

---

[1] Des Maizeaux to Shaftesbury, 10 Feb. 1705, PRO 30/24/27/17, fo. 8ᵛ. Locke's will is printed in *Correspondence*, viii. 419–27.

[2] Locke was himself acquainted with Toland and initially formed a favourable impression of him, though he later came to look on him as boastful and untrustworthy: Limborch to Locke, 25 July/4 Aug. 1693, *Correspondence*, iv. 704–5; Locke to Limborch, 13 Jan. 1694, *Correspondence*, iv. 780; Locke to Molyneux, 3 May, 15 June 1697, *Correspondence*, vi. 105–6, 143–4; Locke to Limborch, 5 Sept. 1699, *Correspondence*, vi. 679. Dealings with Toland in 1694 are recorded in MS Locke f. 29, p. 14. It is most unlikely that Locke would have told Toland anything about any part he may have had in writing the *Letter from a Person of Quality*.

[3] *A Collection of Several Pieces of Mr. John Toland* (1726). There are references to Des Maizeaux's meetings with Toland in Collins to Des Maizeaux, 10 Apr. 1716, 8 Dec. 1717, BL, Add. MS 4282, fos. 118ʳ, 139ᵛ.

[4] Locke possessed copies of both, *LL* 912ᵃ, 1992. For Toland's relations with Shaftesbury and Des Maizeaux, see Blair Worden's introduction to Ludlow, *A Voyce from the Watch Tower*, 42–6; Worden, *Roundhead Reputations*, 106–10.

[5] Shaftesbury to Peter King, Jan. 1705, PRO 30/24/22/2, fo. 35ʳ, printed in Rand, *Shaftesbury*, 326. Le Clerc to Shaftesbury, 9 Jan. 1705 (NS), PRO 30/24/27/19, printed in Barrell, *Shaftesbury*, 66–7.

Remember farr back'.[1] Four weeks later he wrote again to say that 'My recovery has been so slow that I am scarce yett gott up & have been unable to hold any Correspondence with my Friends in Town', and that he had therefore to content himself 'with giving you what I can out of my own head without other assistance'. The relevant part is as follows:

And when my Grand Father quitted the Court & began to be in Danger from it, Mr Lock now shar'd with him in Dangers as before in Honours and advantages. He intrusted him with his Secrettest negotiations & made use of his Assistant Pen in matters that neerly concern'd the State and were fitt to be made publick to raise that spirritt in the Nation which was necessary against the prevailing popish Party. It was for something of this kind that gott Air & out of great tenderness for Mr Lock that my Grand Father in the year 1674 sent him abroad to Travell an improvement which my Grand Father was glad to add to those he had allready given him his Health serv'd as a very just excuse he being Consumptive as early in his life as that was . . .[2]

Most of this is perfectly plausible, though the date of 1674 is evidently wrong and Danby was certainly not trying to strengthen the 'prevailing Popish Party'. Unfortunately it was this last point that Le Clerc seized upon when he reproduced what he took to be the gist of it in his own account, published in French in 1705 and translated into English a year later:

Mr. *Locke* whom this great Man [Shaftesbury] made Privy to his most secret Affairs was joyn'd with him in his Disgrace, and afterwards gave his assistance to some pieces, which his Lordship Publish'd to stir up the *English* Nation, to have a watchful Eye over the Conduct of the *Roman Catholicks*, and to oppose the Designs of that Party.[3]

Le Clerc did not connect the publication of these pieces with Locke's decision to leave England, which was attributed to Shaftesbury's concern for his health.[4] A second edition, described as containing 'some

---

[1] Shaftesbury to Le Clerc, 13 Jan. 1705, PRO 30/24/22/2, fo. 36ʳ; another copy in PRO 30/24/22/5, fo. 373ʳ; printed in Rand, *Shaftesbury*, 327, and (with an incorrect date) in Barrell, *Shaftesbury*, 81–2.

[2] Shaftesbury to Le Clerc, 8 Feb. 1705, PRO 30/24/22/2, fo. 40ʳ⁻ᵛ, printed in Barrell, *Shaftesbury*, 86.

[3] *The Life and Character of Mr. John Locke*, 8. The original reads: 'Mr. *Locke*, à qui ce grand homme avoit fait part de ses plus secretes affaires, fut disgracié aussi bien que lui, & dans la suite contribua à quelques Ecrits, que ce Seigneur fit publier; pour exciter la Nation Angloise à veiller sur la conduite des Catholiques Romains, & à s'opposer aux desseins de ce Parti', 'Eloge de feu Mr Locke', *Bibliothèque choisie*, 6 (1705), 361.

[4] 'In the following Summer 1675, My Lord *Shaftsbury* thought it necessary for Mr. *Locke* to Travel, because he was very much inclin'd to the Phthisick . . .', *The Life and Character of Mr John Locke*, 9.

Enlargements, and many Corrections of the most Material Passages', was published in 1713, but these remarks were left unaltered.[1]

Des Maizeaux was a responsible and conscientious editor, and there is no reason for thinking that he padded out his edition by recklessly attributing to Locke works that there was no evidence he had written. If Collins or King or any of the other surviving members of Locke's circle had objected to the inclusion of any of the writings published in *A Collection of Several Pieces* they would surely have made their objections known, and it is very unlikely that Des Maizeaux would have gone ahead in spite of their opposition. What King thought of *A Collection of Several Pieces* is not known, but Collins clearly approved of it. In March 1721, a year after its publication, he proposed that the works it contained should be included in the second edition of Locke's collected works, currently being prepared by Awnsham Churchill. Churchill's refusal made him livid:

Is it not reasonable to add the undoubted genuin works of Mr L to a new Edition of his works, which will be incompleat without them? And can it do the least injury to Mr Churchil to do Mr Franklin [the publisher of *A Collection of Several Pieces*] so much good as to let him have such a share in Mr Lockes works as his sheets amount to?—Must not Mr Churchil know, that it would be agreeable to me to have those peices added to Mr Lockes works; and that I have reason to be disobligd if he adds them not? And ought he not in civility to me to add them without the least scruple? Is there on any account the least color to reject them?[2]

If Collins wrote in similar terms to Churchill he got nowhere: the second edition (1722) was simply a reprint of the first, as were the third and fourth editions (1727, 1740). *A Collection of Several Pieces* was reissued in 1724 and reprinted in 1739. It was only after Des Maizeaux's death that the works he had edited were included in Locke's collected works, in the fifth edition published in 1751.

By the middle of the eighteenth century the *Letter from a Person of Quality* seems to have become an accepted part of the Locke canon. It was attributed to him in John Oldmixon's *History of England* (1730), in James Ralph's *History of England* (1744), and in the fifth volume of *Biographia Britannica* (1760).[3] No one seems to have expressed any doubts about its

---

[1] *An Account of the Life and Writings of Mr. John Locke*, 14.

[2] Collins to Des Maizeaux, 19 Mar. 1721, BL, Add. MS 4282, fo. 178^{r-v}.

[3] Oldmixon, *History of England*, 585; Ralph, *History of England*, 280 n; *Biographia Britannica*, 2996. There is an inaccurate account of the passage of the bill in Hume's *History of England*, viii. 11–13, but neither Locke nor the *Letter* is mentioned.

inclusion among Locke's works until the second half of the nineteenth century. W. D. Christie's biography of Shaftesbury was published in 1871, and among the documents printed for the first time was an extract from a letter Locke had written to the Earl of Pembroke in November 1684, shortly after he had received news of his expulsion from Christ Church.[1] No one had accused him of writing the *Letter from a Person of Quality*, but he was suspected of being the author of other, more recent libels.[2] This he vehemently denied:

I have often wonderd in the way that I lived, and the make I knew my self of, how it could come to passe, that I was made the author of soe many pamphlets, unlesse it was because I of all my Lords family happend to have been most bred amongst books. This opinion of me I thought time and the contradictions it caryed with it would have cured, and that the most suspitious would at last have been weary of imputeing to me writeings whose matter, and stile have I beleive (for pamphlets have been laid to me which I have never seen) been soe very different, that it was hard to thinke they should have the same author, though a much abler man then me... And it is a very odde fate, that I should get the reputation of noe small writer, without haveing donne any thing for it. For I thinke two or three copys of verses of mine, published with my name to them, have not gaind me that reputation. Bateing those I here solemnly protest in the presence of god, that I am not the author, not only of any libell, but not of any pamphlet or treatise whatsoever in print good bad or indifferent. The apprehension and backwardnesse I have ever had to be in print even in matters very remote from any thing of Libellous or seditious, is soe well known to my freinds, that I am sure I can in this have many compurgators.[3]

A month later Locke repeated these denials to Edward Clarke:

For I tell you again with that truth which should be sacred betwixt freinds that I am not the Author of any treatise or pamphlet in print good bad or indifferent and therefor you may be sure how I am used when people talke of libells. Two or three copys of verses indeed there are of mine in print as I have formerly told you but those have my name to them. But as for libells I am soe far from writeing any that I take care not to read any thing that lookes that way...[4]

These emphatic disclaimers provide one of the strongest arguments against Locke's authorship of the *Letter from a Person of Quality*, and some historians have taken them as conclusive. Christie thought that

[1] Christie, i. 261.
[2] Chudleigh to Middleton, 11/21 Nov. 1684, BL, Add. MS 41810, fo. 188; Wood, *Life and Times*, iii. 117.
[3] Locke to Pembroke, 28 Nov./8 Dec. 1684, *Correspondence*, ii. 664.
[4] Locke to Clarke, 22 Dec. 1684/1 Jan. 1685, *Correspondence*, ii. 672.

'Locke's distinct and decided denial of the authorship...renders it impossible to hold him to be the author.'[1] Fox Bourne also believed that Locke's denial was 'too precise and emphatic to be disputed'.[2] More recent scholars have taken a variety of views. Gough thought that 'Shaftesbury seems to have got Locke to write out an account of his opposition to this bill.'[3] Cranston mentioned Des Maizeaux's attribution but considered that it was 'more likely that the pamphlet was written by Shaftesbury himself with Locke's help'.[4] Laslett thought that 'Desmaizeaux and Collins...were well placed to know what Locke had a hand in'.[5] Haley thought that Locke might have been equivocating in his letter to Pembroke and concluded that the possibility of his involvement 'cannot be so easily ruled out as some would have us believe'.[6] Others have gone considerably further. Ashcraft took the view that the letter to Pembroke 'contains so many prevarications and outright lies that...it merits a unique classification as the most untrustworthy and one of the most puzzling items Locke ever wrote'; he concluded that 'Desmaizeaux's description of the *Letter*'s composition is an accurate one.'[7] Wootton also accepted Des Maizeaux's account, concluding that Locke and Shaftesbury had collaborated in writing the *Letter*, 'but the major role was Shaftesbury's'.[8] Marshall considered it 'extremely likely' that Locke assisted Shaftesbury, 'although perhaps by little more than taking Shaftesbury's "dictation"'.[9] Only de Beer was dismissive: 'Desmaizeaux gives no authority for his statement; there is no stylistic or external evidence to substantiate it.'[10]

There is in fact more common ground on these matters than might appear, for it seems generally to be agreed that (to quote Christie) the *Letter* was 'prepared under the immediate superintendence of Shaftesbury, who may have written much or most of it himself, and would have employed some one else to put it all together and send it to the press'.[11] The person most likely to have done this was Locke, who had regularly performed secretarial services for Shaftesbury, who had several unpublished political writings to his credit, and who seems to have been at St Giles at the time the *Letter* was written. No one else in Shaftesbury's household was so well qualified.

[1] Christie, ii. 207 n.
[2] Fox Bourne, i. 336.
[3] Gough, *John Locke's Political Philosophy*, 186 n.
[4] Cranston, 158.
[5] Introduction to *Two Treatises of Government*, 29 n.
[6] Haley, 392–3.
[7] Ashcraft, *Revolutionary Politics*, 121, 122.
[8] Introduction to Locke, *Political Writings*, 45.
[9] Marshall, *John Locke*, 86.
[10] *Correspondence*, ii. 664 n.
[11] Christie, ii. 207 n.

This sounds plausible, but it has to be asked whether it is consistent with Locke's denials of authorship, which could hardly have been more solemn and emphatic. Locke could be shifty and evasive, especially when it came to questions of authorship, but it is very difficult to believe that he would ever have called upon the Almighty to witness so direct a lie. It is much more likely that any part he may have had in writing the *Letter* did not, in his own eyes at least, amount to authorship. In the seventeenth century 'author' could be used as a synonym for 'writer', but the word also retained its original meaning of 'the person who originates or gives existence to anything'.[1] One example can be found in the Dedication of the Authorized Version of the Bible, where James I is addressed as 'the principal Mover and Author of the work'. Shaftesbury was the principal mover of the *Letter from a Person of Quality* and could with equal justice be described as its author.

It was probably for this reason that Locke did not acknowledge the *Letter* in his will. Eighteen months before his death he received a letter from John Hudson, Bodley's Librarian, enquiring whether he would be willing to donate copies of his published works.[2] He readily complied and instructed his publishers to send copies, though these of course were limited to those published under his own name.[3] Hudson wrote back to thank him, delicately adding that 'I shall not presume to enquire, whether these be all you intended to us'.[4] Seven months later he told Tyrrell that if Locke were to donate his letters to Proast, 'the Present would be yet more valuable'; informing Locke of this, Tyrrell hastened to add that he left it to Locke's discretion.[5] Locke responded by donating various books on travel.[6] Finally, on 15 September 1704, he executed a codicil to his will and for the first time listed those anonymous works—the *Two Treatises of Government*, the three *Letters on Toleration*, the *Reasonableness of Christianity*, and the two *Vindications*—that he was widely believed to have written. He added that 'These are all the Books whereof I am the Author which have been publishd without my name to them'.[7] When he dictated this he knew he did not have long to live—he died six weeks

---

[1] *OED*, s.v. 'Author'.

[2] Hudson to Locke, 6 Feb. 1703, *Correspondence*, vii. 743–4.

[3] Locke to Hudson, 4 Mar. 1703, *Correspondence*, vii. 755. Tyrrell presented them and ensured they were inscribed 'ex Dono Authoris', Tyrrell to Locke, 6 May, 25 July 1703, *Correspondence*, vii. 786, viii. 44.

[4] Hudson to Locke, 20 Apr. 1703, *Correspondence*, vii. 764.

[5] Tyrrell to Locke, 27 Nov. 1703, *Correspondence*, viii. 130.

[6] Tyrrell to Locke, 28 Feb., 4 July, 10 Aug. 1704, *Correspondence*, viii. 220–1, 339, 372–3.

[7] *Correspondence*, viii. 426.

later—and it is difficult to believe that he was still prevaricating. If he did not mention the *Fundamental Constitutions of Carolina*, a work he was known to have had a hand in composing, it must surely have been because he did not consider that his contributions were such as would have entitled him to claim authorship. The same is probably true of the *Letter from a Person of Quality*. Quite simply they were not *his* works, and the disclaimers in his letters to Pembroke and Clarke should be read accordingly.

The picture that emerges from all this is that while Locke may very well, and most probably did, have a significant part in the composition of the *Letter from a Person of Quality*, his role was essentially a secondary one. The *Letter* was written on Shaftesbury's instructions and for his purposes, and its contents reflect his views and not Locke's.

One striking example of this is the emphasis placed on the role of the peerage and the House of Lords:

it must be a great Mistake in Counsels, or worse, that there should be so much pains taken by the Court to debase, and bring low the House of Peers, if a *Military Government* be not intended by some. For the Power of *Peerage*, and a *standing Army* are like two Buckets, the proportion that one goes down, the other exactly goes up; and I refer you to the consideration of all the Histories of ours, or any of our neighbor Northern Monarchies, whether standing forces Military, and Arbitrary government, came not plainly in by the same steps, that the Nobility were lessened; and whether when ever they were in Power, and Greatness, they permitted the least shadow of any of them . . .[1]

These are ostensibly the words of the writer of the *Letter*, but the sentiments were Shaftesbury's. There is little sign that Locke regarded the House of Lords as having a special balancing role within a mixed constitution, though there is nothing to suggest that he was hostile towards the institution as such.[2] His fundamental political ideas were, however, different from Shaftesbury's. He is generally, and correctly, regarded as a defender both of private property and of government by consent, but he never suggested that proprietors *qua* proprietors should have political power, still less that large proprietors should have more power than small ones. Shaftesbury thought precisely this, as can be seen from both the

---

[1] *LPQ* 33, below, p. 374.

[2] The *Two Treatises* were not intended to overthrow what Locke called 'our old Legislative of King, Lords and Commons' (II. 223); after the Revolution he recommended that peace and security could best be preserved 'by restoreing our ancient government, the best possibly that ever was if taken and put togeather all of a peice in its originall constitution', Locke to Edward Clarke, 29 Jan./8 Feb. 1689, *Correspondence*, iii. 545.

Letter from a Person of Quality and the *Fundamental Constitutions of Carolina*. There is a deeply oligarchical thread running through his writings, perfectly exemplified by his speech to the House of Lords on 20 October 1675:

> 'Tis not only your Interest, but the Interest of the Nation that you Maintain your Rights, for let the *House of Commons* and *Gentry* of *England* think what they please, there is no *Prince* that ever governed without a *Nobility* or an *Army*: if you will not have one, you must have t'other, or the *Monarchy* cannot long support, or keep it self from tumbling into a *Democratical Republique*.[1]

Another prominent theme in the *Letter* was the dangers of a standing army. This was a matter to which Locke seems to have paid little attention. Standing armies were never mentioned in the *Two Treatises of Government*, not even among the list of abuses that lead to the dissolution of government, and there is no indication anywhere in his writings or his correspondence that he objected to them as such. He did take some interest in the standing army controversy that arose in the autumn of 1697 after the Treaty of Ryswick had put a temporary end to the war with France, and in December Awnsham Churchill sent him five pamphlets.[2] It is not known what view he took: his friends were engaged on both sides, and the matter was not discussed anywhere in his extant correspondence.[3]

J. G. A. Pocock has described the *Letter from a Person of Quality* as an example of what he called neo-Harringtonianism, 'the first attempt to restate Harringtonian doctrine in a form appropriate to the realities of the

---

[1] *Two Speeches*, 7. A typographical error in the original ('without *Nobility*') has been corrected, following the versions found in *Notes taken in Short-hand of a Speech in the House of Lords*, in *Two Speeches Made in the House of Peers*, and in all the manuscript copies of the speech except NA, SP 29/375/63.

[2] MS Locke f. 10, pp. 368–9 (21 Dec. 1697). The works sent were [Andrew Fletcher], *A Discourse Concerning Militias and Standing Armies*, LL 1141; [John Somers], *A Letter, ballancing the necessity of keeping a land force in times of peace*; [John Trenchard], *A Letter from the Author of the Argument against a Standing army, to the Author of the Ballancing Letter*; [Anon], *The argument against a standing army rectified*; [John Trenchard or Walter Moyle], *The Second part of an Argument, shewing, that a standing army is inconsistent with a free government*, LL 123. Two more works were purchased the following year: LL 1992, 2716ᵃ. For the pamphlet literature, see Schwoerer, 'The Literature of the Standing Army Controversy, 1697–1699', 'Chronology and Authorship of the Standing Army Tracts, 1697–1699'. The classic account of the dispute is Macaulay, *The History of England*, vi. 2736–42; the most recent is Schwoerer, *'No Standing Armies!'*, ch. 8.

[3] De Beer saw a possible allusion in James Johnston to Locke, 2 Feb. 1698, *Correspondence*, vi. 312. See also the reference to 'many things to say to you which I can not do well by a letter', in Andrew Fletcher to Locke, 25 Jan. 1698, ibid. 304.

Restoration'.[1] Locke cannot be described (and was not described by Pocock) as a Harringtonian or a neo-Harringtonian. His own thought was firmly rooted in the natural jurisprudence tradition, and the political theorists he most admired, and was most influenced by, were Hooker and Pufendorf.[2] He does not appear to have paid much attention to Harrington's writings, and what interest he had seems to date from the period before the Restoration and the last decade of his life.[3] If anyone was reading Harrington in the mid-1670s, it is more likely to have been Shaftesbury, who is known to have taken copies of *Oceana* and *The Art of Lawgiving* with him to St Giles in May 1674.[4]

The dangers of standing armies was only one of the themes of the *Letter from a Person of Quality*, and not the most prominent. The main target, as Mark Goldie has pointed out, was the Anglican clergy, especially the bishops.[5] Locke was no friend of the high-flying clergy, but his views on the royal supremacy do not appear to have been the same as Shaftesbury's. Shaftesbury's *Reasons against the Bill for the Test* ends with the objection that 'the Kings Supremacy is justled aside by this Oath, to make better room for an Ecclesiasticall Supremacy', a complaint repeated in the *Letter from a Person of Quality*.[6] The bishops were also accused, in language reminiscent of the attacks on Archbishop Laud, of attempting 'to set the Mitre above the Crown'.[7] Shaftesbury evidently entertained a high view of the royal supremacy, at least where it entailed the subordination of the clergy to the civil power. In his apologia for his part in the Declaration of Indulgence of 1672 he is represented as telling the writer of the *Letter* that 'the power of the King's Supremacy . . . was of

---

[1] *The Machiavellian Moment*, 406. For neo-Harringtonianism, see Pocock, 'Machiavelli, Harrington and English Political Ideologies', 115–21; *The Machiavellian Moment*, 406–16; Introduction to *The Political Works of James Harrington*, 129–33.

[2] *Some Thoughts concerning Education*, § 186; *Some Thoughts concerning Reading and Study for a Gentleman*, ibid. 321–2; Locke to Edward Clarke, 29 Jan./8 Feb. 1686, *Correspondence*, ii. 780; Locke to Lady Peterborough, *c*.Sept. 1697, *Correspondence*, vi. 215; Locke to Richard King, 25 Aug. 1703, *Correspondence*, viii. 58.

[3] There are references to Harrington in Locke's correspondence with William Godolphin in the summer of 1659, *Correspondence*, i. 86, 95, but the only works by Harrington in his library were acquired long afterwards: *The Art of Lawgiving* (1659), *LL* 1387, in 1697 or later, MS Locke e. 3, p. 188; Toland's edition of Harrington's *Works* (1700), *LL* 1388, shortly after its publication, Awnsham Churchill to Locke, 24 Apr. 1700, *Correspondence*, vii. 69. Locke also possessed a copy of Henry Neville's *Plato Redivivus*, which he lent to Tyrrell on 11 May 1681 (MSS Locke f. 5, p. 54; c. 1, p. 412); it is not listed in any of his library catalogues and seems not to have been returned.   [4] PRO 30/24/5/278.

[5] 'Priestcraft and the Birth of Whiggism', 226.

[6] *Reasons against the Bill for the Test*, p. 414 below; *LPQ* 20, below, p. 361.

[7] *Reasons against the Bill for the Test*, p. 412 below; *LPQ* 24, below, p. 366.

another nature then that he had in Civills'.[1] Locke's own views were far less Erastian. In his earliest writings he had allowed the magistrate authority over indifferent things in religious worship, but after 1667 he denied him even this limited role. *Excommunication*, written early in 1674, shows how determined he was to draw the sharpest possible distinction between church and state, not to subordinate one to the other.

Shaftesbury no doubt provided the comments on the other members of the House of Lords and the attacks on Danby and Lauderdale. He must also have been responsible for the *1066 And All That*-style excursions into medieval history—'The *Famous instance* of Hen. 6. who being a soft and weak Prince', etc.—most of which were taken almost verbatim from his speech to the Lords. Locke's own political writings are conspicuously free from historical examples of this kind.

More puzzling is the use made in the *Letter* of the Bible, and in particular of the Old Testament. The writer compared Danby and the bishops to the Egyptians pursuing the Israelites across the Red Sea: 'But it was observable the Hand of *God* was upon them in this whole Affair; their Chariot-wheels were taken off, they drew heavily'.[2] Indeed he had no hesitation in attributing the failure of their schemes to divine intervention: 'and yet the *over ruling hand of God* has blown upon their Politicks, and the Nation is escaped this Session, like *a Bird out of the snare* of the Fowler'.[3] The bishops were even accused of 'seething the Kid in the Mothers milk'—something thrice forbidden by the Mosaic law.[4] Locke was ready enough to quote Scripture when his argument required, but he did not write like this. Nor, one feels, did Shaftesbury, whose outlook was rather more secular than Locke's. No doubt Shaftesbury was ready to adapt his manner to his audience, but the *Letter* was written for country gentlemen, not members of godly conventicles. It may be that some third person was involved, but if he was there is no clue to his identity.

Some of the vocabulary in the *Letter* is also unlike Locke's. The word 'connexture' occurs twice. The *OED* describes it as an erroneous spelling of 'connexure', an old and now obsolete form of 'connexion'. It was not a word Locke seems to have favoured: in the *Essay concerning Human Understanding* 'connexion' was used 155 times (and 'connection' six times), but neither 'connexture' or 'connexure' was used at all.[5]

---

[1] *LPQ* 4, below, p. 341.   [2] *LPQ* 14, below, p. 354; Exod. 14: 25.

[3] *LPQ* 8, below, p. 347; Ps. 124: 7.

[4] *LPQ* 7, below, p. 346; Exod. 23: 19, 34: 26; Deut. 14: 21.

[5] *LPQ* 6, 16, below, pp. 344, 357. Malpas, 'An Electronic Text of Locke's *Essay*'. In the *Two Treatises of Government* 'connection' was used in the First Treatise (§§ 19, 20) and 'connexion' in the Second Treatise (§§ 212, 219); 'connexture' and 'connexure' were not used at all.

All these points deserve to be noted, but while they would surely be enough to discredit any suggestion that the *Letter* was Locke's unaided work, they are quite consistent with Des Maizeaux's account of its composition. As with the *Fundamental Constitutions of Carolina*, Locke's role was probably to put into coherent form material which had been supplied by others. How much of it he wrote himself must remain a matter of conjecture, but there are some passages that could very easily have come from his pen: the peroration, with its claim that the clergy 'have truckt away the Rights and Liberties of the People in this, and all other countries wherever they have had opportunity' in order that '*Priest*, and *Prince* may, like *Castor* and *Pollux*, be worshipt together as Divine in the same temple by Us poor Lay-subjects', has much in common with the vehemently anticlerical additions that he made at around the same time to the copy of the *Essay concerning Toleration* in Adversaria 1661.

THE SELECTION OF JURIES

The Selection of Juries is one of the most recent additions to the corpus of Locke's writings, having been discovered and first published by the editors of this volume in 1997. The only known manuscript is among the Shaftesbury papers; it is in Locke's hand—apart from a few small additions of only a few words each—and though the work is anonymous there can be little if any doubt that Locke was its author.

It is in some respects surprising that Locke should have undertaken a task of this kind. His legal education was minimal at best. As a young man he seems briefly to have contemplated making a career at the Bar, and was even admitted to Gray's Inn, though perhaps he only did so to please his father, an attorney.[1] In any event his heart was not in it and he was soon back in Oxford; in later years he dismissed the 'chicane or wrangling and captious' part of the law as no fit study for a gentleman.[2] His library contained very few books on English law, none of them of any importance.

---

[1] 10 Dec. 1656: *The Register of Admissions to Gray's Inn*, 280; Locke to John Locke, sen., 25 Oct., 15 Nov. 1656, *Correspondence*, i. 41–4.

[2] *Some Thoughts concerning Education*, § 187. For other disparaging remarks about law and lawyers, see Locke to William Carr, 5 Mar. 1660, *Correspondence*, i. 139–40; Locke to Edward Clarke, 29 Jan./8 Feb. 1686, *Correspondence*, ii. 784; Locke to Furly, 30 May 1701, *Correspondence*, vii. 338; *Two Treatises of Government*, II. 12. In 1674 he described 'Multitudes of Lawyers' as a hindrance on trade, *Locke on Money*, 485.

There is, however, nothing about either the style or the content of the tract that renders it unlikely that it was by Locke. The matters covered, though unfamiliar to most modern readers, were well within the grasp of an intelligent layman. Though on a legal topic the tract is conspicuously unencumbered by legal learning; indeed one of the main arguments has an abstract, even metaphysical character, such as might be produced by a sharp-witted and philosophically minded outsider addressing problems of a hitherto unfamiliar kind.

Although the manuscript is undated, it is clear from its content that it was written in the summer or autumn of 1681 while Shaftesbury was in prison facing charges of high treason. Since his dismissal from the chancellorship in November 1673 Shaftesbury had spent much of his time and energy opposing the policies of the King and his ministers, but though he eventually became involved in plans to overthrow the government it is doubtful whether in 1681 he had yet crossed the line dividing faction from treason. He had, however, made many enemies, and some of them were determined to have his head if they could. On the morning of 2 July he was arrested and his papers seized; he was then examined by the Privy Council and committed to the Tower.[1]

Arresting Shaftesbury was easy enough, but obtaining a conviction was another matter. Trying him was not a problem. Peers were entitled to be tried by their fellow peers, but when Parliament was not sitting they were tried in the court of the Lord High Steward, and it was for the King to select the Lords Triers, the peers who would act as a jury.[2] Defendants faced other disadvantages as well: challenges were not permitted and verdicts were by a simple majority. However, before Shaftesbury could be sent for trial he would have to be indicted by a grand jury of commoners, and this was very far from being a formality.

In the seventeenth century the grand jury discharged the function now performed in England by magistrates' courts, namely of deciding whether a prima facie case had been made against the defendant. Grand juries still retained their original power of making presentments on their own knowledge, and only the previous year a Middlesex grand jury at the

---

[1] NA, PC 2/69, p. 315; John Ellis to ——, 2 July 1681, HMC Ormonde, NS, vi. 90–1; Lyttleton to Hatton, 2 July 1681, *Correspondence of the Family of Hatton*, ii. 1. There are five lists of papers taken from Shaftesbury's house in PRO 30/24/6A/349.

[2] Rumour had it that eighteen would be chosen, headed by Hyde, Halifax, Peterborough, and Clarendon—all opponents, Timothy Taylor to Benjamin Herne, 20 Oct. 1681, NA, SP 29/417/46, copy in PRO 30/24/43/69, fo. 11. Only six years earlier Halifax and Clarendon had joined with Shaftesbury in resisting Danby's Test Bill and had been effusively praised in the *Letter from a Person of Quality*.

instigation of Shaftesbury and others had attempted to present the Duke of York as a popish recusant, a ploy the judges foiled by discharging the jury.[1] Usually, however, prosecutions were begun by indictment. Draft indictments, called bills, were drawn up by the court clerks on behalf of the prosecution, and the jury was instructed by the presiding judge to examine them and decide whether a prima facie case had been made. The jury heard the prosecution evidence, usually in private, and could examine witnesses. If not satisfied it returned the non-committal finding of *ignoramus*; if satisfied it found the bill true and endorsed it *billa vera*, whereupon the defendant stood indicted and could be sent to trial. Neither finding constituted a verdict. *Ignoramus* was not an acquittal, and the prosecution was entitled to bring a fresh bill before another grand jury.

It was a fundamental rule of the common law that an indictment could only be presented by a grand jury from the county in which the alleged offence had been committed. This had made perfect sense when grand juries made presentments on their own knowledge, but it lost its point once prosecutions began by indictment and the jurors became judges of evidence given by others. Nevertheless, the rule survived the disappearance of its rationale, and its survival meant that (unless evidence from elsewhere were forthcoming) Shaftesbury would have to be indicted in London or Middlesex.

Criminal jurisdiction in London and Middlesex had several anomalous features. Elsewhere in England indictments were presented and indictable offences tried either at the county quarter sessions or at the twice-yearly assizes.[2] There were, however, no assizes in either London or Middlesex, and serious crimes that elsewhere would have been tried at assizes were tried at the Old Bailey under commissions of gaol delivery, supplemented by general commissions of oyer and terminer.[3] In London these sessions were held eight times a year, usually in January, February, April, May, July, August, October, and December. Each session lasted only a matter of days; trials were conducted with extraordinary rapidity, never lasting more than a day, and usually very much less. Less serious offences were dealt with at quarter sessions and at general sessions of the

---

[1] PRO 30/24/6B/420, 421; PRO 30/24/7/512; Luttrell, i. 49.

[2] For details, see Cockburn, *A History of English Assizes*, ch. 6.

[3] Commissions of gaol delivery appointed justices to deliver the gaol specified—i.e. to try those imprisoned there. Commissions of oyer and terminer appointed justices to inquire into, hear, and determine any offence specified in the commission. Examples from the Home Circuit are reproduced in Cockburn, *Calendar of Assize Records*, 218, 222.

peace; these were held at the Guildhall two or three days before the Old Bailey sessions opened.[1]

A month or so before the sessions of the peace opened the clerk of the peace issued a precept to the sheriffs ordering them to summon a panel of twenty-four good and lawful men (*probi et legales homines*) to serve as grand jurors.[2] In practice the number summoned was invariably greater—usually very much greater—than the twenty-four specified in the precept. When the sessions opened, the names of those attending were recorded, and the grand jury was selected from among them. To take an example from the period of Shaftesbury's imprisonment, in the sessions which opened on 29 August 1681 sixty-two were summoned, forty-five were pricked (i.e. recorded as present), and from these a grand jury of nineteen was selected.[3]

After two (or sometimes three) days the sessions of the peace were adjourned, even if there was still unfinished business, and the Old Bailey sessions opened. The grand jurors were sworn again, this time as the grand jury for the sessions of gaol delivery and oyer and terminer. Usually the same persons were sworn again, though one or two sometimes dropped out for one reason or another. Thus in the sessions of 14 and 17 October 1681 there were nineteen serving on the grand jury at the sessions of the peace but only seventeen at the sessions of gaol delivery and oyer and terminer.[4]

The system worked smoothly so long as sheriffs, judges, and court officials cooperated harmoniously, as usually they did. However, in the early 1680s this cooperation started to break down. The reasons were political. Elsewhere in England most sheriffs were crown appointments, but in London and Middlesex they were elected annually by the City liverymen in Common Hall, the senior London sheriff also acting as sheriff of Middlesex. The office was both time-consuming and

---

[1] Details in *London Sessions Records*, pp. vii–xi; Beattie, 'London Juries', 216–18; Beattie, *Policing and Punishment in London*, 11–17. Middlesex (where most of the population of the metropolis lived) had separate sessions of gaol delivery and oyer and terminer, also held at the Old Bailey; the sessions of the peace were held at Hicks's Hall in Clerkenwell. There were also separate sessions for the City of Westminster which sat in Westminster Hall out of term.

[2] *London Sessions Records*, pp. xxxi–xxxii. A precept from the Home Circuit is reproduced in Cockburn, *Calendar of Assize Records*, 226.

[3] Corporation of London RO, SF 292. The size of the grand jury varied. Since decisions were made by a majority which had to consist of at least twelve jurors, the optimum number was twenty-three, but seventeen or nineteen were most often chosen; odd numbers were preferred to ensure a casting vote. For figures from the Home Circuit, see Cockburn, *Calendar of Assize Records*, 46.   [4] Corporation of London RO, SF 293.

expensive—Burnet put the cost at £5,000 per annum—and it was a sign of the times when Slingsby Bethel, a notoriously parsimonious republican, was elected in July 1680.[1] The other sheriff was Henry Cornish, executed in 1685 for his supposed part in the insurrection plot of 1682. Two equally staunch Whigs, Thomas Pilkington and Samuel Shute, were elected in June 1681 and took up office at the end of September.[2] The King and his ministers knew that these men would obstruct them in every way possible.

It was a fundamental rule in London and elsewhere that it was for the sheriffs alone to return the panel, and the statute 11 Hen. IV, c. 9 laid down that sheriffs were not to return panels at the nomination of anyone else. This created opportunities for abuse if the sheriffs were themselves partial or corrupt, and a later statute, 3 Hen. VIII, c. 12, gave the judges the power to order the sheriffs to make alterations to the panel:

> be it enacted ... that all Panells to be returnyd ... that shalbe made and put in by every Shreve and their Ministers afore any Justice of Gaile delyverye or Justice of Peace ... shalbe reformed by puttyng to and takyng out of the names of the persones which so be enpanelled by every Shrive and their Ministers by discresion of the same Justice before whom such panels shalbe returnyd; And that the same Justice and Justices shall command every Shrive and their ministers in his absens to put other persones in the same panell by their discresions; And that the same panelles so reformyd by the said Justices be good and lawfull ...[3]

This power, it should be noted, was given to justices of the peace and justices of gaol delivery; there was no mention of justices of oyer and terminer. This omission is not easily explained, but it was not a drafting error, for it can also be found in 11 Hen. VII, c. 24 § VI, on which 3 Hen. VIII, c. 12 was based. This created problems for the authorities: justices of the peace had no jurisdiction over treason, and justices of gaol delivery had authority only to deliver the gaol specified in their commission—in London, Newgate. Shaftesbury, of course, was in the Tower. Moreover, according to Sir Edward Coke, whose authority in such matters was not lightly to be disregarded, peers charged with treason could *only* be indicted before commissioners of oyer and terminer or in the King's Bench.[4] The point was made in a contemporary pamphlet which Locke

---

[1] Luttrell, i. 49–50; Burnet, ii. 253.

[2] Luttrell, i. 102–3, 129. Shute was mistakenly called Benjamin Shute in Haley, 657, 764, and in Greaves, *Secrets of the Kingdom*, 37, 96; the source of this is probably a contemporary newsletter printed in *CSPD 1681*, 330. [3] *SR* iii. 32.

[4] Coke, *Third Institute*, 28.

referred to in his tract:

Now no Peer can be indicted legally for Treason or Felony, before any other than Commissioners of *Oyer* and *Terminer*; or in the Kings-bench, as my Lord *Coke* in his third *Institutes*, *p.* 28. saith was adjudged in the Case of *Thomas* Duke of *Norfolk*, in 13 *Eliz.* And then how can this Statute of 3. *H.* 8. be of any use to carry on the present Intrigues, unless the Sheriffs (which no man can believe) will be so far over-awed as to joyn therein, and make a precedent to the ruine of themselves and the whole Nation, by permitting Inquests to be pannelled to inquire before Commissioners of *Oyer* and *Terminer*, to hang the Peers and hazard the Commons.[1]

This was not the only problem the authorities faced. Even when the justices did have jurisdiction to reform the panel, there was the question of how their discretion was to be exercised. The sheriffs were required to select *probi et legales homines* and this meant that the judges were entitled to remove anyone who had been found guilty of perjury, conspiracy, suborning witnesses, bribery, intimidation, etc. Persons who had been excommunicated could also be removed, not being *legales homines*. The judges also took the view that they were entitled to order the removal of persons who had offended against the Conventicles Act (22 Car. II, c. 1), the Elizabethan statute against sectaries (35 Eliz. I, c. 1), or other legislation against nonconformists.

When unsuitable persons were removed from the panel, someone had to nominate their replacements. The statute 3 Hen. VIII, c. 12 is hardly a model of draftsmanship, but it would appear that the 'their' in 'to put other persones in the same panell by their discresions' referred to the sheriffs and their ministers, not to the justices. If so, the justices could order the removal of persons from the panel but had no power to select their replacements: they could only order the sheriffs to find suitable persons, leaving it up to them whom to choose.

Faced with such difficulties the authorities had good reason to proceed cautiously. While Shaftesbury was left waiting, they decided to test the waters by commencing proceedings against one of his supporters, Stephen College. College, a joiner by trade, was probably singled out because he had offended the King by distributing *A Ra-ree Show*, a scurrilous ballad with an engraving depicting Charles as a two-faced trickster.[2] A first attempt to indict him was made at the Old Bailey on

---

[1] *None but the Sheriffs ought to name and return Jurors to serve in Inquests before Commissioners of Oyer and Terminer*, a single-sheet pamphlet published by the Whig printer Richard Baldwin.

[2] *Poems on Affairs of State*, ii. 425–31; Rahn, '*A Ra-ree Show*', 77–98.

8 July, but the grand jury threw out the bill because, in the words of one Court supporter, 'they believed the same witnesses would swear against my Lord Shaftesbury'.[1] Matters did not rest there, however. College had not been acquitted and the authorities were entitled to prefer another bill elsewhere if there was evidence to support it. College's imprudent behaviour at the time of the Oxford parliament provided the pretext, and the King himself insisted that a new bill should be preferred at the forthcoming Oxford assizes.[2]

On 15 July College was indicted at Oxford. On the night of 14 August he was removed from the Tower and taken under armed guard to Oxford.[3] He was tried on 17 August, was convicted in the early hours of the following day, and was executed on 31 August.[4] Shaftesbury's servants did what they could to help College, and several sets of instructions were prepared for him, though attempts to pass them to him proved unavailing.[5] Locke had the closest connections with Oxford, and the movements recorded in his journal point towards his involvement in the case. He left London for Oxford on 9 July, the day after the failed attempt to indict College at the Old Bailey. On 16 July, the day after College was indicted at Oxford, Locke left Oxford for Tyrrell's house at Oakley, where he spent three nights before going on to London. He returned to Oxford on 1 August and remained there until 18 August, the day after College's trial, before returning to London, where he remained until Christmas.[6]

Locke's part in College's defence was noticed by an unsympathetic observer at Christ Church: Humphrey Prideaux later recalled him entertaining Robert West, a Middle Temple barrister who later achieved notoriety for his part in the Rye House Plot:

When West was first taken he [Locke] was very solicitous to know of us at the table who this West was at which one made an unlucky reply that it was the very same person whom he treated at his chamber and caressed at soe great a rate when College was tryed here at Oxford which put the Gentleman into a

---

[1] Arran to Ormonde, 9 July 1681, HMC Ormonde, NS, vi. 95.

[2] Jenkins to Norreys, 11 July 1681, NA, SP 44/62, p. 198.

[3] Luttrell, i. 116–17.

[4] *The Arraignement, Tryal and Condemnation of Stephen Colledge for High-Treason*; Wood, *Life and Times*, ii. 551, 552–4; DWL, MS Morrice P, p. 312; Luttrell, i. 117–18.

[5] PRO 30/24/43/63, fos. 334–5, 336–7, 369; PRO 30/24/6B/433; *A Letter concerning the Tryal at Oxford of Stephen College, August 17. 1681*. See also Prideaux to Ellis, 22 Sept. 1681, BL, Add. MS 28929, fo. 59, *Letters of Humphrey Prideaux*, 93–4.

[6] MS Locke f. 5, pp. 91, 104, 105, 108, 113.

profound silence and the next thing we heard of him was that he was fled for the same.[1]

This was written three years later in a private letter. There is nothing in Prideaux's extant correspondence to show that he was reporting on Locke's activities in 1681.[2]

On 18 July, three days after College's indictment, Halifax and Jenkins ordered Edmund Warcup, a magistrate and an old acquaintance of Shaftesbury, to see if there was sufficient evidence to proceed against him at Oxford.[3] This was indeed the obvious move, and rumours were already circulating that a bill would be preferred there.[4] Shaftesbury himself feared this and sought legal advice. One manuscript in the Shaftesbury papers, dated August 1681, comprises five queries with five answers on the back, signed 'W. Thomson'.[5] These were written by William Thomson, a Middle Temple barrister who had also advised College.[6] The three main points Shaftesbury raised were (i) whether a grand jury could find matters done outside their county; (ii) if the grand jury did find the bill,

---

[1] Prideaux to Ellis, 12 Nov. 1684, BL, Add. MS 28929, fo. 110[r], *Letters of Humphrey Prideaux*, 139–40. On 28 July College was granted permission to converse with West 'as often as he shall desire, in the presence and hearing of the Warder', NA, PC 2/69, p. 331. West was thoroughly untrustworthy and was already passing information to the authorities, Jenkins to Craven, 22 Mar. 1681, NA, SP 44/62, p. 143. Locke was asked by Stringer 'To Enquire of my Lord if he will not have [Richard] Wallopp in stead of West for his Counsill', PRO 30/24/43/63, fo. 501[v]. Shaftesbury chose Wallop, and on 7 July Locke paid him a fee of three guineas, MS Locke f. 5, p. 91.

[2] Prideaux certainly reported on Locke in 1682. Letters of 14 and 19 March and 24 October were sent to Ellis at Ormonde's lodgings at Whitehall and were endorsed with Locke's name and the date of sending: BL, Add. MS 28929, fos. 95, 96, 100. The letters (but not the endorsements) are printed in *Letters of Humphrey Prideaux*, 129–34. This appears to be the first indication that anyone in government circles was paying attention to Locke's activities.

[3] Feiling and Needham, 'The Journals of Edmund Warcup', 257; Warcup to Jenkins, 2 Aug. 1681, NA, SP 29/416/83. Shaftesbury's defence was anxious to discredit Warcup: Stringer asked Locke to 'gett a Copie of the Order of Councill about Warcupp: July 20th 1666 & of his Recantation August 17th 1666. both being entered in the Councill booke', PRO 30/24/43/63, fo. 501[v]. One of the items preserved in the Shaftesbury papers is a copy of the *London Gazette* for 19–26 July 1666, which contains a complaint by Lord Arlington, then Secretary of State, that Warcup had greatly wronged him by using his name to cover some improper financial transactions of his own, PRO 30/24/4/149. Warcup was dismissed from the commission of the peace for Middlesex and imprisoned, something Stringer duly noted, PRO 30/24/43/63, fo. 459. His misdeeds were related in detail in *No Protestant-Plot*, 21–2.

[4] Richard Mulys to ——, 11 July 1681, HMC Ormonde, NS, vi. 97; Humphrey Prideaux to John Ellis, [July] 1681, BL, Add. MS 28929, fo. 56[r], *Letters of Humphrey Prideaux*, 89.

[5] PRO 30/24/6A/368, endorsed 'Mr Thomsons answeres to several queries of mine'.

[6] *The Arraignment, Tryal and Condemnation of Stephen Colledge*, sig. B1[v]. Another set of legal queries, PRO 30/24/6B/403, discussed later, contains a set of answers in the same hand; on fo. 2[v] another (and presumably later) hand has written 'Mr Serj Thompson's

whether the indictment could also be for acts committed elsewhere; and (iii) if a bill were found against a peer by an Oxfordshire grand jury, whether in a trial before the House of Lords evidence could be admitted of acts done elsewhere. To these queries Thomson's answers were reassuringly negative. The two remaining queries concerned the possibility of Shaftesbury bringing an action of *scandalum magnatum* against his detractors, and whether he should demand damages of £20,000. Thomson was not the only lawyer consulted. Another manuscript in the Shaftesbury papers, endorsed 'August 1681 answers to severall Queryes of mine' in the same hand as the endorsement on Thomson's answers, contains five more answers to the same set of queries.[1]

The government was also taking legal advice. On 6 August Jenkins told the Lord Chief Baron that the King wished to have a meeting of all the judges in Whitehall, and five days later a date of 26 August was fixed for them 'to consider of several things his Majesty has to lay before them'.[2] Shaftesbury must have been high on the agenda. On 22 August the Earl of Arran informed his father, the Duke of Ormonde, that 'The Court comes to town on Saturday next and, as it is said, the King intends then to have the opinion of the judges on how they may try my Lord Shaftesbury'.[3] Nothing very positive seems to have emerged, and on 27 August Arran reported that the King and his ministers dared not bring a bill before an Old Bailey jury.[4]

It is not hard to see why. The London and Middlesex sessions of the peace had opened the previous day, and though the jurors selected for the sessions of the peace had no power to indict Shaftesbury for treason, they would in due course sit as jurors at the sessions of gaol delivery and oyer and terminer at the Old Bailey, where a bill could have been preferred. The sheriffs knew this very well, and they returned large, carefully selected panels: fifty for Middlesex and sixty-eight for London.[5] The Middlesex justices invoked their powers under 3 Hen. VIII, c. 12 to reform the panel, but when Bethel refused to comply they did not press

---

opinion about Juries'. Thomson was admitted to the Middle Temple in 1664; he was created serjeant in 1688, was knighted the following year, and died in 1695: *Register of Admissions to the Middle Temple*, i. 171; Baker, *The Order of Serjeants at Law*, 201, 418, 450.

[1] PRO 30/24/6B/434. Another set of questions that raise similar points are in a draft of a letter from Shaftesbury to an unknown addressee, Hampshire RO, 9M73/G220; the letter is undated but references to College show that it was written before he was indicted.

[2] NA, SP 44/62, pp. 246, 254.　　　　　　　　[3] HMC Ormonde, NS, vi. 137.

[4] Arran to Ormonde, 27 Aug. 1681, HMC Ormonde, NS, vi. 141. See also Lyttleton to Hatton, 27 Aug. 1681, BL, Add. MS 29577, fo. 370[r–v].

[5] Newsletter, 30 Aug. 1681, NA, Adm. 77/127.

the point and contented themselves with choosing fifteen from the original panel.[1] Roger Morrice noted with satisfaction that 'the Grand Jury [was] impanneled and sworne without the alteration of one man, so the matter of juries is settled as to the ordinary justices power'.[2]

Late in September Shaftesbury had some more questions, and this time he sent them to Sir William Jones, a former Attorney-General. Sir William returned three answers. The first was that peers could not be indicted for treason at quarter sessions. The second reverted to Shaftesbury's persistent worry that he might be indicted at Oxford; Jones assured him that a statute of 33 Hen. VIII, which enabled indictments to be found before justices of oyer and terminer in counties other than that in which the offence had been committed, had been repealed by 1 & 2 Phil. & Mary, c. 10. The answer to the third question was less reassuring: in cases of treason (unlike felony) a refusal to plead was equivalent to a confession of guilt.[3]

On 6 October the Middlesex quarter sessions opened at Westminster. Another Whig panel was returned, which the under-sheriff was unwilling to alter.[4] Francis Charlton, an old friend of Shaftesbury, was foreman, and most of the rest, Jenkins noted, 'were of that kidney'.[5] In his next letter Jenkins complained that of the forty-nine jurors returned for Middlesex 'but two go to church, the rest are desperate sectaries, most of them Fifth Monarchy men.' Lords Halifax and Hyde, he added, were meeting with Chief Justice Pemberton to see what remedy could be applied.[6] Further exception was taken to Charlton, but the under-sheriff stubbornly refused to alter the panel.[7]

Things were little better at the Old Bailey sessions, which opened on 17 October. The judges noticed that the panel contained 'two fanatics who frequented conventicles and went not to Church' and ordered the sheriffs to strike them off the list. When Pilkington raised objections, Chief Justice North told him that as they had been indicted they were unfit to sit on a grand jury and present indictments against others. He then had 3 Hen. VIII, c. 12 read and informed the sheriffs that it gave the justices authority

---

[1] Luttrell, i. 119.

[2] DWL, MS Morrice P, p. 312; cf. Longford to Ormonde, 3 Sept. 1681, HMC Ormonde, NS, vi. 145.

[3] PRO 30/24/6A/370, headed 'Septemb: 24th 1681 Sir Will Jones his answere to severall queries of mine'.

[4] Luttrell, i. 132; Longford to Ormonde, 9 Oct. 1681, HMC Ormonde, NS, vi. 184.

[5] Jenkins to Conway, 6 Oct. 1681, NA, SP 44/62, p. 331.

[6] Jenkins to Conway, 8 Oct. 1681, NA, SP 44/62, p. 334.

[7] Luttrell, i. 133; Longford to Ormonde, 11 Oct. 1681, HMC Ormonde, NS, vi. 188.

to alter juries 'as they though fit'. On hearing this, Pilkington was prepared to back down, but Shute wished to take counsel's opinion. Much displeased, North was ready to record this as contempt, whereupon the sheriffs retracted and consented to the two names being struck off.[1]

This achieved little. The rest of the panel were occasional conformists who had presciently brought vouchers of their frequenting church, and the judges felt that they had no legal grounds for removing them.[2] The effect of this became clear the next day, 18 October, when a bill was preferred against John Rouse, who had been arrested with College. Much of the evidence against him was given by the witnesses who had already testified against College and would subsequently do so against Shaftesbury. The jury returned a finding of *ignoramus*.[3] The King made his own indignation clear to Sir John Reresby:

The King talked to me a grat while during that evening, walkeing in St. James his Parke . . . The subject was most of the late unjust verdicts and proceeding of the jurys in London and Middlesex, as to which he used this expression, It is a hard case that I am the last man to have law and justice in the whole nation.[4]

On 21 October Jenkins, writing on behalf of Halifax, Conway, and Hyde, summoned Jeffreys and the Common Serjeant to a meeting that same evening.[5] Three days later the Earl of Longford had a meeting with the Attorney-General, who spoke 'with much diffidence of the Grand Jury's finding the bills of indictment against my Lord Shaftesbury'; Longford told Ormonde that the sheriffs' returning such factious juries was 'a mischief the present law cannot remedy'.[6] The following week Longford was told that the sheriffs had relented, but this turned out to be a false report, and in his next letter but one he reported that the grand juries still 'do not please'. 'However,' he added, 'something will be done towards my Lord Shaftesbury's trial, but whether the expedients resolved on will prove effectual is too hard for me who do not understand the law, to undertake.'[7]

Those who did understand the law were considering a variety of increasingly desperate expedients. In October Longford reported

---

[1] Longford to Ormonde, 18 Oct. 1681, HMC Ormonde, NS, vi. 197–8.
[2] John Ellis to —, 18 Oct. 1681, ibid. 199.
[3] Ibid.; Luttrell, i. 137. Rouse was a servant of Sir Thomas Player, and had been involved with payments to the Irish witnesses who were later to testify against Shaftesbury. He was executed in July 1683 for his part in the Rye House Plot.
[4] *The Memoirs of Sir John Reresby*, 234 (19 Oct. 1681).   [5] NA, SP 44/62, p. 343.
[6] Longford to Ormonde, 25 Oct. 1681, HMC Ormonde, NS, vi. 208.
[7] Longford to Ormonde, 1, 8 Nov. 1681, ibid. 215, 220.

'a project now on foot, that the Secondary of the Counter [the sheriffs' prison] may without the Sheriffs make return of a Grand jury in London, a Commission of Oyer and Terminer will be issued for the trial of my Lord Shaftesbury'.[1] In his next letter he informed Ormonde that the judges were considering 'whether the Bailiff of Westminster or his Deputy may not legally return the Grand and Petty Juries'. They met, he added, 'both yesterday morning and last night . . . but their determination (if they have come to any) is yet kept private'.[2] The following week Sir Charles Lyttleton was told that 'the Baylif of Westminster . . . had bene with the Attorney Generall to shew him his pattent of powers about empannelling of juryes upon An especiall commission for Tryalls within his precinct'. He was, however, subsequently informed 'that the Chief Justice says they can proceed no way legally but by A grand jury for the County'.[3] Another suggestion was to present the bill in Southwark, where the panel would be chosen by the sheriff of Surrey.[4]

An even more far-fetched idea was mentioned in Arran's next letter to Ormonde: 'I am credibly informed that if the Grand Jury find an *ignoramus* he will be tried by special commission in the verge of court there being several precedents for it, but this is by way of secret'.[5] It was not kept very secret: the previous week Roger Morrice had noted that 'Wee doe not yet know when any of the Prisoners for Treason will be Tryed a talke of late hath been they should be tryed within the Verge of the Court by a Jury nominated by Court Officers'.[6] There were, however, insuperable legal objections. Cases within the verge—i.e. within twelve miles of the King's place of residence—could be tried by special commission of oyer and terminer but would have to be presented, according to Hale, by 'the good men of the county, wherein the offence was committed'.[7] In Shaftesbury's case this would have meant a London grand jury. According to one contemporary pamphlet,

Lord H———x and the rest of the Conspirators with Mr. *Attorney* put the question, whether by Law, the King might not try *Shaftsbury* by the Court of

---

[1] Longford to Ormonde, 25 Oct. 1681, ibid. 209.
[2] Longford to Ormonde, 29 Oct. 1681, ibid. 211. Roger Morrice had heard a rumour to this effect in September, DWL, MS Morrice P, p. 313, 27 Sept. 1681. The authorities contemplated sending a commission of oyer and terminer to Westminster—where the bailiff was described as 'well affected to the government'—to indict John Rouse, NA, SP 29/417/44.   [3] Lyttleton to Hatton, 8 Nov. 1681, BL, Add. MS 29577, fo. 392ʳ.
[4] Robert Harsnett to Humphrey Prideaux, 10 Nov. 1681, Bodl., MS Tanner 36, fo. 173.
[5] Arran to Ormonde, 12 Nov. 1681, HMC Ormonde, NS, vi. 226.
[6] DWL, MS Morrice P, p. 316, 3 Nov. 1681.
[7] Hale, *Historia Placitorum Coronae*, ii. 10.

Verge: Pemberton gave a very short Answer, *that no such thing could be done*, and the other Judges hearing him so positive, and brisk in it, by their silence, gave consent, or at least none opposed what he had asserted.[1]

This seems to have settled the matter. On 5 November Morrice recorded that 'I believe it is agreed that the E of Shaftsbury &c shall not be tryed within the Verge nor within the Libertys of Westminster'.[2]

When the Michaelmas term began on 24 October, Shaftesbury promptly petitioned the King's Bench to be tried or bailed. Unable to prevaricate on the ground that the Tower lay outside their jurisdiction, the judges replied that bail would be granted if Shaftesbury had not been indicted by the end of term, 28 November.[3] The government could procrastinate no longer. Halifax was of the view that it would be better to release Shaftesbury rather than risk an almost certain finding of *ignoramus* by the grand jury, but he seems to have been in a minority in this.[4] The King felt that even if the jury did not find the bill, Shaftesbury would at least 'go off with a bottle at his tail'.[5] A special commission of oyer and terminer was issued, and the sheriffs were ordered to return a panel. Usually the job was done by secondaries, but on this occasion the sheriffs did it themselves.[6] A panel of thirty-nine was summoned, all thoroughly respectable but all solid Whigs. An unnamed civil servant noted with displeasure, 'I am of Opinion that for Substantiall men they cannot pick out 40 such men in London nor of more Gall and Bitternesse, and they have compassd the whole Town for these'.[7]

On 24 November proceedings opened at the Old Bailey, presided over by Chief Justice Pemberton.[8] The judges made no attempt to remove anyone from the panel. Five of the panel were absent for one reason or another, and three were excused; from the remainder the first twenty-one were sworn in the order they appeared on the list.[9] Sir Samuel Barnardiston, a long-time associate of Shaftesbury, was foreman. The prosecution case was not a strong one. Much of it consisted of

---

[1] *The Second Part of the Growth of Popery and Arbitrary Government*, 315. This was probably written by Robert Ferguson.   [2] DWL, MS Morrice P, p. 316.

[3] Longford to Ormonde, 25 Oct. 1681, HMC Ormonde, NS, vi. 208.

[4] *The Memoirs of Sir John Reresby*, 236 (6 Nov. 1681).

[5] Longford to Ormonde, 15 Nov. 1681, HMC Ormonde, NS, vi. 229. On the battle for public opinion, which left one lasting monument in *Absalom and Achitophel* (published 17 Nov.), see Harth, *Pen for a Party*, 99–102.

[6] Warcup's notes, NA, SP 29/417/110.   [7] NA, SP 29/417/113.

[8] For a detailed account of the proceedings, see Haley, 676–81.

[9] The panel is preserved in Corporation of London RO, SF 294. The panel and the jurors are listed in *The Proceedings against the Right Honourable the Earl of Shaftsbury*.

conversations Shaftesbury had allegedly had with various Irish scoundrels—dubbed the MacShams—who had been imported to further the Popish Plot but had now turned against their former patrons. The jury was well prepared, and it seems that each juror was given a small, pocket-sized book of questions to put to the witnesses.[1] The witnesses were cross-examined and found to give varying and inconsistent accounts; after this, Luttrell wrote, the jury 'withdrew for about two hours, and then came in and returned the bill Ignoramus; at which there was a very great shout, that made even the court shake'.[2] The rejected bill was crossed through and *Ignoramus* was written in large letters on the back.[3] Four days later Shaftesbury was released on bail and went 'very privately home'.[4]

Locke and the Tract on Jury Selection

Locke was never one to draw attention to his activities, and his contributions to Shaftesbury's defence have until recently gone largely unnoticed. One of the items preserved in the Shaftesbury papers is 'Some queries upon the Statute of 3. H. 8 Concerning errecting the Pannels of Juries by Justices &c'.[5] These queries are in the hand of Locke's manservant and amanuensis, Sylvester Brounower, and were corrected by Locke; this strongly suggests that they were drawn up by Locke himself, or at least that he was closely involved in their composition. On the reverse there is a set of replies signed 'W. Thomson'; the hand and signature are the same as in the advice Shaftesbury had obtained in August.

The preamble to 3 Hen. VIII, c. 12 referred to 'grete extorcions and oppressions' of the sheriffs, and in his first query Locke asked whether this meant that the justices could only alter the panel where the sheriffs had been at fault. It did not, Thomson replied, because 'the power given to Justices of Gaol delivery & of the peace is generall and referring it to the discretion of the Court Soe that for reasonable cause shewn against any person they may cause the Sherriffe to strike out such and to returne others.' Thomson returned to the point in his answer to the third

---

[1] Two of these booklets are preserved among the Shaftesbury papers, PRO 30/24/43/63, fos. 375–412, 413–43; a third is in the Bodleian Library, MS Don. f. 7.

[2] Luttrell, i. 146. See also Longford to Ormonde, 26 Nov. 1681, HMC Ormonde, NS, vi. 236–7. [3] Corporation of London RO, SF 294.

[4] Lyttleton to Hatton, 29 Nov. 1681, *Correspondence of the Family of Hatton*, ii. 10; Luttrell, i. 147.

[5] PRO 30/24/6B/403, fo. 1ʳ, described more fully in the Textual Introduction, p. 244, and printed in Appendix VII, below.

query: 'this is a legall discretion and they cannot put out any person without reasonable cause shewn'.

Another issue, raised in the second and sixth query, was whether the statute applied to justices of oyer and terminer. Thomson replied that it did not: 'I conceive the Statute does not extend to give the Justices of Oyer & Terminer any power to reforme the pannells the words of the Statute expressing onely Justices of Gaol delivery & of the peace'. Coke, it may be noted, had been firmly of this view.[1]

A further problem was raised in the third query: whether persons added to the panel were to be nominated by the sheriff or by the justices. Thomson replied that it was the sheriff's job: 'the power of the Sherriff which he had before is not taken away for he is still to returne the Jury & doe all other Acts of his office'. It was this limitation, he added, that made 3 Hen. VIII, c. 12 consistent with 11 Hen. IV, c. 9, which had provided that no one was to be empanelled at the nomination of anyone other than the sheriffs.

We do not know exactly when Locke sought Thomson's opinion, but there can be little doubt that he had his replies in front of him when he wrote the tract on jury selection. He began by arguing, contrary to Thomson's advice, that the discretionary powers granted to the justices in 3 Hen. VIII, c. 12 only applied in cases where 'the present Sherifs are guilty of the same or such like misdemeanors as are mentioned in the preamble of the Statute or that the persons impannelled are such sort of persons as therein are set forth'. This was a weak argument: whatever mischiefs had occasioned the passing of the statute, the powers granted were general, as Thomson had said. Locke was on stronger ground when he argued that the justices' discretion was not 'an extravagant liberty or licence to doe what they please; but their proceedings are to be limited & bounded within the rule of law & Reason, Discretion being a faculty of discerning per legem quid sit justum, & not to be guided by will or private affection Because talis discretio discretionem confundit'.[2] The same account (and the same Latin tags) can be found Coke's *Institutes*[3] and in *Rooke's case*:

Discretion is a Science or Understanding to discern between Falsity and Truth, between Wrong and Right, between Shadows and Substance, between Equity and Colourable Glosses and Pretences, and not to do according to their Wills and private Affections; for as one saith, *Talis discretio discretionem confundit*.[4]

[1] Coke, *Third Institute*, 33.
[2] Below, p. 379.
[3] 'Discretio est discernere per legem, quid sit justum', Coke, *Second Institute*, 56.
[4] 5 Co. Rep. 100 (1598).

The judges would not have disputed this, but they held that non-conformists could be excluded because they had broken the law.[1] Locke disagreed. He objected to this exclusion of 'Dissenters from the Rites & Ceremonys of the church of England' not only because in his view they fell outside the terms of 3 Hen. VIII, c. 12 but also because they were honest, conscientious men who disagreed about 'such things wherein wise & good men have heretofore differed & doe & will always herein more or lesse differ' and who, not being motivated by considerations of 'profit & secular interest', would 'keepe their Oaths lawfully administred & taken'.[2]

The second half of Locke's tract was concerned with the question of who was entitled to exercise these powers. On the face of it justices of oyer and terminer were excluded by the terms of the statute, but Locke was still concerned that they would somehow devise a way of reforming the panel. His fears stemmed from the fact that in London the same jurors presented indictments at the sessions of the peace at the Guildhall and at the sessions of gaol delivery and of oyer and terminer at the Old Bailey. His response was that the identity of a jury (and of the panel from which it was selected) was not fixed by the identity of its members: 'their being the same persons hinders not but that they are 3 destinct Jurys returned upon 3 destinct pannells in obedience to three destinct precepts & pursuant of 3 destinct Commissions'.[3] If there were only one panel, he asked, could it be reformed or not? If it could not, 3 Hen. VIII, c. 12 would be redundant, which was absurd. If it could, the justices of oyer and terminer, though themselves incapable of reforming the panel, would have been able to prefer a bill to a jury selected from a panel whose reform they had previously ordered in their capacity as justices of gaol delivery; this would have made a mockery of their exclusion from the provisions of the Act. Since neither alternative was satisfactory, there had to be more than one panel. Locke was therefore able to conclude that even where the justices of gaol delivery legitimately exercised their powers under 3 Hen. VIII, c. 12, 'this will not concerne nor affect the pannell upon the precept of Oyer & Terminer which must & ought to stand immutable'.[4] The justices of oyer and terminer would have to select their jury from an unreformed panel—one chosen by the Whig sheriffs.

This argument was both subtle and ingenious; whether it would have been effective in practice is less clear. Given that the London jury (or

---

[1] See, for example, Chief Justice North's remarks, reported in Longford to Ormonde, 18 Oct. 1681, HMC Ormonde, NS, vi. 198.   [2] Below, p. 380.
[3] Below, p. 381.   [4] Below, pp. 381–2.

juries) were composed of the same persons, there would only seem to be two criteria for determining how many juries there were: the number of precepts issued and the number of times the jurors were sworn. According to Bowler grand jury precepts were only issued for the sessions of the peace and the sessions of oyer and terminer.[1] Some of the sessions files bear this out, but others contain three grand jury precepts and panels—the file for October 1681 is an example.[2] Either way, there was a separate precept for the sessions of oyer and terminer, which was all Locke needed to establish. On the other hand he had to admit that at the Old Bailey the jurors were usually sworn only once; an examination of the panels preserved in the sessions files indicates that the jurors were sworn at both the sessions of the peace and the sessions of gaol delivery, but not at the sessions of oyer and terminer—unless these happened to be held separately, as in Shaftesbury's case they were.

It is not easy to say exactly when Locke wrote this tract. The only contemporary work mentioned is a 'printed paper', referred to twice; despite the vagueness of the citation this can be identified with virtual certainty as the pamphlet *None but the Sheriffs ought to name and return Jurors to serve in Inquests before Commissioners of Oyer and Terminer.* Unfortunately this is little use in dating Locke's tract, since there is a clear reference to it in a letter written only a week after Shaftesbury's arrest.[3] Locke's own papers confirm his dealing with Thomson but shed little light on the date of the tract. His journal shows that he had dinner with Thomson in July and had further dealings with him in November,[4] but neither this nor the apparent use of Thomson's replies in the tract does much to help in fixing its date; on this evidence the tract could have been written at any time between the second week in July and late November.

---

[1] *London Sessions Records*, pp. xxii–xxiii.

[2] Corporation of London RO, SF 293. Locke quotes from three such precepts at fo. 33^r.

[3] 'Upon the Statute 3 Hen. 8 for correcting pannells of juryes, there was a paper printed, as also of another statute of Hen. 4, in Rastall at large; and the judges in that could not doe ought by reason of the statutes meaning only gaole delivery, whereas the jury was returned on the oyer and terminer commission', William Longueville to Hatton, 9 July 1681, *Correspondence of the Family of Hatton*, ii. 3.

[4] On 7 July he paid two guineas to a Mr T for searching records, and 10s. 'For Mr Thomsons dinner . . . & coach hire'. On 22 November 2s. 6d. was paid to 'M^r T^s man', and on 26 November a fee of ten guineas was paid to 'Mr T', and another 2s. 6d. to 'his man'; their identities are confirmed by Locke's ledger, which records all these transactions, and where the payment on 22 November was initially credited to 'Mr Thomsons man', before the name 'Thomson' is crossed out leaving only the initial, MSS Locke f. 5, pp. 91, 146–7; c. 1, p. 132. Shaftesbury reimbursed Locke for all this expenditure, and for earlier travel to and from Oxford, MS Locke c. 1, p. 167.

Any more precise estimate of the date must be based on internal evidence. One of the most striking features of the tract is that it made no mention of what was undoubtedly Shaftesbury's greatest and most persistent fear, that of being indicted at Oxford like the unfortunate College. Various explanations can be given for this, but the simplest is that the tract was written in the autumn, after it had become clear to everyone—even to the apprehensive Shaftesbury—that this particular danger had passed. Equally absent are any references to the verge, to the Bailiff of Westminster, or to any other of the increasingly desperate expedients that the authorities were known to have been considering. All this indicates that Locke wrote at a time when it had become known that the proceedings would take place at the Old Bailey under a commission of oyer and terminer. This suggests a late date for the tract, possibly well into November.

Locke's intentions can only be surmised. The fact that the manuscript was considerably more neatly written than most of his papers suggests that he intended it for readers besides himself, and the additions show that someone else did look at it. It may only have been written for circulation within Shaftesbury's entourage, but its tone does not suggest this: the tract is clearly an attempt to persuade and not merely to inform. An internal memorandum on the legal issues would have had a very different character, and if Shaftesbury had wanted one there is no reason why he should have sought it from Locke, a layman with no legal training. In fact the main concern of the defence in the autumn was to discredit the prosecution witnesses; except for the set of queries to Thomson in Brounower's hand there is no mention elsewhere in the Shaftesbury papers of the issues which Locke raised. Locke may have written the tract on Shaftesbury's instructions, but it is quite possible that it began as an independent venture of his own.

If the tract had been printed, it would certainly have appeared anonymously, but as far as is known it remained unpublished. It is true that a good number of obscure pamphlets must have disappeared without trace, but we have Locke's solemn assurance, discussed elsewhere in this volume, that he was not the author of 'any pamphlet or treatise whatsoever in print good bad or indifferent'.[1] On this occasion he should be taken at his word. In 1681 Locke was nearing fifty but had published nothing beyond a few poems. In 1661 he had prepared the English Tract on Government for publication, but between then and 1686, when he

---

[1] Locke to Pembroke, 28 Nov./8 Dec. 1684, *Correspondence*, ii. 664; above, p. 111.

ventured very tentatively into print with a French translation of his *New Method of a Commonplace Book*, he appears to have made no attempt to publish anything of his own.[1] His failure to publish the tract may simply have been a consequence of what he himself referred to as the 'apprehension and backwardnesse I have ever had to be in print',[2] but if it was written as late as the middle of November it could also have been overtaken by events.

Several of the points Locke made did, however, appear in more popular form in *The Second Part of No Protestant Plot*, an anonymous pamphlet published a few days before the attempt to indict Shaftesbury:

Nay, at Goal-deliveries, where there is no writ directed to the Sheriffs, yet he is the Officer that is to return the Panel, for so the Law hath constituted him. The *Statute* of the 11 *Hen.* 4. is express to this purpose. Yea, that confidence and power doth the Law place in the Sheriff as to this matter, that in *Inquests* before Commissioners of *Oyer* and *Terminer*, it alloweth not the Judge to except against any whom the Sheriff is pleased to return: and tho' in Juries upon *Goal delivery* the Statute of the 3 *H.* 8. empowers the Judge to reform the Pannel, by excepting against such as they think will be wilfully forsworn and perjured: yet even in that case the Sheriff must still return those who are to supply the places of such as are excepted against.[3]

This was probably written by Robert Ferguson; he subsequently laid claim to it and there is no reason to doubt his word.[4] He was a practised and versatile pamphleteer, but he would have needed assistance on the more technical legal issues, and it would be interesting to know from whom he obtained it. It is tempting to think he read Locke's tract, but the verbal similarities are not so close as to establish direct copying.

[1] 'Methode nouvelle de dresser des recueuils', *Bibliothèque universelle*, 2 (1686), 315–40. In 1669 he composed a lengthy dedication and prefatory epistle for Sydenham's treatise on smallpox (PRO 30/24/47/2, fos. 50–2, 54–61, Dewhurst, *Sydenham*, 101–9), but this too remained unpublished.

[2] Locke to Pembroke, 28 Nov./8 Dec. 1684, *Correspondence*, ii. 664.

[3] *The Second Part of No Protestant Plot*, 25. Although this bore the date of 1682 on the title-page its contents indicate that it was written before the attempt to indict Shaftesbury. A contemporary note in a copy in the Bodleian reads: 'This came abroad a few daies before my Lord Shaftesbury's Bill of Indictment was found Ignoramus', Bodl., Ashm. 733. 1(b). Locke possessed all three parts of *No Protestant Plot* (*LL* 2351–3) and was wrongly suspected of having written the first: Prideaux to Ellis, 25 Oct. 1681, BL, Add. MS 28929, fo. 77^r, *Letters of Humphrey Prideaux*, 115.

[4] Many years later, after Ferguson had become a Jacobite and renounced his former views, he compiled a list of his writings headed 'Its with remorse and shame [I] charge my selfe with having written the following papers', Bodl., MS Smith 31, p. 30. 'No Protestant Plot; in three parts' was one of the works listed. The list is not the original but a copy headed 'A transcript of an original paper put into my hands Octob 8 1706' and endorsed (p. 33) 'Mr F. account of the books good and bad published by him'.

ENTRIES IN COMMONPLACE BOOKS

Locke's commonplace books make up a substantial part of his surviving papers, and the material they contain is of great importance for tracing the development of his thought. He had been using notebooks to record his reading ever since he first came to Oxford, but in about 1660 he seems to have decided that his notes needed to be organized in a systematic way. From this time onwards all his commonplace books were laid out in the manner later described in his *New Method for a Commonplace Book*.[1]

The great majority of the entries in Locke's commonplace books consist of extracts taken from books that he had been reading, but a small proportion are comments by Locke himself. In nearly all cases these entries were distinguished from the others by the initials 'JL' at the end of the entry. The entries made between 1660 and 1675 (considerably more than half the total) are undated, and allocating dates to them can sometimes be difficult; nearly all the entries made from 1679 onwards have the year in which they were made indicated in the margin.[2] All the entries in this volume that are dated in this way were made between 1679 and 1682. Of two entries in Adversaria 1661, 'Pactum' was written at some time in the early 1670s, 'Virtus' certainly not before 1681, but possibly later; the entries in MS Locke f. 24 cannot be later than the spring of 1684, and may have been made several years earlier.

The entries printed here vary considerably in both length and character. Some, such as 'Pactum' in Adversaria 1661, 'Amor', 'Amor Patriae', and 'Patriae Amor' in MS Locke d. 1, and all those in MS Locke f. 24, are private moral reflections which throw welcome light on the outlook of an affable and companionable but ultimately very reserved man who considered that 'The best way to conceale your self is sometimes to be open.'[3]

Several of the entries are on religion. 'Idololatria' expresses a strongly Protestant rejection of the Catholic claim that such practices as kneeling before images of the saints do not constitute idolatry because the

---

[1] There are several closely related systems that Locke used: see below, p. 173.

[2] Some care is needed here. Locke seems to have taken none of his commonplace books with him to France, and for the most part recorded his reading in his journal or on loose sheets of paper; the only commonplace book clearly started in France is MS Locke d. 1. After returning to England he copied many of these notes into his commonplace books; the dates given in the margin of these indicate the time of copying, not when the books were read, which was sometimes several years earlier: for example, the notes on Gabriel Naudé's *Considerations politiques sur les coups d'état* in MS Locke d. 10, pp. 21, 111, 137, 139, are dated 1681, but the book was read in 1676, MS Locke f. 1, pp. 409, 416–17.

[3] 'Malevoli', MS Locke f. 24, fo. 93ʳ, below, p. 394.

intention of the worshipper is not directed towards the image but towards the person it represents. It is a repetition of a point already made in Locke's journal for 15 July 1676, where he defined idolatry as consisting in 'performing outward worship, i.e. bowing, kneeling, prostrating or praying &c. before an image where either the place, time, or other circumstances give the spectator reason to presume that one is imployd in some act of religion or divine worship'.[1] Unlike many of his contemporaries, Locke did not believe that Catholic worship should be prohibited because it was idolatrous, but he clearly had no doubt that it was.

One of the points of contention between Anglicans and Protestant dissenters was the practice of kneeling to receive communion. Locke himself was presumably prepared to do this on the (apparently infrequent) occasions that he took the sacrament. 'Conformitas' records a story from John Covel, who had been chaplain of the Embassy in Constantinople. Covel had found a group of French Protestants in his congregation and had administered the bread to them while they remained standing, explaining that kneeling was not a necessary part of worship; this so moved them that they then knelt to receive the cup. Locke's comment was characteristic: 'This way if it were a litle more practised would perhaps be found not only the most Christian but the most effectuall way to bring men to Conformity.'[2] If, however, someone was not prepared to kneel, he should be free to leave the Church of England and join a congregation where no such requirement was imposed. In 1681 Locke insisted that

> though a man be satisfied in him self by the explication annexd that Kneeling at the Lords Supper is noe sin, yet if its strict injunction & practise be suspected by any to dispose to a superstitious veneration of the Elements . . . & to give an advantage to Popish preists to insinuate & spread their doctrine of transubstantiation whether a sober Christian may not at a time when popery soe threatens & soe nearly surrounds us & is ready by any way it can to find open to enter upon us may not without sin upon this ground withdraw from such a communion to an other . . .[3]

The hostility to Popish priests expressed here can be found in a commonplace-book entry from the following year. 'The Jews, the Romanists & the Turks, who all three pretend to guide them selves by a law reveld from heaven which shews them the way to happynesse, doe yet

---

[1] MS Locke f. 1, p. 321; the entire note is printed in *Essays on the Law of Nature*, 260–3.
[2] MS Locke d. 1, p. 5, below, p. 387.
[3] The 'Critical Notes' against Stillingfleet, MS Locke c. 34, p. 30; passage in Locke's hand.

all of them have recourse very frequently to tradition as a rule of noe lesse authority then their written law.'[1] These traditions are contrived by the clergy of all three religions for their own benefit, and

give occasion to enquireing men to suspect the integrity of their preists & teachers, who unwilling that the people should have a standing known rule of faith and manners, have for the maintenance of their own authority foisted in another of tradition, which will always be in their own power to be varied & suited to their own interest & occasions[2]

Another entry from 1682 expresses Locke's disdain for superstition:

Superstition is made up of apprehension of evill from god, & hopes by formall & outward addresses to him appease him without reall amendment of life ...[3]

Locke had expressed similar views twenty years earlier when writing the English Tract on Government:

But superstition if I understand it aright is a false apprehension of God, or of a false god, attended with a slavish fear of severity and cruelty in him, which they hope to mitigate by a worship of their own invention, and such sacrifices either of the lives of men or beasts or tortures on themselves, as their fears persuaded them are most likely to expiate and satisfy the displeasure of the Deity.[4]

Two of the entries are specifically concerned with toleration. 'Toleratio', dating from 1679, is a succinct restatement of Locke's established position. 'Ecclesia' (1682) starts as a comment on Hooker's account of the church as a supernatural but voluntary society—or, as Locke called it, a society by consent. In the latter respect it resembles the state but has a quite different purpose:

I imagine that the original of this societie is not, from our inclination as he [Hooker] says to a sociable life for that may be fully satisfied in other societies, but from the obligation man by the light of reason findes himself under to own & worship god publiquely in the world[5]

The end of entering into such a society is to obtain the favour of God 'by offering him an acceptable worship'. The bond of association of the society is in part a revealed law, which is unalterable, and in part human laws that depend on consent and so can be changed as circumstances

---

[1] 'Traditio', MS Locke d. 10, p. 163, below, p. 393.
[2] Ibid.
[3] 'Superstitio', MS Locke d. 10, p. 161, below, p. 392.
[4] *Two Tracts*, 147, cf. 235–6.
[5] 'Ecclesia', MS Locke d. 10, p. 43, below, p. 392.

require. Aspects of worship laid down by divine law cannot be modified; those of human origin cannot be imposed:

> noe body can impose any ceremonys unlesse positively & clearly by revelation injoynd, any farther then every one who joyns in the use of them is perswaded in his conscience they are acceptable to god, for if his conscience condemns any part of unrevealed worship he cannot by any sanction of men be obleiged to it.[1]

The implication seems to be that ceremonies that really are positively and clearly enjoined by revelation can be imposed, but the context makes it clear that Locke was referring to imposition by churches, not by the civil magistrate.

WRITINGS PRINTED IN THE APPENDICES

The writings printed in the Appendices fall into three classes: (i) the cancelled portion of the Rough Draft of Locke's *Essay concerning Toleration* in Huntington Library HM 584 (Appendix I); (ii) two works of uncertain authorship whose manuscripts are preserved among Locke's papers, *Philanthropy* and *Queries on Catholic Infallibility* (Appendices II–III); (iii) documents relating to the 1675 Test Bill (Appendices IV–VI), and to Shaftesbury's imprisonment in 1681 (Appendix VII). The first and last of these are discussed in more detail elsewhere.[2] The remarks that follow are concerned with the general problems of attribution, and with the specific problems raised by *Philanthropy* and *Queries on Catholic Infallibility*.

Problems of Attribution

Locke's presence in Shaftesbury's household gave him access to a wide range of potential copyists: servants at Exeter House, clerks working at the Excise Office or for the Council for Trade and Plantations, and no doubt others as well. One consequence of this is the existence of a substantial number of documents that are associated in one way or another with Locke, either by bearing his endorsement or by being preserved among his papers, but which are not in his hand and are of uncertain authorship. Almost all the material of this kind was produced between

---

[1] 'Ecclesia', MS Locke d. 10, p. 43, below, p. 392.

[2] Above, 131–2; below 166–70.

1667 and 1675. Before 1667 Locke was in Oxford, where there were fewer people who could have been requested, or commanded, to act as his amanuensis. Towards the end of his stay in France he engaged a new manservant, Sylvester Brounower, and once Brounower had learned enough English to undertake this kind of work, Locke usually used him as a copyist; when he left Locke's service in 1696 his successors, in particular Timothy Kiplin and William Shaw, acted in his stead. The handwriting of all three is readily identifiable; this is not true of most of the people who did copying for Locke while he was at Exeter House.[1]

Though Locke (in contrast with some contemporaries such as Robert Boyle) preferred to draft material in his own hand, he seems to have been disinclined to make additional copies of works he had already written: if one was needed, the task of producing it was given to someone else.[2] Three of the four surviving manuscripts of the *Essay concerning Toleration* were not written by Locke; neither were the copy of Draft A of the *Essay concerning Human Understanding* in the Shaftesbury papers[3] and two of the manuscripts of the 1668 paper on rates of interest.[4] In all these cases Locke's autograph has survived, either in whole or in part, and there are no problems about authenticity, but there is clearly no guarantee that this will always have happened. One needs to keep in mind the possibility that works by Locke might survive only in copies made by others, and that these manuscripts might not have his name anywhere on them.

The scribal copies of the longer works kept among Locke's own papers usually contain an explicit statement of his authorship.[5] The copy of the *Essays on the Law of Nature* in MS Locke f. 31 ends with the words 'Sic Cogitavit 1664 J. Locke' in Locke's hand, and the copy of the early writings on rates of interest in MS Locke e. 8 has the words 'Sic cogitavit 1668 JL' in Locke's hand at the end of the part written in 1668.[6] The copy of the *Essay concerning Toleration* made in the commonplace book

---

[1] The only earlier manservant who can be identified by name is John Wheelock. If the letters he wrote between 1692 and 1704 (MS Locke c. 23, fos. 84–93) are any guide to his earlier handwriting, he was not responsible for any of the manuscripts used in this edition.

[2] Exceptions are the very carefully written copies of the *Observations upon the Growth and Culture of Vines and Olives*, PRO 30/24/47/35, and the translation of Nicole's *Essays*, Pierpont Morgan Library, New York, MA 232, presented to the Earl and the Countess of Shaftesbury respectively. For his patrons a copy made by Brounower would hardly have been appropriate.   [3] PRO 30/24/47/7.

[4] MS Locke e. 8; BL, Add. MS 32094, fos. 289–93.

[5] One exception is the copy of the *Essay concerning Toleration* in MS Locke c. 28, though this does carry his endorsements on each of its original sheets.

[6] MS Locke f. 31, fo. 119ʳ, *Essays on the Law of Nature*, 214; MS Locke e. 8, fo. 27ᵛ, *Locke on Money*, 192.

Adversaria 1661 ends with the words 'Sic Cogitavit JL 16<u>67</u>' in Locke's hand. In contrast with this, copies of Locke's writings made for use outside his circle seem generally not to have carried his name.[1] Sir William Coventry's copy of the 1668 paper on rates of interest did not originally mention Locke's authorship, though a note apparently by Coventry himself on its first page described it as 'By Mr Locke directed by Lord Ashley'.[2] The copy of the *Essay concerning Toleration* in the Shaftesbury papers is entirely anonymous. It is salutary to reflect that if Locke's papers had been lost, as they easily might have been, then the only surviving copy of the *Essay concerning Toleration* would be one that contains no trace of his hand and gives no indication whatever that he was its author.

In the case of short papers the most valuable source of information—apart from handwriting—is provided by Locke's endorsements. Locke kept most of his loose papers in his desk or in the set of pigeonholes he had ordered to be constructed for his papers.[3] In order to fit into these receptacles they needed to be folded several times, and this was normally done in a way that made the original text invisible. If Locke wanted to see what a bundle of papers contained without going to the trouble of unwrapping it, some note on the outside indicating its contents was required. His procedure was therefore to endorse the document—quite literally—by writing on the back of its final page an identifying description, consisting of a single word or a short phase, and (usually) a date, indicated in his usual way by an underlined two-digit number: for example, the queries on Scottish church government are endorsed '<u>Church</u> Governm^t Q⟨ueries⟩ Concerning the Scotch Discipline <u>68</u>'. In most endorsements one word is underlined, presumably to indicate the letter of the alphabet under which the document was to be filed.

The presence of an endorsement in Locke's hand on a document provides incontrovertible evidence that it passed through his hands, but by itself is neither a necessary nor a sufficient condition of his authorship. The Shaftesbury papers contain scores of documents that were endorsed by him but of which he was manifestly not the author: examples are as varied as draft proposals for a marriage Act, a list of obstructions on the bank of the Thames between the Temple and London Bridge, and an

---

[1] The beginning of the copy of Draft A in the Shaftesbury papers (PRO 30/24/47/7) has been lost, and it is therefore impossible to tell whether it once bore Locke's name or not, or for what use it was intended.   [2] BL, Add. MS 32094, fo. 289^r, *Locke on Money*, 123.

[3] The pigeonholes (so described) are mentioned in notes dated 1675, MS Locke c. 25, fos. 16–18.

inventory of provisions stored at Ashley River in the newly founded colony of Carolina.[1]

A final clue to the authorship of any document is provided by the collection in which it was preserved, though here again matters are less than entirely straightforward. The papers in the Bodleian Library now classed as the Locke MSS include documents that were manifestly written after his death,[2] and may well contain others of an earlier date that were added posthumously. Nevertheless, the fact that a document is now (or was formerly) among Locke's papers is good, albeit not quite conclusive, evidence that he had some connection with it. A document surviving among the Shaftesbury papers, on the other hand, may well have no connection with Locke at all. Unless there is independent evidence of a connection, such as an endorsement in Locke's hand, it is unsafe to assume even that he saw the document, let alone that he had any part in its composition.

Several works that have in the past been attributed with more or less confidence to Locke but which have been excluded from this edition are discussed in the final section of this Introduction.

Philanthropy

This short work is of uncertain authorship. The only known manuscript is a single leaf among Locke's papers, now catalogued as MS Locke c. 27, fo. 30^c; the hand is not identifiable, but there are corrections by Locke, and the verso was endorsed by him, 'Philanthropy 75'. Another copy may once have existed: when Shaftesbury's papers were seized following his arrest in July 1681 one of the documents impounded was described by his secretary, Samuel Wilson, who drew up this particular list, as 'The Sect of Philanthropy'.[3]

Whether Locke wrote *Philanthropy* is uncertain. Some parts agree with his other writings in both style and sentiment, for example the opening sentence:

Mankinde is supported in the way's of Vertue, or Vice, by the Society he is of; & the Conversation he keep's: Example & Fashion being the great Governours of this World.

---

[1] PRO 30/24/5/281, PRO 30/24/5/250, PRO 30/24/48/28.

[2] For example, MSS Locke d. 6 [1709], d. 7 [1714], and d. 8 [*c*.1724], *Summary Catalogue*, 33, 40, 45. These presumably belonged to Peter King.

[3] PRO 30/24/6A/349/5. This was the original title (later deleted) of the copy in MS Locke c. 27, suggesting that the paper seized in 1681 was a different copy.

Others seem less like his usual style:

> The Protestant Religion whilst it was a Sect, & a party, cherish'd, & favour'd each other; increast strangely; against all the power & persecution of the Church of Roome: But since the warmth of that is over, and 'tis embrac't onely as a trewer Doctrine, this last 40 yeares, hath hardly produc't as many Convert's, from the Romish Fopperies . . .

There is nothing implausible in supposing Locke to have drafted a manifesto for a group of Christians wishing to meet together for their own preferred form of worship. In 1688 he did this in an untitled paper, endorsed 'Pacific Christians', the last part of which reads:

> 9 Decency & order in our Assemblys being directed as they ought only to edification, can need but very few & plain rules. Time & place of meeting being setled if any thing else need regulation, the assembly it self or four of the ancientest soberest & discreetest of the brethren chosen for that occasion shall regulate it.
>
> 10 From every brother that after admonition walketh disorderly we withdraw ourselves.
>
> 11 We each of us thinke it our duty to propogate the doctrine & practise of universal charity good will & obedience in all places & on all occasions as god shall give us oportunity.[1]

If the manuscript of this had been in an unknown hand there would probably be some uncertainty about its origin, but as it is in Locke's hand and contains numerous alterations of the kind that he made in his own works, there can no doubt that he was its author.

Even if Locke was not the author of *Philanthropy*, he seems to have had further dealings with whoever was, or with some of his associates: in one of Locke's pocket memorandum books[2] there are comments in his own hand headed 'Philanthropy', apparently on a constitutional document of some kind, presumably emanating from the same source. These comments are undated but appear to have been made towards the end of 1679.[3] They show Locke commenting critically but sympathetically on a radically non-episcopalian form of church government, and resemble in

---

[1] MS Locke c. 27, fos. 80av–80br; Goldie, 306.   [2] MS Locke f. 28, pp. 28–9, 43.
[3] The notes start near the foot of p. 28, continue on the page opposite beneath an earlier note containing a reference to a letter from Nicolas Toinard dated 16 Sept. 1679 (NS), and conclude on p. 43, immediately below the date [16]79 at the head of the page. It appears, therefore, that Locke made these notes at some time between mid–September 1679, when he received Toinard's letter (*Correspondence*, ii. 112), and the end of the year; he was in London from 3 October to 18 or 19 December, when he left for Oxford.

many ways the comments he had made a decade earlier on the draft of the *Fundamental Constitutions of Carolina*.[1]

One conspicuous feature of *Philanthropy* is its anticlericalism. No body of men, the author complains, has any interest in caring for truth:

> the Clergy have pretended to that care, for many hundred's of year's paste, but how well they have perform'd it the world know's; They have found a Mistriss call'd, the present Power that pay's them much better then truth can; Whatever Idoll she injoyn's, they offer us to be worship'd as this great Goddess; and theire Impudence hath beene soe great, that though they vary it as often as the present Power it selfe changeth; yet they affirme it, still to be the same Goddess, truth.

This has parallels both in the *Letter from a Person of Quality*, itself of uncertain authorship, and in one of the additions to the *Essay concerning Toleration* in Adversaria 1661, which was certainly written by Locke; all three passages date from 1675 or thereabouts. Another notable feature is the disparagement of the Quakers, who are described as 'a great instance, how little truth & reason operates upon mankinde, & how great force, society & conversation hath amongst those that maintaine an inviolable freindship & concerne, for all of theire way'. These sentiments are entirely compatible with Locke's authorship of *Philanthropy*: during this time of his life at least, he seems to have regarded the Quakers as irrational and potentially dangerous enthusiasts.[2]

Queries on Catholic Infallibility

Another work of uncertain authorship is a set of queries on the infallibility of the Pope and the Roman Catholic Church. The only known manuscript, MS Locke c. 27, fos. 32–3, is not in his hand, though it is among his papers and does bear his endorsement.[3] Some of the mistakes in the manuscript, such as 'Casmons' for 'Canons', 'Dugenius' for 'Eugenius', and 'dules.' for 'Eccles.', indicate that the copyist was not the author.

Locke's authorship of this piece cannot be entirely ruled out. The kind of queries it contains seem more likely to have been made by a philosopher

---

[1] PRO 30/24/47/3, fo. 1ʳ; Locke's comments are printed in Milton, 'John Locke and the Fundamental Constitutions of Carolina', 120–1.

[2] They are singled out for adverse comment in Draft A, along with Romanists and peripatetics: 'let a Quaker beleive his teacher to be inspird. & you in vaine bring probable reasons against his doctrines', § 42, *Drafts*, i. 71. Compare also the hostile treatment of the Quakers in the original 1667 version of the *Essay concerning Toleration* (below, p. 286) and the derisive remarks in Locke's letters to his father, *Correspondence*, i. 41–4.

[3] On the verso of the second leaf there are the words 'Queries Popery 75'; the first was written by the copyist, the others by Locke.

than by a theologian or an ecclesiastical historian:

1. Whether there be any Infalible Judge on Earth
2. Whether any Church be that Judge
3. Whether the Roman Church be that Church
4. If it be what Capacity, whether the Infallability be in the Pope as the Head or in the Body of the Church, and then whether in the whole Body diffusive or in the Collective in a Councill, and if a Councell be Infalible, then whether it be soe only with the Popes Confirmation; or without it.
5. How shall wee Certainly know whoe must be Members of it Clergie & Laickes or only Clergie; or only Bishopes Presbyters too and Deacons . . .

Locke had long been interested in such matters, and in 1661 had written a short tract denying the necessity of an infallible interpreter of the Scriptures.[1] The author of these *Queries* displays some knowledge of church history, but not more than Locke can reasonably be supposed to have possessed. In one of his commonplace books there is an undated entry taken from an English translation (edition unspecified) of Sarpi's *History of the Council of Trent*, which he seems to have been reading while at Exeter House.[2] His library also contained copies of works by several of the English anti-papal controversialists, notably Chillingworth and Stillingfleet.[3]

However, although Locke could have been the author of these queries, so could many other people in Restoration England. One polemical work published in London in 1675—the date of Locke's endorsement on the manuscript of the *Queries*—has the title *A Letter to a Priest of the Roman Church: wherein the Grounds of their Pretended Infallibility are Called for and Examined, in some Queries*. The queries in MS Locke c. 27 have a fair amount in common with these, but there are no passages that are close enough to indicate direct borrowing.

WRITINGS EXCLUDED FROM THIS EDITION

The writings excluded from this edition that deserve some comment here fall into two classes: those surviving in manuscripts preserved among

---

[1] *An necesse sit dari in ecclesia infallibilem sacro sanctae scripturae interpretem?*, PRO 30/24/47/33; Latin text with translation in 'John Locke's Essay on Infallibility', 316–27; English translation in Goldie, 204–9.

[2] MS Locke d. 11, fo. 14ᵛ. The entry is difficult to date precisely, but is unlikely to be earlier than 1674, since the entry beneath it was taken from J. F. Hertodt's *Crocologia* (Jena, 1671), which Locke was reading in 1674–5. There are no entries in the notebook made between 1676 and 1692.   [3] *LL* 685–6, 2775–8, 2780–1.

Locke's own papers in the Bodleian Library, and those surviving in manuscripts preserved among the Shaftesbury papers in the National Archives.

I. One document of uncertain authorship among Locke's own papers is *The Particular Test for Priests*, written on the first page of a single folded sheet, MS Locke c. 27, fos. 30^a–30^b. The manuscript is not in Locke's hand, but it was endorsed by him, 'Papists Test', on fo. 30^{bv}.[1] The 'Walsh' referred to is undoubtedly Peter Walsh (*c.*1618–1688), an Irish Franciscan who had been excommunicated in 1670 and spent most of his later years in England.[2] In 1674 Walsh published *A Letter to the Catholicks of England, Ireland, Scotland, and all other dominions under his Gracious Majesty Charles II*, a copy of which was briefly in Locke's possession.[3]

Whether or not Locke knew Walsh is uncertain; one person who did was Gilbert Burnet:

He was of Irish extraction, and of the Franciscan order: and was indeed in all points of controversy almost wholly protestant: but he had senses of his own, by which he excused his adhering to the church of Rome. . . . And he observed, not without great indignation at us for our folly, that we, instead of uniting among ourselves and dividing them, according to their maxims, did all we could to keep them united and to disjoint our own body. For he was persuaded, if the government had held an heavy hand on the regulars and the Jesuits, and had been gentle to the seculars, and had set up a distinguishing test, renouncing all sort of power in the pope over the temporal rights of princes, to which the regulars and the Jesuits could never submit, that this would have engaged them into such violent quarrels among themselves, that censures would have been thundered at Rome against all that should take any such test; which would have procured much disputing, and might have probably ended in the revolt of the soberer part of that church.[4]

---

[1] There is another endorsement, 'Te⟨st⟩ [Welch *deleted*] Walsh' on fo. 30^{av}, which is not in Locke's hand. The statement in *Summary Catalogue*, 27 that the manuscript is in Brounower's hand is mistaken.

[2] A detailed but hostile account of Walsh's earlier career is given in Millet, *The Irish Franciscans*, 418–63.

[3] On 14 Mar. 1674 Locke noted in his current memorandum book that he had lent 'Walsh's Epistle' to James Tyrrell, MS Locke f. 13, p. 9. He bought something by a writer named Walsh on 21 March (MS Locke c. 1, p. 53), probably *The History & Vindication of the Loyal Formulary, or Irish Remonstrance* (n.p., 1674); a copy of this (perhaps the same one) was sold to David Thomas on 10 May and paid for on 10 July, MSS Locke f. 13, pp. 21, 23; c. 1, p. 66. Neither work was in Locke's final library, though he did possess copies of two pamphlets by Walsh: *Valesius ad Haroldum* ([London], 1672), *LL* 3044, and *Some Few Questions concerning the Oath of Allegiance: propos'd by a Catholick Gentleman in a Letter to a Person of Learning and Honour* (London, 1674), *LL* 2113.   [4] Burnet, i. 348–9.

The test Burnet described sounds very similar to the document among Locke's papers, and it seems likely that Walsh was its author. He may also have written the manuscript that Locke preserved: the hand of MS Locke c. 27, fo. 30[ar], appears to be the same as that in a copy of Walsh's letter to the Earl of Essex, 4 Aug. 1674, British Library, Add. MS 32094, fos. 377–80.

Among the papers taken away from Thanet House when Shaftesbury was arrested in July 1681 is a document described as 'The Particular Tests for Preists in one sheet'.[1] This is presumably the same work; whether or not it is the same copy is uncertain.

There are copies of the same list of theses (with minor textual variants) at Longleat House and in the Lauinger Library, Georgetown University, Washington,[2] and a rather different list with the same title in the Newberry Library, Chicago.[3]

2. Among the Shaftesbury papers there is a group of undated papers, PRO 30/24/6B/427, 429, and 430, that were probably written in the first half of the 1670s. A number of modern historians have assigned them to the time of the Declaration of Indulgence in March 1672, and supposed that Locke had a part in their composition; though such a dating cannot be ruled out, the grounds for it are not very strong, and evidence for Locke's involvement is weak or non-existent.

PRO 30/24/6B/429 is a proposal for the appointment of a Vicar-General to oversee the reform of the Church of England. This was an office whose holder would have had direct authority over the entire Anglican hierarchy; its only previous occupant had been Thomas Cromwell in the 1530s. The proposal is not in Locke's hand, but it does bear his endorsement: 'Vicar Generall'.

PRO 30/24/6B/427 is an eight-page paper entitled 'Concerning His Majestys Supreame Power Ecclesiastical Establish'd by the Lawes of this Kingdome at this present time in their full force and vigor'. It is not in Locke's hand, and displays a fair amount of legal and historical learning of a kind which he is not known to have possessed. Though not specifically advocating the appointment of a Vicar-General, it mentions Henry VIII's appointment of Cromwell, and remarks that a holder of the post could be 'a lay and married person'.

---

[1] PRO 30/24/6A/349/4. This list is in Henry Starkey's hand.

[2] Longleat House, Thynne papers, vol. 27, fo. 100 (microfilm in the Institute of Historical Research, XR 71/15); Lauinger Library, Georgetown University, Washington DC, Milton House Collection, box 4, folder 28.

[3] Case MS 6A 24, tentatively dated by the Newberry Library to the 1660s.

PRO 30/24/6B/430 is an untitled paper advocating a thoroughly Erastian account of ecclesiastical jurisdiction, concluding that in England it belonged to the civil magistrate 'and in them (whether Clergie or not) to whom the supream magistrate would impart itt'. Cromwell's role as Vicar-General is mentioned as 'an Evident demonstration that Ecclesiasticall Jurisdiction was not tyed to the persons of Clergiemen'. Despite a statement to the contrary in the catalogue of the Shaftesbury papers, the paper is not in Locke's hand.[1]

Maurice Cranston believed that PRO 30/24/6B/429 was drawn up by Locke, and gave a vivid and apparently circumstantial account of its origin:

> Charles told Ashley he would be willing to issue a Declaration of Indulgence provided he could be assured of its legality, and he asked Ashley, with Lauderdale and Clifford, to investigate the constitutional aspects. The task was passed on to Locke, who in turn reported favourably. Religious toleration, his report pointed out, was an ecclesiastical matter, and the King, as Head of the Church of England, was supreme in ecclesiastical jurisdiction.[2]

No source is given for any of this apart from PRO 30/24/6B/429 itself, but the probable origin of his story can be located without much difficulty. In Louise Fargo Brown's biography of Shaftesbury the following account may be found:

> The same day that the duke of York was empowered to attack the Dutch fleet without waiting for a declaration of war, the king asked his foreign committee what was the extent of his powers in ecclesiastical affairs. Lauderdale reminded him that he was supreme governor. Clifford said he had more power than was generally supposed, since he could appoint a vicar general, who was above the archbishop of Canterbury. Ashley thought that through this vicegerent he could declare heresies, excommunicate, and burn.... Ashley, Lauderdale, and Clifford, were directed to look into the question of legality and report. Locke did the spade work, and a paper in his hand on ecclesiastical jurisdiction, deciding for the power of the king, with the extracts from the laws on which it was based, lies among the Shaftesbury papers to-day.[3]

Except for the mention of Locke's involvement this is little more than a précis of the minutes in the Foreign Entry Book for 6 March 1672.[4] Brown's identification of Locke's contribution was, however, different

---

[1] *The Thirty-Third Annual Report of the Deputy Keeper of the Public Records*, 226.
[2] Cranston, 143–4.
[3] *The First Earl of Shaftesbury*, 195–6. Cranston's and Brown's accounts are followed in Lee, *The Cabal*, 186–7.   [4] NA, SP 104/177, fo. 12.

from Cranston's: in a footnote appended to this passage two papers are cited, PRO 30/24/6B/427 and 430.

A very similar account appears in Haley's life of Shaftesbury:

> [Ashley] supported Clifford's view that the King could appoint a Vicar-General and so 'may declare heresies, excommunicate, burn, etc.' He, Clifford and Lauderdale were commissioned 'to consider how the law stands as to this, and what the King has in his power', and John Locke duly provided Ashley with the necessary information, upholding the royal supremacy in ecclesiastical affairs in documents still extant.[1]

No specific identification of these still extant documents is given, but the only items in the Shaftesbury papers mentioned in the sources for the paragraph in which this passage occurs are PRO 30/24/6B/427 and 430.

Yet another variant of the same story was given by Richard Ashcraft:

> The king asked Shaftesbury to provide him with an opinion as to whether he could declare an Act of Indulgence...through the exercise of his royal prerogative. Shaftesbury delegated the responsibility for the answer to this question to Locke, who researched the precedents and supplied Shaftesbury with the necessary information to support the recommendation that the king did possess such power.[2]

In all this two things at least are clear. One is that there is no mention whatever of Locke in the Foreign Entry Book, and any account of his involvement can only be based on the documents in the Shaftesbury papers. The other is that while all four writers are telling more or less the same story,[3] the documents on which their accounts are ostensibly based are different: according to Cranston the paper Locke supplied was PRO 30/24/6B/429; according to Brown and Haley he supplied PRO 30/24/6B/427 and 430; according to Ashcraft, PRO 30/24/6B/429 and 430.

The fact that PRO 30/24/6B/429 bears Locke's endorsement shows that it passed through his hands and suggests that he may have read it,

---

[1] Haley, 297. This account has been followed by later authors, for example Jacob, *Henry Stubbe*, 117.

[2] *Revolutionary Politics*, 111. A footnote adds that 'There are two documents in Locke's hand in the Shaftesbury papers that deal with the king's jurisdiction over ecclesiastical matters (PRO 30/24/6B/429–430...)'.

[3] Yet another variant can be found in Lacey, *Dissent and Parliamentary Politics*, 64: 'Reassured by the report from the Earl of Shaftesbury's secretary, John Locke, who concluded that the King did have the legal right to suspend ecclesiastical laws, Charles and his ministers began their deliberations at the end of 1671.' The sources given for this are Brown and *CSPD, 1671–1672* [actually *CSPD, 1671*], 562–3, which refers to notes made by Joseph Williamson on 11 Nov. 1671 (NA, SP 29/294/15) in which Locke is not mentioned.

but is certainly no indication that he was its author. Its contents give little support to Cranston's account of its origin. Far from reading like a paper drawn up to inform the King and his ministers about the exact extent of the royal prerogative in ecclesiastical matters, it has on the contrary a very unofficial air. The writer was clearly a disappointed man who disliked the bishops and entertained hopes of a second Thomas Cromwell completing what the first had left unfinished. The benefits would be the same as in Henry VIII's reign: 'It will bring a great deale of money, if well managed, unto the Kings treasury: many Colledges being forfeited to the King, and many Ecclesiasticall revennues being Escheated . . .'. Once this had been accomplished a whole field of new opportunities would arise: 'His Majesty will be able to preferr into considerable benefices, and dignities, an active and Learned sort of men, who cannot now get any pre-ferment . . .'. It is difficult not to believe that the writer had himself in mind here, and it is certainly not clear why a layman like Locke who drew a useful part of his income from his position as a non-resident Student of Christ Church should have proposed such a scheme.

It is possible that this paper has some connection with a story circu-lating early in 1675 that Shaftesbury would be made Vicar-General. In his letter to the Earl of Carlisle, Shaftesbury remarked that 'I hear from all quarters of Letters from Whitehall, to give notice that I am comeing up to towne, that a great office with a strange name is preparing for me, & such like. I am ashamed I was thought so easy a fool by those should know me better.'[1] Two copies of the letter have a marginal note 'Vicar Generall' next to this passage.[2] The rumour seems to have been widely known: the Venetian ambassador had heard of it, as had Humphrey Prideaux in Oxford.[3] The prospect of Shaftesbury as a second Thomas Cromwell would have produced apoplexy among the bishops, but it is very difficult to believe that anyone in authority—certainly not Danby—would seriously have contemplated anything of the kind.[4]

PRO 30/24/6B/429 was at least endorsed in Locke's hand. The other two papers have no discernible connection with him at all. Neither looks very much like the kind of paper that Shaftesbury might have carried with him to a meeting of the Committee on Foreign Affairs.

---

[1] 3 Feb. 1675, Bodl., MS Carte 81, fo. 606^r. The copy in Stringer's hand (PRO 30/24/5/284) is badly damaged here.
[2] PRO 30/24/5/294, p. 13; Yale, Osborn Shelves, b. 157, p. 158.
[3] Alberti to the Doge and Senate, 22 Jan./1 Feb. 1675, *CSPV 1673–1675*, 349; Prideaux to Ellis, 24 Jan. 1675, BL, Add. MS 28929, fo. 11^r, *Letters of Humphrey Prideaux*, 29.
[4] Cf. Haley, 369.

PRO 30/24/6B/427 is much too long to read out in full—it amounts to some 5,000 words—and is not well suited to quick reference. PRO 30/24/6B/430, like PRO 30/24/6B/429, has a decidedly unofficial feel to it. It was endorsed by someone other than Locke with the words 'Curious Paper on the Origine of Ecclesiastical Jurisdiction'; the wording of this hardly suggests that the paper had been drawn up by one of Shaftesbury's political staff.

There is therefore no reason to suppose that these documents have any connection with the meetings of the Committee on Foreign Affairs in March 1672, or indeed with the Declaration of Indulgence at all.[1] There is also no reason to suppose that any of them was drafted by Locke, who was hardly an obvious person to consult on delicate questions of constitutional law. It is difficult to regard as credible a theory that supposes that on an issue of such importance the King and his ministers would have bypassed both the law officers and the judges, and sought an opinion from a minor government functionary possessed of no legal training whatever.[2]

Note A. The Toleration Debate, 1667–1668

The list below contains the main works on comprehension and indulgence published in the nine months from the beginning of August 1667 to the adjournment of Parliament on 9 May 1668. Polemical works attacking or defending the Church of England that are not primarily concerned with toleration and works on the position of Catholics or Quakers have not been included. Items are listed in order of publication in so far as this can be determined.

A few of the works (e.g. 1A, 14, 21, 23) are themselves dated, and the relative order of some of the others can be determined by their mention of works already published. The main source of information for publication dates comes from notes made by Thomas Barlow on his own copies, now in the Bodleian Library: most of these are in the volume B 14.15 Linc., but a few are elsewhere. Bodleian shelf-marks for the books owned by Barlow have been given; they include all but four of the works listed here (the exceptions being 10, 14, 15, and 16). Where no

[1] PRO 30/24/6B/431 is endorsed 'Paper concerning the Kings declaration for Indulgence'; it is not in Locke's hand, and no one seems to have attributed it to him.

[2] A fuller discussion of these and other papers wrongly attributed to Locke can be found in Milton, 'Lockean Political Apocrypha'.

other indication is given, dates ascribed to Barlow are taken from notes in his hand on the title-pages of the works concerned.

(1) [John Humfrey], *A Proposition for the Safety & Happiness of the King and Kingdom both in Church and State, and prevention of the Common Enemy. Tendered to the Consideration of his Majesty and the Parliament against their next Session. By a lover of Sincerity & Peace* (London, 1667).

Wing H 77C. 8° F 12(3) Linc. Dated 18 June at the end (p. 94). Published about the beginning of August, Barlow, B 14.15(5) Linc., p. 18. Wrongly ascribed to David Jenkins by British Library Catalogue. For toleration.

(1A) [John Humfrey], *A Proposition for the Safety and Happiness of the King and kingdom, both in Church and State, and prevention of the Common Enemy. Tendered to the Consideration of his Majesty and the Parliament against the tenth of October. By a lover of Sincerity & Peace. The Second Edition revised, corrected and enlarged by the Author. Together with a Reply to the pretended Answer to it* (London, 1667).

Wing H 77D. 8° B 15 Linc. A second edition of (1) containing a reply to (4). Dated 12 October 1667 at end (p. 118). Published 25 October according to notes in Barlow's copy and in B 14.15(5) Linc., p. 18.

(2) [John Corbet], *A Discourse of the Religion of England. Asserting, That Reformed Christianity Setled in its Due Latitude is the Stability and Advancement of this Kingdom* (London, 1667).

Wing C 6252. B 1.4(1) Linc. Probably published in September: described as 'lately printed' in (4), which was published on 10 October. For toleration.

(3) *The Judgement of Mr. Baxter concerning Ceremonies and Conformity. With a Short Reflection upon a Scandalous Pamphlet, Intituled, A Proposition for the Safety and Happiness of the King and Kingdom. In a Letter to a Gentleman of the House of Commons* (London, 1667).

Wing B 1290. B 14.15(5) Linc. Extracts from Baxter's *Five Disputations of Church-Government and Worship* ([London], 1659), put together by an opponent; in part a reply to (1). Against toleration.

(4) [Thomas Tomkins], *The Inconveniences of Toleration, Or An Answer to a late Book, Intituled, A Proposition Made to the King and Parliament, For the Safety and Happiness of the King and Kingdom* (London, 1667).

Two printings: Wing T 1835, 1835A, the latter with the spelling 'Inconveniencies' in the title. B 14.15(1) Linc. is a copy of T 1835A. A reply to (1), but also briefly mentioning (2) at the end, pp. 37–8. Published 10 October (Barlow). Against toleration.

(5) *Votes &c. of the Honourable House of Commons: Febr. 25 &c. 1662. Upon Reading His Majesties Gracious Declaration and Speech, &c.* (n.p. [London], n.d.).

Wing E 2760B. B 14.15(6) Linc. A reprint of a work originally published 1663. This edition was 'reprinted Oct. 19. 1667, when Bill was provided for a toleration of some Non-conformists (and brought into the House by Colonel Birch) that the Members (if any had forgotten) might be reminded of the reason against such toleration', B 14.15 Linc., p. 177; Wing gives a conjectural date for it of 1663.

(6) [Richard Perrinchief], *A Discourse of Toleration: In Answer to a late Book, Intituled, A Discourse Of the Religion of England* (London, 1668).

Wing P 1593B. B 14.15(3) Linc. A reply to (5). Published during the Michaelmas term 1667 (Barlow). Against toleration.

(7) [John Pearson], *Promiscuous Ordinations Are Destructive to the Honour & Safety of the Church of England: (If they should be allowed in it.) Written in a Letter to a Person of Quality* (London, 1668).

Wing P 1005. B 14.15(8) Linc. In part a reply to (1). Published 3 November 1667 (Barlow). Against toleration.

(8) *Dolus an Virtus? Or, An Answer to a Seditious Discourse Concerning The Religion of England: And The Settlement of Reformed Christianity in its due Latitude* (London, 1668).

Wing D 1841; also listed as C 6252A. B 14.15(10) Linc. A reply to (2); also includes the votes of the Commons published separately as (5) at the end. Published November 1667 (Barlow). Latin phrase in title from *Aeneid* II. 390. Against toleration.

(9) *Bentivolyo, or Good Will to all that are Called Unconformists, or To all the People of God* (n.p. [London], 1667).

Wing B 1913. B 14.15(7) Linc. Written 'very near twelve months since the Fire' [2–6 September 1666] (p. 5). Published in London on 13 November 1667 (Barlow). For toleration.

(10) [John Owen], *A Peace-Offering in an Apology and humble Plea for Indulgence and Liberty of Conscience* (London, 1667).

Wing O 790. B 14.15(2) Linc. Published 14 November (Barlow). For toleration.

(11) [John Owen], *Indulgence and Toleration Considered: in a Letter unto A Person of Honour* (London, 1667).

Wing O 763. Precise date of publication uncertain, though probably later than (10). Owen mentions '*Discourses* sent me, published lately about *Indulgence* and *Toleration*' (p. 3); these probably include (4) and (6). For toleration.

(12) [John Corbet], *A Second Discourse of the Religion of England: Further Asserting, That Reformed Christianity, Setled in its Due Latitude, is the Stability and Advancement of this Kingdom. Wherein is included, An Answer to a late Book, Entituled, A Discourse of Toleration* (London, 1668).

Wing C 6263. B 18.5(2) Linc. A successor to (2) and reply to (6). Published at the end of January 1667 [i.e. 1667/8] (Barlow). For toleration.

(13) [Richard Perrinchief], *Indulgence not Justified: Being a Continuation of the Discourse Of Toleration: In Answer to the Argument of a late Book, Entituled A Peace-Offering, or Plea for Indulgence: And to the Cavils Of another, call'd The Second Discourse of the Religion in England* (London, 1668).

Wing P 1594. B 14.15(4) Linc. A successor to (6) and reply to (10) and (12). Attacked in (23), so published not later than early April 1668, and probably rather earlier. Against toleration.

(14) B.P., *A Modest and Peaceable Letter concerning Comprehension, &c.* (London, 1668).

Wing P 7. Dated 18 February 1667 [i.e. 1667/8] at the end (p. 14). Against toleration.

(15) *A Letter to a Member of this Present Parliament, For Liberty of Conscience* (London, 1668).

Wing L 1688. Probably dating from February or March. For toleration.

(16) *A Second Letter to a Member of this Present Parliament, against Comprehension. By the Author of the former Letter for Liberty of Conscience* (London, 1668).

Wing S 2286. A successor to (15) by the same author, probably written soon afterwards. For toleration.

(17) *A Letter of the Presbyterian Ministers In the City of London, Presented the First of Jan. 1645. to the Reverend Assembly of Divines, Sitting at Westminster, by Authority of Parliament, against Toleration. Now Re-printed, with some Animadversions thereon* (London, 1668).

Wing L 1581. B 14.15(9) Linc. Mentioned in (18). The animadversions consist of comments printed in the margin. Against toleration.

(18) J.H. [John Humfrey], *A Defence of the Proposition: Or, Some Reasons rendred why the Nonconformist-Minister who comes to his Parish-Church and Common-Prayer, cannot yet yeeld to other things that are enjoyned, without some Moderation. Being A Full Reply to the Book which is a pretended Answer thereunto* (London, 1668).

Wing H 3676. B 1.4(3) Linc. A successor to (2); mainly a reply to (4), but also mentioning (3), (5), (6), (8), and (17). Attacked in (23), so published not later than early April 1668, and perhaps rather earlier. For toleration.

(19) [Sir Charles Wolseley], *Liberty of Conscience Upon its true and proper Grounds, Asserted & Vindicated. Proving That no Prince, nor State, ought by force to compel Men to any part of the Doctrine, Worship, or Discipline of the Gospel* (London, 1668).

Wing W 3310. B 18.5(4) Linc. Attacked in (23), so published not later than early April 1668. Wing W 3311 is a second edition, also dating from 1668, which also includes both (19) and (20). For toleration.

(20) [Sir Charles Wolseley], *Liberty of Conscience, the Magistrates Interest: Or, To grant Liberty of Conscience to Persons of different perswasions in matters of Religion, is the great Interest of all Kingdoms and States, and particularly of England; Asserted and Proved* (London, 1668).

Wing W 3309. B 18.5(3) Linc. Apparently published shortly after (18); also attacked in (23). For toleration.

(21) *A Proclamation for Inforcing the Laws against Conventicles, and for preservation of the Publick Peace, against Unlawful Assemblies of Papists and Non-Conformists* (London, 1667/8).

Wing C 3346. B 14.15(11) Linc. Proclamation dated 10 March 1668.

(22) *A Few Sober Queries Upon the late Proclamation, for enforcing the Laws against Conventicles, &c. and the late Vote of the House of Commons, For Renewing the said Act for three years more. Proposed to the serious consideration of the Kings majesty, with his two Houses of*

Parliament. By one that earnestly desires the prosperity of England (London, 1668).

Wing F 838. B 14.15(12) Linc. A comment on (21). The vote of the Commons was on 28 April, Milward, 282–3. For toleration.

(23) Abraham Philotheus [Abraham Wright], *Anarchie Reviving, Or, The Good old Cause on the Anvile. Being A Discovery of the present Design to retrive the late Confusions both of Church and State, in several Essays for Liberty of Conscience* (London, 1668).

Wing W 3684. B 1.4(2) Linc. Dated 15 April 1668 at the end (p. 74). A list of the books attacked is given on p. 1, viz. (1), (12), (18), (19), and (20). Against toleration.

Note B. The Persecution of the Japanese Christians

One of the most striking passages in the *Essay concerning Toleration* describes the savage persecution of the Japanese Christians that began in 1614.[1] Locke gave no source for his account, but the details it contains show that it almost certainly derived from a description of Japan made in 1636 by François (or Frans) Caron (1600–73), a Dutchman from a French Protestant family who had lived in Japan between 1619 and 1641. This was first published as *Beschrivinghe van het Machtigh Coninckrijck Iapan . . .* (Amsterdam, 1649).[2]

Locke could have become acquainted with Caron's account of the persecution in at least two different ways:[3]

1. An English translation of the *Beschrivinghe* was published in 1663 as *A true Description of the Mighty Kingdoms of Japan and Siam. Written Originally in Dutch by Francis Caron and Joost Schorten; And now rendred into English by Capt. Roger Manley* (London, 1663). Locke did not own a copy of either this or the subsequent 1669 edition, and there are no records of his reading either.[4]

---

[1] A detailed account of the persecutions is given in Boxer, *The Christian Century in Japan*, ch. 7. Locke mentioned them again in *A Third Letter for Toleration*, 223.

[2] The publication history of Caron's book is described in Boxer's edition, 169–79.

[3] Some of the material in Caron's account was also used (with acknowledgement) in Bernhard Varenius, *Descriptio Regni Japoniae* (Amsterdam, 1649), but he did not include the description of the persecutions. Locke did not own this, nor is there any evidence of his reading it; his copy of the second edition (Cambridge, 1673, *LL* 3050) was bought in 1697, MS Locke f. 10, p. 351.

[4] The only mention of Caron among Locke's papers seems to be in a note taken from Abraham Roger's *La porte ouverte* (Amsterdam, 1670), *LL* 2495: 'Iapan. La description de

2. In the year before Manley's translation appeared, material from Caron's work was included without any acknowledgement in *The Voyages & Travels of J. Albert de Mandelslo . . . into the East-Indies* (London, 1662); though separately paginated, this formed a supplement to a still larger work by Adam Olearius, *The Voyages & Travels of the Ambassadors sent by Frederick Duke of Holstein, to the Great Duke of Muscovy, and the King of Persia . . .* (London, 1662). Mandelslo's account is mentioned in the *Essays on the Law of Nature*,[1] and there are notes on both Olearius and Mandelslo in one of Locke's early commonplace books, dating from about 1662–3.[2] Locke's library contained a copy of the 1662 edition, but he did not buy it until 1682.[3]

Some of the details of Locke's account appear both in Manley's translation of the *Beschrivinghe* and in the translation of Mandelslo,[4] but a few do not. Some of these latter can be found in an account of the persecutions by another Dutch resident in Japan, Reyer Gysbertsz, whose *De Tyrannije ende Wreedheden der Jappanen* (Amsterdam, 1637) was included in the Dutch editions of Caron's *Beschrivinghe*, but was omitted from Manley's translation.

One detail in Locke's account that is not present in Caron does appear in a contemporary contribution to the toleration debate, John Humfrey's *A Proposition for the Safety and Happiness of the King and Kingdom*, published anonymously in the summer of 1667. In the *Essay concerning Toleration* Locke wrote that the persecution

> prevaild not at all to lessen their numbers till they extended the severity beyond the delinquents & made it death not only to the family that enterteind a preist but also to all of both the families that were next neigbours on either hand though they were strangers or enemys to the new religion.[5]

Humfrey's account was as follows:

> In the Kingdom of *Japan* I heard lately there was some Jesuites had crept in and planted the Christian Religion. Their King hearing this, sends a present *terrible* Persecution, whatsoever man is found *Christian*, they execute him presently: This

---

I[apa]n par F: Caron Roger 70/371', MS Locke d. 10, p. 81; the form of citation indicates that it was made in 1683 or later.

[1] 'Mandelslo in nupero illo Olearii itinerario', 172; as von Leyden's note remarks, the allusion is to *Voyages & Travels*, 40–1.   [2] MS Locke f. 14, pp. 55, 93, 112.
[3] *LL* 2128, MS Locke b. 2, fos. 40^r, 41^r. He had already bought a copy of the French translation, *Relation du voyage de Moscovie, Tartarie et de Perse* (Paris, 1656), *LL* 2129, while in France, MS Locke b. 2, fo. 12^r.   [4] Mandelslo, *Voyages & Travels*, 193–4.
[5] Below, p. 300.

not serving the turn, they do not execute the man only, but all the house where he was found to be harboured: This not rooting them quite out neither, the King commands that both that house and the next two houses on both sides of it, should be all put to execution: The terrible dread hereof seizing upon all, there is not a man can escape the discovery, and the Sect is immediately extirpate.[1]

Humfrey's source is unknown, but may have been Caron supplemented by his own imagination. Locke could have been similarly inventive, but it is more likely that this detail was derived from reading Humfrey.

Note C. Peers Mentioned in *A Letter from a Person of Quality*

Peers Signing Protests in the House of Lords

Those Signing All Four Protests

BERKSHIRE	Charles Howard (*c*.1615–1679), 2nd Earl 1669
BUCKINGHAM	George Villiers (1628–87), 2nd Duke 1628. *ODNB*
CLARENDON	Henry Hyde (1638–1709), 2nd Earl 1674. *ODNB*
DELAMERE	George Booth (1622–84), 1st Baron 1661. *ODNB*
DENBIGH	Basil Feilding (*c*.1608–1675), 2nd Earl 1643. *ODNB*
MOHUN	Charles Mohun (1649–77), 3rd Baron 1665
SALISBURY	James Cecil (1646–83), 3rd Earl 1668. *ODNB*
SHAFTESBURY	Anthony Ashley Cooper (1621–83), 1st Baron Ashley 1661, 1st Earl 1672. *ODNB*
WHARTON	Philip Wharton (1613–96), 4th Baron 1625. *ODNB*
WINCHESTER	Charles Paulet (1630/1631–1699), 6th Marquess Mar. 1675, 1st Duke of Bolton 1689. *ODNB*

Those Signing Three Protests

BEDFORD	William Russell (1616–1700), 5th Earl 1641, 1st Duke 1694. *ODNB*
BRIDGEWATER	John Egerton (1623–86), 2nd Earl 1649. *ODNB*
DORSET	Richard Sackville (1622–77), 5th Earl 1652
STAMFORD	Thomas Grey (1653/1654–1720), 2nd Earl 1673. *ODNB*

---

[1] *A Proposition*, 17–18.

General Introduction

Those Signing Two Protests

AILESBURY	Robert Bruce (1626–85), 1st Earl 1664. *ODNB*
BRISTOL	George Digby (1612–77), 2nd Earl 1653. *ODNB*
EURE	Ralph Eure (d. 1707), 7th Baron 1673
GREY OF ROLLESTON	Charles North (1635–91), 1st Baron 1673, 5th Baron North 1677
HALIFAX	George Savile (1633–95), 1st Viscount 1668, Earl 1679, Marquess 1682. *ODNB*
PAGET	William Paget (1609–78), 5th Baron 1629. *ODNB*
SAYE AND SELE	William Fiennes (*c.*1641–1698), 3rd Viscount 1674

Those Signing One Protest

AUDLEY	James Touchet (1612–84), 13th Baron 1633, 3rd Earl of Castlehaven (Ireland) 1631. *ODNB*
FITZWALTER	Benjamin Mildmay (*c.*1646–1679), 14th Baron 1670
HOLLES	Denzil Holles (1598–1680), 1st Baron 1661. *ODNB*
PETRE	William Petre (1625/1626–1684), 4th Baron 1638. *ODNB*

Other Peers Described as Opposing the Bill

BOLINGBROKE	Oliver St John (1634–1688), 2nd Earl 1646
BURLINGTON	Richard Boyle (1612–98), 1st Earl 1665, 2nd Earl of Cork (Ireland), 1643. *ODNB*
CARNARVON	Charles Dormer (1632–1709), 2nd Earl 1643
CREW	John Crew (*c.*1598–1679), 1st Baron 1661. *ODNB*
DEVONSHIRE	William Cavendish (1617–84), 3rd Earl 1628. *ODNB*
HERBERT OF CHERBURY	Edward Herbert (1630–78), 3rd Baron 1655
HEREFORD	Leicester Devereux (1617–76), 6th Viscount 1657
NORTH	Dudley North (1602–77), 4th Baron 1666. *ODNB*
RUTLAND	John Manners (1604–79), 8th Earl 1641. *ODNB*
SANDYS	Henry Sandys (d. *c.*1680), 7th Baron 1669
TOWNSHEND	Horatio Townshend (1630–87), 1st Baron 1661, 1st Viscount 1682. *ODNB*

Peers Described as Supporting the Bill or at least Failing to Oppose It

BERKELEY	George Berkeley (1626/1627–1698), 9th Baron 1658, 1st Earl 1679. *ODNB*
CARLISLE	Charles Howard (1628–85), 1st Earl 1661. *ODNB*
CHESTERFIELD	Philip Stanhope (1633–1714), 2nd Earl 1656. *ODNB*
EXETER	John Cecil (1628–78), 4th Earl 1643
FAUCONBERG	Thomas Belasyse (1627/1628–1700), 2nd Viscount 1653, 1st Earl 1689. *ODNB*
MONTAGUE OF BOUGHTON	Edward Montagu (1616–84), 2nd Baron 1644
NORTHAMPTON	James Compton (1622–81), 3rd Earl 1643. *ODNB*
ROBARTES	John Robartes (1606–85), 2nd Baron 1625, 1st Earl of Radnor 1679. *ODNB*
STAFFORD	William Howard (1612–80), 1st Viscount 1640. *ODNB*
WINCHILSEA	Heneage Finch (1627/1628–1689), 3rd Earl 1639. *ODNB*

TEXTUAL INTRODUCTION

I. HISTORY AND DESCRIPTION OF THE TEXTS

ALL the works included here survive in manuscripts written either by Locke himself or by his contemporaries. Apart from the *Letter from a Person of Quality* none of them was published before the nineteenth century, and none of these later printed editions has any independent textual authority.

AN ESSAY CONCERNING TOLERATION

The *Essay concerning Toleration* poses more complex textual problems than perhaps any other work by Locke. It survives in no fewer than four manuscripts:

H   HM 584 in the Henry E. Huntington Library, San Marino, California.[1]

A   Pages 106–25 and 270–1 of Locke's commonplace book Adversaria 1661, now in private ownership.[2]

O   MS Locke c. 28, fos. 21–32, in the Bodleian Library, Oxford.

P   PRO 30/24/47/1 in the National Archives, Kew.

The first of these is in Locke's hand throughout. The second and third are copies by amanuenses with major additions and alterations in Locke's hand. Only the last is a clean scribal copy without any revisions.

Locke's Autograph

HM 584 consists of two separate documents: (i) a set of twenty-one folded half-sheets gathered into five quires signed A to E, containing a complete text of the *Essay concerning Toleration* on quires B–E together with a fair copy of the first part of this on quire A; (ii) a single half-sheet containing a

---

[1] On the designation of two components of this as H* and F, see below.
[2] There are microfilms in the Bodleian Library, MS Film 77, and the Houghton Library, Harvard University, MS Eng. 860.1.

shorter and apparently earlier version of some of the material found in quires A–E.

The first of these documents was written on several different varieties of paper, as follows:

Quire	Average dimension of leaves	Watermark
A	208 × 149 mm	Coat of arms, resembling Heawood 759, with letters NA in upper circle, lower circle blank
B	205 × 147 mm	Similar to Heawood 759, with AN in upper circle, N in lower circle
C	202 × 147 mm	As quire B
D	198 × 152 mm	Horn, broadly resembling Heawood 2698, with letters PC
E	199 × 144 mm	Circles, resembling Heawood 256, with letters 6[?]AD in upper circle, 2[?] in lower

The measurements given here are approximate: the individual leaves vary slightly in size and are often not precisely rectangular. Each of these sheets was prepared by cutting a foolscap sheet in half so that the chain lines run horizontally and the watermark is at the centre of alternate sheets.

Each quire has a signature letter on its first page. The signature on quire A is placed centrally at the foot of the page, which is otherwise blank, the *Essay* starting on A2; that on quire B is at the foot of the page, a little to the left of centre, and is almost obscured by the text, which was written vertically; those on quires C, D, and E are in the left margin at the foot of the page. The signature letters on quires C, D, and E are in the same ink as the rest of the text on those pages, and were almost certainly written at the same time; the letter on quire B was undoubtedly added later. Each quire has on its final page the endorsement 'Toleration 6̲7̲' followed on the line below by the appropriate signature letter. In quire D this is at the top right of the page, in the others at the top left.

All the quires contain eight leaves, except for quire B, which has ten. Locke numbered the leaves in quires B–E, apart from the first leaf of quire B and the last three leaves of quire E,[1] but except for A2^r the leaves

---

[1] Leaf E6 is now numbered 31; this appears to have been done in very dark pencil, and it is certainly not in Locke's hand.

of quire A were left unnumbered. The relation between Locke's folio numbers and the ordering of the leaves in the manuscript is as follows:

A1	not numbered [fo. i]
A2	fo. 1 [fo. ii]
A3–A8	not numbered [fos. iii–viii]
B1	not numbered [fo. ix]
B2–B10	fos. 1–9
C1–C8	fos. 10–17
D1–D8	fos. 18–25
E1–E5	fos. 26–30
E6–E8	not numbered

Except for A2, Locke's folio numbers have been retained in this edition. The roman numerals used here for quire A and for the first leaf of quire B have been supplied by the editors and do not appear in the manuscript.

The text in quire A (henceforth referred to as the Fair Copy) begins on fo. 2^r and continues nearly to the foot of fo. 6^r; the last two leaves are blank, apart from the endorsement on the final page. The version of the whole *Essay* in quires B–E (the Rough Draft) continues as far as the sixth leaf (fo. 31^r) of quire E; the remainder of the quire is blank apart from the endorsement. Except in the disordered section at the beginning of quire B, described below, Locke used the right-hand pages for the main text, reserving the blank pages opposite for additional material to be inserted as required.

The second document occupies the whole of both sides of a single half-sheet of paper measuring approximately 318×213 mm, apparently of the same type as was used in half-sheets in quire D. The word 'Toleration' is written vertically in the part of the left margin of the first page that would have been outermost when the sheet was folded. The whole of the first page and the first half of the second (as far as 'I conclude then') are crossed through by a single vertical line (Plate 1).

Stages of Composition

The earliest version we possess of the *Essay concerning Toleration* is the one written on the single sheet of paper just described. Its priority is clear from the way in which insertions made in it appear in the main text of the Rough Draft; henceforth it will be referred to as the First Draft.

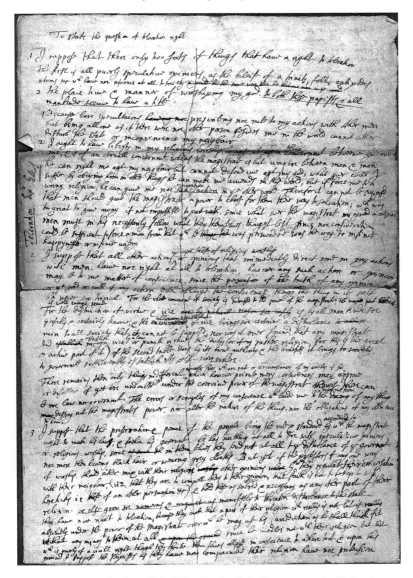

Plate 1. The beginning of the First Draft of *An Essay concerning Toleration*, Huntington Library HM 584. This item is reproduced by permission of the Huntington Library, San Marino, California.

About three-quarters of the material in the First Draft reappears in the Rough Draft, sometimes thoroughly revised but often almost unchanged.

The First Draft, though quite short (just over 1,600 words), is not a fragment: it ends with a set of policy recommendations, just as the final *Essay* does. The theory it presents is, however, very simple and its exposition rather abrupt. Having finished it, Locke seems to have decided that a more elaborate and systematic treatment was needed. He therefore began work on a longer version,[1] this time on folded sheets of paper gathered into quires, starting on what was then the first but is now the second leaf of quire B (Plate 2). The beginning of this is an expanded version of the beginning of the First Draft:[2]

First Draft	Rough Draft, first version
To state the question of toleration right.	The question of toleration stated
1 I suppose that ⟨are⟩ only two sorts of things that have	I ~~suppose~~ *say* that there are only two sorts of things that have in their owne ~~righ~~ nature an absolute &
a right to toleration the first is all puerly speculative opinions, as the beleife of a trinity, fall,	universall right to toleration. The first is all puerly speculative opinions, as the beleife of a trinity, purgatory
antipodes, atoms &c	transubstantion ~~antipodes~~, Christs personall reigne on earth &c

Alterations made by Locke in the First Draft appear in the main text of its successor:

First Draft	Rough Draft, first version
	The other thing that has just claime ~~in all times & place~~ to an unlimited
2 I ought to have liberty in my religious worship, because it is a ~~concernement~~ *thing* betweene god and me, & is of an eternall concernment	toleration, is the place, time, & manner of worshiping my god. Because this is a thing wholy between god & me, & is of an eternall concernment above the reach & extent of polities & government, which are but for my well being in this
wheras the magistrate	world. For the magistrate

---

[1] It is possible that the First Draft was not the only paper that preceded the Rough Draft, and that other material has since been lost. The pages of the Rough Draft vary considerably in appearance, some being untidy and full of deletions, and others very neat—for example, the first page of quire D (fo. 18^r), which marks the start of the second part of the work.   [2] In the texts below, deletions are in ~~strikethrough~~, insertions in *italic*.

is but umpire between man & man	is but umpire between man & man.
he can right me against my neigbour,	He can right me against my neigbour,
but cannot defend me against my	but can not defend me against my
god, what ever evill I suffer by	god. What ever evill I suffer by
obeying him in other things he can	obeying him in other things he can
make me amends in this world, but if	make me amends in this world but if
he force me to a wrong religion, he	he force me to a wrong religion, he
can give me noe ~~satisfaction~~	can make me noe
reparation in the other world.	reparation in the other world.

It would appear, however, that soon after beginning this new version Locke decided that it too was unsatisfactory, and that he needed to start with a more general account of the problem. He therefore added a new sheet of paper on the outside of the quire and used the verso of the first leaf to make yet another beginning (Plate 3):

The Question of toleration stated

In the question of liberty of conscience which has for some years beene soe much bandied among us. One thing that has cheifly perplexd the question kept up the dispute & increasd the animosity hath beene I conceive, this, That both partys have with equall zeale, & mistake too much enlargd their pretensions, whilst one side preach up absolute obedience, & the other claime universall liberty in matters of conscience, without assigneing the matter which has a title to liberty or shewing the boundarys of imposition & obedience.

The material that followed this new beginning grew too long to be contained on the page chosen for it, and it was continued first in the margin of the page itself (B1^v/fo. ix^v), then on the other side of the same leaf (B1^r/fo. ix^r), and finally in the margin of what had originally been the first page (B2^r/fo. 1^r); Locke needed to make use of B2^r because a large part of B1^r had already been used for other additions designed to be inserted into B3^r (fo. 2^r). All the material on B1^r was written vertically rather than horizontally, perhaps to indicate that it was designed to be inserted later on and was not the start of the composition.

The result of all these afterthoughts was a chaotically disordered text, which one imagines that even Locke himself could only have disentangled with some difficulty, and which would have defeated almost any other reader. Locke therefore decided to put together a new quire of paper (designated quire A, either then or subsequently), and to use it for a clean copy of the disordered text that was now filling the opening pages

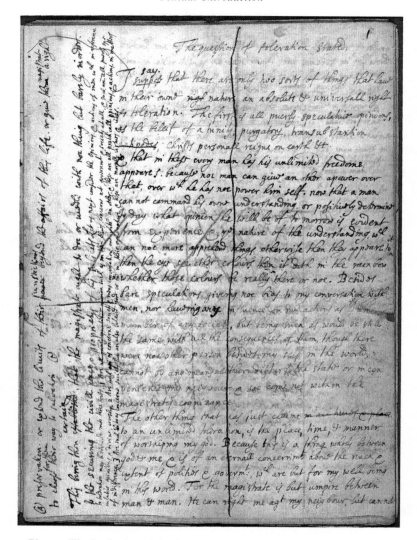

Plate 2. The beginning of the first version of the Rough Draft of *An Essay concerning Toleration*, Huntington Library HM 584, sig. B2^r. This item is reproduced by permission of the Huntington Library, San Marino, California.

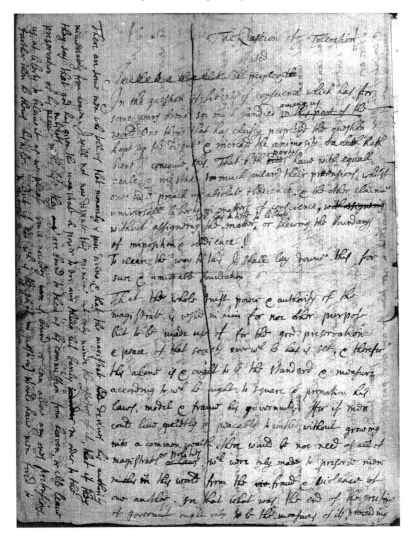

Plate 3. The beginning of the second version of the Rough Draft of *An Essay concerning Toleration*, Huntington Library HM 584, sig. B1ᵛ. This item is reproduced by permission of the Huntington Library, San Marino, California.

of quire B (Plate 4), taking the opportunity while he was doing this to make yet further changes:

Rough Draft, second version	Fair Copy
There are some men who tell us that monarchy is jure divino, & that the magistrate ~~hold~~ derives his authority immediately from heaven. I will not now dispute this opinion but only minde the assertors of it, that if they say	There are some that tell us that Monarchy is jure divino ~~& that the magistrate der~~
	I will not now dispute this opinion but only minde the assertors of it, that if they meane by this (as certainly they must), that the sole supreme arbitrary power & disposall of all things is & ought to be by divine right in a single person,'tis to be suspected they have forgot what country they were borne in, under what laws they live & certainly cannot but be obleigd to declare Magna Charta, to be downe right heresie. If they meane by Monarchy jure divino, not an absolute but limited monarchy, (which I thinke is an absurdity: if not a contradiction) they ought to shew us his charter from
that god has given the magistrate a power to doe any thing but barely in order to the preservation of his ~~people~~ *subjects* in this life, they ~~oug~~ are bound to shew us his commission from heaven, or else leave us at liberty to beleive it as we please since noebody ~~can~~ is bound or can allow any ones pretensions	heaven, & let us see ~~that~~ *where* god hath given the magistrate a power to doe any thing but barely in order to the preservation of his subjects in this life, or else leave us at liberty to beleive it as we please since noe body is bound, or can allow any ones pretensions to a power, (which he himself confesses limited)
farther then he shews his title.	farther then he shews his title.

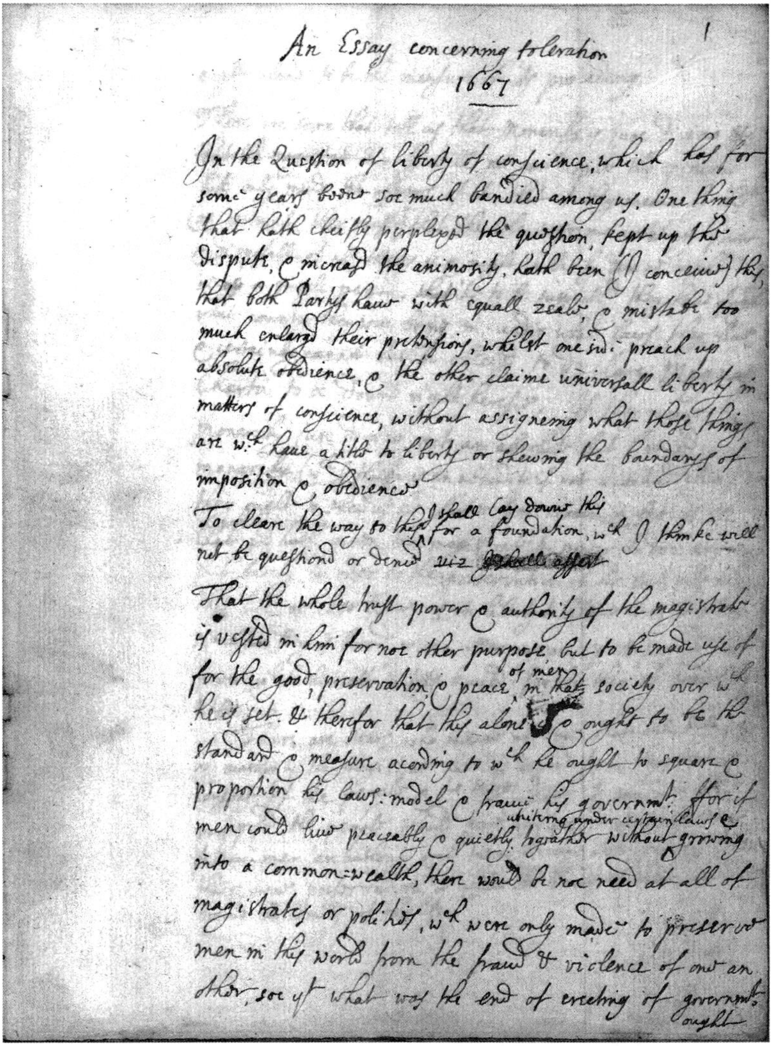

An Essay concerning toleration
1667

In the Question of liberty of conscience, which hath for some years been soe much bandied among us. One thing that hath cheifly perplexd the question, kept up the dispute, & encreasd the animosity, hath been (I conceive) this, that both Partys have with equall zeale, & mistake too much enlargd their pretensions, whilst one side preach up absolute obedience, & the other claime universall liberty in matters of conscience, without assigneing what those things are wch have a title to liberty, or shewing the boundarys of imposition & obedience.

To cleare the way to this I shall lay downe this for a foundation, wch I thinke will not be questiond or denied viz

That the whole trust power & authority of the magistrate is vested in him for noe other purpose, but to be made use of for the good, preservation & peace of men in that society over wch he is set, & therfor that this alone & ought to be the standard & measure acording to wch he ought to square & proportion his laws, model & frame his government. ffor if men could live peaceably & quietly togather without growing into a common-wealth, there would be noe need at all of magistrates or polities, wch were only made to preserve men in this world from the fraud & violence of one an other, soe yt what was the end of erecting of governmt ought

Plate 4. The beginning of the Fair Copy of *An Essay concerning Toleration*, Huntington Library HM 584, sig. A2ʳ. This item is reproduced by permission of the Huntington Library, San Marino, California.

The Fair Copy only replaces the badly disorganized text at the start of the *Essay*, extending as far as line 7 of B3^r. From this point onwards the Rough Draft was sufficiently well ordered to be easily understood by someone familiar with Locke's methods of composition.

It is therefore possible to distinguish four successive strata of text in the opening pages of the *Essay*:

1. The First Draft.
2. The first version of the Rough Draft, beginning on B2^r.
3. The second version of the Rough Draft, beginning on B1^v.
4. The Fair Copy, in quire A.

In what follows, the First Draft and the Fair Copy will be designated as **F** and **H*** respectively, reserving the siglum **H** for the Rough Draft.

The date 1667 appears at the end of **H**, 'Sic Cogitavit Atticus, 166_7_', and in the title of **H***, 'An Essay concerning toleration 166_7_'; it does not appear at the start of **H** or anywhere in **F**. The most cautious inference from this would be that **H*** and at least the later parts of **H** were written at some time between 1 January 1667 and 24 March 1668, but the circumstances of Locke's life and the events of the toleration debate of 1667–8 together make it extremely unlikely that **F** was begun before the summer of 1667; the most probable date for the main part of the work is late 1667 or early 1668.

Other Manuscript Copies

None of the other manuscripts of the *Essay* was written by Locke, though two of the three contain alterations and additions in his hand.

1. Unlike the other manuscripts, **A** is not a separate document or group of documents. It consists of three successive entries in one of Locke's large commonplace books, generally known as Adversaria 1661. The longest of these, on pages 106–25, is a copy of the *Essay* made by an amanuensis; his identity is not known, but he was also responsible for the copy of Draft A of the *Essay concerning Human Understanding* in the Shaftesbury papers, which was probably written around the same time.[1] It would be rather unkind to describe the handwriting as semi-literate, but the writer was certainly not a professional copyist and may well have been Locke's current manservant or one of the other servants at

---

[1] PRO 30/24/47/7; described in *Drafts*, i. 287–93.

Exeter House. The text was carelessly written and contains frequent corrections and alterations in Locke's hand; usually these restore the original reading of Locke's autograph, but not always. At the end of the main part of the *Essay* (before the two additions that occur only in this manuscript) there are the words 'Sic Cogitavit JL 16<u>67</u>' in Locke's hand.

Because of its position in Adversaria 1661, this copy of the *Essay* can be dated with reasonable precision. Locke's method for locating entries in his commonplace books was as follows.[1] Each entry was assigned a keyword (usually in Latin, whatever the language of the entry), and this was placed in the margin at the start of the entry; the appropriate page for the entry was determined by the first letter and first subsequent vowel of the keyword: entries with the keyword 'Toleratio' were placed on the page used for 'To' entries, those on the church (keyword 'Ecclesia') on the page for the 'Ee' entries, and so on. When Locke wished to make a new entry, he found the page with the relevant two-letter heading and added the new entry immediately below those that were already there. If the heading had not been used before or if the relevant pages were full, he would turn forward in the notebook to find the first blank left-hand page and use this; this new page might follow immediately after its predecessor, but it could be a hundred or more pages later on. If an entry was so long that it needed to be continued on a new left-hand page, then Locke did the same.

It is clear from this that the mere page number of an entry gives little information about when it was made: the entry 'Virtus', included in this volume among the entries in the commonplace books, was written on pages 10–11 of Adversaria 1661 but was made at least ten years later than the long entry containing Draft A of the *Essay concerning Human Understanding* that begins on page 56. The main rules for dating entries are (i) all the entries under a particular heading are in strict chronological order, and (ii) the *first* entries on each left-hand page (including parts of entries begun on earlier pages) are also in strict chronological order.

One clue to the date of the copy of the *Essay concerning Toleration* in Adversaria 1661 is provided by the presence on pages 56–89 and 94–5 of Locke's autograph of Draft A of the *Essay concerning Human Understanding*; since Locke tells us himself in Draft A that a passage on page 80 was written on 11 July 1671,[2] the copy of the *Essay concerning Toleration*

---

[1] The system described here is the basic one set out in Locke's 'Methode nouvelle de dresser des recueils' (1686) and used in the majority of the commonplace books; a different though related system was used for the two volumes of Lemmata, MSS Locke d. 10 and d. 11: see Milton, 'Locke's Medical Notebooks', for a fuller account.

[2] Draft A, § 27, *Drafts*, i. 43.

on pages 106–25 must have been made some time after this. As it also comes after notes on pages 96–104 taken from works by François Bernier and Sir Samuel Morland[1] that were published in the winter of 1671–2, a *terminus a quo* of very late in 1671 can be established. A rather less precise *terminus ante quem* is suggested by entries on pages 144 and 146 which were taken from the 1656 edition of Herbert of Cherbury's *De Veritate*, a work discussed at some length in Draft B of the *Essay concerning Human Understanding*. Draft B is certainly later than Draft A, but its precise period of composition is not known, though it is likely that the later parts of it date from 1672.[2] The most likely date for this copy of the *Essay concerning Toleration* is therefore early in 1672, perhaps around the time of the Declaration of Indulgence (15 March).

The copy of the *Essay concerning Toleration* in Adversaria 1661 is followed by two additions that are unique to this manuscript. The first, of some 200 words, comes immediately after the end of the main part of the *Essay* on page 125 and is in the same hand; there are no corrections by Locke. It seems reasonable to presume that it was copied at the same time as the main part of the *Essay* or very soon afterwards. Blank spaces left by the copyist show that he was following a manuscript, but what this was and when it was written can only be surmised. The second addition is considerably longer—just over 1,500 words—and was written several years later. The text begins on page 125 immediately below the first addition, but then continues on pages 270 and 271; it contains numerous deletions and alterations and is in Locke's hand throughout. Given Locke's method of filling his commonplace books, this later portion (and presumably therefore the addition as a whole) must be later than the first entries on any of the intervening pages. Most of these are filled with material on plantations in the West Indies and elsewhere that presumably date from Locke's time as secretary to the Council for Trade and Plantations, a post he took up on 15 October 1673.[3] The pages immediately before pages 270–1 contain notes on several works by the biblical scholar

---

[1] *A Continuation of the Memoirs of Mr Bernier* (London, 1672) and *Tuba Stentoro-phonica* (London, 1671), listed in the Term Catalogues for 20 Nov. 1671 and 7 Feb. 1672 respectively (i. 86, 97). Locke's copy of Morland was apparently sold to John Strachey on or before 16 March 1672, MS Locke f. 48, p. 15.

[2] Draft B is dated 1671 at the beginning, but this could indicate any time up until 24 March 1671/2. Writing a work as long as Draft B must have taken some considerable time, and as all the references to *De Veritate* (*Drafts*, i. 111–14) are on interleaved pages inserted into the manuscript they may well date from 1672 rather than 1671.

[3] The copy of the report of the Irish Council of Trade has the date 25 Mar. 1673 at the end (p. 231), but this is the date of the original report, not when it was copied into the notebook.

John Lightfoot; these cannot be dated directly, but entries in Locke's ledger and elsewhere show transactions with Shaftesbury involving Lightfoot's works in 1673–5.[1] A date of 1674 or 1675 for the Lightfoot entries in Adversaria 1661 seems most likely. As all the entries in Adversaria 1661 from page 272 onwards were made in 1679 or subsequently, a date of 1675 for the second addition to the *Essay concerning Toleration* would seem quite plausible, perhaps in the summer or autumn, around the time of the composition of the *Letter from a Person of Quality*.[2]

2. The copy of the *Essay* in MS Locke c. 28, fos. 21–32 (**O**) is the only one still remaining among Locke's papers. Like the copy in Adversaria 1661 it is a scribal copy in an unidentified hand, and it too contains additional material found nowhere else. It was written on loose sheets of paper which are now bound into a guardbook of philosophical manuscripts; the folio numbers used here were added by the staff of the Bodleian Library when this was done.

The original text was written on five single sheets, each folded to make two leaves measuring approximately 327 × 210 mm, and signed from A to E by Locke at the foot of each front page. Sig. A is now designated as fos. 21 and 24, sig. B as fos. 25–6, sig. C as fos. 27–8, sig. D as fos. 29–30, and sig. E as fos. 31–2; except in the case of fo. 21^v the original text was written only on the recto side of each leaf. There is also an unsigned sheet (fos. 22–3) which was inserted by Locke into quire A; this is of the same size as the others and has the same watermark, but the paper is noticeably thicker. It contains no part of the original text but has two of the three long additions in Locke's hand that are unique to this manuscript, the third being on the otherwise blank verso of fo. 28. Locke had already numbered the pages before he inserted the sheet containing fos. 22–3, the numbers running continuously from page 1 (fo. 21^r) to page 17 (fo. 31^r); he did not assign any numbers to fos. 22–3.

The final page of each of the folded sheets making up the original copy has the word 'Toleration' at the foot of the page, together with the appropriate signature letter written twice, on either side of the centre-line. Each of these pages also has the words 'Toleration | 67' written vertically near the right-hand edge of the page with the corresponding signature letter near the left-hand edge; as the dirt on the final page shows, this writing is on the part of the manuscript that would have been

---

[1] Adversaria 1661, pp. 266, 268; MS Locke c. 1, pp. 4, 39, 53, 81–2; PRO 30/24/47/30, fos. 16^r, 17^r.

[2] There is no sign that Locke took Adversaria 1661 (or indeed any of his commonplace books) when he went to France in November 1675.

outermost when the paper was folded. All these endorsements are in Locke's hand.

The writer of **O** either paid little attention to the meaning of what he was copying, or lacked intelligence, or both. The text he produced is littered with absurd misreadings: 'forreign' for 'inforceing', 'leagues' for 'laws', 'destinction' for 'destruction' (orthographically less bizarre, but hardly belonging in the phrase 'destruction & extirpation of all dissenters at once'), and—perhaps most grotesquely of all—'Measure of France' instead of 'Massacre of France'. The handwriting is cramped and rather old-fashioned, and the spelling idiosyncratic ('scociety' being used invariably for 'society').

O contains several distinct groups of alterations and additions: (i) a small number of corrections in the hand of the original copyist, presumably made while the manuscript was being copied, or immediately afterwards; (ii) a rather larger number of corrections and short alterations made by Locke himself, possibly on more than one occasion; (iii) certainly three and possibly four alterations in a third, unidentified hand, designated in the textual apparatus as Hand B;[1] (iv) a set of large deletions and additions made by Locke. These large deletions and additions are one of the most conspicuous features of the manuscript: three passages amounting to nearly 1,100 words were crossed out and three more of just over 700 words added. The material deleted includes some of the oldest parts of the work, some passages going right back to the First Draft; the significance of the changes for the development of Locke's theory of toleration is discussed in the General Introduction. It is clear that these changes were made after at least some of the corrections in categories (i) and (ii), since the deleted passages had already been corrected, but otherwise there is nothing in the manuscript that gives any indication of when they were made. None of the additions in Hand B occurs in any of these deleted passages.

3. The copy of the *Essay* in the Shaftesbury papers (**P**) is contained in two booklets, each of 20 leaves measuring approximately 244 × 190 mm, with the text written on the right-hand pages only. The first pages of both booklets (fos. 1, 21) are blank, apart in each case from a title ('Essay on Toleration Part 1'; 'Essay on Toleration Part 2') written in what appears to be a much later (nineteenth-century?) hand; the final pages of the second booklet (fos. 35–40) are also blank. The text is a fair copy in the hand of an unknown amanuensis, with no new material and only a handful of minor corrections, all in the hand of the original copyist.

---

[1] The changes in Hand B are all very short: the replacement of the word 'growing' by 'entering', the addition of 'or' and 'either they' at paragraph ends, and possibly the insertion of 'ill' before 'treatment'.

P was much more carefully written than either **A** and **O**. These two manuscripts were both produced by copyists who appear to have worked mechanically, giving little if any attention to the meaning of what they were copying, and though most of the mistakes they introduced were corrected subsequently by Locke, by no means all were. **P**, by contrast, was written in a neat and easily legible hand by someone who gives the clear impression of having been thinking about what he was doing. Unlike the other manuscripts it does not bear Locke's name anywhere, and the absence of any of his characteristic endorsements indicates that it was not kept among his papers.

P may perhaps have been given by Locke to Ashley, but it would be quite wrong to describe it as a presentation copy: the copies of his works that Locke made for this purpose were in his own hand and clearly identified him as the author.[1] A presentation copy would presumably also have contained a dedication to his patron. Among Locke's papers there is a fragmentary draft dating from 1668 of a dedication for the paper on interest, and in 1669 he wrote a much longer dedication for Sydenham's projected treatise on smallpox.[2] If anything comparable was drafted for the *Essay concerning Toleration* it has not survived.

Several recent writers on Locke have described the four manuscripts of the *Essay concerning Toleration* as four 'drafts'.[3] As a characterization of **A**, **O**, and **P** this is entirely mistaken. All three manuscripts are copies made by amanuenses after Locke had finished—or at least largely finished—work on the manuscript from which they are all derived. The only material that can accurately be described as drafts of the *Essay* are the deleted and discarded sections of Huntington Library HM 584.

Relations between the Manuscripts

The fact that the Huntington manuscript is in Locke's hand and that (alterations and additions aside) the other manuscripts are not creates a

---

[1] PRO 30/24/47/35, the manuscript of *Observations upon the Growth and Culture of Vines and Olives* dedicated to Shaftesbury; Pierpont Morgan Library, New York, MA 232, the translation of Nicole's *Essais de morale* dedicated to his wife (microfilm, Bodl., MS Film 70).

[2] MS Locke b. 3, fo. 1ʳ, *Locke on Money*, 202; PRO 30/24/47/2, fos. 60–3, Dewhurst, *Sydenham*, 101–2. In neither case was the addressee named, but there can be little doubt that in both it was Ashley.

[3] Cranston, 111; Haley, 224; Ashcraft, *Revolutionary Politics*, 88n; Marshall, *John Locke*, 49–50.

strong presumption that it is the original from which all the others were derived. This is confirmed by an examination of the manuscripts themselves. Even the Fair Copy contains a small number of additions and alterations, and the later parts of the Rough Draft were extensively revised, with frequent deletions and alterations, and with large additions inserted on the pages opposite. Almost all of these changes appear in the main texts of the other manuscripts. There is no doubt whatever that **A**, **O**, and **P** were copied directly or indirectly from HM 584—from the Fair Copy **H*** for as long as it was available, and thereafter from the Rough Draft **H**. In what follows, **A**, **O**, and **P** will therefore be collectively referred to as the derived manuscripts.

The only writer to have addressed the question of the relation between the four manuscripts was C. A. Viano, who came to the conclusion that **H** came first, and was followed in order by **A**, **P**, and **O**, each having been copied from its predecessor.[1] Except in respect of the primacy of **H**, this is certainly wrong.

A valuable clue to the relations between the other manuscripts is given by their treatment of a passage that occurs towards the end of the *Essay*. On fo. 24^r of **H** Locke originally wrote (Plate 5):

Whereby we may see 'twill be a hazardous attempt for those who designe it, to bring this Island to the condition of a gally where the greater part shall be reducd to the condition of slaves, be forcd with blows to row the vessell, but share in none of the ladeing or be allowd soe much as a cabin unlesse they will make chaines, for all those who are to be usd like Turks & persuade them to stand still whilst they put them on.

At some time after he had written this, he decided to delete the part from 'to bring this Island' onwards[2] and replace it with new material added on the blank page opposite (Plate 6):

If they are not much the greater number, to compell dissenters by force & ill usage to be true to that government & serviceable to that interest, which instead of an equall protection affords them noe other treatment but disgrace, punishment & persecution: Unlesse those who would thus inforce an uniformity will make chains for all those to whome they will allow noe liberty & perswade them also to stand still whilst they put them upon 'em . . .

---

[1] 'La storia dell'*Essay*, perciò, continua a svolgersi da *M* [H] a *H* [A] a *RO* [P] per finire a *LC* [O]', 'L'abbozzo originario e gli stadi di composizione di "An Essay concerning Toleration" ', 311.

[2] He also omitted to delete the last clause, '& persuade them to stand still whilst they put them on', which also appears (slightly altered) in the added material.

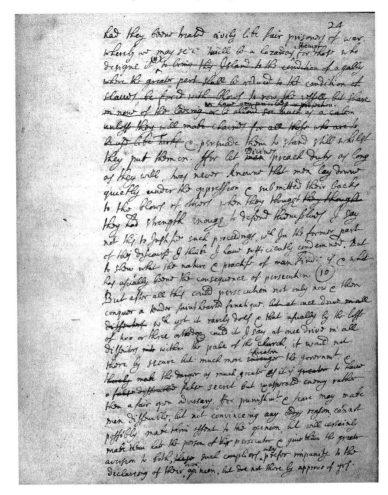

Plate 5. *An Essay concerning Toleration*, the 'Galley' passage, first version, Huntington Library HM 584, fo. 24[r]. This item is reproduced by permission of the Huntington Library, San Marino, California.

The derived manuscripts fall into two groups here: **O** and **P** follow the earlier state of **H**, **A** the revised state.[1] This passage alone is enough to

---

[1] When **O** was copied, Locke had already altered the text of **H** by replacing the phrase 'or be allowd soe much as a cabin' with 'nor have any priviledg or protection'; both **O** and **P** have this revised reading.

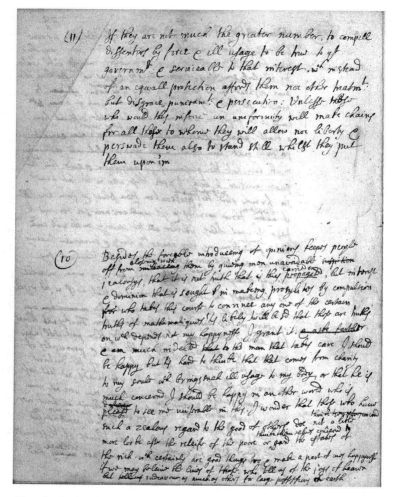

Plate 6. *An Essay concerning Toleration*, the 'Galley' passage, second version, Huntington Library HM 584, fo. 23ᵛ. This item is reproduced by permission of the Huntington Library, San Marino, California.

establish the conclusion—confirmed by numerous other passages[1]—that neither **O** nor **P** could have been copied from **A**, and that **A** could not

---

[1] That **A** was not derived from either **O** or **P** is clear from the passages mentioned later in connection with the relation between **O** and **P**. That neither **O** nor **P** derives from **A** is

have been copied from either **O** or **P**. It also makes it extremely unlikely that **A**, **O**, and **P** were all derived from a lost copy of **H*** and **H**, since this would presumably have contained either the original Galley passage or its replacement, but not both.[1]

The strongest evidence that **A** was copied directly from **H*** and **H**, and not from some lost intermediate, comes from the way in which additions made in **H** were reproduced in **A**. On fo. 22^r of **H** there is a passage which in its earliest state describes the Catholics as the common enemy to 'our church & all christian liberty'. The phrase 'protestant professions &' was then added above the words 'christian liberty'; no caret marking the insertion point was provided, though the context makes it clear that the words were meant to be inserted after 'all'. Finally, the phrase 'christian liberty' was deleted by underscoring, leaving the words still easily legible. **O** and **P** follow the final state of **H**, with the superfluous '&' retained and used to link this to the next sentence. The copyist of **A** originally wrote 'our church and all christian liberty protestant professions and', which makes no sense at all; the words 'christian liberty' and the second 'and' were then deleted, either by the original copyist or (more probably) by Locke himself. It would seem that the copyist of **A** was following **H** without thinking about the meaning of what he was writing and misunderstood where the insertion was meant to go.

Two more sets of changes are hardly explicable except on the assumption that **A** was copied directly from **H*** and **H**. The first is in the third paragraph of the *Essay*. In **H*** Locke originally wrote: 'For if men could live peaceably & quietly togeather without growing into a Common-wealth . . .'. He then decided to add the phrase 'uniteing under certaine laws &', indicating the insertion point by a caret after the word 'without'. The caret is almost obscured by the tail of the first 'g' in 'growing', and it seems that the writer of **A** failed to notice it: he inserted

confirmed by the following passages: me to a **H*OP**, to **A** [fo. v^r]; injury **HOP**, injureing **A** [fo. 1^v]; could **HOP**, would **A** [fo. 12^r]; factions **HOP**, factors **A** [fo. 13^r]; fencd **HOP**, freed **A** [fo. 16^r]; is possible **HOP**, possible **A** [fo. 16^r]; the fairer **HOP**, fairer **A** [fo. 17^r]; any of them **HOP**, them **A** [fo. 21^r]; yet it **HOP**, it **A** [fo. 24^r]; defineing **HOP**, desireing **A** [fo. 31^r].

[1] There are eighteen places where **AOP** agree against **H** or **H*** (ignoring cases where the same word appears on either side of a page-break and is in effect being used as a catchword). They can be analysed as follows: spelling corrected (3), superfluous word omitted (4), wrongly deleted but still legible word replaced (1), stylistic variation (its/it is) (1), change from singular to plural (3), deletion ignored (2), insertion ignored (1), deletion and replacement ignored (2), addition inserted in a different place (1). There are no changes of a kind that would require the postulation of a sub-archetype derived from **H/H*** from which the other MSS would have been copied.

the phrase before 'without' instead of after it, thereby destroying the sense of the passage. When Locke subsequently read through A he added the word 'without' before 'uniteing', but failed to delete the superfluous 'without' before 'growing'.[1]

The second example is even clearer. On fo. 21^r of H Locke had originally written of the Catholics that

this is certaine a severe hand over them, cannot (as in other dissenting partys) make them cement with the Fanatiques . . .

He then decided to add the phrase 'that toleration can not make them divide amongst them selves nor' after 'certaine', and to delete the following 'cannot'; the first six words ('that toleration can not make them') were inserted between the lines, the remainder ('divide amongst them selves nor') in the margin. In A, before Locke corrected it, the passage is badly garbled:

this is certaine that toleration can not make them a severe hand over them as in other dissenting partys divide amongst them selves nor make them cement with the Fanatics . . . [2]

It is clear what has gone wrong: the writer of A had failed to understand that the interlinear and the marginal parts of the insertion belonged together, and had added them separately. This makes it virtually certain that he was working from H, since it is very unlikely that another manuscript would have divided the insertion in precisely this way.

An example of a deleted passage in H appearing in A occurs on fo. 10^r. Locke wrote that if public societies could subsist without the legal enforcement of the second table of the Ten Commandments, the lawmaker

ought not to prescribe any rules about them, or endeavour to reclaime out of vice with the sword of justice but leave the practise of them intirely to the discretion & consciences of his people.

He then deleted the phrase 'or endeavour to reclaime out of vice with the sword of justice'. All three derived manuscripts follow the final state of H, but in A the words 'of Justice' appear before 'but', though they were subsequently deleted. The only possible explanation for their presence is that the copyist of A was working from a manuscript that contained the passage deleted from H; this surely must have been H itself, where the deleted passage is easily legible and the words 'of justice' form the start of a new line.

---

[1] O and P follow the revised text of H*, though in O 'growing' was subsequently replaced by 'entering'; the change is in Hand B. [2] Adversaria 1661, p. 119.

The writer of **A** was often unable to read individual words in the manuscript he was copying, and accordingly left a blank space for Locke to insert the correct reading. In two of these cases a mark (× or †) appears in the same place in **H** (fos. 11^r, 14^r): presumably this was inserted by the copyist in order to make the place easier to find.

When Locke corrected **A** he sometimes—though not always—went back to **H*** or **H** to check what he had written. For example, on fo. 23^v of **H** he originally wrote that:

> I wonder that those who have such a zealous regard to the good of others doe not a litle more looke after the releife of the poore or gard the estates of the rich . . .

and then added the phrase 'thinke them selves concernd to' before 'gard'. The writer of **A** overlooked this addition,[1] but Locke inserted the missing words, which he could hardly have done without referring back to **H**. Other phrases inserted by Locke in **A** include 'make use of any means that could not reach but would rather', 'and the actions flowing from them have a title', 'soe numerous as', and 'for malcontents to molest you', as well as a large number of individual words.[2] It is unlikely that he could have done all this from memory.

Further evidence that Locke went back to **H** when he was correcting **A** emerges if the former manuscript is examined carefully. A small number of the additions in **H** are in a very much darker ink than the remainder of the manuscript, and in more than half of these the words or phrases added were also later insertions by Locke in **A**. Two straightforward examples are the addition of 'civill' before 'good' on fo. 5^r of **H** and 'being' before 'secret malecontents' on fo. 25^r. A slightly more complex case occurs further down fo. 25^r: Locke originally wrote the word 'have', then altered it to 'be' as a result of making changes earlier in the sentence, and then finally after still further revisions went back to 'have'. **O** and **P** have 'be'; so originally did **A**, but Locke crossed it out and replaced it by 'have'.[3] It would seem, therefore, that most (and perhaps all) of these changes in dark ink in **H** were made in 1671 or 1672, when Locke was revising **A**.

If, as seems virtually certain, **A** was copied directly from **H*** and **H**, then it is necessary to postulate the existence of a document—now lost—that contained the first addition on page 125. This might have been

---

[1] Adversaria 1661, p. 121.　　　　[2] Adversaria 1661, pp. 109, 110, 115, 118.
[3] Not all the changes in dark ink in **H** have anything corresponding in **A**. On fo. 16^r Locke originally wrote that by using force the magistrate 'does in parte cross what he pretends to doe, which is the safety of all', but subsequently deleted 'doe' and inserted 'to promote' after 'is'. The earlier version appears in all the derived manuscripts.

nothing more than a single sheet of paper, which could easily have become separated from the other parts of HM 584.

O and P were certainly not derived from A, but their relations to H/H* are not quite so easy to determine. There are four possibilities: (i) O and P were both derived independently from H/H*; (ii) P was derived from O; (iii) O was derived from P; and (iv) both O and P were derived from a lost intermediate.

Possibility (i), that O and P were derived independently from H/H*, can be ruled out. There are sixty places where O and P agree against H/H*, and although many of these involve very minor differences of wording, quite a number involve changes that are in varying degrees unlikely to have been made more than once. Examples include:

his charter H*A, this charter OP [fo. iii^r]; then it doth in the rainbow H*A, in the rainbow then it doth OP [fo. v^r]; at the sacrament HA, in the sacrament OP [fo. 1^v]; flowing HA, following OP [fo. 4^r]; dangerous opinions HA, opinions OP [fo. 13^r]; pretenses of conscience HA, pretences OP [fo. 14^r]; place or posture HA, posture OP [fo. 14^r]; breake & suppresse HA, suppress OP [fo. 15^r]; can never HA, never OP [fo. 19^r]; different HA, differing OP [fo. 22^r]; I thinke by the way HA, (by the way) I thinke OP [fo. 22^r]; animosity HA, animosities OP [fo. 22^r]; all history HA, history OP [fo. 22^v]; drive in all dissenters HA, drive all dissenters OP [fo. 24^r]; much more threaten HA, more threaten OP [fo. 24^r]; their owne opinion HA, their opinion OP [fo. 24^r]; the right HA, right OP [fo. 26^r]; the other HA, but the other OP [fo. 26^r].

Taken in isolation perhaps none of these would be decisive: taken together they make it virtually certain that O and P were not derived independently from H/H*.

One piece of evidence that strongly favours possibility (ii), that P was derived from O, is that in a significant number of places P agrees with alterations made by Locke in O, rather than with either H/H* or the original state of O (in the following examples the revised state of O has been designated as o):

preservation H*O, preservation & welfare oP [fo. iii^r]; then H*O, to it then oP [fo. v^r]; uncontrould HO, uncontroulable oP [fo. 3^r]; the ineffectuall persecution HO, the ineffectuall force of persecution oP [fo. 23^r]; 'twill be a H, it will be O, it would be an oP [fo. 24^r]; for those who designe HO, if any should designe oP [fo. 24^r]; retaine their persuasion HO, retaine their perswasion, & continue in an opinion different from you oP [fo. 25^r].

Taken together, these changes seem to rule out both possibility (iii), that O was derived from P, and possibility (iv), that O and P were derived independently from a lost intermediate. By far the most natural explanation would appear to be possibility (ii), that **P** was copied from **O** after Locke had made these alterations.

Further evidence that **O** was not derived from **P** comes from one of the very few places where **P** agrees with neither the original nor the corrected state of **O**.[1] On fo. 12^r of **H** Locke wrote that he 'would faine know' what government in the world did not tolerate some vices; **O** has the same reading, but **P** merely has 'would know'. The text of **P** makes perfect sense, and the writer of **O** manifestly failed to bring a very acute intelligence to what he was doing: if he had been working from **P**, it is unlikely that he would have noticed anything wrong, and it is scarcely credible that he would have been able to guess the missing word.

Though **P** usually follows the corrected text of **O** it does not invariably do so. In another passage on fo. 12^r of **H** Locke mentioned the power that the magistrate has over property rights. Here the three manuscripts have the following readings:[2]

for the magistrate haveing a power to appoint ways of transferring proprietys . . . (H)

For the Magistrate haveing a power of transferring proprieties . . . (O, first state; P)

For the Magistrate haveing a power of makeing rules of transferring proprieties . . . (O, second state, altered by Locke)

It seems that when **O** was copied, the phrase 'to appoint ways' was inadvertently omitted, and that this was not corrected by the copyist. **P** follows this shortened version, but when revising **O** Locke noticed that something was wrong and added the phrase 'makeing rules of' before 'transferring'. In all there are over twenty places where **P** follows the original text of **O** rather than the revised text. This number of changes is far too great to be the result of mere oversight by the copyist of **P**, and the most likely explanation is that Locke read through **O** at least twice, once (presumably) soon after the manuscript had been written in order to rectify copying errors (though he took the opportunity make a few small changes), and then at some later time to make further and more extensive revisions of content. **P** would have been copied after the first set of changes had been made but before the second.

There is, however, one potentially serious objection to this conclusion that **P** was copied from **O**, which is that there are over forty places where

---

[1] The others are: hath **HAO**, has **P** [fo. 19^r]; thinke **HAO**, thinkes **P** [fo. 29^r].

[2] Minor differences of spelling in **O** and **P** have been ignored. A follows **H** here, except for a (subsequently corrected) miscopying of 'transferring' as 'transforming'.

it agrees with **H*** or **H** against **O**. Some of the differences are stylistic— the copyist of **O** frequently replaced Locke's 'has' by 'hath', while the copyist of **P** preferred 'has'—but most appear to be the result of deliberate emendation. Unlike the writer of **O**, who was careless and frequently introduced changes that made Locke's argument either ungrammatical or nonsensical or both, the writer of **P** seems to have been thinking about what he was doing. It would not have required more than fairly ordinary intelligence to realize that 'their ground concernment in an other world' should read 'their grand concernment' (fo. 8^r) or to discern what was wrong with 'will be much improved be the discountenanceing of popery' (fos. 21^r–22^r). On other occasions, however, the correction required would have been less obvious. For example, in one place (fo. 3^r) both **H** and **P** describe polygamy and divorce as practices that could be regarded as 'lawfull or unlawfull &c', while there is a blank space of about 1 cm in **O** in place of '&c', presumably because the copyist could not read the manuscript he was following; the appearance of the word in **P** would be due to intelligent conjecture. Another instance occurs on fo. 23^r of **H**: Locke wrote that 'I desire noe body to goe farther then his owne boosome for an experiment whether ever violence gaind any thing upon his opinion ...'. **P** follows **H**, but in **O** the word 'experience' is used in place of 'experiment'. If **P** was copied from **O** one would have to assume that the writer felt that the word 'experience' was wrong in this context, and that 'experiment' would be better. This is not implausible. It is very significant that none of the instances where **P** agrees with **H*** or **H** against **O** provides strong—still less conclusive—evidence that **P** was not derived from **O**. If **P** had been derived independently from **H/H*** then one would expect to find at least a few readings in it that could not possibly have come from **O**, and there are none.

In the remainder of the discussion it will be assumed that **A** and **O** were copied directly from **H**, and that **P** was copied from **O** after Locke had made some (but not all) of the small changes, and before he added the entirely new material on fos. 22 and 28. If this is correct, then the changes made by Locke in **O** can be divided into two groups: those made before **P** was copied and those made afterwards. The former are mostly corrections of misreadings by the copyist, though there are a few minor alterations of wording. The latter are more extensive and involve changes in doctrine as well as improvements of exposition.

The discussion so far has been entirely concerned with the relationships between the manuscripts, and no attempt has been made to determine when **O** and **P** were copied, or when any of the various changes in **O** were made. One reason for supposing that **O** was copied before **A** is that in several places **A** incorporates changes made in **H** that **O** and **P** do not. Some of these, including the Galley passage, have already been mentioned; others are (the revised state of **H** has been designated as **h**):

the power **HOP**, this power h**A** [fo. 12^r]; their opinion **HOP**, their owne opinion h**A** [fo. 24^r]; severall men **HOP**, severall (I thinke I may say most) men **h**, severall I thinke I may say most men **A** [fo. 25^r].

Taken together with the Galley passage and the additions in dark ink that appear in both **H** and **A**, these changes show that **O** was the first copy to be made, and that it was copied before Locke had finished making changes in **H**.

In both **O** and **P** the *Essay* has the same title that it had in **H***: 'An Essay concerning Toleration 1667'.[1] The presence of the date in **O** is arguably of small significance, since its copyist seems merely to have transcribed mechanically (if inaccurately) whatever was in front of him, but its retention in **P** does suggest an early date for this manuscript. **P** is a fair copy apparently designed to be read by Ashley or by other people associated with the government: it is difficult to believe that if it had been made for this purpose in (say) 1672 it would have proclaimed on its opening page that it had been written five years previously.

If **P** was copied in 1667 or early 1668 then this provides a *terminus ante quem* for the first group of changes in **O**. The large additions and deletions in **O** cannot be dated precisely, and such evidence as there is points in different directions. If—as is possible but by no means certain—the additional sheet (fos. 22–3) on which the first and second of them were written is of the same paper as the rest of the manuscript, then it is likely that it was inserted soon after the main text had been copied; given the very large number of different kinds of paper used by Locke over the years, it is difficult to believe that if he had made the insertion several years later he would have had a stock of exactly the right paper to hand, or indeed that he would have been bothered to choose it if he had. In other respects a date after the copying of **A** seems preferable: it is not easy

---

[1] In both **O** and **P** the phrase 'Sic Cogitavit Atticus 1667' (to judge from the ink, a later addition in **H**) is missing at the end. In **A** there is no title, but at the end Locke added 'Sic Cogitavit JL 1667'. The words 'Toleration 67', in Locke's hand, appear in the margin of the first page; the subsequent pages all have 'Toleration' or 'Toleratio', usually in Locke's hand.

to see why Locke would have instructed a copyist to transcribe into one of his commonplace books a version of the *Essay* that had already been superseded. As has already been mentioned in the General Introduction, a relatively late date for these additions is also suggested by their content, which shows a significant shift away from the views that Locke had maintained in 1667 and towards those expressed in the *Epistola de Tolerantia*.

Choice of Copy-Text

The usual practice when preparing a critical edition is to use as copy-text the last version containing authorial revisions, but there are several reasons why this is not feasible here. In the first place, neither the copy in Adversaria 1661 (**A**) nor the copy in MS Locke c. 28 (**O**) retains Locke's spelling and punctuation, and both are full of corrupt readings which he apparently did not notice and therefore did not correct. Secondly, it is not clear which of these manuscripts actually contains the latest version, or indeed that in the strict sense there is a latest version. The situation is quite unlike that occurring with the *Essay concerning Human Understanding*, where there is a succession of printed editions each derived from its predecessor; among the derived manuscripts of the *Essay concerning Toleration* there is instead a divergent tradition of independently revised texts.

It might seem from this that the best option would be to assemble a text based on Huntington Library HM 584 (i.e. **H*** for as long as it is available, and **H** for the remainder), but incorporating the changes subsequently introduced by Locke into **A** and **O**. There are, however, two disadvantages with this.

The first is that it is not clear that all the revisions in these manuscripts supersede the readings in Locke's autograph. A considerable number of the changes made by Locke in **A** and **O** were to correct earlier miscopyings, and though the revised text usually agrees with the original in **H*** or **H**, sometimes it does not. For example, on fo. 5^r of **H** Locke described the magistrate as 'not being made infallible in reference to others, by being made a governor over them'. The copyist of **A** left out the phrase 'being made infallible in reference to others, by', thereby destroying the sense of the passage. Locke must have noticed this, since he restored the missing phrase, though without the words 'in reference'. There are three possibilities here: (i) Locke was aiming merely to restore the original sense of the passage and did so without going back to check what he had written in **H**; (ii) he looked at **H** but inadvertently copied the missing phrase incorrectly; (iii) he deliberately chose to omit these words. It is not at all clear which explanation should be preferred.

A more complex example occurs on fo. 25^r of **H**. Locke originally wrote that men never take their opinions from those 'of whose freindship to them as well as knowledg in the thing they are well assurd'; he then inserted the word 'not' before 'well assurd'. Even with this correction the passage is not very elegantly expressed, and it is not surprising that Locke chose to revise it. He therefore deleted 'freindship to them as well as knowledg in the thing', replacing it by 'knowledg freindship & sincerety', so that the passage now read 'of whose knowledg freindship & sincerety they are not well assurd'. **O** and **P** follow this second state of **H**. **A** originally had the same reading, but Locke subsequently deleted 'are' and 'well assurd', replacing them with 'have' and 'a good opinion'. In **H** he made yet another change, deleting 'they are not well assurd' and inserting 'they have not very good thoughts'. If the first state of **H** is set aside, there are three variants:

are not well assurd (**H**, second state; **A**, first state; **OP**).

have not a good opinion (**A**, second state).

have not very good thoughts (**H**, third state).

The first of these was rejected twice by Locke, but it is not clear that either of the others should be seen as constituting his true preference. There seem to be three possibilities: (i) when Locke revised **A** he referred back to **H** but the final alteration to **H** had not yet been made; (ii) he referred back to **H** but decided not to adopt the reading there and to choose something different; (iii) he changed **A** without (on this occasion) referring back to **H**. On the third hypothesis there is no way of telling which manuscript has the later reading; on the first hypothesis the final reading of **H** would be later, on the second the final reading of **A**.

The second disadvantage of an eclectic text incorporating all the changes in **A** and **O** is that such a text would not correspond to anything that Locke himself had produced, or reflect his thinking about toleration at any particular time. If one sets aside the very small number of insertions in dark ink that seem to have been made around 1671–2, a text based on **H***** and **H** would be a record of Locke's thoughts in 1667–8; a text based on all the manuscripts would be a purely synthetic one, assembled from material written at very different (and in some cases quite uncertain) times.

It has therefore been decided to use as the copy-text the final state of Locke's autograph, i.e. H* for as long as it is available and **H** thereafter, recording in the textual apparatus additions and deletions in these two manuscripts, variant readings in the superseded portion of **H**, and later changes made in the derived manuscripts. Readings from the First Draft **F** have been included in the textual apparatus when this corresponds closely to H* or **H** but not otherwise; complete texts of the First Draft and the long additions in **O** and **A** have been given separately.

The Preservation of the Manuscripts

The endorsements on the quires of Huntington Library HM 584 indicate that Locke intended to keep them together among his own papers. It appears from the pattern of dirt on the final page of each quire that its pages were folded once about a vertical axis in such a way as to leave the endorsement easily visible, and the set was then stored together in a packet or bundle. The sheet containing the First Draft was folded twice horizontally, making it about the same size as the folded quires, and it was presumably kept with them.

The quires are currently neither stitched nor bound, though holes left by stitching that has since been removed are clearly visible; it is clear from the variable number and position of these holes that the quires were never bound together. In quire A the top-edges and fore-edges of the leaves are now gilded, suggesting that it had once been included in a bound volume; probably it was selected for this as an easily legible sample of a work by the famous Mr Locke. When, where, and by whom this was done is not now known.

All the parts of the manuscript were listed as item 2467 in Maggs Brothers' catalogue 427 (Autumn 1922), and sold to Henry E. Huntington; since that time they have been in the Huntington Library.

Adversaria 1661 remained among Locke's papers in the keeping of the King family until the middle of the twentieth century, when it was sold to Arthur A. Houghton, Jr.[1] It is now in private ownership in France.

The copy of the *Essay* in MS Locke c. 28 has remained among Locke's papers to the present day, and has been in the Bodleian Library since 1942.

---

[1] The earlier history of this manuscript is described by Peter Nidditch in *Draft A of Locke's Essay concerning Human Understanding*, 198–200.

The copy among the Shaftesbury papers remained in the hands of the family until it was deposited in the Public Record Office by the seventh Earl in 1871.

Publication

The *Essay concerning Toleration* was never published in Locke's lifetime, and though Peter King must have had access to more than one copy it was not among the works that he chose to have published after Locke's death. The list of conclusions at the end of the *Essay* and the long addition in Locke's hand in Adversaria 1661 were published in 1829 in Lord King's *Life of John Locke*,[1] but the work as a whole did not appear in print until H. R. Fox Bourne's 1876 biography.[2] King had used the copy in Adversaria 1661, which was then still among Locke's papers and therefore in his own possession; by 1876 these were no longer accessible to outsiders, and Fox Bourne used the only manuscript available to him, PRO 30/24/47/1, which had recently been deposited in the Public Record Office.

In 1950 J. W. Gough printed the long additions (and some of the smaller changes) in MS Locke c. 28 in an appendix to his *John Locke's Political Philosophy*.[3] The existence of all four manuscripts of the *Essay* seems first to have been made public in Maurice Cranston's 1957 biography and in the catalogue of the Lovelace Collection that Philip Long published two years later.[4]

In 1961 C. A. Viano included an English version of the *Essay* in his edition of Locke's writings on toleration.[5] The text he printed was an eclectic one based mainly on MS Locke c. 28, but with its obvious copying errors corrected from readings in the other manuscripts. Viano consulted all four manuscripts, but though he was fully aware of the importance of the Huntington Library manuscript, as Locke's autograph, he made no attempt to reproduce its text, contenting himself with recording among his footnotes some details of its variant readings. He

---

[1] The conclusions, from 'But to shew the danger ...' to the end of the work, are in King (1829), 156; the text shows that they were taken from the copy in Adversaria 1661. The longer addition in Adversaria 1661 is in King (1829), 287–91, where it is combined with 'Sacerdos', an entry in the same volume (p. 93) dating from 1698; see Milton, 'Locke's *Essay on Toleration*', 53–6.   [2] Fox Bourne, i. 174–94.

[3] pp. 197–9; this appendix was not retained in the second edition of 1973.

[4] Cranston, 111; *Summary Catalogue*, 29.

[5] *Scritti editi e inediti sulla tolleranza*, 81–103.

also printed a complete text of the First Draft, the first time that any part of this had been published.[1]

Viano's edition was followed some years later by Kimimasa Inoue's edition: John Locke, *An Essay concerning Toleration and Toleratio*. Like Viano, Inoue used MS Locke c. 28 as his copy-text. His notes contained rather more information about the readings in the other manuscripts than Viano's had done, but neither edition could claim to be a critical one.

In recent years the *Essay* has been reprinted in collections of Locke's political writings edited by David Wootton and by Mark Goldie.[2] Both editions provide modernized texts based on MS Locke c. 28, though with editorial corrections where this is manifestly defective.

WRITINGS ON CHURCH AND STATE, 1668–1674

Queries on Scottish Church Government

These queries are written in Locke's hand on a single sheet of paper measuring approximately 227×169 mm, now preserved among the Shaftesbury papers in the National Archives, PRO 30/24/47/30, fo. 45 (Plate 7). They have not previously been published.

The only indication of the date of these queries is given by Locke's endorsement: 'Church Government Q[ueries] Concerning the Scotch Discipline 68'. This probably indicates that they were written in the year beginning 25 March 1668, though a date between 1 January and 24 March cannot be excluded.[3]

Notes on Samuel Parker's Discourse of Ecclesiastical Politie

The surviving portion of Locke's notes on Parker's *Discourse* are preserved on three folded sheets of paper, now collected together in MS Locke c. 39, fos. 5–10; fos. 6, 8, 9^v, and 10 are blank, apart from Locke's

---

[1] *Scritti editi e inediti sulla tolleranza*, 104–7.

[2] *Political Writings*, ed. Wootton, 186–210; Goldie, 135–59; Goldie also printed the additions to the *Essay* in Adversaria 1661 as 'Toleration A', 231–5.

[3] In his endorsements Locke seems normally to have reckoned the year as beginning on 25 March. Dual dates indicating both years (e.g. 69/70) are quite common in the endorsements added to incoming letters, but much rarer in those on other documents. Of the ten surviving letters dated between 1 January and 24 March that Locke received while at Exeter House, six have dual dates (letters *240, 242, 251, 282, 285, 286*), and four (*252, 261, 268, 287*) old-style dates with the year ending on 24 March.

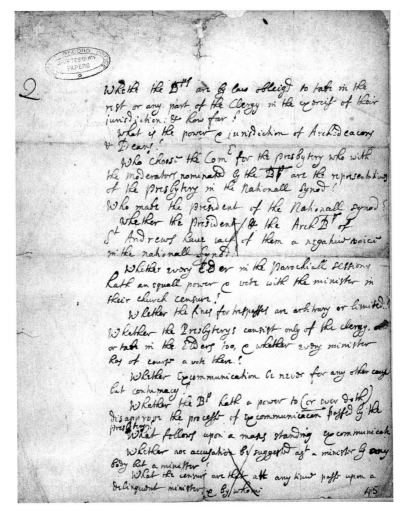

Plate 7. Queries on Scottish Church Government. The National Archives, PRO 30/24/47/30, fo. 45^r, reproduced by permission of the National Archives

endorsement on fo. 8^v: 'Q[uerie]s on S. Ps discourse of toleration. <u>69</u>'. The leaves of fos. 5–6 each measure approximately 299 × 194 mm, those of fos. 7–8 approximately 230 × 172 mm, those of fos. 9–10 approximately 342 × 233 mm. None of the leaves is numbered. The same paper appears to have been used for fos. 7–8 and fos. 9–10, the former being a half-sheet, the latter a full sheet; the paper used for fos. 5–6 has an entirely different watermark.

The notes on fo. 5 are all in the left-hand column of the page. They are not explicitly linked to any passages in Parker's *Discourse*, but relate to the account in his first chapter of the foundations of civil and ecclesiastical government; they do not include any critical comments by Locke himself. Since these notes are on different paper from those on fo. 7 and fo. 9 it is not certain that they were made at the same time or for the same purpose. The notes on fo. 7 relate to pages 11–29 of the Parker's book, and those on fo. 9 to pages 144–53; though one cannot be certain, it would seem quite likely that these two sheets are stray survivors from a considerably fuller body of notes that have since been lost. Variations in the colour of the ink in the notes on fo. 7 show that they were not all made at the same time.

Locke's endorsement on fo. 8ᵛ indicates that the notes on fo. 7 were made before 25 March 1669/70; it is not possible to say for certain that they were made before 31 December 1669, though it is quite likely that they were.

The comments on fos. 7 and 9 were first printed by Cranston, and subsequently by Goldie.[1] Those on fo. 5 have not previously been printed.

Excommunication

This is contained on a single folded sheet, MS Locke c. 27, fos. 29ᵃ–29ᵇ, the leaves measuring approximately 318 × 212 mm. The first part of the text is in an unidentified hand, with additions by Locke.[2] From the heading 'The Paralel' onwards all the text is in Locke's hand, and there can be no doubt that he was the author of the whole work. The date of writing is provided by Locke's endorsement: '<u>Excommunication</u> 7¾' on fo. 29ᵇᵛ, the dual dating indicating the first three months of 1674.

Excommunication was first printed with a few minor omissions by King, and more recently in full by Goldie, under the title 'Civil and Ecclesiastical Power'.[3]

---

[1] Cranston, 131–3; Goldie, 211–15.

[2] The hand resembles that of the copy in MS Locke d. 9, p. 87 of Locke's queries on poisonous fish extracted from an (otherwise lost) letter to Sir Peter Colleton dated May 1675, *Correspondence*, viii. 428–9, and the entries in MS Locke c. 44, pp. 1–23 relating to ecclesiastical patronage, made in 1672–3 while Locke was Secretary for Presentations.

[3] King (1829), 297–304; Goldie, 216–21.

A LETTER FROM A PERSON OF QUALITY, TO HIS FRIEND
IN THE COUNTRY

Four editions of *A Letter from a Person of Quality* were published in Locke's lifetime. Two of these (Wing S 2897, Wing S 2897aA) have the date of 1675 on the title-page and are the only editions with any claim to textual authority. In 1689 and 1693 the *Letter* was included in *State Tracts*, a Whig compilation of anti-government writings from the 1670s and 1680s; the text was taken from Wing S 2897aA. Two early manuscripts exist in the British Library: Egerton MS 3383, fos. 59ʳ–68ᵛ, and Add. MS 74273. The former certainly derives from Wing S 2897aA, but it is not certain whether the latter derives from Wing S 2897 or is an independent copy.

The 1675 Printed Editions

Both these editions are quarto pamphlets of 40 leaves, with nearly identical title-pages. Wing S 2897 is in bibliographical respects the more straightforward of the two 1675 editions. It is gathered in twos with each leaf correctly signed (A, A2; B, B2; etc.), though three pages were incorrectly numbered.[1]

Wing S 2897aA evidently had a much more complex and troubled printing history, with more than one compositor apparently involved, and possibly more than one printing house. While the gatherings from C onwards are in twos with each leaf correctly signed (C, C2; D, D2; etc.), the first signed gathering (pages 1–8) consists of a whole sheet signed A, A2, B, with the final leaf unsigned. This gathering is in a different typeface from the remainder of the work, and it would seem that its compositor was inexperienced, or working much too quickly, or both. The printer was certainly in a hurry, since he started running off sheets before anyone had corrected the proofs. In the copies printed before any corrections were made, these first eight pages contain nine incorrect, missing, or repeated words; thirteen turned letters; ten letters displaced, missing, or in the wrong font; and fifty spelling errors, many

---

[1] A full bibliographical description of both editions is given below, pp. 232–3. The fact that each gathering is only a half-sheet suggests that they were printed by half-sheet imposition, a procedure that would have saved time by allowing printing to begin when only four pages had been composed, as opposed to eight in full-sheet imposition.

of them gross.[1] These are not the only manifestations of incompetence: some of the lines of type are not straight, and many individual letters were not squarely set, or were allowed to protrude too far above the level of their surroundings, or not far enough. It is a truly abysmal piece of printing.

Someone at the time seems to have drawn a similar conclusion, because in the majority of the copies examined by the present editors most though not quite all of these errors have been corrected. There are also two hybrid copies in the Bodleian Library in which the first gathering was printed from an uncorrected outer forme (pages 1, 4, 5, 8) and a corrected inner one (pages 2, 3, 6, 7).[2]

In the remainder of S 2897aA, from gathering C onwards, only page 24 was corrected, with five small changes of spelling and punctuation. Copies with the corrected state of this page appear to be considerably more common than those with the uncorrected one, but no attempt seems to have been made to keep the corrected sheets of this and gathering A together: among the copies of S 2897aA examined by the editors examples have been found of each state of page 24 bound together with each state of the first gathering.[3]

Gatherings C–I of S 2897aA were considerably better printed than gathering A, for the most part as well as S 2897. Differences of spelling between the two editions in this part of the *Letter* suggest strongly that different compositors were involved: one of the most noticeable is the frequent doubling in S 2897 of the letter *l* in words such as civill, illegall, monarchicall, penall, quallity, withall, etc., where S 2897aA almost always has the modern spelling. The compositor(s) of S 2897 also had a strong preference for the ending '-or' in words such as endeavor, favor, and honor, while both the compositors of S 2897aA generally preferred '-our'.

The title-page of S 2897aA closely resembles that of S 2897 (Plate 8), but was less skilfully set up, with the rules composing the border misaligned and joined together in a way that left more obvious gaps.

One of the most conspicuous differences between the 1675 printings can be found in the printer's ornaments at the head of the first page.

---

[1] For example: enes, ihose, rhose, ar, ophosed, aoainst, htve, lioht, hfi, iim, ohe, ahe, hio, miiigate, clamouo, rf, artileoy, thtnk, Scoth, Pesbytery, ornce, principlbs, besidei, rhe, arricles, draad, mhnage.   [2] Bodl., Firth e. 9 (1); G. Pamph. 1359 (9).

[3] For example, pp. 1–8 uncorrected, p. 24 uncorrected, CUL, Syn. 5. 67. 9; pp. 1–8 uncorrected, p. 24 corrected, Bodl., G. Pamph. 1125 (10); pp. 1–8 corrected, p. 24 uncorrected, Bodl., G. Pamph. 1793 (6); pp. 1–8 corrected, p. 24 corrected, Bodl., G. Pamph. 1374 (10).

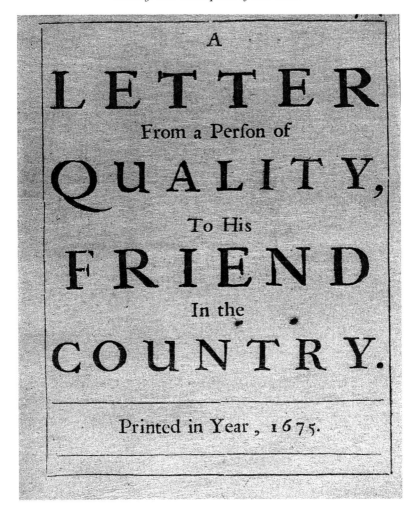

A

LETTER

From a Perſon of

QUALITY,

To His

FRIEND

In the

COUNTRY.

Printed in Year, 1675.

Plate 8. *A Letter from a Person of Quality*. Wing S 2897, title-page. The National Archives, SP 116/413, reproduced by permission of the National Archives

(Plates 9, 10, 11). In S 2897 there is a row of thirty-eight of them, with a question mark between the thirty-fourth and thirty-fifth. In the uncorrected state of S 2897aA there are twenty-three quite different and somewhat larger ornaments, with a colon placed between the

(1)

A
Letter from a Perfon of Quality, to His
Friend in the Country.

S I R,

His Seffion being ended, and the Bill of the *Teft* neer finished at the Committee of the whole Houfe ; I can now give you a perfect Account of this STATE MASTER-PIECE. It was firft hatch't (as almoft all the Mifchiefs of the World have hitherto been) amongft the *Great Church Men,* and is a Project of feveral Years ftanding, but found not Minifters bold enough to go through with it, until thefe *new ones,* who wanting a better Bottom to fupport them, betook themfelves wholly to this, which is no fmall Undertaking if you confider it in its whole Extent.

Firft, to *make a diftinct Party* from the reft of the Nation of the High Epifcopal Man, and the Old Cavalier, who are to fwallow the hopes of enjoying all the Power and Office of the Kingdom , being alfo tempted by the advantage they may recieve from overthrowing the *Act of Oblivion,* and not a little rejoycing to think how valiant they fhould prove, if they could get any to fight the Old Quarrel over again ; Now they are poffeft of the Arms, Forts, and Ammunition of the Nation.

Next they defign to *have the Government of the Church Sworne to as Unalterable,* and fo Tacitely owned to be of Divine Right, which though inconfiftent with the Oath of Supremacy ; yet the Church Men eafily break through all Obligations whatfoever, to attain this Station, the advantage of which, the Prelate of *Rome* hath fufficiently taught the World.

Then in requital to the Crown , they declare the Government *abfolute* and *Arbitrary,* and allow Monarchy as well as Epifcopacy to be *Jure Divino,* and not to be bounded, or limited by humane Laws.

A   And

Plate 9. *A Letter from a Person of Quality.* Wing S 2897, p. 1. The National Archives, SP 116/413, reproduced by permission of the National Archives

thirteenth and fourteenth. When the first sheet was corrected, these ornaments were replaced by a row of thirty-three smaller ones, with two much smaller colons placed one above the other between the thirteenth and fourteenth; presumably this was done to facilitate identification of

(1)

A

Letter from a Perſon of Quality, to His Friend in the Country.

SIR,

This Seſſion being ended, and the Bill of *Teſt* near finiſhed at the Committee of the whole Houſe, I can now give you a perfect Account of this STATE MASTER-PIECE. It was firſt hatch'd (as almoſt all the Miſchiefs of the World had hitherto been) amongſt the *Great Church-Men*, and is a Project of ſeveral Years ſtanding; but found not Miniſters bold enough to go through with it, until theſe *new enet* who wanting a better Bottom to ſupport them, betook themſelves wholly to this, which is no ſmall Undertaking, if you conſider it in its whole Extent.

Firſt, To *make a diſtinct Party* from the reſt of the Nation of the High Epiſcopal Man, and the Old Cavalier, who are to ſwallow the hopes of enjoying all the Power and Office of the Kingdom, being alſo tempted by the advantage they may receive from overthrowing the *Act of Oblivion,* and not a little rejoycing to think how valiant they ſhould prove, if they could get any to fight the Old Quarrel over again; Now they are poſſeſs'd of the Arms, Forts, and Ammunition of the Nation.

Next they deſign to *have the Government of the Church Sworn to as Unalterable,* and ſo Tacitely owned to be of Divine Right, which though inconſiwith the Oath of Supremacy; yet the Church-Men eaſily break through all Obligations whatſoever, to attain this Station, the advantage of which, the Prelate of *Rome* hath ſufficiently taught the World.

Then in requital to the Crown, they declare the Government *abſolute* and *Arbitrary,* and allow Monarchy as well as Epiſcopacy to be *Jure Divino,* and not to be bounded, or limited by humane Laws.

A   And

Plate 10. *A Letter from a Person of Quality.* Wing S 2897aA, p. 1, uncorrected state. Cambridge University Library, Syn. 5. 67. 9, reproduced by permission of the Syndics of Cambridge University Library

the corrected sheets. These smaller ornaments closely resemble those used in S 2897.

Neither edition contains any indication of where or by whom it was printed or published, but it is clear that one must have been set up from the other: they correspond page for page on twenty-six pages (pages 1, 5,

(1)

A

Letter from a Perſon of Quality, to His Friend in the Country.

S I R ;

THis Seſſion being ended, and the Bill of *Teſt* near finiſhed at the Committee of the whole Houſe ; I can now give you a perfect Account of this S T A T E M A S T E R-P I E C E. It was firſt hatch'd (as almoſt all the Miſchiefs of the World had hitherto been) amongſt the *Great Church-Men*, and is a Project of ſeveral Years ſtanding, but found not Miniſters bold enough to go through with it, until theſe *new ones*, who wanting a better Bottom to ſupport them, betook themſelves wholly to this, which is no ſmall Undertaking, if you conſider it in its whole Extent.

First, To *make a diſtinct Party* from the reſt of the Nation of the High Epiſcopal Man, and the Old Cavalier, who are to ſwallow the hopes of enjoying all the Power and Office of the Kingdom, being alſo tempted by the advantage they may receive from overthrowing the *Act of Oblivion*, and not a little rejoycing to think how valiant they ſhould prove, if they could get any to fight the Old Quarrel over again ; Now they are poſſeſs'd of the Arms, Forts, and Ammunition of the Nation.

Next they deſign to *have the Government of the Church Sworn to as Unalterable*, and ſo Tacitely owned to be of Divine Right, which though Inconſiſtent with the Oath of Supremacy ; yet the Church-Men eaſily break through all Obligations whatſoever, to attain this Station, the advantage of which, the Prelate of *Rome* hath ſufficiently taught the World.

Then in requital to the Crown, they declare the Government *abſolute* and *Arbitrary*, and allow Monarchy as well as Epiſcopacy to be *Jure Divine*, and not to be bounded, or limited by humane Laws.

A   And

Plate 11. *A Letter from a Person of Quality*. Wing S 2897aA, p. 1, corrected state. Cambridge University Library, Bb*. 10. 19[8], reproduced by permission of the Syndics of Cambridge University Library

6, 9, 13–34) and line for line on twelve (pages 5, 13, 16, 23–8, 30–2).[1] Given this, one might expect that their measures (line-widths) would be

[1] Some utterly unimportant features were faithfully copied: in both editions page numbers are indicated by numerals between round brackets placed centrally at the head

the same, at least for those pages that either exactly or very nearly correspond line for line. In fact only two pages (13, 17) have the same measure in both editions: otherwise the measures in S 2897aA are invariably narrower than their equivalents in S 2897:

Pages	Gathering/leaf	Measure, S 2897	Measure, S 2897aA
1–8	A, B	119 mm	114 mm
9–12	C	119 mm	113 mm
13	D1^r	119 mm	119 mm
14–16	D1^v–2^v	119 mm	112 mm
17	E1^r	119 mm	119 mm
18–20	E1^v–2^v	119 mm	111 mm
21–2	F1	119 mm	107 mm
23–7	F2^r–G2^r	113 mm	107 mm
28–34	G2^v–I1^r	109 mm	107 mm

The greatest difference occurs in the two pages (21, 22) at the start of gathering F, where the measure in S 2897aA is 12 mm narrower than in S 2897. Page 21 contains exactly the same text in both editions, apart from five minor differences of punctuation and spelling, and except in one place they correspond line for line. When the two pages are compared, it is immediately apparent that the text in S 2897aA is very much more compressed: there are three places in the first four lines where a comma is inserted between two words without a space afterwards, and line 27 was set as follows:

Liturgie was not so sacred;being made by Men the other day,& thought

In S 2897 the line is spaced normally, with the word 'and' instead of the ampersand. If S 2897aA had been set first, it is not clear why the text should have needed to be so ruthlessly compressed. The most natural explanation is that S 2897 was printed first, and that S 2897aA was set up from it.

The same conclusion is suggested by an examination of gatherings A and B. Here the difference in the measures is only 5 mm but the text in S 2897aA appears much more cramped. This is not wholly attributable to the incompetence of the compositor: even if he had been much more careful, the resulting pages would still have looked worse than their equivalents in S 2897. The roman typeface in this part of S 2897aA is slightly broader than that used in S 2897, so that a text that would

of the page immediately above the text, except on p. 27 and p. 29 where there is an intervening line-space.

naturally occupy a rather larger space had to be squeezed into one that was significantly smaller. Some more room was found on the pages printed from the inner forme (2, 3, 6, 7) by adding an extra line, but though this helped, it did not eliminate the problem.[1] From gathering C onwards a narrower typeface was used, similar if not identical to that used in S 2897, and though the difference in the measures is often greater, the unsightly compression so apparent in gathering A is for the most part avoided.

The different use of ampersands in S 2897 and S 2897aA also suggests that the latter was set up from the former. In S 2897 the italic form alone is used, in two Latin phrases, once in the word *&c.*, and twice in the proper name *Say & Seal*. In S 2897aA these are retained, but the non-italic form is also used on eight occasions. One of these, on page 21, has already been mentioned. The others are on page 17 and—most strikingly of all—near the foot of page 3, where an ampersand is used four times in as many lines (Plate 12). The extreme compression of the text here is very conspicuous, and the only plausible explanation for this cluster of ampersands is that the compositor had somehow to get a certain amount of text onto the page, and was starting to run out of space.[2]

All these considerations point strongly towards the priority of S 2897. Further evidence is provided by a number of places where it and the two states of S 2897aA all have different readings:

(1) On page 1:

S 2897	which though inconsistent | with the Oath of Supremacy
S 2897aA (uncorrected)	which though inconsi- | with the Oath of Supremacy
S 2897aA (corrected)	which though inconsi- | stent with the Oath of Supremacy

The simplest explanation for the unfinished word in the uncorrected state of S 2897aA is that the compositor was following S 2897 but reached the end of the line before he was able to set the whole of 'inconsistent';

---

[1] The normal number of lines on a full page in both editions is 38. In S 2897 pp. 2, 3, 4, 5 and 20 have 39 lines, while pp. 8, 9, 27, and 29 have 37. Most pages in S 2897aA have the same number of lines as their equivalents in S 2897, the exceptions being pp. 2, 3, 6, 7, and 34, which have one more line, and p. 11, which has two more.

[2] The division between p. 3 and p. 4 nearly coincides in the two editions: the last word on p. 3 in S 2897, 'Discourse', is the first word on p. 4 in S 2897aA.

one reason for this is that the line-width on this page in S 2897aA is 5 mm less than in S 2897. He therefore broke the word, but when he began setting the next line he simply copied it directly from S 2897, forgetting that the unfinished word had still to be completed.

(2) On page 2:

S 2897	And as the topstone of the whole Fabrique, a pretence shall be taken
S 2897aA (uncorrected)	And as the topstone of the whole Fabrique,a pretence shall be taken
S 2897aA (corrected)	And as the topstone of the whole Fabrick, a pretence shall be taken

The only plausible explanation for these variants is that S 2897 was printed first and S 2897aA was set from it. The compositor of S 2897aA followed the spelling of S 2897 but in doing so left no space after 'Fabrique'; as on page 1, he was attempting to set text that had occupied a line of 119 mm in one 5 mm narrower. The corrector made the required space by altering the spelling to 'Fabrick'.

(3) On page 2:

S 2897	And yet that *Bartholomew day* was fatal to our Church, and Religion, in throw-|ing out a very great Number of *Whorthy, Learned, Pious, and Orthodox Divines*
S 2897aA (uncorrected)	And yet that *Bartholomew* day was fatal to our Church | and Religion, in throwing out e very great Number of *Whorthy, Learned,|Pious, aad Orthodox Divines*
S 2897aA (corrected)	And yet that *Bartholomew day* was fatal to our Church | and Religion, in throwing out every great Number of *Worthy, Learned,|Pious, aad Orthodox Divines*

There are four variant readings here. Two of them, the comma after 'Church' in S 2897 and the mis-spelling of '*and*' in both states of S 2897aA, are of no value for determining the priority of the editions. In the case of the other variants it is the difference between the two states of S 2897aA that provides the necessary clue. (i) Clearly the correct reading in the second line is 'a very great Number', as in S 2897. The only

(3)

Book of *Common Prayer* thereby eſtabliſhed; you ſhall plainly find it could not be Printed, and diſtributed ſo, as one Man in forty could have ſeen, and read the Book they did ſo perfeɛlly Aſſent and Conſent to.

But this Matter was not compleat until *the Five Mile Aɛt*, paſſed at *Oxford*, wherein they take an opportunity to introduce the Oath in the terms they would have ie : This was then ſtrongly ophoſed by the L. Treaſurer *Southampton*, Lord *Wharton*, L. *Aſhley*, and others, not only in the concern of thoſe poor Miniſters that were ſo ſeverely handled, but as it was in it ſelf, a moſt Unlawful, and Unjuſtifyable Oath ; however, the zeal of that time aoainſt all *Nonconformiſts* eaſily paſſed the Aɛt.

This Aɛt was ſeconded the ſame Seſſions at *Oxford*,by another Bill in the Houſe of Commons, to htve impoſed that Oath on the *whole Nation* ; and the Providence by which it was thrown out,was very remarquable; For Mr. *Peregrine Bertie* , being newly choſen, was that morning introduced into the Houſe by his Brother the now Earl of *Lindſay* and Sir *Tho. Osborn* now L.Treaſurer,who all Three gave their Votes againſt that Bill;and the Numbers were ſo even upon that diviſion, that their three Votes carried the Queſtion againſt it. But we owe that Right to the Earl of *Lindſey* , and the L.Treaſurer as to acknowledg that they have ſince made ample ſatisfaɛtion, for whatever oʇʇence they gave either the Church or Court in that Vote.

Thus our *Church* became *Triumphant*, and continued ſo for divers yea rs, the diſſenting *Proteſtant* being the only *Enemy*, and therefore only perſecuted, whileſt the Papiſts remained undiſturbed, being by the Court thought Loyal, and by our Great Biſhops not dangerous they differing only in Doɛtrine, and Fundamentals ; but as to the Government of the Church , that was in their Religion in its h gheſt Exaltation.

This Dominion continued unto them,until the L.*Clifford*,a man of a da̶ ̶ ing and *ambitious ſpirit* , made his way to the chief Miniſtery of Affairs by other,and far different meaſures,and took the opportunity oʇthe War with *Holland*,the *King* was then engaged in , to propoſe *the Declaration of Indulgence*, that the Diſſenters of all ſorts, as well Proteſtants ar Papiſts, might be at reſt.and ſo vaſt a number of People,not be made deſperate,at Home,while the *King* was engaged with ſo potent an Enemy abroad. This was no ſooner propoſed,but the E.of *Schaftsbury*,a man as daring but more able(though of principles & intereſt,diametrically oppoſite to the other)preſently cloſed with it,& perhaps the opportunity I have had by my converſation with them both,who were men of diverſion,& oʇfree and open Diſcourſes where they had a confidence; may give you more lioht into both their Deſigns,& ſo by conſequence the aimes of their Parties , then you will have from any other han i. My L.*Clifford* did in expreſs Terms,tell me one day in private

A 2   Diſcourſe :

Plate 12. *A Letter from a Person of Quality*. Wing S 2897aA, p. 3, uncorrected state. Cambridge University Library, Syn. 5. 67. 9, reproduced by permission of the Syndics of Cambridge University Library

remotely plausible explanation for the two variant readings in S 2897aA is that S 2897 is the first edition, that the compositor of S 2897aA was following it but mis-set 'a very' as 'e very', and that though the corrector saw that this was wrong, he assumed—without checking the original or paying any attention to the sense of the passage—that 'e very' should have been 'every'. (ii) The word 'Worthy' was set as '*Worthy*' in the corrected state of S 2897aA, but as '*Whorthy*' in both S 2897 and the uncorrected state of S 2897aA. It is most unlikely that two compositors would independently have chosen such an unusual spelling, and even if there were no other evidence, this alone would make it virtually certain that S 2897 was not set from the corrected state of S 2897aA.

The evidence set out above provides very strong evidence that S 2897 was printed first, and that S 2897aA was set up from it. The same conclusion is suggested by the one major textual difference between the two editions. On page 8, S 2897 has a description of how

the main thing design'd for a Bill voted in the former Session, *viz. the marrying our Princes to none but Protestants*, was *rejected* and carried in the Negative by the unanimous Votes of the *Bishops Bench*; <u>for I must acquaint you that our great Prelates were so neer an Infallibility, that they were always found in this Session of one mind in the *Lords House*</u>; yet the Lay Lords, not understanding from how excellent a Principle this proceeded, commonly called them for that reason *the dead Weight* . . . [1]

In both states of S 2897aA the clause underlined here is missing. It is not hard to see how this could have happened by chance if S 2897aA had been set from S 2897. In S 2897 the passage omitted in S 2897aA is separated from the surrounding text by two semicolons, one two lines below the other but displaced from it horizontally by only about 6 mm; it is easy to see how a compositor as careless as the person who set up the first gathering in the uncorrected state of S 2897aA could have paused at the first semicolon and then inadvertently resumed setting at the second. It is less easy to give a plausible account of how such a passage could have come to be inserted. The omission of the underlined clause changes the meaning of the whole passage: in S 2897 the lay peers called the bishops 'the dead Weight' because of their invariable practice of voting with the court; as the text stands in S 2897aA it would seem that they were so described merely because they had voted against a bill on royal marriages.

External evidence also suggests that S 2897 was the first edition. Considerably fewer copies of it seem to have survived, as one would expect if a large number had been seized and destroyed by the authorities.[2] All four copies of the *Letter* in the State Papers are of this edition, and the

---

[1] Below, p. 348.
[2] Of the thirty copies examined by the present editors, only eleven are of the first edition, and four of these are in the State Papers: NA, SP 9/247/53; SP 30, case F (two copies); SP 116/413.

most likely explanation for their presence there is that they came from the batch of thirty copies taken from Katharine Knight on 10 November. The officials of the Stationers' Company reported that the copies they had examined were too well printed for a private press.[1] It is unlikely that they would have said this about S 2897aA, even in its corrected state.

Taken all together, the evidence presented here leaves no doubt whatever that S 2897 was printed first, and that S 2897aA was derived from it. In the discussion that follows, they will therefore be referred to as the first and second editions.

The text of the second edition is generally inferior to that of the first. In its corrected state it contains a total of forty differences of wording, of which twenty-nine are in the first gathering. The attack on Lauderdale on page 7 provides a good illustration of these differences. In the first edition this reads:

But his Grace of *Scotland*: was least to be executed of the Three, for having fall'n from *Presbitery, Protestaant* Religion, and all principles of Publick good and private friendship, and become the Slave of *Clifford* to carry on the Ruine of all that he had professed to support, does now also quit even *Clifford*'s generous Principles, and betake himself to a sort of Men, that *never forgive any Man the having once been in the right*; and such Men, who would do the worst of things by the worst of means, enslave their country, and betray them, under the mask of Religion, which they have the publick Pay for, and charge off; so seething the Kid in the Mothers milk.[2]

There are five obvious faults here: the colon after 'Scotland', 'executed' instead of 'excused', 'charge off' instead of 'charge of', and the mis-spellings 'Presbitery' and 'Protestaant'. Only the last of these was properly corrected in the second edition, the uncorrected state of which introduced a flood of new errors:

But his Grace of *Scotland*: was least to be executed of the Tree, for having fall'n from *Pesbytery, Protestant* Religion, and all principles of Publick good and prvate friendship, and become the Slave of *Clifford* to carry on the Rnine of all he had professed to support, does now also quit even *Clifford*'s generous Principles, and betake himself to a sort of Men, that *never forgive any Man the havingornce been in the righr*; and such Men,who would do the worst of things by the worst of means, enslave their country,and betray them,under the mask of Religion,which they have publick Pay for,and the charge off, so seeching the Kid in the Mothers milk.

The compression of the text caused by the narrower measure is clearly apparent. There are three substantive changes: the removal of 'that'

---

[1] Above, p. 95.   [2] Below, p. 346

206

before 'he had professed' and 'the' before 'publick Pay', and the addition of 'the' before 'charge off'. The corrector removed most of the new spelling errors—though 'seeching' was left—but he retained the three substantive changes and added a fourth by using '*he*' rather than '*the*' in '*he having once*'. The three main errors in the first edition—the colon after 'Scotland', 'executed' instead of 'excused', 'charge off' instead of 'charge of'—remained uncorrected.

The great majority of the variants in the second edition are simply corruptions of the text in the first, but there are a few places where the first edition is faulty and the second has a better reading:

First edition	Second edition
That the Princes of the Blood-Royal should all Marry Protestants	That the Prince of the Blood-Royal should only Marry Protestants
whether it were meant all for an Oath, or some of it a Declaration, and some an Oath?	whether it were meant all for an Oath, or some of it for a Declaration, and some an Oath?
one of the eminentest of those were for the Bill added the words *by Law*	one of the eminentest of those that were for the Bill, added the words *by Law*[1]

All these changes appear to be conjectures, possibly even unconscious ones. There is nothing in the second edition that shows any sign of having been introduced by anyone involved in writing the *Letter*.

No direct evidence has emerged for the exact date at which the second edition went on sale, but all the circumstantial evidence suggests that it was rushed into print to cash in on the demand created by the public condemnation and burning of the first edition on 10 November.[2] It gives every appearance of having been composed and printed in a great hurry, and whoever organized its printing evidently had no qualms about selling defective copies to the public.

As mentioned in the General Introduction, Henry Bridges and John Marlow admitted to having printed part of the *Letter*.[3] This may only

---

[1] *LPQ* 7 (italics suppressed), 15, 23, below, pp. 345, 356, 365. In the first passage the singular 'Prince' in the second edition is clearly a printer's error.

[2] On the day after the *Letter* was burned, one of Sir Ralph Verney's correspondents told him that 'It was first sold for 12^d and is now valued at 20^s. Could I possibly have gotten one at a reasonable rate I would have sent it you', William Fall to Verney, 11 Nov. 1675, Buckinghamshire RO, M11/29, unfoliated. A few days later another correspondent told him that 'I cannot get sight of the seditious booke, but I am promised fair ...', William Denton to Verney, 15 Nov. 1675, ibid. It would appear that the second edition was not yet on sale when these letters were written.   [3] Above, p. 96.

mean that they printed one of the 1675 editions, but the more natural interpretation is that they were responsible for part (but not all) of one of them. If so, it is much more likely that they were involved with the second edition than with the first. The first edition uses the same typeface throughout and contains nothing suggesting that it was the work of more than one printer. In the second edition gathering A is not in the same typeface as the remainder of the work: the differences are most apparent in capital M and R but are also discernible in other letters such as lower-case o, p, and d. Together with the difference in format, this strongly suggests that this gathering was set up and printed in a different printing house.

If the second edition was the work of two different printers, the question arises whether either of them had also been responsible for the first edition. No one could suppose that gathering A of the second edition was set up by the printer of the first, but it is possible that gatherings C–I were: the typeface of these is not obviously distinguishable from that of the first edition. The printer's ornaments used in the corrected state of the second edition also appear to be of the same type as those used in the first, though differently arranged. There is, however, one very serious objection to such a conclusion: if gatherings C–I of the second edition were set up in the same printing house as the first, the greater part as a line-for-line reprint, why should the line-widths have been systematically reduced?[1]

In addition to their part in printing the *Letter*, Bridges and Marlow also admitted to having printed 'the Earl of Shaftesbury's speech in the pamphlet *Two Speeches*, &c., for Thos. Sawbridge'. This is a reference to *Two Speeches. I. The Earl of Shaftsbury's Speech in the House of Lords the 20th. of October, 1675. II. The D. of Buckinghams Speech in the House of Lords the 16th. of November 1675.* The printing history of this is quite complex: there are two editions that claim on their title-pages to have been published in Amsterdam in 1675, though no publisher's name is given in either case and it is almost certain that both were printed in London.[2] The printer's ornaments in the commoner—and almost

---

[1] In this respect it is instructive to compare the two editions of the *Letter* with the first and second editions of *Some Thoughts concerning Education*, both published in 1693 by Awnsham and John Churchill; the second is a line-for-line reprint of the first with a virtually identical title-page. The very inconspicuous differences between them are described in *Some Thoughts concerning Education*, 52–4.

[2] The two editions are not distinguished in Wing (S 2907) or the *English Short-Title Catalogue*. The commoner is a quarto, gathered in fours, with three gatherings, p. 5 being signed B and p. 13 signed C; examples are Bodl., B 2.1(2) Linc., and PRO 30/24/5/292.

certainly earlier—of the two editions are very similar to those used in the first edition of the *Letter* and the corrected state of the second, while the typeface closely resembles that used in gathering A of the second edition.

Another political tract associated with Shaftesbury that appeared around this time was *Two Seasonable Discourses Concerning this present Parliament.*[1] According to its title-page this was published in Oxford in 1675, but here again it is virtually certain that the imprint is false and that the book was printed in London.[2] Like the second edition of the *Letter*, it seems to have been the work of more than one printer: pages 1–4 (the second half of gathering A, which begins with a blank preliminary leaf and the leaf with the title-page) are less well printed than those that follow; their typeface resembles that of gathering A of the second edition of the *Letter*, whereas gatherings B and C were printed with type similar to that used in the remainder of the second edition. Both the *Two Speeches* and the *Two Seasonable Discourses* also resemble the *Letter from a Person of Quality* in matters of layout, such as the style and positioning of page numbers.

Unless further evidence is forthcoming it is not possible to be definite about the circumstances in which the second edition of the *Letter from a Person of Quality* was printed. There are three possibilities:

1. The second edition was printed by the same printers as the first. This is wholly unbelievable in the case of the first gathering, and not at all likely in the case of the others.

2. The second edition was printed by a different printer—or more probably printers—but was still authorized by Shaftesbury. Either the original printer declined to do any more work, presumably because of the rumpus caused by the publication of the first edition, or else Shaftesbury decided that a new printer would be more difficult for the authorities to track down.

3. The second edition was a pirate edition, issued without any authorization by Shaftesbury, and presumably without his knowledge.

The other is also a quarto in fours but has only two gatherings, with p. 9 signed B; the only example examined by the editors is BL, 8122. e. 2 (1). Since this edition incorporates the corrections listed in the erratum slip in the other, it is presumably the later of the two.

[1] Wood remarked that 'though no name is set to them [the *Two Seasonable Discourses*], yet it was very well known to all, that *Shaftesbury* wrot them', *Athenae Oxonienses*, ii. 545.

[2] Madan, *Oxford Books*, no. 3054. Thomas Barlow noted in the margin of p. 10 of his copy of the *Two Speeches* (Bodl., B 2.1(2) Linc.), 'See a booke, call'd ... *Two seasonable Discourses concerning this present Parliament, Oxford printed* (thats false, and in fraudem) *1675*'; cf. Wood, *Athenae Oxonienses*, ii. 545.

The last of these possibilities deserves to be taken seriously: the public burning of the first edition had both increased demand and reduced supply, and though such a venture would have been very risky, the potential profits would have been extremely tempting.[1] Taken overall, however, the evidence described above does suggest that Shaftesbury ordered the printing of the second edition. Bridges and Marlow admitted to having printed the *Two Speeches*, which must have been authorized by Shaftesbury, as well as part of the *Letter from a Person of Quality*, and it would seem more likely that they were involved with the second edition of the *Letter* than the first. If they were responsible for any part of the second edition, then piracy would seem to be ruled out.

Later Editions, 1689–1808

No further editions of the *Letter* were printed until after the Revolution. Early in 1689 it was included in *State Tracts*,[2] along with both the *Two Speeches* and the *Two Seasonable Discourses*. The text of the *Letter* seems to have been taken from the first copy that came to hand—which by ill fortune happened to be the uncorrected state of the second edition[3]—but though the editor must have been working in a hurry, he made a real attempt not only to correct its numerous typographical errors but also to emend the text where its readings appeared to be faulty.

One example of this occurs in the account of the Declaration of Indulgence on page 6, where the uncorrected state of the second edition reads:

Notwithstanding, the Bishops attain'd their Ends fully, the *Declaration* being *Cancelled*, and the great Seal being broken off from it, The Parliament having passed an Act in favor of the dissenters, and yet the sense of both Houses sufficiently declared against all the Indulgence but by *Act of Parliament* ...[4]

The only substantive difference from the first edition here is the unnecessary though not positively ungrammatical insertion of the word

---

[1] Ventures of this sort were far from unknown: there were two pirated editions of Marvell's *The Rehearsal Transpros'd*, one printed in 1672 and the other in 1673 (for details, see D. I. B. Smith's edition, pp. xxvii–xxviii, xxix–xxxi). Locke possessed a copy of the former (*LL* 1931).

[2] *State Tracts: Being a Collection of Several Treatises Relating to the Government. Privately Printed in the Reign of K. Charles II*, 41–56. No publisher is indicated but it was entered in the Stationers' Company register (iii. 343) on 18 January 1689, on behalf of Jacob Tonson.

[3] In a passage on p. 5 the uncorrected state has: '*and that power of our Church should come into the hands of a* Bishop Prince ...'. *State Tracts* follows this; the first edition and the corrected state of the second both have 'Popish Prince'. [4] Below, p. 344.

'the' before 'Indulgence'. Whoever was responsible for preparing the text of *State Tracts* apparently saw nothing wrong in this, but he altered 'an Act' to 'no Act', presumably on the grounds that Parliament had not passed an Act in favour of the dissenters. Shaftesbury would hardly have made such an elementary mistake, and the reading in the first and second editions is almost certainly a corruption.

The most substantial changes in *State Tracts* were due neither to carelessness nor to emendatory sagacity, but to caution. As originally published the *Letter* contained some savage criticism of Danby, Lindsey, Finch, and Lauderdale. The remarks on Finch and Lauderdale were left unaltered, but those on Danby and Lindsey were systematically revised. A sarcastic comment on the vote they gave in 1665 against the extension of the oath in the Five Mile Act to the whole nation was omitted entirely:

But we owe that Right to the Earl of *Lindsey*, and the Lord Treasurer, as to acknowledg that they have since made ample Satisfaction for whatever offence they gave either the Church or Court in that Vote.[1]

A derisive remark about the ability of the two leaders of the court party was retained, but with the reference to Danby excised:

The Keeper [Finch] and ——— are of a just size to this affair, for it is a certain Rule with the Church-Men, to endure (as seldom as they can) in business, Men abler than themselves.[2]

The reason for these changes is not hard to discern. In 1689 Lauderdale and Finch had been dead some years but Danby and Lindsey were very much alive.[3] Similarly motivated changes were made elsewhere. Several disparaging remarks about the bishops were cut, as were unfavourable comments on some of the peers who for various reasons had failed to oppose the Test Bill. Again the reason is a simple one: in 1689 three of those named—Berkeley, Chesterfield, and Fauconberg—were still alive.

Locke returned from Holland in February 1689, nearly a month after *State Tracts* had been entered in the Stationers' Company register. There is no reason for thinking that he was in any way involved in its publication, though he did purchase a copy for his library.[4]

---

[1] *LPQ* 3, below, p. 340.

[2] *State Tracts*, 44; *LPQ* 7 (below, p. 346) has 'The Keeper and the Treasurer'.

[3] Another Tory mentioned unfavourably in the *Letter* (p. 31) who voted for the accession of William and Mary was the Earl of Winchilsea (d. 28 Aug. 1689). In *State Tracts* the passage mentioning him is retained, but he is referred to merely as the 'Earl of *W*.'.

[4] *LL* 2759, bought on 10 Sept. 1689, MS Locke b. 2, fo. 115ʳ. Locke recommended it in 'Some Thoughts concerning Reading and Study for a Gentleman', *Some Thoughts concerning Education*, 323.

A second edition of *State Tracts* was published in 1693. There are minor variations in the text of the *Letter*, but none that suggests any editorial revision.

The next publication of the *Letter* was in 1720 when Pierre Des Maizeaux included it in *A Collection of Several Pieces of Mr. John Locke*. Des Maizeaux was a conscientious editor who made a real (and often successful) effort to produce a better text. He was acquainted with the earlier *State Tracts* edition, and he was not impressed by the work of his anonymous predecessor:

> This Piece [the *Letter*] was grown very scarce. It is true it was inserted, in the year 1689, in the first volume of the *State Tracts*; but in such a manner, that it had been far better not to have reprinted it at all. And indeed, among numbers of lesser faults, there are several whole periods left out; and many places, appear to be designedly falsified. It is likely all this was occasion'd by the Compiler's making use of the first printed Copy that fell into his hands: without giving himself the trouble to look out for more exact ones. That I might not be guilty of the same fault, I have sought after all the editions I cou'd possibly hear of: and have luckily met with two printed in the year 1675, both pretty exact, tho' one is more so than the other. I have collated them with each other, and with that contain'd in the State Tracts.[1]

Des Maizeaux's methods were those of his age: though he discovered that there were two 1675 editions, he seems to have made no attempt to ascertain their order.[2] By modern editorial standards this was a fatal error, but he himself did not see things this way—as his account makes clear, he approached his task in the manner of a classical scholar editing a text from two independent manuscripts:

> In short, that this piece might appear with the best advantage, I have taken the same care, as if I had been to publish some Greek or Latin Author from ancient Manuscripts. And truly, when a man undertakes to republish a Work that is out of print, and which deserves to be made more easy to be come at; be it either ancient or modern, it is the same thing: the Publick is equally abused, if instead of restoring it according to the best editions, and in the most correct manner that is possible, the editor gives it from the first copy he chances to light upon, without troubling himself whether that copy be defective or no.[3]

---

[1] *A Collection of Several Pieces of Mr. John Locke*, sigs. A7ᵛ–A8ᵛ.

[2] Des Maizeaux's description of the two editions as 'both pretty exact, tho' one . . . more so than the other' seems to indicate that he used a copy of the corrected state of the second edition. He never mentioned the existence of the uncorrected state; perhaps he was fortunate enough not to have come across an example, though the number of surviving copies indicates that they were far from uncommon. Unawareness of the uncorrected state would partly explain his harsh comments on the *State Tracts* edition.

[3] *A Collection of Several Pieces of Mr. John Locke*, sig. A8ᵛ.

Further insight into his method of working is provided by the survival among his papers of a mutilated copy of the 1689 *State Tracts* edition, with extensive corrections and instructions to the printer in his hand.[1] There are two series of annotations, one in an ink that has faded and turned brown, the other in a darker ink that is still nearly black. That the notes in brown ink were made first is indicated by the fact that quite a number of them are crossed out in black ink, while the reverse never occurs. It seems that Des Maizeaux began by collating the text in *State Tracts* against the first edition (these are the notes in brown ink), and then repeated the process with a copy of the second edition. The result was that on several occasions he altered his copy of *State Tracts* to give the reading of the first edition, and then deleted the alteration when he saw that the other 1675 edition agreed with *State Tracts*. For example, on page 6 of the first edition the statement is made that 'there were no general Directions given for prosecuting the *Nonconformists*'. In the second edition (and in *State Tracts*) 'prosecuting' was changed to 'persecuting', an inferior reading though not an absurd one. In his copy of *State Tracts*, Des Maizeaux first altered the word to 'prosecuting' and then changed it back to 'persecuting'. Other examples of a similar sequence of corrections can be given.[2]

Where the two 1675 editions contained different readings, Des Maizeaux exercised his own judgement. About one-third of his readings were taken from the second edition, and although some of these are indeed better, others are not. For example, on page 4 the first edition describes Shaftesbury as replying 'half angry' to a question posed by the author of the *Letter*; the second edition has 'all angry', a much inferior reading. On page 5 Shaftesbury explained that the Archbishop of Canterbury '*might become, not only* Alterius Orbis, *but* Alterius Religionis Papa'; the second edition has 'Alterius Regionis Papa'. Admittedly the

---

[1] BL, Add. MS 4224, fos. 228–43. These are leaves cut out of the 1689 edition and then in most cases cut horizontally in two. They are not 'The original proof sheets with corrections', as stated in Schwoerer, *'No Standing Armies!'*, 109 n: they are not proof sheets, and the fact that they are in folio indicates that they cannot possibly have been taken from either of the 1675 editions.

[2] On p. 1 of the first edition the conspiracy unmasked in the *Letter* is described as having been 'hatch't amongst the great Church Men'; in the second edition the spelling was changed to 'hatch'd', and this was followed in *State Tracts*. Des Maizeaux corrected the spelling to that of the first edition but then crossed out his correction. In an account of the Lords debate on p. 15 the question was raised whether the proposed oath 'were meant all for an Oath, or some of it a Declaration, and some an Oath?'; in the second edition and *State Tracts* 'for' was inserted before 'a Declaration'. Des Maizeaux deleted the word and then restored it.

allusion is rather obscure, but there can be little doubt that the first edition preserves the correct reading.[1]

Although Des Maizeaux poured much scorn on the *State Tracts* edition, there are several places where he took readings from it. In the first edition the opening sentence of the *Letter* begins: 'This Session being ended, and the Bill of the *Test* neer finished at the Committee of the whole House . . . '. The second edition and *State Tracts* both have 'Bill of *Test*', and *State Tracts* also has 'being' instead of 'neer' finished, a reading that not only has no textual authority but is also factually wrong—the Test Bill had not been reported from committee when Parliament was prorogued. Des Maizeaux retained 'Bill of *Test*'—he either failed to notice that the first edition had a different reading or else did not think the change worth making—but he dithered about whether to prefer 'neer' or 'being', first deleting the latter and inserting the former, and then writing 'stet' to indicate a preference for the original reading.

It is quite likely that some of these departures from the 1675 editions were unintended and came about because Des Maizeaux prepared his copy for the press by marking up pages removed from *State Tracts*. The disadvantage of this way of proceeding is that the reading in *State Tracts* became the default reading: any errors in it that Des Maizeaux failed to notice would have gone to the printer and (unless subsequently detected) would have appeared in his edition. A possible example can be found in the interview with Clifford, who explained how some addition 'might be easily and undiscernedly made to the Forces now on foot'.[2] The second edition follows the first here, but both *State Tracts* and *A Collection of Several Pieces* have 'undiscernably', which is certainly incorrect: Clifford's point was that the additions to the armed forces would not be noticed, not that they could not be.

By no means all the changes that Des Maizeaux made in his copy of *State Tracts* finally appeared in his edition. On page 23, where the first and second editions describe the Country Lords 'standing up in a clump together', *State Tracts* has 'standing up in a lump together', which is clearly wrong. Des Maizeaux deleted 'lump' and inserted 'clump' in the margin. He seems, however, subsequently to have had second thoughts, because in the published text the entire phrase was omitted; perhaps he thought it inelegant, or perhaps the English idiom escaped him.

---

[1] Pope Urban II is said to have described the Archbishop of Canterbury as 'quasi alterius orbis papa': see p. 342, below.   [2] *LPQ* 4, below, p. 341, italics reversed.

Des Maizeaux was quite ready to suggest emendations in places where it seemed to him that the earlier editions were defective. Both the 1675 editions describe on page 6 how 'some of the most Confiding Justices, were made use of to try how they could receive the Old Persecution'. The word 'receive' is retained in *State Tracts* but it is clearly erroneous; Des Maizeaux altered it to 'revive'. Another plausible alteration was suggested for a passage on page 27 of the first edition, where the peers opposing the bill pleaded 'that they might not be deprived by this dark way of proceeding of that Liberty was necessary to them as Men'. Both the second edition and *State Tracts* follow the first edition here, though an attentive reader should have realized that something had gone wrong. Des Maizeaux added 'which' after 'Liberty', which is clearly an improvement and probably correct; the same reading can be found in one of the early manuscript copies of the *Letter*, British Library Add. MS 74273, discussed below.

Another of the responsibilities of an editor—as Des Maizeaux saw them—was to remove irregularities of spelling and punctuation, and generally to revise the accidentals of the text in accordance with the standards expected by his readers. He found the frequent use of capitals and italics in the two 1675 editions particularly deplorable:

As for what concerns the Impression it self, in order to make it more beautiful, I have been obliged to recede, in several respects, from our usual way of printing; which, if I am allow'd to speak freely, is extreamly vicious. It is a matter of wonder, that in such a Country as this, where there is so much encouragement for Printing, there shou'd prevail a sort of Gothick taste, which deforms our English Impressions, and makes them not a little ridiculous. For can any thing be more absurd, than so many capital Letters, that are not only prefix'd to all nouns substantives; but also often to adjectives, pronouns, particles, and even to verbs? And what shall we say of that odd mixture of Italick, which instead of helping the Reader to distinguish matters the more clearly, does only perplex him; and breeds a confusion shocking to the eye?[1]

His own text was thoroughly reformed in accordance with these principles. The result was a handsome volume, free from 'Gothick' irregularities and fit for a gentleman's library.

Des Maizeaux supplied his readers with a number of explanatory footnotes, some of considerable length, which were subsequently incorporated into the editions of Locke's works. They have not been reproduced here.

---

[1] *A Collection of Several Pieces of Mr. John Locke*, sigs. Aa8ᵛ–Bb1ʳ. These remarks ostensibly apply to all the material Des Maizeaux reprinted and not only to the *Letter from a Person of Quality*, but they are more applicable to the *Letter* than to anything else.

Unused sheets from the 1720 edition were reissued in 1724 with a new title-page describing this as the second edition; copies are very rare, and it is likely that only a few were produced.[1] A true second edition was printed in 1739, this time in folio; the punctuation was systematically revised and more italics were removed, but otherwise the text does not differ significantly from that of the 1720 edition.

Des Maizeaux died in 1745. In 1751 the *Letter* was included in the fifth edition of *The Works of John Locke*, along with all the other material that Des Maizeaux had edited; it has been retained in all the subsequent editions of Locke's collected works. As the *Letter* was reprinted during the eighteenth and early nineteenth centuries the text underwent further modernization in accordance with the literary taste of the age: the italics and capitals that Des Maizeaux had complained of were almost entirely suppressed, the punctuation was systematically revised, several passages were reworded, and a few new errors were introduced. One change that first appeared in the seventh edition of 1768 almost certainly rectifies a previously unnoticed error. On page 16 of the first edition there is this passage:

> For in our *English* Government, and all bounded Monarchys, where the Prince is not absolute, there every individual Subject is under the fear of the King, and His People, either for breaking the Peace, or disturbing the common Interest that every Man hath in it, or if he invades the Person or Right of his Prince, he invades his whole People, who have bound up in him, and derive from Him, all their Liberty, Property, and Safety...[2]

This was followed (with minor variations of punctuation and spelling) in all the manuscripts and early printed versions, but it is clear that something is wrong: the passage makes much more sense when 'or' in 'or if he invades...' is replaced by 'for'.

Though Des Maizeaux's text was used in editions of Locke's works, the publishers of parliamentary histories preferred to go back to *State Tracts*. In 1741 the *Letter* was included in *A Collection of the Parliamentary Debates in England*, and in the following year in *The History and Proceedings of the House of Lords*.[3] The text of the former seems to have been taken predominantly from the 1693 edition of *State Tracts*, but with some readings apparently from Des Maizeaux's edition, that of the latter

---

[1] Yolton, *John Locke: A Descriptive Bibliography*, 366–7.   [2] Below, p. 357.
[3] *A Collection of the Parliamentary Debates in England, from the Year M,DC,LXVIII. To the Present Time*, i. 71–115; *The History and Proceedings of the House of Lords, from the Restoration in 1660, to the Present Time*, i. 129–60.

from the 1741 edition.[1] In 1808 the *Letter* appeared again in the fourth volume of *Cobbett's Parliamentary History of England*, the text having been taken from the 1742 edition.[2]

Manuscript Copies of the Letter

Two contemporary manuscript copies of the *Letter* are preserved in the British Library.

1. Egerton MS 3383 is a volume of miscellaneous political writings, preserved among the papers of the first Duke of Leeds, formerly the Earl of Danby. Folios 58–73 are a separate booklet with leaves measuring 299 × 195 mm, containing copies (in the same hand) of the *Letter from a Person of Quality* (fos. 59ʳ–68ᵛ) and Shaftesbury's speech of 20 October 1675 on *Shirley* v *Fagg* (fos. 69ʳ–72ᵛ); on the front cover (fo. 58ʳ) there is a note 'For Sir Oliver Sᵗ George, Janr. 2ᵈ 1676/7'.[3] The text of the *Letter* was taken from one of the corrected copies of the second edition,[4] and provides therefore a *terminus ante quem* for its publication (though in fact there can be little if any doubt that it was printed very soon after the first edition went on sale). The manuscript appears to have been written by a professional copyist, but the job was not very carefully done: several passages were accidentally omitted and there are a large number of smaller errors. The passages that had been omitted were added in the margin in another hand; the person who did this also made a few other changes, but most of the copying errors remained uncorrected. The marginal insertions were taken from a copy of the second edition, presumably the one that the original copyist had used. There are no major

---

[1] The most significant new reading in both editions is that the reference to 'the Earl of *W.*' [i.e. Winchilsea] in *State Tracts* is wrongly expanded as 'the Earl of Wharton': *A Collection of the Parliamentary Debates*, i. 111; *The History and Proceedings of the House of Lords*, i. 157. Both editions also restore the passage near the end of the *Letter* that had described the dignified clergy as 'the most dangerous sort of Men alive to our *English* Government'.

[2] Appendix V, cols. xxxvii–lxviii; its origins are indicated by the reference to 'the earl of Wharton', col. lxiv.

[3] Oliver St George of Carrickdrumrusk (d. 1696); created baronet (Ireland) 5 Sept. 1660: Burke, *Extinct and Dormant Baronetcies*, 461.

[4] The manuscript does not contain the passage on p. 8 of the first edition that was omitted in the second, and where the corrected and uncorrected states differ it follows the former even when neither is manifestly incorrect: for example, on p. 7 the uncorrected state has '*never forgive any Man the havingornce* [sic] *been in the right*'; the corrected state and the manuscript have '*he*' instead of '*the*' after '*Man*'. The manuscript has none of the distinctive readings of the uncorrected state.

divergences from the second edition, but in small ways the text was frequently and sometimes quite wilfully changed.[1] The punctuation was frequently altered and often improved, and a few of the more obvious errors in the printed text were rectified.

2. The other manuscript, Add. MS 74273, is a very recent acquisition by the British Library (1999), and is of uncertain provenance. It consists of twelve unsewn and unbound bifolia, each measuring 195 × 152 mm; the text of the *Letter* is written in a small, very neat hand on the first forty-seven pages. Since the text includes material omitted in the second edition, it cannot have been taken from it; whether it derives from the first edition or from an earlier manuscript is rather less clear.

It is by no means unlikely that some copies of the *Letter* circulated in manuscript prior to publication, and that Add. MS 74273 is one of these. That Shaftesbury was ready to publicize his own thoughts in this fashion is attested by the survival of so many copies of his letter to the Earl of Carlisle, his *Reasons against the Bill for the Test*, and his speech in the Lords on 20 October.[2] The *Letter* is much longer than any of these, but not too long for a few copies to have been made. Unlike the writings just mentioned, it was a party tract, not a speech or letter associated with Shaftesbury alone, and though it is not known whether he discussed the *Letter* with the other leaders of the country party, it would have been courteous to have let them see a copy before publication. The existence of such copies would explain the curious postscript printed in italics at the end of the published letter: 'Sir, I have no more to say, but begg your Pardon for this tedious Trouble, and that you will be very careful to whom you Communicate any of this.' It is easy to see why a privately circulated manuscript might have contained an injunction of this kind, but it seems out of place in a printed pamphlet on sale to the general public and intended for as wide a readership as possible.

The other possibility is that Add. MS 74273 was copied from the first edition. The public burning on 10 November provided excellent

---

[1] To give only one example, the words on p. 25 of the second edition, 'but they must say with the Lord of *Southampton* upon the occasion of this Oath in the Parliament of *Oxford* . . .' were altered to 'but they must say with the Lord Treasurer Southampton upon the occasion of this oath at Oxford in the parliment held there . . .', BL, Egerton MS 3383, fo. 65ᵛ.

[2] On copies of the letter to Carlisle and the speech of 20 October, see the General Introduction, pp. 80, 92. Another widely circulated writing was the letter to [John?] Bennett on the Dorset by-election, dated 28 Aug. 1675: copies in BL, Add. MS 41568, fo. 3ʳ; Bodl., MS Don. b. 8, pp. 523–4; Hampshire RO, 9M73/G199/7; PRO 30/24/5/288; Wiltshire and Swindon RO, 9/34/15; also recorded in HMC, 9th Report, Appendix, Part II, 450a. It is printed in Christie, ii. 216–18.

publicity—far better than anything Shaftesbury himself could have arranged—and at the same time destroyed a good many copies that could otherwise have been sold. Prices rose dramatically, but copies were still difficult to obtain. It would not therefore be surprising if someone who had not managed to purchase a printed copy borrowed one and commissioned a professional scribe to make a copy.

Both of these rival accounts are quite plausible, and it is not easy to say which is correct. Although there are a large number of differences between the manuscript and the printed text, the great majority can be equally well explained by either hypothesis. For example, in the first edition Shaftesbury is quoted as saying that no government can exist

without a standing Supream Executive power, fully enabled to Mitigate, or wholly to suspend the Execution of any penal Law, in the Intervalls of the *Legislative* power, which when assembled, there was no doubt but <u>wherever there lies a *Negative* in passing of a Law, there the address or sense known of either of them to the contrary, (as for instance of either of our two Houses of *Parliament* in *England*) ought to determine that Indulgence, and</u> restore the Law to its full execution . . .[1]

In the manuscript the passage underlined here is missing and in its place there are the words 'that they might either confirm that Indulgence or'. The simplest explanation is that the copyist was following an earlier version which had this shorter reading, but it is also possible that he was unable to understand the convoluted—and possibly corrupt—passage found in the first edition and therefore discarded it in favour of something shorter of his own devising.

When they differ, the readings in Add. MS 74273 are generally worse than those in the first edition, but not always. One place where the text of the first edition is clearly corrupt and the manuscript has a better reading occurs in the attack on Lauderdale already mentioned: in place of 'executed' in the first edition the manuscript has 'excused'. Another is on page 26: where the first edition has 'the Debates of the proceeding days', the manuscript has 'preceding'. The copyist may have been following an earlier and uncorrupted text, but since in each case it is quite clear what the correct word is, he may have guessed it himself: in both cases the reading in Add. MS 74273 is also found in both Egerton MS 3383 and *State Tracts*, where it can only be due to deliberate or unconscious emendation.[2]

---

[1] *LPQ* 4, below, p. 342, italics reversed.
[2] The change from 'executed' to 'excused' was also made by an early reader in the margin of a copy of the second edition owned by one of the editors.

A less straightforward example can be found on page 8 of the first edition, which reads:

Besides this, the great Ministers of State did in their common publick assure the partie, that all the places of Profit, Command, and Trust, should only be given to the old *Cavalier* . . . [1]

The phrase 'in their common publick' is evidently wrong: a noun has either been left out after 'publick' or else misread as 'publick'. Add. MS 72473 has 'in their common talke'. This is clearly better, but it is far from certain that it is the correct reading, and other solutions have been proposed. In *State Tracts* 'publick' was retained but 'talk' added after it, a change that Des Maizeaux retained. Two unknown readers of the second edition, which has the same reading as the first, inserted 'discourse' or 'discourses' after 'publicke' in their own copies.[2]

Two more examples are of particular interest because they occur in the reports of the protests made in the House of Lords, which are independently recorded in the Lords Journal. As printed in the first edition the second protest states that the Test Bill would 'stick at the very *root of* Government'.[3] Both the manuscript and the Lords Journal have 'strike at', which is obviously the right reading; unfortunately it is so obvious that the change was also made quite independently by both the copyist of Egerton MS 3383 and the editor of *State Tracts*. The other example occurs on page 13, where the first edition has a reference to '*the assistance of the* House of Peers', while both Add. MS 74273 and the Lords Journal have 'Assistants', which is certainly correct;[4] here too the required emendation was made by the editor of *State Tracts*, though not by the copyist of Egerton MS 3383.

If Add. MS 74273 was not derived from the first edition but from an earlier and less corrupt manuscript, one might expect it to contain better readings in some of those places where the text of the first edition is evidently faulty but where the correct reading is not readily apparent. One such passage can be found on page 15 of the first edition. The issue was whether the oath set out in the Test Bill was purely an oath, or partly a declaration and only partly an oath:

There was no small pains taken by the Lord Keeper and the Bishops, to prove that it was brought in; the two first parts were only a *Declaration*, and not an *Oath* . . . [5]

---

[1] Below, p. 347.

[2] Huntington Library, 92417, 'discourse'; editor's copy, 'discourses'.

[3] *LPQ* 10, below, p. 350, italics reversed. The second edition follows the first here.

[4] The Assistants of the House of Lords were the judges and law officers, who could be summoned by a writ of assistance but did not have the right to vote: see Adair and Greir Evans, 'Writs of Assistance, 1558–1700'.   [5] Below, p. 356.

Something is clearly wrong here. In the manuscript the wording and punctuation are altered only slightly, but enough to change the meaning:

> There was no small paines taken by the Lord Keeper and the Bishops, to prove, that as it was brought in, the 2 first parts were only a Declaration, & not an oath . . .

This is very much better. The changes would probably occur to most editors if they considered the passage for long enough, but they eluded both Des Maizeaux and the editor of *State Tracts*, and it is very difficult to believe that they would have occurred to a copyist while he was writing. It would seem more likely that this reading was present in the text from which Add. MS 74273 was copied; if so, this cannot have been the first edition.

A second case is simpler in that it concerns only a single word. On page 22 of the first and second editions there is a reference to 'the *Stat. 25. Hen. 8. cap.* 19 confirmed and received by 1. *Eliz.*'. Something is clearly wrong here: no lawyer would ever describe one statute as receiving another. Either 'revived' or 'renewed' would be far better. Both are possible: 'revived' is palaeographically closer and legally more accurate, and it was the reading chosen by the editor of *State Tracts*, whom Des Maizeaux should have followed but did not; 'renewed' has independent support in that it was used in a speech by Shaftesbury from which this part of the *Letter* was copied with only minor changes.[1] Add. MS 74273 has 'continued', which is much better than 'received' but not as good as either 'revived' or 'renewed'; this suggests that someone—the copyist of Add. MS 74273 or perhaps the copyist of an earlier manuscript from which it had been derived—was following an archetype that had 'received', saw that it must be wrong, and made a conjecture of his own. Whether this was the first edition or an earlier manuscript that already contained the corrupt reading can only be surmised.

Further evidence comes from the lists of signatories to the protests made in the House of Lords. The *Letter* includes the full text of four of these, and at the end of each the names of the peers who signed it are set out in tabular form. In the first edition the list signing the first protest is as follows:[2]

Buckingham	Aylisbury	Howard E. of Berks	Shaftsbury
Bridgwater	Bristol	Mohun	Clarendon
Winchester	Denbigh	Stamford	Grey Roll.

---

[1] See Appendix V; also below, p. 364.
[2] *LPQ* 10, below, p. 350, italics suppressed.

Salisbury	Pagitt	Hallifax	Say & Seal
Bedford	Holles	De la mer	Wharton
Dorset	Peter	Eure	

In the manuscript the table is divided between two pages (15–16), there are twenty-four names, as compared with twenty-three in the first edition, and their order is quite different:

Buckingham	Winchester	Bedford	Grey Roll	Aylsbury
Bridgwater	Salisbury	Dorset	Say & Seal	Bristoll
[*Page-break*]				
Denbigh	Hollis	Wharton	Mohun	Hallifax
Paget	Peter	Howard	Stamford	Delamere
Eure	Shaftsbury	Clarendon	Berks	

One cannot conclude merely from the arrangement of the table in five columns rather than four that it was not copied from the printed version,[1] but the radically different order of the names does suggest this. The presence of an extra name in Add. MS 74273 also requires some explanation, especially since 'Howard' and 'Berks' are in fact the same person, Charles Howard, Earl of Berkshire. It is difficult to see why anyone copying the entry '*Howard* E. of *Berks*' in the first edition should have made such a mistake, and it would seem more likely that the manuscript was copied from a predecessor in which the text was less clear. In the original manuscript of the protest the signatures of the protesting peers are in three columns, but the Earl of Berkshire signed as 'Howard E of Berks' in a large bold hand, the name spreading across two columns.[2] At some stage in the transmission of this list a copyist seems to have misunderstood this as a reference to two different people, Lord Howard and the Earl of Berkshire.

The second and fourth protests were signed by only twelve and sixteen peers respectively, and their names appear in the same order in Add. MS 74273 and the first edition. In the list of peers signing the third protest, however, another complex rearrangement can be seen. In the first edition their names are set out as follows:[3]

Bucks	Denbigh	Hallifax	Holles
Winton	Berks	Audley	De la mer
Bedford	Clarendon	Fitswater	Grey Roll.
Dorset	Aylisbury	Eure	

---

[1] In Egerton MS 3383, which was certainly copied from the second edition, there are six columns (fo. 61^v).   [2] HLRO, Manuscript Journal, 21 Apr. 1675.
[3] *LPQ* 12, below, p. 352, italics reversed.

Salisbury	Shaftsbury	Wharton
Bridgwater	Say & Seal	Mohun

In the manuscript the names are the same but their order is quite different:

Buckingham	Berks	Fitzwater	Grey Roll	Say & Seal
Winchester	Clarendon	Eure	Dorset	Wharton
Bedford	Hallifax	Hollis	Salisbury	Mohun
Denbigh	Audley	Delamere	Shaftsbury	
Bridgwater	Alesbury			

Again the question arises: if the copyist of the manuscript had merely wished to add another column, why should he have shuffled the names so thoroughly that it takes some little time to check that none had been left out or included twice?

The evidence set out above does not point decisively in favour of any hypothesis concerning the origin of Add. MS 74273. The opinion of the present editors is that it was probably not copied from the first edition but from an earlier manuscript, presumably now lost. If this is correct—and the case is clearly far from conclusive—this earlier manuscript is unlikely to have been the original manuscript of the *Letter*, but rather a copy that already contained some of the corrupt readings found in the first edition.

Other Manuscript Sources

It is clear that a considerable part of the *Letter from a Person of Quality* was put together from pre-existing documents. Manuscript copies of a number of these survive and are of considerable value for removing corruptions from the printed text.

1. Four protests, amounting to some 1,300 words in all, were quoted verbatim in the *Letter*, and these may be checked against the original protests in the Lords Journal.[1] Doing so reveals several places where the texts given in the *Letter* are defective. In the fourth protest the first edition has:

and whereas also, upon debate of the same, the *Bill* was ordered, the Third of this instant *May*, that there shall be nothing in this *Bill* . . .[2]

---

[1] Each protest was entered into the Journal by the clerk and then subscribed by each of the protesting peers. In this edition comparisons have been made with the original manuscript Journal, but the printed version is generally accurate.

[2] *LPQ* 13, below, p. 353, italics reversed.

There is something clearly wrong here, but in the second edition the only change made was the removal of the comma after 'ordered'. In *State Tracts* 'the Bill' was altered to 'it', a change that Des Maizeaux retained. This is better, but the Journal gives the correct reading:

And whereas also upon debate of the same bill, It was ordered the third of this instant May, That there shall be nothing in this Bill... [1]

A comparison with the Lords Journal also shows that printers of the 1675 editions completely misunderstood the extent of the fourth protest. In both editions the protests were distinguished from their surroundings by being printed in italics, but this protest was divided into two paragraphs, with the first ten lines of the second set in roman type, leaving the reader quite unclear where the protest began and what exactly it contained.

Shaftesbury subscribed to all four protests and is likely to have been actively involved in their drafting. He would probably have retained copies for his own purposes, and the texts of the protests in the *Letter* were presumably taken from these and not from the Lords Journal. This would explain one curious difference between the *Letter* and the Journal. The *Letter* gives the names of sixteen peers signing the fourth protest, whereas the printed Journal lists only fifteen, Lord Paget's name being omitted. In the manuscript Journal the signature of one peer has been so heavily crossed out that it is now indecipherable; presumably this was Paget, who had changed his mind since signing. [2]

There are other differences between the texts of the protests in the *Letter* and in the Lords Journal. The title of the bill is given (correctly) in the Journal as 'An Act to prevent the dangers which may arise from Persons disaffected to the Government', but the *Letter* has 'danger'. [3] This is probably a corruption that occurred at some stage in the copying or printing of the *Letter*, but it is doubtful whether all the differences between the *Letter* and the Journal can be so explained. These include:

A Letter from a Person of Quality [4]	*Lords Journal* [5]
the priviledges of Sitting	the Priviledge of sitting
the Priviledges and birth-right	the Priviledge and Birthright
the undoubted priviledg of each Peer	the undoubted Priviledge of every Peere

[1] HLRO, Manuscript Journal, 4 May 1675; *LJ* xii. 677. The readings in the two manuscripts of the *Letter* differ only in accidentals from those in the 1675 editions.

[2] *LPQ* 14, below, p. 354; *LJ* xii. 677; HLRO, Manuscript Journal, 4 May 1675.

[3] The two manuscript copies of the bill differ here: Bodl., MS Rawl. A 162, fo. 54ʳ has 'Dangers'; BL, Add. MS 41656, fo. 79ʳ has 'Danger'.

[4] *LPQ* 10–13, below, pp. 349–54, italics suppressed.

[5] HLRO, Manuscript Journal, 21, 26, 29 Apr., 4 May 1675.

to receive the countenance	to receive so much as the Countenance
we humbly apprehend	we do in all Humility apprehend
liberty to debate	Liberty of debates
any Conference or Committee	any Conferences or Committees
the first enacted Clause	the first enacting Clause
upon them as Members	upon the members

Some of these differences may have arisen because the clerk inadvertently departed from the text given him by the peers who had organized the protest, and some from carelessness in the composition, copying, and printing of the *Letter*, but it is also possible that the author of the *Letter* had been supplied with a text of the protest that differed significantly from the one given to the clerk.

2. The content of the Test Bill and its progress in the House of Lords were obviously of great interest to many outside the House, and any oaths that might be imposed were a matter of particular concern. The declaration and oath contained in the bill were recorded in several contemporary letters and other documents, including four of the copies of the *Reasons against the Bill for the Test*.

In the *Letter from a Person of Quality* the text of the oath is as follows:

I A. B. do declare that it is not Lawful upon any pretence whatsoever, to take up Armes against the King, and that I do abhorr that Traiterous position of taking Armes by His authority, against His Person, or against those that are commission'd by Him in pursuance of such Commission; And I do swear that I will not at any time endeavor the Alteration of the Government, either in Church or State, so help me God.[1]

This differs in several small respects from the version given in the two surviving copies of the bill: both omit 'up' in the phrase 'take up Armes' and both have 'Commissions' in place of 'Commission'.[2] 'Commissions' is almost certainly correct: nearly all the other manuscript and early printed sources for the oath have the plural here.[3] It would seem that the singular in the *Letter from a Person of Quality* is a copying or printing

---

[1] *LPQ* 9, below, p. 349, italics suppressed; the texts of the first and second editions are identical here. [2] Bodl., MS Rawl. A 162, fo. 54ʳ; BL, Add. MS 41656, fo. 79ʳ.

[3] Bodl., MS Rawl. D 924, fo. 300ʳ; William Ball to Francis Parry, 6 Nov. 1675, BL, Add. MS 41568, fo. 2ʳ; BL, Harleian MS 5277, fo. 33ᵛ; Hampshire RO, 9M73/G197, pp. 49–50; HMC Portland, iii. 352; Marvell to Hull Corporation, 22 Apr. 1675, *Poems and Letters*, ii. 148–9; NA, SP 29/370/111; PRO 30/24/5/294, p. 11; Surrey History Centre, LM/1331/60, p. 1; Yale, Osborn Shelves, b. 157, unfoliated. Both copies of Orrery's account of his conversation with Danby have 'Commission': National Art Library, MS Forster 47. A. 47, p. 20; BL, Add. MS 70500, fo. 95ʳ. The plural is found in the nearly identical oath in the Five Mile Act, 17 Car. II, c. 2.

error. In contrast with this, it is almost certain that Shaftesbury did intend the words 'take up Armes': the phrase is repeated later in the *Letter* and is alluded to in this form both in the *Letter* and in the *Reasons against the Bill for the Test*.[1] Whether it is historically accurate is another matter—most of the sources for the oath do not include the word 'up', though a few do.[2]

The fullest account of the debates on the Test Bill is found in the *Letter from a Person of Quality* itself, but some additional information is provided by other contemporary sources, including the manuscript minutes from which the Lords Journal was derived.[3] One unsuccessful amendment that attracted particular interest was proposed by the Marquess of Winchester. In the *Letter* it is given as follows:

I do swear that I will never by Threats, Injunctions, Promises, Advantages, or Invitation, by or from any person whatsoever, nor from the hopes, or prospect of any Gift, Place, Office, or Benefit whatsoever, give my Vote other then according to my Opinion and Conscience, as I shall be truly, and really persuaded upon the debate of any business in Parliament; so help me God.[4]

The version given in the manuscript minutes differs in several respects: 'Invitation' appears as 'Invitations', and 'my Vote' as 'any Vote'.[5] 'Invitations' seems preferable, as all the other items in the list are in the plural, and it is also the reading given in three independent witnesses to the amendment; all these, however, agree with the *Letter* in having the reading 'my Vote'.[6]

3. The *Letter from a Person of Quality* also contains material taken from speeches given by Shaftesbury. Manuscripts have survived of two of

---

[1] *LPQ* 16, 17, 18, below, pp. 356, 357, 359; *Reasons against the Bill for the Test*, p. 412.

[2] 'Take up arms': Bodl., MS Rawl. D 924; BL, Add. MS 41568; BL, Harleian MS 5277; Hampshire RO, 9M73/G197, pp. 49–50; Surrey History Centre, LM/1331/60. 'Take arms': Bodl., MS Rawl. A 162; BL, Add. MSS 41656, 70500; HMC Portland, iii. 352; Marvell to Hull Corporation; National Art Library, MS Forster 47. A. 47; NA, SP 29/370/111; PRO 30/24/5/294; Yale, Osborn Shelves, b. 157. The word 'up' is not present in the oath in the Five Mile Act.

[3] *LPQ* 19, 20, 23, 26, below, pp. 360–1, 361, 364–5, 368; HLRO, Manuscript Minutes (Feb. 1674–May 1678), 12, 21 May 1675; Bodl., MS Rawl. D 924, fo. 300ʳ; Bodl., MS Don. b. 8, pp. 519–20; *Reliquiae Baxterianae*, pt. III, § 298.

[4] *LPQ* 28, below, p. 370; apart from one minor difference in spelling, the texts of the first and second editions are identical here.

[5] HLRO, Manuscript Minutes (Feb. 1674–May 1678), 12 May 1675.

[6] Bodl., MS Don. b. 8, p. 519; BL, Harleian MS 5277, fo. 42ᵛ; *Reliquiae Baxterianae*, pt. III, § 296. Elsewhere in the amendment, MS Don. b. 8 and *Reliquiae Baxterianae* have 'hopes or prospects', MS Harl. 5277 'hope or prospect', and HLRO, Manuscript Minutes, xix, 'hopes or prospect'.

these, 'The Earle of Shaftesbury's Speech in the House of Lords against the Test' and the *Reasons against the Bill for the Test*; they are discussed in more detail in a later section of this Introduction. Though these manuscripts are of considerable value for correcting errors in the text of the *Letter*, they need to be used with some caution. They are copies made by unknown amanuenses of writings which, though in some sense ancestral to the *Letter*, are by no means identical with any part of it, and there is no question of automatically preferring any reading they contain.

One passage where the first edition has a reading that may be defective can be found on page 24: 'The Bishops alleadged that *Priesthood* and the *Power* thereof, and the *Authorities* belonging thereunto were derived immediately from *Christ* . . .'. The other printed editions and manuscripts all follow the first edition here, except in accidentals, but five of the six manuscripts of the *Reasons against the Bill for the Test* have the word 'authority' (the sixth[1] does not have the passage in this form). The singular seems intrinsically the better reading and it would seem likely that the plural in the *Letter from a Person of Quality* is a corruption.

A less straightforward example can be found on page 19 of the first edition:

And it is not out of the way to suppose, that if any King hereafter, shall contrary to *the petition of Right*, demand, and levie Money by Privy-Seal, or otherwise, and cause Souldiers to enter, and distrain for such like illegall Taxes . . .[2]

There is nothing obviously amiss here, but all the manuscripts of the *Reasons against the Bill for the Test* have 'demand loan money' instead of 'demand, and levie Money'. There can be no doubt that this is the original reading of the *Reasons against the Bill for the Test*, but it is not possible to say whether Shaftesbury or someone else involved in the compilation of the *Letter* authorized the change, or whether it was made inadvertently by a copyist or by the printer.

Another complicated situation can be found further down the same page:

These instances may seem somwhat rough, and not with the usual *reverence* towards the Crown, but they alleadged, they were to be excused, when all was concerned, And without speaking thus plain, it is refused to be understood . . .[3]

The overall point is reasonably clear, but nobody would call the passage well written. Who are the 'they' in 'but they alleadged', and what exactly

---

[1] Bodl., MS Rawl. D 924 has 'the Preisthood & the Power belonging thereuntto'.
[2] Below, p. 360.
[3] *LPQ* 19, below, p. 360. The later editions and the manuscripts all have the same text as the first edition, with minor variations in accidentals.

is meant by 'it is refused to be understood'? The version in the *Reasons against the Bill for the Test* is shorter and very much clearer:

This may seeme somewhat a rude instance towards the Crown, but it cannot be explained without speaking thus plain . . . [1]

The writer of the *Letter* must have decided to expand this rather abrupt statement, but either he or his copyist(s), or possibly the printer, made a mess of it.

Another passage where the text of the *Letter* may be defective occurs in the report of Shaftesbury's speech on page 21:

He humbly conceived the *Liturgie* was not so sacred, being made by Men the other day, and thought to be more differing from the dissenting *Protestants*, and less easy to be complyed with, upon the advantage of a pretense well known unto us all, of making <u>*alterations* as might the better *unite* us</u>; in stead whereof, there is scarce one alteration, but *widens* the breach . . . [2]

Most of this is the same in the two reports of the speech, but the passage underlined is given differently in each: the copy in the Malmesbury papers has '*Making Abatements as may better invite them*', while John Oldmixon's *History of England* has '*making Abatements as might the better invite them*'.[3] It seems likely, though not certain, that Oldmixon preserved the original reading.

The Composition of the Letter *and its Transmission to the Printer*

It is clear from the evidence described above that the *Letter* was put together from several already existing documents, with bridging passages and other new material supplied by the assembler. If Locke was given the task, then to judge by his (admittedly rather later) practice elsewhere, it is very unlikely that he would have copied the whole work out in his own hand. Either he would have incorporated leaves from the earlier manuscripts into the new work,[4] or else he would have passed on the job of

---

[1] This is the version in Bodl., MS Rawl. A 191. Leicestershire RO, DG7/PP30 and Surrey History Centre, LM/1331/60 differ only in accidentals, while PRO 30/24/5/294 and Yale, Osborne Shelves, b. 157 omit 'somewhat'. The text in Bodl., MS Rawl. D 924 is corrupt here.   [2] Below, p. 363.

[3] Hampshire RO, 9M73/G201/1, p. 2, underlined in MS; *The History of England, During the Reigns of the Royal House of Stuart*, 590, italics in original.

[4] The manuscript of *Some Considerations* includes sheets taken from the 1668/1674 autograph, MS Locke d. 2, fos. 28–37; *Locke on Money*, 126–8. In 'Of Ethick in General', MS Locke c. 28, fos. 146–52, a passage on fo. 151$^{r–v}$ taken over from Draft B (*Drafts*,

copying them to a clerk or a servant in the household. It is impossible to say whether Shaftesbury supervised the composition of the *Letter* at all closely, but he would undoubtedly have wished to check and approve the finished version. Unless time were very short one can assume that a fair copy would have been provided for him, and one would also have been needed for the printer. This could have been the one presented to Shaftesbury, but only if he had approved it without making any alterations—it can safely be presumed that he would not have sent a manuscript with anything in his own quite easily recognizable hand to the printing house, where it might be seized by the authorities and traced back to him; the same is probably true for Locke also. It is much more likely that the printer was supplied with a fair copy in a not very easily traceable hand—either that of a member of Shaftesbury's household or that of a professional copyist whose discretion could be relied on; Ann Brewster's landlord, the former Cromwellian officer who could write 'three or four very good hands', is a strong candidate.[1] If an outsider had been used there is no reason why he should have been told anything about the origins of the work he was copying.

All this copying and recopying would have given plenty of opportunities for errors to creep in. There were copyists in the late seventeenth century who took great care and managed to produce work with very few errors, the writer of the copy of the *Essay concerning Toleration* in the Shaftesbury papers being an example, but they were a small minority: the copyists of Egerton MS 3383 and the other scribal copies of the *Essay concerning Toleration* were unfortunately more typical. There can therefore be little doubt that the manuscript of the *Letter* that was sent to the printer contained many more-or-less trivial errors, and probably a fair number of more intractable corruptions.

One manifestly corrupt passage can be found on page 6 of the first edition. It describes how

those good and sober Men, who had really long feared the Encrease and continuance of *Popery*, had hitherto received, began to believe the Bishops were in earnest . . .[2]

Something is certainly wrong here, but it is far from clear what should be done about it. In Add. MS 74273 the words 'had hitherto received' were omitted, but though this restores both grammar and sense to the passage,

i. 269–70) was copied by Brounower, the newer material in the remainder of the manuscript being in Locke's hand.

[1] General Introduction, p. 97.   [2] Below, p. 344.

it is very unlikely that this was the original reading; if it had been, then the intrusion of the phrase into the first edition would be extremely difficult to explain. The second edition, Egerton MS 3383, and *State Tracts* followed the first here, but Des Maizeaux recognized that something was amiss. His solution was to replace 'continuance' with 'countenance'— i.e. favour or support—and delete 'of', so that his text reads: 'those good and sober Men, who had really long feared the increase and countenance, *Popery* had hitherto received, began to believe the Bishops were in earnest'. This is an improvement, but it is still not right. The passage ought, one feels, to read: 'those good and sober Men, who had really long feared the Encrease of Popery, and the countenance it had hitherto received, began to believe the Bishops were in earnest'. Unfortunately there is no authority whatever for so drastic a change.

Another difficult passage occurs on page 34 of the first edition:

for if that be true, I am sure Monarchy is not to be bounded by humane Laws, and the 8. *chap.* of 1. *Samuel*, will prove (as many of our Divines would have it) the great Charter of the Royal Prerogative, and our *Magna Charta* that says *Our Kings may not take our Fields, our Vineyards, our Corn, and our Sheep* is not in force, but *void* and *null*, because against divine Institution ... [1]

All the printed and manuscript versions say the same, though with minor variations of punctuation and spelling. There is, however, nothing about fields, vineyards, corn, and sheep in Magna Carta;[2] the reference to these was taken from 1 Samuel 8: 14–17, the prophet's warning to the people of Israel of the consequences of choosing to be ruled by a king:

And he will take your fields, and your vineyards, and your oliveyards, even the best of them, and give them to his servants. And he will take the tenth of your seed, and of your vineyards, and give to his officers, and to his servants ... He will take the tenth of your sheep: and ye shall be his servants.[3]

It seems likely therefore that something has gone wrong with the text of the *Letter*. It might at first sight appear that the reference to fields,

---

[1] Below, p. 376.

[2] One cannot be sure which part of Magna Carta the writer of the *Letter* had in mind, but it was probably clause 39 (clause 29 in the 1225 version): 'No free man shall be taken or imprisoned or disseised or outlawed or exiled or in any way destroyed ... except by lawful judgment of his peers or by the law of the land.' Holt, *Magna Carta*, app. 6.

[3] The passage was a famous one and had been discussed from various points of view by James I (*Political Writings*, 66–70), Hobbes (*De Cive*, xi. 6; *Leviathan*, 105), Filmer (*Patriarcha and Other Writings*, 35–7), and Harrington (*Political Works*, 462, 604, 640). It was also discussed in Sidney's *Discourses concerning Government* (III. 3), but is not mentioned in the extant part of the *Two Treatises of Government*.

vineyards, corn, and sheep has simply been displaced from earlier in the sentence, but if it is put back there without any other changes being made, the passage would then read:

for if that be true, I am sure Monarchy is not to be bounded by humane Laws, and the 8. *chap.* of 1. *Samuel*, that says *Our Kings may not take our Fields, our Vine-yards, our Corn, and our Sheep*, will prove (as many of our Divines would have it) the great Charter of the Royal Prerogative, and our *Magna Charta* is not in force, but *void* and *null*, because against divine Institution . . .

This is still not satisfactory: 1 Samuel 8: 14–17 is not a prohibition against kings taking fields, vineyards, and so on, but a warning that this is what they will do. It seems likely, therefore, that in the original version of the *Letter* 1 Samuel was quoted more accurately, as 'Our Kings will take our Fields . . .', and that the quotation was first inadvertently displaced and then altered because in its new position it no longer made sense.

Another possibly corrupt passage occurs on page 16 of the first edition. It begins:

There is a Law of 25 *Edw.* 3. that Armes shall not be taken up against the *King*, and that it is Treason to do so, and it is a very just and reasonable Law; but it is an idle question at best, to ask whether Armes in any case can be taken up against a lawful Prince, because it necessarily brings in the debate in every Man's mind . . . [1]

Most people who had read thus far would presume that the debate would have been whether the prince was indeed a lawful one. The *Letter*, however, continues quite differently:

how there can be a distinction then left between Absolute, and Bounded Monarchys, if *Monarchs* have only the fear of *God*, and no fear of humane Resistance to restrain them.

This seems to come from an entirely different discussion. It is tempting to conclude that there is a lacuna here, and that a significant quantity of text has been lost.

Choice of Copy-Text

The first edition has been taken as the copy-text. Standard editorial practice is that the first edition of any work should be taken as the copy-text except where there are good reasons for thinking that any manuscript

---

[1] Below, p. 356.

copies or later editions contain authorial changes or corrections. There are no such reasons here. None of the changes in the second edition gives any appearance of having been made by Shaftesbury or any of his associates. It is possible that Add. MS 74273 does not derive from the first edition, and therefore that at least some of its better readings are authentic and not merely the result of intelligent emendation, but even if this could be conclusively established there would be no grounds for using it as the copy-text. Even if it is independent of the first edition, it is manifestly not ancestral to it, and it undoubtedly contains a considerable number of copying errors. In any case the first edition is the text that Shaftesbury caused to be issued to the public.

Bibliographical Descriptions

The first edition, Wing S 2897

[within single rules] A | LETTER | From a Person of | QUALITY, | To His | FRIEND | In the | COUNTRY. | [rule] | Printed in Year, 1675. | [rule]

Collation: 4° (209 × 166 mm): π^2 A–I² [$2 signed, I2 unsigned], 20 leaves.

Contents: π1 blank; π2^r: title (verso blank); A–I: text; I2 blank.

Pagination: 40 pages, pp. [4], 1–34, [2], p. 3 misnumbered p. 7, p. 33 misnumbered p. 29, p. 34 misnumbered p. 32.

Copies examined: All Souls College, Oxford, Codrington Library, BW 3. 13 (17); Bodleian Library, B 2. 1 (1) Linc.; British Library, 4103 dd. 2; Leicester University Library, SCM 05531; National Archives, SP 30, case F [two copies]; National Archives, SP 116/413; National Archives, SP 9/247/53; Senate House Library, University of London, [G. L.] 1675; Senate House Library, University of London, B. P. 368 (2); Yale University, Beinecke Library, British Tracts 1675 Sh. 13.

The second edition, Wing S 2897aA

[within single rules] A | LETTER | From a Person of | QUALITY, | To His | FRIEND | In the | COUNTRY. | [rule] | Printed in Year, 1675. | [rule]

Collation: 4° (214 × 169 mm): π^2 A⁴ C²–I² [$2 signed; A3 mis-signed B; A4, I2 unsigned], 20 leaves.

Contents: π1 blank; π2^r: title (verso blank); A–I: text; I2 blank.

Pagination: 40 pages, pp. [4], 1–34, [2], p. 7 misnumbered p. 6.

Copies examined:

Printed from uncorrected outer and inner formes of sheet A: Bodleian Library, Pamph. C. 134 (9); Bodleian Library, G. Pamph. 1125 (10); Cambridge University Library, Syn. 5. 67. 9; Huntington Library, 92417.

Printed from uncorrected outer and corrected inner formes of sheet A: Bodleian Library, Firth e. 9 (1); Bodleian Library, G. Pamph. 1359 (9).

Printed from corrected outer and inner formes of sheet A: All Souls College, Oxford, Codrington Library, BW 3. 11 (4); Bodleian Library, G. Pamph. 1374 (10); Bodleian Library, G. Pamph. 1793 (6); British Library, E 1959 (9); Cambridge University Library, Bb*. 10. 19^8; Christ Church, Oxford, 3. Z. 14 (3); Christ Church, Oxford, 4. A. 215 (4); Christ Church, Oxford, 7. Z. 39 (7); House of Lords Record Office, Main Papers, 8 Nov. 1675, no. 296; House of Lords Library, Case Q3; Huntington Library, 10646; Senate House Library, University of London, [B. L.] 1675 [letter]; Editor's copy.

THE SELECTION OF JURIES

This tract is preserved among the Shaftesbury papers in the National Archives in PRO 30/24/47/30, the file of miscellaneous papers that also contains the *Queries on Scottish Church Government*. It is written on two sheets of paper (fos. 32–5), each folded in half to make two leaves, and apart from a few very short additions is in Locke's hand throughout (Plate 13).[1] The sheets have different watermarks and differ slightly in size, the leaves of fos. 32–3 measuring approximately 302 × 188 mm, those of fos. 34–5, 289 × 193 mm. The two sheets nevertheless clearly belong together; apart from the evident continuity of the text, the catchword at the foot of fo. 33^v is identical with the first word of fo. 34^r. The last three pages (fos. 34^v–35) are blank. Locke numbered the pages, so despite the absence of a title and the rather abrupt beginning there is no reason to think that anything has been lost. The tract was first printed by the editors of this volume in 1997.[2]

The *Queries on Jury Selection*, PRO 30/24/6B/403, are described in a later section.

---

[1] These additions are written, almost certainly by the same writer, in a distinctively legal hand; they add nothing of significance.

[2] Milton and Milton, 'Selecting the Grand Jury: A Tract by John Locke'.

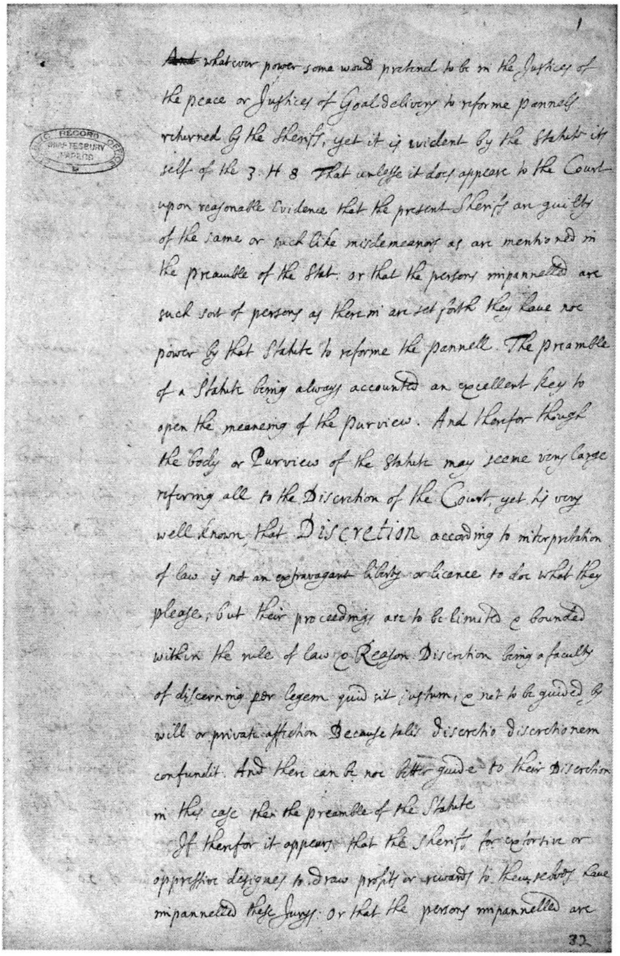
1

~~And~~ whatever power some would pretend to be in the Justices of
the peace or Justices of Goaldelivery to reforme pannells
returned by the Sherif, yet it is evident by the Statute it
self of the 3 H 8 That unlesse it does appeare to the Court
upon reasonable Evidence that the present Sherifs are guilty
of the same or such like misdemeanors as are mentioned in
the preamble of the Stat. or that the persons impannelled are
such sort of persons as therein are set forth they have noe
power by that Statute to reforme the pannell. The preamble
of a Statute being always accounted an excellent key to
open the meaning of the purview. And therfor though
the body or Purview of the Statute may seeme very large
referring all to the Discretion of the Court, yet tis very
well known that Discretion according to interpretation
of law is not an extravagant liberty or licence to doe what they
please, but their proceedings are to be limited & bounded
within the rule of law & Reason. Discretion being a faculty
of discerning per legem quid sit justum, & not to be guided by
will or private affection Because talis discretio discretionem
confundit. And there can be noe better guide to their Discretion
in this case then the preamble of the Statute
If therfor it appears that the Sherifs for extortive or
oppressive designes to draw profit or rewards to themselves have
impannelled these Jurys. Or that the persons impannelled are

32

Plate 13. The Selction of Juries. The National Archives, PRO 30/24/47/30, fo. 32r, reproduced by permission of the National Archives

ENTRIES IN COMMONPLACE BOOKS

The entries printed in this volume come from five commonplace books, Adversaria 1661, MS Locke c. 42, MS Locke d. 1, MS Locke d. 10, and MS Locke f. 24, and from the loose reading notes now collected together in MS Locke c. 33.

1. The commonplace book Adversaria 1661 has been mentioned already in connection with the *Essay concerning Toleration*. Despite its title little if any of the material it contains in fact dates back to 1661: the earliest entries organized according to Locke's system of commonplacing cannot have been made before 1668 and were probably made two or three years later.[1] The notebook seems to have remained in England while Locke was abroad: the earliest stratum of entries it contains are undated but appear from their position in the manuscript to have been made between *c.*1670 and *c.*1675; most of the later entries are dated and were made in 1679–81 or 1691–1700.

Neither of the entries printed here is dated. 'Pactum' is in Locke's hand and appears from its position to have been made in the early 1670s. 'Virtus' is immediately below another entry dated 1681 and cannot therefore have been made before that year. It is in the hand of Locke's manservant Sylvester Brounower, and though it is not signed with Locke's initials it does contain several alterations in his hand; there can be little if any doubt that he was the author.[2]

'Virtus' was first printed by King, and subsequently by Fox Bourne, Wootton, and Goldie.[3] 'Pactum' has not previously been printed.

2. MS Locke c. 33 is not a commonplace book, but consists of two separate series of notes on loose sheets of paper, bound together by the staff of the Bodleian Library after the purchase of the Lovelace Collection. The first series (fos. 1–16) was made during Locke's final months in France and soon after his return to England, the second (fos. 17–42) while he was in Holland. Many of these notes were subsequently copied into Locke's commonplace books; when this was done Locke normally deleted the note with a single vertical line. The notes printed here are themselves undated, but the dates on other notes nearby show that they were all made in March 1679, a month or so before Locke's return to England. All three were first printed by Goldie.[4]

3. MS Locke c. 42 is a pair of notebooks now bound together, though separately paginated; the first (c. 42A) was used for medicine, the second (c. 42B) for ethical and other topics. Locke seems to have started using both of them soon after he arrived back in England in 1679. Most of the entries they contain were taken from his journal or from other notes made

---

[1] Milton, 'The Dating of "Adversaria 1661"', 105–17.

[2] If the entry does belong to the 1690s, it cannot have been made later than 1696 when Brounower left Locke's service.

[3] King (1829), 292–3; Fox Bourne, i. 162–4; *Political Writings*, ed. Wootton, 240–2; Goldie, 287–8.　　　　　　　　　　　　　　　　　　　　[4] Goldie, 273–4.

while he was in France; the entries printed here were copied from notes originally made in MS Locke c. 33.

4. MS Locke d. 1 is another notebook used for ethical topics. Most of the relatively small number of entries it contains, including all those printed here, are dated 1679, but there are also a few from 1692. The notebook seems to have been begun while Locke was still in France, and most if not all of the entries date from the period before his return to England on 30 April.[1] The entries 'Amor Patriae' and 'Patriae Amor' seem from their content to have been written when he was reflecting on his return home.

'Conformitas' can be dated more precisely to the beginning of 1679.[2] The report came from the Cambridge scholar John Covel, who had been chaplain to the Levant Company in Constantinople and was on his way back to England when Locke met him in Paris in the autumn of 1678.[3] Though Covel was the source of the story, the account itself can reasonably be attributed to Locke.

With the exception of 'Idololatria', all the entries included here have already been published. 'Amor Patriae' and 'Patriae Amor' were first printed by King, 'Toleratio' by Inoue, 'Conformitas' by Ian Harris, and 'Amor' by Goldie.[4]

5. MS Locke d. 10 is a large notebook ('Lemmata Ethica') begun in 1659 or 1660 and used during three periods of Locke's life: *c.*1660–*c.*1667, 1681–2, and 1693–1701. All the entries printed here are dated 1682. They were first printed by King in the second edition of his *Life*, and subsequently by Goldie.[5]

---

[1] All the books quoted in the 1679 entries in MS Locke d. 1 were bought during Locke's last six months in France, with the exception of Sir Robert Talbor, Πυρετολογια *A Rational Account of the Cause and Cure of Agues* (London, 1672), *LL* 2828ᵃ. Locke bought a copy of this in December 1680 (MS Locke c. 1, p. 129; Locke to Toinard, 13 Dec. 1680, *Correspondence*, ii. 318), and it is mentioned in a list of books left in London in 1693, MS Locke b. 2, fo. 154ʳ; otherwise there seems to be no record of it among Locke's papers. Notes in his journal show that he was reading the other books cited in the 1679 entries in MS Locke d. 1 between Dec. 1678 and Feb. 1679: MSS Locke f. 3, pp. 380–1; f. 28, p. 33; BL, Add. MS 15642, pp. 1, 5, 6, 18; there are no records of Locke reading any of these works after his return to England.

[2] There is a cross-reference in Locke's journal for 1 Jan. 1679 (NS): 'And how the Nonconformist Protestants were induced by him [Covel] to take the Sacrament kneeleing v: Conformity', BL, Add. MS 15642, p. 1, *Locke's Travels in France*, 253.

[3] Locke to Toinard, 11 Nov. 1678, *Correspondence*, i. 632; MSS Locke f. 3, p. 386; f. 28, p. 80; biographical details in *Correspondence*, ii. 22–3.

[4] King (1829), 291–2; *An Essay concerning Toleration and Toleratio*, ed. Inoue, 47; Goldie, 274–7; Harris, *The Mind of John Locke*, 365.

[5] King (1830), ii. 99–102; Goldie, 291–3.

6. MS Locke f. 24 is a set of quires of paper stored in a parchment box; they were clearly designed to be bound into a small notebook, but in the event this was not done. Most of the entries are on medicine and appear to have been made while Locke was in Holland in 1684 and 1685, with a smaller amount of material from the following years, the last datable entry having been made in 1688.[1] There are also a smaller number of earlier entries, all now crossed through, on ethical topics; these were mostly culled from Locke's reading, but there are a few of his own composition signed with his initials, all of which are printed here. These ethical entries are unlikely to be very much earlier than the medical ones, but whether they were made before or after Locke left England in 1683 is not known. They have not previously been printed.

WRITINGS PRINTED IN THE APPENDICES

The Cancelled Part of the Rough Draft of An Essay concerning Toleration

This is printed in Appendix I. The manuscript has already been described in an earlier section of this Introduction.

Philanthropy, or The Christian Philosophers

Two documents are printed in Appendix II. The first is contained on a single leaf, MS Locke c. 27, fo. 30^c, measuring approximately 295×183 mm; the hand is unidentifiable, but the verso was endorsed by Locke, 'Philanthropy 75'; there are also corrections in Locke's hand. The second is an entry in the pocket memorandum book MS Locke f. 28, pp. 28, 29, 43, and is in Locke's hand throughout. This was subsequently crossed through, presumably by Locke himself, though not so heavily as to prevent it from being fairly easily legible. The keyword 'Philanthropoy' (*sic*) occurs in the left-hand margin at the start of the entry, and again where it continues on pages 29 and 43. Parts of the text are underlined, presumably to indicate quotations from the document on which Locke was commenting.

Philanthropy was first printed in 1972 by Mario Sina, and subsequently by Milton, Wootton, and Goldie.[2] The comments in MS Locke f. 28 have not previously been printed.

---

[1] On fo. 18^v there is an extract from Claude Gendron to Locke, 29 Sept./9 Oct. 1688, *Correspondence*, iii. 503.

[2] Sina, 'Testi teologico-filosofici Lockiani', 59–61; Milton, 'Philanthropy or the Christian Philosophers'; *Political Writings*, ed. Wootton, 232–4; Goldie, 225–6.

Queries on Catholic Infallibility

These queries are printed in Appendix III. They are written in an unidentified hand on a single folded sheet of paper, MS Locke c. 27, fos. 32–3, the individual leaves measuring approximately 299 × 187 mm. The sheet is endorsed 'Queries <u>Popery</u> 75' on its final page, the last two words being in Locke's hand.

The queries were first printed by Sina, and subsequently by Goldie.[1]

Papers relating to the Test Bill

Three writings associated with the Test Bill are printed here: Shaftesbury's *Reasons against the Bill for the Test* in Appendix IV, his speech in the House of Lords in Appendix V, and the Test Bill itself in Appendix VI.

1. Though not printed, Shaftesbury's *Reasons against the Bill for the Test* was widely circulated in manuscript, and six copies are known to exist:

(i) Bodleian Library, MS Rawlinson A 191, fos. 3^r–4^r (**T**). This is a single sheet folded to make two leaves, each measuring approximately 303 × 186 mm; it is now among the Pepys papers and was presumably acquired by Pepys himself, though it is not in his hand. The title is 'Reasons against the Bill for the Test'. On fo. 4^v there is a note: 'May 1675 Reasons against the Test at present under debate in the House of Lords'.

(ii) Bodleian Library, MS Rawlinson D 924, fos. 297^r–300^r (**R**). This occupies pages 1–7 of a 44-page quarto booklet containing speeches, verses, and other political material from the time of Charles II, the leaves measuring approximately 237 × 172 mm. The title is 'Reasons Against the oath of the Bill Intituled an act to prevent Dangers which May arise from persons ill affected to the Government'. It is followed (fo. 300^r) by copies of the oath both as originally proposed in the bill and as revised after debate. The latest datable item in the booklet is a short poem on the prorogation of Parliament on 23 November 1675 (fos. 308^v–10^v); the copy of the *Reasons against the Bill for the Test* is unlikely to be much later than this, and may well be earlier.

(iii) Leicestershire Record Office, DG7/PP30 (**L**). This is a single sheet folded to make two leaves, each measuring approximately 293 × 192 mm. It has the same title as the copy in the Pepys papers. In a space below the title there is a note in the hand of Daniel Finch, later second Earl of

---

[1] Sina, 'Testi teologico–filosofici Lockiani', 62–4; Goldie, 226–30.

Nottingham: 'given out to be fram'd by Lord Shaftesbury & intended to have bin spoken by him in Parliament. but They are rather a collection of all the arguments that were used by the severall Lords that spoke against the Test, & here putt together in one entire discourse.'

It is likely that the manuscript was acquired by Heneage Finch, Daniel's father—as Lord Keeper and one of the chief promoters of the bill he would have been very interested in the activities of its opponents. The texts of this copy and the one in the Pepys papers are quite close, and it can reasonably be presumed it too was made in 1675. The text was written in a neat, old-fashioned hand, with a large number of secretary-hand forms.

(iv) Surrey History Centre, Woking, LM/1331/60 (**S**). This is a single sheet folded to make two leaves, each measuring approximately 230 × 176 mm. The first page is headed 'The test in the house of Peers', and is followed first by a copy of the oath proposed in the Test Bill, and then by a copy of the *Reasons against the Bill for the Test*, under the title 'Reasons against the oath in the Bill entituled an Act to prevent dangers that may arise from persons disaffected to the Government By the Earle of Shaftesbury'. The manuscript was neatly written in a late seventeenth-century hand, probably by a professional copyist, and was presumably made in 1675 or soon afterwards. It was preserved among the papers of the More Molyneux family of Loseley Park, Surrey.[1]

(v) National Archives, Shaftesbury papers, PRO 30/24/5/294 (**N**). This is a folio gathering of eight leaves, each measuring 325 × 212 mm. The speech, which occupies pages 1–10 of the booklet, has the title 'Reasons against the Bill for the Test by the Earl of Shaftesbury. 1675'. It is followed by copies in the same hand of the proposed oath and Shaftesbury's letter to the Earl of Carlisle. This is the only version of the *Reasons against the Bill for the Test* to have been printed, in Christie's life of Shaftesbury.[2]

(vi) Beinecke Rare Books and Manuscript Library, Yale University, Osborn Shelves b. 157 (**Y**). This copy was added at the back of a volume previously used for extracts from Coke's *Institutes*, and is followed by copies of the oath and the letter to Carlisle. The pages measure 197 × 123 mm; in this part of the manuscript they are not numbered, but if they had been the speech would occupy pages 141–55. The title, 'Reasons against the Bill for the Test by the Earl of Shaftesbury A°. 1675',

---

[1] Sir William More (*c*.1644–1684) was elected MP for Haslemere on 7 June 1675, Henning, iii. 96. His sympathies were with the court party, and he was not an associate of Shaftesbury.　　　　　　　　[2] Christie, vol. ii, app. VI, pp. lxxvii–lxxxi.

is nearly identical to that of the copy among the Shaftesbury papers. There is no indication in the manuscript of when it was written, but both spelling and handwriting suggest a date well before 1700.

Textual variations between these six manuscripts show clearly that none of them can have been copied from any of the others. They fall into two families, which may be termed Family A (**L, R, S, T**) and Family B (**N, Y**). Apart from one large and presumably inadvertent omission in **Y**, the texts of the two manuscripts in Family B are nearly identical; both were presumably derived directly or indirectly from an archetype that also included the oath in the Test Bill and the letter to Carlisle.

In those places where material in the *Letter from a Person of Quality* was taken from the *Reasons against the Bill for the Test* the text of the *Letter* is closer to that of the manuscripts in Family A:[1]

T (Family A)	N (Family B)	*A Letter from a Person of Quality*
An other Instance. Put Case a future King of England should be of the same temper with Henry 6.th & should be taken prisoner by any accident by Spaniard Dutch or French which should then be of over growing power enough to give them thoughts of vast Empire, and in Prosecution of that should both with the person & Commission of the King invade England for a Conquest	The other Instance, put case a future King of England should be of the same Temper with Henry the 6th: and should be taken Prisoner by any accident, by Spaniard, Dutch, or French, which should then be an Overgrowing Power, and should both with the Person and Commission of the King Invade England	and if the case should be put, that a future King of England of the same temper with Hen. 6. or Charl. 6. of France, should be taken prisoner by Spaniard, Dutch, or French, whose overgrowing power should give them thoughts of vast Empire, and should, with the person and commission of the King, invade England for a Conquest[2]

[1] Very occasionally the text in the *Letter from a Person of Quality* is closer to that of the manuscripts in Family B. In the discussion of unlawful eviction by soldiers of a standing army all four Family A manuscripts read 'and shooting and even killing those who shall violently endeavour to enter his house'. In both Family B manuscripts and the *Letter from a Person of Quality* the words 'shooting and even' were omitted.

[2] Bodl., MS Rawl. A 191, fo. 3ᵛ; PRO 30/24/5/294, pp. 5–6; *LPQ* 18, below, pp. 358–9, italics suppressed.

Since the endorsement on fo. 4ᵛ of **T** shows that this manuscript had already been put into circulation by May 1675, when the bill was still under debate in the Lords, it is highly probable that the version of the *Reasons against the Bill for the Test* in Family A is the earlier of the two. The differences between the texts in Family A and Family B are too great to have been caused by scribal carelessness, and it would seem likely that someone—either Shaftesbury or one of his associates—decided that revisions were needed. When this was done is not known, but none of the new material in the manuscripts of Family B appears in the *Letter*:

T (Family A)	**N** (Family B)	*A Letter from a Person of Quality*
I beseech your Lordshipps consider how dangerous a thing it is, that by oath and Act of Parliament	I beseech your Lordshipps Consider how dangerous a Thing it is That by Act of Parliament, and your Oaths, they should be secured	To which was replied, that it was a dangerous thing to secure by Oath, and Act of Parliament
they be secured in the Exercise of an authority in the Kings Country and over his Subjects which being received from Christ himselfe cannot be altered or limited by his Laws	in the Exercise of an Authority in the Kings Country, and over his Subjects, which being received from Christ cannot be altered.	those in the exercise of an Authority, and power in the King's Country, and over His Subjects, which being received from Christ himself, cannot be altered, or limitted by the King's Laws;
	How must we again be preistridden? when the Church shall by Act of Parliament and your Oaths be thus seperate and set above the Civill Power. This do's indeed set the Mitre above the Crown.	
and whether this be not directly to sett the mitre above the Crowne.		and that this was directly to set the Mitre above the Crown.[1]

The manuscripts in Family A can in turn be divided into two classes: **L** and **T** have closely resembling texts, as do **R** and **S**. These may be termed Family A(i) and Family A(ii) respectively. A collation of the

---

[1] Bodl., MS Rawl. A 191, fo. 3ᵛ; PRO 30/24/5/294, p. 7; *LPQ* 24, below, p. 366, italics suppressed.

manuscripts shows that where the Family A(i) and Family A(ii) differ, the readings in Family B are much closer to the former.[1] Both the surviving manuscripts in Family A(ii) were carelessly copied, but even the lost sub-archetype from which they were derived must have had a text that is generally inferior to that in Family A(i). There are many minor examples of this, and one blatant one:

T Family A(i)	**S** Family A(ii)	**N** Family B
and for the distinction	& for the distinction	and for the distinction
of power and the	of power &	of power, and the
manner of Exercise	manner of	manner of Exerciseing
there can be noe such		it; there can be no such
distinction here for		distinction here: for
power and the manner		power, and the manner
of excercise	exercise,	of Exercise
are so interwoven	are so inter woven	are so interwoven

Here the text in the Family A(ii) manuscripts is manifestly corrupt. Elsewhere it seems to have undergone a deliberate attempt at improvement. In one part of his speech Shaftesbury warned of the dangers that might arise if an incapable monarch should come to the throne. In **L**, **N**, and **Y** the passage begins (with minor variations of spelling): 'The other Instance, put case a future King of England should be of the same temper with Henry the 6th'.[2] The abrupt 'put case'—which looks very much like a note for a speaker—must surely have been the original reading, but in both the manuscripts of Family A(ii) it was changed to 'suppose'. In the

---

[1] For example: proceeding **LNTY**, procedure **RS**; into possession **LNTY**, in possession **RS**; take the possession **LNTY**, retake the possession **RS**; the man **LNTY**, that man **RS**; who are commissioned **LNTY**, that are commissioned **RS**; those that refuse **LNTY**, them that refuse **RS**; and yet **LNTY**, and **RS**; when taken prisoner **LNTY**, was taken prisoner **RS**; other **LNTY**, otherwise **RS**; should both **LNTY**, should **RS**; put case **LNTY**, suppose **RS**; overgrowing power **LNTY**, overgrown power **RS**; disloyal to him **LNTY**, disloyall **RS**; denied me **LNTY**, denied by them **RS**; Civil Authority **LNTY**, Civil Government **RS**; Being and Ends **LNTY**, End and Being **RS**; answered me **LNTY**, answered **RS**; bore him witness **LNTY**, bears him witness **RS**; very Nature **LNTY**, Nature **RS**; or in whole **LNTY**, or whole **RS**; the manner **LNTY**, manner **RS**; King in Parliament **LNTY**, King and Parliament **RS**; to England **LNTY**, for England **RS**; extreamly invade **LNTY**, invade **RS**; of being sworn **LNTY**, being sworn **RS**; justled aside by this Oath **LNTY**, justled aside **RS**. In two places the readings of the MSS in Family B follow Family A(ii) and not Family A(i): members of both Houses of Parliament **NRSY**, members of both houses **LT**; not to take away **NRSY**, not take away **LT**. In the former 'houses' would have been correct for someone addressing Parliament and was probably the reading in Shaftesbury's own notes; later copyists presumably thought some expansion was needed for the general reader.

[2] **T** has 'An other Instance . . .', but otherwise has the same text, except in accidentals.

Letter from a Person of Quality the passage was again altered: 'and if the case should be put, that a future King of England . . .'.[1]

Where there are differences between the two branches of Family A the text of the *Letter from a Person of Quality* is noticeably closer to that of Family A(i):

T Family A(i)	S Family A(ii)	*A Letter from a Person of Quality*
or thought but that if they had ⟨done⟩[2] other	or thought that if they had don otherwise	or thought but that, if they had done other
to take the possession	to retake possession	to take the possession
the man in possession	that man in possession	the man in Possession
who are commissioned	that are commissioned	who are Commissioned
over growing power	overgrown power	overgrowing power
And the Kings supremacy is justled aside by this oath	and the Kings Supremacy is Justled aside	but the King's Supremacy is justled aside by this Oath

It is clear, therefore, that the writer of the *Letter from a Person of Quality* was working from a manuscript that was much closer to those in Family A(i) than to those in either Family A(ii) or Family B.

2. Only one manuscript of Shaftesbury's speech in the House of Lords against the Test Bill is known, a fair copy in the hand of an unidentified copyist that was presumably once kept with Shaftesbury's own papers but is now among the Malmesbury papers in the Hampshire Record Office, 9M73/G201/1. The text occupies all four pages of a single folded sheet, the leaves measuring approximately 189 × 154 mm; at the head of the first page is the title: '1675 The Earle of Shaftesbury's Speech in the H. of L. against the Test.'

In 1730 the speech was printed in John Oldmixon's *History of England*.[3] Oldmixon's account of the debates in the House of Lords was taken for the most part from the *Letter from a Person of Quality*, which he quoted extensively and ascribed to Locke, but his source for this speech must have been an independent manuscript, since his text is nearly identical to that of the copy in the Malmesbury papers.

---

[1] *LPQ* 18, below, p. 358, italics suppressed.
[2] This word is missing in **T**, and has been supplied from **L**.
[3] *The History of England, During the Reigns of the Royal House of Stuart*, 590.

3. No text of the Test Bill itself now exists among the records of the House of Lords, but at least two copies have survived elsewhere.

(i) Bodleian Library, MS Rawl. A 162, fos. 54^r–55^r. MS Rawl. A 162 is a very large folio paperbook, the leaves measuring approximately 369 × 231 mm, which was used for recording the texts of unsuccessful bills from the reigns of Charles II and James II. The copy of the Test Bill must have been made at least ten years after the events of 1675, since the bill recorded on fos. 49^r–51^r had its first reading in the House of Lords on 30 June 1685.[1]

(ii) British Library, Add. MS 41656, fos. 79^r–80^r is a single folded sheet, the leaves measuring approximately 313 × 209 mm. It was preserved among the papers of the Townshend family, but otherwise nothing is known of its history. The text is written in a neat seventeenth-century hand, and was subsequently checked and corrected by the copyist.

There are minor differences between the two texts, but none of any great significance.

Queries on Jury Selection

PRO 30/24/6B/403 is a single folded sheet of paper, the leaves measuring approximately 300 × 285 mm. It contains a set of queries about jury selection on the first page in the hand of Locke's manservant, Sylvester Brounower, together with replies written overleaf by the barrister William Thomson. Both the queries and the replies are printed in Appendix VII.

II. TRANSCRIPTION OF MANUSCRIPTS AND PRESENTATION OF PRINTED TEXTS

THE TRANSCRIPTION OF MANUSCRIPTS

The works edited from manuscript fall into six classes:

1. Works surviving in a single manuscript written by Locke. These include the First Draft of the *Essay concerning Toleration*, the second addition to the *Essay concerning Toleration* in Adversaria 1661, all the additions to the *Essay concerning Toleration* in MS Locke c. 28, the *Queries on Scottish Church Government*, the Notes on Samuel Parker, the second

---

[1] An Act for the better Preservation of His Majesty's Person and Government, *LJ* xiv. 68.

part of *Excommunication*, the Philanthropy comments, *The Selection of Juries*, and all but one of the entries in Locke's commonplace books.

2. Works surviving in a single manuscript not written by Locke. These are the first addition to the *Essay concerning Toleration* in Adversaria 1661, the entry 'Virtus' in the same commonplace book, the first part of *Excommunication*, *Philanthropy*, the *Queries on Catholic Infallibility*, and the *Queries on Jury Selection*.

3. Works surviving in two manuscripts both written by Locke. There are only two of these: the entries 'Iustitia' and 'Politia', which occur in both MS Locke c. 33 and MS Locke c. 42B.

4. Works surviving in two or more manuscripts, none written by Locke or by the original author if this was someone other than Locke. The examples here are the Test Bill and Shaftesbury's *Reasons against the Bill for the Test*.

5. Works surviving in one or more manuscript copies, not written by Locke, and in one or more early printed editions. The one example of this is Shaftesbury's speech in the House of Lords.

6. Works surviving in two or more manuscripts, some written by Locke and some by other people. The only example here is the *Essay concerning Toleration*.

Though there are two contemporary manuscripts of the *Letter from a Person of Quality*, the main authorities for this work are the early printed editions. It is therefore discussed in the next section.

1. Works Surviving in a Single Manuscript Written by Locke

In the case of the works edited from a single manuscript in Locke's hand, the text reproduced here is the final version, incorporating all additions, deletions, and alterations. The original spelling, capitalization, and punctuation have been retained, with the exceptions noted below. The transcript in Appendix I of the discarded portion of the Rough Draft of the *Essay concerning Toleration* is printed without any editorial emendations.

Spelling. Manuscript forms for words such as 'ag^{n}', 'ag^{t}', 'y^{e}', 'y^{t}', etc. have been replaced by the usual printed forms,[1] as have suffixes such as '-c$\overline{on}$' (-tion) and '-m^{t}' (ment); the dots resembling a colon that sometimes

---

[1] Manuscript contractions have sometimes been retained in the textual apparatus: forms such as 'y^{e}' and 'y^{t}' can easily be confused with each other by careless copyists, and to print them as 'the' and 'your' would obscure this.

follow the last of these have been treated as part of the abbreviation rather than as a punctuation mark. Standard contractions and abbreviations such as 'B^P' (Bishop), 'K' (King), 'Lds' (Lords), 'nāāl' (natural), 'p^t' (part), 'sp^t' (spirit), 'S^r' (Sir), 'X' and 'X^t' (Christ) have been expanded; if there is any uncertainty about the correct reading, the unexpanded form has been given in the textual apparatus. Diphthongs such as 'æ' have been given as separate letters. Ordinal numbers indicated by numerals, as '1st', '2^d', etc. have been retained, though Locke's practice of underlining numerals in the text—for example, '1°'—has not. The ampersand has also been kept, though without any distinction being made between '&' and Locke's more usual form, which resembles a Greek rho; 'ff' at the beginning of words has been transcribed as 'F'. Double hyphens, as in 'Arch = deacon', have been represented by single hyphens. The abbreviation for *id est*, which takes a variety of forms such as '.i.e' and 'i.e', has been given throughout as 'i.e.'

Locke's handwriting is generally clear, and except in passages that were subsequently deleted it is seldom difficult to discern what he intended. A few words can sometimes be hard to distinguish from one another, the commonest example being 'these' and 'those', especially when the former is written with a secretary-hand 'e'; here the general sense of the passage has been taken as a guide. In cases such as 'vertue'/'virtue' where there is no difference of meaning and Locke used both forms, the modern spelling has been preferred where the manuscript reading is uncertain.

Locke often left a small space between two words (or between two parts of the same word), leaving it uncertain whether his intention had been to write one word or two; examples are 'noe body'/'noebody', and 'common wealth'/'commonwealth'. When Locke's own preferred usage is clear it has been followed; otherwise general seventeenth-century usage has been taken as a guide.

Locke sometimes left an apparent break in a word that he is extremely unlikely to have regarded as two words, e.g. 'im position' and 'hind er'; he also sometimes left no discernible break between words that he would surely have regarded as distinct, e.g. 'atonce' and 'astate'. All such words are given in their usual form in the text.

Capitalization. Most of Locke's capital letters (for example, A, B, D, E, F, G) are entirely different from the lower-case forms and cannot be confused with them. In the case of a few letters (notably P, but also O, U, and V) where the resemblance is closer he frequently added a dot inside the capital letter to remove any ambiguity. Locke often began words with a letter which appears intermediate in both formation and size between the capital and the lower-case forms—this is particularly common in the case of the letters C, M, and S, but it also affects K, L, N, and W. Such letters have been represented here by the lower-case form, except when they occur at the beginning of a sentence or in a context where Locke's practice elsewhere makes it reasonable to presume that he would have used a capital. There is no visible difference between Locke's capital I and capital J: the latter has been used when he normally used a lower-case 'j' when writing the word without using capitals (e.g. 'justify'), or in words where the letter 'J' would have been in general use in the late seventeenth century (e.g. 'Jew').

Punctuation. Manuscripts in Locke's own hand range in neatness and legibility from very neatly written presentation copies intended for the Earl or Countess of Shaftesbury to scrawled drafts of letters and other writings. The punctuation in these presentation copies—carefully considered and unmodified by any printing-house conventions—provides the best guide we have to Locke's own preferred practice. When he was writing for himself alone his approach was much more casual. The less carefully a manuscript was written, the less systematic and consistent its punctuation tends to be, and in the case of the rougher drafts such punctuation as there is tends to be scanty, irregular, and occasionally bizarre. The manuscripts used in this volume are of broadly average quality in this respect: the least tidy are the First Draft and the discarded part of the Rough Draft of the *Essay concerning Toleration*, the neatest the Fair Copy of the *Essay* and the tract on jury selection. Differences of ink strongly suggest that some of the punctuation in the undeleted part of the Rough Draft was added later.

Perhaps the clearest evidence of Locke's somewhat casual attitude towards punctuation is provided by a passage in the First Draft of the *Essay* that was recopied with only two minor changes of wording in the Rough Draft, and then again without any further alterations in the Fair Copy. The punctuation changes each time (line-breaks are indicated by the solidus, /):

First Draft	*Rough Draft*	*Fair Copy*
wheras the magistrate is	For the magistrate is	For the magistrate/ is
but umpire between	but umpire between/	but umpire between
man & man/ he can	man & man. He can	man & man. He can
right me against my	right me against my	right me against my
neigbour, but cannot	neigbour but can not/	neigbour, but cannot
defend me against my	defend me against my	defend me against my
god, what ever evill I/	god. What ever evill I	god/ What ever evill I

suffer by obeying him	suffer by obeying/ him	suffer by obeying him
in other things he can	in other things he can	in other things/ he can
make me amends in this	make me amends in this	make me amends in this
world, but if he force	world/ but if he force	world, but if he force
me to a/ wrong religion,	me to a wrong religion,	me/ to a wrong religion,
he can give me noe	he can make me/ noe	he can make me noe
reparation in the	reparation in the	reparation in/ the
other world.	other world.	other world.

It is apparent that most of the differences of punctuation here arise from a general (though by no means universal) disinclination on Locke's part to provide punctuation marks at the end of a line—for example, after 'man & man' in the First Draft, 'this world' in the Rough Draft, and 'against my god' in the Fair Copy. An upper point ' · ' has been used as an editorial stop in places where there is no punctuation mark in the manuscript but the sense of the passage requires a semicolon, colon, or full stop.

Locke often used a light point as a punctuation mark. Such marks have been represented either by a comma or by a full stop in accordance with his normal usage if this can clearly be discerned, otherwise as the sense of the passage seems to require.

Interlinear insertions by Locke frequently end with a full stop which if retained would disrupt the sense of the complete passage. Such stops have been omitted, but their presence is recorded in the textual apparatus.

Deviant punctuation marks such as '..' ',,' and '?.' have been silently reformed to standard forms, as have such oddities as a question mark incorporating a comma rather than a full stop.

Emphasis and underlining. Words and phrases written in larger letters than usual, presumably for emphasis, have been set in bold type. Underlinings in passages where this was not intended as a sign of deletion have been retained; usually this is a sign of quotation from another document.

Lineation. The original lineation of the manuscripts has not been retained and has only been recorded where it is of some relevance to understanding their readings. The catchwords that Locke occasionally employed have not been recorded. Hyphens used to break a word at the end of a line have neither been reproduced nor recorded in the textual apparatus, except in those very few cases where Locke's usual practice was to hyphenate the word in question. Places where a word has been divided between two lines without a hyphen are not indicated in the textual apparatus if there is no uncertainty whether one word or two was intended.

Locke usually began paragraphs without any indentation, so it is not always clear where paragraph breaks occur; in such cases editorial judgement has been exercised. Numbers for paragraphs placed in the left margin have been moved to the left-hand edge of the text.

Deletions. Locke indicated his deletions in a variety of ways. The commonest was by drawing one or two horizontal lines through the deleted material; normally this left it quite easily legible, as did occasional deletions made by drawing a line under the passage (underscoring)—indeed in the later case it is not always possible to be certain that deletion was intended. Sometimes, however, deleted passages were much more heavily obscured, either by a series of loops written over the text or by a second text written on top of the first. Especially in the last case, the original writing can be very difficult and sometimes impossible to read—presumably this is what Locke was aiming at when he took the trouble to delete material in this way. Deletions by underscoring or overwriting are indicated in the textual apparatus.

Locke often altered individual letters within words by overwriting, and in such cases it is not always possible to discern both readings or to determine which came first. All doubtful readings are noted in the textual apparatus.

All changes made to the text as originally written have been recorded in the textual apparatus, with the following exceptions:

1. Deletions of words that had accidentally been written twice. These usually, though not invariably, occur when a word was written at the end of one line and again at the start of the next.

2. Deletions of apparently incomplete words where they are followed without a break by the same word written in full.

3. Corrections made to words that had either been mis-spelt or were apparently regarded by the writer as insufficiently legible.

4. Deletions of a few letters only where the original reading is no longer discernible. Longer illegible deletions have been mentioned in the textual apparatus.

In general corrections and deletions are recorded when they provide evidence of a change in thought or expression, but not when they merely correct errors of writing, or when no change of content can now be discerned.

Emendation. In a relatively small number of cases the text has been emended by the editors.

On a few occasions a word was accidentally omitted. For example, in the manuscript the second sentence of the first draft of the *Essay concerning Toleration* reads, 'I suppose that there only two sorts of things that have a right to toleration'. In the text printed here the word 'are' has been added, between angle brackets: 'I suppose that there ⟨are⟩ only two sorts of things . . .'. If a blot has obscured part of a word, or damage to the paper has made a word at the end of a line incomplete, the text has been emended, with the conjectured letter(s) indicated in the textual apparatus by being enclosed in angle brackets.

Occasionally a word or small group of words was written twice by mistake, but this was not detected and the second occurrence was not deleted. In such cases the appropriate correction has been made in the text and the original reading given in the textual apparatus.

No emendations have been made merely in order to eliminate unusual spellings or to correct defective grammar; if an unfamiliar spelling is one that might mislead a modern reader, an explanatory note has been provided. Merely eccentric spellings that could hardly cause misunderstanding—as in a description in the first draft of the *Essay concerning Toleration* of the Quakers being distinguished from other subjects only by 'the beare keeping on their hats'—have been left unaltered and unannotated.

2. Works Surviving in a Single Manuscript not Written by Locke

The rules given above apply with a small number of modifications to manuscripts that are not in Locke's hand. In these manuscripts deletions and other corrections in the hand of the copyist would have been caused by his misreading or mistranscribing the manuscript from which he was working, and not by any change of thought on Locke's part. Slips of this kind have not been recorded, except in a few cases where the change is of sufficient interest to deserve comment. For example, in *Excommunication* the copyist originally wrote that religious worship 'conteins in it both the wayes of expressing our honour and adoration of the trinity'.[1] He then deleted 'trinity' and replaced it by 'deity'. This seems a curious mistake for a copyist to make, and it raises the question of whether the original manuscript (presumably in Locke's hand) had the word 'trinity' deleted in such a way as to leave it easily legible.

[1] MS Locke c. 27, fo. 29^ar.

In those cases where the survival of Locke's autograph makes it possible to check, none of his copyists—not even Brounower—followed exactly his punctuation or spelling, and many of them evidently preferred their own way of doing things. It can safely be assumed that the same is true of those works that survive only in a single scribal copy. The widespread occurrence of un-Lockean spellings in the manuscript of *Philanthropy* (Appendix II) does not by itself constitute evidence that this work is not by Locke.

In the case of works, or parts of works, that survive only in single manuscripts not written by Locke, the editors have allowed themselves rather more emendatory discretion, especially where manuscripts in which Locke himself made no corrections are concerned. The writers he used as amanuenses varied in competence, and some of them manifestly failed to understand the meaning of what they were copying. The first addition to the *Essay concerning Toleration* in Adversaria 1661 contains some manifestly corrupt readings, such as 'endearement' where 'endeavour' is clearly the correct word, and strange mis-spellings such as 'mothod' for 'method'. Since Locke is unlikely to have written—and certainly cannot have intended—these and similar absurdities, the text has been corrected whenever the true reading is obvious, and the corrupt manuscript reading recorded in the textual apparatus.

Any alterations in these manuscripts that were certainly or probably made by Locke have been recorded.

3. Works Surviving in Two Manuscripts Written by Locke

Two of the three entries in MS Locke c. 33 were copied by Locke into the commonplace book MS Locke c. 42B, and in each case minor revisions were made. MS Locke c. 42B has been used as the copy-text, and all the material variants in MS Locke c. 33 have been recorded in the textual apparatus. In a few places a reading in MS Locke c. 33 has been preferred; in each case the reading in MS Locke c. 42B has been recorded in the apparatus.

4. Works Surviving in Two or More Manuscripts, None Written by Locke

All six manuscripts of the *Reasons against the Bill for the Test* (Appendix IV) are scribal copies which exhibit considerable variations of spelling and punctuation. There is no reason to suppose that any of these manuscripts consistently follows the original in these respects, and it is therefore quite inappropriate to treat any of them as a copy-text. The following editorial principles have therefore been adopted.

When an old spelling has been consistently used—for example, 'soldiers' is spelt as 'souldiers' in all six manuscripts, as well as in the *Letter from a Person of Quality*—it has been retained. When various divergent spellings have been used—e.g. 'maintain', 'maintaine', and 'mainteyne'—the form closest to modern usage has been preferred. The punctuation of the manuscripts has been followed where it is consistent and not seriously misleading. When, as frequently happens, the manuscripts have different punctuation, the variant that makes the sense of the passage clearest has been preferred. Variant readings that are unquestionably due to scribal miscopying have not been recorded in the textual apparatus.

The text of the Test Bill (Appendix VI) is preserved in two manuscripts, neither of which is an official copy, though both were carefully written and apparently preserve the original text of the bill with reasonable accuracy. The editorial policy set out in the preceding paragraphs has been followed here.

5. Works Surviving in One or More Manuscripts, None Written by Locke, and in One or More Early Printed Editions

Only one manuscript of Shaftesbury's speech in the House of Lords (Appendix V) is known, but a version is also preserved in John Oldmixon's *History of England*. The two texts are nearly identical, except in respect of accidentals such as italicization. The contents of the speech are so close to the report in the *Letter from a Person of Quality* that the text of the *Letter* can be used as a guide to possible corruptions in the two texts of the speech (and indeed vice versa). When the speech was adapted for use in the *Letter* the first-person references it contained were changed to the third person, and the present tense was changed to the past, so that 'I beg' became 'he begg'd'. Such changes have not been recorded in the textual apparatus; all other substantive differences between the manuscript, the text printed by Oldmixon, and the first edition of the *Letter* have been recorded. Differences in accidentals between the manuscript and Oldmixon's text have not been recorded.

6. Works Surviving in Two or More Manuscripts, Some Written by Locke

Though superficially similar, the issues involved in editing a work like the *Essay concerning Toleration* are very unlike those that confront an editor of a text from classical antiquity, where the task is to reconstruct, as far as possible, the text of the archetype from which the surviving manuscripts are descended. In the case of the *Essay* the archetype—Locke's autograph—itself survives and does not need to be reconstructed. Readings in the derived manuscripts are occasionally of value where Locke's writing is unclear, but are of interest mainly when they can be used for determining the relations between the manuscripts or when they illustrate Locke's activity in correcting and revising the text.

Departures from the copy-text. The copy-text for the *Essay concerning Toleration* is the Fair Copy **H*** for as long as it exists, and the Rough Draft **H** thereafter. In a small number of places the reading of another manuscript has been preferred to that of **H*** or **H**. These fall into three classes:

1. In a few places a reading in either the First Draft or the discarded part of the Rough Draft has been adopted. An example of this occurs on fo. v^r of **H***, where Locke wrote that the understanding 'can noe more apprehend things otherwise then they appeare, then the eye see other colours then it doth in the rainbow'. In **H** the words 'to it' had been inserted after 'appeare'. **O** originally followed **H***, but when Locke revised it he inserted the same two words in the same place. It would seem that their omission in **H*** was an oversight, and they have therefore been included in the text printed here.

Occasionally it has been possible to use a reading from the First Draft **F** to correct the text of the Rough Draft. On fo. 2^r of **H** the text reads 'men must in this necessary follow'. The sense clearly requires the adverb 'necessarily', which is the reading of both **F** and the derived manuscripts **O** and **P**; **A** originally followed **H**, but the word was then altered to 'necessarily', probably by Locke.

2. Sometimes a change made by Locke in one of the derived manuscripts has been adopted. For example, in **H** (fo. 31^r) one of the numbered proposals at the end of the work is given as 'makeing the termes church communion as large as may be'; **A**, **O**, and **P** all have '... of church communion', the 'of' in **A** having been inserted by Locke. Clearly the latter is the correct reading—what seems to have happened is that Locke started to write 'termes of communion', got as far as the fifth

letter of the last word before deciding that he needed to add the adjective 'church', and deleted not only the unfinished word but also (inadvertently) its predecessor.

A more complex example occurs two pages earlier: in **H** Locke originally wrote that the Japanese rulers allowed Christianity to grow up quietly among them 'fill the doctrine of the church of Rome' gave them suspicions that religion was merely a cover for Spanish imperial aggression. In the four manuscripts the readings are as follows:

fill the doctrine of the church of Rome (**H**, first state)

fill the doctrine of popish preists (**H**, second state)

and fill the doctrine of popish preists (**A**, first state)

till the doctrine of popish preists (**A**, second state, altered by Locke)

till the doctrine of popish priests (**O**, first state; **P**)

till the doctrines of the popish priests (**O**, second state, altered by Locke)

Of these variants, 'fill' is clearly a slip of the pen which the present editors would have corrected even if Locke himself had not already done so in **A**. The plural 'doctrines' is a late change in **O** that has been recorded in the textual apparatus, though excluded from the main text. The insertion of 'the' before 'popish priests' in **O** looks at first sight like another late change, but it is arguable that it is a return to what Locke intended when he crossed out 'the church of Rome' in **H**; the word has therefore been included in the main text. The text adopted in this edition is therefore not quite the same as that of any of the manuscripts: 'till the doctrine of the popish preists'.

3. In a very small number of cases a reading from one of the derived manuscripts has been preferred to the reading of **H** even though there are no alterations by Locke in any of the derived manuscripts. Most of these are mere slips of the pen. For example, on fo. 7^r of **H** Locke refers to 'actions flowing from any of these opinion'. **A** follows **H** here, but **O** and **P** have 'opinions', which is clearly better. If Locke habitually used a spelling that diverges from present-day usage, this has been employed in the correction—for example, on fo. 23^r **H** has 'knowled', and this has been altered to 'knowledg'. If Locke used both modern and older spellings, the former has been preferred.

There are no places in the main part of the *Essay* in which it has been necessary to introduce an editorial emendation unsupported by any of the manuscripts, and only a small number in either the First Draft or the additions to **A** and **O**.

Recording of variants. As originally written, the derived manuscripts **A**, **O**, and **P** contain literally thousands of variants of capitalization, spelling, and punctuation, none of them in any way due to Locke himself. Some indication of their number and variety may be obtained from a comparison of the opening lines of the *Essay*:

H*   In the Question of liberty of conscience, which has for some years beene soe much bandied among us, One thing that hath cheifly perplexed the question, kept up the dispute, & increasd the animosity, hath been (I conceive) this, . . .

A   In the Question of liberty of Conscience which has for some years beene soe much bandied among us one thing that hath cheifly perplexed the question kept up the dispute and increasd the animosity hath been I conceive this . . .

O   In the Question of Liberty of Conscience wich has for some yeares bin so much Bandied amongst us One thing that hath cheifly perplexed the Question Kept up the dispute & increased the Animosity hath bene I conceive, this . . .

P   In the Question of Liberty of Conscience, which has for some years been so much Bandied amongst us, one thing that hath cheifly perplexed the Question, Kept up the dispute, & increased the Animosity, hath been I conceive this, . . .

The writer of **A** seems to have tried following Locke's spelling, though not his punctuation; the writer of **O** manifestly made no attempt to reproduce either. The only variant here of the slightest significance, and the only one recorded in the textual apparatus, is: among **H*****A**, amongst **OP**, and even this is of small importance.

All additions, deletions, and other alterations made by Locke in **H** and **H*** are recorded in the textual apparatus, with the exceptions already described in the section on works surviving in one manuscript. Editorial policy with respect to variant readings in the derived manuscripts is as follows:

The following variants have been recorded:

1. All substantive differences between the manuscripts that provide evidence of the relation between them, even when these appear to have been caused merely by carelessness on the part of the copyist.

2. All substantive additions or alterations made by Locke, except those noted in (4) below.

The following variants have not been recorded:

1. Mere variations of capitalization, spelling, and punctuation. Variants such as 'another'/'an other' or 'thereby'/'there by' have been treated as mere differences of spelling. Spellings which are now reserved for quite separate words but which in the seventeenth century were alternative spellings of the same word, such as 'than'/'then' (with the meaning *than*), have been treated similarly.

2. Minor textual variants caused by scribal miscopying that are of no value for determining the relation between the manuscripts.

3. Corrections made by the copyists themselves of earlier misreadings on their own part.

4. Corrections made by Locke of minor misreadings by the copyists when these merely restore the text to the reading in **H**.

5. Corrections of earlier misreadings which cannot be attributed with any confidence either to Locke or to the original copyist. These all involve only very small alterations, usually only of one or two letters.

Textual Apparatus

The conventions used in the textual apparatus broadly follow those employed in previous volumes of the Clarendon Edition. Where the text is derived from more than one manuscript, the note begins with a lemma indicating the relevant portion of text and closed with a single square bracket. If there is only one manuscript no lemma is used. The following examples are all taken from the *Essay concerning Toleration* but the same conventions have been used elsewhere.

Insertions are indicated by reverse and normal primes preceding and following the inserted material:

of men in] A, O, P | ʻof menʼ in **H*** | of **H**

Here **H*** (copied from **H**) originally read 'in', but Locke then inserted the words 'of men'. A, O, and P follow the revised reading of **H***.

In **H*** and **H** everything is in Locke's hand, so it is not necessary to indicate who was responsible for insertions. In the derived manuscripts changes in Locke's hand are identified explicitly:

an] H, A, P | ʻin their senseʼ an **O** *add. JL*

Here **H**, **A**, and **P** have the reading given in the lemma, while in **O** there is an addition in Locke's hand. Changes in the derived manuscripts that are left unattributed are either probably or certainly the work of the copyist.

Unless indicated otherwise, insertions are interlinear, with the insertion point indicated either by the immediate proximity of deleted material or by a caret. If nothing has been deleted but no caret is present, its absence has been noted.

Deletions are indicated by square brackets enclosing the deleted material:

relation] A, O, P | [weale] relation H

If a deleted passage contained words that had already been deleted on an earlier occasion, this is indicated by a second pair of brackets nested inside the first:

but] H*, A, O, P | [`further then as it refers to the [peace] good of the publique.'] but H

This indicates that in H Locke inserted the phrase 'further . . . publique', deleting the word 'peace' immediately after writing it, but later deleted the entire insertion.

Deletions that appear from the manuscript to have been made sequentially are indicated by separate groups of brackets. The note

injunction] A, O, P | [discipline] [severity] `injunction' H

indicates that in H Locke first wrote the word 'discipline', but then immediately deleted it and replaced it with 'severity', which follows it on the same line; he subsequently deleted 'severity' and inserted 'injunction' in the space above the line. Sometimes insertions were subsequently deleted: the note

losse] A, O, P | [losse] [`restraint'] `losse' H

indicates that Locke originally wrote 'losse', then deleted it and inserted 'restraint' above the line, before finally deciding that the first word was better after all.

Alterations by overwriting are indicated by doubled brackets:

their] H*, A, O, P | [[his]]their H

This indicates that in H the word 'his' was altered to 'their' by over-writing, rather than by the deletion of the one word and its replacement by the other.

Editorial insertions are enclosed in angle brackets. For the most part these are conjectural continuations of words that Locke deleted before he had finished writing them, for example:

fraud] H*, A, O, P | [vio⟨lence⟩] fraud H

The missing letters here are easy enough to guess, especially as 'fraud' is followed by '& violence'. Other conjectures are less certain, for example:

soe] A, O, P | [wh⟨olly⟩] soe H

The identification of the incomplete word is suggested, though not proved, by the sense of the passage in which it occurs: 'the Fanatiques, (whose principles & worship & tempers are soe utterly inconsistent) ...'.

Editorial deletions are enclosed in braces. Superfluous words usually occur because Locke inadvertently wrote a word twice, but are sometimes a result of imprecisely executed insertions and deletions. This example occurs in the First Draft:

{to} [society]/ to

As mentioned below, the solidus / indicates a line-break. Locke started by writing 'to society', but having done so immediately decided that 'to government' would be better; he therefore deleted 'society' before adding the new phrase but forgot to delete 'to' on the previous line.

Uncertain readings are indicated by dots placed beneath the letters that are doubtful:

them] A, O, P | the'm' [ene⟨mies⟩] H

Here the word enclosed in square brackets was so heavily deleted that it is now almost illegible, and its identification is far from certain.

Illegible passages of a few letters only are indicated by dots placed beneath blank spaces, the number of dots being approximately equal to the number of illegible letters:

heard] O, P | heard [of] H | [h⸳⸳d] 'heard' A *alt. JL*

Only the first and last letter of the deleted word in A can now be read. Longer illegible passages are described in the textual apparatus.

Line-breaks are indicated by a solidus (/):

one an other] A, O, P | 'one'/ 'an' other [men]. H *additions on line at line-end and in margin, no carets*

Page-breaks are indicated by a doubled solidus (//):

> understanding] H, A, O, P | understanding// understanding, H*

When the reading in the lemma does not coincide precisely with the reading in any of the manuscripts, this is reported as follows:

> to promote] ed. | ʿto promoteʾ H | *om.* A, O, P

This indicates than an insertion in H—perhaps a late one—was not included in any of the derived manuscripts. The use of 'ed.' in such cases is not a sign of editorial emendation, but in a few places such emendations have been required. In the second addition in Adversaria 1661 Locke wrote 'within a church whereof his is not professor or member'. It is clear that this was a slip of the pen, and the text has accordingly been corrected, with the emendation recorded by:

> he] ed. | his A

Two other features of the method of recording variants used here should be noted. One is that variants in capitalization, spelling, and punctuation in the derived manuscripts have generally not been recorded. For example, in H* (fo. vi^r) Locke wrote that if God should wish to have men forced to heaven, it would be by the inward constraints of his own spirit on their minds 'which are not to be wrought on by any humane compulsion'. H had a different text. All three derived manuscripts follow H*, but O and P differ from it in accidentals:

> which are not to be wrought on by any humaine Compulsion (O).

> which are not to be wrought on by any Humane Compulsion (P).

These differences are not recorded in the textual apparatus, in which the variants are recorded as follows:

> which ... compulsion] H*, A, O, P | ʿwhich compulsion works not on.ʾ H

When a passage was altered in Locke's autograph, but no further substantive variants were introduced in any of the derived manuscripts, these are listed immediately after the lemma, for example:

> companys] A, O, P | [a party] ʿcompanysʾ H

Nevertheless, the accidentals of the word or phrase in the lemma are those of Locke's autograph, and not generally those of the derived manuscripts, which frequently diverge from this—in the case cited here, A has 'companyes', while O and P have 'Companies'.

Editorial comment. Bold capitals are used as sigla for manuscripts and to indicate editorial emendations, as set out above. All other editorial material is in italics, except for the short vertical line used to separate the readings of the different manuscripts. The following abbreviations have been used:

add.	added
alt.	altered
del.	deleted
foll.	followed
illeg.	illegible
not in	used to indicate absence in an earlier manuscript of material found in a later one
om.	omitted; used to indicate absence in a later manuscript of material found in an earlier one

THE PRESENTATION OF PRINTED TEXTS

The only printed text included here is *A Letter from a Person of Quality*.

Editorial Principles

The general policy has been, with some exceptions noted below, to reproduce the text of the first edition, retaining the original spelling, punctuation, italicization, capitalization (including the use of small capitals), and paragraphing. Catchwords, used routinely by the printers of both 1675 editions, have not been recorded. End-line hyphens have not been reproduced or recorded, unless it is clear that the word was intended to be hyphenated (e.g. 'Lambeth-House'). Ligatures have been neither reproduced nor recorded. The long 's' has been rendered as 's'. The letter 'j' has been printed as 'i' in Latin words, and when used in capital form as a personal pronoun. The letter 'l' used to indicate sums in sterling (e.g. 500 *l*.) has been consistently italicized in order to distinguish it from the numeral '1'. Errors in pagination have been corrected.

On pages 1–13 the paragraphs are not separated by a line-space, whereas on pages 14–34 they are, with the exception of the last paragraph on page 18. These variations have not been reproduced.

Manifestly erroneous spellings—'whorthy', 'govenrment', 'dispoxing', 'vavity', 'Protestaant', and 'thrid'—have been silently corrected.

Departures from the copy-text. The first edition was not seen carefully through the press and in many places its text is probably or certainly corrupt. There are therefore a considerable number of places where the editors have decided not to follow it, and have preferred to take readings from one of the manuscripts or one of the later editions. It should be emphasized that, with the possible exception of Add. MS 74273, none of these other sources has any independent authority, in that they all derive directly or indirectly from the first edition. Nevertheless, they are of considerable value where the first edition appears to be corrupt, since they provide evidence of what a number of contemporaries thought the correct readings ought to be.

It was common in the seventeenth century for punctuation to be largely provided by the printer, and presumably this was done here. For the most part the punctuation of the first edition is unobjectionable enough, but in a few places the syntax of the sentence is obscured, as on page 2: 'a pretence shall be taken from the Jealousies they themselves have raised, and a real necessity from the smallness of their Partie to encrease, and keep up a standing Army'. The second edition follows the first here, as does Egerton MS 3383, but in Add. MS 74273, *State Tracts*, and Des Maizeaux's edition the comma after 'encrease' was moved to after 'Partie'. The same change has been made in this edition, and the variant readings recorded in the apparatus.

In accordance with the practice of his time, the compositor of the first edition had frequent recourse to capital letters, occasionally in places where they seem entirely unnecessary, as on page 2: 'for you know That sort of Men are taught rather to obey'. When these superfluous capitals do not appear either in the manuscripts or in the other early printed editions they have been suppressed, though the reading of the first edition has been recorded.

The compositor of the first edition also made considerable use of italic type, both for emphasis and to indicate quotations. Only one change has been made: the Latin phrase 'in terminis' at the foot of page 12 was printed as 'in *terminis*', presumably because the compositor recognized that the second word was not English but thought that the first word was; in this edition both words have been put in italics.

In a few places readings have been taken from other contemporary writings used in the compilation of the *Letter*, including the copies of the

Test Bill, Shaftesbury's speech in the House of Lords, the *Reasons against the Bill for the Test*, and the Lords Journals.

Recording of variants. Several policies have been adopted here, reflecting the different characters of the various printed and manuscript texts.

1. All material variants in the second edition (2) have been recorded in the apparatus; formal variants (spelling, italicization, capitalization and semantically non-significant punctuation) have not.

2. The edition of the *Letter* in *State Tracts* (3) contains several valuable emendations that were retained in subsequent editions, but its main importance is as a historical document. Both the politically motivated excisions and those material variants that may constitute improvements to the text have been recorded in the apparatus; other material variants and formal variants have not.

3. Manuscript alterations made by Des Maizeaux in his copy of *State Tracts* (D) have been recorded when they are of value for the correction of possibly corrupt passages in the first edition, or where they throw light on his editorial methods, but not otherwise.

4. Material variants in *A Collection of Several Pieces of Mr. John Locke* (4) have been recorded when they are of value for the correction of possibly corrupt passages in the first edition, as have significant errata (4er).

5. One emendation has been taken from the seventh (1768) edition of Locke's works (7); otherwise readings from this have not been included.

6. Variant readings in Add. MS 74273 (B) have been recorded, with the exception of obvious corruptions caused by miscopying.

7. Variant readings in Egerton MS 3383 (E) have been recorded when they furnish clear evidence of its derivation from the second edition, or are of value for the emendation of corrupt readings or punctuation, but not otherwise. When there is no mention of E in the textual apparatus, its readings agree with 2, except in respect of italicization, and sometimes capitalization.

8. Variant readings in those passages in the Lords Journal (J) that also appear in the *Letter from a Person of Quality* have been recorded. For this purpose the original manuscript of the Journal in the House of Lords Record Office has been used.

9. Variant readings in Shaftesbury's *Reasons against the Bill for the Test* and his speech in the House of Lords have been recorded when they are directly relevant to the text of the *Letter from a Person of Quality*, but not otherwise. The full texts of both works are given in Appendices IV and V.

Textual Apparatus

Notes are given by means of a lemma, closing with a single square bracket, followed by variant readings:

the] 1, **B** | *om.* 2–4

This indicates that the word 'the' is present in the first edition and Add. MS 74273, but was omitted from the second edition, *State Tracts*, and *A Collection of Several Pieces*.

The second edition is cited as 2 when there is no difference between the uncorrected and corrected states of any of its leaves; when these have different readings they are cited as **2u** and **2c** respectively.

Editorial emendations are indicated by **ed.**

The symbols used for manuscript alterations are those described in the previous section of this Introduction.

TEXTS

AN ESSAY CONCERNING
TOLERATION

Sigla

A   Adversaria 1661, pp. 106–25

F   Huntington Library HM 584, First Draft

H*   Huntington Library HM 584, quire A

H   Huntington Library HM 584, quires B–E

O   Bodleian Library, MS Locke c. 28, fos. 21–32

P   National Archives, PRO 30/24/47/1

An Essay concerning toleration
16<u>67</u>

In the Question of liberty of conscience, which has for some years beene
soe much bandied among us, One thing that hath cheifly perplexed the 5
question, kept up the dispute, & increasd the animosity, hath been (I
conceive) this, that both Partys have with equall zeale, & mistake too
much enlargd their pretensions, whilst one side preach up absolute
obedience, & the other claime universall liberty in matters of conscience,
without assigneing what those things are which have a title to liberty or 10
shewing the boundarys of imposition & obedience

To cleare the way to this I shall lay downe this for a foundation, which
I thinke will not be questiond or denied· I shall assert

That the whole trust power & authority of the magistrate is vested in
him for noe other purpose, but to be made use of for the good, preserv- 15
ation, & peace of men in that society over which he is set, & therefor
that this alone is & ought to be the standard & measure acording to which
he ought to square & proportion his laws: model & frame his government·
For if men could live peaceably & quietly togeather without uniteing
under certain laws & growing into a common-wealth, there would be noe 20
need at all of magistrates or polities, which were only made to preserve
men in this world from the fraud & violence of one an other, soe that

---

Numbers in square brackets are folios of HM 584. Fo. i^r is blank, except for signature letter A
at foot. Fo. ii^r was numbered 1 *by Locke; none of the other pages in quire* A *is numbered. The
folio numbers i–ix have been supplied by the editors; all other folio numbers except the last
(fo. 31) are Locke's*   2–3 An...1667] H* | An...1667 O, P | The Question of
Toleration stated H | *no title in* A, *but keyword* Toleration 67 *in Locke's hand in margin*
4 In] H*, A, O, P | [In the one thing that hath perplex the] / In H   5 among us]
H*, A | [in this part of the world] 'among us' H | amongst us O, P   hath] H*, A, O, P |
has H   6 hath] H*, A, O, P | [[to]]on both] ha[[s]]th H   7 Partys] H*, A, O, P
| [sides] 'partys' H   8 preach] H*, H, O, P | preached A   10 what... liberty]
H*, A, O, P | the matter 'which has a title to liberty' H   11 obedience] H*, A, O, P |
obedience. I H   12 I...this] H, A, O, P | 'I...this' H*   a] H*, A, O, P | sure &
unmoveable H   12–13 which... denied] H*, O, P | which I thinke will 'not' be
denied A *add. JL* | *not in* H   13 [*2nd*] I...assert] ed. | [viz] I...assert H* *pencil
shading over last three words* | viz [I...assert] A | viz O, P | *not in* H   16 of men in]
A, O, P | 'of men' in H* | of H   is] H*, A, O, P | [has] is H   17 that] H*, A, O, P
| *not in* H   19 peaceably & quietly] H*, A, O, P | quietly & peacably H
19–20 without...growing] P | without 'uniteing under certain laws &' growing H* |
without growing H | 'without' uniteing under certaine lawes and without groweing A *alt.*
JL | without Uniteing Under Certain Lawes & [growing] 'entering' O *apparently added in
Hand B*   21 or polities] H*, A, O, P | [or laws] 'or polities' H   were] H*, H, A, P
| are O   22 fraud] H*, A, O, P | [vio⟨lence⟩] fraud H

269

what was the end of erecting of government, [*fo. iii^r*] ought alone to be the measure of its proceeding

There are some that tell us that Monarchy is jure divino· I will not now dispute this opinion but only minde the assertors of it, that if they
5 meane by this (as certainly they must), that the sole supreme arbitrary power & disposall of all things is & ought to be by divine right in a single person, 'tis to be suspected they have forgot what country they were borne in, under what laws they live & certainly cannot but be obleigd to declare Magna Charta, to be downe right heresie. If they meane by
10 Monarchy jure divino, not an absolute but limited monarchy, (which I thinke is an absurdity: if not a contradiction) they ought to shew us his charter from heaven, & let us see where god hath given the magistrate a power to doe any thing but barely in order to the preservation of his subjects in this life, or else leave us at liberty to beleive it as we please
15 since noe body is bound, or can allow any ones pretensions to a power, (which he himself confesses limited) farther then he shews his title.

There are others who affirme that all the power & authority the magistrate hath is derivd from the grant & consent of the people, & to those I say it can not be suppdd the people should give any one or more
20 of their fellow men an authority over them for any other purpose then their owne preservation, or extend the limits of their jurisdiction beyond the limits of this life

[*fo. iv^r*] This being premisd that the magistrate ought to doe or medle with noething but barely in order to secureing the civill peace &

---

1 erecting] H*, A, O, P | the erecting H   alone] H*, A, O, P | only H   2 measure] H*, A, O, P | measures H   3 [*1st*] that] H*, A, O, P | men who H   divino] A, O, P | divino [& that the magistrate der⟨ives⟩] H* | divino, & that the magistrate [hold⟨s⟩] derives his authority immediately from heaven. H   4–12 they … where] A, O, P, *with variants noted below* | they … [that] 'where' H* | they/ they say that H   6 single] H*, O, P | [simple] 'single' A *alt. JL*   7 'tis] O, P | [that] 'tis H* | its [suspected] A   were] H*, A, P | are O   11 is] H*, A, P | *om.* O   his] H*, A | this O, P   12 hath] H*, A, O, P | has H   13–14 of his subjects] H* | of his [people] 'subjects' H | of his subject[ion]s A | '& welfare' of his subjects O *add. JL* | & welfare of his subjects P   14 or] H*, A, O, P | they [oug⟨ht⟩] are bound to shew us his commission from heaven, or H   it] H*, H, A, P | *om.* O   15 is] H*, A, O, P | [can] is H   15–16 to … limited)] H*, A, O, P | *not in* H   17 who affirme] A, O, P | who [believe] affirme H* | assert H   19 those] H*, A, O, P | these H   or more] H*, A, O, P | 'or more' H   20 their] H*, A, O, P | [his]their H   fellow] H*, A, O, P | [number a power] of their fellow H   an authority] H*, A, O, P | a'n' [jurisdiction] 'authority' H   21 jurisdiction] H*, A, O, P | [power] 'jurisdictions' H   22 limits] H*, A, O, P | affairs H   life] *foll. in* H *by* or give the[m] 'magistrate' a right to choose 'for them' their way to salvation (5) *with space about 3 cm deep at foot of page*   23 premisd] H*, A, O, P | then [establishd] 'certain' H   24 secureing] H*, O, P | the secureing H | 'secureing' A *inserted by Locke in space left by copyist*

proprietys of his subjects, Let us next consider the opinions & actions of men, which in reference to toleration divide them selves into 3 sorts

1 Are all such opinions & actions as in them selves concerne not government or society at all, & such are all puerly speculative opinions, & Divine worship   5

2 Are such as in their owne nature are neither good nor bad but yet concerne society & mens conversations one with an other, & these are all practicall opinions & actions in matters of indifferency

3 Are such too as concerne society, but are also good or bad in their owne nature & these are morall virtues & vices   10

1 I say that the first sort only viz speculative opinions & Divine worship are those things alone which have an absolute & universall right to toleration. 1st Puerly speculative opinions as the beleife of the trinity, purgatory transsubstantion, Antipodes, Christs personall reigne on earth, &c, & that in these every man has his unlimited freedom appears. Because 15 bare speculations give noe bias to my conversation with men, nor haveing any influence on my actions as I am a member of any society, but being

1 proprietys] H*, H, A | propriety O, P   2 divide them selves] H*, A, O, P | may be divided H   3] H*A | three H, O, P   sorts] H*, H, P | [parts] `sorts' A *alt. JL* | sorts. `either they' O *addition on line in Hand B*   3 all] H*, A, O, P | [all puerly speculative opinion⟨s⟩] H   opinions & actions] H*, A, O, P | *not in* H   4 or] H*, A, O, P | & H 5 worship] H*, H, A, P | Worshipp. `or' O *addition on line in Hand B*   6 as . . . yet] H*, A, O, P | [opi⟨nions⟩] as H   their] H*, A, P | the O   7 conversations] H*, A, O, P | conversation H   9 good] H*, A, O, P | beleivd good H   10 [*2nd*] &] H*, H, A, P | or O   11 1] H*, A, O, P | H *has heading* The question of toleration stated. *at top of page, marking start of original composition*   say] H*, A, O, P | [suppose] `say.' H | suppose F 11–12 the . . . have] H*, A, O, P | there are only two sorts of things that have in their owne [righ⟨t⟩] nature H | there are only two sorts of things that have F       12 absolute &] H, A, O, P | `absolute &' H*   13 1st] H*, A, O, P | The first is all H   [*2nd*] the] H*, A, O, P | a H, F   14 Antipodes] H*, F, A, O, P | [Antipodes] H *del. by underscoring* 15 has] H*, H, A, P | hath O   15–272.11 Because . . . noe] H*, A, O, P *with variants noted below. In* H *the order of the sentences is different:* because noe man can give an other a power over that, over which he has noe power him self. now that a man can not command his owne understanding, or positively determine to day what opinion he will be of to morrow is evident from experience & the nature of the understanding, which can noe more apprehend things otherwise then they appeare `to it' then the eye see other colours then it doth in the rainbow whether those colours be really there or noe. Besides bare speculations giving noe bias to my conversation with men, nor haveing [noe]any influence on my actions as I am member of any society, but being such as would be still the same with all the consequences of them, though there were noe other person besides my self in the world, cannot by any means either disturb the state or inconvenience my neigbour, & soe come not within the magistrats cognizance.   16 give] H*, A, O, P | gieveing H   conversation] H*, H, A, P | conservation O   17 [*1st*] any] H*, A, O, P | [noe]any H   on] H*, H, A, P | one O   a] O, P | *not in* H, H*, A

271

such as would be still the same with all the consequences of them though there were noe other person besides my self in the world cannot by any means either disturbe the state or inconvenience my neigbour & soe come not within the magistrates cognizance. Besides noe man can give an other
5 man power, (& it would be to noe purpose if god should) over that over which he has noe power himself, now that a man cannot command his owne understanding, [*fo. v'*] or positively determin today what opinion he will be of tomorrow, is evident from experience, & the nature of the understanding, which can noe more apprehend things otherwise then they
10 appeare to it, then the eye see other colours then it doth in the rainbow whether those colours be really there or noe.

The other thing that has just claim to an unlimited toleration is the place time & manner of worshiping my god. Because this is a thing wholy between god & me & of an eternall concernment above the reach & extent
15 of polities & government which are but for my well being in this world. For the magistrate is but umpire between man & man. He can right me against my neigbour but cannot defend me against my god. What ever evill I suffer by obeying him in other things he can make me amends in this world, but if he force me to a wrong religion, he can make me noe
20 reparation in the other world. To which let me adde that even in things of this world over which the magistrate has an authority, he never does, & it would be unjustice if he should, any farther then it concerns the good of the publique injoyne men the care of their private civill concernments, or force them to a prosecution of their owne private interests,
25 but only protects them from being invaded & injurd in them by others,

<hr>

4 magistrates] H*, H, P | magistrate A, O   5 man] H*, A, O, P | a H   (& . . . over] H*, A, O, P | over H   7 understanding] H, A, O, P | understanding// understanding H*   8 [*2nd*] the] H*, H, A, P | 'the' O *add. JL*   10 to it] P | 'to it' H, O *add. JL* | *om.* H*, A   eye] H*, H, O, P | eyes A   then . . . rainbow] H*, H, A | in the Rainebowe then it doth O, P   11 really] H*, H, O, P | 'realy' A *add. JL* at line-end noe] *foll. in* O *by addition in Locke's hand on fo.* 22' I . . . societie *printed below, p. 308*   12 has] H*, H, A, P | hath O   to] H*, A, O, P | [in all times & place⟨s⟩] to H   an] H, A, O, P | [tole⟨ration⟩] an H*   13 god.] H, F | god H*, A | God. O | God, P   14 me &] H*, A, P | me, & is H, F | [[one]]me '&' O *alt. JL*   15 government] H*, H, A, P | Governments O   17 god.] H, A | god H* | god, F | God O | God. P   19 me to a] H*, H, F, O, P | to A   20–273.20 To . . . end] H*, A, O, P *with variants noted below* | 'To . . . end' H   21 magistrate] H*, A, O, P | [magistrate] 'he' H   22 unjustice] H*, H, A | injustice O, P   22–23 any . . . publique] H*, A, O, P | 'any farther then it refer to the good of the publique' H   23 private] H*, O, P | 'private' H, A *add. JL in both MSS*   24 interests] H*, A, O, P | interest H   25 but] H*, A, O, P | ['further then as it refers to the [peace] good of the publique.'] but H   from being] H*, A, O, P | 'from being' H   in them] H*, A, O, P | 'in them' H

(which is a perfect toleration)· & therefor we may well suppose he hath noe thing at all to doe with my private interest in an other world, & that he ought not to prescribe me the way or require my diligence in the prosecution of that [*fo. vi^r*] good which is of a far higher concernment to me then any thing within his power, haveing noe more certain or more 5 infallible knowledg of the way to attain it then I my self, where we are both equally inquirers both equally subjects, & wherein he can give me noe security, that I shall not, nor make me any recompense if I doe miscarry. Can it be reasonable that he that cannot compell me to buy a house should force me his way to venture the purchas of heaven, that he that can not in 10 justice prescribe me rules of preserveing my health, should injoyne me methods of saveing my soule, he that cannot choose a wife for me should choose a religion. But if god (which is the point in question) would have men forcd to heaven, it must not be by the outward violence of the magistrate on mens bodys, but the inward constraints of his owne spirit on 15 their minds, which are not to be wrought on by any humane compulsion, The way to salvation not being any forced exterior performance, but the voluntary & secret choise of the minde, & it cannot be supposd that god would make use of any means, which could not reach but would rather crosse the attainment of the end. Nor can it be thought that men should 20 give the magistrate a power to choose for them their way to salvation

1 (which ... toleration)] H⁺O | `which ... toleration'. H | which ... toleration: A | (which ... Toleration.) P    2 private interest] H⁺, A, O, P | [concernment] `private interest' H   &] H⁺, A, O, P | [nor ough⟨t⟩ to] & H   3 require] H⁺, A, O, P | [compell] `exact' H    4 that] H, A, O, P | that// that H⁺    5–6 [*1st*] more ... infallible] H⁺, A, O, P | certaine`r' `or more infallible' H    6–7 where ... subjects] H⁺, A, O, P | `where ... subjects' H   8 me] H⁺, H, O, P | [mee] A   9 me] H⁺, H, O, P | *om.* A   buy a house] H⁺, A, O, P | [keepe my estate] `buy a house' H *del. by underscoring*    10 venture ... of] A, O, P | `venture the' purchas `of' H⁺ | [gain] `purchas' H   11 rules] H⁺, A, O, P | [methods] `rules' H *del. by underscoring*    12 a wife for me] H⁺, H, O, P | [me] a wife for A    should] H⁺, A, O, P | shall he H    16 which ... compulsion] H⁺, A, O, P | `which compulsion works not on.' H   17 to salvation] H⁺, A, O, P | thither H   exterior] H⁺, A, O, P | [& unwilling] `exterior' H    performance] H⁺, A, O, P | performances [of] H    18 choise] H⁺, A, O, P | [perf⟨ormance⟩] [consent] `choise' H   19–20 make ... end] H⁺, O, P | make [choise] `use' of any means which could not reach `but did rather crosse the attainment of the end.' H | `make use of any means that could not reach but would rather' rather crosse the attainment of the end. A *add.* JL   20–21 Nor ... salvation] H⁺, A, O, P *with variants noted below* | [Therefor it cannot be supposd that men should give the magistrate a power to choose for them their way to salvation,] H *del. by underscoring;* [5] *in margin*   21 the magistrate] H⁺, H, F, O, P | `the' magistrates A *add.* JL

which is too great to give away, [*fo. 2ʳ*] if not impossible to part with, since
whatever the magistrate injoynd in the worship of god, men must in
this necessarily follow what they them selves thought best, since noe
consideration could be sufficient to force a man from or to that, which he
5 was fully perswaded, was the way to infinite happinesse or infinite misery.
Religious worship being that homage which I pay to that god I adore in a
way I judg acceptable to him, & soe being an action or commerce passeing
only between god & my self, hath in its owne nature noe reference at all to
my governor or to my neigbour, & soe necessarily produces noe action
10 which disturbs the community. For [*fo. 1ᵛ*] kneeling or siting at the
sacrament can in its self tend noe more to the disturbance of the government, or injury of my neigbour, then siting or standing at my owne
table; weareing a cope, or surplice in the church, can noe more alarme, or
threaten the peace of the state, then wearing a cloak, or coat in the market;
15 being rebaptisd noe more make a tempest in the common wealth then it
doth in the river, nor then barely washing my self would doe in either.
[*fo. 2ʳ*] if I observe the friday with the Mahumetan, or the Saturday
with the Jew, or the sunday with the Christian, whether I pray with or
without a forme, whether I worship God in the various & pompous
20 ceremonies of the papists, or in the plainer way of the Calvinists. I see noe
thing in any of these, if they be donne sincerely & out of conscience, that
can of its self make me, either the worse subject to my prince, or worse
neigbour to my fellow subject. unlesse it be, that I will out of pride, or

---

1 is] H*, A, O, P | [was] [`is a power'] H *addition del. by underscoring* | was F   away,]
foll. by full stop in H*, *which ends here.* Endorsement Toleration 67/ A *on fo.* viiiᵛ. *The
undeleted part of* H *begins 6 lines from the top of fo.* 2ʳ   2 whatever] H, F, A, P | what
soever O   3 necessarily] F, O, P | necessary`ly' A *add. JL* | necessary H
4 to . . . man] F, O, P | `to . . . man' H | to force `a man' A *add. JL*   5 misery.] *foll. in*
H *by deleted addition on fo.* 1ᵛ [`Nor doe I finde that the doctrine of Christianity does
invest the magistrate with any new power or give him any more jurisdictions in matters
of religion, then he had before from the nature of government in generall, or the
constitution of that society he is is intrusted with'] (1) *in margin and at start of addition*
6 Religious] A, O, P | [Besides] religious H   7 acceptable] A, O, P | [pleasein⟨g⟩]
acceptable H   or] A, O, P | [where] or H   10 For] H, O, P | [ffar] `for' A
alt. JL   10–16 kneeling . . . either] A, O, P *with variants noted below* | `kneeling . . . either'
H, *addition on fo.* 1ᵛ, (2) *in margin and at start of addition*   10 at] H, A | in O, P
12 injury] H, O, P | injureing A   13 cope] H, O, P | cap[e] A   alarme] H, A, P |
`in its own nature' alarume O *add. JL*   14 peace] A, O, P | [state] peace H   coat]
H, A, P | a Coate O   market] A, O, P | [exchange] `market' H   15 common wealth]
A, O, P | [state] `common wealth' H       16  [2nd] in] A, O, P | `in' H   17 if] H, O, P
| For if A   20 papists] H, P | papist A, O   Calvinists] O, P | Calvinist H, A
22 worse] A, O, P | `worse' H

overweeningnesse of my owne opinion, & a secret conceit of my owne infalibility, takeing to my self some thing of a god like power, force & compell others to be of my minde, or censure & maligne them if they be not. This indeed often happens, but tis not the fault of the worship, but the men. & is not the consequence [*fo. 3ʳ*] of this or that forme of ₅ devotion, but the product of depravd ambitious human nature, which successively makes use of all sorts of religion, as Ahab[1] did of keepeing a fast: which was not the cause, but means, & artifice to take away Naboths viniard. which miscariages of some professors doe noe more discredit any religion, (for the same happens in all) then Ahabs rapine does fasting. ₁₀

From what is premisd I thinke will follow.

1 That in speculations & religious worship every man hath a perfect uncontrould liberty, which he may freely use without or contrary to the magistrates command, without any guilt or sin at all: provided always that it be all donne sincerely & out of conscience to god according to the ₁₅ best of his knowledg & perswasion. But if there be any ambition, pride, revenge, faction, or any such aloy that mixes its self with what he calls conscience, soe much there is of guilt, & soe much he shall answer for at the day of judgment

2 I say all practicall principles, or opinions by which men thinke ₂₀ themselves obleigd to regulate their actions, with one an other. [*fo. 2ᵛ*] As that men may breed their children or dispose of their estates as they

---

1 &] H, O, P | or A   2 takeing] A, O, P | [&] takeing H   3 &] H, A | or O, P
5 forme] A, O, P | [kinde] 'forme' H   7 successively] A, O, P | [often] 'successively'
H   religion] H, O, P | religions A   keepeing] A, O, P | [fasting] keepeing H
11 will follow] H, O, P | [comes after] will follow A | *foll. in* O *by addition*
Twill . . . worship *in Locke's hand on fo. 22'; printed below, p. 308*   12 1] A, O, P | *not
in* H   13 uncontrould] H, A | uncontroul[[ed]]able O *alt. JL* | Uncontroulable P
16 ambition] A, O, P | [mixture] ambition H   17 what] H, A, P | [[what]]which]
'that which' O *alt. JL*   19 judgement] *foll. in* H *by passage del. by overwriting;* Quaere
in margin Whether it will not hence also follow, that any man or party keepeing within the
former rules may not lawfully by force [. . . .] defend them selves against the magistrate that
would by force impose any thing on them in opinion or worship, where neither of them
directly tend to the disturbance of his government since in this he 'would then' invades them
in that, over which he has noe power nor 'doe' they owe him any more subjection then they
doe to a foraigne prince, whose subjects they are not.   20 say] A, O, P | [suppose]
'say' H   by] A, O, P | [that] [[m⟨en⟩]]by H   21 with] H, A, P | [which] 'with' O *alt.*
JL   one an other] A, O, P | 'one'/ 'an' other [men]. H *additions on line at line-end and in*
margin, no carets   21–276.1 As . . . fit] A, O, P | {as,} [that faith is not to be kept with
hereticks, that a man is bound to propagate & publish his religion & endeavour to gain
proselyts to it] 'As . . . fit.' H *addition on fo. 2ᵛ, (5) in margin and at start of addition*

---

1 1 Kgs. 21: 1–16.

please, That men may worke or rest when they thinke fit, that polygamy & divorce are lawfull or unlawfull &c. [*fo. 3^r*] These opinions [*fo. 4^r*] & the actions flowing from them with all other things indifferent, have a title also to toleration; but yet only soe far, as they doe not tend to the
5 disturbance of the state, or doe not cause greater inconveniences, then advantages to the community. For all these opinions, except such of them, as are apparently destructive to humane society, being things either of indifferency or doubt, & neither the magistrate, or subject being on either side infallible, he ought noe farther to consider them, then as the
10 makeing laws, & interposeing his authority in such opinions may conduce to the wellfare & safety of his people. But yet noe such opinion has any right to toleration, on this ground, that it is a matter of conscience, & some men are perswaded that it is either a sin or a duty. Because the conscience, or persuasion of the subject, cannot possibly be a measure by
15 which the magistrate can, or ought to frame his laws, which ought to be suited to the good of all his subjects, not the persuasions of a part: which often happening to be contrary one to another must produce contrary laws. & there being noe thing soe indifferent which the consciences of some or other, doe not check at,[1] a toleration of men in
20 all that which they pretend out of conscience they cannot submit to, will wholy take away all the civil laws, & all the magistrates power, & soe there will be noe law, nor government if you deny the magistrates authority in [*fo. 5^r*] indifferent things, over which it is acknowledgd on all hands that he has jurisdiction. And therefor the errors, or scruples of any ones

---

2 &c] H, A, P | *blank space of about 1 cm in* O   2–4 [*2nd*] & ... also] **ed.** | `&' [with] the actions flowing from them `with [with] all other things indifferent,' have a title ⟦t⟨o⟩⟧also **H** | with all other things indifferent `& the actions flowing from them have a title' also **A** *add. JL* | & the actions following from them with all other things indifferent have a title also **O, P**        5 not] **P** | [not] **H, A** *del. with single line in* **H** | `not' **O** *add. JL*   6 the] **A, O, P** | the the **H**   7 society] **H, O, P** | societys **A**   8 indifferency] **H, O, P** | indifferences **A**   11 people.] *foll. in* **H, A** *by* ×× *placed vertically*   has] **H, A, P** | hath **O**   16 [*1st*] the] **A, O, P** | `the' **H**        persuasions] **A, O, P** | [phansys] `persuasions' **H** *del. by underscoring*   a] **H, O, P** | *om.* **A**   17 which] **A, O, P** | [which often happening to be contrary one] which **H**   one to another] **A, O, P** | `one to another' **H** (*no caret*)        18 the] **A, O, P** | ⟦some⟧the **H**        19 men in] **A, O, P** | `men in' **H**   20 which they] **A, O, P** | [men] `which they' **H**        22 deny] **O, P** | [take away] `deny' **H** | deny deny **A**   23 indifferent] **H, A, P** | different **O**   24 has] **H, P** | hath **A, O**

---

[1] check at: to stop short (as if checked), pull up, *OED* check; a term originally from falconry.

conscience, which lead him to, or deterr him from the doeing of any thing, doe not destroy the magistrates power nor alter the nature of the thing which is still indifferent. For I will not doubt here to call all these practicall opinions in respect of the Law maker indifferent, though perhaps they are not soe in them selves. For however the magistrate be ₅ perswaded in him self of the reasonablenesse, or absurdity; necessity, or unlawfulnesse of any of them, & is possibly in the right· yet whilst he acknowledges him self not infallible, he ought to regard them in makeing of his laws, noe otherwise, then as things indifferent, except only as that being injoynd, tolerated, or forbidden, they carry with them the civill ₁₀ good & wellfare of the people. Though at the same time he be obleigd strictly to suit his personall actions, to the dictates of his owne con-science, & persuasion in these very opinions. For not being made infal-lible in reference to others, by being made a governor over them, he shall hereafter be accountable to god for his actions as a man, according as they ₁₅ are suited to his owne conscience & perswasion; but shall be accountable for his laws & administration as a magistrate, according as they are intended to the good, preservation, & quiet of all his subjects in this world as much as is possible, which is a rule soe certaine & soe cleare, that he can scarce erre in it unlesse he doe it wilfully. ₂₀

[*fo. 6'*] But before I proceed to shew the limits of restraint & liberty in reference to these things, It will be necessary to set downe the severall degrees of imposition, that are, or may be usd in matters of opinion.

1 The prohibiting to publish or vent[1] any opinion.

2 Forceing to renounce or abjure any opinion. ₂₅

3 Compelling to declare an assent to the contrary opinion

There are answerable to these the same degrees of toleration

From all which I conclude

---

1 deterr] **O, P** | deterrs **H, A**   2 magistrates] **H, O, P** | magistrate **A**
3 still] **A, O, P** | 'still' **H**   indifferent.] *foll. in* **H, A** by ×× *placed vertically*
7 &...right.] **A, O, P** | '&...right' **H**   10 civill] *ed.* | 'civill' **H, A** *add. JL in both MSS* | *om.* **O, P**   13–14 being...by] **H, O, P** | 'being made infallible to others by' **A** *add. JL*   15 hereafter] **A, O, P** | [after] hereafter **H**   17 a] **O, P** | ⟦m⟨agistrate⟩⟧a **H** | *om.* **A**   18–19 in this world] **A, O, P** | 'in this world' **H**
20 erre] **A, O, P** | [except] erre **H**   21 restraint] **O, P** | [obe⟨dience⟩] restraint **H** | restraint[s] **A** *deletion not certain*   22 these] **H, A** | those **O, P**

---

[1] vent: to give outlet, expression or utterance, *OED* vent, 3b.

1 That the magistrate may prohibit the publishing of any of these opinions when they tend to the disturbance of the government because they are then under his cognizance & jurisdiction

2 That noe man ought to be forcd to renounce his opinion, or assent
5 to the contrary, because such a compulsion can not produce any reall effect to that purpose for which it is designd· it can not alter mens minds it can only force them to be hyppocrits, & by this way the magistrate is soe far from bringing men to imbrace the truth of his opinion, that he only constrains them to lye for their owne. Nor does this
10 injunction at all conduce to the peace or security of the government but quite the contrary. because hereby the magistrate does not make any one [*fo. 7ʳ*] to be one jot the more of his minde, but to be very much more his enemy.

3 That any actions flowing from any of these opinions, as also in all other
15 indifferent things, the magistrate has a power to command or forbid soe far as they tend to the peace, safety or security of his people, whereof though he be judg, yet he ought still to have a great care, that noe such laws be made, noe such restraints establishd, for any other reason, but because the necessity of the state, & the wellfare of the people cald for
20 them. & perhaps it will not be sufficient, that he barely thinks such impositions, & such rigor necessary, or convenient, unlesse he hath seriously & impartially considerd, & debated whether they be soe or noe: & his opinion (if he mistake) will noe more justifye him in the makeing of such laws, then the conscience, or opinion of the subject, will excuse him,
25 if he disobey them; if consideration, & enquiry could have better informd either of them. And I thinke it will easily be granted, that the makeing of laws to any other end, but only for the security of the government &

---

2 when...government] A, P | 'when...government' H | when 'in them selves' they tend to the disturbance of the Government O *add. JL*   3 they are then] A, O, P | [it]they [is] 'are then' H   jurisdiction] *foll. in* H by [as a matter which may disturbe the government]   6 effect] H, O, P | effects A   to...can not] A, P | 'to...can not' [or] H | to that purpose for which it is designed it can O   7 can] H, A, P | can not O   force them] A, O, P | [mak⟨e⟩] [by this way.] force [men] 'them' H   7–8 the...is] A, O, P | yᵘ ᵉ [are] 'magistrate is' H   9 constrains them] A, O, P | [forc⟨es⟩] constrains [him]them H   their] A, O, P | [his]their H   10 injunction] A, O, P | [discipline] [severity] 'injunction' H   11 not] A, O, P | 'not' H   14 opinions] O, P | opinion H, A   16 tend] H, O, P | [tend ['give'] power] 'tend' A *second insertion by Locke*   security] A, O, P | [any other bene⟨fit⟩] security H   21 rigor] A, O, P | rigo[rs]r H   or] A, O, P | [&]or H *order of writing not certain*   22 they] H, O, P | it A   26 the] A, O, P | [such] the H   27 security] A, O, P | [preservati⟨on⟩] security H

278

protection of the people in their lives, estates, & libertys, i.e. the preservation of the whole, will meet with the severest doome at the great
trybunall, not only because the abuse of that power & trust which is in the
lawmakers hands, produces greater & more [*fo. 8ʳ*] unavoidable mischeifs
then any thing else to man kinde; for whose good ŏnly governments were 5
instituted, but also, because he is not accountable to any tribunall here.
Nor can there be [*fo. 7ᵛ*] a greater provocation to the supreme preserver
of mankinde, then that the magistrate should make use of that power,
which was given him only for the preservation of all his subjects, &
every particular person amongst them, as far as it is practicable; should 10
misuse it to the service of his pleasure, vanity, or passion, & imploy it to
the disquieting or oppression of his fellow men, between whome &
himself in respect of the King of Kings there is but a small & accidentall
difference. [*fo. 8ʳ*]

4 That if the magistrate in these opinions or actions by laws & 15
impositions endeavour to restrain, or compell men, contrary to the
sincere perswasions of their owne consciences; they ought to doe what
their consciences require of them, as far as without violence they can;
but withall are bound at the same time quietly to submitt to the
penaltys the law inflicts on such disobedience. for by this means they 20
secure to them selves their grand concernment in an other world, &
disturb not the peace of this; offend not against their allegiance either to
god or the king but give both their due the interest of the magistrate &
their owne being both safe. & certainly he is an hyppocrite, & only
pretends conscience & aims at something else in this world, who will not 25

4 lawmakers] A, O, P | [magistrates] ʿlawmakersʾ H   hands] H, A, P | hand O   &
more] A, O, P | & more// & more H   unavoidable] H, O, P | ʿunʾavoydable A *alt.*
JL   5 then...else] A, O, P | ʿthen...elseʾ H   7–13 Nor...difference] A, O, P,
with variants noted below | ʿNor...differenceʾ H, *first four words added at paragraph-end,
remainder on fo. 7ᵛ*; (7) (*no caret) at line-end and at start of addition*   9 his] A, O, P |
[the] his H   12 disquieting or] A, O, P | ʿdisquieting orʾ H   13 in respect] O,
P | ʿin respect [of]ʾ H | ʿin respectʾ A *inserted by Locke in space left by copyist*
16 endeavour to] A, O, P | ʿendeavour toʾ H   18 require] A, O, P | [perswade]
require H   19 withall] A, O, P | with/ all H   quietly] A, O, P | ʿquietlyʾ H
20 penaltys] H | penalty A, O, P   law] A, O, P | ʿlawʾ H   on] A, O, P | [for] [s⟨uch⟩]on
H   21 secure] H, A, P | ʿsecureʾ O *inserted by Locke in space left by copyist*   grand]
H, A, P | ground O   22–23 offend...due] A, O, P *with variants noted below* | ʿ[&]
offend[s]...dueʾ H *final three words in margin*   22 their allegiance] O, P | [[his]]their
[duty] ʿallegianceʾ H |the ʿirʾ allegiance due A   23 king] O, P | kings H | king[s] A
give] O, P | give[s] H, A   24 an] H, A | a O, P

by obeying his conscience, & submiting also to the law, purchase heaven
for himself & peace for his country though at the rate of his estate,
liberty, or life its self. But here also the private person, as well as the
magistrate in the former case, must take great care that his conscience,
5 or opinion doe not mislead him, in the obstinate persuit or flight of
any thing as necessary or unlawfull, which in truth is not soe,
least by such an error, or wilfulnesse, he come to be punished for the
same disobedience in this world & the other too. For liberty of conscience being the great priviledg of the subject, as the right of imposeing
10 is the great [*fo. 7ᵛ*] prerogative of the magistrate, they ought the more
narrowly to be watcht, that they doe not mislead either magistrate,
or subject: because of the faire praetenses they have. those wrongs
being the most dangerous, most carefully to be avoided, & such
as god will most severely punish, which are donne under the specious
15 semblances & appearances of right. [*fo. 9ʳ*]

3 I say There are, besides the two former, a third sort of actions, which
are thought good or bad in them selves viz the Dutys of the second table[1]
or trespasses against it or the morall vertues of the philosophers. These
though they are the vigorous active parte of religion, & that where in
20 mens consciences are very much concernd, yet I finde, that they make
but a litle part of the disputes of liberty of conscience. I know not
whether it be, that if men were more zealous for these, they would be lesse
contentious about the other. But this is certaine, that the countenanceing
vertue is soe necessary a prop to a state, & the allowance of some vices

---

1 by] A, O, P | [purchase heaven for himself] by **H**   also] A, O, P | ˋalsoˊ **H**   to] H,
A, P | ˋtoˊ O *add. JL*   2 at] H, A, P | as O   5 doe] H, A, P | [[to]]doe O *alt.
JL*   not] H, O, P | ˋnotˊ A *add. JL*   in] A, O, P | [to that] [& make] in H   6 not
soe] O, P | not ˋsoeˊ **H** (*no caret*) | not A   7 least] A, O, P | [ˋleastˊ] [& soe he be
p⟨unished⟩] [ˋhap⟨pen⟩ˊ] least **H**   8–15 For...right] A, O, P, *with variants noted
below* | ˋForˊ...ˋrightˊ **H** *first part added at foot of page, remainder on fo. 7ᵛ; (6) in
margin and at start of addition*   9 the right] A, O, P | [liberty] ˋthe rightˊ **H**
13 to] H, A | are to O, P   14 as god will] O, P | as god [doth] ˋwillˊ **H** | ˋgodˊ will A
add. JL (no caret)   15 appearances] H, O, P | appeareance A   16 I say] A, O,
P | ˋI sayˊ **H**   17 thought] H, A, P | [thought] O *del. JL*   18 or...it] A, O, P
| ˋor...itˊ **H**   morall] A, O, P | [virtues] morall H   of] A, P | [& vices] of H | ˋ& vicesˊ
of O *add. JL*   19 vigorous] A, O, P | [most] vigorous **H**   &] A, O, P | [& our
devotion to god] & **H**   21 part] H, O, P | ˋpartˊ A *add. JL*   23 contentious] H,
P | contentions A, O   is] H, A, P | ˋisˊ O *add. JL*   the countenanceing] A, O, P | ˋthe
countenanceingˊ **H**   24 allowance] H, A, P | allowances O   some vices] A, O, P |
ˋsomeˊ viceˋsˊ **H** | vice F

---

[1] The last six of the Ten Commandments, Exod. 20: 12–17.

brings soe certaine a disturbance & ruin to society, that it was never
found that any magistrate did; nor can be suspected, that he ever will,
establish vice by a law, or prohibit the practise of virtue. which does by
its owne authority, & the advantages it brings to all goverments sufficiently
establish its self every where. Yet give me leave to say, however strange it 5
may seeme, that the Lawmaker hath noe thing to doe with morall virtues
& vices, nor ought to injoyne the dutys of the 2^d table any otherwise, then
barely as they are subservient to the good & preservation of mankinde
under government· For could publique societys well subsist, or men
enjoy peace or safety, [*fo. 10^r*] without the inforceing of those dutys, by 10
the injunctions & penaltys of laws, It is certaine the Law maker ought not
to prescribe any rules about them. but leave the practise of them intirely
to the discretion & consciences of his people. For could even these morall
vertues & vices be seperated from the relation they have to the weale of
the publike, & cease to be a meanes to setle or disturbe mens peace & 15
proprietys, they would then become only the private & super-politicall
concernment between god & a mans soule, wherein the magistrates
authority is not to interpose. God hath appointed the magistrate his vice
gerent in this world, with power to command; but tis but like other
deputys, to command only in the affairs of that place where he is vice 20
gerent· who ever medle in the concernments of the other world, have noe
other power, but to intreate, & perswade. The magistrate hath noe
thing to doe with the good of mens soules or their concernments in an
other life but is ordeind, & intrusted with his power, only for the quiet &

---

1 a] F, A, O, P | [&] a H   4 its] H, F, O, P | [his] 'its' A *alt. JL*
5 establish...self] H, F, A, P [Establish its selfe] 'deserve the countenance of the
Magistrate' O *alt. JL*   give] A, O, P | [even ⟨....⟩ these m] give H   7 dutys] H, O,
P | duty A   any] A, O, P | [more then] any H   9 societys] H, O, P | society A
10 enjoy] A, O, P | ejoy H   or] H, A, P | [or]and O *alt. JL*   safety] A, O, P | safety//
safety H | In H *fo. 9^v has endorsement* Toleration 67/ B   *in* H *signature* C *in direction
line*   inforceing] H, A, P | [[forreign]inforceing O *alt. JL*   11 penaltys] H, O, P |
penalty A   maker] ed. | make`r' H | makers A, O, P   12 but] O, P | [or endeavour
to reclaime out of vice with the sword of justice] but H | [of Justice] but A
the] A, O, P | the[m] H   13 even] H, O, P | ever A   these] H, A | those O, P
14 relation] A, O, P | [weale] relation H   15 &] A, O, P | [[or]]& H *order of writing
not certain*   16 become] A, O, P | [only] become H   19 *in* H *del. and illeg.
word in margin*   20 of] H, A, P | [[in]]of O *alt. JL*   21–22 who...perswade]
O, P | [god sends [only] Ambasadors with instructions 'only' to [per⟨suade⟩] treat &
persuade in things of the other world] 'who...perswade' H *add. in margin;* (3) *in text and
above start of addition* | ['only'] who...perswade A   21 concernments] A, O, P |
[affairs] concernments H   22 magistrate] H, A, P | Magistrat 'as magistrate' O
add. JL   24 his] H, A, P | [the] 'his' O *alt. JL*

comfortable liveing of men in society one with an other, as has beene
already sufficiently proved

And it is yet farther evident, that the magistrate commands not the
practice of vertues, because they are vertues, & obleige the conscience, or
5 are [*fo. 11ʳ*] the dutys of man to god & the way to his mercy & favour but
because they are the advantages of man with man, & most of them the
strong ties & bonds of society; which cannot be loosend, without shat-
tering the whole frame. For some of them, which have not that influence
on the state, & yet are vices & acknowledged to be soe as much as any, as
10 coviteousnesse, disobedience to parents, ingratitude malice, reveng, &
severall others, the magistrate never draws his sword against· nor can it
be said, that these are neglected, because they can not be knowne, when
the secretest of them revenge & malice put the distinction in judicature
betweene man slaughter & murther.¹ Yea even charity its self, which is
15 certainly the great duty both of a man, & a christian hath not yet in its full
latitude, an universall right to toleration: since there are some parts, &
instances of it, which the magistrate hath absolutely forbidden, & that,
for ought I could ever heare, without any offence to the tenderest consciences. for who doubts that to releive with an almes the poore though
20 beggars (if one see them in want) is, if considerd absolutely, a vertue &
every particular mans duty, yet this is amongst us prohibited by a law &
the rigor of a penalty.² & yet noe body in this case complains of the

---

1 has] H, A | hath O, P   5 are] A, O, P | are// are H   &... favour] A, O, P |
'&... favour' H   6 most of them] A, O, P | 'most of them' H   9 [*1st*] &...
any] A, O, P | '&... any.' H   12 these] H, A | those O, P   13 revenge] A, O,
P | [malice &] revenge H   put] A, P | ['every day'] put H (*no caret*) | [b]'p'ut O *alt.*
JL   in judicature] A, O, P | 'in judicature' H   14–283.19 Yea... society *del. by*
Locke in O   15 [*1st*] a] H, A, P | 'a' O *add. JL*   its] H, A, P | [the] 'its' O *alt. JL*
16 right] A, O, P | righ H   19 to] H, O, P | 'to' A *add. JL*   with an almes] A, O,
P | 'with an almes' H   though] A, O, P | [in want] though H   20 if one see] ed. |
[[in]]If 'one']/ [want] 'if one' see H | if [twere] 'one' see A *add. JL* | if one sees O, P   in
want] H, O, P | 'in want' A *add. JL*   21 a] H, O, P | *om.* A   22 in] A, O, P |
[complaines] in H

---

¹ Originally murder meant a secret killing, but this particular usage had become obsolete
long before Locke wrote. Medieval English law did not distinguish between degrees of
felonious homicide, but from the early 16th century onwards such homicides were divided
into two kinds, murder and manslaughter, the difference being that murder required that
the defendant acted with malice aforethought, while manslaughter did not. The basic
distinction was between deliberate and accidental killings: 'malice' did not mean spite or
malevolence and 'aforethought' did not mean premeditation. For the law in Locke's day,
see Hale, *Historia Placitorum Coronae*, i. 449–70.
² It is not clear what law Locke had in mind. There were no provisions to this effect
either in the two current statutes for the relief of the poor, 43 Eliz. I, c. 2, and 14 Car. II, c.
12, or in 39 Eliz. I, c. 4, An Acte for punishment of Rogues Vagabonds & sturdy Beggars.

violation of his conscience, or the losse of his liberty, which certainly, if it were an unlawfull restraint upon the conscience could not be over-lookd by soe many tender & scrupulous men. God does sometimes, (soe much does he take care of the preservation of governments), make his law in some degrees submit, & comply with mans, his law forbids the vice, but the law of man often makes [*fo. 12ʳ*] the measures of it. There have beene common wealths that have made theft lawfull for such as were not caught in the fact, & perhaps 'twas as guiltlesse a thing to steale a horse at Sparta,[1] as to win a horse race in England. for the magistrate haveing a power to appoint ways of transferring proprietys, from one man to another, may establish any, soe they be universal, equall & without violence, & suited to the interest & welfare of that society, as this was at Sparta, who being a warlike people found this noe ill way, to teach their citizens, vigilancy, boldnesse & activity. this I only note by the by, to shew how much the good of the common wealth is the standard of all human laws, when it seemes to limit & alter the obligation even of some of the laws of god. & change the nature of vice & vertue. hence it is that the magistrate who could make theft innocent could not yet make perjury or breach of faith lawfull because distructive to humane society.

From this power therefor that the magistrate hath over good & bad actions I thinke it will follow

1 That he is not bound to punish all, i.e. he may tolerate some vices, for I would faine know what government in the world doth not [*fo. 11ᵛ*]

---

1 losse] A, O, P | [losse] ['restraint'] 'losse' H   2 were] H, A, P | was O restraint] A, O, P | [force upon] restraint H   conscience] H, O, P | consciences A 3 scrupulous] H, O, P; *in H there is a mark* † *here, perhaps made by the copyist of* A *to mark an indecipherable word* | 'scrupulous' A *inserted by Locke in space left by copyist* 6 measures] H, A | measure O, P   8 'twas] A, O, P | ['twas] [a man contracted noe more guilt] 'twas H   at] A, O, P | [race] at H   9 in] H, O, P | here in A 10 to...of] H, A | of 'makeing rules of' O *add. JL* | of P   transferring] H, O, P | trans[forming]'ferring' A   proprietys] A, O, P | [the] proprietys H   11 soe] A, O, P | [that] soe H   15 laws] H, A, P | [leagues] 'laws' O *alt. JL*   16 &] O, P | '&' A *added by Locke on line* | [& determine] H   17–19 hence...society] A, O, P | 'hence...society' H *add. partly at paragraph-end, remainder in margin*   18 [*1st*] could] H, O, P | would A   19 lawfull] H, O, P | 'lawfull' A *add. JL* 20 this] A | th[e]is H | the O, P   22 [*1st*] he] A, O, P | the [magistrat] he H 23 faine] H, A, O | *om.* P   not] H *has del. addition on fo. 11ᵛ*: 1 [that he is not bound to punish all vices [or tolerate all virtues] considerd absolutely, & I would faine know what government in the world ever did soe.] *no caret; del. numeral* (8) *in margin and at start of addition*

---

[1] Plutarch, *Vita Lycurgi*, xvii. 3.

2 That he ought not to command the practice of any vice, because such an injunction can not be subservient to the good of the people, or preservation of the government [*fo. 12*^r]

3 That if it can be supposd that he should command the practise of any
5 vice, the conscienscious & scandalizd subject is bound to disobey his injunction, but submit to his penalty. as in the former case

These I suppose are the limits of imposition & liberty, & these three severall sorts of things wherein mens consciences are concernd have right to such a latitude of toleration as I have set downe & noe more, if they are
10 considerd separately & abstractly in them selves [*fo. 13*^r]

But yet there are two cases, or circumstances which may still upon the same grounds vary the magistrates usage of the men that claime this right to toleration.

1 Since men usually take up their religion in grosse, & assume to them
15 selves the opinions of their party all at once in a bundle. it often happens, that they mix with their religious worship, & speculative opinions, other doctrines absolutely destructive to the society wherein they live, as is evident in the Roman Catholicks that are subjects of any prince but the Pope. These therefor blending such opinions with their religion, rever-
20 encing them as fundamentall truths, & submiting to them as articles of their faith, ought not to be tolerated by the magistrate in the exercise of their religion unlesse he can be securd, that he can allow one part,

---

1–3 2 . . . government] A, O, P | ʽ2 . . . government' H *added on fo. 11*^v; (8) *at end of previous paragraph and at start of addition*   2 such . . . not] A, O, P | [noe vice can] ʽsuch . . . not' H   4–6 *paragraph heavily deleted by Locke in* O   4 3] A, O, P | [[2]]3 H   if] A, O, P | [he] if H   can be supposd] A, O, P | [should happen] ʽcan be supposd' H   6 as . . . case] A, O, P | [because noe man can be br] ʽas . . . case' H *add. at paragraph-end*   7–10 These . . . selves] *In* H *this paragraph written with a much finer pen, perhaps a later addition*   8 sorts] A, O, P | sortʽs' H   things] A, O, P | thingʽs' H   wherein . . . concernd] A, O, P | ʽwherein . . . concernd' H   have] H, O, P | ʽhave' A *add. JL*   right] A, O, P | [ʽright to'] [soe much & noe more] right H   9 of . . . downe] A, O, P | ʽof . . . downe' H   if] A, O, P | [toleration] if H   11 are . . . circumstances] H, A, P | [are two] ʽis a' case[s or circumstances] O *alt. JL*   12 men] A, O, P | [severall] men H   12–13 claime . . . toleration] A, O, P | [professe them.] [ʽare dissenters.'] ʽclaime . . . toleration.' H   14 1] H, A, P | ʽ1' O *add. JL*   assume] A, O, P | [at once] assume H   15 it] A, O, P | [th⟨ey⟩] it H   16 &] A, O, P | [opi⟨nions⟩] & H   17 they] H, A, P | theʽy' O *alt. JL*   live] H, O, P | [have] ʽlive' A *alt. JL*   is] H, A, P | i[n]s O *alt. JL*   18 subjects] A, O, P | [members of any government] subjects H   21 ought] A, O, P | [cannot] ought H   be] H, A, P | ʽbe' O *add. on line by Locke*   by . . . magistrate] A, O, P | ʽby . . . magistrate' H   22 unlesse] A, O, P | [one part of it which you cannot seperate from the other.] unlesse H

284

without the spreading of the other, & that the propagation of these dangerous opinions may be seperated from their religious worship, which I suppose is very hard to be donne.

2 Since experience vouches the practise, & men are not all saints that pretend conscience, I thinke I shall not injure any party, if I say, that 5 most men, at least factions of men, when they have power sufficient, make use of it right or wrong for their owne advantage, & the establishment of them selves in authority, few men forbeareing to graspe at dominion that have power to seize & hold it. When therefor men heard them selves into companys with distinctions from the publique, & a 10 stricter confederacy with those of their owne denomination [*fo. 14ʳ*] & party, then other their fellow subjects. whether the destinction be religious or ridiculous it matters not, otherwise then as the ties of religion are stronger, & the pretenses of conscience fairer, & apter to draw partisans, & therefor the more to be suspected & the more heedfully to be 15 watchd· When, I say, any such destinct party is growne, or growing soe numerous as to appeare dangerous to the magistrate, & seeme visibly to threaten the peace of the state. The magistrate may & ought to use all ways either of polisie or power that shall be convenient, to lessen break & suppresse the party & soe prevent the mischeife. For though their 20 seperation were really in noe thing but religious worship, & he should use as the last remedy force & severity against them, who did noe thing but worship god in their owne way, yet did he not really persecute their religion, or punish them for that more then in a battle, the conqueror kils

---

1 spreading of the] A, O, P | 'spreading of the' H   [*3rd*] the...these] H, A | [the propagation of] th⟦o⟧ese O *alt. JL* | the Propagation of those P   2 dangerous] H, A | *om.* O, P   may...from] H, A, P | [may...from] 'will not be imbibd & espoused by all those who communicate with them in' O *alt. JL*   4–287.8 Since...dispute] *del. by Locke in* O, *and replaced by two passages in Locke's hand on fo. 28ᵉ* And that which...any occasion *and* The objection...I dare affirm *both printed below, pp. 309 and 309–10*   4 men] H, A, P | man O   5 not] H, O, P | 'not' A *add. JL*   if] A, O, P | [of 'religious' men], if H   6 factions] H, O, P | factors A   sufficient] A, O, P | [enough] sufficient H   9 &] A, O, P | [on it] & H   10 companys] A, O, P | [a party] 'companys' H   11 with] A, O, P | [one] with [an other,] H   12–13 be religious] H, A, P | b⟦y⟧e Religions O *probably alt. JL*   13 it] H, A, P | *om.* O   14 pretenses of conscience] H | [pret....] 'pretenses' of conscience A *alt. JL* | pretences O, P   15 partisans] O, P | [prosylites] 'partisans' H | [partis....] 'partisans' A *alt. JL*   15–16 [*2nd*] &... watchd] O, P | '&...watchd' H | and the more heedfully 'to be' watchd A *add. JL*   16–17 soe...as] H, O, P | 'soe...as' A *add. JL*   17–18 [*1st*] to...state] O, P | [to be able to disturbe the state] 'to...state' H | to appeare dangerous to the magistrate and seeme visibly [soe numerous as] to threaten the peace of the state A   19 polisie] A | politie H | policy O, P   that] A, O, P | [to lessen, breake & suppresse the p⟨arty⟩] that H   22 severity] H, F, O, P | 'severity' A *inserted by Locke in space left by copyist*

men for weareing white ribbons in their hats, or any other badg about them; but because, this was a marke that they were enemys & dangerous. Religion i.e. this or that forme of worship, being the cause of their union, & correspondence; not of their factiousnesse, & turbulancy. For the
5 praying to god in this or that place or posture, does noe more make men factious, or at enemity one with an other, nor ought otherwise to be treated, then the wearing of hats or turbants, which yet either of them may doe by being a note of distinction, & giveing men an oportunity to number their forces, know their strength, be confident of one another, &
10 readily unite upon any occasion. Soe that they are not [*fo. 15*ʳ] restraind, because of this, or that opinion, or worship: but because such a number of any opinion whatsoever, who dissented, would be dangerous. The same thing would happen if any fashon of clothes distinct from that of the magistrate, & those that adhere to him, should spread its self, & become
15 the badg of a very considerable part of the people, who there upon grew into a very strict correspondence & freindship one with another. might not this well give the magistrate cause of jealoussy, & make him with penaltys forbid the fashon; not because unlawfull, but because of the danger it might occasion? Thus a lay cloke may have the same effect with
20 an ecclesiasticall coule or any other religious habit.

And perhaps the Quakers, were they numerous enough to become dangerous to the state, would deserve the magistrates care, & watchfulnesse to breake & suppresse them, were they noe other way destinguished from the rest of his subjects, but by the bare keepeing on their hats, as
25 much, as if they had a set forme of religion seperate from the state. In which case noe body would thinke, that the not standing bare were a thing the magistrate leveld his severity against, any otherwise, then as it united a great number of men who though they dissented from him in a very indifferent & triviall circumstance; yet might thereby endanger the
30 government. & in such case he may endeavour to suppresse, & weaken

---

2 that they] H, F | that the A | they O, P   4 correspondence] H, F, O, P | correspondences A   5 place or] H, F, A | *om.* O, P   15 badg] H, F, O, P | body A   a very] H, F, A, P | `a´ [e]very O *alt. JL*          16 grew] H, A, P | grow O 18 with penaltys] A, O, P | `with penaltys´ H | *not in* F   19 danger] O, P | danger[ous] H, A | dangerous consequence F   might] A, O, P | migh H   a . . . may] O, P | a [cloke] lay cloke may H | a cloke may F | `a´ lay clocke my A *add. JL*          20 coule] H, F, O, P *foll. in* H *by a small deleted cross, also deleted in margin* | `coule´ A *inserted by Locke in space left by copyist*   23 breake &] H, F, A | *om.* O, P   were] H, F, A, P | where O   28 men] A, O, P | [men dissenting] [men] [togeather] `men´ H | men togeather F          29 might] F, A, O, P | migh H          30 he] A, O, P | `he´ H

286

or dissolve any party of men, which religion or any other thing hath united [*fo. 16*'] to the manifest danger of his government by all those means, that shall be most convenient for that purpose, whereof he is to be judg, nor shall he be accountable in the other world, for what he does directly in order to the preservation & peace of his people according to 5 the best of his knowledg.

Whether force & compulsion be the right way to this end I will not here dispute, but this I dare affirme, that it is the worst, the last to be usd, & with the greatest caution. for these reasons.

1 Because it brings that upon a man, which that he might be fencd from 10 is the only reason why he is a member of the Common wealth, viz violence. For were there noe feare of violence, there would be noe government in the world, nor any need of it.

2 Because the magistrate in useing of force, does in parte cross what he pretends to, which is to promote the safety of all. For the preservation as 15 much as is possible of the propriety quiet & life of every individuall being his duty; he is obleigd not to disturb, or destroy some, for the quiet, or safety of the rest, till it has beene tried, whether there be not ways to save all. For soe far as he undoes or destroys any of his subjects, for the security of the rest, soe far he opposes his owne designe, which is professed & 20 ought to be only for preservation to which even the meanest have a title. Twould [*fo. 17*'] be but an uncharitable, as well as unskilfull way of cure, & such as noe body would use or consent to, to cut of soe much as an ulcerd toe, though tending to a gangren, till all other gentler remedys had provd unsuccessfull; though it be a part as low as the earth, & far distant 25 from the head.

I can see but one objection that can be made to this, & that is, that by the application of gentler remedys, such slow methods may make you lose

1 [*1st*] or] A, O, P | [that party by all means] or H   4 does] H, F, O, P | 'does' A *add. JL*   8 dispute] A, O, P | [debate] dispute H   9 for these reasons] A, O, P | 'for these reasons' H *add. on line at paragraph-end*   10 might] H, A, P | may O fencd] H, O, P | freed A   11 [*1st*] is] A, O, P | [was] 'is' H   12 [*2nd*] there] A, O, P | [in the world], there H   15 [*1st*] to] ed. | to [doe] H | to doe A, O, P   to promote] ed. | 'to promote' H | *om.* A, O, P   16 is] H, O, P | *om.* A   18 has] H, A, P | hath O   19 for] A, O, P | [though the meanest] for H   21 preservation] H, A, P | the preservation O   22 Twould] A, O | Twould// Twould H, P an] H, O, P | [a thing] A   23 [*2nd*] to] H, O, P | 'to' A *add. JL*   24 toe] H, O, P | [for] 'toe' A *alt. JL*

the oportunity of those remedys that if timely would be effectuall. whereas in your faint way of proceeding the maladie increases, the faction grows strong gathers head, & becomes your masters.

To this I answer. That partys & factions grow slowly & by degrees,
5 have their times of infancy & weakenesse, as well as full growth, & strength, & become not formidable in an instant: but give sufficient time for experimenting other kinde of cures, without any danger by the delay. But if the magistrate chance to finde the dissenters soe numerous, as to be in a condition to cope with him, I see not what he can gaine by
10 force & severity, when he thereby gives them the fairer pretence to embody, & arme & makes them all unite the firmer against him. but this bordering something upon that part of the question, which concerns more the interest of the magistrate then his duty, I shall refer to a fitter place. [*fo. 18^r*]

15 Hitherto I have only tracd out the bounds that god hath set to the power of the magistrate & the obedience of the subject, both which are subjects & equally owe obedience to the great King of Kings who expects from them the performance of those dutys which are incumbent on them in their severall stations & conditions, the sum whereof is that

20 1 There are some opinions & actions that are wholy seperate from the concernment of the state, & have noe direct influence upon mens lives in society, & those are, all speculative opinions & religious worship, & these have a cleare title to universal toleration, which the magistrate ought not to intrench on

25 2 There are some opinions & actions, which are in their naturall tendency absolutely destructive to humane society, as that faith may be

---

1 remedys...be] **A, O, P** | [that would be otherwise] 'remedys...be' **H**
2 whereas...proceeding] **O, P** | [whilst]'whereas...proceeding' **H** | whereas... proceedings **A**   your] **H, A, P** | [your] 'this' **O** *alt. JL*   [*2nd*] the] **A, O, P** | [whilst] the **H**   3 gathers] **O, P** | [&] gathers **H** | and gathers **A**   becomes] **O, P** | become **H, A**   5 times] **H, A** | time **O, P**   7 by...delay] **A, O, P** | [at all] 'by...delay.' **H** *add. in margin*   8 soe] **A, O, P** | [numerous & strong] soe **H**
10 when he thereby] **O, P** | [but] 'when he thereby' **H** | when there by **A**   the] **H, O, P** | *om.* **A**   11 [*2nd*] &] **A, O, P** | [against him] & **H**   makes] **H, A** | make **O, P**   this] **A, O, P** | 'this' **H** (*no caret*)   13 [*1st*] the] **H, A, P** | 'the' **O** *add. JL*
14 **H** *fo. 17^v has endorsement* Toleration 67/ **C**   15 *in* **H** *signature* D *in direction line*   Hitherto] *preceded in* **H** *by del. paragraph* [Hitherto I have been the bounds of imposition & obedience & shewing]   23 which] **A, O, P** | [& these the] which **H** *del. by underscoring*   25 in their] **H, O, P** | [wholy] [in either] 'in their' **A** *alt. JL*

288

broken with hereticks, that if the magistrate doth not reforme religion the subjects may, that one is bound to broach[1] & propagate any opinion he beleives himself & such like, & in actions all manner of fraud & injustice &c· And these the magistrate ought not to tolerate at all.

3 There is a third sort of opinions & actions which in them selves doe 5 not inconvenience or advantage humane society, but only as the temper of the state & posture of affairs may vary their influence to good or bad, as that polygamy is lawfull or unlawfull, That flesh or fish is to be eaten [*fo. 19ʳ*] or absteind from at certain seasons. & such other practicall opinions & all actions conversant about matters of indifferency· And 10 these have a right to toleration soe far only as they doe not interfere with the advantages of the publique or serve any way to disturbe the government

And thus far of toleration as it concerns the magistrates duty. Haveing shewd what he is bound in conscience to doe, it will not be amisse to 15 consider a litle what he ought to doe in prudence.

But because the dutys of men are conteind in generall established rules, but their prudence is regulated by circumstances relateing to them selves in particular, it will be necessary in shewing how much toleration is the magistrates interest, to come to particulars. 20

To consider therefor the state of England at present· There is but this one question in the whole matter & that is whether toleration or imposition be the readyest way to secure the safety & peace & promote the welfare of this kingdom

As to secureing your safety & peace, there is but one way which is 25 that your freinds at home be many & vigorous, & your enemys few &

---

1 doth not reforme] H, P | 'doth not' reforme A *insertion by Locke in space left by copyist* | doth not 'make a publique' reform⟦e⟧'ation in' O *alt. JL*   2 one is] H, O, P | [is] one 'is' A *alt. JL*   to broach &] H, P | to broach '&' A *add. JL* | [to broach] 'publiquely to teach' & O *alt. JL*   5 of] H, O, P | 'of' A *add. JL*   7 bad] A, O, P | [evill] bad H   10–11 And these] H, A | [And] O | *om.* P   17 established] O, P | establish H, A   18 their prudence] A, O, P | the'ir' prudence [of men] H   19 selves] A, O, P | 'selves' H (*no caret*)   in shewing] A, O, P | [to] in [cosidering] ['stateing'] [the interest] 'in shewing' H   23 safety &] O, P | 'safety &' H | safety '&' A *add. JL*   23–24 promote the] A, O, P | 'promote the' H   24 this] H, O, P | his A   25 your] H, P | yᵉ A | yᵉ O   safety &] H, A, P | [Safety, and] O   26 at home] A, O, P | 'at home' H (*no caret*)   [2nd] your] H, A, P | yᵉ O

---

[1] to broach: to give vent or publicity to, *OED* broach.

contemptible. or at least that the inequality of their number make it very
dangerous & difficult for malecontents to molest you

As to promoteing the welfare of the Kingdome which consists in riches
& power, to this most immediately conduces the number & industry of
5 your subjects.

What influence toleration hath on all these cannot be well seene
without considering the different Partys now among us. [*fo. 20ʳ*] which
may well be comprehended under these two Papist & Fanatique.

1 As to the Papists, tis certaine that severall of their dangerous opinions
10 which are absolutely destructive to all governments but the popes ought
not to be tolerated in propagateing those opinions, & who soever shall
spread or publish any of them the magistrate is bound to suppresse soe
far as may be sufficient to restrain it. [*fo. 19ᵛ*] And this rule reaches not
only the Papists but any other sort of men amongst us. for such restraint
15 will something hinder the spreading of those doctrines, which will always
be of ill consequence & like serpents can never be prevaild on by kinde
usage to lay by their venom.

2 Papists are not to enjoy the benefit of toleration because where they
have power they thinke them selves bound to deny it to others. For it
20 is unreasonable that any should have a free liberty of their religion, who
doe not acknowledg it as a principle of theirs that noe body ought to
persecute or molest an other because he dissents from him in religion.
For toleration being setled by the magistrate as a foundation whereon to

1–2 or...you] O, P | 'or...you' H | or...for 'malecontents to molest you' A
add. JL   1 that the] A, P | th⟦e⟧at the H | the that O   4 to] A, O, P | [&]
to H   6 hath] H, A, O | has P   7 us] *in H foll. by half a blank line appar-
ently indicating end of paragraph, but text continues on fo. 20ʳ without a break*   8 Papist]
H | Papist[s] A *deletion not certain* | Papists O, P   Fanatique] H, A | Fanatiques O, P
9 dangerous] A, O, P | 'dangerous' H   10 which...popes] A, O, P |
'which...popes' H   11 in...opinions] O, P | 'in propagateing those opinions'
H (*no caret*) | 'in propagateing' these opinions A *insertion by Locke in space left by
copyist*   12 any of them] O, P | any 'of' them H | ['any'] [either] 'any of them' [by
indulgence] A *both alterations by Locke*   suppresse] A, O, P | [punish] 'suppresse' H
13–291.4 And...able] A, O, P, *with variants noted below* | 'And...able' H *added on fo.*
19ᵛ; (9) *in margin and at start of addition; change of handwriting shows second paragraph added*
later   14 for...restraint] O, P | [which can never be t⟨amed⟩] 'for...restraint' H |
for...restraints A   16 like] A, O, P | [can never be tamd by kinde usage.] like H
can] H, A | *om.* O, P   18 Papists] A, O, P | Papist H   enjoy] A, O, P | [be
tolerated] enjoy H   19 thinke...[*ıst*] to] A, O, P | 'thinke...to' H
21 acknowledg it as] O, P | [make it] ['allow it'] 'acknowledg it as' H | it as A   a] H,
A, P | 'a' O *add. JL*   22 persecute] A, O, P | [be]persecute H   because he] A, O,
P | [that] 'because he' H   23 setled] A, O, P | [made] 'setled' H

establish the peace & quiet of his people, by tolerateing any who enjoy the benefit of this indulgence, which at the same time they condemne as unlawfull, he only cherishes those who professe themselves obleigd to disturbe his government as soone as they shall be able [*fo. 20^r*]

3 It being impossible either by indulgence or severity to make Papists whilst Papists freinds to your government being enemys to it both in their principles & interest, & therefor considering them as irreconcileable enemys of whose fidelity you can never be securd, whilst they owe a blinde obedience to an infalible pope, who has the keys of their consciences tied to his girdle, & can upon occasion dispense with all their oaths promises & the obligations they have to their prince espetially being an heritick & arme them to the disturbance of the government I thinke they ought not to enjoy the benefit of toleration

Because toleration can never, but restraint may lessen their number or at least not increase it, as it does usually all other opinions which grow & spread by persecution, & recommend them selves to bystanders by the hardships they under goe· men being forward to have compassion for sufferers & esteeme for that religion as pure, & the professors of it as sincere which can stand the test of persecution· But I thinke it is far otherwise with Catholiques who are lesse apt to be pittyed then others because they [*fo. 21^r*] receive noe other usage then what the cruelty of their owne principles & practises are knowne to deserve· most men judging those severitys they complain of, as just punishments due to

---

1 enjoy] A, O, P | [only] enjoy H   2 at] A, O, P | [they] at H   3 who] H, A, P | 'who' O *add. JL*   5 3] A, O, P | ⟦2⟧3 H   indulgence] A, O, P | [toleration] [to] 'indulgence.' H   Papists] H, A, P | Papist's' O *add. JL*   6 Papists] A, P | Papist H | Papist's' O *add. JL*   7 [2nd] &] A, O, P | [you are in this respect either to tolerate them ⟦in⟧or at once rid your hands of them, for all severitys short of that may make them more miserable & you noething the more secure.] & H   9 obedience] A, O, P | 'obedience' H (*no caret*)   an] H, A, P | any O   has] H, A, P | hath O   11 the] A, O, P | 'the' H (*no caret*)   12 an] H, A, P | 'in their sense' an O *add. JL*   I] H, A, P | *om.* O   14 Because] A, O, P | [1] Because H   restraint] A, O, P | [severity] 'restraint' H   16 to bystanders] A, O, P | [by] [& their] 'to bystanders' H   17–18 forward . . . for] O, P | [apt to thinke] 'forward . . . for' H | 'forward' . . . for A *insertion by Locke in space left by copyist*   18 as pure] A, O, P | [pure] 'as pure' H [2nd] as] A, O, P | 'as' H (*no caret*)   19 stand] A, O, P | [endure] 'stand' H   20 Catholiques] A, O, P | [Popery] Catholiques H   lesse] H, O, P | lest A   be] H, O, P | *om.* A   21 they] A, O, P | they// they H   22 knowne] A, O, P | [apt] 'knowne' H   most] A, O, P | [& they are reputed by most] most H   23 judging] A, O, P | [lookeing upon] 'judging' H   they] A, O, P | [that are usd to them] they H   as just] A | [rather] [as] just H *second deletion not certain* | just O, P

them as enemys to the state rather then persecutions of conscientious men for their religion which indeed it is not. [*fo. 20ᵛ*] Nor can they be thought to be punishd meerly for their consciences who owne them selves at the same time subjects of a foraigne & enemy Prince. [*fo. 21ʳ*] besides
5 the principles & doctrines of that religion are lesse apt to take inquisitive heads & unstable minds, men commonly in their voluntary changes doe persue liberty & enthusiasme, wherein they are still free & at their owne disposall rather then give them selves up to the authority & impositions of others. this is certaine that toleration can not make them divide
10 amongst them selves nor a severe hand over them, (as in other dissenting partys) make them cement with the Fanatiques, (whose principles & worship & tempers are soe utterly inconsistent) & by that meanes increaseing the number of the united malecontents make the danger greater. adde to this that popery haveing beene brought in upon the
15 ignorant & zealous world by the art & industry of their clergy, & kept up by the same artifice backd by power & force, it is the most likely of any religion to decay where the secular power handles them severely, or at least takes from them those incouragements & supports they receivd by their owne Clergy.

20 But if restraint of the Papists doe not lessen the number of our enemys in bringing any of them over to us yet it increases the number it strengthens the hands of our freinds, & knits all the Protestant partys firmer to our assistance & defence. For the interest of the King of England as head of the Protestants will be much improvd by the [*fo. 22ʳ*]
25 discountenanceing of popery amongst us. The different partys will

---

1 them] A, O, P | the`m' [ẹnẹ⟨mies⟩] H        2–4 Nor...Prince] A, O, P, *with variants noted below* | `Nor...Prince' H *added on fo. 20ᵛ;* (8) *in margin and at start of addition*   2 can] A, O, P | [indeed] ⟦are⟧can H   3 meerly] A, O, P | `meerly' H
4 &] H, A, P | *om.* O   5 lesse] H, O, P | `lesse' A *add. JL*        6 unstable] H, A, P | [unfa]`un'stable O *alt. JL*   7 persue] A, O, P | [rather] persue H
9–10 that...nor] O, P | `that...nor' H that...them *added between lines, remainder in margin* | that toleration can not make them [a secure hand over them as in other dissenting partys] divide amongst them selves nor A   10–11 a...partys)] H, O, P |
`a...partys' [the] A *add. JL*   10 as] A, O, P | [cannot] (as H   11 &] H, O, P |
[and] A   12 soe] A, O, P | [wh⟨olly⟩] soe H   13 number] H, A | numbers
O, P   the united] O, P | [dissatisfied] `the' united H (*no caret*) | the `united' A
add. JL   14–15 upon...world] O, P | [& continued in the world] `upon...world' H
| upon the ignorant and `zealous world' A *insertion by Locke in space left by copyist*
15 their] A, O, P | [the world] their H   16 by...backd] A, O, P | `[& kept up]
by...backd' H   21 any of] H, O, P | *om.* A   it...number] A, O, P |
`it...number' H        [*2nd*] it] H, A, P | [it] `&' O *add. JL on line*   22 partys] H, A |
party O, P   23 assistance] A, O, P | [interest, alliance] `assistance' H   24 by]
H, A, P | be O   25 different] H, A | differing O, P

sooner unite in a common freindship with us, when they finde we really seperate from & set our selves against the common enemy both to our church & all protestant professions. This will be an hostage of our freindship to them, & a security that they shall not be deceivd in the confidence they have of us, & the sincerity of the accord we make 5 with them.

All the rest of dissenters come under the opprobrious name of Phanatiques, which I thinke by the way might with more prudence be laid aside & forgotten then made use of· for what understanding man in a disordered state would finde out & fix notes of distinction, a thing to be 10 coveted only by those that are factious, or by giveing one common name to different partys teach those to unite whome he is concernd to divide & keep at a distance one among another.

But to come to what is more materiall, I thinke it is agreed on in all hands, that it is necessary the Fanatiques should be made usefull & 15 assisting & as much as possible firme to the goverment as it now stands. both as to secure it from disturbance at home & defend it against invasions from abrode which noe thing can possibly bring to passe but what is able to alter their mindes & bring them over to your profession· or else if they doe not part with their opinions, yet may persuade them to lay 20 by their animosity, & become freinds to the state though they are not sonnes of the church.

What efficacy force & severity hath to alter the opinions [*fo. 23ʳ*] of mankinde [*fo. 22ᵛ*] though all history be full of examples, & there is scarce an instance to be found of any opinion driven out of the world by 25

---

2 selves] A, O, P | sel⟦f⟧ves H   to] A, O, P | 'to' H   3 protestant . . . This] ed. | 'protestant professions {&}' [christian liberty]. This H *del. by underscoring* | [christian liberty] protestant professions [and] this A | Protestant professions, and this O, P   5 confidence] A, O, P | [trust] confidence H   sincerity of the] A, O, P | 'sincerity of the' H   5–6 we . . . them] A, O, P | [betweene us.] 'we . . . them.' H *add. at paragraph-end*   8 I . . . way] A | I thinke 'by the way' H | (by the way) I thinke O, P   10 a] A, O, P | [&] 'a' H   12 whome] H, O, P | where A   [*3rd*] to] A, O, P | to to H 14 in] H, A | *om.* O, P   15 it] H, A, P | 'it' O *add. JL*   the] H, O, P | *om.* A 16 [*3rd*] as] A, O, P | [of] as H   17 both] A, O, P | [which I see that all agree in the end] both H   as] H, A | [as] O | *om.* P   it against] A, O, P | [from] 'it against' H 18 noe] A, O, P | [certainly can be brought to passe but by one or both of those ways wh⟨ich⟩ noe] noe H   19 your] H, A, P | [your] 'our' O *alt. JL*   20 doe] A, O, P | [can] 'doe' H   21 animosity] H | 'animosity' A *inserted by Locke in space left by copyist* | animosities O, P   become freinds] H, O, P | [bree . . . frauds] 'become freinds' A *alt. JL*   22 sonnes] A, O, P | [me⟨embers⟩] sonnes H   24–294.2 though . . . too] A, O, P, *with variants noted below* | 'though . . . too' H *added on fo. 22ᵛ;* (2) *in margin and at start of addition*   24 all] H, A | *om.* O, P

persecution but where the violence of it at once swept away all the professors too. [*fo. 23ʳ*] I desire noe body to goe farther then his owne boosome for an experiment whether ever violence gaind any thing upon his opinion, whether even arguments managd with heate doe not loose
5 some thing of their efficacy, & have not made him the more obstinate in his opinion, soe chary is humane nature to preserve the liberty of that part where in lyes the dignity of a man, which could it be imposd on would make him but little different from a beast. I aske those who in the late times soe firmely stood the ineffectuall persecution them selves &
10 found how little it obteind on their opinions, & yet are now soe forward to trye it upon others, whether all the severity in the world could have drawne them one step nearer to a hearty & sincere imbraceing the opinions that were then uppermost, let them not say it was because they knew they were in the right, for every man in what he beleives, has soe
15 far this persuasion that he is in the right. But how litle this obstinacy or constancy depends upon knowledg, may appeare in those gally slaves who returne from Turky,[1] who though they have endured all manner of miserys rather then part with their religion, yet one would guesse by the lives & principles of most of them, that they had noe knowledg of the
20 doctrine & practise of christianity at all. who thinks not that those pore captives who (for renounceing a religion they were not over instructed in

2 too] *foll. in* H *by del. caret with numeral* (2)   3 experiment] H, A, P | Experience O
6 chary] H, O, P | 'chary' A *inserted by Locke in space left by copyist*   humane
nature] A, O, P | [the] 'humane' nature [of man] H   7 part] A, O, P | 'part' H
which] O, P | [[to]]which H | [to] which A   8 I] A, O, P | [paine & feare 'not'
convinceing [noe bodys reason] 'any bodys reason' cannot possibly make him assent to the
opinion, but will certainly make him hate the person of his persecutor & give him the
greater aversion to both.] I H   9 the . . . persecution] ed. | the 'ineffectuall [force
of]' persecution H | [the] ineffectual [the] persecution A | the ineffectuall 'force of'
persecution O *add. JL* | the ineffectuall force of persecution P | *In* H XV *written
faintly in margin*   10 it . . . on] O, P | it [alterd] 'obteind on' H | 'it obteined' on A
inserted by Locke in space left by copyist   are] A, O, P | [would] are H   12 drawne]
A, O, P | [forcd] 'drawne' H   to] A, O, P | 'to' H (*no caret*)   14 knew they] A,
O, P | 'knew they' H   15 [2nd] this] H, A, P | his O   15–16 or
constancy] A, O, P | 'or constancy.' H   16 may] A, O, P | [or conviction] may H
17 have] A, O, P | 'have' H (*no caret*)   18 part] H, O, P | [then] 'part' A *alt. JL*
19 knowledg] A, O, P | knowled⟨g⟩ H   21 captives] A, O, P | [people] 'captives' H
over] A, O, P | [very] over H   in] A, O, P | [of] 'in' H

---

[1] On accounts of captivity of English prisoners in Muslim countries, see Matar, *Turks, Moors and Englishmen in the Age of Discovery*, 181–4.

nor dureing the injoyment of their freedome at home over zealous for)
might have regaind their liberty, for changeing their opinion would not
(had their chains given them leave) have cut the throats of those cruell
patrons who used them soe severly to whome they would yet have donne
noe violence had [*fo. 24ʳ*] they beene treated civily like fair prisoners of 5
war. Whereby we may see 'twill be a hazardous attempt for those who
designe it, [*fo. 23ᵛ*] If they are not much the greater number, to compell
dissenters by force & ill usage to be true to that government & serviceable
to that interest, which instead of an equall protection affords them noe
other treatment but disgrace, punishment & persecution: Unlesse those 10
who would thus inforce an uniformity will make chains for all those to
whome they will allow noe liberty & perswade them also to stand still
whilst they put them upon 'em· [*fo. 24ʳ*] For let Divines preach duty as
long as they will, twas never knowne that men lay downe quietly under
the oppression & submitted their backs to the blows of others when they 15
thought they had strength enough to defend themselves. I say not this to
Justifie such proceedings, which In the former part of this discourse I
thinke I have sufficiently condemned. But to shew what the nature &

---

1 dureing the] A, O, P | [in the] 'dureing the' H   over] ed. | over H | ever A, P |
'were' [[e]]over O *alt. JL*   2 might] A, O, P | migh H   *in H letter* q *in margin next
to this passage*   for...opinion] A, O, P | 'for...opinion.' H   3 leave...cut] P |
leave) cut H | cut A | leave) 'have' cut O *add. JL*   4 who...severly] A, O, P |
'who...severly.' H   yet] O, P | 'yet' H | [not] 'yet' A *alt. JL*   5 violence] A, O, P |
[injury] 'violence' H   had] A, P | had// had H | [he] 'had' O *alt. JL*   6 'twill be a]
H, A | it [will be] 'would be an' O *alt. JL* | it would be an P   attempt] A, O, P | 'attempt'
H   for...designe] H | for those who [deserve] 'designe' A *alt. JL* | [for those who] 'if
any should' designe O *alt. JL* | if any should designe P   7–13 If...'em] ed. |
'If...'em' H *added on fo.* 23ᵛ; (11) *in margin and at start of addition. Replaces deleted passage:*
[to bring this Island to the condition of a gally where the greater part shall be reducd to the
condition of slaves, be forcd with blows to row the vessell, but share in none of the ladeing
[or be allowd soe much as a cabin] *(deletion not certain)* 'nor have any priviledg or
protection.' *(no caret)* unlesse they will make chaines, for all those who are to be usd like
Turks] & persuade them to stand still whilst they put them on. *Locke should have deleted the
last phrase after making the addition on fo.* 23ᵛ. A *follows revised state of* H *with minor variations
of punctuation and spelling;* Gally *in Locke's hand in margin.* O *follows earlier state of* H: to
bring this Island to the Condition of a Gally where the greater parte shalbe reduced to the
Condition of slaves, Be forced with blowes to Rowe the Vessell, but share in none of the
Ladeing, nor have any priviledge or protection unless they will make Chaines for all those
who are to be used Like Turkes, & perswade them to stand still whilst they put them on.
P *has the same text as* O *with minor variations of punctuation and spelling*   11 those] A |
th[[em]]ose H   13 Divines] A, O, P | [men] 'Divines' H   17 this] A, O, P |
th[[e]]is H

practise of man kinde is & what has usually beene the consequence of persecution. [*fo. 23ᵛ*]

Besides the forcible introduceing of opinions keepes people off from closeing with them by giveing men unavoidable jealousys, that it is not
5 truth that is thus carried on, but interest & dominion that is sought in makeing prosylites by compulsion· for who takes this course to convince any one of the certain truths of mathematiques? tis likely twill be said that those are truths on which depends not my happynesse· I grant it, & am much indebted to the man that takes care I should be happy but tis hard
10 to thinke that that comes from charity to my soule which brings such ill usage to my body, or that he is much concernd I should be happy in an other world who is pleased to see me miserable in this. I wonder that those who have such a zealous regard to the good of others, doe not a litle more looke after the releife of the poore or thinke them selves concernd
15 to gard the estates of the rich, which certainly are good things too & make a part of ones happynesse if we may beleive the lives of those, who tell us the joys of heaven but endeavour as much as others for large possessions on earth. [*fo. 24ʳ*]

But after all this could persecution not only now & then conquer a
20 tender faint hearted fanatique, which yet it rarely does & that usually by the losse of two or three orthodox, could it I say at once drive in all dissenters within the pale of the church, it would not there by secure but much more threaten the government & make the danger as much greater as it is to have a false secret but exasperated enemy rather then a fair open
25 adversary. For punishment & feare may make men dissemble, but not convinceing any bodys reason, cannot possibly make them assent to the

3–18 Besides . . . earth] A, O, P, *with variants noted below* | `Besides . . . earth' H *add. on fo. 23ᵛ; insertion point marked by* (10) *(without caret) at end of previous paragraph;* (10) *at start of addition*   4 closeing with] A, O, P | [imbraceing] 'closeing with' H   jealousys] A, O, P | [suspition] jealousys H   it] H, A, P | *om.* O   5 carried on] O, P | [propagated] 'carried on' H | carried 'on' A *add. JL (no caret)*   6 for] A | [wh⟨o⟩]for H | *om.* O, P   7 twill] H, A | it will O, P   8 depends] H, A | depend O, P   &] A, P | [& aske farther] & H | a⟦m⟧nd O *alt. JL*   9 to] A, O, P | [that] [ta⟨kes⟩]to H   12 pleased] A, O, P | [pleasd] *del. by underscoring* ['delighte⟨d⟩'] H   13 [*2nd*] a] A, O, P | ['thinke them selves concernd'] a H   14–15 thinke . . . to] O, P | 'thinke . . . to' H, A *add. JL in both MSS*   17 endeavour] A, O, P | [tell us] endeavour H   20 which] A, O, P | [but at once drive in all dissenters] which H   yet] H, O, P | *om.* A   21 it] H, A, P | 'it' O *add. JL*   in] H, A | *om.* O, P   22 within] A, O, P | [into] within H   23 much] H, A | *om.* O, P   threaten] A, O, P | [endanger] 'threaten' H   make] A, O, P | [thereby] make H   24 as] A, O, P | [&]as H   to] A, O, P | [greater] to H   false] A, O, P | [false] [dissembled] false H   26 convinceing] H, O, P | convince`ing' A *alt. JL*   them] A, O, P | [him]them H

opinion, but will certainly make them hate the person of their persecutor & give them the greater aversion to both, such compliers only prefer impunity to the declareing of their owne opinion, but doe not there by approve of yours. [*fo. 25ʳ*] feare of your power not love of your government is that which restrains them, & if that be the chaine that ties 5 them to you it would certainly hold them suerer were they open dissenters, then being secret malecontents, because it would not only be some thing easier, to be worne but harder to be knockd of. at least this is certaine that compelling men to your opinion any other way then by convinceing them of the truth of it, makes them noe more your freinds, 10 then forceing the pore Indians by droves into the rivers to be baptisd made them Christians.

Though force cannot master the opinions men have, nor plant new ones in their breasts, yet courtesy freindship & soft usage may, for severall (I thinke I may say most) men whose businesse or lazynesse 15 keepe them from examineing take many of their opinions upon trust, even in things of religion, but never take them from any man of whose knowledg freindship & sincerety they have not very good thoughts· which it is impossible they should have of one that persecuts them. 20

But inquisitive men though they are not of an others minde because of his kindenesse yet they are the more willing to be convincd & will be apt

---

1 them] A, O, P | ⟦him⟧them H   their] A, O, P | ⟦his⟧their H   2 them] A, O, P | ⟦him⟧them H   such] A, O, P | [these] such H   only] A, O, P | ʻonlyʼ H   3 owne] A | ʻowneʼ H | *om.* O, P   4 yours] H, A, P | [yours] ʻoursʼ O *alt. JL*   [*1st*] your] H, A, P | yᵗᵒʳᵉ O *alt. JL*   [*2nd*] of your] H, P | o⟦r⟧f your A *alt. JL* | of yᵗᵒʳᵉ O *alt. JL*   5 is] A, O, P | [only hold] is H   6 would] A, O, P | w⟦ill⟧ould H   suerer] A, O, P | [faster] ʻsuererʼ H   7 being] ʻbeingʼ H, A *add. JL in both MSS* (*no caret*) | *om.* O, P   it] A, O, P | [they] ʻitʼ H   8 [*1st*] to] A, O, P | [but] to H   at] A, O, P | [at] [but I th⟨ink⟩] at H   9 opinion] A, O, P | [discipline] ʻopinionʼ H   10 [*1st*] them] A, O, P | [of] them H   truth] A, O, P | [goodnesse] truth H   13 Though] A, O, P | [Force therefor not mastering mens opinions let us see what soft usage will doe, & here, though I am not of any ones minde because] Though H   15 (I...most)] A | ʻ(I...most)ʼ H | *om.* O, P   16 many] A, O, P | [severall] ʻmanyʼ H   17 in] A, O, P | [of] ʻinʼ H   never] A, O, P | [cannot] ʻneverʼ H   18 of] H, O, P | [knowledge] ʻofʼ A *alt. JL*   knowledg...sincerety] A, O, P | [freindship] [to them as well as knowledg in the thing] ʻknowledg...sineretyʼ H   18–19 they...thoughts] *ed.* | [they are ʻnotʼ well assurd] ʻthey...thoughtsʼ H | they [are] ʻhaveʼ not [well assurd] ʻa good opinionʼ A *alt. JL* | they are not well assured O, P   19 it is] A | [opinion] it is H *del. by underscoring* | its O, P   have] *ed.* | [have] [ʻbeʼ] ʻhaveʼ H | [be] ʻhaveʼ A *alt. JL* | be O, P   21 an others minde] A, O, P | [mens] ʻan others' mind⟦s⟧eʼ H   22 apt] H, A, P | aptʻerʼ O *alt. JL*

to search after reasons that may persuade them to be soe whome they are
obleigd to love

    Since force is a wrong way to bring dissenters off from their persua-
sions, & by drawing them to your opinion you cement them fast to the
5 state, it will certainly prevaile much lesse with those to be your freinds
who stedfastly retaine their persuasion· [*fo. 26ʳ*] he that differs in an
opinion is only soe far at a distance from you but if you use him ill for that
which he beleives to be the right he is then at perfect enmity, the one is
barely a seperation the other a quarrell. Nor is that all the mischeife
10 which severity will doe among us as the state of things is at present, for
force & harsh usage will not only increase the animosity but number of
enemys. For the Fanatiques taken all togeather being numerous, &
possibly more then the hearty freinds to the state religion,[1] are yet
crumbled into different partys amongst them selves, & are at as much
15 distance one from another as from you, if you drive them not farther of
by the treatment they receive from you, for their bare opinions are as
inconsistent one with another as with the church of England. People
therefor that are soe shatterd into different factions are best securd by
toleration since being in as good a condition under you, as they can hope
20 for under any, tis not like they should joyn, to set up any other, whom
they can not be certain will use them soe well. But if you persecute them
you make them all of one party & interest against you, tempt them to
shake of your yoak & venture for a new government wherein every one
has hopes to get the dominion them selves or better usage under others,
25 who cannot but see that the same severity of the Government which
helpd them to power & partisans to get up, will give others the same

---

1 persuade] A, O, P | ⟦br⟨ing⟩⟧persuade H   soe] ed. | [of his opinion] `soe´ H |
of his opinion A, O, P   whome] O, P | who⟦se⟧me [person & conversation] H | whose
`person´ A *add. JL*    3 Since] A, O, P | [Since force [can not bring] `is´ [men]
`dissenter´ off from their opinions & soe make them fast freinds to the government]
Since H   4 you] O, P | *om.* H, A   6 stedfastly] A, O, P | `stedfastly´ H (*no
caret*)   persuasion] H, A | perswasion. `& continue in an opinion different from you.´ O
add. JL | perswasion, & continue in an opinion different from you. P; H *fo. 25ᵛ has
endorsement* Toleration 67 / D   *in* H *fo. 26ʳ has signature* E *in direction line*   in] A, O, P |
[from you] in H   8 [*1st*] the] H, A | *om.* O, P   9 [*1st*] the] H, A | but the O, P
10 will] A, O, P | [doth] will H   12 the] A, O, P | [all the] the H
16 treatment] H, A, P | `ill´ treatment O *addition perhaps in Hand B*   22 tempt
them] A, O, P | `tempt them.´ H (*no caret*) | *not in* F   25 of the Government] A, O,
P | `of the Government´ H *add. in margin, no caret*

---

[1] On the number of dissenters, see the General Introduction, p. 12.

desire & same strength to pull them downe, & therefor it may be expected they will be cautious how they exercise it. But if you thinke the different [*fo. 27*^r] partys are already grown to a consistency & formd into one body & interest against you. whether it were the hardships they sufferd under you made them unite or noe, when they are soe many as 5 to equall or exceed you in number as perhaps they doe in England, force will be but an ill & hazardous way to bring them to submission.

If uniformity in England be soe necessary as many pretend, & compulsion be the way to it, I demand of those who are soe zealous for it, whether they really intend by force to have it or noe. If they doe not, it is not 10 only imprudent but malicious under that pretense, by ineffectuall punishments to disquiet & torment their brethren. for to shew how litle persecution if not in the extremest degree has beene able to establish uniformity, I shall aske but this one plaine question, Was there ever a free toleration in this kingdom. If there were not I desire to know of any of the 15 Clergy who were once sequesterd, how they came to be turnd out of their liveings & whether impositions & severity were able to preserve the Church of England & hinder the growth of puritans even before the war. If therefor violence be to settle uniformity tis in vain to mince the matter. that severity which must produce it cannot stop short, of the totall destruction 20 & extirpation of all dissenters at once, & how well this will agree with the doctrine of christianity the principles of our church & reformation from popery, I leave them to judg who can thinke the Massacre of France[1] worthy their imitation, And desire [*fo. 28*^r] them to consider if death for noe thing lesse can make uniformity were the penalty of not comeing to 25 common prayer, & joyneing in all our church worship, how much such a law would settle the quiet & secure the government of the Kingdom.

1 strength] A, O, P | [weapons] `strength.' H    therefor it may] ed. | there`for' `it' may H for *inserted on line;* it *inserted after* may *but caret before* | therefor may it A, O, P 2 [*1st*] they] A, O, P | `they' H   4 against you] A, O, P | `against you' H    5 you] *foll. in* H *by idle caret* unite] A, O, P | [soe] `unite' H   many] A, O, P | [numerous] `many' H    6 exceed] A, O, P | [far] exceed H    8 as] A, O, P | [in England] as H    11 imprudent] A, O, P | [foolish] `imprudent' H   12 for] A, O, P | [whether therefor] for H   15 in this kingdom] A, O, P | [in England. If there were not I desi⟨re⟩] [Except in the late times & there never establish but carried out [in] in England] `in this kingdom' H    19 mince] H, O, P | `mince' A *inserted by Locke in space left by copyist*   20 destruction] H, O, P | destinction O   22 of] H, O, P | `of' A *add. JL*    our] A, O, P | [pr⟨otestant⟩] our H    23 can] A, O, P | [thi⟨nk⟩] can H    Massacre] H, A, P | [Measure] `Massacre' O *alt. JL*   24–25 for... uniformity] A, O, P | `for... uniformity.' H   27 [*3rd*] the] H, O, P | this A

---

[1] The St Bartholomew's Day massacre, 1572.

The Romish religion that had beene but a litle while planted & taken
but small roote in Japan[1] (for the pore converts had but litle of the
efficacious truths & light of christianity conveyd to them by those teachers who make ignorance the mother of devotion, & knew very litle beyond
5 an ave marie, or pater noster.) could not be extirpated but by the death of
many thousands, which too prevaild not at all to lessen their numbers till
they extended the severity beyond the delinquents & made it death not
only to the family that enterteind a preist but also to all of both the
families that were next neigbours on either hand though they were
10 strangers or enemys to the new religion. And invented exquisite
lingering torments worse then a thousand deaths which though some had
strength enough to endure 14 days togeather yet many renouncd their
religion, whose names were all registerd with a designe that when the
professors of Christianity were all destroyd, these too should be butcherd
15 all on a day, never thinkeing the opinion rooted out beyond possibility
of spreading again, as long as there were any alive who were the least
acquainted with it or had almost heard any thing of Christianity more
then [*fo. 29ʳ*] the name. Nor are the Christians that trade there to this day
sufferd to discourse fold their hands or use any gesture that may shew the
20 difference of their religion. If any one thinke uniformity in our church
ought to be restord though by such a method as this, he will doe well to
consider how many subjects the King will have left by that time it is
donne. There is this one thing more observeable in the case, which is,
That it was not to set up uniformity in religion, (for they tolerate seven or
25 eight sects & some soe different as is the beleife of the mortality or
immortality of the soule, nor is the magistrate at all curious or inquisitive

2 in] H, O, P | `in' A *add. JL on line*   had] A, O, P | [were] [[bu⟨t⟩]]had H   litle]
H, A | a little O, P   3 truths] A, O, P | truth`s' H   light] A, O, P | [spirit]
`light' H   6 to] A, O, P | [till the] to H   7 they] A, O, P | [the persecution grew
soe hot that it] they H   &...death] A, O, P | `&... death' H   8 that] O, P | [but]
that H | *om.* A   preist] A, O, P | [preist] [Romish] preist H   all of] A, O, P | `all of' H
9 neigbours] A, O, P | `neigbours' H      11 lingering] A, O, P | [`lingering
t⟨orments⟩'] [torments] [worse then a thousand deaths,] [of long durations which]
lingering H   had] A, O, P | [endurd for 14] had H   13 with] A, O, P | [in a book]
with H   that] A, O, P | `that' H      17 heard] O, P | heard [of] H | [h. .d] `heard' A
alt. JL   19 fold their hands] A, O, P | `fold their hands' H   gesture] *foll. in* H *by*
idle caret   20 thinke] H, A, O | thinkes P   22 it is] A, O, P | [they have] `it is' H
25 of] A, O, P | `of' H      26 is the magistrate] A, O, P | [are] `is the magistrate' H
at all] H, O, P | `at all' A *add. JL*

[1] Possible sources for Locke's account of the persecution are discussed in the General
Introduction, Note B.

what sect his subjects are of, or does in the least force them to his religion) nor any aversion to Christianity which they sufferd a good while quietly to grow up among them, till the doctrine of the popish preists, gave them jealousys that religion was but their pretense but empire theire designe, & made them feare the subversion of their state, which suspition 5 their owne preists improved all they could to the extirpation of this growing religion

But to shew the danger of establishing uniformity [*fo. 30ʳ*]

To give a full prospect of this subject there remaine yet these following particulars to be handled   10

1° To shew what influence Toleration is like to have upon the number & industry of your people on which depends the power & riches of the kingdom

2° That if force must compell all to an Uniformity in England to consider what party alone, or what partys are likelyest to unite to make a 15 force able to compell the rest.

3° To shew that all that speake against toleration seeme to suppose that severity & force are the only arts of government & way to suppresse any faction, which is a mistake

4° That for the most part the matters of controversy & destinction be- 20 tween sects, are noe parts or very inconsiderable ones and appendixes of true religion

5° To consider how it comes to passe that Christian religion hath made more factions wars, & disturbances in civil societys then any other, & whether tolleration & Latitudinisme[1] would prevent those evills.   25

1 sect] H, P | sect[ş] A | sects O   in] A, O, P | [at] in H   2 any] A, O, P | [to] any H   3 among] H, O, P | amongst A   till] O, P | [ ] fill H | [and fill] 'till' A *alt.* | *JL*   doctrine] H, A, P | Doctrine`s' O *add. JL*   the popish preists] ed. | [the church of Rome] 'popish preists' H | 'the' popish priests O *add. JL* | popish priests A, P   4 gave] A, O, P | [made] gave H   jealousys] ed. | [reason to feare] [the] 'jealousys' H | jealousy A, O, P   5 them] H, O, P | 'them' A *add. JL*   6 priests] A, O, P | preist H   8 But . . . uniformity] *written in darker ink in* H, *probably added later; remainder of page (about 5 cm) blank*   12 your] H, A, P | yᵉ[ᵒʳ]ᵉ O *probably alt. JL*   21 sects] A, O, P | [partys] [factions] [of]sects H   and] O, P | [or]and H | and 'but' A *add. JL*   24 wars] A, O, P | [d⟨isturbances⟩]wars H   25 &] A, O, P | [or]& H   evills] *foll. in* H *by* [But of these when I have more leisure] *on separate line*

[1] For the origins of the term, see *A Brief Account of the new Sect of Latitude-Men Together with some reflections upon the New Philosophy*; Burnet, i. 331–41. The best modern account is Spurr, ' "Latitudinarianism" and the Restoration Church'.

6° That Toleration conduces noe otherwise to the setlement of a government then as it makes the majority of one minde & incourages vertue in all, which is donne by makeing & executeing strict laws concerning vertue & vice, but makeing the [*fo. 31ʳ*] termes of church communion as
5 large as may be, i.e. that your articles in speculative opinions be few & large, & ceremonys in worship few & easy. which is Latitudinisme.

7° That the defineing & undertakeing to prove severall doctrines which are confesd to be incomprehensible[1] & to be noe otherwise knowne but by revelation, & requireing men to assent to them in the termes proposd by
10 the Doctors of your severall churches, must needs make a great many atheists.

But of these when I have more leisure:

Sic Cogitavit Atticus[2] 1667

1–6 *written in lighter ink in* H, *probably added later*   3 strict] H, A, P | `strict′ O *inserted by Locke in space left by copyist*   4 *in* H *folio number written in pencil, not by Locke*   of] O, P | [of commu⟨nion⟩] H | `of′ A *add.* JL   7–11 *written in darker ink in* H, *probably added later*   7 defineing] H, O, P | desireing A   9 revelation] H, O, P | re`ve′lation A *alt.* JL   [*1st*] to] A, O, P | [to consent] to H   12 But...leisure] H, O, P *written in lighter ink in* H | But...leisure A *in Locke's hand, preceded by illegible sentence deleted by overwriting, also in Locke's hand*   of] H, A, P | `of′ O *inserted on line, probably by Locke*   13 Sic...1667] H *written boldly in darker ink* | Sic Cogitavit JL 1667 A *in Locke's hand, foll. by the additions printed below* | *om.* O, P | H *fo. 33ᵛ has the endorsement* Toleration 67/ E

[1] Presumably a reference to the description of the Trinity in the Athanasian Creed as 'The Father incomprehensible, the Son incomprehensible: and the Holy Ghost incomprehensible'. Cf. *A Third Letter for Toleration*, 232: 'What think you of St. *Athanasius's* Creed? Is the sense of that so *obvious and expos'd* to every one who seeks it, which so many Learned Men have explain'd so different Ways, and which yet a great many profess they cannot understand?'
[2] Locke's friend Elinor Parry used the name Atticus for him in several letters of around this time: *Correspondence*, i. 261, 298, 307, 311, 318.

THE FIRST DRAFT OF *AN ESSAY CONCERNING TOLERATION*

This is written on the two sides of a single sheet of paper now kept with the quires of paper that contain the Rough Draft and the Fair Copy of the *Essay concerning Toleration* in Huntington Library HM 584. Folio numbers have been supplied by the editors.

[*fo. 1ʳ*]

To state the question of toleration right.

1 I suppose that there ⟨are⟩ only two sorts of things that have a right to toleration.

⟨1⟩ the first is all puerly speculative opinions, as the beleife of a trinity, fall, antipodes atoms &c which have noe reference at all to society   5

2 the place time & manner of worshiping my god.

1 Because bare speculations prescribeing noe rule to my actions with other men but being all one as if there were noe other person besides me in the world cannot either disturb the state or inconvenience my neigbour   10

2 I ought to have liberty in my religious worship, because it is a thing betweene god and me, & is of an eternall concernment wheras the magistrate is but umpire between man & man· he can right me against my neigbour, but cannot defend me against my god, what ever evill I suffer by obeying him in other things he can make me amends in this world, but   15 if he force me to a wrong religion, he can give me noe reparation in the other world. Therefor it can not be supposd that men should give the magistrate a power to choose for them their way to salvation; which was too great to give away if not impossible to part with, since what ever the magistrate injoyned in religion men must in this necessarily follow what   20 they themselves thought best, since noe consideration could be sufficient

---

5 'which...society [& would be the same were there but that one man in the world]' *added at paragraph-end*   6 god] *foll. by* In both these papists & all mankinde seeme to have a title *underscored by Locke, presumably to indicate deletion*   7 [haveing noe] prescribeing   11 [concernment] 'thing'   16 [*1st*] 'he' (*no caret*)   [satisfaction] 'reparation'   20 injoyne'd'   'in religion' *apparently added at line-end*

An Essay Concerning Toleration

to force a man from or to that which he was perswaded was the way to infinite happynesse or infinite misery.

2 I suppose that all other actions except those of religious worship or opinions that immediately direct me in my actions with men. have noe
5 right at all to toleration, how ever any such action or opinion may be to me matter of conscience, since the persuasion of the truth of any opinion or the good or evill of any action doth obleige the conscience, though the thing in its self be never soe trivial. For the whole concerment of society is intrusted to the power of the magistrate, the morall part whereof is well
10 enough secur'd.

For the distinction of virtue & vice is by all man kinde soe perfectly & certainly knowne, & the establishment of vice brings soe certaine a disturbance & ruin to all society that it cannot be suppos'd, nor was it ever found, that any magistrate did establish vice by a law or punish virtue.
15 the dutys (or rather religion, for this is the great & active part of it) of the second table does by its owne authority & the benefits it brings to governments sufficiently establish its self everywhere.

There remains then only things indifferent, except those which are part or circumstances of my worship of god, which however private mens
20 consciences may approve or disallow of yet are undoubtedly under the coercive power of the magistrate otherwise there can be noe law nor government· The errors or scruples of my conscience which leade me to or deter me from the doeing of any thing destroy not the magistrates power, nor alter the nature of the thing, nor the obligations of my
25 obedience to him.

3 I suppose that the preservation & peace of the people being the rule & standard according to which the magistrate ought to make his laws, & fashion his government, he has noething at all to doe with speculative opinions or religious worship, since in them selves they tend not at all to
30 the disturbance of the government noe more then haveing black hair, or wearing grey cloaths. But yet if the professors of any one way of worship, should either mix with their religion other opinions by which they

---

1 'or to' (*no caret*)   [though⟨t⟩ the] [*1st*] was   3 'except...worship'
6 ⟦an⟨y⟩⟧the   8–10 'For...secur'd' *added at paragraph-end*   9 ⟦th⟧where'of'
11 [are by naturall reason soe easily] is   12 [encourageing] ['allowance']
'establishment'   13 [to all] &   14 [establish] [injoyn] 'establish'   'by a law'
(*no caret*)   15 [if y] rather   16 {to} [society]/ to   18–19 'except...
god'   20 undoubt'edly'   23 'or...from'   [may] destroy   24–25 'nor...
him' *last two words on new line, rest of phrase probably also added*   27 [by]
'according to'   29 [as such th] in   32 religio⟦us⟧n [worship]   [where] by
'which'

regulate their conversation with their neigbour, (viz, that they are to
compell others to their opinion, that faith is not to be kept with hereticks
i.e. those of an other persuasion &c), & hold those as sacred & necessary
as any other part of their religion. they have noe right to toleration,
because they make that a part of their religion which really is not, but is 5
absolutely under the power of the Magistrate over which he may use his
jurisdiction as he shall think fit without any injury to them at all, since he
medles not with their religion but that which is puerly of a civill right
though they thinke them selves obleigd in conscience to adhere to it &
upon this ground I suppose the Papists as they have now compounded 10
their religion have noe pretension [*fo. 1ᵛ*] to toleration farther then the
magistrate shall thinke convenient.
  Or else if the professors of any worship shall grow soe numerous &
unquiet as manifestly to threaten disturbance to the state. the magistrate
may take all ways he shall thinke convenient either by art or power to 15
prevent the mischeife. & though he should use force & severity if that
were a fit way to weaken them, yet did he not really persecute their
religion or punish them for that, noe more then in a battle the conqueror
kills men for weareing white ribbons in their hats or any other badg, but
because this was a marke that they were enemys & dangerous. religion 20
i.e. this or that forme of worship being the cause only of their union &
correspondence; not of their factiousnesse or turbulency, for the praying
to god in this or that place or posture or any other part of religious
worship does noe more in its self make men at enmity one with an other
or produce seditions then the weareing of hats & turbants, which either of 25
them may doe by being a note of destinction, & giveing men an oportunity to number their forces know their strength be confident of one an
other, & upon any occasion readily unite soe that they are not restraind
because of this or that opinion but because such a number of opinion
what soever that dissented would be dangerous 30
  the same thing therefor would happen if a fashon of clothes distinct
from that of the magistrate & those that adhere to him, should be taken
up at first by a few & by degrees spread its self & become the badge of a

---

4 [or else grow soe numerous & unquiet as manifestly to threaten disturbance to the
state] they   6 [really] absolutely   7 [& upon this ground] since
15 [by] either   [force] `power'   17 [pros⟨ecute⟩] persecute       19 [`or a⟨ny⟩'
but because] or   24 [pr⟨oduce⟩] make   25 `or...seditions'   27 [stren⟨gth⟩]
forces   [&] be   28–30 `soe...dangerous' *added at paragraph-end*   31 [the
greatest] [by degrees people [her⟨e⟩] in England should take up a new] ⟨a⟩ fashon
32 [which] should   [come to be worne by] ⟨be⟩

very considerable part of the people, who held a very strict correspondence & freindship one with an other, might not this well give the
magistrate cause of jealousy, make him forbid the fashon not because
unlawfull, but because of the dangerous consequence, thus a cloke may
5 have the same effects with a coule or any other religious way or habit· &
perhaps the Quakers were they numerous enough to be dangerous to the
state would deserve the magistrates care & watchfulnesse to breake &
suppresse them were they noe other wais destinguishd from the rest of his
subjects but by the beare keeping on their hats, as much as if they had a set
10 forme of religion seperate from others, in which case noe body would
thinke that the not standing bare were a thing the magistrate leveld his
severity against any other wise then as it united a great number of men
togeather, who though they dissented from him in a very indifferent or
triviall circumstance yet might thereby indanger his government· & in
15 such a case the magistrate noe question has a power & right to weaken,
restraine or breake any party of men which religion or any other thing hath
united to the manifest danger of his government· but whether severity &
force, the bare forbiding of their opinion practices or strict imposeing of
his owne worship or any other milder method be the readiest way to
20 suppresse them he only is to be judg. & shall not be accountable in the
other world for what he does directly in order to the praeservation & peace
of his people according to the best of his knowledg.

I conclude then

1 That Papists & all other men have a right to toleration of their religious
25 worship & speculative opinions

2 The Papists haveing adopted into their religion as fundamentall truths,
severall opinions, that are oposite & destructive to any government but
the popes, have noe title to toleration

3 Considering the Papists as a certaine number of men now in England
30 suppose $\frac{1}{10}$, or $\frac{1}{5}$ or $\frac{1}{2}$ of the nation,[1] they are noe lesse dangerous to the

---

5 [a surplice.] any   *On the line below there are the deleted words* Quakers hats *and three
lines further down the underscored and probably deleted words* Papists at present *It is likely that
both phrases were written before the texts that surrounds them as reminders for topics needing
further discussion*   8 [had] 'were'   10 o⟦r⟧f   15 ⟦t⟨o⟩⟧&   18 'bare'
19 'or...method.'   22 [judgment] 'knowledg.' *added at line-end; text deleted by
single vertical line as far as this point*   26 [mixt other doc⟨trines⟩] adopted
27 ⟦cer⟨tain⟩⟧severall

---

[1] As with the number of dissenting Protestants, only approximate figures can be given:
for a discussion, see Bossy, *The English Catholic Community 1570–1850*, 188–94. The

state whether tolerated or persecuted, but as they are there by better or worse armed, since their very principles make them irreconcilable to the state, & therefor are not to be tolerated.

4 Considering the Papists as a changeable body of men growing or decreaseing, soe they ought to be tolerated & suppressed proportionably 5
as either of these usages may serve to lessen their number & weaken their party.

5 That all other dissenters from you if they be more in number then you, but crumbled into different partys amongst them selves, are best securd by toleration, since being in as good a condition under you as they can hope 10
under any, tis not like they should joyne to set up any other which they cannot be certaine will use them soe well. but if you persecute them you make them all of one party & interest against you, to shake of your yoake & venture for a new government where in every one has hopes to get the dominion them selves or better usage under others. If the dissenters be all 15
of one opinion & fewer then you they ought to be tolerated in their religious worship & speculative opinions, if they have not the mixture of any dangerous practicall principles· And if they be more then you force will be but an ill & hazardous way to bring them to submission

ADDITIONS TO *AN ESSAY*
CONCERNING TOLERATION

MS Locke c. 28

Three passages were added by Locke to the copy of the *Essay* in MS Locke c. 28, in one case replacing another deleted passage. All are in Locke's hand; none of them appears in any other manuscript.

2 [by] their   5 [&] soe   6 'usages.' (*no caret*)   7 *foll. on separate line*
by [And these perhaps may be rules for other partys as well as Papist.]   12 [secure]
'certaine'   15 [gov⟨ernment⟩] dominion   16 ough⟨t⟩   18–19 'And . . .
submission' *written vertically in margin*

Compton Census gave a figure of 11,870 communicants for the province of Canterbury, to which should be added a substantial figure for the province of York, where the proportion of Catholics was considerably higher. Bossy (ibid. 189, 422) and Miller (*Popery and Politics*, 9–12) suggest an overall figure of about 60,000 for the later 17th century, which would make Catholics about 1.2% of the population.

(*a*) MS Locke c. 28, fo. 22ʳ, designed to be added after 'whether those colours be really there or noe' on fo. 21ᵛ (above, p. 272). The passage is keyed by the numeral (1) at the beginning, with a corresponding numeral and caret at the point of insertion on fo. 21ᵛ.

I must only remarke before I leave this head of speculative opinions that the beleif of a deitie is not to be recond amongst puerly speculative opinions for it being the foundation of all morality & that which influences the whole life & actions of men without which a man is to be
5 counted noe other then one of the most dangerous sorts of wild beasts & soe uncapeable of all societie

(*b*) MS Locke c. 28, fo. 22ʳ, designed to be added after 'From what is premisd I thinke will follow', on fo. 21ᵛ (above, p. 275). The passage is keyed by the numeral (2) at the beginning, with a corresponding numeral and caret at the point of insertion on fo. 21ᵛ.

Twill be said that if a toleration shall be allowd as due to all the parts of religious worship it will shut out the Magistrates power from makeing laws about those things over which it is acknowledged on all hands that
10 he has a power viz things indifferent as many things made use of in Religious worship are, viz weareing a white or a black garment, Kneeleing or not Kneeleing, &c. To which I answer that in religious worship noething is indifferent for it being the useing of those habits gestures &c & noe other which I thinke acceptable to god in my worshiping of him,
15 however they may be in their own nature perfectly indifferent, yet when I am worshiping my god in a way I thinke he has prescribd & will approve of I cannot alter omit or adde any circumstance in that which I thinke the true way of worship. And therefor if the magistrate permit me to be of a profession or church different from his tis incongruous that he should
20 prescribe any one circumstance of my worship, & tis strange to conceive upon what grounds of Uniformity any different profession of Christians can be prohibited in a christian Country where the Jewish religion (which is directly opposite to the principles of Christianity) is tolerated, & would it not be irrationall where the Jewish religion is permitted, that the
25 Christian magistrate upon pretence of his power in indifferent things, should enjoyn or forbid any thing or any way interpose in their way or manner of worship

2 [barely] `puerly'    7 [to] if    9 acknowledg⟨ed⟩    10 things] *foll. by idle caret*    11 [as] `viz'   13–14 &c `[& noe] other' *deleted caret before* &c *undeleted one afterwards*    17 [or] omit `or adde'   [to] in   18 `t'he `magistrate' [worship god in a way in o] be   21 [of Religion] `of Uniformity'    22 `christian'

(*c*) MS Locke c. 28, fo. 28ᵛ. These two passages are separated in the manuscript by a space of about 2 cm, and were designed to replace a long deleted passage on the Quakers and other Protestant dissenters on fos. 26ʳ–27ʳ (above, pp. 285–7). In the margin next to the first passage there are the words 'v. p. 7' [fo. 26ʳ] followed by the bracketed numeral (7). At the end of the paragraph on fo. 26ʳ Locke originally wrote the bracketed numeral (2), which was then overwritten to turn it into '(3)', and finally deleted and replaced by '(7)'; in the left margin there are the words 'p. 12 (7)', p. 12 being fo. 28ᵛ.

And that which may render them yet more incapeable of toleration is when ⟨to⟩ these doctrines dangerous to government they have the power of a neighbour prince of the same religion at hand to countenance & backe them upon any occasion.

The objection usually made against Toleration That the Magistrates 5 great businesse being to preserve peace & quiet of the government He is obleiged not to tolerate different religions in his country since they bring destinctions wherein men unite & incorporate into bodys seperate from the publique, they may occasion disorder conspiracys & seditions in the commonwealth & endanger the government 10
    I answer if all things that may occasion disorder or conspiracy in a commonwealth must not be endurd in it All discontented & active men must be removd, & whispering must be lesse tolerated then preaching as much likelier to carry on & foment a conspiracy. & if all numbers of men joynd in an union & corporation destinct from the publique be not to be 15 sufferd all charters of Towns espetially great ones are presently to be taken away. Men united in religion have as litle & perhaps lesse interest against the government then those united in the priviledges of a Corp-oration. this I am sure they are lesse dangerous as being more scatterd & not formd into that order. And the mindes of men are soe various in 20 matters of religion & soe nice & scrupulous in things of an eternall concernment that where men are indifferently tolerated & persecution & force does not drive them togeather, they are apt to devide & subdivide into soe many litle bodys & always with the greatest enmity to those they

---

2 [to] these   [dangerous] doctrines   6 [the] quiet   7 bring] **ed.** |
being **O**   8 destinction's'   9 [give] occasion   [of] `disorder'
11 [sedition] disorder   12 [active] discontented   14 [corporations or] numbers
15 [united & incorp⟨orated⟩] joynd   17 [the] religion   20 m⟦a⟧en [is] `are'
22 [they] [*1st*] &   [does] [*2nd*] &

last parted from or stand nearest to, that they are a guard one upon an other & the publique can have noe apprehensions of them as long as they have their equall share of common justice & protection. & if the Example of Old Rome (where soe many different opinions gods & ways of worship
5 were promiscuously tolerated) be of any weight we have reason to imagin that noe Religion can become suspected to the state of ill intention to it till the government first by a partiall usage of them different from the rest of the subjects declare its ill intentions to its professors, & soe make a state business of it. And if any rationall man can imagin that force &
10 Compulsion can at any time be the right way to get an opinion or religion out of the world or to breake a party of men that unite in the profession of it. This I dare affirme.

Adversaria 1661

In Adversaria 1661 there are two separate additions to the *Essay concerning Toleration*, neither of which appears in any other manuscript. (*a*) The first, on p. 125, follows on immediately after the main part of the *Essay* and is in the same hand; it was therefore almost certainly copied at the same time, in 1671–2. (*b*) The second starts on p. 125 immediately below the first addition and continues on pp. 270–1. Unlike its predecessor it is in Locke's hand, and was added some years later, probably around 1675.

(*a*) Adversaria 1661, p. 125.

me thinks the clergy should like ambasadors endeavour to entreate convince and perswade men to the truth rather then thus solicit The
15 magistrate to force them into theire fold· this was the way that gaind admittance for christianity and spread the religion they professe soe far into the world: whereas whilst they once a weeke uncharitably preach against: and the rest of the weeke as impudently raile at theire dissenting bretheren and doe not endeavour by the meekeness and tender methods
20 of the gospell and by the soft cords of love to draw men to them: but would have even those compeld under theire jurisdiction whom they never take care to instruct in theire opinions· for I think I may say

---

4 'opinions'   5 [may] be   8 [that religion] its   10 [[a]]the   [out] or
12 This...affirme] *phrase appears on both fo. 27ʳ and fo. 26ᵛ*   13 endeavour] ed. |
endearemt A   17 a weeke] ed. | aweeke A   19 methods] ed. | mothods A
21 'even'   [his Juri⟨sdiction⟩] theire   [they never] whom

that preaching a sermon once a weeke at rovers[1] perhaps learned perhaps otherwise doth very little towards instructing men in the knowledg of faith which after many years hearing one may be still ignorant of and is seldome effectuall to perswade them to good lives. this makes some men suspect that tis not the feeding of the sheep but the benefit of the fleece that makes these men endeavour by such methods to enlarge theire fold: this I am sure is quite contrary to the first way which nursd up christianity

(*b*) Adversaria 1661, pp. 125, 270–1.

Though the Magistrate have a power of commanding or forbiding things indifferent which have a relation to religion, yet this can only be within that church whereof he him self is a member, who being a lawgiver in matters indifferent in the Commonwealth under his jurisdiction as it is purely a civil society, for their peace, is fitest also to be lawgiver in the religious society (which yet must be understood to be only a voluntary society & dureing every members pleasure) in matters indifferent for decency & order[2] for the peace of that too. But I doe not see how hereby he hath any power to order & direct even matters indifferent in the circumstances of a worship or within a church whereof he is not professor or member. Tis true he may forbid such things as may tend to the disturbance of the peace of the commonwealth to be donne by any of his people, whether they esteem them civil or religious. this is his proper businesse but to command or direct any circumstances of a worship as part of that religious worship which he himself doth not professe nor approve is altogeather without his authority & absurd to suppose. Can any one thinke it reasonable yea or practicable that a Christian Prince should direct the forme of Mahumetan Worship the whole religion being thought by him false & prophane & vice versa· & yet it is not impossible that a Christian prince should have Mahumetan Subjects who may deserve all civil freedom. & defacto the Turke hath Christian subjects.

---

1 a weeke] ed. | aweeke A   2 perhaps {perhaps} *separated by blank space sufficient for about one word*   3 ⟦p⟧knowledg   hearing] ed. | hearein A   7 fold[s] 9 [bid]   forbiding   10 [with]   which   13 [is fitest]   for   [for]   in 14–15 ʿ(which ... pleasureʿ⟨⟩⟩ *two carets, after* society *and at end of sentence*   16 too] *foll. by idle caret*   18 he] ed. | his A   21 [publiq⟨ue⟩] civil 23 ʿnotʿ   26 [which] [*2nd*] the

---

[1] at rovers: without any aim or object; at random, haphazard, *OED* rovers.
[2] decency & order: 1 Cor. 14: 40. Cf. *Two Tracts*, 146; *A Third Letter for Toleration*, 13.

As absurd would it be that a Magistrate either Popish, Protestant, Lutheran, Presbyterian Quaker &c should prescribe a forme to any or all of the differing churches in their way of worship. The reason whereof is because religious worship being that homage which every man pays to his
5 god, he cannot doe it in any other way [*p. 270*] nor use any other rights, ceremonys, nor formes even of indifferent things then he him self is perswaded are acceptable & pleaseing to that god he worships, which depending upon his opinion of his god & what will best please him, it is impossible for one man to prescribe or direct any one circumstance of it
10 to an other, & this being a thing different & independent wholy from every mans concerns in the civil society which hath noething to doe with a mans affairs in the other world, the magistrate hath here noe more right to intermedle then any private man, & hath lesse right to direct the forme of it then he hath to prescribe to a subject of his in what manner he shall
15 doe his homage to another prince to whom he is feudatory, for some thing which he holds immediately from him, which whether it be standing kneeling or prostrate, bareheaded or bare footed whether in this or that habit &c concerns not his allegiance to him at all, nor his well government of his people. For though the things in them selves are perfectly indif-
20 ferent, & it may be trivial· yet, to the worshiper when he considers them as required by his god or forbidden, pleaseing or displeasing to the Invisible power he addresses to, they are by noe meanes soe, & till you have alterd his opinion (which perswasion can only doe) you can by noe meanes, nor without the greatest tyrany prescribe him a way of worship.
25 Which was soe unreasonable to doe that we finde litle bustle about it, & scarce any attempts towards it by the Magistrates in the severall societys of mankinde till Christianity was well growne up in the world & was become a nationall religion. & since that it hath been the cause of more disorders tumults & bloudshed then all other causes put togeather.
30 But far be it from any one to thinke Christ the author of these disorders, or that such fatal mischeifs are the consequence of his doctrine though they have grown up with it· Anti christ hath sowne these tares in the feild of the church.[1] The rise whereof hath been only hence, that the clergy by degrees as Christianity spread asserting dominion laid claime to

---

4 to his] **ed.** | `his'` to **A**   5 270 *in margin at foot of p. 125*   13 [prescribe the] direct   14 [matt⟨er⟩] what   19 [may] are   22 [app⟨eals⟩]   addresses   24 [his [f⟨orm⟩] worship] him   25 [attem⟨pt⟩] bustle   34 asserting] *reading unclear, possibly* affecting

---

[1] Matt. 13: 25. Locke alluded to the parable again in the *Third Letter for Toleration*, 315.

a preisthood derived by succession from Christ & soe independent from the civill power, receiveing (as they pretend) by the imposition of hands & some othere ceremonys agreed on (but variously) by the preisthoods of the severall factions, an indelible character particular sanctity & a power immediately from heaven, to doe severall things which are not lawfull to be donne by other men, the cheif whereof are· 1° to teach opinions concerning god, a future state & ways of worship· 2° to doe & performe them selves certain rights[1] exclusive of others. 3° To punish dissenters from their doctrines or rules· Whereas it is evident from Scripture[2] that all preisthood terminated in the Great high preist Jesus Christ who was the last preist. 2° There are noe foot steps in Scripture of any soe set apart with such powers as they pretend to after the Apostles time nor that had any indelible character. 3° That it is to be made out that there is noe thing which a preist can doe which an other man without any such ordination, (if other circumstances of fitnesse & an appointment to it, not disturbeing peace & order concur) may not lawfully performe & doe, & the church & worship of god be preserved, as the peace of the State may by Justices of peace & other officers, who had noe ordination or laying on of hands to fit them to be Justices, & by takeing away their commissions may cease to be soe. soe Ministers as well as Justices are necessary one for the administration of religious publique worship, the other of civil justice, but an indellible character, peculiar sanctity of the function, or a power, immediately derived from heaven is not necessary or as much as convenient for either. [*p. 271*]

But the clergy (as they call them selves of the Christian religion in imitation of the Jewish preisthood[3]) haveing almost ever since the first ages of the church laid claim to this power seperate from the civil

---

1 [on] [*2nd*] 'from' 3 [severall factions] preisthoods 4 'particular sanctity' 5 [was not] [were] 'are' 6 [to t⟨each⟩] 1° 9 [there] it 10 the *smudged, perhaps deleted* 11 ⟦I⟨n⟩⟧There 16 [which another] may 21 [civil] religious 23 'not' 25 [preisthood of] clergy 26 [laid clai⟨m⟩] the 27 [seperate] power

[1] i.e. rites.

[2] Presumably Heb. 7: 23–5, 10: 11–12; for a contemporary exposition, see Owen, *Exercitations on the Epistle to the Hebrews, Concerning the Priesthood of Christ*, especially Exercitations VII and VIII. In the *Reasonableness of Christianity* (p. 120) Locke commented that 'I do not remember that he [Jesus] any where assumes to himself the Title of a Priest, or mentions any thing relating to his Priesthood . . .'.

[3] 'For Clergy signifies those, whose maintenance is that Revenue, which God having reserved to himselfe during his Reigne over the Israelites, assigned to the tribe of Levi . . .', *Leviathan*, 336.

313

government as received from god himself, have wherever the civil magistrate hath been Christian & of their opinion & superior in power to the clergy & they not able to cope with him pretended this power only to be spirituall & to extend noe farther, but yet still pressed as a duty on the
5 Magistrate to punish & persecute those who they disliked & declared against· & soe whom they excommunicated their under officer the Magistrate was to execute, & to reward princes for thus doeing their drudgery, they have (when ever princes have been serviceable to their ends) been carefull to preach up monarchy jure divino, for common
10 wealths have hitherto been lesse favourable to their power. But notwithstanding the jus divinum of Monarchy, when any prince hath dared to dissent from their doctrines or formes, or been lesse apt to execute the decrees of the hirarchy they have been the first & forwardest in giveing chek to his authority & disturbance to his government. And princes on
15 the otherside being apt to hearken to such as seeme to advance their authority, & bring in religion to the assistance of their absolute power, have been generally very ready to worry those sheepe who have ever soe litle stragled out of those shepheards folds, where they were kept in order to be shorne by them both, & to be howld[1] on both upon subjects &
20 neigbours at their pleasure, & hence have come most of those calamitys which have soe long disturbd & wasted Christendom. Whilst the Magistrate being perswaded it is his duty to punish those the clergy please to call hericticks scismaticks or fanatick, or else being taught to apprehend danger from dissenters in religion thinks it his interest to
25 suppresse them, persecutes all who observe not the same formes in religious worship which is set up in his country. The People on the other side findeing the mischeifs that fall on them for worshiping god according to their owne perswasions enter into confederacys & combinations to secure them selves as well as they can, soe that oppression & vexation on
30 one side, self defence & desire of religious liberty on the other, creat dislikes jealousys apprehensions & factions which seldom faile to breake out into downright persecution, or open war.

---

1 [&] `as'      2–3 [but their interest weak & not] `& superior . . . not'   5 [from whom] who   7 & [the better]   9 [cried] been   10 [very litle] `lesse' 12 [not] been      16 [power] absolute      17 [like ⟨ . . . . . . ⟩ mastives] to 18 those] *perhaps* these      19 on [upon]      20 [all] `most of'   21 [either] the   22 [& suppresse] those   the[y] `clergy'      23 [fanaticks] scismaticks [then] taught      26 The] `y^{er} *on line, probably added later*   29 [&] `on' 31 [persecution] &

[1]Meaning obscure; not in *OED*.

But notwithstanding the liberality of the Clergy to princes where they have not strength enough to deale with him be very large, yet when they are once in a condition to strive with him for mastery, then is it seen how far their spirituall power extends & how in ordine ad spiritualia[1] absolute temporall power comes in. Soe that ordination that begins in preisthood [5] if it be let alone will certainly grow up to absolute empire, & though Christ declares him self to have noe Kingdom of this world,[2] his successors have (when ever they can but grasp the power) a large commission to execute & that rigorously civil dominion. The Popedom hath been a large & lasting instance of this. And what presbytery could doe even in [10] its infancy when it had a litle humbled the Magistrate let Scotland shew.[3]

---

[1] in ordine ad spiritualia. Cf. *Two Tracts*, 154; *A Second Letter concerning Toleration*, 53; Hobbes, *Behemoth*, 41. [2] John 18: 36.

[3] Stories of clerical tyranny exercised by the Presbyterians in Scotland found a ready readership in England after the Restoration. In the English Tract on Government (*Two Tracts*, 157) Locke cited *The Burthen of Issachar* (London, 1646), written by the exiled bishop of Ross, John Maxwell; this was reprinted in 1663 as *Presbytery Displayd*. On 20 March 1674 Locke bought a copy of the work (under its original title) for Shaftesbury, MS Locke f. 48, p. 9; National Art Library, Forster MS 48. G. 3/22.

WRITINGS ON CHURCH
AND STATE,
1668–1674

QUERIES ON SCOTTISH CHURCH GOVERNMENT

PRO 30/24/47/30, fo. 45.

[*fo. 45*^r]

Q Whethe⟨r⟩ the Bishops are by law obleigd to take in the rest or any part of the Clergy in the exercise of their jurisdiction: & how far?[1]

What is the power & jurisdiction of Arch-deacons & Deans?[2]

Who choose the Commissioners for the Presbytery who with the Moderators nominated by the Bishop are the representatives of the 5 Presbytery in the Nationall Synod?[3]

Who make the President of the National Synod?[4]

Whether the President & the ArchBishop of St Andrews have each of them a negative voice in the nationall Synod?[5]

Whether every Elder in the Parochiall sessions hath an equall power & 10 vote with the minister in their church censure?[6]

---

4 Com^{rs}   8–9 Whether...Synod? *crossed through with a light vertical line, perhaps* indicating deletion

[1] According to the 1662 Act of Restitution bishops were to exercise their functions 'With advice and assistance of such of the Clergie as they shall find to be of knoun loyaltie and prudence' (*Acts of the Parliaments of Scotland*, vii. 372).
[2] Both deans and archdeacons had been formally re-established in 1661–2, but the posts had little significance, and were often held by the ministers of parishes within the diocese. The disciplinary responsibilities of archdeacons in England were exercised by presbyteries in Scotland.
[3] The Act establishing the national synod laid down that presbyteries were to be represented by their moderators and by 'one presbiter or minister of each meeting [presbytery] To be choysen and elected by the moderator & plurality of presbiters of the same' (*Acts of the Parliaments of Scotland*, vii. 465).
[4] The Archbishop of St Andrews was to preside (*Acts of the Parliaments of Scotland*, vii. 465).
[5] This question wrongly presumes that the President and the Archbishop of St Andrews might be distinct, which may explain why Locke later deleted it. Approval by the President and by the majority of the synod was required for any decision (*Acts of the Parliaments of Scotland*, vii. 465).
[6] Parochial sessions, or kirk-sessions as they were usually called, were attended by the minister (as chairman) with the elders and deacons of the parish.

Whether the fines for trespasses are arbitrary or limited?[1]

Whether the Presbyterys consist only of the clergy, or take in the Elders too, & whether every minister has of course a vote there?[2]

Whether Excommunication be never for any other cause but
5 contumacy?[3]

Whether the Bishop hath a power to (or ever doth) disapprove the processe of excommunication passed by the Presbytery?[4]

What follows upon a mans standing excommunicate[5]

Whether noe accusation be suggested against a minister by any body
10 but a minister?[6]

What the censures are that att any time passe upon a delinquent minister, & by whome[7]

[*fo. 45[v]*] In the triall for Ordination[8] what is meant an Homely,[9] a common head,[10] addition & Exercise?[11]

---

2 [and] / or *first word blotted and presumably deleted*   7 'passed...Presbytery'
9-12 Whether...whome *crossed through with a light vertical line, perhaps indicating deletion*
9 [noe]any   11 [an]att

---

[1] Not known.

[2] Every minister had a vote in his presbytery, but since the Restoration the elders had been excluded, Foster, *Bishop and Presbytery*, 72.

[3] Excommunication could be for a variety of offences, including drunkenness, swearing, sabbath-breaking, and witchcraft, ibid. 81.

[4] 'A sentence of greater excommunication [was] pronounced after the bishop had examined the process, and had given his consent', Hunter, *The Diocese and Presbytery of Dunkeld*, ii. 53.

[5] There were two forms of excommunication: 'lesser excommunication, which was suspension from Church privileges, and greater excommunication. The latter sentence was indeed a terrible one. Such a person was forbidden to leave the parish, to enter the house of any other person, or to have any contact with other parishioners.' Foster, *Bishop and Presbytery*, 81.   [6] Not known.

[7] Minor disciplinary matters were the responsibility of the presbytery, but suspension or deprivation remained in the hands of the bishop.

[8] A candidate for the ministry went through two separate series of trials, the first for a licence to preach, and the second (usually several years later) for ordination and presentation to a benefice; both sets of trials were organized by a presbytery, though ordination itself remained in the hands of the bishop. See ibid. 45.

[9] A private sermon before the ministers assembled at a meeting of the presbytery, Hunter, *The Diocese and Presbytery of Dunkeld*, ii. 7.

[10] A theological disputation, usually in Latin, on a set theme, Foster, *Bishop and Presbytery*, 74–5.

[11] An exercise was 'the Explicatory and Analytick Part' of the exposition of a passage of Scripture; the addition, 'the Raising of Observations and Doctrines from the Text', Hunter, *The Diocese and Presbytery of Dunkeld*, ii. 19.

Whether the Bishop can suspend or depose noe minister without the concurrence of the Presbytery or Synod?[1]

Endorsed by Locke: <u>Church</u> Government / Q Concerning the Scotch Discipline / <u>68</u>

---

3 <u>Church</u> Government *in darker ink than remainder of endorsement*

---

[1] The concurrence of the presbytery or (diocesan) synod was not legally required.

NOTES ON SAMUEL PARKER'S
DISCOURSE OF ECCLESIASTICAL POLITIE

MS Locke c. 39, fos. 5–10. The quotations from Parker's *Discourse* printed here in italics have been supplied by the editors, and do not appear in the manuscript.

[*fo. 5ʳ*]

Society is necessary to the preservation of humane nature

Goverment necessary to the preservation of Society· The end whereof is peace

One Supreme necessary in every City for the preservation of the government· 1° because there can not be two suprems; 2° because 5 coordinate distinct powers may command the same person contrary obedience which he cannot be obliged to

This supreme is the Civil magistrate

The Civil magistrate must have under his power all that may concerne the end of government i.e. peace. 10

Religion & Conscience are more apt to disturbe the peace then even vice it self, 1° because men are most apt to mistake because backd, with zeale the glory of god & the good of mens soules martyrdom they make men more resolute confident turbulent &c. where as vice discoverd is out of countenance

Ergo It is necessary the magistrate should have power over mens 15 consciences in matters of religion.

This power is to be exercised with the most severity & strictnesse, because ordinary severity will not doe.

Fathers have an absolute power over their children

This paternall power grew into severall monarchys 20

These monarchs by this paternall right were also preists.

Soveraignty & preisthood joyntly vested in the same person for first 2500 years

Ecclesiasticall supremacy exercised by the Jewish Kings though the preisthood were vested in other persons.

Christ haveing noe temporall power exercised none, nor could give the magistrate none about his religion which was to be propagated by patience & submission 5

[*fo. 5ᵛ*] but instead of civil coercive power to keepe up ecclesiastical discipline there was given the church a miraculous power to punish as well as eject offenders by excommunication· this lasted in the church till the magistrate became Christian & then ceased as noe longer necessary, because then the government of religion resolved in the magistrate & was 10 restord though the preists commissioned by our saviour kept the ministerial function & soe the Christian magistrate hath again the power over religion

First then 'tis absolutely necessary to the Peace and Tranquillity of the Commonwealth, which, though it be the prime and most important end of 15 *Government, can never be sufficiently secured, unless Religion be subject to the Authority of the supreme Power, in that it has the strongest influence upon humane affairs; and therefore if the Sovereign Power cannot order and manage it, it would be but a very incompetent Instrument of publique happiness, would want the better half of it self, and be utterly weak and ineffectual* 20 *for the ends of Government.*[1]

[*fo. 7ʳ*] Q p. 11. §. 4. 5. 6. 8 10
Whether Prooves any thing but that the magistrates businesse being only to preserve peace, those wrong opinions are to be restraind that have a direct tendency to disturbe it? and this is by every sober man to be allowd 25

...as true Piety secures the publique weal by taming and civilizing the passions of men, and inuring them to a mild gentle and governable spirit: So superstition and wrong notions of God and his Worship are the most powerful engines to overturn its settlement. And therefore unless Princes have Power to bind their subjects to that Religion that they apprehend most advantageous to 30 *publique Peace and Tranquillity, and restrain those Religious mistakes that tend to its subversion; they are no better than Statues and Images of*

---

1   though {though}   3 Christ] X   'could' (*no caret*)   give] gave *MS*
10–11 '& ...restored'   12 'Christian' (*no caret*)   [still] 'again'   22 Q. . . 10]
in margin   23 'Whether' *addition in darker ink* (*no caret*)   ⟦noe⟧ any
24 'wrong'   25 '? and ...allowd' *addition on line in darker ink*

[1] Parker, *A Discourse of Ecclesiastical Politie*, 11–12.

Authority, and want that part of their power that is most necessary to a right discharge of their Government.[1]

p 12. Whether assigneing those ill effects that follow to <u>mistakes</u>. p. 18 <u>wrong notions of god & his worship</u> he does not suppose the magistrates power to proceed from his being in the right.   5

    Whether by <u>binde the subject to his religion</u>, he means that whether the magistrates opinion be right or wrong he has power to force the subject to renownce his owne opinions however quiet & peaceable & declare assent & consent to those of the magistrate? & if soe why Christ & the Apostles directed not their discourses, & addressed their miracles to 10 the princes & magistrates of the world to perswade them, whereas by preaching to & converting the people they according to this doctrine under a necessity of being either Seditious or Martyrs.

For if Conscience be ever able to break down the restraints of Government, and all men have licence to follow their own perswasions, the mischief is infinite, and 15 *the folly endless. . . . there never yet was any Common-wealth, that gave a real liberty to mens Imaginations, that was not suddainly overrun with numberless divisions and subdivisions of Sects: as was notorious in the late Confusions, when Liberty of Conscience was laid as the Foundation of Settlement.*[2]

p 21 Whether subdivision of opinions into small sects be of such danger 20 to the government

. . . and because the Church of Rome by her unreasonable Impositions has invaded the Fundamental Liberties of mankind, they presently conclude all restraints upon licentious Practices and Perswasions about Religion under the hated name of Popery.[3]
    25

p. 24 What fundamentall libertys of mankinde were invaded by the church of Rome that will not be in the same condition, under the civill magistrate according to his doctrine? since the power of the church of Rome was allowd, & their decrees inforcd by the will of the civill magistrate

But . . . 'tis enough at present to have proved in general the absolute necessity 30 *that Affairs of Religion should be subject to Government; and then if they*

---

3 p 12] *in margin*   th<u>o</u>se *possibly* these   `mistakes . . . 18' *addition in fainter ink*
3, 4, 6 *Locke's underlining, indicating quotations from Parker*   8 [to assent] `to'
9 magistrate?] *note up to this point in a dark ink, similar to that used for addition on fo. 5*
20 p 21] *in margin*   26 p 24] *in margin*   27 [accord⟨ing⟩] *under*

[1] Ibid.   [2] Ibid. 21–2.   [3] Ibid. 24.

be exempt from the Jurisdiction of the Civil Power, I shall demand, Whether
they are subject to any other Power, or to none at all? If the former, then
the Supreme Power is not Supreme, but is subject to a Superiour in all matters of
Religion, or rather (what is equally absurd) there would be two Supreme
Powers in every Commonwealth; for if the Princes Jurisdiction be limited to 5
Civil Affairs, and the concerns of Religion be subject to another Government,
then may subjects be obliged to (what is impossible) contradictory
commands. . . . But seeing no man can be subject to contradictory obligations, 'tis
by consequence utterly imposible to be subject to two Supreme Powers.[1]

p. 25 §10 The end of government being publique peace tis noe question 10
the supreme power must have an uncontroulable right to judg & ordeyne
all things that may conduce to it? but yet the question will be whether
Uniformity establishd by a law be (as is here supposd) a necessary
means to it? i.e. whether it be at all dangerous to the magistrate that he
beleiveing free will, some of his subjects should beleive predestination, or 15
whether it be more necessary for his government to make laws for
weareing surplices, then it is for wearing vests?

And hence the Wisdom of Providence . . . so ordered Affairs, that no man could
be born into the World without being subject to some Superiour: every Father
being by Nature Vested with a Right to govern his Children. And the first 20
Governments in the world were establisht purely upon the natural Rights of
Paternal Authority, which afterward grew up to a Kingly Power by the
encrease of Posterity . . . and hence it came to pass that in the first ages of the
World, Monarchy was its only Government . . .[2]

p. 29 §11 Whether allowing the paternall right of government (which is 25
asserted not proved) that paternall monarchy descended [*fo. 7ᵛ*] upon death
of the father it descended wholy to the eldest sonne, or else all the brothers
had an equall power over their respective issues? if the first then
Monarchy is certainly jure naturali, but then there can be but one
rightfull monarch in the whole world i.e. the right heire of Adam, if the 30
second, all governments whether monarchicall or other is only from the
consent of the people.

[*fo. 9ʳ*]

---

10 p . . . 10] *in margin*   11 [us] must *deleted word very uncertain*   15 [his] some
16 [nece⟨ssary⟩] more   25 p . . . 11] *in margin*   27 [upon] all
29 [the] Monarchy

[1] Ibid. 25–6.   [2] Ibid. 29.

p.144

Q

The vulgar are apt to be superstitious & to have wrong conceits in religion. Doctrines of religion are very powerfull to incline men to obedience or disturbance. The opinions in religion influence more forcibly then any, ergo, it is the magistrates interest to take care what particular doctrines of religion are taught, & above all things to looke to the doctrines & articles of mens beleif. p 144 §. 3.[1]

Whether hence it will follow that the magistrate ought to force men by severity of laws & penaltys to force men to be of the same minde with him in   5 the speculative opinions in religion, or worship god with the same ceremonys? That the magistrate should restraine seditious doctrines who denys but because he may then has he power over   10 all other doctrines to forbid or impose, if he hath not the argument is short, if he hath how far is this short of Mr Hobbs's doctrine?

  15

There is the same phanatick spirit that mixes it self with all the religions in the world. 153.[2]

Whether this Fanatick spirit be not the same passion fird with religious zeale whose phanatick heats he in the same § accuses of haveing committed such dire outrages massacres & butchery   20 & donne such mischeifs among men, & if it mixes its self with all religions I desire him to examin though he be of the church of England what spirit that is which sets him soe zealously to stir up   25 the magistrate to persecute all those who dissent from him in those opinions or ways of worship the publique support whereof is to give him preferment?

Endorsed by Locke (fo. 8ᵛ): Qs On S.Ps discourse of toleration. 69

---

1 p. 14⟨4⟩   2 [have wrong opinions in religion] be   3–4 '&...religion' (*no*
caret)   18 in] is *MS*   20 'massacres...butchery' (*no caret*)
22 [be] mixes   23 [consid⟨er⟩] examin   23–24 'though...England'
25 [furiously] 'zealously'   28 [communion] ways

---

[1] 'But secondly, Nothing more concerns the Interest of the Civil Magistrate, than to take care, what particular Doctrines of Religion are taught within his Dominions; because some are peculiarly advantageous to the Ends of Government, and others as naturally tending to its disturbance...' (ibid. 144).
[2] 'In brief, Fanaticism is both the greatest, and the easiest Vice that is incident to Religion; 'tis a Weed that thrives in all Soils, and there is the same Fanatick Spirit, that mixes it self with all the Religions in the World.' (ibid. 153).

EXCOMMUNICATION

MS Locke c. 27, fos. 29ᵃ–29ᵇ. The first part of the text is in an unidentified hand, with additions by Locke; from the heading 'The Paralel' onwards all the text is in Locke's hand.

[*fo. 29ᵃʳ*]

There is 2 fold Society of which allmost all men in the world are Members and that from the 2 fold concernment they have to attaine a 2 fold happinesse, viz: That of this world and that of the other· and hence there arises these 2 following Societys, viz: Religious & Civill

Civill Society or the State	Religious Society or the Church.
1 The End of Civill Society is Civill Peace and prosperity or the preservation of the Society and every Member theereof in a free and peaceable enjoyment of all the good things of this life that belong to each of them, but beyond the concernments of this life this society hath noething to doe at all	1 The end of Religious Society is attaining happinesse after this life in another world.
2 The termes of Communion with or being a part of this Society is promise of obedience to the laws of it	2 The terms of Communion or Condition of being Members of this Society is promise of obedience to the laws of it
3 The proper matter circa quam¹ of the laws of this	3 The propper matter of the laws of this

---

5 Civill Society *in large bold letters* 'or…state' *add. JL in much smaller letters* 5–6 Religious…Church *in large bold letters* 8 [re] attaining 14–16 [this life this Society] 'the…all' *add. JL* 17–20 [*LH column*] 2…it *in Locke's hand* 18 'with' (*no caret*) [*LH column*] [ad⟨mission⟩] being [*RH column*] Conditions[s] 19 [*RH column*] ⟦ar⟨e⟩⟧is

¹ about which

327

Society are all things tending
to the end above mentioned
i.e. Civill happinesse and are
in effect allmost all morall
5 and indifferent things which
yet are not the propper matter
of the laws of this Society till
the doeing or omitting of any
of them come to have a
10 tendency to the end above
mentioned

15 4 The means to procure
obedience to the lawes of this
Society and thereby preserve
it is force or punishment
i.e. The Abridgement of any
20 ones share of the good things
within the Reach of this
Society and sometimes
a totall deprivation as in
Capitall punishments
25 [*fo. 29^{av}*]

30

And this I think is the whole

Society are all things tending
to the attainement of future
bliss which are of these 3 sorts.
1 Credenda[1] or matters of faith
and opinion which terminate in
the understanding. 2. Cultus
Religiosus[2] which conteins in
it both the wayes of expressing
our honour and adoration of
the deity & of addresse to him
for the obteining any good
from him. 3 Moralia or the right
management of our actions in
respect of our selves and others

4 The means to preserve
obedience to the laws of
this society are the hopes and
feares of happinesse and misery
in another world. But though
the laws of this Society be in
order to happinesse in another
world and so the penaltys annext
to them are also of another
world yet the society being
[*fo. 29^{av}*] in this world and to be
continued here there is some
means necessary for the
preservation of the Society here
which is the expulsion of such
members as obey not the laws
of it or disturbe its order.

And this I think is the whole

5 [*RH column*] [and t⟨erminate⟩] which   6 [come] 'are' *alt. JL*   [*LH column*] [to be]
the   8 [injoying or forbid⟨ing⟩] doeing   10 [trinity] deity   15 [preserve
Civ⟨il⟩] procure   17 [f]ar'e' *alt. JL*   21–22 [of this world] 'within … Society.'
del. by underscoring, addition by Locke   22 [and] 'an'next   24 society[s]
25 *at the top of fo. 29^{av} the two columns are headed* Civill Society *and* Church *respectively*   [of]
/ in   29 [all those who live] such   31 'or … order.' *add. JL*

[1] things to be believed   [2] religious worship

end latitude and extent of Civill power and Society	end latitude and extent of Ecclesiasticall power and religious Society.

This being as I suppose the destinct bounds of Church and State let us a little Compare them togeather   5

The Paralel

1 The end of civil society is present enjoyment of what this world affords	1 The end of church communion, future expectation of what is to be had in the other world
2 An other end of civil society is the preservation of the Society or Government its self for its owne sake	2 The preservation of the society in religious communion is only in order to the conveying & propagateing those laws & truths which concern our well being in an other world 15

3 The termes of Communion must be the same in all Societys.

4 The Laws of a Commonwealth are muteable being made within the Society by an authority not destinct from it nor exterior to it	4 The Laws of Religious Society bateing[1] those which are only subservient to the order necessary to their execution are immutable not subject to any authority of the Society but only proposed by & within the Society, but made by a lawgiver without the Society & Paramount to it 25
5 The proper meanes to procure obedience to the law of the Civil Society & thereby atteine the end civil happynesse is	5 The proper inforcement of obedience to the laws of Religion is the rewards & punishments of the other world· But civil

6 *heading in large bold letters; remainder of manuscript in Locke's hand*   7 [RH column] ⟦2⟧1   17 [RH column] of {of}   18–20 'bateing...execution' *added in a much fainter ink*   19 ⟦b⟧made   21–22 [&] 'not...but'   23 ⟦the⟧'&'   26–29 [The proper meanes to attein the end of Civil Society] 'The...happynesse' *del. by underscoring*   26–27 [meanes to attein the end of [civil Society] Religious Society] 'inforcement...Religion'   27 [Civil] law

[1] excepting

force or punishment. 1ˢᵗ it is
effectuall & adequate means
for the preservation of the
society & of civil happynesse
5 is the immediate & natural
consequence of the execution
of the law· 2° It is just, For
the breach of laws being mostly
the prejudice & diminution
10 of another mans right & always
tending to the dissolution of
the society in the continuance
whereof every mans particular
right is comprehended, it is just
15 that he who hath impaired an
other mans good should suffer
the diminution of his owne.
3 Tis within the power of the
society which can exert its owne
20 strength against offenders, the
sword being put into the
magistrates hand to that purpose.
But civil Society hath noething to
doe without its owne limits which
25 is civil happynesse

30

punishment is not soe·
1° Because, it is ineffectuall
to that purpose, for punishment
is never sufficient to keepe men
to the obedience of any law, where
the evil it brings is not certainly
greater, then the good which is
obteined or expected from the
disobedience. And therefor noe
temporal worldly punishment can
be sufficient to perswade a man to
that or from that way which he
beleives leads to everlasting
happynesse or misery. 2° Because
it is unjust, in reference both to
Credenda & Cultus that I should
be dispoiled of my good things of
this world where I disturbe not in
the least the injoyment of others.
for my faith or religious worship
hurts not an other man in any
concernment of his. And in moral
transgressions the 3ᵈ & great part
of Religion the Religious Society
cannot punish because it then invades the civil Society, & wrests the
Magistrates sword out of his hand.
in Civil Society one mans good is
involved & complicated with an
other, but in religious Societys
every mans concerns are seperate,
& one mans transgression hurts
not an other any farther then he
imitates him, & if he erre he errs at

1–2 '1ˢᵗ...means'   3 [yᵉ immedi⟨ate⟩] [1ˢᵗ] the   [*RH column*] [but] [[to]]for
4 [[f⟨or⟩]]to   5 [is] '[being] is'   10 [tis ju⟨st⟩]   &   [[p⟨unishment⟩]]
wor⟨l⟩dly   13 [imagins]beleives   15 [both]in   17 [punished] dispoiled
22 [concern] in   23 '& great'   26 [So⟨ciety⟩] civil   28–331.1 'in...
cost' *interlinear addition without caret, continued after* religious *in margin of fo.* 29ᵇʳ

330

his owne private cost. Therefore I thinke noe external punishment i.e. deprivation or diminution of the good of this life belongs to the

6 Church membership is perfectly voluntary & may end when ever any one pleases, without any prejudice to him but in Civil Society it is not soe.

Church. Only because for the propagation of the truth (which every Society beleives to be its owne Religion) it is equity, it should remove those two

[*fo. 29^{br}*] evils which will hinder its propagation. 1° Disturbance within, which is contradiction or disobedience of any of its members to its doctrines & discipline· 2° Infamy without which is the scandalous lives, or disallowed profession of any of its members· And the proper way to doe this which is in its power, is to exclude, & disowne such vitious members.

But because religious societys are of two sorts, wherein their circumstances very much differ· The exercise of their power is also much different.

It is to be considered that all man kinde, (very few or none excepted) are combined into civil societies in various formes, as force, chance, Agreement or other accidents have happend to contrive them. There are very few also that have not some Religion. And hence it comes to passe that very few men but are members both of some church & of some common wealth· & Hence it comes to passe

1 That in some places the Civil & Religious Societys are coextended, i.e. Both the Magistrate, & every subject of the same common wealth is also member of the same church. And thus it is in Muscovy. Where they have all the same civil laws & the same opinions & religious worship

2 In some places the Commonwealth though all of one religion is but a part of the church, or religious Society which acts & is acknowledged to be one entire society, & soe is it in Spaine & all the principalitys of Italy.

6–7 [it is] (which [if] 'every' [religious]   7 [But in a] without   11 'of...
members' *insertion in margin, no caret*   13 [& that is] And   'proper'
19 *preceded by* [1] *in margin*   20 [& Common⟨wealth⟩] in   21–22 'There...
Religion'   23 member's'   26 [Every subj⟨ect⟩] Both   [state is als⟨o⟩]
same   27–28 'Where...worship' *apparently added later*   27 Whe[[n]]re
28 'civil' (*no caret*)   30–31 'or...society.' (*no caret*)   31 [Germany.] Italy

3 In some places the Religion of the Commonwealth i.e. the publique establishd religion is not received by all the subjects of the Common wealth, & thus the Protestant religion in England, the Reformed in Brandenburg,[1] the Lutheran in Sweden.

5 4 In some places the Religion of part of the people is different from the Governing part of the civil Society, & Thus the presbiterian Independent Anabaptist quaker, Papist & Jewish in England, the Lutheran & Popish in Cleve[2] &c. & in these two laste the Religious Society is part of the Civil.

10 There are also 3 things to be considered in each religion, as the matter of their Communion

   1 Opinions or Speculations or Credenda

   2 Cultus religiosus

15   3 Mores.[3]

Which are all to be considered in the exercise of Church power, which I conceive does properly extend noe farther then Excommunication, which is to remove a scandalous or turbulent member.

20 1 In the first case there is noe need of Excommunication for immorality, because the civil law hath or may sufficiently provide against that by penall laws enough to suppress it, for the Civil Magistrate hath morall actions under the dominion of his sword, & therefor tis not like he will turne away a subject out of his country, for a fault which he can compell 25 him to reforme. But if any one differ from the Church in fide aut Cultu[4]

---

3 th⟦is⟧us   4 Sweden. [& here the]   7 Anabaptist [& &]   `Papist' (*no*
caret)   `& Jewish' *add. in margin*   16 [power] exercise   21 or may] [& doth]
`or may.'   provide] provided *MS*   24 [when he] for

---

[1] The Electors of Brandenburg had been Calvinists since the reign of Johann Sigismund (1572–1619; Elector, 1608; converted 1613), but the majority of the population were Lutherans.

[2] Locke was familiar with the situation in Cleves since his visit there in 1665–6. The Duchy of Cleves had come under the rule of the Electors of Brandenburg in 1614. The religious situation in this and the other German states since the Peace of Westphalia (1648) was that 'the official or dominant faith enjoyed the *exercitium religionis publicum* (churches with spires and bells); those with rights dating from before 1624 could enjoy the *exercitium religionis privatum* (chapels without bells); those without such rights had only the *exercitium religionis domesticum* (prayers in the family home) and the right to visit churches in a neighbouring principality', Whaley, 'A Tolerant Society?', 179–80.

[3] morals, or customs   [4] in faith or worship

I thinke first the civil Magistrate may punish him for it, where he is fully perswaded that it is likely to disturbe the civil peace, otherwise not. But the religious society may certainly excommunicate him, the peace whereof may by this means be preserved, but noe other evil ought to follow him upon that excommunication as such, but only upon the consideration of the publique peace, for if he will silently conceale his opinion or carry away his opinion [*fo. 29^{bv}*] or differing worship out of the Verge[1] of that Government I know not by what right he can be hindered.

2 In the 2^d case I thinke the Church may excommunicate for faults in faith & worship, but not those faults in manners which the Magistrate hath annexed penaltys to for the preservation of Civil Society & happynesse

3 The same also I thinke ought to be the rule in the 3^d case

4 In the 4th case I thinke the church hath power to Excommunicate for matters of faith, Worship or manners, though the Magistrate punish the same immoralitys with his sword, because the church cannot otherwise remove the Scandal which is necessary for its preservation & the propagation of its doctrine. And this power of being judges who are fit to be of their Society the magistrate cannot deny to any Religious Society, which is permitted within his dominions. This was the state of the church til Constantine.

But in none of the former Cases is Excommunication capeable to be denounced by any church upon any one but the members of that church, it being absurt to cut of that which is noe part: Neither ought the Civil Magistrate to inflict any punishment upon the score of excommunication but to punish the fact[2] or forbeare, just as he findes it convenient for the preservation of the civil peace & prosperity of the common wealth,

---

6 [carry away his opi⟨nion⟩] silently   7 [is] 'his'   10 [Scan⟨dal⟩] faults
12 [the] Civil   16 [mode] Worship   19–22 'And...Constantine.'
24 [....h] church   25 [impossible] 'absurt'   [not a] 'noe'   27–28 [it
tends to the disturbance] 'he...preservation'   28 [2nd] ⟦his⟧the

---

[1] The verge of court was the area with twelve miles of the royal court that lay under the jurisdiction of the Lord High Steward. In the 17th century the term was widely used in metaphorical senses derived from this: the range, sphere, or scope of something, *OED* verge.   [2] deed

(within which his power is confined) without any regard to the excommunication at all.

Endorsed by Locke on fo. 29^{bv}:   E   <u>Excommunication</u>   7¾

1 [his] which   2 *foll. by* [And this power of being judges who are fit to be of their Society] *remainder of page blank*

A LETTER FROM A PERSON OF QUALITY, TO HIS FRIEND IN THE COUNTRY

Sigla

I		The first edition, Wing S 2897
2		The second edition, Wing S 2897aA
	2u	The uncorrected state of the second edition
	2c	The corrected state of the second edition
3		*State Tracts* (1689), 41–56
4		*A Collection of Several Pieces of Mr. John Locke*, ed. P. Des Maizeaux (1720), 57–149
	4er	Errata in *A Collection of Several Pieces*
7		*The Works of John Locke*, seventh edition (1768)
B		British Library, Additional MS 74273
D		British Library, Additional MS 4224, fos. 228–43; Des Maizeaux's corrections to his copy of *State Tracts*
E		British Library, Egerton MS 3383, fos. 59–68
J		House of Lords Record Office, Manuscript Journals
M		Hampshire Record Office, 9M73/G201/1, 'The Earle of Shaftesbury's Speech in the H. of L. against the Test'
Old.		John Oldmixon, *The History of England, During the Reigns of the Royal House of Stuart* (1730)

The following manuscripts of Shaftesbury's *Reasons against the Bill for the Test* are also cited:

L	Leicestershire Record Office, DG7/PP30
N	The National Archives, PRO 30/24/5/294, pp. 1–10
R	Bodleian Library, MS Rawlinson D 924, fos. 297–300
S	Surrey History Centre, Woking, LM/1331/60
T	Bodleian Library, MS Rawlinson A 191, fos. 3–4
Y	Beinecke Library, Yale University, Osborn Shelves, b. 157, pp. 141–55

A Letter from a Person of Quality,
to His Friend in the Country

SIR,

This Session being ended, and the Bill of the *Test* neer finished at the 5
Committee of the whole House; I can now give you a perfect Account of
this STATE MASTER-PIECE. It was first hatch't (as almost all the Mischiefs
of the World have hitherto been) amongst the *Great Church Men*, and is a
Project of several Years standing, but found not Ministers bold enough to
go through with it, until these *new ones*, who wanting a better Bottom to 10
support them, betook themselves wholly to this, which is no small
Undertaking if you consider it in its whole Extent.

First, to *make a distinct Party* from the rest of the Nation of the High
Episcopal Man, and the Old Cavalier, who are to swallow the hopes of
enjoying all the Power and Office of the Kingdom, being also tempted by 15
the advantage they may receive from overthrowing the *Act of Oblivion*,[1]
and not a little rejoycing to think how valiant they should prove, if they
could get any to fight the Old Quarrel over again; Now they are possest of
the Arms, Forts, and Ammunition of the Nation.

Next they design to *have the Government of the Church Sworne to as* 20
Unalterable, and so Tacitely owned to be of Divine Right; which though
inconsistent with the Oath of Supremacy, yet the Church Men easily
break through all Obligations whatsoever, to attain this Station, the
advantage of which, the Prelate of *Rome* hath sufficiently taught the
World. 25

Then in requital to the Crown, they declare the Government *absolute*
and *Arbitrary*, and allow Monarchy as well as Episcopacy to be *Jure*
Divino, and not to be bounded, or limited by humane Laws.

[*p. 2*] And to secure all this they resolve to take away the Power, and
opportunity of *Parliaments* to alter any thing in Church or State, only 30
leave them as an *instrument* to raise Money, and to pass such Laws, as the

---

5 [*2nd*] the] 1, B | *om.* 2–4   neer] 1–2, B | being 3–4 | [being] [`neer'] `being' D | *om.*
E   8 have] 1, 4, B, D | had 2–3   15 Office] 1–4 | offices B   21 Right;]
ed. | Right, 1–2 | *Right*; 3 | Right: D, 4 | right, B   22 Supremacy,] B, E |
Supremacy; 1–4

[1] 12 Car. II, c. 11, *SR* v. 226–34.

Court, and Church shall have a mind to; The Attempt of any other, how necessary soever, must be no less a Crime then Perjury.

And as the topstone of the whole Fabrique, a pretence shall be taken from the Jealousies they themselves have raised, and a real necessity from
5 the smallness of their Partie, to encrease and keep up a standing Army, and then in due time the Cavalier and Church-man, will be made greater *fools*, but as errant *Slaves* as the rest of the Nation.

In order to this, The *first step* was made in the *Act for Regulating Corporations*,[1] wisely beginning that in those lesser Governments which
10 they meant afterwards to introduce upon the Government of the Nation, and making them Swear to a Declaration, and beleif of such propositions as they themselves afterwards upon debate, were enforced to alter, and could not justifie in those words; so that many of the Wealthyest, Worthyest, and Soberest Men, are still kept out of the Magistracy of
15 those places.

The *next step* was in the *Act of the Militia*,[2] which went for most of the cheifest Nobility and Gentry, being obliged as Lord-Lieutenants, Deputy-Lieutenants, *&c.* to Swear to the same Declaration and Beleif, with the addition only of these words *In pursuance of such Military*
20 *Commissions*, which makes the Matter rather worse then better; Yet this went down smoothly as an Oath in fashion, a testimony of Loyalty, and none adventuring freely to debate the matter, the humor of the Age like a strong Tide, carries Wise and good Men down before it: This Act is of a piece, for it establisheth a *standing Army* by a Law, and swears Us
25 into a *Military Government*.

Immediately after this, Followeth the *Act of Uniformity*,[3] by which all the Clergy of *England* are obliged to subscribe, and declare what the Corporations, Nobility, and Gentry, had before Sworn, but with this additional clause of the Militia Act omitted: This the Clergy readily
30 complyed with; for you know that sort of Men are taught rather to obey,

---

3 [*1st*] the] 1–4 | A B | to the E   5 Partie, to encrease] ed. | Partie to encrease, 1–2 | Party, to encrease 3–4, B, D   9 beginning that] B | beginning, that 1–3 | beginning that, 4, D   12 they] 3–4 | *not in* 1–2, B   14 [*2nd*] of] 1–4 | in B   16 *the*] 1 | the 2c, B, D, E | *om.* 2u, 3–4   went for] 1–4 | passed; For B   18 Deputy-Lieutenants, *&c.*] 1–4 | and Deputy Lieutenants, B   Declaration] 2–4 | Declaration, 1 | declaration B   21 a] 1–4 | & a B   23 carries] 1–4 | carried B   24 of a] 1–4 | a master B   27 of *England*] 1–3 | of England 4, D | *not in* B   30 that] 2–4, B | That 1

---

[1] 13 Car. II, st. 2, c. 1, *SR* v. 321–3.   [2] 14 Car. II, c. 3, *SR* v. 358–64.
[3] 14 Car. II, c. 4, *SR* v. 364–70.

then understand, and to use that *Learning* they have, to *justify*, not to *examine* what their Superiors command: And yet that *Bartholomew day*[1] was fatal to our Church, and Religion, in throwing out a very great Number of *Worthy, Learned, Pious, and Orthodox Divines*, who could not come up to this, and other things in that Act; And it is upon this occasion 5 worth your knowledg, that so great was the Zeal in carrying on this Church affair, and so blind was the Obedience required, that if you compute the time of the passing this Act, with the time allowed for the Clergy to subscribe the Book of *Common Prayer* thereby established; you shall plainly find it [*p. 3*] could not be Printed, and distributed, so as one 10 Man in forty could have seen and read the Book they did so perfectly Assent and Consent to.[2]

But this Matter was not compleat until *the Five Mile Act* passed at *Oxford*,[3] wherein they take an opportunity to introduce the Oath in the terms they would have it: This was then strongly opposed by the 15 L. Treasurer *Southampton*,[4] Lord *Wharton*, L. *Ashley*, and others not only in the Concern of those poor Ministers that were so severely handled, but as it was in it Self, a most Unlawful, and Unjustifyable Oath; however, the Zeal of that time against All *Nonconformists*, easily passed the Act. 20

This Act was seconded the same Session at *Oxford* by another Bill in the House of Commons, to have imposed that Oath on the *whole Nation*; and the Providence by which it was thrown out, was very remarquable; for Mr. *Peregrine Bertie*, being newly chosen, was that morning introduced into the House by his Brother the now Earl of *Lindsey*, and 25 Sir *Tho. Osborn* now L. Treasurer, who all Three gave their Votes against that Bill;[5] and the Numbers were so even upon the division, that

2 their] 1–4 | *not in* B   3 a very] 1, 3–4, B, E | e very 2u | every 2c   5 it is] ed. | it is, 4, D | it is an Oath 1–3 | it is an oath B   10 distributed, so] ed. | distributed so, 1–4 | distributed, so, B | distributed so E   21 Session] 3–4, B | Sessions 1–2   27 [*2nd*] the] 1, 4, B, D | that 2–3

[1] 24 Aug. 1662.

[2] This was no exaggeration: see Burnet, i. 327–8; Green, *Re-establishment*, 145–7. Locke mentioned this in *A Third Letter for Toleration*, 213.

[3] 17 Car. II, c. 2, *SR* v. 575. Parliament sat from 9 to 31 Oct. 1665; the session was held at Oxford because of the plague.

[4] Thomas Wriothesley (1607–67), fourth Earl of Southampton, Lord Treasurer 1660–7. *ODNB*.

[5] Peregrine Bertie (*c*.1635–1701), second son of Montagu Bertie, second Earl of Lindsey; elected MP for Stamford 21 Oct. 1665, Henning, i. 644–5. Robert Bertie (1630–1701), MP for Boston 1661–6, third Earl of Lindsey 1666, Henning, i. 645–6. Danby, then Sir Thomas Osborne, had been elected MP for York on 16 January 1665.

their three Votes carried the Question against it. But we owe that Right to the Earl of *Lindsey*, and the Lord Treasurer, as to acknowledg that they have since made ample Satisfaction for whatever offence they gave either the Church or Court in that Vote.

5   Thus our *Church* became *Triumphant*, and continued so for divers years, the dissenting *Protestant* being the only *Enemy*, and therefore only persecuted, whilest the Papists remained undisturbed, being by the Court thought Loyal, and by our Great Bishops not dangerous, they differing only in Doctrine, and Fundamentalls; but, as to the Govern-
10 ment of the Church, that was in their Religion in its highest Exaltation.

This Dominion continued unto them, untill the L. *Clifford*,[1] a Man of a *daring* and *ambitious spirit*, made his way to the cheif Ministery of Affairs by other, and far different measures, and took the opportunity of the War with *Holland*, the *King* was then engaged in, to propose *the*
15 *Declaration of Indulgence*,[2] that the Dissenters of all sorts, as well Pro-testants as Papists, might be at rest, and so vast a number of People, not be made desperate, at Home, while the *King* was engaged with so potent an Enemy abroad. This was no sooner proposed, but the E. of *Shaftsbury*, a Man as daring but more Able, (though of principles and interest,
20 Diametrically opposite to the other) presently closed with it, and perhaps the opportunity I have had by my conversation with them both, who were Men of diversion, and of free and open Discourses where they had a confidence, may give you more light into both their Designs, and so by consequence the aimes of their Parties, then you will have from any other
25 hand. My *L. Clifford* did in express Terms, tell me one day in private Discourse; [*p. 4*] *That the King, if He would be firm to Himself, might settle what Religion He pleased, and carry the Government to what height He would; for if Men were assured in the Liberty of their Conscience, and undisturbed in their Properties, able and upright Judges made in*
30 Westminster-Hall to *judg the Causes of* Meum *and* Tuum, *and if on the*

   1–4 But . . . Vote] 1–2, 4, B, D | *om.* 3   2 Treasurer,] 4, B, D, E | Treasurer 1–2   7 undisturbed,] 2–4, B | undisturbed 1   9 and] 1–4 | not in B 18 *Shaftsbury*,] 2–4 | *Shaftsbury* 1 | Shaftsbury, B | Shaftsbury E   19 of] 1–4 | not of B   interest,] 1–2, 4 | Interest, 3 | interests with, But B   23 confidence,] E | confidence; 1–2, 4 | Confidence, 3 | confidence) B   24 aimes] 1–2 | aims 3–4 | aime B   29 made] 1–4 | *not in* B

---

[1] Thomas Clifford (1630–73), first Lord Clifford of Chudleigh, Lord Treasurer 1672–3. *ODNB*.
[2] His Majesty's Declaration to all his loving subjects, 15 Mar. 1672 (Kenyon, *Stuart Constitution*, 382–3).

other hand the Fort of Tilbury[1] *was finished to bridle the City, the Fort of* Plymouth *to secure the West, and Armes for* 20000 *in each of these, and in* Hull *for the Northern parts, with some addition, which might be easily and undiscernedly made to the Forces now on foot, there were none that would have either Will, Opportunity, or Power to resist. But he added withall, he* 5 *was so sincere in the maintenance of Propriety, and Liberty of Conscience, that if he had his Will, though he should introduce a Bishop of* Durham, *(which was the Instance he then made, that See being then vacant)*[2] *of another Religion, yet he would not disturb any of the Church beside, but suffer them to dye away, and not let his change (how hasty soever he was in it)* 10 *overthrow either of those principles, and therefore desired he might be thought an honest Man as to his part of the Declaration, for he meant it really.*[3] The L. *Shaftsbury* (with whom I had more freedom) I with great assurance, asked what he meant by the *Declaration,* for it seemed to me (as I then told him) that it assumed *a Power to repeal and suspend all our Laws,* to 15 *destroy the Church, to overthrow the Protestant Religion, and to tolerate Popery;* He replyed half angry, *That he wondered at my Objection, there being not one of these in the Case: For the King assumed no power of repealing Laws, or suspending them, contrary to the will of his Parliament, or People, and not to argue with me at that time the power of the King's Supremacy,* 20 *which was of another nature then that he had in Civills, and had been exercised without exception in this very case by His Father, Grand Father, and* Queen Elizabeth, *under the Great Seal to Forreign* Protestants, *become subjects of* England, *nor to instance in the suspending the Execution of the two Acts of* Navigation *and* Trade, *during both this, and the last* Dutch *War*[4] 25 *in the same words, and upon the same necessity, and as yet, without Clamour*

---

1 *other*] 2–4 | *Other* 1 | other **B**   4 *undiscernedly*] 1–2 | *undiscernably* 3–4 |
undiscernedly **B**   *were*] 1–4 | would be **B**   6 *Propriety,*] 1 | *Property,* 2 | *Property*
3–4 | Property **B, E**   10 *them*] 1–4 | *not in* **B**   *let*] 1, 4, **D** | *om.* 2 | *by* 3 |
let **B**   17 *half*] 1, **B**, **D** | *all* 2–4   19 *suspending*] 1–4 | suspending of **B**
22 *Grand*] 1, 2c–4 | *Great* 2u | Grand **B, E**   23 *become*] 1, 3–4 | *beceme* 2u | *became* 2c
| become **B** | became **E**   24 *nor*] 1–2 | *not* 3–4 | nor **B**

---

[1] 'I went over to see the new begun *Fort of Tilbery*, a Royal work indeede, & such as will one day bridle a greate Citty to the purpose, before they are aware', *The Diary of John Evelyn,* iii. 609 (21 Mar. 1672).
[2] John Cosin died in January 1672; his successor, Nathaniel Crewe, was not appointed until August 1674.
[3] A proposal of this kind in Clifford's hand, entitled 'The Scheme', is in BL, Add. MS 65138, fos. 75ʳ–76ʳ; printed in Hartmann, *Clifford of the Cabal,* 153–5.
[4] Orders in Council suspending the Navigation Act (12 Car. II, c. 18) were made on 8 March 1665 and 10 May 1672, NA, PC 2/58, p. 68; PC 2/63, pp. 237–8.

that ever we heard; *But, to pass by all that, this is certain, a Government could not be supposed whether* Monarchical, *or other of any sort, without a standing* Supream Executive power, *fully enabled to Mitigate, or wholly to suspend the Execution of any penal Law, in the Intervalls of the* Legislative
5 *power, which when assembled, there was no doubt but wherever there lies a* Negative *in passing of a Law, there the address or sense known of either of them to the contrary, (as for instance of either of our two Houses of* Parliament *in* England) *ought to determine that Indulgence, and restore the Law to its full execution: For without this, the Laws were to no purpose made, if the*
10 *Prince could annull them at pleasure; and so on the other [p. 5] hand, without a Power always in being of dispensing upon occasion, was to suppose a constitution extreamly imperfect and unpracticable, and to cure those with a* Legislative *power always in being, is, when considered, no other then a perfect Tyranny. As to the Church, he conceived the Declaration was extreamly their*
15 *Interest; for the narrow bottom they had placed themselves upon, and the Measures they had proceeded by, so contrary to the Properties, and Liberties of the Nation, must needs in short time, prove fatall to them, whereas this led them into another way to live peaceably with the dissenting and differing* Protestants, *both at home and abroad, and so by necessary and unavoidable*
20 *Consequences, to become the Head of them all; For that place is due to the* Church of England, *being in favor, and of neerest approach to the Most powerful Prince of that* Religion, *and so always had it in their hands to be the Intercessors and Procurers of the greatest Good and Protection, that partie throughout all* Christendom, *can receive. And thus the A. Bishop of*
25 Canterbury *might become, not only* Alterius Orbis, *but* Alterius Religionis Papa,[1] *and all this addition of Honor and Power attaind without the least loss or diminution of the Church; It not being intended that one Living, Dignity, or Preferment should be given to Any but those, that were strictly Conformable. As to the* Protestant Religion, *he told me plainly, It was for the*

---

1 *is*] 1–3 | *was* 4, D | is B   2 *other of any*] 1–2 | *of any other* 3–4 | other of any B   5–8 *wherever . . . determine*] 1–4 | they might either confirm B   8 *and*] 1–4 | or B   22 *it*] 1–4 | *not in* B   25 Alterius Religionis] 1 | Alterius Regionis 2–3 | alterius regionis 4 | Alter B   27 *or*] 1, 2c–4 | *of* 2u | or B, E   *Living,*] 3 | *living* 1–2 | *living,* 4 | living B   29 *plainly*] 1–4 | *not in* B

---

[1] At the Council of Bari (1098) Urban II is said to have made Anselm sit beside him, saying, 'Let us put him in our world, for he is as it were Pope of the other sphere' ('Includamus hunc in orbe nostro quasi alterius orbis papam'). In his *Life of St Anselm* Eadmer credits Urban with the phrase 'velut alterius orbis apostolicum et patriarcham jure venerandum censeamus'; Southern (p. 104) suggested this to be the true origin of the better-known phrase used by William of Malmesbury, as given above. See also Milton, *Catholic and Reformed*, 337.

342

preserving of that and that only that he heartily joyned in the Declaration; *for besides that, he thought it his Duty to have care in his Place and Station, of those he was convinced, were the People of* God *and feared Him, though of different persuasions; he also knew nothing else but Liberty, and Indulgence that could possibly (as our case stood) secure the* Protestant Religion in England; *and he beg'd me to consider, if the Church of* England *should attain to a rigid, blind, and undisputed Conformity, and that power of our Church should come into the hands of a* Popish Prince, *which was not a thing so impossible, or remote, as not to be apprehended; whether in such a case, would not all the Armes and Artillery of the Government of the Church, be turned against the present Religion of it, and should not all good* Protestants *tremble to think what Bishops such a Prince was like to make, And whom those Bishops would condemn for Hereticks, and that Prince might burn; Whereas if this which is now but a* Declaration, *might ever by the Experience of it, gain the Advantage of becoming an Established Law, the true* Protestant Religion *would still be kept up amongst the Cities, Towns, and Trading places, and the Worthyest, and Soberest (if not the greatest) part of the Nobility, and Gentry, and People:* As for the *toleration of Popery* he said, *It was a pleasant Objection, since he could confidently say that the* Papists *had no advantage in the least by this* Declaration, *that they did not as* fully *enjoy, and with less noise, by the favor of all the Bishops before. It was the Vanity of the* L. Keeper,[1] *that they were named [p. 6] at all, for the whole advantage was to the dissenting* Protestants, *which were the only Men disturb'd before; and yet he confest to me, that it was his opinion, and always had been, that the* Papists *ought to have no other pressure laid upon them, but to be made uncapable of Office, Court, or Armes, and to pay so much as might bring them at least to a ballance with the* Protestants, *for those chargable Offices they are lyable unto; and concluded with this that he desired me seriously to weigh, whether Liberty and Propriety were likely to be maintained long in a Countrey like Ours, where Trade is so absolutely necessary to the very being, as well as prosperity of it, and in this Age of the World, if Articles of Faith and Matters of Religion should become the only accessible ways to our Civil Rights.*

Thus Sir, You have perhaps a better account of the *Declaration*, then you can receive from any other hand, and I could have wisht it a longer

---

1 [*1st*] *that*] 2 | *That* 1 | *that*, 3–4 | that, B   8 Popish] 1, 2c, 4, D, B, E | Bishop 2u, 3   10 [*1st*] *of the*] 1, 4, D | *and* 2u, 3 | *the of* 2c | of the B, E   12 *whom*] 1, 2c–4 | *when* 2u | whom B, E   21 *before*] 1, D | before B | *om.* 2–4   26 *a*] 1, 4, D | a B | *om.* 2–3   27 *unto*] 1–4 | to B   33 Thus] 1, 2c, B, E | Thus, 3–4 | This 2u

---

[1] Sir Orlando Bridgeman, Lord Keeper 1667–72. *ODNB*.

continuance, and better Reception then it had: for the Bishops took so great Offence at it, that they gave the Alarum of *Popery* through the whole Nation, and by their Emissaries the Clergy (who by the Connexture and Subordination of their Government, and their being
5 posted in every Parish, have the Advantage of a quick dispersing their Orders, and a sudden and universal Insinuation of whatever they please) raised such a cry, that those good and sober Men, who had really long feared the Encrease and countenance *Popery* had hitherto received, began to believe the Bishops were in earnest, their Eyes opened, though late,
10 and therefore joyned in heartily with them; so that at the next meeting of Parliament, the *Protestants* Interest was run so high, as an Act came up from the *Commons* to the *H. of Lords* in favor of the dissenting Protestants, and had passed the *Lords*, but for want of time.[1] Besides, another excellent *Act* passed the Royal Assent for the *Excluding all*
15 *Papists from Office*,[2] in the Opposition of which, the L. Treasurer *Clifford* fell, and yet to prevent his ruine, this Session had the speedier End. Notwithstanding, the Bishops attain'd their Ends fully, the *Declaration* being *Cancelled*, and the great Seal being broken off from it, The Parliament having passed no Act in favor of the Dissenters, and yet the sense
20 of both Houses sufficiently declared against all Indulgence but by *Act of Parliament*: Having got this Point, they used it at first with seeming Moderation, there were no general Directions given for prosecuting the *Nonconformists*, but here and there some of the most Confiding Justices,

---

2 so great] 1–4 | such **B**   8 and . . . received,] ed. | and continuance of *Popery*, had hitherto received, 1–3 | and countenance, Popery had hitherto received, 4 | of Popery, **B** 9 in] 1, 2c–4, **B**, **E** | in an 2u   earnest, **B** | earnest; 1–4   13 time.] 2–4 | time, 1 | time; **B**   16 his] 1, 3–4, **B**, **E** | this 2   Session] 4, **B**, **D**, **E** | Sessions 1–3   19 no] 3–4 | an 1–2, **B** | [an] no **D**   20 all] 1, 2c, 4, **B**, **D**, **E** | all the 2u, 3   22 prosecuting] 1, **B** | persecuting 2–4 | p[ro]ʼerʼsecuting **D**

---

[1] This is inaccurate. A bill entitled 'An Act for the Ease of his Majesties Protestant Subjects, Dissenters from the Church of England' was introduced into the Commons on 6 March 1673 and received its second and third readings on 7 and 19 March (*CJ* ix. 263, 264, 271); for the debates, see *The Parliamentary Diary of Sir Edward Dering*, 122–6, 137–8. In the Lords the bill received its first reading on 21 March and was sent to committee (24–6 March) where it was heavily amended; it received its third reading on 27 March (*LJ* xii. 561, 566, 571–3, 576). The Commons found many of these amendments hard to accept (*LJ* xii. 579–80) and were still debating them when the session was adjourned on 29 March. There are copies of the bill and the Lords' amendments in Bodl., MS Tanner 43, fos. 189ʳ⁻ᵛ, 191ʳ⁻4ʳ. The bill is discussed in Thomas, 'Comprehension and Indulgence', 212–15; Sykes, *From Sheldon to Secker*, 77–8; Spurr, 'The Church of England, Comprehension and the Toleration Act of 1689', 935; Miller, *After the Civil Wars*, 219–20.

[2] An Act for preventing Dangers which may happen from Popish Recusants, 25 Car. II, c. 2, *SR* v. 781–4, commonly known as the Test Act 1673.

were made use of to try how they could revive the Old Persecution; for as yet the Zeal raised against the *Papists*, was so great, that the worthyest, and soberest, of the Episcopal party, thought it necessary to unite with the dissenting *Protestants*, and not to divide their Party, when all their Forces were little enough. In this posture [*p. 7*] the *Session of Parliament* that began *Oct.* 27. 1673. found Matters, which being suddenly broken up, did nothing.[1]   5

The next Session, which began *Jan 7.* following, the *Bishops* continued their *Zeal against the Papists*, and seem'd to carry it on by joyning with the Countrey Lords, in many excellent Votes in order to a Bill, as 10 in particular, *That the Princes of the Blood-Royal should only Marry Protestants*,[2] and many others, but their favor to dissenting *Protestants* was gone, and they attempted a Bargain with the Countrey Lords, with whom they then joyned not to promote any thing of that nature, except *the Bill for taking away Assent and Consent, and renouncing the Covenant.*[3] 15

This Session was no sooner ended without doing any thing, but the whole Clergy were instructed to declare that there was now no more danger of the *Papists*: The *Phanatique* (for so they call the dissenting *Protestant*) is again become the *only dangerous Enemy*, and the Bishops had found a *Scotch* Lord, and two new Ministers, or rather Great Officers 20 of *England*, who were desperate and rash enough, to put their Masters business upon so narrow and weak a bottom; And that *old Covenanter Lauderdale*,[4] is become the *Patron of the Church*, and has his Coach and

---

1 revive] **4, D** | receive **1–3, B**   5 enough.] **B, D, 4** | enough; **1–2** | enough: **3**
5 *Session*] ed. | *Sessions* **1–3** | Session **4, B, D**   8 Session,] **4, D** | Sessions **1–2** |
Sessions, **3** | Session **B**   9 their] **1, 3–4, B** | the **2**   it on by] ed. | it on, by **B** | on in
1–2 | on, in **3–4, D**   10 [*1st*] in] **B** | *om.* **1–4**   11 *Princes* **1, 3–4** | *Prince* **2** |
Princes **B**   *Blood-Royal*] **1–4** | Royall blood **B**   *only*] **2–3** | *all* **1, 4, D** | all **B**
15 *Bill*] **3–4** | *bill* **1–2** | Bill **B**

---

[1] Parliament was adjourned on 4 November, *LJ* xii. 593.

[2] An Act for the better Securing the Protestant Religion; draft printed in HMC, 9th Report, Appendix, Part II, 45b–46a. It received a first reading on 21 February 1674 but made no further progress, *LJ* xii. 647.

[3] An Act for composing differences in Religion and inviting sober and peaceably minded Dissenters into the Service of the Church; draft printed in HMC, 9th Report, Appendix, Part II, 44b. The bill received its first and second readings on 13 and 19 Feb. 1674 (*LJ* xii. 636, 644) but lapsed when Parliament was prorogued on 24 February. See also Thomas, 'Comprehension and Indulgence', 215–16; Sykes, *From Sheldon to Secker*, 79–80; Spurr, 'The Church of England, Comprehension and the Toleration Act of 1689', 935–6.

[4] John Maitland (1616–82), second Earl and first Duke of Lauderdale. He was named in 1643 as one of the commissioners for the Solemn League and Covenant, and was one of those ordered to carry it to Westminster. *ODNB*.

table fil'd with Bishops. The Keeper[1] and the Treasurer are of a just size to this affair, for it is a certain rule with the Church Men, to endure (as seldom as they can) in business, Men abler then themselves. But his Grace of *Scotland* was least to be excused of the Three, for having fall'n
5 from *Presbytery, Protestant* Religion, and all principles of Publick good and private friendship, and become the Slave of *Clifford* to carry on the Ruine of all that he had professed to support, does now also quit even *Clifford*'s generous Principles, and betake himself to a sort of Men, that *never forgive any Man the having once been in the right*; and such Men, who
10 would do the worst of things by the worst of means, enslave their country, and betray them, under the mask of Religion, which they have the publick Pay for, and charge of; so seething the Kid in the Mothers milk.[2] Our Statesmen and Bishops being now as well agreed, as in Old *Laud*'s time, on the same principles, with the same passion to attain their
15 end, they in the first place give orders to the Judges in all their Circuits to quicken the Execution of the Laws against Dissenters; a *new Declaration* is published directly contrary to the former, most in words against the *Papists*, but in the Sense, and in the close, did fully serve against both, and in the Execution, it was plain who were meant. A *Commission* besides,
20 comes down directed to the principal Gentlemen of each County, *to seize the Estates of* both *Papists* and *Phanatiques*, mentioned in a List annexed, wherein by great misfortune, or skill, the Names of the *Papists* of best quality and fortune [*p. 8*] (and so best known) were mistaken, and the Commission render'd ineffectual as to them.[3]

---

1 Bishops] 1–2, 4, **B, D** | that Party 3   the Treasurer] 1, 4, **B, D** | Treasurer 2 | ———3   4 *Scotland*] 3 | *Scotland:* 1–2 | Scotland 4, **B, D** | Scotland, E   excused] 3–4, **B, E** | executed 1–2   7 that] 1, 4, **B, D** | *om.* 2–3   9 [*1st*] *the*] 1–2u, 3 | *he* 2c | the 4, **B, D** | he E   12 [*1st*] the] 1, 4, **B, D, E** | *om.* 2–3   charge of] ed. | charge off 1 | the charge off 2 | the Charge of 3 | the charge of 4 | charg of B   16 Laws] 1, 3–4, **B** | Law 2 | lawes E   a] 1–4 | and a **B**   20 County] 3–4, **B, E** | country 1 | countrey 2 22 [*2nd*] the] 1, **B** | *om.* 2–4

---

[1] Heneage Finch (1621–82), Baron Finch of Daventry, subsequently Earl of Nottingham. *ODNB.*   [2] Exod. 23: 19, 34: 26; Deut. 14: 21.
[3] Proclamations against papists had been issued on 20 November 1673, 14 January 1674, and 10 June 1674, NA, SP 44/36, p. 297; Steele, *Proclamations*, i. 434–5. On 6 March 1674 the judges were ordered to 'cause the Laws against Popish Recusants to be put in execution', NA, PC 2/64, p. 188. On 3 June Justices of the Peace were ordered to use 'utmost endeavour' to discover and apprehend seminary priests and Jesuits, NA, PC 2/64, pp. 234–5. On 3 February 1675 the Privy Council ordered the laws against recusants to be executed 'with more care and Diligence then of late they have bin', and the Attorney General was asked 'whether any persons of quality who are suspected to be Popish Recusants have bin omitted to be presented', NA, PC 2/64, p. 364; Steele, *Proclamations*, i. 437. These instructions were taken from the recommendations of the meeting at Lambeth

Besides this, the great Ministers of State did in their common publick talk assure the partie, that all the places of Profit, Command, and Trust, should only be given to the old *Cavalier*; no Man that had served, or been of the contrary Party, should be left in any of them; And a direction is issued to the Great Ministers before mentioned, and Six or seven of the Bishops to meet at *Lambeth-House*, who were like the Lords of the Articles in *Scotland*,[1] to prepare their compleat Modell for the ensuing *Session of Parliament*.

And now comes this *memorable Session of Aprill* 13. 75. then which never any came with more expectation of the Court, or dread and apprehension of the People; the Officers, Court Lords, and Bishops, were clearly the major Vote in the *Lords House*, and they assured themselves to have the Commons as much at their dispose when they reckoned the number of the Courtiers, Officers, Pensioners encreased by the addition of the Church and Cavalier party, besides the Address they had made to Men of the best quality there by hopes of Honor, great employment, and such things as would take. In a word, the *French* King's Ministers, who are the great Chapmen of the World, did not out-doe ours at this time, and yet the *over ruling hand of God* has blown upon their Politicks, and the Nation is escaped this Session, like *a Bird out of the snare* of the Fowler.[2]

In this Session the Bishops wholly laid aside their Zeal against *Popery*. The Committee of the whole House for Religion, which the Country Lords had caused to be set up again by the example of the former Sessions, could hardly get, at any time, a day appointed for their Sitting,

---

1–2 publick talk] 3 | publick 1–2 | publick talk, D, 4 | talk B   2 of] 1, 3–4, B, E | of the 2   9 75.] 1–3, B | 1675 4, D   then] E | then, 1–2 | than B, 3–4   15 had] 1, 4, B, D | *om.* 2–3   Men] 1 | men 2–4 | the men B 21 Session] 3–4, B | Sessions 1–2

on 26 January 1675, described in the General Introduction, p. 77. On 10 February the King issued a 'Declaration for Suppressing Popery & Conventicles', NA, PC 2/64, p. 372.

[1] The Lords of the Articles were the members of the Committee of the Articles in the Scottish parliament. They decided which (public) bills should come before the parliament as a whole, and thereby largely controlled its business. The method for determining the membership of the committee had varied in the past, but in 1663 it was settled by statute (*Acts of the Parliaments of Scotland*, vii. 449): the bishops would choose eight members from among the nobility, who would in turn choose eight bishops; the bishops and nobles so chosen would then act together to select eight members each from among the representatives of the shires and the burghs. Since the bishops were royal nominees, the king (or in practice his commissioner) could determine the election: as Lauderdale observed, 'nothing can come to the Parliament but through the articles, and nothing can pass in articles but what is warranted by his Majestie: so that the king is absolute master in Parliament both of the negative and affirmative', *Lauderdale Papers*, i. 173–4.   [2] Ps. 124: 7.

and the main thing design'd for a Bill voted in the former Session, *viz. the marrying our Princes to none but Protestants*, was *rejected* and carryed in the Negative by the unanimous Votes of the *Bishops Bench*; for I must acquaint you that our great Prelates were so neer an Infallibility, that they
5 were always found in this Session of one mind in the *Lords House*; yet the Lay Lords, not understanding from how excellent a Principle this proceeded, commonly called them for that reason *the dead Weight*, and they really proved so in the following business, for the third day of this Session this *Bill of Test* was brought into the Lords House by the Earl of
10 *Lindsey* L. High Chamberlain, a person of great quality, but in this imposed upon, and received its first reading[1] and appointment for the second without much opposition; the Country Lords being desirous to observe what weight they put upon it, or how they designed to manage it.

[*p. 9*] At the second reading,[2] the L. Keeper, and some other of the
15 Court Lords, recommended the Bill to the House in Set and Elaborate *Speeches*, the *Keeper* calling it *A moderate Security to the Church and Crown*, and that no honest Man could refuse it, and whosoever did, gave great suspition of Dangerous, and *Anti-Monarchicall* Principles; the other Lords declamed very much upon the Rebellion of the late Times, the
20 great number of *Phanatiques*, the dangerous principles of rebellion still remaining, carrying the Discourse on as if they meant to trample down the *Act of Oblivion*,[3] and all those whose Securities depended on it. But the Earl of *Shaftsbury* and some other of the Country Lords, earnestly prest that the Bill might be laid aside, and that they might not be engaged
25 in the debate of it; or else that that Freedom they should be forced to use in the necessary defence of their Opinion, and the preserving of their Laws, Rights, and Liberties, which this Bill would overthrow, might not be misconstrued: For there are many things that must be spoken upon the debate, both concerning Church and State, that it was well known

---

2 *Princes*] 1 | *Prince* 2–4 | Princes B   3–5 for...*Lords House;*] 1 | *om.* 2–3 | for...Lord's House: 4, D | For...found of one mind in this session of one mind in the Lords House, B   10 *Lindsey*] 1, 2c, 4, D | *Lindsay* 2u | Lindsey B | Lindsay E | *L.* 3   High Chamberlain] 1–2 | high Chamberlain 4, B | High Chamberlain of England E | *C.* 3   14 other] 1, 3–4, B | others 2   16 calling] 1–4 | calld B   18 Principles;] 3 | Principles, 1–2 | Principles. 4, D | Principles: B   19 declamed] ed. | declame 1–2, D | declaim 3 | declam'd 4 | declaime B   22 it.] 3–4 | it, 1–2 | it; B, E   29 the] 1–4 | *not in* B

---

[1] 15 April, *LJ* xii. 659.   [2] 20 April, *LJ* xii. 664.
[3] An Act of free and general pardon, indemnity and oblivion, 12 Car. II, c. 11 (1660), *SR* v. 226–34.

they had no mind to hear. Notwithstanding this, the great Officers and Bishops called out for the Question of referring the Bill to a Committee; but the Earl of *Shaftsbury*, a Man of great Abilities, and knowledg in Affairs, and one that, in all the variety of changes of this last Age, was never known to be either bought or frighted out of his publick Principles, at Large opened the mischievous, and ill designs, and consequences of the Bill, which as it was brought in, required all Officers of Church and State, and all Members of both Houses of *Parliament*, to take this Oath following.

I A. B. *do declare that it is not Lawful upon any pretence whatsoever, to take up Armes against the King, and that I do abhorr that Traiterous position of taking Armes by His authority, against His Person, or against those that are commission'd by Him in pursuance of such Commission, And I do swear that I will not at any time endeavor the Alteration of the Government, either in Church or State, so help me God.* The Earl of *Shaftsbury* and other Lords, spake with such convincing Reason, that all the Lords, who were at liberty from Court-Engagements, resolved to *oppose* to the uttermost, *a Bill of so dangerous consequence*; and the debate lasted Five several days before it was committed to a Committee of the whole House, which hardly ever happened to any Bill before. All this and the following debates, were managed cheifly by the Lords, whose Names you will find to the following *Protestations*; the *First* whereof, was as followeth.[1]

[*p. 10*] *We whose Names are under Written being Peers of this Realm, do according to our Rights and the ancient Usage of* Parliaments, *declare that the Question having been put whether the Bill (entitled an Act to prevent the dangers which may arise from Persons disaffected to the Government) doth so far intrench upon the Priviledges of This House; that it ought therefore to be cast out. It being resolved in the Negative, We do humbly conceive that any Bill which imposeth an Oath upon the* Peers *with a Penalty, as this doth, that upon the refusal of that Oath,* They shall *be made uncapable of Sitting and Voting in this* House, *as it is a thing unpresidented in former Times, so is it, in Our humble Opinion, the highest Invasion of the Liberties and Priviledges of*

---

[1] 21 April, *LJ* xii. 665.

the Peerage, *that possibly may be, and most destructive of the Freedom, which they ought to enjoy as Members of* Parliament, *because the priviledge of Sitting and Voting in* Parliament *is an Honor they have by Birth, and a Right so inherant in them, and inseparable from them, as that nothing can take it away, but what by the Law of the Land, must withal take away their Lives, and corrupt* their Blood; *upon which ground we do here enter our Dissent from that Vote, and our Protestation against it*

Buckingham	*Aylisbury*	*Howard* E. of *Berks*	*Shaftsbury*
Bridgwater	*Bristol*	*Mohun*	*Clarendon*
Winchester	*Denbigh*	*Stamford*	*Grey Roll.*
Salisbury	*Pagitt*	*Hallifax*	*Say & Seal*
Bedford	*Holles*	*De la mer*	*Wharton*
Dorset	*Peter*	*Eure*	

The *next Protestation* was against the Vote of committing the Bill in the words following;[1]

The Question being put whether the Bill Entituled An Act to prevent the Dangers, which may arise from Persons disaffected to the Government, should be commited, It being carried in the Affirmative, and We after several days *debate, being in no measure Satisfied, but still apprehending that this Bill doth not only subvert the Priviledges and birth-right of the* Peers, *by imposing an Oath upon them with the penalty of losing their Places in* Parliament; *but also, as We humbly conceive, strike at the very* root of *Government*; *it being necessary to all Government to have freedom of Votes and Debates in those, who have power to alter, and make Laws, and besides, the express words of this Bill, obliging every Man to abjure all Endeavors to alter the Government in the Church,* [*p. 11*] *without regard to any thing that rules of Prudence in Government, or Christian compassion to* Protestant *Dissenters, or the necessity of Affairs at any time, shall or may require. Upon these Considerations, We humbly conceive it to be of dangerous consequence to have any* Bill *of this*

2 *priviledge*] **ed.** | *priviledges* **1–2** | *Priviledges* **3** | *privilege* **4** | Priviledges **B** | priviledg **E** | Priviledge **J**   5 *withal*] **3–4** | *withal,* **1–2** | withall **B, E** | withal **J**   8–13 *The same names occur in a different order in* **B** *and* **E**; *see Textual Introduction*, p. 222.   20 *Priviledges*] **2–3** | *Priviledges,* **1** | *privileges* **4** | Priviledges **B** | Priviledge **J**   21 *Places*] **1–3** | places **4, B** | Place **E, J** | Places **D**   22 *strike*] **3–4** | stick **1–2** | strike **B, E** | does strike **J**   26 *Church,*] **3** | *Church*; **1–2** | Church, **4, E** | Church or state **B** | Church **J**   *in*] **ed.** | in **J** | *in the* **1–4** | in the **B**   29 *conceive*] **1–4** | conceive **B** | conceiving **J**

[1] 26 April, *LJ* xii. 669.

Nature, so much as Committed, and do enter our Dissents from that Vote and Protestation against it,

Buckingham	*Bristol*	*Shaftsbury*	
Winton	*Howard of Berks*	*Wharton*	
Salisbury	*Clarendon*	*Mohun*	5
Denbigh	*Stamford*	*De la mer*	

Which Protestation was no sooner entred and subscribed the next day, but the great Officers and Bishops raised a *storm* against the Lords that had Subscrib'd it; endeavouring not only some severe proceedings against their *persons*, if they had found the House would have born it, 10 but also to have taken away *the very liberty of Entring Protestations with Reasons*; but that was defended with so great Ability, Learning, and Reason, by the L. *Holles*, that they quitted the Attempt, and the Debate ran for some hours either wholly to raze the Protestation out of the Books, or at least some part of it, the Expression of *Christian compassion to* 15 *Protestant Dissenters* being that, which gave them most offence; but both these ways were so disagreeable to the honor and priviledg of the House, and the Latter to common Sense and Right, that they despaired of carrying it, and contented themselves with having voted *That the Reasons given in the said Protestation, did reflect upon the Honor of the House, and* 20 *were of dangerous consequence.*[1] And I cannot here forbear to mention the *Worth, and Honor, of that Noble Lord Holles*, suitable to all his former life, that whilst the Debate was at the height, and the Protesting Lords in danger of the *Tower*, he begg'd the House to give him leave to put his Name to that *Protestation*, and take his Fortune with those Lords, be- 25 cause his sickness had forced him out of the House the day before, so that not being at the Question, he could not by the rules of the House Sign it. This Vote against those twelve Lords begat the next day this following *Protestation* signed by 21.[2]

Whereas it is the undoubted priviledg of each Peer in Parliament *when a* 30 *Question is past contrary to his Vote and judgment, to enter his Protestation against it, and that in pursuance thereof, the* Bill *entituled An Act to prevent the dan[p.12]gers which may arise from persons disaffected to the Government, being conceived by some Lords to be of so dangerous a Nature, as that it was*

---

1 [*1st*] *and*] 1–4 | & B | *om.* J   14 ran] B, 3–4 | run 1–2   24 *Tower,*] 3 |
Tower; 1–2 | Tower, 4, B, D, E   25 *Protestation*] ed. | *Protest* 1–4 | Protestation B
30 *each*] 1–4 | each B | every J   31 *past*] 1–4 | past B | put E | passed J

     [1] 29 April, *LJ* xii. 671.   [2] 29 April, *LJ* xii. 671.

351

not fit to receive the countenance of a Commitment, those Lords did protest
against the Commitment of the said Bill, and the House having taken
exceptions at some expressions in their Protestation; those Lords who were
present at the Debate, did all of them severally and voluntarily declare, That
5 they had no intention to reflect upon any Member, much less upon the whole
House, which, as is humbly conceived, was more then in strictness did consist
with that absolute freedom of Protesting, which is inseparable from every
Member of this House, and was done by them meerly out of their great Respect
to the House, and their earnest desire to give all satisfaction concerning
10 themselves, and the clearness of their intentions: Yet the House not satisfied
with this their Declaration but proceeding to a Vote, that the Reasons given in
the said Protestation do reflect upon the honor of the House, and are of
dangerous consequence; which is in our humble Opinion, a great discounten-
ancing of the very liberty of Protesting. We whose Names are under Written,
15 conceive our selves, and the whole House of Peers, extreamly concerned that
this great Wound should be given (as we humbly apprehend) to so essential a
priviledg of the whole Peerage of this Realm, as their liberty of Protesting, do
now (according to our unquestionable Right) make use of the same liberty to
enter this our Dissent from, and Protestation against the said Vote,

20 Bucks	Denbigh	Hallifax	Holles
Winton	Berks	Audley	De la mer
Bedford	Clarendon	Fits Water	Grey Roll.
Dorset	Aylisbury	Eure	
Salisbury	Shaftsbury	Wharton	
25 Bridgwater	Say & Seal	Mohun	

After this Bill being committed to a Committee of the whole House,
the first thing insisted upon by the Lords against the Bill, was, that there
ought to be passed some *previous Votes* to secure the Rights of *Peerage*,
and Priviledg of *Parliament* before they entred upon the debate, or
30 Amendments of such a Bill as this; and at last two *previous Votes* were
obtained, which I need not here set down, because the next Protestation
hath them both *in terminis.*[1]

---

1 *the*] 1–4 | the B | so much as the J   2 *Commitment*] 1–4 | Commitment B |
committing J   5 *no*] 3–4 | *not* 1–2 | not B | no J   15 *conceive*] 1–4 | conceive B
| conceiving J   16 *humbly*] 1–4 | humbly B | do in all Humility J   17 *as*] 1–4 |
as B | as is J   20–25 *The names below are in a different order in* B; *see Textual
Introduction*, p. 223.   27 Bill,] 3–4, B | Bill; 1–2 | bill, E   30 *previous*] 2–4 |
previous 1, B   32 *in*] 4, D | in 1–3, B

---

[1] 4 May, *LJ* xii. 677.

[*p. 13*] Whereas upon the debate on the Bill *entituled An Act to prevent the Dangers which may arise from Persons disaffected to the Government,* It was ordered by the house of Peers the 30*th. of Aprill* last, *that no Oath should be imposed by any Bill, or otherwise, upon the Peers with a penalty in case of Refusal, to lose their Places, and Votes in* Parliament, *or liberty to* 5 *debate therein;*[1] *and whereas also, upon debate of the same Bill, it was ordered, the Third of this instant* May, *that there shall be nothing in this Bill, which shall extend to deprive either of the Houses of* Parliament, *or any of their Members, of their just ancient Freedom, and priviledg of debating any Matter or business which shall be propounded, or debated in either of the said* 10 *Houses, or at any Conference or Committee, of both, or either of the said Houses of* Parliament, *or touching the Repeal, or Alteration of any Old, or preparing any new Laws, or the redressing any publick Grievance; but that the said Members of either of the said Houses, and the Assistants of the* House of Peers, *and every of them, shall have the same freedom of Speech, and all other* 15 *Priviledges whatsoever, as they had before the making of this Act.*[2]

Both which Orders were passed as Previous directions unto the Committee of the whole House, to whom the said Bill was committed, to the end that nothing should remain in the said Bill, which might any ways tend towards the depriving of either of the Houses of *Parliament,* or 20 any of their Members, of their ancient freedom of Debates, or Votes, or other their priviledges whatsoever: Yet the House being pleased, upon the report from the Committee, to pass a Vote, That all Persons who have, or shall have Right to sit and Vote in either House of *Parliament,* should be added to the first enacted Clause in the said Bill, whereby an 25 Oath is to be imposed upon them as Members of either House, which Vote *We whose names are under Written being Peers of this Realm, do humbly conceive, is not agreeable to the said two Previous Orders,* and it having been humbly offered, and insisted upon by divers of us, that the

3 last] 1–4, J | 75 B   5 and] ed. | or 1–4 | or B | and J   5–6 to debate] 1–4 | to debate B | of debates J   same Bill, it was ordered,] ed. | same Bill, it was ordered, J | same, the Bill was ordered 1–2 | same, it was ordered 3 | same, it was order'd, 4 | same, the Bill was ordered B | same, [the Bill] 'it' was ordered D   10 Matter] 1–3 | matter 4 | matter B | matters E | Matters J   11 Conference] 1–4 | conference B | Conferences J   Committee] 1–4 | Committee B | Committees J   13 any] 1–4 | any B | of any J   14 Assistants] 3 | assistance 1–2 | assistants 4 | Assistants B, J   17 unto] 1–4, B | to J   22 other] 1–4, B | any other J   23 from the] 1–4, B | of the said J   25 enacted] 1–4, B | enacting J   26 them as] 1–4, B | the J   27 are] 1 | om. 2–3 | are 4, B, D, J   this] 1 | the 2–3 | the 4 | this B, J

[1] 30 April, *LJ* xii. 673.   [2] 4 May, *LJ* xii. 674.

Proviso in the late Act *Entituled An Act for preventing Dangers, that may happen from* Popish *Recusants*,[1] might be added to the Bill depending, *Whereby the Peerage of every Peer of this Realm, and all their Priviledges, might be preserved in this Bill, as fully as in the said late Act*: Yet the House
5 not pleasing to admit of the said Proviso, but proceeding to the passing of the said Vote, *We do humbly upon the Grounds aforesaid, and according unto our undoubted Right, enter this our Dissent from, and Protestation against the same.* [*p. 14*]

Bucks	*Berks*	*Denbigh*	*Eure*
10	*Bedford*	*Bridgwater*	*Dorset*	*De la mer*
Winton	*Stamford*	*Shaftsbury*	*Pagitt*[2]
Salisbury	*Clarendon*	*Wharton*	*Mohun*

This was their last Protestation; for after this they alter'd their Method, and reported not the Votes of the Committee, and parts of the
15 Bill to the House, as they past them, but took the same Order as is observed in other Bills, not to report unto the House, untill they had gone through with the Bill, and so report all the Amendments together.[3] This they thought a way of more Dispach and which did prevent all Protestations, untill it came to the House; for the Votes of a Committee, though
20 of the whole House, are not thought of that weight, as that there should be allowed the entering a Dissent from them, or Protestation against them.

The Bill being read over at the Committee, the Lord Keeper objected against the form of it, and desired that he might put it in another Method, which was easily allowed him, that being not the Dispute. But it
25 was observable the Hand of *God* was upon them in this whole Affair; their Chariot-wheels were taken off, they drew heavily:[4] A Bill so long design'd, prepared, and of that Moment to all their Affairs, had hardly a sensible Composure.

The first part of the Bill that was fallen upon, was, whether there
30 should be an Oath at all in the Bill, and this was the only part the Court-Partie defended with Reason: for the whole Bill being to enjoyn an Oath,

---

1 *that*] 1–4 | that B | which E, J   2 *Recusants*,] 3–4 | *Recusants*; 1–2 | Recusants,
B, E, J   20 the] 1–4 | a B   21 from] B | of 1–4   23 in] 1–4 | into B
29 upon,] 3–4, E | upon; 1–2 | upon B

[1] 25 Car. II, c. 2, *SR* v. 781–4, commonly known as the Test Act 1673.
[2] A name, presumably Paget's, is heavily erased in the manuscript Journal in the HLRO. Paget's name was not included in the Protest in the printed *Lords Journal*.
[3] 7 May, *LJ* xii. 682; NA, SP 29/370/111–13.   [4] Exod. 14: 25.

the House might reject it, but the Committee was not to destroy it. Yet the *Lord Hallifax* did with that quickness, Learning, and Elegance, which are inseparable from all his Discourses, make appear, that as *there really was no Security to any State by Oaths*, so also, no private Person, much less States-Man, would ever order his Affairs as relying on them; no Man would ever sleep with open Doors, or unlockt up Treasure, or Plate, should all the Town be sworn not to Rob; So that the use of multiplying Oaths had been most commonly to Exclude, or disturb some honest Consciencious Men, who would never have prejudiced the Government. It was also in[*p. 15*]sisted on by that Lord and others, that the Oath imposed by the Bill, contained Three Clauses, the two former Assertory, and the last Promissory, and that it was worthy the Consideration of the Bishops, Whether *Assertory Oaths*, which were properly appointed to give testimony of a matter of Fact, whereof a Man is capable to be fully assured by the evidence of his Senses, be lawfully to be made use of to Confirm, or Invalidate Doctrinal Propositions, and whether that Legislative power, which imposes such an Oath, doth not necessarily assume to it self an Infallibility? And, as for *Promissory Oaths*, It was desired that those Learned Prelates would consider the Opinion of *Grotius de jure Belli & pacis, lib.* 2. *cap.* XIII. who seems to make it plain that those kind of Oaths are forbidden by our *Saviour Christ, Mat.* 5. 34, 37.[1] and whether it would not become the Fathers of the Church, when they have well weighed that and other places of the *New Testament*, to be more tender in multiplying Oaths, then hitherto the great Men of the Church have been? But the Bishops carried the Point, and an Oath was ordered by the major Vote.

The next thing in Consideration, was about the *Persons* that should be enjoyned to take this Oath; and those were to be, *all such as enjoyed any beneficial Office or Employment, Ecclesiastical, Civil, or Military*; and no farther went the Debate for some hours, until at last the Lord Keeper

---

5 as] 1–4 | *not in* B   them;] B | it, 1–3 | it; 4   6 Doors] 1–3 | doors 4 | *not in* B   23 *Testament,*] 3 | *Testament*; 1–2 | Testament, 4, B   25 Bishops] 1–2, 4, B | B. 3   30 farther] 1–4 | further B, E

---

[1] 'What is said in the teachings of Christ and the writings of St James against taking oaths does not properly apply to oaths of assertion, of which there are some examples in the writings of the Apostle Paul, but to future and uncertain promises. This is clearly shown in the words of Christ: "Again, ye have heard that it hath been said by them of old time, Thou shalt not forswear thyself, but shalt perform unto the Lord thine oaths: But I say unto you, Swear not at all" [Matt. 5: 33–4]. And the reason, which James adds, "lest ye fall into condemnation" [Jas. 5: 12]...', Grotius, *De Jure Belli ac Pacis*, II. xiii. 21, § 1.

rises up, and with an eloquent Oration, desires to add *Privy Counsellors, Justices of the Peace,* and *Members of both Houses*; The two former particularly mentioned only to usher in the latter; which was so directly against the two Previous Votes, the first of which was enroll'd amongst
5 the standing Orders of the House, that it wanted a Man of no less assurance in his Eloquence to propose it, and he was driven hard, when he was forced to tell the House, that they were *Masters of their own Orders,* and Interpretation of them.

The next consideration at the Committee was *the Oath it self,* and it
10 was desired by the Countrey Lords, that it might be clearly known, whether it were meant all for an Oath, or some of it for a Declaration, and some an Oath? If the latter, then it was desired it might be distinctly parted, and that the Declaratory part should be subscribed by it self, and not sworn. There was no small pains taken by the Lord Keeper and
15 the Bishops, to prove that as it was brought in, the two first parts were only a *Declaration,* and not an *Oath*; and though it was replyed that to declare upon ones Oath, or to abhorr upon ones Oath, is the same thing with *I do Swear*; yet there was some diffi[*p. 16*]culty to obtain the dividing of them, and that the Declaratory part should be only Subscribed,
20 and the rest Sworn to.[1]

The Persons being determin'd, and this division agreed to, the next thing was the parts of the *Declaration,* wherein the first was; I A. B. *do declare that it is not lawful upon any pretence whatsoever, to take up Armes against the King.* This was lyable to great Objections; for it was said it
25 might introduce a great change of the Government, to oblige all the Men in great Trust in *England,* to declare that exact Boundary, and Extent, of the Oath of *Allegiance,* and inforce some things to be Stated, that are much better involv'd in Generals, and peradventure are not capable of another way of expression, without great wrong on the one side, or the
30 other. There is a Law of 25 *Edw.* 3.[2] that Armes shall not be taken up against the *King,* and that it is Treason to do so, and it is a very just and reasonable Law; but it is an idle question at best, to ask whether Armes in any case can be taken up against a lawful Prince, because it necessarily brings in the debate in every Man's mind, how there can be a distinction

---

11   for] 2–4 | [for] `for´ D | *not in* 1, B   15 the Bishops] 1–2, 4, B, D | that
Party 3   as it . . . in,] B | it . . . in; 1–3 | it . . . in, E | *om.* 4, D   17 or . . . Oath] 1–4 |
not in B   28 involv'd] 1–4 | enclosed B

[1] 7 May, NA, SP 29/370/111–13.
[2] The Treasons Act 1351, 25 Edw. III, st. 5, c. 2, *SR* i. 320.

then left between Absolute, and Bounded Monarchys, if *Monarchs* have only the fear of *God*, and no fear of humane Resistance to restrain them. And it was farther urged, that if the chance of humane Affairs in future Ages, should give the *French King* a just Title and Investiture in the Crown of *England*, and he should avowedly own a design by force, to 5 change the Religion, and make his Government here as Absolute as in *France*, by the extirpation of the Nobility, Gentry, and principal Citizens of the *Protestant* Party, whether in such, or like Cases, this *Declaration* will be a Service to the Government, as it is now establisht: Nay, and it was farther said, that they overthrow the Government that suppose to 10 place any part of it above the fear of Man: For in our *English* Government, and all bounded Monarchys, where the Prince is not absolute, there every individual Subject is under the fear of the King, and His People, either for breaking the Peace, or disturbing the common Interest that every Man hath in it, for if he invades the Person or Right of his 15 Prince, he invades his whole People, who have bound up in him, and derive from Him, all their Liberty, Property, and Safety: As also the Prince himself, is under the fear of breaking that Golden Chain and Connexture between Him and his People, by making his interest contrary to that they justly and rightly claim: And therefore neither our Ancestors, 20 nor any other Country free like ours, whilst they preserv'd their Liberties, did ever suffer any *mercenary, or standing Guards to their Prince*, [*p. 17*] but took care that his Safety should be in Them, as theirs was in Him. Though these were the Objections to this Head, yet they were but lightly touch'd, and not fully insisted upon, until the debate of the second 25 Head, where the Scope of the Design was opened clearer, and more distinct to every Man's capacity.

The second was, *And that I do abhorr that Trayterous Position of taking Armes by His Authority against His Person*. To this was objected, That if this be meant an Explanation of the Oath of Allegiance to leave men 30 without pretense to oppose where the individual person of the King is, then it was to be considered, that the proposition as it is here set down is universal, and yet in most cases the position is not to be abhorred by honest or wise men: For there is but one case, and that never like to happen again, where this position is in danger to be Trayterous, which 35 was the Case of the *Long Parliament*, made perpetual by the King's own

---

3 farther] 1–2, 4 | further 3, B, D, E   7 Nobility,] 1–3 | nobility, 4 | Nobility & B | nobility E   10 farther] 1–2, 4 | further 3, B, E   15 it, for] ed. | it, or 1–2 | it; or 3–4, B, D | it; for 7   32 proposition] 1 | position 2 | Position 3–4 | Proposition B

Act,[1] by which the Government was perfectly altered, and made inconsistent with its self; but it is to be supposed the Crown hath sufficient warning, and full power to prevent the falling again into that danger. But the other cases are many, and such as may every day occurr, wherein
5 this position is so far from Traiterous, that it would prove both necessary and our duty. The *Famous instance* of *Hen.* 6. who being a soft and weak Prince, when taken Prisoner by his Cousin *Edward* 4. that pretended to the Crown, and the great Earl of *Warwick*, was carryed in their Armies, gave what orders and Commissions they pleased, and yet all those that
10 were Loyal to him adhered to his Wife and Son, fought in a pitcht battel against him in person, and retook him:[2] This was directly taking up Armes by His Authority against his person, and against those that were Commission'd by Him, and yet to this day no Man hath ever blamed them, or thought but that, if they had done other, they had betray'd their
15 Prince. The great Case of *Charles* 6. *of France*, who being of a weak and crazie Brain, yet govern'd by himself, or rather by his Wife, a Woman of passionate, and heady humour, that hated her Son the *Dolphin*, a vigorous and brave Prince, and passionately loved her Daughter; so that She easily (being pressed by the Victory of *Hen.* 5. *of England*) comply'd to
20 settle the Crown of *France* upon Him, to marry her Daughter to Him, and own his Right, contrary to the Salique Law.[3] This was directly opposed with Armes and Force by the *Dolphin*, and all good *French Men*, even in his Father's life time. A third instance is that of *King James* of blessed Memory, who when he was a Child, was seized, and taken
25 Prisoner by those, who were justly thought no friends to His [*p. 18*] Crown or Safety,[4] and if the case should be put, that a future *King of England* of the same temper with *Hen.* 6. or *Charl.* 6. of *France*, should be taken prisoner by *Spaniard*, *Dutch*, or *French*, whose overgrowing power should give them thoughts of vast Empire, and should, with the person

---

1 perfectly] 1–4 | *not in* B   6 The] 1–4 | There is the B   [*2nd*] and] 1–4, L, N, R, S, T, Y | *not in* B   14 other] 1–2, L, N, T, Y | otherwise 3–4, B, R, S   15 The] 1–4 | A second instance is the B

[1]   An Act for the preventing the inconveniences happening by the long intermission of Parliament, 16 Car. I, c. 1, *SR* v. 54–7.
[2]   Henry VI was captured at the battle of Northampton in July 1460 and remained under the control of the Earl of March (the future Edward IV) and the Earl of Warwick until he was recaptured by the Queen's forces at the second battle of St Albans in February 1461.
[3]   In January 1421 Charles VI disinherited Charles, his third and only surviving son, in favour of his daughter Catherine, the wife of Henry V.
[4]   In August 1582 James was seized and kept prisoner in Ruthven Castle; he managed to escape in June 1583.

and commission of the King, invade *England* for a Conquest, were it not
suitable to our Loyalty to joyn with the Son of that King, for the defence
of His Fathers Crown and Dignity, even against his Person and Commission? In all these and the like Cases it was not justified, but that the
strict Letter of the Law might be otherwise construed, and when wisely 5
considerd, fit it should be so, yet that it was not safe either for the
Kingdom, or person of the King and His Crown, that it should be in
express words Sworn against; for if we shall forswear all Distinctions,
which ill Men have made ill use of, either in *Rebellion*, or *Heresy*, we must
extend the Oath to all the particulars of Divinity, and Politiques. To this 10
the aged Bishop of *Winchester*[1] reply'd, That *to take up Armes in such cases,
is not against, but for the person of the King:* But his Lordship was told that
he might then as well, nay much better, have left it upon the Old Oath of
Allegiance, then made such a wide gapp in his new *Declaration*.

The third and last part of the Declaration was *or against those that are* 15
Commissioned by him. Here the mask was plainly pluckt off, and *Arbitrary
Government* appear'd bare-faced, and a *standing Army* to be established by
Act of Parliament, for it was said by several of the Lords, That *if whatever
is by the King's Commission, be not opposed by the King's Authority, then a
standing Army is Law when ever the King pleases*; and yet the King's 20
Commission was never thought sufficient to Protect, or justify any man,
where it is against his Authority, which is the Law;[2] this allowed alters
the whole Law of *England*, in the most essential and Fundamental parts
of it, and makes the whole Law of *property* to become *Arbitrary*, and
without effect, whenever the King pleases. 25

For instance, if in a Suit with a great Favourite, a man recovers House
and Lands, and by course of Law be put into Possession by the Sheriff,
and afterwards a Warrant is obtain'd by the interest of the person, to
command some Souldiers of the standing Army to take the possession
and deliver it back, in such a case, the man in Possession may justify 30

---

10 all the] 1, 4, B, D, T | all 2–3, R, S | the L | *om.* N, Y   15 *or . . . are*] 1–4 | only
against these that were B   19 *opposed*] 1–3 | opposed 4, B | to be opposed D   *the
King's*] 1–3 | the King's 4, D | his B   22 this allowed] 1–2 | this allowed, 3 | This
allowed, 4, D | This, being allowed, B   26 [*1st*] a] 1, B | *om.* 2–4   29 [*2nd*]
the] 1–4, L, N, T | *not in* B, R, S

[1] George Morley (1597–1684), Bishop of Worcester 1660, Bishop of Winchester 1662.
ODNB.
[2] Cf. *Two Treatises*, II. 206: 'For the King's Authority being given him only by the Law,
he cannot impower any one to act against the Law, or justifie him, by his Commission in so
doing.'

to defend himself, and killing those who shall violently endeavour to enter his house; the party, whose house is invaded, takes up Armes by the King's Authority against those, who are Commissioned by him. And it is the same case, if the Souldiers had been Commissioned to defend the
5 House against the Sheriff, when he first endeavored to take the [*p. 19*] possession according to Law, neither could any Order, or Commission of the King's, put a stop to the Sheriff, if he had done his duty in raising the whole force of that County to put the Law in execution; neither can the Court, from whom that Order proceeds, (if they observe their oaths, and
10 duty) put any stop to the execution of the Law in such a case, by any command or commission from the King whatsoever; Nay, all the Guards, and standing forces in *England*, cannot be secured by any Commission from being a direct Riot, and unlawful Assembly, unless in time of open War and Rebellion: And it is not out of the way to suppose,
15 that if any King hereafter, shall contrary to *the petition of Right*, demand, and levie Money by Privy-Seal, or otherwise, and cause Souldiers to enter, and distrain for such like illegall Taxes, that in such a case any Man may by Law defend his house against them; and yet this is of the same nature with the former, and against the words of the Declaration. These
20 instances may seem somwhat rough, and not with the usual *reverence* towards the Crown, but they alleadged, they were to be excused, when all was concerned, And without speaking thus plain, it is refused to be understood; and, however happy we are now, either in the present Prince, or those we have in prospect, yet the suppositions are not ex-
25 travagant, when we consider, Kings are but Men, and compassed with more temptations then others; And, as the Earl of *Salisbury*, who stood like a Rock of Nobility, and *English* Principles, excellently replyed to the Lord Keeper, who was pleased to term them *remote Instances*, that they would not hereafter prove so, when this Declaration had made the
30 practise of them Justifiable.

These Arguments enforced the Lords for the Bill to a change of this part of the *Declaration*, so that they agreed the second, and third parts of it, should run thus; *And I do abhorr that Trayterous position of taking Armes by His Authority, against his Person, or against those, that are*

---

1 to defend] 1–4, B | the defending E, L, N, R, S, T, Y   2 house;] 2 | house, 1, E | House, 3 | house. 4 | House. D | house: B   5 [*2nd*] the] 1–3 | *not in* 4, B 11 from . . . whatsoever] 1–4 | whatsoever from the King B   21 towards] 1–4, L, N, R, S, T, Y | toward E | to B   23 however happy] 1–4, L, N, S, T, Y | how happy soever B, R   25 compassed] 1–4 | encompassed B   34 *Armes*] ed. | *Armes against* 1 | *Arms against* 2 | *Arms* 3 | *arms* 4 | Armes B | armes E | *arms* [`against'] D

360

commissioned by Him according to Law, in time of Rebellion, or War, acting in pursuance of such Commission.[1] Which mends the matter very little; for if they mean the King's Authority, and his lawful Commission, to be two things, and such as are capable of Opposition, then it is as dangerous to the Liberties of the Nation, as when it ran in the former words, and we are only cheated by new Phrasing of it: But if they understand them to be one and the same thing, as really and truly they are, then we are only to abhorr the Treason of the position of taking Armes by the King's Authority against the King's Authority, because it is Non-sense, and [*p. 20*] not practicable; and so they had done little but confest, that all the Clergy and many other Persons, have been forced by former Acts of this present *Parliament*, to make this Declaration in other words, that now are found so far from being Justifiable, that they are directly contrary to *Magna Charta*, our Properties, and the Establish'd Law and Government of the Nation.

The next thing in course was, the Oath it self, against which the Objection lay so plain, and so strong at the first entrance, *Viz.* That *there was no care taken of the Doctrine, but only the Discipline of the Church.* The Papists need not scruple the taking this Oath; for Episcopacy remains in its greatest Lustre, though the Popish Religion was introduced, but the King's Supremacy is justled aside by this Oath, and makes better room for an *Ecclesiastical One*, in so much that with this, and much more, they were inforced to change their Oath, and the next day bring it in as followeth: *I do swear that I will not endeavour to alter the Protestant Religion or the Government either of Church or State.* By this they thought they had salved all, and now began to call their Oath *A Security for the Protestant Religion, and the only good design to prevent Popery*, if we should have a Popish Prince. But the Countrey Lords wondred at their confidence in this, since they had never thought of it before, and had been but the last preceeding day of the Debate by *pure Shame* compell'd to this Addition; for it was not unknown to them, that some of the *Bishops* themselves had told some of the *Roman Catholick Lords* of the House, that *care had been taken that it might be such an Oath, as might not bear upon them.* But let it be whatever they would have it, yet the Countrey Lords thought the

5

10

15

20

25

30

4   to] 2–4, B | to are 1   5   ran] B | run 1–4   6   are] 4, B, D | *not in* 1–3
8   [*2nd*] the] 1, 3–4, B | *om.* 2   9   because it] 1–4 | which B   14   *Charta,*] 3–4 |
Charta 1–2 | Charta, B, E   22   that] 1, 4, B, D | *om.* 2–3   23–24   followeth:]
2–4 | followeth. 1 | followeth, B | followeth; E   30   to] 2–4, B | to to 1 | to make E

[1]   10 May, NA, SP 29/370/138.

addition was unreasonable, and of as dangerous consequence as the rest of the Oath. And it was not to be wondred at, if the addition of the best things, wanting the Authority of an express divine Institution, should make an Oath *not to endeavor to alter*, just so much worse by the addition.

5 For as the Earl of *Shaftsbury* very well urg'd, that it is a far different thing to believe, or to be fully persuaded of the truth of the Doctrine of Our Church; and to swear *never to endeavor to alter*; which last, must be utterly unlawful, unless you place an *Infallibility* either in the Church, or Your Self, you being otherwise obliged to alter, when ever a clearer, or

10 better light comes to you; and he desir'd leave to ask, where are the Boundaries, or where shall we find, how much is meant by the *Protestant Religion*. The Lord Keeper thinking he had now got an advantage, with his usual Eloquence, desires it might not be told in *Gath*, nor published in the Streets of *Askalon*,[1] that a Lord of so great Parts, and Eminence,

15 and pro[*p. 21*]fessing himself for the Church of *England*, should not know what is meant by the *Protestant* Religion. This was seconded with great pleasantness by Divers of the Lords the Bishops; but the Bishop of *Winchester*, and some others of them were pleased to condescend to instruct that Lord, that the *Protestant* Religion was comprehended in 39

20 *Articles*, the *Liturgie*, the *Catechisme*, the *Homilies*, and the *Canons*. To this the Earl of *Shaftsbury* replied, that he begg'd so much Charity of them to believe, that he knew the *Protestant* Religion so well, and was so confirmed in it, that he hoped he should *burn* for the witness of it, if Providence should call him to it: But he might perhaps think some things

25 *not necessary*, that they accounted *Essential*, nay he might think some things *not true*, or agreeable to the Scripture, that they might call *Doctrines of the Church*: Besides when he was to swear *never to endeavor to alter*, it was certainly necessary to know *how far the just extent of this Oath was*; but since they had told him that the Protestant Religion was in those

30 5 *tracts*, he had still to ask, whether they meant those whole Tracts were the *Protestant* Religion, or only that the Protestant Religion was contained in all those, but that every part of those was not the Protestant Religion. If they meant the former of these then he was extreamly in the dark to find the Doctrine of *Predestination* in the 17. and 18. *Art.* to be

35 owned by so few great Doctors of the Church, and to find the 19. *Art.* to

---

7 *alter*] 1–4 | alter it B, E | these 1–4, M, Old.   12 he had now] 1–4 | now he had B   32 those] B, E | these 1–4, M, Old.   34 17. *and* 18.] ed. | 18. *and* 17. 1–2 | 18 and 17 3 | 18th and 17th 4 | 17 & 18 B, E | seventeenth & eighteenth M, Old.

[1] 2 Sam. 1: 20.

362

define *the Church* directly as the *Independents* do: Besides the 20. *Art.* stating the Authority of the Church is very dark, and either contradicts it self, or says nothing, or what is contrary to the known Laws of the Land; besides several other things, in the 39 *Articles*, have been Preached, and Writ against by Men of great Favor, Power, and Preferment in the Church. He humbly conceived the *Liturgie* was not so sacred, being made by Men the other day, and thought to be more differing from the dissenting *Protestants*, and less easy to be complyed with, upon the advantage of a pretense well known unto us all, of making *alterations* as might the better *unite* us; in stead whereof, there is scarce one alteration, but *widens* the breach, and no *ordination* allow'd by it here, (as it now stands last reformed in the *Act of Uniformity*) but what is *Episcopall*; in so much that a *Popish Priest* is capable, when converted, of any Church preferment without *Reordination*; but no *Protestant Minister* not Episcopally ordain'd, but is required to be reordain'd; as much as in us lies *unchurching* all the *forreign Protestants*, that have not Bishops, though the contrary was both allow'd, and practis'd from the beginning of the Reformation till the time of that Act, and several Bishops made of [*p. 22*] such, as were never ordain'd Priests by Bishops. Moreover the *Uncharitableness* of it was so much against the Interest of the *Crown, and Church of England* (casting off the dependency of the whole Protestant partie abroad) that it would have been *bought* by the *Pope* and *French King* at a vast summ of Money; and it is difficult to conceive so great an advantage fell to them meerly by chance, and without their help; so that he thought to endeavor to alter, and restore the Liturgy to what it was in *Queen Elizabeths* days might consist with his being a very good Protestant.

As to the *Catachisme*, he really thought it might be mended, and durst declare to them, it was not well that there was not a better made.

For the *Homilies* he thought there might be a better Book made, and the 3. *Hom.* of *Repairing* and *keeping clean of Churches*, might be omitted.

What is yet stranger then all this, The *Canons* of our Church are directly the *old Popish Canons*, which are still in force, and no other; which will appear, if you turn to the *Stat.* 25. *Hen.* 8. *cap.* 19 confirmed

---

4 Preached] 1–2 | preached 3–4 | preached against **B** | preach'd **M, Old.** 11 now] 1–4, **M, Old.** | *not in* **B** 19 never] 1–4, **M, Old.** | not **B** 19–24 Moreover . . . help] 1–4, **B** | *not in* **M, Old.** 31 of] 1–4 | *not in* **B, M, Old.**

and renewed by 1. *Eliz.*[1] where all those Canons are establish'd, untill an alteration should be made by the King in pursuance of that Act; which thing was attempted by *Edward the 6th.* but not perfected, and let alone ever since, for what reasons the Lords the Bishops could best tell; and it
5 was very hard to be obliged by Oath *not to endeavour to alter* either the English Common-Prayer book, or the Canon of the Mass. But if they meant the latter, *That the Protestant Religion is contein'd in all those, but that every part of those is not the Protestant Religion,* then he apprehended it might be in the Bishops Power to declare *ex post facto* what is the
10 Protestant Religion or not, or else they must leave it to every Man to judge for himself, what parts of those books are or are not, and then their Oath had been much better let alone. Much of this nature was said by that Lord, and Others, and the great Officers, and Bishops were so hard put to it, that they seemed willing, and convinced to admit of *an Expe-*
15 *dient.* The *Lord Wharton* an Old and Expert Parliament Man of eminent Piety and Abilities, beside a great Friend to the Protestant Religion, and Interest of *England,* offer'd as a cure to the whole Oath, and what might make it pass in all the 3 parts of it, without any farther debate, the addition of these words at the latter end of the Oath, *Viz.* [*p. 23*] *as the*
20 *same is or shall be establish'd by Act of Parliament,* but this was not endured at all, when the Lord *Grey* of *Rollston,* a worthy and true *English* Lord, offered another Expedient, which was the addition of these words, *by force or fraud,* to the beginning of the Oath, and then it would run thus, *I do swear not to endeavor by force or fraud to alter;* this was also a *cure* that
25 would have passed the whole Oath, and seemed as if it would have carried the whole House, the Duke of *York* and the Bishop of *Rochester*[2] both seconding it; but the Lord Treasurer, who had privately before consented to it, speaking against it, gave the word and sign to that party, and it being put to the question, the major Vote answered all arguments, and the
30 L. *Grey's* Proposition was laid aside.

Having thus carried the question, relying upon their strength of Votes, taking advantage that those expedients that had been offered, extended to the whole Oath, though but one of the 3 Clauses in the Oath had been

---

1 renewed] **M, Old.** | received 1–2, 4, **D** | revived 3 | continued **B**   18 farther]
1, 4 | further 2–3, **B**   22 these words] 3–4, **B** | words 1–2   26 House, the] 3,
B | House. The 1–2 | House; the 4, **D**

[1] 25 Hen. VIII, c. 19, An Act for the submission of the Clergy to the King's Majesty, was repealed by 1 & 2 Phil. & Mary, c. 8, § III, and revived by 1 Eliz. I, c. 1, § II.
[2] John Dolben (1625–86), Bishop of Rochester 1666, Archbishop of York 1683. *ODNB.*

debated, the other two not mentioned at all, they attempted strongly at
nine of the Clock at night to have the whole Oath put to the question, and
though it was resolutely opposed by the Lord *Mohun*, a Lord of great
courage, and *resolution* in the Publick Interest, and one whose own personal merits, as well as his Fathers, gave him a just title to the best favors 5
of the Court; yet they were not diverted but by as great a disorder as ever
was seen in that House proceeding from the rage those unreasonable
proceedings had caused in the Country Lords, they standing up in a
clump together, and crying out with so loud a continued Voice, *Adjourn*,
that when silence was obtain'd, Fear did what Reason could not do, cause 10
the question to be put only upon the first Clause concerning *Protestant
Religion*, to which the Bishops desired might be added, *as it is now
established*, and one of the eminentest of those that were for the Bill added
the words *by Law*; so that, as it was passed, it ran, *I A. B. do swear that I
will not endeavor to alter the Protestant Religion now by Law established in* 15
the Church of England.[1] And here observe the words *by Law* do directly
take in the *Canons* though the Bishops had never mentioned them. And
now comes the consideration of the latter part of the Oath which com-
prehends these 2 Clauses, viz. *nor the Government either in Church or
State*, wherein the Church came first to be considerd. And it was objected 20
by the Lords against the Bill, that it was [*p. 24*] *not agreeable to the King's
Crown and Dignity, to have His Subjects sworn to the Government of the
Church equally as to Himself*; That for the Kings of *England* to swear to
maintain the Church, was a different thing from enjoyning all His
Officers, and both His Houses of Parliament to swear to them. It would 25
be well understood, before the Bill passed, what the *Government of the
Church* (we are to swear to) is, and what the *Boundaries* of it, whether it
derives no Power, nor Authority, nor the exercise of any Power, Authority, or Function, but from the *King as head of the Church*, and from
God as through him, as all his other Officers do? 30
  For no Church or Religion can justify it self to the Government, but
the *State Religion*, that ownes an entire dependency on, and is but a
branch of it; or the *independent Congregations*, whilst they claim no other
power, but the exclusion of their own members from their particular

  6 of the] 1–4 | at the **B** | at E   8–9 in a clump] 1–2, **D** | in a lump 3, **B** | *om.* 4
9 Voice,] 2–3 | voice, 4, **B** | Voice 1   *Adjourn*,] 1–3 | *adjourn*, 4 | Adjourn,
Adjourn; **B**   13 that] 2–3, **B** | *not in* 1 | who 4, **D**   21 Bill,] 2–4, **B** | Bill 1

[1] 12 May, NA, SP 29/370/155.

Communion, and endeavor not to set up a Kingdom of Christ to their own use in this World, whilest our Saviour hath told us, that His Kingdom is not of it; for otherwise there would be *Imperium in imperio*, and two distinct Supream Powers inconsistent with each other, in the
5 same place, and over the same persons. The Bishops alleadged that *Priesthood* and the *Power* thereof, and the *Authority* belonging thereunto were derived immediately from *Christ*, but that the *license of exercising that Authority* and Power in any Country is derived from the *civil Magistrate*: To which was replied, that it was *a dangerous thing to secure by*
10 *Oath, and Act of Parliament those in the exercise of an Authority, and power in the King's Country, and over His Subjects, which being received from Christ himself, cannot be altered, or limitted by the King's Laws*; and that this was directly to set the *Mitre above the Crown*. And it was farther offered, that *this Oath was the greatest attempt that had been made against*
15 *the King's Supremacy since the Reformation*; for the King in Parliament may alter, diminish, enlarge, or take away any Bishoprick; He may take any part of a Diocess, or a whole Diocess, and put them under Deans, or other Persons; for if this be not lawful, but that Episcopacy should be *jure divino*, the maintaining the Government as it is now, is unlawful; since
20 the Deans of *Hereford*, and *Salisbury*, have very large tracts under their jurisdiction, and several Parsons of Parishes have Episcopal jurisdiction; so that at best that Go[*p. 25*]vernment wants alteration, that is so imperfectly settled.[1] The Bishop of *Winchester* affirmed in this debate several times, that there was no Christian Church before *Calvin* that
25 had not Bishops; to which he was answered that the *Albigenses* a very numerous People, and the only visible known Church of true beleivers, of some Ages, had no Bishops. It is very true, what the Bishop of *Winchester* replyd, that they had some amongst them, who alone had power to ordain, but that was only to commit that power to the Wisest, and
30 Gravest Men amongst Them, and to secure ill, and unfit Men from being admitted into the Ministery; but they exercis'd no jurisdiction over the others. And it was said by divers of the Lords, that they thought Episcopal Government best for the Church, and most suitable for the Monarchy, but they must say with the Lord of *Southampton* upon the

---

2 hath] 1–4 | *not in* B   6 *Authority*] ed. | authority L, N, S, T, Y | *Authorities* 1–3 | authorities 4, D | Authorities B   19 Government] 2c–4, B | Government: 1 | Government, 2u | government, E

[1] Maps showing ecclesiastical jurisdictions, including the peculiars describe here, can be found in Humphery-Smith, *The Phillimore Atlas and Index of Parish Registers.*

occasion of this Oath in the Parliament of *Oxford, I will not be sworn not to take away Episcopacie*, there being nothing, that is not of Divine Precept, but such circumstances may come in humane affairs, as may render it Eligible by the best of Men.[1] And it was also said, that *if Episcopacy be to be received as by Divine Precept, the King's Supremacy is overthrown*, and 5 so is also the opinion of the Parliaments both in *Edw.* 6. and *Queen Elizabeths* time; and the constitution of our Church ought to be altered, as hath been shewd. But the Church of *Rome* it self hath contradicted that Opinion, when She hath made such vast tracts of ground, and great numbers of Men exempt from Episcopal jurisdiction. The Lord *Wharton* 10 upon the Bishops claim to a Divine Right, asked a very hard question, *viz. whether they then did not claim withall, a power of Excommunicating their Prince*, which they Evading to answer, and being press'd by some other Lords, said they never had done it. Upon which the Lord *Hallifax* told them that that might well be; for since the Reformation they had 15 hitherto had too great a dependance on the Crown to venture on that, or any other Offence to it: and so the debate passed on to the third Clause, which had the same exceptions against it with the two former, of being unbounded How far any Man might meddle, and how far not, and is of that extent, that it *overthrew all Parliaments*, and left them capable of 20 nothing but giving Money. For what is the business of Parliaments but the alteration, either by adding, or taking away some part of the Government, either in Church or State? and every new Act of Parliament is an alteration; and what kind of Government [*p. 26*] in Church and State must that be, which I must swear upon no alteration of Time, emergencie 25 of Affairs, nor variation of humane Things, never to endeavor to alter? Would it not be requisite that such a Government should be given by God himself, and that with all the Ceremonie of Thunder, and Lightening, and visible appearance to the whole People, which God

---

4 it Eligible] ed. | it eligible B, T | it not Eligible 1–2, S | it not eligible 3–4 | it not eligied R | the contrary Eligible L, N, Y   27 should] 1–4 | *not in* B   28 with all] B, 3–4 | withall 1, E | withal 2

---

[1] This refers to the debates on the Five Mile Act. According to Burnet (i. 401), 'The earl of Southampton spoke vehemently against it in the house of lords; he said he could take no such oath himself: for, how firm soever he had always been to the church, yet, as things were managed, he did not know but he himself might see cause to endeavour an alternation.' According to another contemporary account, Southampton said that 'hee approves of the Government of the Church & thinks it a good one & perhaps the best, & wishes well to it, and for the good of it would not have such things prest, but hee would not bee bound to sweare never to endeavor an alternation of it', Bodl., MS Carte 80, fo. 757ᵛ, printed in Robbins, 'The Oxford Session of the Long Parliament of Charles II', 222.

vouchsafed to the Children of *Israel* at Mount *Sinai*? and yet you shall no where read that they were sworn to it by any Oath like this: nay on the Contrary, the Princes and the Rulers, even those recorded for the best of them, did make several variations. The Lord *Stafford*, a Noble Man of
5 great Honor and Candour, but who had been all along for the Bill, yet was so far convinced with the debate, that he freely declared, there ought to be an addition to the Oath, for preserving the freedom of debates in Parliament. This was strongly urged by the never to be forgotten, Earl of *Bridgwater*, who gave reputation, and strength to this *Cause of England*; as
10 did also those worthy Earls, *Denbigh*, *Clarendon*, and *Aylisbury*, Men of great Worth and Honor. To Salve all that was said by these, and the Other Lords, The Lord Keeper and the Bishops urged, that there was a Proviso, which fully preserved the Priviledges of Parliament, and upon farther enquiry there appearing no such, but only a Previous vote, as is
15 before mention'd, they allow'd that that Previous vote should be drawn into a *Proviso*, and added to the Bill, and then in their opinion the Exception to the Oath for this cause was perfectly removed; but on the other side it was offered, that a positive absolute Oath being taken, a Proviso in the Act could not dispence with it without some reference in the body of
20 the Oath, unto that Proviso; but this also was utterly denied, untill the next day, the debate going on upon other matters, the Lord Treasurer, whose authority easily obtained with the major Vote, reassumed what was mentioned in the Debates of the preceding days, and allow'd a reference to the Proviso, so that it then past in these words, *I A. B. do swear that I*
25 *will not endeavor to alter the Protestant Religion now by Law Establisht in the Church of England, nor the Government of this Kingdom in Church, or State, as it is now by Law established, and I do take this Oath according to the meaning of this Act and the Proviso contain'd in the same, so help me God.*[1]

[*p. 27*] There was a passage of the very greatest observation in the
30 whole debate, and which with most clearness shewd what the great Men and Bishops aimed at, and should in order have come in before, but that it deserved so particular a consideration, that I thought best to place it here by it self, which was, that upon passing of the Proviso for preserving the Rights, and Priviledges of Parliaments made out of the Previous
35 Votes, It was excellently observ'd by the Earl of *Bullingbrook*, a Man of great Abilitie, and Learning in the Laws of the Land, and perfectly

---

2 Oath] 2–4, B | oath 1   14 farther] 1–4 | further B, E   20 unto] 1–4 |
to B   23 preceding] 3–4, B, E | proceeding 1–2

[1] 21 May, NA, SP 29/370/227–8.

stedfast in all good *English* Principles, that *though that Proviso did preserve the freedom of Debates and Votes in Parliament, yet the Oath remain'd notwithstanding that Proviso* upon all Men, that shall take it, as a prohibition either by Speech, or Writing, or Address, to endeavor any alteration in Religion, Church, or State; nay also upon the *Members* of 5 *both Houses* otherwise then as they speak, and vote in open Parliaments or Committees: for this Oath takes away all *private Converse* upon any such affairs even one with another. This was seconded by the Lord *De la mer*, whose Name is well known, as also his Worth, Piety, and Learning; I should mention his great Merits too, but I know not whether that be 10 lawful, they lying yet unrewarded. The Lord *Shaftsbury* presently drew up some words for preserving the same Rights, Priviledges, and Freedoms, which Men now enjoy by the Laws established, that so by a side Wind we might not be deprived of the great Liberty we enjoy as *English Men*, and desired those words might be inserted in that Proviso before it 15 past. This was seconded by many of the forementioned Lords, and prest upon those terms, that they desired not to countenance, or make in the least degree any thing lawful, that was not already so, but that they might not be deprived by this dark way of proceeding of that Liberty which was necessary to them as Men, and without which Parliaments would be 20 renderd useless. Upon this all the great Officers showd themselves, nay the D. of *Lauderdail* himself, though under the Load of two Addresses,[1] opened his mouth, and together with the Lord Keeper, and the Lord Treasurer, told the Committee in plain terms, that they intended, and design'd to prevent Caballing, and conspiracies against the Government; 25 that they knew no reason why any of the King's Officers should consult [*p. 28*] with Parliament Men about Parliament business, and particularly mention'd those of the Armie, Treasury, and Navy; and when it was Objected to them, that the greatest part of the most knowing Gentry were either Justices of the Peace, or of the Militia, and that this took away all 30 converse, or discourse of any alteration, which was in truth of any business in Parliament, and that the Officers of the Navy, and Treasury,

---

3 it,] **B** | *not in* 1–2 | it 3–4   19 which] **B, D, 4** | *not in* 1–3   25 Government;] 2–3 | Government 1 | Government: 4, **D** | Government, **B** | government; **E**

---

[1] On 14 April the Commons voted him to be 'a person obnoxious and dangerous to the Government'; the address was sent to the King on 23 April, the King replied on 7 May, and a second address was sent on 31 May: *CJ* ix. 316, 322–3, 332, 347–8; NA, SP 29/369/256; NA, SP 29/370/116–17; BL, Add. MS 33051, fos. 202–4; BL, Add. MS 32094, fos. 358–60; BL, Harleian MS 5277, fos. 34^r–35^r; *Debates*, ed. Grey, iii. 24–33, 107–12; Dering, *Diaries and Papers*, 60, 68–9, 79–80, 95–6.

might be best able to advise what should be fit in many cases; and that withall none of their Lordships did offer any thing to salve the inconvenience of Parliament Men being deprived of discoursing one with another, upon the matters that were before them. Besides it must be again
5 remembred, that nothing was herein desired to be countenanced, or made lawful, but to preserve that which is already Law, and avowedly justified by it; For without this addition to the Proviso, the Oath renderd Parliaments but a *Snare* not a *Security* to the People; Yet to all this was answerd sometimes with passion, and high words, sometimes with Jests,
10 and Raillery (the best they had) and at the last the major Vote answered all objections, and laid aside the addition tendered.

There was another thing before the finishing of the Oath, which I shall here also mention, which was an *additional Oath* tendered by the Marquess of *Winchester*, who ought to have been mentioned in the first,
15 and chiefest place for his conduct, and support in the whole debate, being an expert Parliament Man, and one whose Quallity, Parts and Fortune, and owning of good Principles, concurr to give him one of the greatest places in the esteem of good Men. The additional Oath tenderd, was as followeth, *I do swear that I will never by Threats, Injunctions, Promises,*
20 *Advantages, or Invitations, by or from any person whatsoever, nor from the hopes, or prospect of any Gift, Place, Office, or Benefit whatsoever, give my Vote other then according to my Opinion and Conscience, as I shall be truly, and really persuaded upon the debate of any business in Parliament; so help me God.*[1]

25 [*p. 29*] This Oath was offerd upon the occasion of swearing Members of Parliament, and upon this score only, that if any new Oath was thought fit (which that Noble Lord declared his own Judgment perfectly against) this certainly was (all considerations, and circumstances taken in) most necessary to be a part, and the nature of it was not so strange if they
30 considerd the *Judges* Oath, which was not much different from this. To this the Lord Keeper seemed very averse, and declared in a very fine Speech, that it was an *Useless Oath*; for all Gifts, Places, and Offices, were likelyest to come from the King, and no Member of Parliament in either

---

6 which] **4, D** | that **1–3, B**   11 aside] **3–4, B, E** | a side **1–2**   17 [*1st*] of]
1–4 | *not in* **B**   20 *Invitations*] ed. | *Invitation* **1–3** | *invitation* **4, D** | invitation **B** |
Invitations **J**   29 part] **1–4** | part of it **B**

---

[1] There are copies of this proposed oath in HLRO, MS Minutes, XIX (Feb. 1674–May 1678), 12 May 1675; Bodl., MS Don. b. 8, p. 519; BL, Harleian MS 5277, fo. 42ᵛ; *Reliquiae Baxterianae*, pt. III, § 296.

House, could do too much for the King, or be too much of His side, and that Men might lawfully, and worthily, have in their Prospect, such Offices, or Benefits from Him. With this the Lords against the Bill, were in no tearms satisfied, but plainly spoke out *that Men had been, might, and were likely to be, in either House, too much for the King, as they call'd it,* and 5 that whoever did endeavour to give more power to the King, then the Law and constitution of the Government had given, especially if it tended to the Introducing an *Absolute* and *Arbitrary* Government might justly be said to do too much for the King, and to be corrupted in his judgment by the prospect of advantages, and rewards; Though, when it is considered 10 that every deviation of the Crown towards Absolute power, lessens the King in the love, and affection of his People, makeing Him become less their Interest, a wise Prince will not think it a Service done Him.

And now remains only the last part of the Bill, which is the penalty different according to the quallifications of the Persons: *All that are, or* 15 *shall be Privy Counsellors, Justices of the Peace, or possessors of any beneficial Office, Ecclesiastical, Civill, or Military, are to take the Oath when summoned, upon pain of* 500l. *and being made uncapable of bearing Office, the Members of both Houses are not made uncapable, but lyable to the penalty of* 500l. *if they take it not.*[1] Upon all which the considerations of the Debate 20 were, That those Officers, and [*p. 30*] Members of both Houses are of all the Nation the most dangerous to be sworn into a mistake, or change of the Government, and that, as to the Members of both Houses, the penalty of 500l. was directly against the latter of the 2. Previous Votes, and although they had not applied the penalty of Incapacity unto the 25 Members of both Houses, because of the first Previous Vote in the Case of the Lords, neither durst they admit of a Proposition made by some of themselves, *that those that did not come up, and Sit as Members, should be lyable to the taking the Oath, or penalty, untill they did so*: Yet their Ends were not to be compassed without invading the latter Previous Vote, and 30 contrary to the Rights and Priviledges of *Parliament* enforce them to swear, or pay 500l. every Parliament, and this they carried through with so strong a Resolution, that having experienced their misfortunes in replys for several hours, not one of the party could be provoked to speak

---

1 of] 1–4 | on B   12–13 less their Interest, a] 3 | less their Interest, A 1 | less their Interest. A 2 | less their Interest; a D, 4er | less their interest, a E | less, there, a B | less in their interest; a 4   15 Persons:] ed. | Persons 1 | Persons. 2–3 | persons: 4, D | Persons, B   24 latter] 1–4 | letter B

[1] 31 May, NA, SP 29/370/278–9.

one word. Though, besides the former arguments, it was strongly urged, that this Oath ought not to be put upon Officers with a heavier penalty then the *Test* was in the Act of the immediate preceding Session against the *Papists*, by which any Man might sit down with the loss of his Office,

5 without being in the danger of the penalty of 500*l.* and also that this Act had a direct retrospect (which ought never to be in Penall Laws) for this Act punishes Men for having an Office without taking this Oath, which office, before this Law pass, they may now lawfully enjoy without it. Yet notwithstanding it provides not a power, in many cases, for them to part

10 with it, before this Oath overtake them; For the clause *whoever is in Office the* 1. *September* will not relieve a Justice of the Peace, who, being once Sworn, is not in his own power to be left out of commission; and so might be instanced in several other cases; as also the members of the House of Commons were not in their own power to be unchosen; and as to the

15 Lords, they were subjected by it to the meanest condition of Mankind, if they could not enjoy their Birthright, without playing Tricks sutable to the Humour of every Age, and be enforced to swear to every fancie of the present times. Three years ago it was *All Liberty and Indulgence*, and now it is *Strict and Rigid Conformity* and what it may be, in some [*p. 31*] short

20 time hereafter, without the Spirit of Prophesying might be shrewdly guest by a considering Man. This being answerd with silence, the Duke of *Buckingham*, whose Quality, admirable Wit, and unusual pains, that he took all along in the debate against this Bill, makes me mention Him in this last place, as General of the partie, and coming last out of the Field,

25 made a Speech late at night of Eloquent, and well placed Non-sense, showing how excellently well he could do both ways, and hoping that might do, when Sense (which he often before used with the highest advantage of Wit, and Reason) would not; but the Earl of *Winchilsea* readily apprehending the Dialect, in a short reply, put an end to the

30 Debate, and the major Vote *ultima ratio Senatuum, & Conciliorum,*[1] carried the Question as the Court, and Bishops would have it.

This was the *last Act* of this *Tragi-Comedy*, which had taken up sixteen or seventeen whole days debate, the House sitting many times till eight or nine of the Clock at night, and sometimes till Midnight; but the business

---

2 not] 4, D | *not in* 1–3, B   28 *Winchilsea*] 1–2 | *Winchelsea* 4, D | Winchelsey B | *W.* 3

[1] The ultimate argument of senates and councils. Similar phrases were in common use: 'ultima ratio regum' was cast on the artillery pieces of Louis XIV, and Marvell used 'ultima ratio cleri' in *The Rehearsal Transpros'd*, 94.

of *priviledg* between the two Houses gave such an interruption, that this Bill was never reported from the Committee to the House.

I have mention'd to You divers Lords, that were Speakers, as it fell in the Debate, but I have not distributed the Arguments of the debate to every particular Lord. Now you know the Speakers, your curiosity may 5 be satisfied, and the Lords I am sure will not quarrel about the division. I must not forget to mention those great Lords, *Bedford*, *Devonshire*, and *Burlington*, for the Countenance and support they gave to the *English* Interest. The Earl of *Bedford* was so brave in it, that he joyn'd in three of the Protests; So also did the Earl of *Dorset*, and the Earl of *Stamford*, a 10 Young Noble Man of great hopes, The Lord *Eure*, the Lord *Viscount Say and Seal*, and the Lord *Pagitt* in two; the Lord *Audley* and the Lord *Fitzwater* in the *3d*. and the Lord *Peter*, a Noble Man of great Estate, and always true to the maintenance of Liberty, and Property, in the first. And I should not have omitted the Earl of *Dorset*, Lord *Audley*, and the Lord 15 *Peter* amongst the Speakers: for I will assure you they did their parts excellently well. The Lord *Viscount Hereford* was a steady Man among the Countrey [*p. 32*] Lords; so also was the Lord *Townsend*, a Man justly of great Esteem, and power in his own countrey, and amongst all those that well know him. The Earl of *Carnarvon* ought not to be mention'd in 20 the last place, for he came out of the Countrey on purpose to oppose the Bill, stuck very fast to the Countrey partie, and spoke many excellent things against it. I dare not mention the *Roman Catholick* Lords, and some others, for fear I hurt them; but thus much I shall say of the *Roman Catholick* Peers, that if they were safe in their Estates, and yet kept out of 25 Office, their Votes in that House would not be the most unsafe to *England* of any sort of Men in it. As for the absent Lords, the Earl of *Ruttland*, Lord *Sandys*, Lord *Herbert* of *Cherbury*, Lord *North*, and Lord *Crew*, ought to be mentiond with Honor, having taken care their Votes should maintain their own interest, and opinions; but the Earls of *Exceter*, and 30 *Chesterfield*, that gave no proxies this Session, the Lord *Montague* of *Boughton*, that gave his to the Treasurer, and the Lord *Roberts* his to the Earl of *Northampton*, are not easily to be understood. If you ask after the Earl of *Carlisle*, the Lord *Viscount Falconbridge*, and the Lord *Berkely* of *Berkley* Castle, because you find them not mentioned amongst their old 35 Friends, all I have to say, is, That the Earl of *Carlisle* stept aside to receive his Pention, the Lord *Berkely* to dine with the Lord Treasurer, but the

---

1 between] 1–4 | betwixt **B**   14 Property,] 2–4 | Property 1, **B**, **E**
30–374.5 but . . . bottom] 1–2, 4, **B** | *om.* 3   31 Session] 4 | Sessions 1–2 | sessions **B**

Lord *Viscount Falconberg*, like the Noble Man in the Gospel,[1] went away
sorrowfull, for he had a Great Office at Court; but I despair not of giving
you a better account of them next Session, for it is not possible when they
consider that *Cromwell's* Major General, Son in law, and Friend,[2] should
5 think to find their Accounts amongst Men that set up on such a bottom.

Thus Sir, You see the Standard of the *new Partie* is not yet set up, but
must be the work of another Session, though it be admirable to me, how
the *King* can be enduced to venture His Affairs upon such *weak Counsels*,
and *of so fatal consequences*; for I believe it is the first time in the World,
10 that ever it was thought adviseable, after fifteen years of the highest
Peace, Quiet, and Obedience, that ever was in any Countrey, that there
should be a *pretense* taken up, and a reviving of former miscarriages,
especially after so many Promises, and Declarations, as well as Acts of
Oblivion, and so much [*p. 33*] merit of the Offending partie, in being the
15 Instruments of the King's Happy Return, besides the putting so vast a
number of the King's Subjects in utter despair of having their crimes
ever forgotten; and it must be a great Mistake in Counsels, or worse, that
there should be so much pains taken by the Court to debase, and bring
low the House of Peers, if a *Military Government* be not intended by
20 some. For the Power of *Peerage*, and a *standing Army* are like two
Buckets, the proportion that one goes down, the other exactly goes up;
and I refer you to the consideration of all the Histories of ours, or any of
our neighbor Northern Monarchies, whether standing forces Military,
and Arbitrary government, came not plainly in by the same steps, that the
25 Nobility were lessened; and whether when ever they were in Power, and
Greatness, they permitted the least shadow of any of them: Our own
Countrey is a clear instance of it; For though the *White Rose* and the *Red*
chang'd fortunes often to the ruine, slaughter and beheading of the great
Men of the other side; yet nothing could enforce them to secure them-
30 selves by a standing force: But I cannot believe that the King Himself will
ever design any such thing; for He is not of a temper Robust, and
Laborious enough, to deale with such a sort of Men, or reap the
advantages, if there be any, of such a Government; and I think, He can
hardly have forgot the treatment his *Father* received from the Officers of

---

3 Session] **4** | Sessions 1–2 | sessions **B**   24 plainly] 1–4 | *not in* **B**
33 Government;] 3 | Government, 1–2, **B** | Government. **4, D**

[1] Matt. 19: 22; Mark 10: 22; Luke 18: 23.
[2] Thomas Belasyse (1627/1628–1700), second Viscount Fauconberg, *ODNB*, m.
(second wife) Mary Cromwell, daughter of Oliver Cromwell.

his Army, both at *Oxford*, and *Newark*;[1] 'Twas an hard, but almost an even choice to be the Parliaments *Prisoner*, or their *Slave*; but I am sure the greatest prosperity of his Armes could have brought him to no happier condition, then our King his Son hath before him whenever he please. However, This may be said for the honor of this Session, that there is no Prince in Christendom that hath at a greater expence of Money, maintained for two Months space, a Nobler, or more useful dispute of the Politiques, Mistery, and secrets of Government, both in Church and State, then this hath been; Of which noble design no part is owing to any of the Countrey Lords, for they several of them begg'd, at the first entrance into the Debate, that they might not be engaged in such disputes, as would unavoidably produce divers things to be said, which they were willing to let alone. But I must bear them witness, and so will you, having read this, that they did their parts in it, when it came to it, and spoke plain like *old English* Lords.

[*p. 34*] I shall conclude with that, upon the whole matter, is most worthy your consideration, That the *design* is *to declare us first into another Government more Absolute, and Arbitrary, then the Oath of Allegience, or old Law knew*, and then make us *swear unto it*, as it is so established: And less then this the Bishops could not offer in requital to the Crown for parting with its Supremacy, and suffering them to be sworn to equal with it self. Archbishop *Laud* was the first Founder of this Device; in his Canons of 1640.[2] you shall find an Oath very like this, and a Declaratory Canon preceding, *that Monarchy is of divine Right*, which was also affirmed in this debate by our Reverend Prelates, and is owned in Print by no less Men then A. Bishop *Usher*,[3] and B. *Sanderson*;[4] and I am afraid it is the avowd opinion of much the greater part of our dignified Clergie: If so, I am sure they are the most dangerous sort of Men alive to our *English* Government, and it is the first thing that ought to be lookt into, and strictly examin'd by our Parliaments, 'tis the *leaven* that corrupts the

5

10

15

20

25

30

6 that] ed. | *not in* 1–4, B   10 they] 1–3, B | *om.* 4, D, E   16 that] 1–3, B | what 4 | [that 'which'] 'what' D   24 preceding,] 2–4, B | preceding 1 | preceding; E 27 If so,] 1–2, 4, B, D | and 3 | if so E   28 they are] 1–2, 4, B, D | it is 3 Men] 1–2, 4, D | men B | Opinion 3   29 that] ed. | *not in* 1–4, B

[1] This refers to the angry scenes between Charles I and Prince Rupert's officers that followed the surrender of Bristol on 10 September 1645. This passage is discussed in Pocock, 'Machiavelli, Harrington and English Political Ideologies in the Eighteenth Century', 121.
[2] See Kenyon, *Stuart Constitution*, 150–3.
[3] James Ussher (1581–1656), Archbishop of Armagh 1625. *ODNB*.
[4] Robert Sanderson (1587–1663), Bishop of Lincoln 1660. *ODNB*.

whole lump; for if that be true, I am sure Monarchy is not to be bounded by humane Laws, and the 8. *chap.* of 1. *Samuel,* that says *Our Kings will take our Fields, our Vineyards, our Corn, and our Sheep,* will prove (as many of our Divines would have it) the great Charter of the Royal
5 Prerogative, and our *Magna Charta* is not in force, but *void* and *null,* because against divine Institution;[1] and you have the *Riddle* out, why the Clergy are so ready to take themselves, and impose upon others such kind of Oaths as these, they have placed themselves, and their possessions upon a better, and a surer bottom (as they think) then *Magna Charta,* and
10 so have no more need of, or concern for it: Nay what is worse, they have truckt away the Rights and Liberties of the People in this, and all other countries wherever they have had opportunity, that they might be owned by the Prince to be *Jure Divino,* and maintain'd in that Pretention by that absolute power and force, they have contributed so much to put into his
15 hands; and that *Priest,* and *Prince* may, like *Castor* and *Pollux,* be worshipt together as Divine in the same temple by Us poor Lay-subjects; and that *sense* and *reason, Law, Properties, Rights,* and *Liberties,* shall be understood as the Oracles of those Deities shall interpret, or give signification to them, and ne'r be made use of in the world to oppose the
20 absolute and free Will of either of them.

Sir, I have no more to say, but begg your Pardon for this tedious Trouble, and that you will be very careful to whom you Communicate any of this.

FINIS.

2–3 that...*Sheep*] *in all the editions and MSS this clause occurs after* our *Magna Charta (line 5)*   3 *will*] ed. | *may not* 1–4 | may not **B**   prove] 1–4 | *not in* **B**
4 would] 1–2, 4, **B, D** | will 3   6 [*2nd*] the] 1–2, 4, **B, D** | some of the 3
9 [*2nd*] a] 1–4 | `a' **B** | *om.* **E**   20 absolute and free Will] **D,** 4 | Absolute, and Freewill 1–2 | Absolute and Free-will 3 | absolute and freewill **B, E**   23 *FINIS.*] 1–2 | FINIS. **B** | *om.* 3–4, **E**

---

[1] The text of this passage is discussed above, pp. 230–1.

THE SELECTION OF JURIES

THE SELECTION OF JURIES

PRO 30/24/47/30, fos. 32–4.

[*fo. 32ʳ*] whatever power some would pretend to be in the Justices of the peace or Justices of Goal delivery to reforme pannels returned by the Sherifs, yet it is evident by the Statute its self of the 3. H. 8[1] That unlesse it does appeare to the Court upon reasonable Evidence that the present Sherifs are guilty of the same or such like misdemeanors as are mentioned in the preamble of the Statute or that the persons impannelled are such sort of persons as therein are set forth they have noe power by that Statute to reforme the pannell. The preamble of a Statute being always accounted an excellent key to open the meaneing of the purview. And therefor though the body or Purview of the Statute may seeme very large refering all to the Discretion of the Court, yet tis very well known that **Discretion** according to interpretation of law is not an extravagant liberty or licence to doe what they please; but their proceedings are to be limited & bounded within the rule of law & Reason˙ Discretion being a faculty of discerning per legem quid sit justum,[2] & not to be guided by will or private affection Because talis discretio discretionem confundit.[3] And there can be noe better guide to their Discretion in this case then the preamble of the Statute

If therefor it appears that the Sherifs for extorsive or oppressive designes to draw profits or rewards to them selves have impannelled these Jurys: Or that the persons impannelled are [*fo. 32ᵛ*] men of ill fame & such as probably make noe conscience of an oath there may be reason to reforme the pannell. But every breach of law, or repeated breaches of law espetially of some penall laws the observation of which is not rigorously exacted will not render a man suspected of being guilty of wilfull perjury which the Statute takes notice of. For at this rate every one that eats flesh on Fridays or that doth not exactly keep lent or observe all the holy days will be made incapeable.

---

1 [And] whatever   12 **Discretion** *written in emphatic style*

[1] An Act agaynst Shreifs for abuses, 3 Hen. VIII, c. 12, *SR* iii. 32.
[2] through the law what is just.
[3] such discretion confounds discretion.

And as to the Dissenters from the Rites & Ceremonys of the church of England (which hath been objected) they cannot be brought within the meaning of that Act. Because the Dissent is in such things wherein wise & good men have heretofore differed & doe & will always herein more or
5 lesse differ. And the dissent being soe much against the profit & secular interest of the Dissenters it can not be presumed to proceed from any thing but impulse of conscience: wherein although they may erre & therefor be or be thought weake: yet there can be noe reason to conclude them wicked, but rather that they feare & therefor will keepe their Oaths
10 lawfully administred & taken. Besides that Dissenters cease not thereby to be free men of England but are equally with others capeable of the same priviledges & lyable to the same burthens & services & the law makes noe such destinction nor is there any reason for it

From all which it follows that if the Court should command the
15 Sherifs to reforme the pannell where there is noe fault which this Statute of 3 H. 8 takes notice of the Sherifs may refuse to obey & stand to their owne pannell without any forfeiture of 20^{li} [*fo. 33^r*]

But if the Sherifs should yeild them selves guilty of haveing returned such persons in their pannells as <u>for the singular advantage benefit &</u>
20 <u>gain of the said Sherifs or their ministers will be wilfully forsworne &</u>
<u>perjured by the sinister labour of the said Sherifs & their ministers</u>[1] which is the only cause wherein the law provides & allows the reformation of the pannell by the command of the Bench. If (I say) the Sherifs should be prevailed on by the Court to lay soe deepe an infamy &
25 soe lasting a disparagement on them selves & those cittizens whose names they strike out of the pannell yet they are farther to consider. That this power of Reforming pannells is given only to the Justices of the peace (who in the precept which they send forth are stiled Justiciarii Domini Regis ad pacem in dictâ civitate conservand⟨am⟩.)[2] & to the Com-
30 missioners or Justices of Goal delivery (who in the precept they send forth are stiled Justic⟨iarii⟩ Domini Regis ad Gaolam de Newgate de

---

10–13 'Besides...it' *added at paragraph-end and in margin*   10 [the] Dissenters   19–21 *Underlined by Locke; marginal note:* Vid preamble of the Stat: 3 H. 8 in the printed paper   28 [& the Justices] (who

[1] 3 Hen. VIII, c. 12, *SR* iii. 32. The printed paper mentioned in the marginal note is *None but the Sheriffs ought to name and return Jurors to serve in Inquests before Commissioners of Oyer and Terminer*: see above, pp. 122–3, 134.
[2] Justices of our Lord the King for keeping the peace in the said city.

prisonar⟨ibus⟩ in eadem existent⟨ibus⟩ deliberand⟨um⟩ Assignat⟨um⟩).[1]
But the Commissioners or Justices of Oyer & Terminer have noe power
at all to reforme the pannell returned upon & annexed to their precept,
wherein they are stiled Justic⟨iarii⟩ Domini Regis ad inquirend⟨um⟩ pro
dicto Domino Rege de quibuscunque prodicionibus &c[2]   5

To understand this aright we must know that in the Citty of London
though it be the practise that the same men who are returned & sworne of
the Grand Jury at the Sessions of the peace at Guild hall be also the grand
Jury of Goal delivery & of Oyer & Terminer at the old bayly yet their
being the same persons hinders not but that they are 3 destinct Jurys   10
returned upon 3 destinct pannells in obedience to three destinct precepts
& [*fo. 33ᵛ*] pursuant of 3 destinct Commissions: viz the Commission of
the peace (which in London is heald by charter & the Sessions there upon
begins at Guild hall & adjourns to the Old bayly) the Commission of Goal
delivery & the Commission of Oyer & Terminer which are begun and   15
held at the Old bayly. And the Sherifs might if they pleased returne upon
each destinct pannell different men did not the ease of the people (when
the businesse can as well or better be dispatchd by the same men serveing
in these different Jurys) recommend & warrant this practise both in
London & at the Contry Assizes where the same persons who are of the   20
grand Jury are returned upon 3 severall pannells as matters doe happen

One thing farther must be observed to avoid confusion. viz that the
Justices of Goal delivery & the Justices of Oyer & Terminer being the
same persons, when the same Jurors names are returned upon the two
destinct pannells of Goal delivery & of Oyer & Terminer the said Jurors 25
are usually sworne but once. Because the Commissioners or Justices sit
there in both capacitys. But yet this hinders not but that they are still two
destinct Jurys

These therefor being destinct pannells with the same names in them, if
the Justices of Goal delivery who are the same with those of Oyer &   30
Terminer should by vertue of the Statute 3. H. 8 finde reason to command the pannell upon the precept of Goal delivery to be reformed, &
the Sherifs finde reason to submit to it, yet this will not concerne nor

---

2 ‘Comʳˢ or’   5 de…&c *added in another hand*   13 [which begins at
G⟨uildhall⟩] &   20 [grand J⟨ury⟩] persons   21 as…happen *added in another
hand*   24 ‘names’   26 ‘usually’

[1] Justices of our Lord the King for the delivery of prisoners held in the Gaol at
Newgate.
[2] Justices of our Lord the King for inquiry into all kinds of treasons etc. against the said
King.

affect the pannell upon the precept of Oyer & Terminer which must & ought to stand immutable as returned by the Sherifs [*fo. 34ʳ*] as appeares by the Statute 11 H. 4 whereby it is absolutely injoyned that noe body shall be returned upon <u>any nomination to the Sheriff by any person of the</u>

5 <u>names which by him should be impannelld.</u>[1] And if any one will looke into the preamble of that Statute he shall finde that that law was particularly made to hinder the <u>Justices</u> from makeing any such alterations in pannells, or nominateing any one to be put into them, which is so absolutely provided against, that if it should happen at any time to be

10 donne all proceedings thereupon are made void as appears by the same law. Soe that whatever may happen to the pannell of Goal delivery the Court has noe power to alter or reforme any thing in the pannell of Oyer & Terminer but the law is directly against it, & therefor that pannell as once returned by the Sherifs must stand. Besides if Commissioners to

15 enquire should have such power over pannells great part of the miserys practised by Empson & Dudley c Inst. 4 may be practised again[2]

---

3 H. 4] *followed by* [in the printed paper] *deleted, square brackets in text;* vid. printed paper *added in margin*   4–5 *underlined by Locke*   4 ⟦Sherifs⟧Sherrif *probably not altered by Locke*   12 'or reforme'   13 th⟦e⟧at

[1] 11 Hen. IV, c. 9, *SR* ii. 166. Locke's quotation is slightly abridged.

[2] Richard Empson and Edmund Dudley were ministers of Henry VII executed for treason by Henry VIII. Their notorious oppressions were mentioned in Coke's *Fourth Institute*, 40–1, 196–9, and in numerous contemporary tracts: *The English-mans right*, 6; *The Triumph of Justice over Unjust Judges*, 12–20; *The Second Part of No Protestant Plot*, 21–2; *The Third Part of No Protestant Plot*, 33. For further contemporary references, see Scott, *Algernon Sidney and the Restoration Crisis*, 192–3. Locke could have read about them in Bacon's *The Historie of the Reigne of King Henry the Seventh*, a copy of which he had at Christ Church in July 1681, *LL* 162.

ENTRIES IN COMMONPLACE
BOOKS

Pactum

Adversaria 1661, p. 16. Undated, written *c*.1670–1673.

Pactum   Deale not with people litigious or poore· from one their owne necessity will give you trouble from the other their disposition. JL

Amor   5

MS Locke d. 1, p. 57. Dated 1679

Amor   All men have a stock of love laid up in them by nature which they cannot forbeare to bestow on some thing or other. we should therefor take care to choose fit & worthy objects of our love least like women that want children the proper objects of their affection we grow fond of litle 10 dogs & munkys   JL

Patriae Amor

MS Locke d. 1, p. 53. Dated 1679.

Patriae Amor   Is from the Idea of setlement there & not leaveing it again· The minde not being satisfied with any thing that suggests often to 15 it the thoughts of leaveing it which naturally attends a man in a strange country. For though in generall we thinke of dyeing & soe leaveing the place where we have set up our rest in this world Yet in particular defering & puting it off from time to time we make our stay there eternall, because we never set precise bounds to our abode there & never thinke of 20 leaveing it in good earnest v. pl. p. 57. Amor   JL

Amor Patriae

MS Locke d. 1, p. 57. Dated 1679.

Amor Patriae) The remembrance of pleasures & conveniencys we have had there. The love of our freinds whose conversation & assistance may 25 be pleasant & usefull to us & the thoughts of recommending our selves to

---

7 [naturall] stock   [[by nature]]as it were] by   9 [[least]]& not] 'least'
14 [thoughts] 'Idea'   19 [it] our   20 [of leaveing it] to   26 [if] the
'thoughts of' (*no caret*)

our old acquaintance by the improvements we shall bring home either of
our fortunes or abilitys or the increase of esteeme we expect from haveing
traveld & seen more then others of the world & the strange things in it· all
these preserve in us in long absence a constant affection to our country &
5 a desire to returne to it. But yet I thinke this is not all nor the cheife cause
that keeps in us a longing after our countrys. Whilst we are abroad we
look on our selves as strangers there & are always thinkeing of departing·
we set not up our rest, but often see or thinke of the end of our being
there & the minde is not easily satisfied with any thing it can reach to the
10 end of. But when we are returnd to our country where we thinke of a
lasting abode wherein to set up our rest an everlasting aboad for we
seldome thinke of any thing beyond it, we doe not propose to our selves
an other country whither we thinke to remove & establish our selves
afterwards· This is that I imagin that sets man kinde soe constantly upon
15 desires of returning to their country because they thinke noe more of
leaveing it again & therefor men maried & setled in any place are much
more cold in those desires. And I beleive when any one thinkes often of
this world as of a place wherein he is not to make any long abode where he
can have noe lasting fixed setlement, but that he sees the bounds of his
20 stay here & often reflects upon his departure, he will presently upon it
put on the thoughts of a stranger, be much more indifferent for the
particular place of his nativity, & noe more fond of it then a traveller is of
any forain country when he thinks he must leave them all indifferently to
returne & setle in his native soile   JL v. pl. p. 53 Patria

25   Conformitas

MS Locke d. 1, p. 5. Dated 1679.

Conformitas. Severall protestants not of the Church of England resident
at Constantinople, had leave of Sir J. Finch[1] the English Ambasador
there to have a roome in his house to meet to pray in· they being most of
30 the French church. But at last it was thought fit that if they would
continue in that priviledg they should come & receive the sacrament in
his chappell administerd there by his chaplain according to the discipline

---

11 [ab⟨ode⟩] everlasting   13   whither] whether *MS*   17 `often'
19 [aboad] setlement   23 ⟦ . . . ⟧any

[1] Sir John Finch (1626–82) *ODNB*, English ambassador at Constantinople 1672–82,
younger brother of Heneage Finch, Shaftesbury's successor as Lord Keeper.

of the Church of England. Of which they haveing notice they accordingly came. But presented them selves to receive it according to the severall fashons of their churches or perswasions of their owne mindes some siting & some standing though the Ambasador & all the usuall congregation of the English there had received it kneeling. However the chaplain thought he could not refuse it any one that came solemly & seriously to receive it for any posture he presented him self in, & therefor administred the bread to them all. which significant declaration that kneeling was noe essentiall part of receiveing the Lords supper & noe necessary part of worship had soe powerfull an effect upon them, that when he came afterwards to give them the cup, they of their own accords received it every one kneeling. This way if it were a litle more practised would perhaps be found not only the most Christian but the most effectuall way to bring men to Conformity. Mr Covell[1]

Idololatria

MS Locke d. 1, p. 81. Dated 1679.

Idololatria   That it is not terminateing the worship of the minde on an Idol but performeing outward acts of worship before an Idol that is Idolatry seems cleare by what god says I have 7000 who have not bent their knee before Baal.[2] It is not said that have not directed their worship & terminated it on the Idol Baal. Bending the knee made them guilty. And I aske how any one could be found guilty of Idolatry in a judicial proceeding (for it was to be punishd with death[3]) if that which denominated the action, & made it truly & formally Idolatry were only an internall act of the minde that terminated it amisse. This would be a hard thing for witnesses to prove   JL

Iustitia

MS Locke c. 33, fo. 11[r]; copy in MS Locke c. 42B, p. 60. Entry in MS Locke c. 33 written on 25 March 1679.

---

8 [it] the   10 [th] had   12 way] was *MS*   20 [And I ask] It
21 'it'   23 [if it] (for   24 [that which] denominated   26 prove [it]

---

[1] John Covel (1638–1722) *ODNB*, Chaplain at Constantinople, subsequently Master of Christ's College, Cambridge. Biographical note in *Correspondence*, ii. 22–3.
[2] 1 Kgs. 19: 18.   [3] Deut. 17: 2–5.

Iustitia   Since most of the wrong judgments that are given in the world are rather the faults of the will then of the understanding to have justice well administred care should be taken to choose rather upright then learned men   JL

5   Pietas

MS Locke c. 33, fo. 10ᵛ. Written in March 1679.

Pietas   Education not generation gives the obligation & the affection for the children taken prisoners when men make war against their parents & country as heartily as any 454.[1] we see the same in the Janisarys.[2]   JL

10   Politia

MS Locke c. 33, fo. 11ʳ; copy in MS Locke c. 42B, p. 6. Entry in MS Locke c. 33 written on 25 March 1679.

Politia   The Kings of Canada are elective but the sons never faile to succeed their fathers when they are heirs to their vertues, otherwise not.
15 & their Kings are rather obeyd by consent & persuasion then by force & compulsion the publique good being the measure of their authority Sagard $\overline{1005}$ p. 418.[3] And this seems to have been the state of regall authority in its Original at least in all this part of the world   JL

                                         Toleratio

20 MS Locke d. 1, pp. 125–6. Dated 1679.

Toleratio. Noe man has power to prescribe to an other what he should beleive or doe in order to the saveing his own soule, because it is only his

---

2 [*2nd*] of] *MS Locke c.42B* | *not in MS Locke c.33*   13 of] *MS Locke c.42B* | [of the] *MS Locke c.33*   14 heirs] *MS Locke c.33* | heyers *MS Locke c.42B*   vertues,] *MS Locke c.33* | vertues *MS Locke c.42B*   not.] *MS Locke c.33* | not *MS Locke c.42B*   15 & persuasion] *MS Locke c.42B* | '& persuasion' *MS Locke c.33* by force &] *MS Locke c42B* | *not in MS Locke c.33*   17 have been] *MS Locke c.42B* | be *MS Locke c.33*   22 [his] only 'h'is

---

[1] Page reference to Gabriel Sagard, *Histoire du Canada* (Paris, 1636), LL 2526, a work Locke bought and read while in France: MS Locke c. 33, fo. 11; cf. Journal, 2 Jan. 1679 (NS), BL, Add. MS 15642, p. 1.
[2] The elite troops of the Ottoman sultans, forcibly recruited for the most part from the children of their Christian subjects.   [3] Sagard, *Histoire du Canada*, 418.

owne private interest & concerns not another man. god has noe where
given such power to any man or society, nor can man possibly be supposd
to give it an other absolutely over him. 1 Because men in all states being
liable to error as well governors as those under them Doctors as Schol-
lers, it would be unreasonable to be put under the absolute direction of 5
those who may erre in a matter of that concernement eternall concernement where in if they misguide us they can make us noe reparation·
2° Because such a power can by noe meanes serve to the end for which
only it can be supposd to be given, viz to keepe men in the right way to
salvation· For supposeing all the different pretenders to this power were 10
nearer agreed in the matters they prescribe, or could consent to resigne
all their pretentions to this power to one certain guide, neither of which is
ever like to happen. yet the power of useing force to bring men in faith &
opinions & uniformity in worship could not serve to secure mens salvation even though that power were in its self infallible, because noe 15
compulsion can make a man beleive against his present light & perswasion be it what it will, though it may make him professe indeed. but
profession without sincerity will litle set a man forwards in his way to any
place but that where he is to have his share with Hippocrites. & to doe
any thing in the worship of god which a man judges in his owne con- 20
science not to be that worship he requires & will accept is soe far from
serveing or pleaseing god in it, that such a worshiper affronts god only to
please men. For even the circumstances of the worship of god cannot be
indifferent to him that thinkes them not soe, nor can the time, habit
posture &c be at pleasure used or omitted by one who thinkes either 25
acceptable or displeaseing to the god he worships

But though noe body can have a right to force men to receive such
doctrins or to practise such ways of worship yet this will not hinder the
power of every society or profession of religion to establish within them
selves confessions of faith & rules of decency & order, which yet are not 30
to be imposed on any one with constraint. It only forbids that men should
be compeld into that communion or any one be hinderd from with-
drawing from it whenever anything comes to be establishd in it which he

---

1 [concernment wherein] interest   3 'absolutely' (*no caret*)   5 [*2nd*] 'be'
(*no caret*)   6 [where in they] of   11 prescribe] *Followed by about twelve words of
illegible material, deleted first by overwriting and then by crossing through. A few words are barely
legible:* supposeing . . . it . . . those freedoms . . . guide *in the first stratum of text;* both which are
never . . . *in the second*   12 [both 'neither of' which are] neither   13 {to} [beleive
certaine doctrines &] in   22 [him] [*2nd*] 'god'   30 'confessions of faith &'
31 [with] on   [noe body] It   32 ⟦b⟨e⟩⟧or 'any one' *addition at line-end*

judges contrary to the end for which he enters in to such a communion or religious society i.e. the beleiveing & owneing certain truths [*p. 126*] which are taught & professed there, & the worshiping of god in a way acceptable to him· Sic argumentatus est Atti⟨cus⟩: de quo videndum[1]

5 ## Virtus

Adversaria 1661, pp. 10–11. Undated; written 1681 or later.

Virtus   Vertue as in its obligation it is the will of God, discovered by naturall reason, & thus has the force of a Law so in the matter of it, it is nothing else but doeing of good, either to our selfs or others, & the
10 contrary here unto vice is nothing else but doeing of harme. thus the bounds of Temperance are prescribed by our health, Estates & the use of our time: Justice, truth & mercie, by the good or Evil they are like to produce, since every body allows one may with justice deny another the possession of his own sword, when there is reason to beleeve, he would
15 make use of it to his owne harme· but since men in society are in a farr different state than when considerd single & alone the instances & measures of vertue & vice are very different under these two con- sideration⟨s⟩· for though as I said before the measures of Temperance to a solitary man be none but those above mentioned, yet if he be a member
20 of a society, it may according to the station he has in it, receive measures from reputation & example so that that which would be no vicious excess in a retired obscurity may be a very great one amongst people, who think ill of such excess, because by lessening his esteem amongst them it makes a man uncapable of haveing that Authority & doeing that good, which
25 otherwise he might. for esteem & reputation, being a sort of Morall Strength whereby a man is enabled to do as it were by an augmented force, that which others of equall naturall parts & natural power cannot doe without it, he that by any intemperance weakens this his morall strength does himselfe as much harme as if by intemperance he weakened
30 the naturall strength either of his mind or body & so is equally vicious by doeing harme to himself· this if well considerd will give us better boundarys of vertue & vice than curious Questions stated with the nicest

---

7 Virtus...obligation in *Locke's hand*   `it' *probably added by Locke, replacing a deleted and illegible word, perhaps* y^t   16 [e] state   23 [least ning] `lessening'   27 `natural' *probably added by Locke*

---

[1] Sic...videndum: Thus Atticus has argued, concerning which see. A reference to the *Essay concerning Toleration.*

destinctions. that being always the greatest vice whose consequences draw after it the greatest harme· & therefore the injurys & mischiefs done to societys are much more culpable then those done to private men though with greater personall agravations· & so many things naturally become vices amongst men in societys, which without that would be 5 innocent actions· thus for a man to cohabite & have children by one or more women who are at their owne dispos⟨al⟩ & when they think fit to part again I see not how it can be condemd as a vice, since no body is harmd supposeing it done among persons considerd as seperate from the rest of mankind· but yet this hinders not but it is a vice of deep dye when 10 the same thing is done in a societie, wherein modestie the great vertue of the weaker sex, has often other rules & bounds set by custom & reputation than what it has by direct instances of the Law of nature in a solitude or an estate seperate from the opinion of this or that societie. For if a woman by transgressing those bounds which the received opinion of 15 her country or religion & not nature or reason have set to modesty, has drawn any blemish on her reputation she may run the risque of being [*p. 11*] exposd to infamy & other mischiefs amongst which the least is not the danger of looseing the comforts of a conjugall settlement & therewith the chief end of her being, the propagation of mankinde   JL   20

Ecclesia

MS Locke d. 10, p. 43. Dated 1682.

Ecclesia. Hookers description of the church /1. §15[1] amounts to this· That it is a supernatural but voluntary societie wherein a man associates himself to god angels & holy men. The original of it he says is the same as 25

2 [being] [*2nd*] the	7 dispos⟨al⟩ /	10 when / {when} *the two words separated*
by half a blank line	17 'run'	18 {exposed} // exposd 20 JL *in*
Locke's hand		

[1] 'The Church being a supernaturall societie, doth differ from naturall societies in this, that the persons unto whome we associate our selves, in the one are men simplye considered as men, but they to whome wee be joyned in the other, are God, Angels, and holie men. Againe the Church being both a societie and a societie supernaturall, although as it is a societie it have the selfe same originall grounds which other politique societies have, namely, the naturall inclination which all men have unto sociable life, and consent to some certaine bond of association, which bond is the lawe that appointeth what kinde of order they shall be associated in: yet unto the Church as it is a societie supernaturall this is peculiar, that part of the bond of their association which belong to the Church of God, must be a lawe supernaturall, which God himselfe hath revealed concerning the kinde of worship which his people shall doe unto him,' *Of the Laws of Ecclesiastical Polity*, I. xv. 2.

of other societies viz an inclination unto sociable life & a consent to the bond of association which is the law & order they are associated in. That which makes it supernatural is, that part of the bond of their association is a law revealed concerning what worship god would have donne unto him,
5 which natural reason could not have discoverd, soe that the worship of god soe far forth as it hath any thing in it more then the law of reason doth teach may not be invented of men. From whence I thinke it will follow· 1° That the church being a supernatural societie, & a societie by consent The secular power which is puerly natural nor any other power
10 can compel one to be of any particular church societie there being many such to be found. 2° That the end of entering into such societie being only to obtein the favour of god by offering him an acceptable worship. noe body can impose any ceremonys unlesse positively & clearly by revelation injoynd, any farther then every one who joyns in the use of
15 them is perswaded in his conscience they are acceptable to god. for if his conscience condemns any part of unrevealed worship he cannot by any sanction of men be obleiged to it. 3° That since a part only of the bond of this association is a revealed law this part alone is unalterable, & the other which is humane depends wholy upon consent & soe is alterable & a man
20 is held by such laws or [*p. 44*] to such a particular societie noe longer then he himself doth consent. 4° I imagine that the original of this societie is not, from our inclination as he says to a sociable life for that may be fully satisfied in other societies, but from the obligation man by the light of reason findes himself under to own & worship god publiquely in the
25 world   JL

Superstitio

MS Locke d. 10, p. 161. Dated 1682.

Superstitio Superstition is made up of apprehension of evill from god, & hopes by formall & outward addresses to him to appease him without
30 reall amendment of life   JL

---

4 [god] worship   14 [unlesse] any   28 Superstitio] *at head of column, next to an earlier entry on the same topic, or an earlier part of the same entry*   29 '& outward'

Traditio

MS Locke d. 10, p. 163. Dated 1682.

Traditio   The Jews, the Romanists & the Turks, who all three pretend
to guide them selves by a law reveld from heaven which shews them the
way to happynesse, doe yet all of them have recourse very frequently to ₅
tradition as a rule of noe lesse authority then their written law. Whereby
they seeme to allow, that the divine law (however god be willing to
reveale it) is not capeable to be conveyd by writeing to mankinde distant
in place time languages & customes, & soe through the defect of language
noe positive law of righteousnesse can be that way conveyd sufficiently & ₁₀
with exactnesse to all the inhabitants of the earth in remote generations,
& soe must resolve all into naturall religion, & that light which every man
has borne with him. Or els they give occasion to enquireing men to
suspect the integrity of their preists & teachers, who unwilling that the
people should have a standing known rule of faith and manners, have for ₁₅
the maintenance of their own authority foisted in another of tradition,
which will always be in their own power to be varied & suited to their
own interest & occasions   JL. Q whether the Bramines besides their
book of Hanscrit,[1] make use also of Tradition & soe of others who pretend to a revealed religion? JL   ₂₀

Aestimatio

MS Locke f. 24, fo. 4ʳ. Undated; written before the spring of 1684. Entry crossed
through with a single vertical line.

Æstimatio. Majora credi de absentibus Major e longinquo reverentia.
Tacit.[2] Raise noe great expectation before hand of what you would have ₂₅

---

8 'by writeing'   [poste⟨rity⟩] mankinde   13 [t⟨hem⟩]him   15 manner's'

[1] Presumably an inaccurate reference to the Hindu scriptures, written in Sanskrit. In
1681 Locke had been reading Abraham Roger, *La porte ouvert pour parvenir à la connoissance du Paganisme caché: ou la vraye representation de la vie, des moeurs, de la réligion, et
du service divin des Bramines...* (Amsterdam, 1671), *LL* 2496, cited in Adversaria 1661, pp.
96, 272, 276, 296. There are earlier notes on the subject dating from about 1670 or 1671 in
Adversaria 1661, pp. 18, 102, 154–5, taken from Arnoldus Montanus, *Atlas Japannensis*
(London, 1670), and from the English translation of several works by François Bernier.
[2] There are two separate passages in Tacitus here: *maiora credi de absentibus* (greater
things are believed of what is not present), *Histories*, 2. 83; *maior e longinquo reverentia*
(greater reverence for what is at a distance), *Annals*, 1. 47

please. Imagination & desire beget & increase one an other to a degree that enjoyment seldome answers. JL

Conversatio

MS Locke f. 24, fo. 31^r. Undated; written before the spring of 1684. Entry
5 crossed through with a single vertical line.

Conversatio. In conversation gain esteem goodwill knowledg & where it is worth while interest. vertue & abilitys gain esteem. goodwill good will˙ for knowledg talke with every man of that wherein he hath skill by which commonly you learne & obleige him at once, men being generally pleased
10 more with teaching then learning. Obligations & usefulnesse gives one interest, the first with gratefull men, the other with all. JL

Malevoli

MS Locke f. 24, fo. 93^r. Undated; written before the spring of 1684. Entry crossed through with a single vertical line.

15 Malevoli. To guard your self against the malitious envious, curious, which are the greatest part of men, Keepe not allways in the same tract. The best way to conceale your self is sometimes to be open. JL

Mos

MS Locke f. 24, fo. 99^r. Undated; written before the spring of 1684. Entry
20 crossed through with a single vertical line.

Mos. Judg of fashons by thy self, follow them with others. JL

6 [all] conversation	[men should endeavour to] gain,	9 [many] men
15 [preserve] 'guard'	16 [trait] tract	

APPENDICES

APPENDIX I

THE ROUGH DRAFT OF
AN ESSAY CONCERNING TOLERATION

The portions of text below are given in the order in which they occur in the manuscript, Huntington Library HM 584. All this material has been deleted by a single vertical line; this was presumably done when the Fair Copy was made. The letters A, B, C, etc. in the margin have been supplied by the editors and do not appear in the manuscript.

The order in which Locke intended this part of the manuscript to be read is indicated by his transcription of them in the Fair Copy, namely D E C G H I B F A. The order in which they were written is less easy to establish but is certainly not the same; perhaps the most likely order is I D B C G E F A, with H having been written either after G or after A.

The first leaf of quire B was not numbered by Locke, and is here designated as fo. ix. The second and third leaves were numbered 1 and 2 by Locke, and these numbers are used here.

[*fo. ix^r*]

A   heaven it must not be by the ~~the~~ outward violence of the magistrate on mens bodys, but the inward constraint of his owne spirit on their minds, ‘which compulsion works not on.’ the way thither not being any forcd ~~& unwilling~~ ‘exterior’ performances ~~of~~ but the voluntary & secret ~~perf consent~~ ‘choise’ of the minde. & it cannot be supposd that god would make ~~choise~~ ‘use’ of any means   5 which could not reach ‘but did rather crosse the attainment of the end.’

B   To which let me adde that even in things of this world over which the ~~magistrate~~ ‘he’ has an authority, he never does & it would be unjustice if he should ‘any farther then it refer to the good of the publique’ injoyn men the care of their ‘private’ civill concernments or force them to a prosecution of their owne private   10 interest ‘~~further then as it refers to the [peace] good of the publique~~.’ but only protects them ‘from being’ invaded & injurd ‘in them’ by others ‘which is a perfect toleration’. & therefor we may well suppose he hath noe thing at all to doe to with my ~~concernment~~ ‘private interest’ in an other world ~~nor ough to~~ & that he ought not to prescribe me the way or ~~compell~~ ‘exact’ my diligence in the pro-   15 secution of that good which is of a far higher concernment to me, then any thing within his power, haveing noe certaine ‘r’ ‘or more infallible’ knowledg of the way to attain it then I my self ‘where we are both equally inquirers both equally

All the writing on fo. ix^r is done vertically, from top to bottom. Between sections A and B there is a space of about 2 cm, containing the words ‘Anthony / O Father Father’ in a childish hand. Locke’s writing breaks in order to avoid this, indicating that it was already on the paper when he came to use it

subjects', & where in, he can give me noe security that I shall not, nor make me any recompense if I doe miscarry. can it be reasonable that he that cannot compell me to ~~keepe my estate~~ 'buy a house' should force me his way to ~~gain~~ 'purchas' heaven. that he that can not in justice prescribe me ~~methods~~ 'rules' of preserveing
5   my health, should injoyn me methods of saveing my soule. he that cannot choose a wife for me shall he choose a religion

There are others assert that all the power & authority the magistrate hath is C derivd from the grant & consent of the people & to these I say it can not be supposd the people should give any one 'or more' of th⟦is⟧eir ~~number a power~~ of
10   their fellow men a'n' ~~jurisdiction~~ 'authority' over them for any other purpose then their owne (4)

[*fo. ix*^{v}]

The Question of Toleration stated   D

~~In the one thing that hath perplex the~~
15   In the question of liberty of conscience which has for some years beene soe much bandied ~~in this part of the world~~ 'among us' One thing that has cheifly perplexd the question kept up the dispute & increasd the animosity ⟦to⟧ ~~on both~~ hath beene I conceive, this, That both ~~sides~~ 'partys' have with equall zeale, & mistake too much enlargd their pretensions, whilst one side preach up absolute obedience,
20   & the other claime universall liberty in matters of conscience, ~~with assigneing~~ without assigneing the matter 'which has a title to liberty' or shewing the boundarys of imposition & obedience. I
To cleare the way to this I shall lay downe this for sure & unmoveable foundation
25   That the whole trust power & authority of the magistrate is vested in him for noe other purpose but to be made use of for the good preservation & peace of that society over which he ~~has~~ is set, & therefor this alone is & ought to be the standard & measure according to which he ought to square & proportion his laws, model & frame his government For if men could live quietly & peacably togeather without
30   growing into a common wealth, there would be noe need at all of magistrates ~~or laws~~ 'or polities', which were only made to preserve men ~~in this~~ in this world from the ~~vio~~ fraud & violence of one another. soe that what was the end of the erecting of government ought only to be the measures of its proceeding

There are some men who tell us that monarchy is jure divino, & that the E
35   magistrate ~~hold~~ derives his authority immediately from heaven. I will not now dispute this opinion but only minde the assertors of it, that if they they say that

398.34–399.6 *Sections E and F written vertically in the margin. No break between sections in MS, but F preceded by a mark × and followed by* this ought to come in in *[sic] the first* ⟨pro⟩position *(word blotted)* god has given the magistrate a power to doe any thing but barely ~~ind order~~ in order to the preservation of his ~~people~~ 'subjects' in this life, they ~~oug~~ are bound to shew us his commission from heaven, or else leave us at liberty to beleive it as we please since noebody ~~can~~ is bound or allow any ones pretensions farther then he shews his title.   5

F But if god (which is the point in question) would have men forcd to

[*fo. 1*^{r}]

G (4) preservation. or extend the limits of their ~~power~~ 'jurisdictions' beyond the affairs of this life, or give ~~them~~ 'magistrate' a right to choose 'for them' their way to salvation (5)   10

H This being then ~~establishd~~ 'certain', that the magistrate ought to doe or medle with noe thing but barely in order to the secureing the civill peace & propretys of his subjects. Let us next consider the Opinions & actions of men which in reference to toleration may be divided into three sorts. 1 Are ~~all puerly speculative opinion~~ such as in them selves concerne not government & society at all, &   15 such are all puerly speculative opinions, & divine worship. 2 Are such ~~opi~~ as concerne society & mens conversation one with an other, & these are all practicall opinions, & actions, in matters of indifferency. 3 Are such ~~the~~ too as concerne society, but are also beleivd good or bad in their owne nature, & these are morall virtues & vices.   20

I   The question of toleration stated.

I ~~suppose~~ 'say.' that there are only two sorts of things that have in their owne ~~righ~~ nature an absolute & universall right to toleration. The first is all puerly speculative opinions, as the beleif of a trinity, purgatory, transubstantion ~~antipodes~~, Christs personall reigne on earth &c.   25
    & that in these every man has his unlimited freedome, appeares: because noe man can give an other a power over that, over which he has noe power him self. now that a man can not command his owne understanding, or positively determine to day what opinion he will be of to morrow is evident from experience & the nature of the understanding, which can noe more apprehend things otherwise   30 then they appeare 'to it' then the eye see other colours then it doth in the rainbow whether those colours be really there or noe. Besides bare speculations giveing

---

8 Sections G and H both in margin of fo. 2^r. (4) at start of G links it to end of Section C. [5]
in margin at end of Section I indicates that deleted text there was to be replaced by last sentence of
Section G   13 Let us] remainder of section H written with a much finer pen; perhaps a
later addition   21 the original beginning of the Essay

noe bias to my conversation with men, nor haveing ⟦noe⟧any influence on my
actions as I am member of any society, but being such as would be still the same
with all the consequences of them, though there were noe other person besides
my self in the world, cannot by any means either disturb the state or incon-
5 venience my neigbour, & soe come not within the magistrates cognizance.

The other thing that has just claime ~~in all times & place~~ to an unlimited
toleration, is the place, time, & manner of worshiping my god. Because this is a
thing wholy between god & me, & is of an eternall concernment above the reach &
extent of polities & goverment, which are but for my well being in this world. For
10 the magistrate is but umpire between man & man. He can right me against my
neigbour, but can not [*fo. 2ʳ*] defend me against my god. What ever evill I suffer
by obeying him in other things he can make me amends in this world but if he
force me to a wrong religion, he can make me noe reparation in the other world.
<u>Therefore it cannot be supposd that men should give the magistrate a power to</u>
15 <u>choose for them their way to salvation</u>, which ~~was~~ 'is a power' too great to
give away,

14–15 *deleted numeral* 5 *in the margin next to this underscored passage, indicating that it was
to be replaced by last part of Section G*   16 **H*** *ends here*

APPENDIX II

PHILANTHROPY, OR THE CHRISTIAN PHILOSOPHERS, AND PHILANTHROPY COMMENTS

I. PHILANTHROPY

MS Locke c. 27, fo. 30^c.

Philanthropoy or The Christian Philosopher's

Mankinde is supported in the way's of Vertue, or Vice, by the Society he is of; & the Conversation he keep's: Example & Fashion being the great Governours of this World. The 1st Question, every man ought to aske in all thing's he doth, or undertakes; is, how is this acceptable to God? But the first Question most men 5 aske, is, how will this render me to my Company, and those, whose esteeme I valew? He that askes neither of these Question's, is a Melancholy Rogue; & allway's of the most dangerous, & worst of men. This is the foundation of all the Sect's, & order's, either of Religion, or Philosophy, that have beene in the World. Men are supported, & delighted, with the freindship, & protection, they enjoy, 10 from all the rest of the same way: & as these are more or less really perform'd amongst them; soe the Party increaseth or diminisheth. The Protestant Religion whilst it was a Sect, & a party, cherish'd, & favour'd each other; increast strangely; against all the power & persecution of the Church of Roome: But since the warmth of that is over, and 'tis embrac't onely as a trewer Doctrine, this last 15 40 yeares, hath hardly produc't as many Convert's, from the Romish Fopperies: The greater Clergy playnly inclineing to goe back to theire Interest, which is highest exalted in that Religion: but the greatest parte of the Laity, having an abhorrence to their cruelty and Ambition; as well as theire Interests Contrary; have divided themselves into Sect's and churches, of new, & different names, & 20 way's; that they may keep up some warmth, and heate, in opposition to the common

---

1 *preceded on the previous line by* [The Sect of Philanthropy or] *in the hand of the copyist, which is deleted by being overwritten by* [The Philosophers religion], *in Locke's hand; before* Philanthropoy *there are the words* [The Sect of] *in the hand of the amanuensis, overwritten by* Or the Philosof *by Locke*
2 *preceded on previous line by* [The reason or⟨..........⟩] *overwritten by* [The cause of the ⟨......⟩] Vice. [by nothing more], 4 [same] ʻ1st' 9 [hath] ʻhave' *probably alt. by Locke* 12 ʻ& a party' 18 Religio⟨n⟩ *letter lost at line end* ⟦&⟧but 19 [it] ʻtheir ... Ambition' *added in hand not that of Locke or the copyist*

401

enemy: who otherwise was like to finde us all asleep. The Quaker's are a great instance, how little truth & reason operates upon mankinde, & how great force, society & conversation [*fo. 30^{ct}*] hath amongst those that maintaine an inviolable freindship & concerne, for all of theire way. 'Tis a trew Proverb, what is every man's
5 buisness, is noe man's. This befall's truth, she hath noe Sect, noe Corporation, 'tis made noe man's Interest, to owne her: There is noe body of men noe council sitting, that should take care of him, that suffer's for her; the Clergy have pretended to that care, for many hundred's of year's paste, but how well they have perform'd it the world know's; They have found a Mistriss call'd, the present Power that pay's them
10 much better then truth can; Whatever Idoll she injoyn's, they offer us to be wor-ship'd as this great Goddess; and theire Impudence hath beene soe great, that though they vary it as often as the present Power it selfe changeth; yet they affirme it, still to be the same Goddess, truth. Neither is it possible that the greatest parte of that sorte of men should not either flatter the Magistrate, or the People: in both truth
15 suffer's. Learning is a trade that most men apply themselves to with paynes and charge; that they may hereafter live, & make advantage by it: 'Tis naturall for trade, to goe to the best Markett: Truth, and mony; Truth, & Hyre; did never yet long agree. These thought's, moov'd us to endeavour to associate our selves, with such as are lover's of truth, and virtue; that we may encourage, assist, and supporte each
20 other, in the way's of them; and may possibly become some help in the preserving truth, Religion, & virtue amongst us; whatever Deluge of misery, & mischeife may overrun this parte of the world. We intermeddle not with any thing that concernes, the Just, & legall power of the Civill Magistrate; the government & Law's of our Country, cannot be injur'd by such as love truth, virtue, & justice; we thinke our
25 selves obleig'd to lay downe our lives, and fortunes; in the defence of it. Noe man can say he loves God, that loves not his neighbour: Noe man can love his neighbour, that loves not his Country: 'Tis the greatest charity to preserve the Law's, & right's of the nation, whereof we are. A Good man, & a charitable man, is to give to every
30 man his due. From the King upon the throne, to the Beggar in the streete.

---

1 [[is]]was   7 [he] should   9 present] Preas^t.   10 `Idoll'    11 [in the name of] `as' *inserted on line*   12 `it'    present] preas$^t$.    12 `it self changeth'   13 `truth' *perhaps add. by Locke*   18 [joyne together, &] endeav-our   29 *numeral 2 in the left margin next to the last line*

II. PHILANTHROPY COMMENTS

MS Locke f. 28, pp. 28–9, 43.

[*p. 28*]

Philanthropoy   Q If the conduct of this society be to reside in The Elder & his
associates whether 10 will not be enough. p. 3 espetially the elders of provinces 5
makeing a part of their body

p 4 <u>Over every number of men not lesse then ten nor exceeding 15</u> leg:[1] 20. or
rather. 50

p. 5. <u>There must be 3 parts of 5 consenting</u> adde within 1 Month of the vacancy.
or els it is to be referd to the way of Election of the next superior order   10

[*p. 29*]

p 6. Q whether there be any other difference between those ordaynd to preach &
judg by the Elders of 10–50–250 have any other difference but that of extent of
their authority it being as large I suppose as that of those who Elect them   15

Q whether it will not be best that those ordeynd to preach or judg should not be
soe annually

⟨p.⟩8 <u>Lastly</u> adde as it is to preserve a perfect union charity & freindship one
amongst another

Q Whether the congregations of 10 50 & 250 are not too litle & would not be 20
better changed into 10–100–1000 considering the number of officers & that those
of 50 meet but once a month & 250 but once a quarter

p 9 In the instructive part there seems wanting the Catechiseing of children

[*p. 43*]   25

p. 11. The Elder & his colledg to be only judges of communications which to be
further communicated & which kept constantly

---

4 [security] conduct Th⟨e⟩   5-6 'espeti/ally...body'   7 *underlined in MS*
9 *underlined in MS*   'adde'   18 *underlined in MS*   25 Philanthropoy *in*
margin   27 ⟦secret⟧constantly *alteration in lighter ink*

---

[1]legatur *or* legenda: it should be read.

403

APPENDIX III

QUERIES ON CATHOLIC INFALLIBILITY

MS Locke c. 27, fos. 32–3.

[*fo. 32ʳ*]

Queries

1 Whether there be any Infalible Judge on Earth

2 Whether any Church be that Judge

3 Whether the Roman Church be that Church

5   4 If it be what Capacity, whether the Infallability be in the Pope as the Head or in the Body of the Church, and then whether in the whole Body diffusive or in the Collective in a Councill, and if a Councell be Infalible, then whether it be soe only with the Popes Confirmation; or without it.

  5 How shall wee Certainly know whoe must be Members of it Clergie &
10 Laickes or only Clergie; or only Bishopes Presbyters too and Deacons, or Choropiscopy[1] at least for wee finde all these usually Subscribing

  6 Or let the Councell be as they would have it) how shall I be sure they are Infalible, for are they soe absolutely Infalible as they cannot determine falsly in rebus fidei[2] doe what they will.

15   7 How shall I know when they determin aright, and what is required to a Synodicall Constitution˙ must all concurre in the Votes, or will the Major part serve the turne.

  8 What makes a Councell Generall, must all the Bishoppes of the Christian world be called.

20   9 When they are all called must they all come, Or else it is noe Generall Councell

---

3 [Church] Judge

---

[1] *Chorepiscopy*, The institution that existed in the early church of appointing a country or suffragan bishop to superintend churches at a distance from the city where the bishop of the diocese resided, *OED*. Locke used the word in his Critical Notes against Stillingfleet, MS Locke c. 34, p. 97.

[2] In matters of faith.

10 Whoe must call the Generall Councill the Pope or the Christian Kings, and Emperours, and how shall I be assured which of them must.

11 How farre are those determinations Infalible, whether in matters of fact as well as faith.

12 And if in matters of faith then whether in fundamentalls only or in Super-   5
Structures.

13 How shall I Infalible know which pointes are fundamentall which not.

14 But admitt all these were determined, and our Infalible Judge were a Generall Councell with the Pope yet in a time of Schisme where there are two or three Popes at once Cle. 3. Greg. 7. Gelasus. 2. Greg. 8. Celastin. 2. Honorius. 2.   10
Anacletus 2. Innocent. 2. Victor. 4 Alex. 3. Clem. 7. Urban. 6. Dugenius. 4. Felix. 5.[1] you may see Gautior the Jessuites Booke[2] a large Cataloge more, and these Warring one against another for 40. or 50. yeeres together: soe that the Learned'st Clergymen alive know not which was St Peters true Successor and thus sayth reason there may be againe: then I aske how I shall know which is the Infalible   15
Judge Or by what Rule a Romanist may tell when a troath is defined and when not· Since Sextus the 5th. defined one Bible to be true Anno. 1590. and Clemens the 8th another 2. yeares after and each of them Prohibited and Condemned all but his owne;[3] and these two Bibles containe many Contradictions each to other, and Certainly Contradictory Propositions cannot both be Gospell and if not then   20
either one of these two was not really (whence inconveniency enough will followe) or they were both true Popes, and soe both these definitions true, and soe noe true Papist hath any true Bible.

15 But suppose there be no schisme and all agreed on the Pope and a Generall Councell Mett, how shall I be sure that he that is reputed Pope is soe indeed   25
seeing by their owne Principles Secrett Symony makes him Non⟨e⟩, Soe the Bull

---

[1] The popes listed are Clement III (antipope 1080, 1084–1100) and Gregory VII (1073–85); Gelasius II (1118–19) and Gregory VIII (antipope 1118–21); Celestine II (antipope 1124) and Honorius II (1124–30); Anacletus II (antipope 1130–8) and Innocent II (1130–43); Victor IV (antipope 1159–64) and Alexander III (1159–81); Clement VII (antipope 1378–94) and Urban VI (1378–89); Eugene IV (1431–47) and Felix V (antipope 1439–49); the dates are taken from Kelly, *The Oxford Dictionary of Popes*.

[2] Jacques Gaultier, *Table chronographique de l'estat du Christianisme, depuis la naissance de Jesus-Christ, jusques à l'année M.D.CVIII.* (Lyon, 1609, and subsequent editions); Latin translation as *Tabula Chronographica Status Ecclesiae Catholicae* (Lyon, 1616). Among much other information this provides lists of popes and antipopes for each century.

[3] Following the decision of the Council of Trent that the Vulgate was the sole authoritative text of the Bible, Sixtus V decided that an official edition should be produced, and that all previous editions should be discarded. Unfortunately the resulting text, issued shortly before his death (27 August 1590), contained several serious imperfections, notably the omission of Num. 30: 11–13; a commission of cardinals forbade its sale on 9 September. An extensively revised edition was issued by Clement VIII in 1592. For a fuller account, see Crehan, 'The Bible in the Roman Catholic Church', 207–13.

of Pope Julius 2^d Super Simoniaca Papae Electione si contigeritt,[1] and that he was not Simoniacall it is Impossable for me to know; the Election of Sextus. 5.[2] was Notoriously Simoniacall for Cardinall d'essy[3] whome he bribed and promised to obey and defend against any opposite faction &c.: sent all these Obligations
5 subscribed by Sextus 5. his owne hand to Phillip then [*fo. 32^v*] King of Spaine whoe in the yeere. 1599. sent to Roome to bid the Cardinalls who had bin Elected before Sextus the 5. come to the See, to come to a Councell at Sevill in Spaine[4] where the Originall writeing was produced and the Crime was Evidently proved and if soe all the Cardinalls which were made by this Sextus were in reality noe
10 Cardinalls, and then all the Popes which have been realy are no Popes.

16. But admit the Pope were certainly knowne to be such that neither he nor any of his Predecessors came in by Simony, yet how shall I know whether those Bishopes, who with him make up a Councill are Bishopes Indeed, for if they be no Bishopes then it is noe Councill. And that they are true Bishopes it is for ever
15 impossible for any Papist certainly to know, for if he that did Ordaine them did not intend it when he gave Orders, And whether he did or noe God only knowes, then by their owne Principles, they are noe Bishops and by consequence noe Councell.

17. How shall I know that the Pope and Bishops soe mett (at Trent[5] for
20 Example) are Christians for if not then they are noe Legislative Councill or Church representative and that they are Christians it is Impossable for any Catholick to know with any Infalible certainty, for if they be not Baptized then I am sure with them they are noe Christians, and if the Preist that Baptized them did not intend to doe it then by the Cannon of the Trent Councells they are not
25 baptized.[6] Now what the Preist intended when he Administred that Sacrament tis impossible that any (Save God that knowes the hart) should certainly know without immediate Revelation which they pretend not to and consequently tis impossible that any of them should certainly know that ever there was a Pope or a Bishop or a Preist since our Saviours dayes, Nay Impossable that they should
30 know whether there be now one Christian in their Church and therefore much less that there is or hath bin a Lawfull Councill.

---

[1] The Bull of Pope Julius II, Super Simoniaca Papae Electione si Contigerit, was issued on 19 January 1505. There is an account in Creighton, *A History of the Papacy*, v. 82–3.

[2] Sixtus V (1585–90).

[3] Louis [Luigi] D'Este (1538–86), cr. 1561, Migne, *Dictionnaire des Cardinaux*, col. 881.

[4] It has not been possible to discover the events on which this account is based, but some confusion is apparent. The King of Spain when Cardinal d'Este died was Philip II, who died in 1598. In 1599 the king was Philip III (reigned 1598–1621).

[5] The council responsible for initiating the Counter-Reformation; it sat in 1545–8, 1551–2, and 1562–3.

[6] At the Council of Trent it decreed that 'If any say that, when a minister effect or confer the sacraments, they do not need the intention of at least doing what the church does, let him be anathema.' Session 7, 3 Mar. 1547, De sacramentis in genere, Canon 11, in *Decrees of the Ecumenical Councils*, 685.

18. But admit all these doubts were cleerely resolved & a Councell (in their owne sence Lawfull) sitting and determining matters in controversy yet how shall wee know certainly that these are their determinations specially since the Greek Church neere 300 yeeres since accused the Roman for forceing a Cannon into the Niceene Councells in behalfe of the Popes being head of the Universall Church, 5 which could never be found in the Authentick Coppies though the Affrican Bishops sent to Constantinople, Alexandria and Antiock to serch for them. Codex. Can. Eccles. afri. Iustel. p: 39. 40.[1] wee must rely on the honnesty of the amanuensis or of those persons that convey them to us. and those are Certainly not infalible, and wee know there are Indices Expurgatorij foysting in and 10 Blotting out of Manuscripts.[2]

19. But admitt all this cleered yet when I have indeed the Genuine Canons and am sure of it, how shall I be assured of the true meaning of them for wee know that Vega and Soto[3] (two famous and Learned men in the Councell of Trent) writt and defended contradictory opinions, yet Each thinketh the Canon of the Councill 15 to determine on his side, Now of necessity one of them must mistake the Doctrine of the Councell unlesse you will say the Councell determined contradictions and then the Councell is not infalible it selfe, and if either of them mistooke the Councill, then it was not an infalible Guide to him, now if Learned Men whoe were Members of the Councell (such as disputed much in it) could not infalibly know 20 the meaning of it how can I whoe am neither. [*fo. 33ʳ*]

20. What necessity of an Infalible Judge at all, the Christian World had noe such Judge for 325 yeeres for the Nicene Councell[4] was the first Generall and if they understood Scripture and were saved then when they had no such thing why may not wee now, and if they were not saved, the Church of Roome must Blott 25 out many hundreds and thousands of Saintes and Martirs out of her Matirology.

Till these 20 Questions be infalibly resolved it seemes impossible that any man should have any infalible knowledge of the Church of Roomes infalibility.

Endorsed on fo. 33ᵛ: Queries   Popery/ 75[5]

---

5 [Creed] Councills   8 Eccles] dules   12 Canons] Casmons
14 Vega] Voga

[1] *Bibliotheca Juris Canonici Veteris*. There is nothing relevant on p. 39 or p. 40; the Codex Canonum Ecclesiae Africanae is on pp. 305–492 of vol. i.
[2] It was a frequent Protestant complaint that the Inquisition not only compiled lists of banned books—the *Indices Expurgatorii*—but defaced and altered manuscripts, including ancient ones: see James, *A Treatise of the Corruption of Scripture*. One such work in Locke's library (*LL* 2552) was the 1638 edition of Sir Edwin Sandys, *Europae Speculum*; see pp. 180–9.
[3] Andrés de Vega (1498–1549) and Domingo de Soto (*c.*1495–1560), mentioned by Laud, *A Relation of the Conference between William Lawd ... And Mr. Fisher the Jesuite*, 49. See also Milton, *Catholic and Reformed*, 246.
[4] The first Council of Nicaea, called by Constantine in 325.
[5] 'Queries' in the hand of the copyist, remainder in Locke's hand.

APPENDIX IV

REASONS AGAINST THE BILL
FOR THE TEST

Sigla

L   Leicestershire Record Office, DG7/PP30

N   The National Archives, PRO 30/24/5/294, pp. 1–10

R   Bodleian Library, MS Rawlinson D 924, fos. 297–300

S   Surrey History Centre, Woking, LM/1331/60

T   Bodleian Library, MS Rawlinson A 191, fos. 3–4

Y   Beinecke Library, Yale, Osborn Shelves, b. 157, pp. 141–55

Reasons against the Bill for the Test

1 It is a great step to the overthrowing the Act of Oblivion and reviving distinction between Partys against a designe so much now avowed and talked of.

That it is in other Acts doth not justify the matter, for those were but steps to
5 the same end, and I should rather think that after 15 years, those should be repealed, then that it should be now enjoyned to be taken by all the Officers of the Nation, and even by the members of both Houses of Parliament.

2 It is against the nature of an Oath, which ought to be simple and plain, but this is of a dark, intricate and perplexed meaning, and therefore is a snare to the
10 consciences of well meaning men.

---

1 Reasons...Test.] L, T | Reasons against the Bill for the Test by the Earl of Shaftsbury. 1675. N | Reasons Against the oath of the Bill Intituled an act to preventt Dangers which May arise from persons ill affected to the Government. R | Reasons against the oath in the Bill entituled an Act to prevent dangers that may arise from persons disaffected to the Government By the Earle of Shaftsbury S | Reasons against the Bill for the Test by the Earl of Shaftsbury. A° 1675. With a Letter to the Earl of Carlisle Y   2 [*2nd*] the] L, S, T, Y | of the N, R   2–3 reviving...of] T | the revieveing...of L | distinguishing of Partyes N, Y | Promoting Distinctions betweene persons against a Designe so much now Avoided R | revieveing distinctions again between partyes, a design so much avoided & talked of S   4 but] L, N, Y | *om.* R, S, T 6 be now] L, T | now be N, Y | be R | now by S   7 Houses of Parliament] N, R, S, Y | houses L, T   10 well meaning] L, R, S, T | good N, Y

3 It is needless, for it either means no more then the Oath of Allegiance, or where it attempts more, or goes to explaine it, is pernicious and dangerous.

4 It is directly establishing a standing Army by Act of Parliament, for if whatever be by the Kings Commission be by the Kings authority, then a standing Army is Law, for the Kings authority is nothing but the Law in other words. Besides it 5 alters the whole Law of England in one of the most fundamentall parts of it, for the Kings Commission was never thought to protect or justify any man in any proceeding when it was against his authority which is the Law.

5 It is against the property of the subject, of which I give this instance, that if any one shall in a suit with a man in great favour at Court (as may happen hereafter) 10 recover House and Lands, and shall by order of Law be put into possession by the sherriff, and afterwards a warrant is obtained by the interest of the Favourite to command some souldiers of the standing Army to take the possession and deliver it back, I conceive that by the Law the man in possession may justify the defending himself by arms and shooting and even killing those who shall violently 15 endeavour to enter his house, and yet in this case the party whose house is invaded takes up arms by the Kings authority against those who are Commissioned by him.

For another Instance, put the case that any King hereafter shall contrary to the Petition of Right, demand Loan money by Privy Seale or otherwise of private 20 persons, and shall send souldiers to break open the houses of those that refuse to pay, and distrain their money goods and plate, It is lawfull in such a case as the Law now stands to defend his house against such Invasion, and yet it is of the same nature with the former, and against the words of this Oath.

I do not say, it is wisely done or well done of any man to take that course, but if 25 it be not allowed lawfully to be done, it goes very farre in changing our Law, and some circumstances may make it wise and necessary where the present violence may justly be apprehended to be designed very farre, or the delay may give him

1 it either] **L, R, T** | either it maintains and **N, Y** | either it **S**   3–4 whatever be] **L, N, S, Y** | whatsoever is **R, T**   8 proceeding] **L, N, T, Y** | procedure **R, S** when] **L, N, Y** | where **R, S, T**   9 give] **L, N, S, Y** | give you **R, T**   that] **L, R, S, T** | *om.* **N, Y**   10 one] **L, R, T** | Man **N, Y** | *om.* **S**   shall in a] **L, S, T** | should be in **R** | at **N** | in a **Y**   a man in great] **L, S, T** | a Great Man in **R** | one in greater **N** | one in great **Y**   11 recover] **L, S, T** | shall recover **N, Y** | & shall Recover **R**   into] **L, N, T, Y** | in **R, S**   12 [*1st*] the] **N, S, T, Y** | *om.* **L, R**   13 take the] **L, N, T, Y** | retake **R, S**   14 that] **S, T, Y** | *om.* **L, N, R**   [*2nd*] the] **L, N, T, Y** | that **R, S**   15 shooting and even] **L, R, S, T** | *om.* **N, Y**   17 who] **L, N, T, Y** | that **R, S**   21 open] **L, R, S, T** | up **N, Y**   those] **L, N, T, Y** | them **R, S**   22 [*1st*] and] **L, R, S, T** | And shall **N, Y**   [*2nd*] and] **L, N, R, S** | or **T, Y**   23 to…house] **L, S, T** | to Protect his house **R** | for those Men to defend their Houses **N, Y**   Invasion] **N, S, T, Y** | Invasions **L, R**   yet] **L, N, T, Y** | *om.* **R, S**   25–410.2 I…of] **L, R, S, T** *with variants noted below* | *om.* **N, Y**   26 lawfully] **L, T** | lawfull **R, S**   Law] **L, T** | Laws **R, S**   27 where] **L, T** | as when **R** | when **S**

hopes to procure contrary orders from the Court, besides several others which at present I do not think of. This may seem somewhat a rude instance towards the Crown but it cannot be explained without speaking thus plain, and it cannot be denied me, but that however happy we are now, Kings being but men, the
5 suppositions are not extravagant.

6 It is against the safety of the Kings Crown which I shall explaine by two Instances.

The one that is well known to you all (and what hath been may very well be supposed to be hereafter) I mean that famous instance of Henry the 6th who being
10 a soft and weak Prince when taken prisoner by his cousin Edward the 4th that pretended to the Crown, and that Bustling Earle of Warwicke, was carried in their Armyes gave what orders and Commissions they pleased, whilst all those that were Loyall to him, as a Man adhered to his wife and son, and fought a pitch Battle against him and retook him. This was directly taking up armes by Henry
15 the 6th his Authority against his person and against those that were Commissioned by him, and yet to this day no man hath ever blamed them, or thought but that if they had done other they had betrayed their Prince and been disloyall to him.

The other Instance, put case, a future King of England should be of the same
20 Temper with Henry the 6th and should be taken prisoner by any accident by Spaniard, Dutch or French, which should then be of overgrowing power enough to give them thoughts of vast Empire, and in prosecution of that, should both with the Person and Commission of the King invade England for a Conquest, were it not suitable with our Loyalties to joine with the son of that Prince for the

1 Court] L, T | the Court R, S   2 at…of] S | I doe not at present remember L | I Doe not Thinke of R | at present I doe not thinke on T   somewhat] L, R, S, T | *om.* N, Y   4 me] L, N, T, Y | by them R, S   that] L, T | *om.* R, S   4–5 the suppositions] R, S, T | the suspitions L | these Suppositions N, Y   6 by] L, N, Y | only by R, T, | one by S   8 that is well] L | is N, Y | *om.* R, S | that T   to] L, N, Y | unto R | by S | one to T   what hath been] R, T | what L | that which hath been S | *om.* N, Y   10 when] L, N, T, Y | was R, S   11 and…Warwicke] L, T | & by the Blustring Earle of Warwick R | & that blustering Earle of Warwick S | *om.* N, Y   11–12 in their Armyes] L | in the Armyes R, S | in their Armes T | up and down in the Army N, Y   13 as a] L, T | as one N, Y | even to a R | to a S   14 him] L, N, R, Y | him in person T, S   14–16 This…him] L, R, S, T *with variants noted below* | *om.* N, Y   15 [*1st*] his] R, S | *om.* L, T   [*2nd*] against] S, T | *om.* L, R   16–17 or…that] L, T | or thought but N, Y | but though R | or thought that S   17 other] L, N, T, Y | otherwise R, S   17–18 to him] L, N, T, Y | *om.* R, S   19 The other] L, N, Y | Another R, S, T   put case] L, N, T, Y | suppose R, S   20 by any accident] L, N, T, Y | accidentally R | *in* S *the phrase* by an accident *is placed before* be taken prisoner   21 of overgrowing] L, T | an overgrowing N, Y | of overgrown R, S   21–22 enough…that] L, R, S, T | and N, Y   22 both] L, N, T, Y | *om.* R, S   23 for a Conquest] L, R, S, T | *om.* N, Y

defence of his Fathers Crown and Dignity even against the Person and Commission of the King.

And here you must take my instance as I put it. A King as Henry the 6th was acting purely out of fear and weakness, so that every mans conscience in the Nation bore him witness that he did what was most loyall and safe for his person 5 and Interest.

In both these Cases, as I cannot justify them by the strict Letter of the Law they stand in need of the Kings Pardon, yet I do not think it safe either for the Person of the King or his Crown and Dignity that it should be expressly sworne against. And if you will forswear all distinctions which ill men have made ill use of 10 either in Rebellion or Heresy you must extend the Oath to all the particulars of Divinity and Politics.

Thus much for the Oath in generall, and the first part of it, but for the latter part of it, it is infinitely more extravagant then the former, neither doth the alteration of the words from Endeavour the alteration of the Government either 15 in Church or State, to Endeavour the subversion of the Government either in Church or State mend the matter at all, but seems to give something when indeed it gives nothing at all, nor makes it one jott easier to swallow. For.

1 It is against the Kings Crown and Dignity that his subjects should be sworne to the Government of the Church equall as to himself. The Kings of England 20 have always been sworne to maintain the Church, and their people have sworne Faith and true Allegiance to them. But I cannot think it safe for the King to permit by Act of Parliament, much less to enjoyn his great officers and both Houses of Parliament to swear to the Church equall as to himself. And it were a question not unfit to be asked, what the Government of the Church, we are to 25 swear to is? Whether it derives no Power, nor Authority, nor the Exercise of

---

3–9 And . . . King] L, N, R, S, T *with variants noted below* | *om.* Y   3 And] L, N | But R, S, T   4–5 in the Nation] L, R, S, T | *om.* N   5 bore] L, N, T | bears R, S   that] L, R, S, T | that in fighting against him N   most . . . safe] L | most loyall to his prince, & Safest N | both safe & Loyall both R | loyall & safe both S | most loyall and safe even T   7 justify them] R, S | but justify but L, N | justifie but T   11 all . . . of] T | the particulars of L | all particulars both of all R | all particulars of S | *om.* N, Y   14–18 then . . . swallow] L, R, S, T *with variants noted below* | *om.* N, Y   15–17 Endeavour . . . State] ed. | Endeavour the alteration of the Governement either in Church or State; To endeavour the subversion of the governement either in Church or State L | endeavoring any alterations either in Church or state R | endeavouring any alteration in gouverment either in Church or State S | Endeavour any alteration of Goverment in Church or State to Endeavour the alteration of the Goverment either in church or state T   18 easier] L, T | the easier R, S   22 Faith and true] L, T | faith & R, S | *om.* N, Y   24 equall as] ed. | as L, N, Y | equall R, T | equally as S   25 unfit to be asked] N, S, T, Y | fitt to bee asked L | unfitt to aske R   what] L, R, S, T | What is N, Y   26 is] L, R, S, T | *om.* N, Y   the . . . of] T | the exercize, nor the L | the excersice of the R | the exercise of her S | *om.* N, Y

Preisthood, nor function, but from him as head of the Church, and from God as
through him. For if they derive a power seperate and independent from the King,
I am sure it is not safe for the King to permit his subjects to be sworne to them. If
any shall say that the Preisthood and the power thereof and the authority
5 belonging thereto are derived immediately from Christ, but the Licence of
Exercising that authority and power in the Kings Dominions and over his subjects is derived from the Civil Authority. I beseech your Lordships consider how
dangerous a thing it is, that by Oath and Act of Parliament they be secured in the
exercise of an Authority in the Kings Country and over his subjects which being
10 received from Christ himselfe cannot be altered or limited by his Laws. And
whether this be not directly to set the Mitre above the Crown.

2 It is against the very Nature, Being and Ends of Parliament, and so subverts
the foundation of our Government. For what is the business of Parliaments, but
an alteration either by adding or taking away some part of the Government either
15 in Church or State. If it be answered me, that it is allowed to alter parts, but not
the whole, or to make alterations about the exercise of the power, and not to take
away the power it self either in part, or in whole, Pardon me if I say, this is not
sense. For if I may alter part, I desire to be told how many or where I must stop,
and for the distinction of power and the manner of Exercise, there can be no such
20 distinction here. For power and the manner of exercise are so interwoven, that
whoever can prescribe the manner, can absolutely enervate the power.

1 him] L, R, S, T | the King N, Y   1–2 and . . . him] L, R, S, T | *om.* N, Y
3 I . . . is] R, S | It is L, N, Y | I measure it is T   4 [*2nd*] the] R, S, T | *om.* L,
N, Y   5 thereto] L, N, S, Y | thereunto R, T   5–7 immediately . . . derived]
L, N, R, S, Y *with variants noted below* | *om.* T   5–6 of Exercising] L, N, Y | of the
Exercise & R | & exercise of S   6 and power] L, N, Y | *om.* R, S   7 Authority] L, N,
T, Y | Government R, S   8 Oath . . . Parliament] L, T | oaths and that of Parliament R |
oath & out of parliament S | Act of Parliament, and your Oaths N, Y   be] L, R, S, T |
should be N, Y   10 himselfe] L, R, S, T | *om.* N, Y   or . . . Laws] T | by his Laws
L | & limited by any Laws R | or limited to his laws S | *om.* N, Y   10–11 And . . . to]
L, R, S, T | How must we again be preistridden? when the Church shall by Act of
Parliament and your Oaths be thus seperate and set above the Civill Power. This do's
indeed N, Y   12 very] L, N, T, Y | *om.* R, S   Being and Ends] L, N, T, Y |
End and Being R, S   Parliament] L, T | Parliaments N, S, Y | a Parliament R
13 Parliaments] L, N, S, Y | Parliament R, T   14 an alteration] L, R, S, T | to
make alterations N, Y   [*2nd*] either] L, S, T | *om.* R, N, Y   15 me] L, N, T, Y |
om. R, S   parts] L, N, T, Y | parte R, S   16 alterations] L, N, R, Y | alteration
S, T   and] L, N, T, Y | but R, S   [*2nd*] to] N, R, S, Y | *om.* L, T   17 [*2nd*] in]
L, N, T, Y | *om.* R, S   this] L, N, T, Y | that R | it S   17–18 not sense] L, S, T |
no sense R | nonsense N, Y   18 part] L, R, S, Y | any part N | parts T   be] L, R,
S, T | know, and to be N, Y   many] L, R, S, T | much N, Y   or] L, N, T, Y | & R, S
19–20 [*2nd*] and . . . power] L, N, T, Y *with variants noted below* | *om.* R, S
19 Exercise] L, T | exerciseing it N, Y   20 the] L, N, T, Y | *om.* R, S
21 prescribe] L, R, S, T | prevail in N, Y

3 It is against the Kings Supremacy, and the greatest attempt that hath been made against it since the Reformation, for I beg, before we are made to take this Oath, that we may understand whether the King in Parliament may not alter, diminish, enlarge or take away any Bishoprick. And whether after this Oath I may safely in Parliament consent to it? Whether he may take away any part of a 5 Diocesse or the whole diocesse, and put them under Deans or any other persons? Because if it be not lawfull for the King and Parliament to do it, I scruple the maintaining the Government as it is, when the Dean of Hereford and the Dean of Salisbury have very large Tracts of Land under their Jurisdiction, as fully as any Bishops have their Dioceses under them, and severall parsons of Parishes have 10 Episcopall Jurisdiction; Nay (I fear) some Laymen have it too, and yet I hope are in a state of Salvation. If not I should be loath to swear to such a Government of the Church, that is so imperfectly settled.

My Lords I would not be mistaken in this discourse, for I think Episcopall Government best for the Church, and most suitable to England. But I must say 15 with the great Lord of Southampton upon the occasion of this Oath in the Parliament at Oxford, I will not be sworne never to alter it, though as yet I am perswaded I am the farthest imaginable from consenting to it. But there is nothing that is not made necessary to our Religion by Divine precept, but such Circumstances may come in human affairs as may render the contrary eligible by 20 the best of men. And if the Government of our Church be look't upon as such, I am sure that opinion doth not only extreamly invade the Kings Supremacy, but

---

3 in] L, N, T, Y | & R, S   4 diminish, enlarge] L, T | Inlarge Diminish R | diminish N, S, Y   4–5 I...Parliament] L, R, S, T | in Parliament I may safely N, Y   5 he] L, R, S, T | the King N, Y   away any] L, T | any N, R, S | away Y 5–6 a...diocesse] L | a Diocess R | a Diocess or whole diocess N, Y | a diocess or a whole diocess S | Diocesses or whole Diocesses T   8 [*1st*] the] L, N, S, Y | of the R, T when] L, R, S, T | *om.* N, Y   9 large...Land] L, N, Y | lately acted R | large tracts S | large tract T   10 Bishops...Dioceses] T | Bishop have their Dioces L | Bishops have their Diocess N, Y | Bishop in their Diocesse R | Bishop hath his diocess S 11 have it too] L, R, T | too, have it N, Y | have it heere S   13 that is] N, T, Y | this is L | which is S | *om.* R   14–15 Episcopall Government best] L, T | the episcopall Government is the best R | the Episcopall government best S | Episcopacy the best Government N, Y   15 to] L, N, T, Y | for R, S   16 great Lord of] N, Y | great Lord L, T | Good & Great Earle of R | a good & great Earle of S   [*2nd*] the] R, S, T | *om.* L, N, Y   in] T, Y | [at] 'in' N | at L, S, R   17 it] L, R, S, T | the Church Government as now Constituted N, Y   though...am] N, Y | though as I am yet L | as yet R, S, T   18 the farthest] N, S, Y | furthest L | the further R | the furthest T   But] L, R, S, T | *om.* N, Y   19 that is not] R, S, Y | that is L, N | is not T   20 Circumstances] L, R, S, T | Circumstance N, Y   the contrary] L, N, Y | it not R, S | it T   21 [*2nd*] the...Church] ed. | our Government of our Church L | our Government of the Church R, T | the government of the Church S | our Church Government N, Y   as such] L, R | as so S, T | to be so divine as not to be altered, and therefore fit for us all to swear allegiance to it N, Y   22 extreamly] L, N, T, Y | *om.* R, S

differs from the Opinion of the Parliaments both in Edward the 6ths and Queen Elizabeths time. And it must follow that there is no Salvation, but where there is Episcopacy, which if our Church themselves did really believe, they would not leave so many parishes (as I have before mentioned to your Lordships) in so ill a
5 state in England. Nay the Church of Rome it self, that is the great Mother of that Opinion, gives her self the Lye when she hath such vast tracts of ground and such great numbers of men exempt from Episcopall Jurisdiction.

But my Lords I had almost forgot one thing which is, how scandalous this Oath will appear, not only at home, but abroad to all forreign Protestants, when this
10 part of being sworn to the Government of the Church doth not secure our Doctrine at all, for Episcopacy remains, though the popish Religion were introduced, and the Kings Supremacy is justled aside by this Oath, to make better room for an Ecclesiasticall Supremacy.

1 Parliaments] **L, R, S** | Parliament **N, T, Y**   2 time] **N, R, T, Y** | times **L, S**   that] **R, S, T** | *om.* **L, N, Y**   3 our] **R, S, T** | the **L, N, Y**   really believe] **R, S, T** | believe really **L** | beleive **N, Y**   4 parishes] **L, R, S, T** | Partyes **N, Y**   in] **L, R, S, T** | to rest in **N, Y**   6 [*1st*] such] **L, R, Y** | so **N, S, T**   7 numbers] **S, T, Y** | number **L, N** | *reading of* **R** *not clear*   9 not...abroad] **L, R, S, T** | *om.* **N, Y**   10 [*1st*] of] **L, N, T, Y** | *om.* **R, S**   11 remains] **L, S, T** | would remain **N, Y** | might stand **R**   12 by this Oath] **L, N, T, Y** | *om.* **R, S**   12–13 to...room] **ed.** | which makes better **L** | to make Roome **R** | to make way **N, Y** | and makes room **S** | and makes better **T**

APPENDIX V

SHAFTESBURY'S SPEECH IN THE HOUSE OF LORDS

Sigla

M   Hampshire Record Office, 9M73/G201/1

Old.   John Oldmixon, *The History of England, During the Reigns of the Royal House of Stuart*

1   *A Letter from a Person of Quality*, first edition

1675 The Earle of Shaftesbury's Speech in the H. of L. against the Test.

I beg so much Charity of you to believe that I know the Protestant Religion so well, & am so confirm'd in it, that I hope I shou'd burn for the Witness of it, if Providence shou'd call me to it. But I may perhaps think some things not ne- 5 cessary which you account Essential: Nay I may think some things not True or agreable to Scripture, which you may call Doctrines of the Church. Besides, when I am to swear *never to endeavour to alter*, it is certainly necessary to know how far the Extent of this oath is; but since you have told me that the Protestant Religion is in those five Tracts, I have still power to ask, Whether you mean those whole 10 Tracts were the Protestant Religion, or only that the Protestant Religion is contain'd in all these, but that every part of These are not the Protestant Religion? If you mean the former of These, then I am extreamly in the dark to find the Doctrine of Predestination in the seventeenth & eighteenth Articles, to be own'd by so few great Doctors of the Church & to find the nineteenth Article to define 15 the Church directly as the Independants doe. Besides, the twentieth Article stating the Authority of the Church, is very dark, & either contradicts itself, or says nothing, or what is contrary to the known Laws of the Land. Further, several

---

1–2 1675 . . . Test.] **M** | *om.* **Old.**, 1   6 some things] **Old.**, 1 | 'some things' **M**
7 Scripture] **M, Old.** | the Scripture 1   which] **M, Old.** | that 1   9 Extent] **M,**
Old. | *just extent* 1   you] *side-note in* **M**: Morley Bp of Winton   10 power]
M, Old. | *om.* 1   12 these] **M, Old.** | those 1   14 seventeenth & eighteenth]
M, Old. | 18. *and* 17. 1   18 Further] **M, Old.** | besides 1

other things in the thirty nine Articles have been preach'd and written against by Men of great Favour, Power, & Preferment in the Church.

I humbly conceive the Liturgy is not so sacred, being made by Men the other day, & thought to be more differing from the Dissenting Protestants, & less easy
5 to be comply'd with, upon the Advantage of a Pretence well known to us all, of *Making Abatements as might the better invite them*, instead of which, there's scarce one Alteration but widens the Breach, & no ordination allow'd by it here (as it now stands last Reform'd by the Act of Uniformity) but what is Episcopal. So that a popish Priest, when converted, is capable of any Church Preferment,
10 without Reordination; but a Protestant Minister, not Episcopally ordain'd, is requir'd to be re-ordain'd. As much as in us lies, Unchurching all the Foreign Protestants that have not Bishops; though the contrary was both allow'd & practis'd from the Beginning of the Reformation to the Time of that Act, & several Bishops made of such as were never ordain'd Priests by Bishops; & I
15 think, *to endeavour to alter* and restore the Liturgy to what it was in Queen Elizabeth's days, may consist with my being a very good Protestant. As to the Catechism, I really think it may be amended, and dare declare to you, it is not well that there is not a better made. For the Homilies, I believe there may be a better book made; and Homily the third of Repairing and keeping clean churches
20 may be omitted. What is yet stranger than all this, the Canons of our Church are directly the old popish Canons, which are full in force, & no other, as will appear if you turn to Stat. 25 Hen. VIII. cap. 10. confirm'd & renew'd by 1 Eliz. where all those Canons are establish'd, till an Alteration shall be made by the King in pursuance of that act; which was attempted by Edward VI. but not perfected, and
25 let alone ever since, for what reason the Lords the Bishops can best tell; and it is very hard to be oblig'd by Oath not *to endeavour to alter* either the English Common-Prayer or the Canon of the Mass # # # #

---

1 written] **M, Old.** | Writ 1   5 [*2nd*] to] **M, Old.** | unto 1
6 *Abatements . . . them*] **Old.** | *Abatements as may better invite them* **M** | alterations as might the better *unite* us 1   of which] **M, Old.** | whereof 1   8 So] **M, Old.** | in so much 1
9 when . . . capable] **M, Old.** | is capable, when converted 1   10 a] **M, Old.** | no 1
is] **M, Old.** | but is 1   13 to] **M, Old.** | till 1   14 &] **M, Old.** | Moreover the *Uncharitableness* of it was so much against the Interest of the *Crown, and Church of England* (casting off the dependency of the whole Protestant partie abroad) that it would have been *bought* by the *Pope* and *French King* at a vast summ of Money; and it is difficult to conceive so great an advantage fell to them meerly by chance, and without their help; so that 1
17 amended] **M, Old.** | mended 1   18 believe] **M, Old.** | thought 1   [*2nd*] there]
Old., 1 | *illeg. in* **M**   19 churches] **M, Old.** | *of Churches* 1   20 stranger] 1 |
stronger **M, Old.**   21 full] **M, Old.** | still 1   as] **M, Old.** | which 1
22 Stat.] **M, Old.** | the *Stat.* 1   10] **M, Old.** | 19 1   renew'd] **M, Old.** | received 1
23 till] **M, Old.** | untill 1   24 which] **M, Old.** | which thing 1   25 reason]
M, Old. | reasons 1   27 Common-Prayer] **M, Old.** | Common-Prayer book 1
####] *M* | *om.* **Old.,** 1

APPENDIX VI

THE TEST BILL

Sigla

U   Bodleian Library, MS Rawlinson A 162, fos. 54^r–55^r

X   British Library, Additional MS 41656, fos. 79^r–80^r

An Act to prevent the Dangers which may arise from Persons disaffected to the Government

For the more plaine and express Declaration of the Loyalty and good affections of all those who do or shall hold any Office or Employment Ecclesiasticall Civil or Military or shall sit and vote as Members of either House of Parliament **Be it** 5 Enacted by the Kings most Excellent Majesty by and with the advice and consent of the Lords Spirituall and Temporall and of the Commons in this present Parliament Assembled, and by the Authority of the same **That no person** being a Peer of this Realm shall hereafter be capable of holding any Office or Employment Ecclesiasticall Civil or Military, within the Kingdom of England, 10 Dominion of Wales, Towne of Berwick upon Tweed or in the Islands of Jersey and Guernsey, unless he or they shall within   months after their Grant and admittance thereinto before three of the Lords of his Majesty's Privy Counsell for the time being or such other persons as shall by his Majesty be authorized to administer the same, take and subscribe the Declaration and Oath herein after 15 mentioned, which Declaration and Oath they have power hereby to tender and administer. And the said Declaration and Oath shall be in these words following.

> **I A. B.** doe declare that it is not Lawfull upon any pretence whatsoever to take Arms against the King, and that I doe abhor that Trayterous Position of taking Arms by his Authority against his Person, or against those that are 20 Commissioned by him in pursuance of such Commissions, And I doe sweare that I will not at any time endeavour the Alteration of the Government either in Church or State.

---

1 Dangers] U | Danger X   may] X | *om.* U   7–8 [*1st*] of . . . same] U | &c. X
12 and] U | [&] 'or' X   15 [*1st*] and] X | *om.* U   16 power hereby] U | hereby
power X   20 that] X | who U

And be it further Enacted that no Person under the Degree of a Peer of this Realme shall hereafter be capable of holding any Office or Employment Ecclesiasticall Civil or Military unless he or they shall within   months after their Grant or admittance thereinto take and subscribe the Declaration and Oath
5 aforesaid before some Justice of Peace of the County or place where such person shall be inhabiting, which Oath any one Justice of the Peace of the County or place where any such person shall be inhabiting shall be enabled to Administer.

And all and every person and persons being Peers of this Realme and under that Degree and now having or holding any such Offices or Employments shall
10 before the   day of   take and subscribe the said Declaration and Oath before such persons and in such manner respectively as is herein before appointed in cases where any Peer of the Realme or person under that Degree shall be admitted into any Office or Employments hereafter to be granted.

And be it further Enacted that where any Peer of this Realme having any such
15 Office or Employment shall take and subscribe the said Declaration and Oath before three of the Lords of the Councell, That in every such case the Clerk of the Councell attending shall be obliged to enter the Memoriall thereof in the Councell Book there to remaine, and if the said Declaration and Oath shall be tendred to any Peer by virtue of a speciall commission so to doe, that then and in
20 such case the Commissioner or Commissioners shall certify the taking and subscribing thereof under their hands and seales unto the Clerk of the Councell attending who is hereby required to enter the same as aforesaid.

And where any person under the Degree of a Peer of the Realme shall take and subscribe the said Declaration and Oath in manner before appointed, That then
25 and in such case the Justice of the Peace before whom the same shall be done shall give a Certificate under his hand and seale to the person so takeing and subscribeing the same, Which Certificate shall be brought to the next Quarter sessions and there read in open Court, & afterwards entred by the Clerk of the Peace amongst the Records of that Sessions gratis.

30 **And** be it further Enacted That no person being a Peer of this Realme shall after the Royall Assent to this Bill actually given be admitted to sit or vote in the House of Peers in this Parliament or in any other Parliament hereafter to be summoned, who shall not first take and subscribe this said Declaration & oath above mentioned, the said Oath to be administred in such manner as the Oath of
35 Obedience is accustomed to be; And that no person shall after the Royall Assent to this Bill actually given be admitted to sit or vote as a Member of the House of Commons in this Parliament, or in any other Parliament hereafter to be summoned, who shall not first take and subscribe the Declaration and Oath above mentioned, the said Oath to be administred in such manner as the Oath of
40 Obedience is accustomed to be.

---

2 hereafter be] X | be hereafter U   4 thereinto] U | thereunto X   8 this] U
| the X   10 said] U | *om.* X   34 [*1st*] the] X | & the U

And if any shall presume to sit and vote in either House without having first taken and subscribed the Declaration and Oath above mentioned, such person shall be punished as he ought to be who shall presume to sit in Parliament, without any right or authority so to doe.

APPENDIX VII
QUERIES ON JURY SELECTION

PRO 30/24/6B/403. The queries printed here in the left-hand column are in the hand of Sylvester Brounower, and were presumably drafted or dictated by Locke. The replies in the right-hand column are in the hand of the barrister William Thomson. In the manuscript Brounower's queries are on the front of the sheet and Thomson's replies on the back.

Some Queries upon the Statute of 3. H. 8
Concerning errecting the Pannells of Juries by Justices &c:

1 whereas the recitall of the Statute
mentions the oppressions of
5 Sheriffs & their officers to be the
reason of making the Statute,
whether the Court can alter the
panell where no fault appears to be
in the Sheriff. &c.

10

15

1. I conceive the Court may alter the
pannell where noe fault appeares in
the Sheriffes for tho the preamble of
the Statute mentions the reason of
makeing the law to be the miscarriages of Sherriffs yett the power
given to Justices of Gaol delivery &
of the peace is generall and referring
it to the discretion of the Court Soe
that for reasonable cause shewn
against any person they may cause
the Sherriffe to strike out such and to
returne others.

2. The power being given to Justices
of Goal Delivery & of the peace,
whether Justices of Oyer & Ter-
20 miner have any power to proceed
by a Jury so impannelld.

2. I conceive the Statute does not extend to give the Justices of oyer &
Terminer any power to reforme the
pannells the words of the Statute
expressing onely Justices of Gaol
delivery & of the peace And this law
cannot be extended to any other in
equity however not to Justices of

2 C 'Concerning' *add. in margin, probably by Locke*

oyer and Terminer because their
commission is distinct and of a
superior nature.

3. whether the persons to be
added to such Jury ought to be
nominated by the Sheriff or by
the Justices no mention being
made in the Statute by whom the
persons to be added shall be
named.

3. I conceive upon reformeing the
pannells even at Gaol delivery & of
the peace upon strickeing out any
person the Sherriffs shall nominate
others for thoe those Courts have
power to reforme the pannells at
their discretion yet this is a legall
discretion and they cannot put out
any person without reasonable cause
shewn and the power of the Sherriff
which he had before is not taken
away for he is still to returne the Jury
& doe all other Acts of his office but
these Courts seeme to have a new
power of excepting and dissaloweing
of persons returned if they have
reasonable cause for it And this
makes the Statute of 11th of H 4
and the Statute of 3. H 8.
consistent which otherwise would
be repugnant for by 11th of H 4th
the Sherriffs are not to returne any
Jury at the nomination of any one
whatsoever.

4. whether the Court have any
means to compell the Sheriff to
returne the Panell corrected by
the Justices other then 20^{li} to be
sued for according to the act.

4. I conceive the penalty of 20^{li} is all
the Sherriff cann incurr if he refuse
to doe any thing required by this
Statute.

5. whether in inquiryes of Treason
the Justices can proceed
according to this act, Since the
Statute of 1. &. 2. Ph. & Mar. c.
10. has appointed all treasons to
be tried according to the Court of
the Common law.

5 The Statute of 1 & 2. Phil: &
Mary. is onely as to the manner of
tryalls not to returneing of Juryes.

421

6. whether by the Statute 11 H 4th the Sherifs only must not returne Jurys in London in our Case that of 3 H. 8. being only concerning Goal delivery & our case being of oyer & Terminer so that these two Statutes of 11 H. 4 & 3 H. 8 are consistent

The last Query is answered before

W: Thomson

8 [consistute] `consistent' *alt. JL*

BIBLIOGRAPHY

MANUSCRIPT SOURCES

Beinecke Rare Book and Manuscript Library, Yale University

Osborn Shelves, b. 120: Miscellaneous political papers, 17th century.
Osborn Shelves, b. 157: Miscellaneous legal and political papers, 17th century.
Osborn Shelves, fb. 155: Commonplace book of John Browne.
OSB MSS 6: Danby papers.

Bodleian Library, Oxford

Lovelace Collection

MS Locke b. 1: Bills and other papers relating to Locke's expenditure.
MS Locke b. 2: Papers relating to Locke's books.
MS Locke b. 3: Papers relating to money and the coinage.
MS Locke b. 4: Miscellaneous papers.
MS Locke b. 5: Deeds relating to Locke's land and other personal papers.
MS Locke c. 1: Locke's ledger, 1671–1702.
MS Locke c. 23: Letters from correspondents, surnames V–Z.
MS Locke c. 25: Personal papers.
MS Locke c. 26: Papers relating to Locke's land.
MS Locke c. 27: Theological papers.
MS Locke c. 28: Philosophical papers.
MS Locke c. 29: Medical papers.
MS Locke c. 30: Papers on trade and the colonies.
MS Locke c. 31: Miscellaneous papers.
MS Locke c. 33: Notes on books read by Locke.
MS Locke c. 34: Critical notes on works by Edward Stillingfleet, *c*.1681.
MS Locke c. 42B: General commonplace book.
MS Locke c. 44: Records of ecclesiastical patronage handled by Locke, 1672–3; volume used for other purposes after 1689.
MS Locke d. 1: General commonplace book, 1679, 1692.
MS Locke d. 3: Writings against Malebranche and Norris.
MS Locke d. 9: Medical commonplace book, *c*.1665–*c*.1669.
MS Locke d. 10: 'Lemmata Ethica', General commonplace book, *c*.1660–*c*.1667, 1681–2, 1693–1701.
MS Locke d. 11: 'Lemmata Physica', Medical commonplace book, *c*.1659– *c*.1675, 1693–1701.

MS Locke e. 3: Catalogue of Locke's library, 1697 and later.
MS Locke e. 8: Copy of the 1668 tract on rates of interest.
MS Locke f. 1: Journal, Nov. 1675–Dec. 1676.
MS Locke f. 2: Journal, 1677.
MS Locke f. 3: Journal, 1678.
MS Locke f. 4: Journal, 1680.
MS Locke f. 5: Journal, 1681.
MS Locke f. 7: Journal, 1683.
MS Locke f. 9: Journal, 1686–8.
MS Locke f. 10: Journal, 1689–1704.
MS Locke f. 12: Accounts and notes on Locke's land, 1664–72.
MS Locke f. 13: Pocket memorandum book, 1674.
MS Locke f. 14: Commonplace book, *c*.1659–*c*.1666.
MS Locke f. 15: Pocket memorandum book, 1677–8.
MS Locke f. 19: Medical commonplace book, *c*.1662–*c*.1669.
MS Locke f. 21: Medical notebook, *c*.1669–*c*.1672, 1679–81.
MS Locke f. 22: Medical notebook, *c*.1665–6.
MS Locke f. 24: Medical notebook, *c*.1684–*c*.1688.
MS Locke f. 25: Chemical notebook, 1663–7.
MS Locke f. 26: Draft B of *An Essay concerning Human Understanding*, 1671.
MS Locke f. 27: Pocket memorandum book, 1664–6.
MS Locke f. 28: Pocket memorandum book, 1678–85.
MS Locke f. 29: Pocket memorandum book, 1683–1702.
MS Locke f. 31: Scribal copy of the *Essays on the Law of Nature*.
MS Locke f. 48: Pocket memorandum book, 1672.

Other Collections

MS Carte 38: Ormonde correspondence, 1673–9.
MS Carte 59: Miscellaneous Ormonde papers.
MS Carte 72: Newsletters to Ormonde, 1660–85.
MS Carte 80: Wharton papers.
MS Carte 81: Wharton papers.
MS Carte 228: Miscellaneous papers from the Wharton and Huntingdon collections.
MS Carte 243: Ormonde correspondence, 1670–81.

MS Don. b. 8: Commonplace book of Sir Robert Haward.
MS Don. f. 7: Questions for Shaftesbury's grand jury, 1681.

MS Rawlinson A 162: Bills introduced into the House of Lords, 1662–85.
MS Rawlinson A 185: Pepys papers.
MS Rawlinson A 191: Pepys papers.
MS Rawlinson D 924: Miscellaneous papers on English history.

MS Smith 31: Miscellaneous papers collected by Thomas Smith.

MS Tanner 36: Papers on English history, 1681.
MS Tanner 43: Sancroft papers.
MS Tanner 290: Miscellaneous papers, 17th century.

Microfilms of Manuscripts in Other Libraries or in Private Hands

MS Film 70: Translation of Pierre Nicole's *Essais de morale* [Pierpont Morgan Library, New York, MA 232].
MS Film 77: Locke's commonplace book Adversaria 1661.
MS Film 79: Locke's 1667 memorandum book.

British Library, London

Additional MS 4222: Birch papers.
Additional MS 4224: Birch papers.
Additional MS 4282: Des Maizeaux papers.
Additional MS 4288: Des Maizeaux papers.
Additional MS 4290: Des Maizeaux papers.
Additional MS 5714: Locke's medical case notes, 1667–70.
Additional MS 15642: Locke's journal, 1679.
Additional MS 19526: Historical collections of Henry Gregory.
Additional MS 21947: Letters to the Duke of Richmond and Lennox, 1661–70.
Additional MS 25124: Letter book of Henry Coventry.
Additional MS 28728: Letters and papers of Locke and Nicolas Toinard.
Additional MS 28929: Letters from Humphrey Prideaux to John Ellis.
Additional MS 29577: Letters from Sir Charles Lyttelton to Lord Hatton, 1657–83.
Additional MS 32094: Miscellaneous documents and papers collected by Sir John Malet, 1660–76.
Additional MS 33051: Newcastle papers.
Additional MS 36916: Aston newsletters, 1667–72.
Additional MS 40860: Diary of the Earl of Anglesey, 1671–5.
Additional MS 41568: Parry newsletters, 1675, 1679.
Additional MS 41656: Townshend papers.
Additional MS 41810: Middleton correspondence, 1683–8.
Additional MS 46470: Locke's 1669 memorandum book.
Additional MS 63057: Early version of Burnet's *History of My Own Time*.
Additional MS 65138: Clifford papers, 1669–72.
Additional MS 70500: Cavendish papers, 1661–95.
Additional MS 74273: Manuscript copy of *A Letter from a Person of Quality*.

Egerton MS 2539: Letters from Sir John Nicholas to his father, 1666–9.
Egerton MS 3383: Leeds papers.

Harleian MS 5277: Papers relating to proceedings in Parliament, 1670–7.

Lansdowne MS 1039: Miscellaneous papers collected by White Kennett.
Stowe MS 207: Essex correspondence.
Stowe MS 208: Essex correspondence.

Centre for Buckinghamshire Studies, Aylesbury

M11/29: Verney papers (microfilm).

Christ Church, Oxford

XII. b. 104–19 Disbursement books, 1661–76.

Corporation of London Records Office

SF 292–4: Sessions files, Aug.–Nov. 1681.

Hampshire Record Office, Winchester

Malmesbury Papers

9M73/G197: Manuscript treatise: 'Respecting the Life and Character of the 1st
  East of Shaftesbury', early eighteenth century.
9M73/G201/1: Shaftesbury's speech against the Test Bill, 1675.
9M73/G201/2: Shaftesbury's speech in the House of Lords, 20 Oct. 1675.
9M73/G220: Legal queries from the Earl of Shaftesbury, 1681.
9M73/G237/8, 9: Two letters from Shaftesbury to Thomas Stringer, undated.
9M73/G238: Letters from the third Earl of Shaftesbury to Thomas Stringer,
  1698–1702.
9M73/G242: Locke's power of attorney, 11 Nov. 1675.

Houghton Library, Harvard University

Microfilms of Manuscripts in Other Libraries or in Private Hands
MS Eng. 860.1: Locke's commonplace book Adversaria 1661.

House of Lords Record Office

Minutes of committees 1672–85.
Manuscript journals.
Manuscript minutes, vol. 19 (Feb. 1674–May 1678).

Microfilms of Manuscripts in Other Libraries or in Private Hands
Braye MS 96 [Beinecke Library, Yale, Osborn Shelves, fb. 155].

Bibliography

Huntington Library, San Marino, California

EL 8416: Shaftesbury's speech in the House of Lords, 20 Oct. 1675.
HM 584: Locke's autograph of *An Essay concerning Toleration*.

Lauinger Library, Georgetown University, Washington DC

Milton House Collection, box 4, folder 28: 'The particular test for Priests'.

Leicester, Leicestershire, and Rutland Record Office, Leicester

Finch papers

DG7/Ecc. 2: Minutes of meetings, January 1675.
DG7/PP 30: Reasons against the Bill for the Test.
DG7/PP 36: Draft of the King's speech to Parliament, 13 Apr. 1675.

Longleat House, Wiltshire

Coventry papers

Vol. 83: Letter book of Henry Coventry (Microfilm, Institute of Historical Research, University of London, XR 60/67).

Thynne papers

Vol. 27: Documents collected by George Harbin (Microfilm, Institute of Historical Research, University of London, XR 71/15).

The National Archives, Kew

Shaftesbury Papers

PRO 30/24/4/149: The *London Gazette*, no. 72, July 1666.
PRO 30/24/4/236: Shaftesbury's household, 1672.
PRO 30/24/5/250: Notes on obstructions on the Thames quayside, 1673.
PRO 30/24/5/257: Draft letter from Shaftesbury relating to ecclesiastical patronage, 4 Aug. 1673.
PRO 30/24/5/264: Orders for Shaftesbury's household.
PRO 30/24/5/278: List of books taken to country, May 1674.
PRO 30/24/5/281: Draft of a Marriage Bill, endorsed by Locke.
PRO 30/24/5/284: Letter from Shaftesbury to the Earl of Carlisle, 3 Feb. 1675.
PRO 30/24/5/286: Orders for Shaftesbury's household, 1675.
PRO 30/24/5/288: Letter from Shaftesbury to Bennett, 28 Aug. 1675.
PRO 30/24/5/293: 'Book of memorandums', relating to gardening and agriculture.

PRO 30/24/5/294: Reasons against the Bill for the Test; letter from Shaftesbury to the Earl of Carlisle, 3 Feb. 1675.

PRO 30/24/6A/349: Lists of papers taken from Shaftesbury's house, 2 July 1681.

PRO 30/24/6A/368: Thomson's answers to Shaftesbury's queries, 1681.

PRO 30/24/6A/370: William Jones's answers to Shaftesbury's queries, 1681.

PRO 30/24/6A/385: Copy of Locke's Epitaph for Shaftesbury.

PRO 30/24/6B/393: Letter from Shaftesbury to the Earl of Carlisle, 3 Feb. 1675.

PRO 30/24/6B/403: Queries on Juries with Thomson's replies.

PRO 30/24/6B/417: Copy of letter from [Jane Stringer?] to Madam [Elizabeth Ashley Cooper?], undated.

PRO 30/24/6B/420: Presentment of the Duke of York as a recusant.

PRO 30/24/6B/421: Reason of Grand Jury for presenting the Duke of York.

PRO 30/24/6B/427: Paper on ecclesiastical jurisdiction.

PRO 30/24/6B/429: Paper advocating appointment of a Vicar-General.

PRO 30/24/6B/430: Paper on ecclesiastical jurisdiction.

PRO 30/24/6B/431: Paper on the Declaration of Indulgence, *c*.1672.

PRO 30/24/6B/433: Papers relating to Stephen College.

PRO 30/24/6B/441: Thomas Stringer's memoir of Shaftesbury.

PRO 30/24/7/512: Presentment of the Duke of York as a recusant.

PRO 30/24/21/221: Letter from the third Earl of Shaftesbury to John Wheelock, 10 Jan. 1713.

PRO 30/24/22/2: Letter book of the third Earl of Shaftesbury, 1689–1706.

PRO 30/24/22/5: Letter book of the third Earl of Shaftesbury, 1704–5.

PRO 30/24/27/17: Letters from Pierre Des Maizeaux to the third Earl of Shaftesbury, 1701–5.

PRO 30/24/27/19: Letters from Jean Le Clerc to the third Earl of Shaftesbury, 1705.

PRO 30/24/42/59: Papers relating to Locke's work as Secretary for Presentations, 1672–3.

PRO 30/24/43/63: Papers relating to the Popish Plot and Shaftesbury's imprisonment, 1678–81.

PRO 30/24/43/69: Papers relating to Shaftesbury's imprisonment, 1681.

PRO 30/24/44/77: Correspondence of the third Earl of Shaftesbury.

PRO 30/24/45/80: Letters to the third Earl of Shaftesbury.

PRO 30/24/47/1: Copy of *An Essay concerning Toleration*.

PRO 30/24/47/2: Medical papers relating to Locke, Sydenham, and Shaftesbury, 1666–74.

PRO 30/24/47/3: *The Fundamental Constitutions of Carolina*, 1669.

PRO 30/24/47/7: Copy of Draft A of *An Essay concerning Human Understanding*.

PRO 30/24/47/22: Papers relating to Locke and Christ Church.

PRO 30/24/47/30: Miscellaneous Locke papers.

PRO 30/24/47/33: Latin disputation (1661) by Locke, *An necesse sit dari in Ecclesia SS^{ae} scripturae interpretem?*

PRO 30/24/47/35: Copy in Locke's hand of *Observations upon the Growth and Culture of Vines and Olives*, 1680.

PRO 30/24/48/28: Notes on provisions at Ashley River, 1670.

PRO 30/24/49/8: Papers relating to the Council for Trade and Plantations.

State Papers

SP 29: State Papers, Charles II.

SP 44: Domestic entry books.

SP 104/177: Committee for Foreign Affairs, Entry Book.

Other Collections

Adm. 77: Greenwich Hospital newsletters.

CO 5/286: Carolina Entry Book.

CO 388/5: Board of Trade papers 1696–8.

PC 2: Privy Council registers.

National Art Library, Victoria and Albert Museum, London

Forster Manuscripts

MS Forster 47. A. 47: Orrery's diary, 1675.

MS Forster 48. G. 3: Miscellaneous Locke papers.

Newberry Library, Chicago

Case MS 6A 24: 'The Particular Test for Priests'.

Olin Library, Washington University, St Louis

William Keeney Bixby papers 15/104, 132: Correspondence of Locke and the third Earl of Shaftesbury, 1703.

Surrey History Centre, Woking

More Molyneux Papers

LM/1331/60: Reasons against the Bill for the Test.

Somers papers

371/14/J/1: Shaftesbury's speech in the House of Lords, 20 Oct. 1675.

Dr Williams's Library, London

Baxter Treatises.
MS Morrice P: Roger Morrice's Entering Book 1677–86.

Wiltshire and Swindon History Centre, Chippenham

Savernake Estate

9/34/15: Copies of letters concerning Lord Digby and the Dorset by-election, 1675.

EARLY PRINTED WORKS (TO 1800)

This section includes more recent editions of works written before 1800.

The Acts of the Parliaments of Scotland, ed. T. Thomson *et al.*, 12 vols. (Edinburgh, 1814–75).

The Arraignment, Tryal, and Condemnation of Stephen Colledge for High-Treason, in Conspiring the Death of the King, the Levying of War, and the Subversion of the Government (London, 1681). Wing A 3761.

BAXTER, RICHARD, *Additional Notes on the Life and Death of Sir Matthew Hale* (London, 1682). Wing B 1180.

——*Reliquiae Baxterianae: Or, Mr. Richard Baxter's Narrative of The most Memorable Passages of his Life and Times Faithfully Publish'd from his own Original Manuscript, By Matthew Sylvester* (London, 1696). LL 228. Wing B 1370.

——*Calendar of the Correspondence of Richard Baxter*, ed. N. H. Keeble and Geoffrey F. Nuttall, 2 vols. (Oxford, 1991).

Bentivolyo, or Good Will to all that are Called Unconformists, or To all the People of God (n.p., 1667). Wing B 1913.

Bibliotheca Juris Canonici Veteris, ed. Guillaume Voelle and Henri Justel, 2 vols. (Paris, 1661).

Biographia Britannica; Or, the Lives of the Most eminent Persons Who have flourished in Great Britain and Ireland, From the earliest Ages, down to the present Times, 6 vols. (London, 1747–66).

BLACKSTONE, WILLIAM, *Commentaries on the Laws of England*, 4 vols. (Oxford, 1765–8).

BOYLE, ROBERT, *The Correspondence of Robert Boyle*, ed. Michael Hunter, Antonio Clericuzio, and Lawrence M. Principe, 6 vols. (London, 2001).

Bibliography

A Brief Account of the new Sect of Latitude-Men Together with some reflections upon the New Philosophy (London, 1662). Wing P 754.

BULSTRODE, SIR RICHARD, *Memoirs and Reflections upon the Reign and Government of King Charles the Ist and King Charles the II^d* (London, 1721).

BURNET, GILBERT, *The Life and Death of Sir Matthew Hale*, 2nd edn. (London, 1682). Wing B 5828.

—— *An Enquiry into the Reasons for Abrogating the Test imposed on all Members of Parliament. Offered by Sa. Oxon.* (n.p., 1688). *LL* 2200. Wing B 5813.

—— *Burnet's History of My Own Time*, ed. Osmund Airy, 2 vols. (Oxford, 1897–1900).

—— *A Supplement to Burnet's History of My Own Time*, ed. H. C. Foxcroft (Oxford, 1902).

Calendar of the Clarendon State Papers Preserved in the Bodleian Library, ed. O. Ogle, W. H. Bliss, W. D. Macray, and F. J. Routledge, 5 vols. (Oxford, 1869–1970).

CARON, FRANÇOIS, and SCHOUTEN, JOOST, *A True Description of the Mighty Kingdoms of Japan and Siam* (London, 1663). Wing C 607.

—— *A True Description of the Mighty Kingdoms of Japan and Siam*, ed. C. R. Boxer (London, 1935).

COKE, SIR EDWARD, *The Second Part of the Institutes of the Lawes of England* (London, 1642). Wing C 4948.

—— *The Third Part of the Institutes of the Laws of England* (London, 1644). Wing C 4960.

—— *The Fourth Part of the Institutes of the Laws of England* (London, 1644). Wing C 4929.

The Collection of Autograph Letters and Historical Documents formed by Alfred Morrison, The Bulstrode Papers: 1667–1675 (n.p., 1897).

A Collection of the Parliamentary Debates in England, from the Year M,DC,LXVIII. To the Present Time, 21 vols. (London, 1741–2).

The Compton Census of 1676: A Critical Edition, ed. Anne Whiteman (London, 1986).

[CORBET, JOHN], *A Discourse of the Religion of England. Asserting, That Reformed Christianity setled in its Due Latitude is the Stability and Advancement of this Kingdom* (London, 1667). Wing C 6252.

—— *A Second Discourse of the Religion of England: Further Asserting, That Reformed Christianity, Setled in its Due Latitude, is the Stability and Advancement of this Kingdom. Wherein is included, An Answer to a late Book, Entituled, A Discourse of Toleration* (London, 1668). Wing C 6263.

Correspondence of the Family of Hatton, ed. E. M. Thompson, Camden Society, 2nd ser., 22, 23 (London, 1878).

DALTON, MICHAEL, *The Countrey Justice* (London, 1635).

Debates of the House of Commons, From the Year 1667 to the Year 1694, ed. Anchitell Grey, 10 vols. (London, 1763).

Bibliography

DERING, SIR EDWARD, *The Parliamentary Diary of Sir Edward Dering 1670–1673*, ed. Basil Duke Henning (New Haven, 1940).

—— *The Diaries and Papers of Sir Edward Dering, Second Baronet, 1644 to 1684*, ed. Maurice F. Bond (London, 1976).

Dolus an Virtus? Or, An Answer to a Seditious Discourse Concerning The Religion of England: And The Settlement of Reformed Christianity in its due Latitude (London, 1668). Wing D 1841.

EADMER, *The Life of St Anselm*, ed. and trans. R. W. Southern (London, 1962).

The English-mans right. A Dialogue between a Barrister at law and a Jury-man (London, 1680). Wing H 1185.

Essex Papers, ed. Osmund Airy, Camden Society, 2nd ser., 47 (London, 1890).

EVELYN, JOHN, *The Diary of John Evelyn*, ed. E. S. de Beer, 6 vols. (Oxford, 1955).

A Few Sober Queries Upon the late Proclamation, for enforcing the Laws against Conventicles, &c. and the late Vote of the House of Commons, For Renewing the said Act for three years more. Proposed to the serious consideration of the Kings majesty, with his two Houses of Parliament. By one that earnestly desires the prosperity of England (London, 1668). Wing F 838.

FILMER, SIR ROBERT, *'Patriarcha' and Other Writings*, ed. Johann P. Sommerville (Cambridge, 1991).

F., R. [Robert Ferguson], *A Sober Enquiry into the Nature, Measure, and Principle of Moral Virtue, in Distinction from Gospel-Holiness* (London, 1673). Wing F 760.

Forgery Detected and Innocency Vindicated (London, 1673). Wing F 1558.

GAULTIER, JACQUES, *Table chronographique de l'estat du Christianisme, depuis la naissance de Jesus-Christ, jusques à l'année MDLI* (Lyon, 1651).

GROTIUS, HUGO, *De Jure Belli ac Pacis Libri Tres*, trans. Frank W. Kelsey (Oxford, 1925).

HALE, SIR MATTHEW, *Historia Placitorum Coronae*, 2 vols. (London, 1736).

HARRINGTON, JAMES, *The Political Works of James Harrington*, ed. J. G. A. Pocock (Cambridge, 1977).

His Majesties Declaration to All His loving Subjects, December 26, 1662 (London, 1662). Wing C 2988.

His Majesties Declaration for Enforcing a late Order Made in Council (London, 1675). Wing C 2965.

The History and Proceedings of the House of Lords, from the Restoration in 1660, to the Present Time, 8 vols. (London, 1742–3).

HOBBES, THOMAS, *Leviathan* (London, 1651). LL 1465. Wing H 2246.

—— *Behemoth, Or the Long Parliament*, ed. Ferdinand Tönnies (London, 1889).

HOOKER, RICHARD, *Of the Laws of Ecclesiastical Politie*, ed. W. Speed Hill *et al.*, 3 vols. (Cambridge, Mass., 1977–81).

Bibliography

Hume, David, *The History of England, From The Invasion of Julius Caesar To The Revolution in 1688*, 8 vols. (London, 1768).

[Humfrey, John], *A Proposition for the Safety & Happiness of the King and Kingdom both in Church and State, and prevention of the Common Enemy. Tendered to the Consideration of his Majesty and the Parliament against their next Session. By a lover of Sincerity & Peace* (London, 1667). Wing H 77C.

—— *A Proposition for the Safety and Happiness of the King and kingdom, both in Church and State, and prevention of the Common Enemy. Tendered to the Consideration of his Majesty and the Parliament against the tenth of October. By a lover os Sincerity & Peace. The Second Edition revised, corrected and enlarged by the Author. Together with a Reply to the pretended Answer to it* (London, 1667). Wing H 77D.

—— *The Authority of the Magistrate About Religion, Discussed, In a Rebuke to the Prefacer of a late Book of Bishop Bramhalls* (London, 1672). Wing H 3669.

Insolence and Impudence triumphant; Envy and Fury enthron'd: the Mirrour of Malice and Madness, in a late Treatise Entituled, A Discourse of Ecclesiastical Polity, &c. (n.p., 1669). Wing I 226.

James VI and I, *Political Writings*, ed. Johann P. Sommerville (Cambridge, 1994).

James, Thomas, *A Treatise of the Corruption of Scripture, Councils and Father by the Prelats, Pastors, and Pillars of the Church of Rome, For the Maintenance of Popery* ... (London, 1611).

J.H. [John Humfrey], *A Defence of the Proposition: Or, Some Reasons rendred why the Nonconformist-Minister who comes to his Parish-Church and Common-Prayer, cannot yet yeeld to other things that are enjoyned, without some Moderation. Being A Full Reply to the Book which is a pretended Answer thereunto* ([London], 1668). Wing H 3676.

The Judgement of Mr. Baxter Concerning Ceremonies and Conformity. With a Short Refelection upon a Scandalous Pamphlet, Intituled, A Proposition for the Safety and Happiness of the King and Kingdom. In a Letter to a Gentlemen of the House of Commons. (London, 1667). Wing B 1290.

Laud, William, *A Relation of the Conference between William Lawd* ... *And Mr. Fisher the Jesuite* ... (London, 1639).

Lauderdale Correspondence, 1660–77, ed. J. Dowden, Miscellany of the Scottish History Society, 1 (Edinburgh, 1893).

The Lauderdale Papers, ed. Osmund Airy, Camden Society, 2nd ser., 34, 36, 38 (London, 1884–5).

Le Clerc, Jean, 'Eloge de feu Mr Locke', *Bibliotheque Choisie*, 6 (1705), 342–411.

—— *The Life and Character of Mr. John Locke*, trans. T.F.P., Gent. (London, 1706).

433

Bibliography

LE CLERC, JEAN, *An Account of the Life and Writings of Mr. John Locke* (London, 1713).

A Letter concerning the Tryal at Oxford of Stephen College, August 17. 1681. (London, 1681). Wing L 1356.

A Letter of the Presbyterian Ministers In the City of London, Presented the First of Jan. 1645. to the Reverend Assembly of Divines, Sitting at Westminster, by Authority of Parliament, against Toleration. Now Re-printed, with some Animadversions thereon (London, 1668). Wing L 1581.

A Letter to a Member of this Present Parliament, For Liberty of Conscience (London, 1668). Wing L 1688.

A Letter to a Priest of the Roman Church: Wherein the Grounds of their Pretended Infallibility Are Called for and Examined, in some Queries (London, 1675). Wing L 1695.

Letters addressed from London to Sir Joseph Williamson, ed. W. D. Christie, Camden Society, 2nd ser., 8, 9 (London, 1874).

LOCKE, JOHN, 'Methode nouvelle de dresser des recueuils', *Bibliothèque universelle*, 2 (1686), 315–40.

—— *A Second Letter concerning Toleration* (London, 1690). *LL* 2945. Wing L 2755.

—— *A Third Letter for Toleration* (London, 1692). *LL* 2947. Wing L 2765.

—— *Posthumous Works of Mr. John Locke* (London, 1706).

—— *A Collection of Several Pieces of Mr. John Locke, Never before printed, or not extant in his Works*, ed. Pierre Des Maizeaux (London, 1720).

—— *A Collection of Several Pieces of Mr. John Locke. Publish'd by Mr. Desmaizeaux, under the Direction of Anthony Collins, Esq.* (London, 1739).

—— *The Works of John Locke*, 7th edn. (London, 1768).

—— *An Early Draft of Locke's Essay, Together with Excerpts from his Journals*, ed. Richard I. Aaron and Jocelyn Gibb (Oxford, 1936).

—— *Locke's Travels in France, 1675–1679*, ed. John Lough (Cambridge, 1953).

—— *Essays on the Law of Nature*, ed. W. von Leyden (Oxford, 1954).

—— *Scritti editi e inediti sulla tolleranza*, ed. C. A. Viano (Turin, 1961).

—— *Two Tracts on Government*, ed. Philip Abrams (Cambridge, 1967).

—— *Two Treatises of Government*, ed. Peter Laslett, 2nd edn. (Cambridge, 1967).

—— *Epistola de Tolerantia*, ed. Raymond Klibansky, trans. J. W. Gough (Oxford, 1968).

—— *An Essay concerning Toleration and Toleratio*, ed. Kimimasa Inoue (Nara, 1974).

—— *An Essay concerning Human Understanding*, ed. Peter H. Nidditch (Oxford, 1975).

—— *The Correspondence of John Locke*, ed. E. S. de Beer, 9 vols. (Oxford, 1976–).

—— 'John Locke's Essay on Infallibility', ed. John C. Biddle, *Journal of Church and State*, 19 (1977), 301–27.

—— *Draft A of Locke's Essay concerning Human Understanding*, ed. Peter H. Nidditch (Sheffield, 1980).

—— *A Paraphrase and Notes on the Epistles of St Paul*, ed. Arthur W. Wainwright, 2 vols. (Oxford, 1987).

—— *Some Thoughts concerning Education*, ed. John W. Yolton and Jean S. Yolton (Oxford, 1989).

—— *Drafts for the 'Essay concerning Human Understanding' and Other Philosophical Writings*, i, ed. Peter H. Nidditch and G. A. J. Rogers (Oxford, 1990).

—— *Locke on Money*, ed. Patrick Hyde Kelly, 2 vols. (Oxford, 1991).

—— *Political Writings*, ed. David Wootton (Harmondsworth, 1993).

—— *Political Essays*, ed. Mark Goldie (Cambridge, 1997).

—— *Ensayo y carta sobre la tolerancia*, ed. and trans. Carlos Mellizo (Madrid, 1999).

—— *The Reasonableness of Christianity*, ed. John C. Higgins-Biddle (Oxford, 1999).

—— *Writings on Religion*, ed. Victor Nuovo (Oxford, 2002).

London Sessions Records, 1605–1685, ed. Dom Hugh Bowler, Catholic Records Society, 34 (London, 1934).

LUDLOW, EDMUND, *A Voyce from the Watch Tower*, ed. A. B. Worden, Camden Society, 4th ser., 21 (London, 1978).

LUTHER, MARTIN, *Luther's Works*, ed. Jaroslav Pelikan and Helmut T. Lehmann, 55 vols. (St Louis, 1958–67).

LUTTRELL, NARCISSUS, *A Brief Historical Relation of State Affairs from September 1678 to April 1714*, 6 vols. (Oxford, 1857).

Magdalen College and King James II, 1686–1688, ed. J. R. Bloxham (Oxford Historical Society, 1886).

MANDELSLO, JOHAN ALBRECHT VON, *The Voyages & Travels of J. Albert de Mandelslo . . . into the East-Indies* (London, 1662). *LL* 2128. Wing O 269.

[MARVELL, ANDREW], *An Account of the Growth of Popery and Arbitrary Government in England* ('Amsterdam' [London?], 1677). *LL* 1935. Wing M 860.

MARVELL, ANDREW *The Poems and Letters of Andrew Marvell*, ed. H. M. Margoliouth, 3rd edn., rev. Pierre Legouis, 2 vols. (Oxford, 1971).

—— *The Rehearsal Transpros'd and The Rehearsal Transpros'd, The Second Part*, ed. D. I. B. Smith (Oxford, 1971).

MASHAM, DAMARIS, 'Lady Masham's Account of Locke', ed. Roger Woolhouse, *Locke Studies*, 3 (2003), 167–93.

Middlesex County Records, ed. John Cordy Jeaffreson, 4 vols. (London, 1892).

MILTON, JOHN, *Complete Prose Works of John Milton*, ed. Don M. Wolfe *et al.*, 8 vols. (New Haven, 1953–82).

MILWARD, JOHN, *The Diary of John Milward, Esq., Member of Parliament for Derbyshire, September 1666 to May 1668*, ed. Caroline Robbins (Cambridge, 1938).

Mr. Baxter Baptiz'd in Bloud; or, A Sad History of the unparallel'd cruelty of the Anabaptists in New England. Faithfully Relating the Cruel, Barbarous and Bloudy Murther of Mr. Baxter an Orthodox Minister, who was kill'd by the Anabaptists, and his Skin most cruelly flead off from his Body (London, 1673). Wing B 1170.

Bibliography

None but the Sheriffs ought to name and return Jurors to serve in Inquests before Commissioners of Oyer and Terminer (London, 1681). Wing N 1226.

No Protestant-Plot: or The present pretended Conspiracy of Protestants against the King and Government. Discovered to be a Conspiracy of the Papists Against the King and his Protestant-Subjects (London, 1681). *LL* 2351. Wing F 756.

Notes taken in Short-hand of a Speech in the House of Lords on the Debates of appointing a day for Hearing Dr. Shirley's Cause, Octob. 20. 1675. (n.p., n.d.). Wing S 2897A.

OLDMIXON, JOHN, *The History of England, During the Reigns of the Royal House of Stuart* (London, 1730).

OLEARIUS, ADAM, *The Voyages & Travels of the Ambassadors sent by Frederick Duke of Holstein, to the Great Duke of Muscovy, and the King of Persia* ... (London, 1662). *LL* 2128. Wing O 269.

[OWEN, JOHN], *A Peace-Offering in an Apology and humble Plea for Indulgence and Liberty of Conscience* (London, 1667). Wing O 790.

—— *Indulgence and Toleration Considered: in a Letter unto A Person of Honour* (London, 1667). Wing O 763.

—— *Truth and Innocence Vindicated: In a Survey of a Discourse Concerning Ecclesiastical Polity; And the Authority of the Civil Magistrate over the Consciences of Subjects in Matters of Religion* (London, 1669). Wing O 817.

—— *Exercitations on the Epistle to the Hebrews, Concerning the Priesthood of Christ* (London, 1674). Wing O 753B.

A Pacquet of Advices and Animadversions, Sent from London To the Men of Shaftsbury (London, 1676). Wing N 400, N 401.

P. B., *A Modest and Peaceable Letter concerning Comprehension, &c.* (London, 1668). Wing P 7.

PARKER, SAMUEL, *A Discourse of Ecclesiastical Politie: Wherein The Authority of the Civil Magistrate Over the Consciences of Subjects in Matters of Religion is Asserted; The Mischiefs and Inconveniences of Toleration are Represented, And All Pretenses Pleaded in Behalf of Liberty of Conscience are Fully Answered* (London, 1670). Wing P 459.

—— *A Defence and Continuation of the Ecclesiastical Politie* (London, 1671). Wing P 457.

—— *A Free and Impartial Censure of the Platonick Philosophie, Being a Letter Written to his much Honoured Friend Mr. N.B.* (Oxford, 1666). Wing P 463.

A Particular Account of the Proceedings at the Old-Bayly, the 17 & 18 of this Instant October: with relation to the Earl of Shaftsbury, and others, Prisoners in the Tower; and Mr. Rouse, who was Indicted of High Treason &c (London, 1681). Wing P 586.

[PEARSON, JOHN], *Promiscuous Ordinations Are Destructive to the Honour & Safety of the Church of England: (If they should be allowed in it.) Written in a Letter to a Person of Quality* (London, 1668). Wing P 1005.

Bibliography

PEPYS, SAMUEL, *The Diary of Samuel Pepys*, ed. Robert Latham and William Matthews, 11 vols. (London, 1970–83).

[PERRINCHIEF, RICHARD], *A Discourse of Toleration: In Answer to a late Book, Intituled, A Discourse of the Religion of England* (London, 1668). Wing P 1593B.

—— *Indulgence not Justified: Being a Continuation of the Discourse of Toleration: In Answer to the Argument of a late Book, Entituled A Peace-Offering, or Plea for Indulgence: And to the Cavils of another, call'd The Second Discourse of the Religion in England* (London, 1668). Wing P 1594.

PHILOTHEUS, ABRAHAM [ABRAHAM WRIGHT], *Anarchie Reviving, Or, The Good old Cause on the Anvile. Being A Discovery of the present Design to retrive the late Confusions both of Church and State, in several Essays for Liberty of Conscience* (London, 1668). Wing W 3684.

Poems on Affairs of State, ed. G. deF. Lord *et al.*, 6 vols. (New Haven, 1963–70).

PRIDEAUX, HUMPHREY, *Letters of Humphrey Prideaux to John Ellis*, ed. E. M. Thompson, Camden Society, 2nd ser., 15 (London, 1875).

The Proceedings against the Right Honourable the Earl of Shaftsbury, at the Old Baily, On Thursday the Twenty fourth of November, 1681 (London, 1681). Wing P 3553A.

The Proceedings at the Sessions House in the Old-Baily, London, on Thursday the 24th day of November, 1681. Before His Majesties Commissioners of Oyer and Terminer, upon the Bill of Indictment for High-Treason against Anthony Earl of Shaftsbury. Published by his Majesties Special Command (London, 1681). Wing P 3564.

A Proclamation for Inforcing the Laws against Conventicles, and for preservation of the Publick Peace, against Unlawful Assemblies of Papists and Non-Conformists (London, 1667/8). Wing C 3340.

A Proclamation For the better Discovery of Seditious Libellers (London, 1675). Wing C 3451.

RALPH, JAMES, *The History of England: during the reigns of K. William, Q. Anne, and K. George I*, 2 vols. (London, 1744, 1746).

The Register of the Privy Council of Scotland, ed. P. Hume Brown *et al.*, 3rd ser., 15 vols. (Edinburgh, 1908–).

RERESBY, SIR JOHN, *The Memoirs of Sir John Reresby*, ed. Andrew Browning (Glasgow, 1936).

SANDYS, SIR EDWIN, *Europae Speculum. Or, A View or Survey of the State of Religion in the Westerne parts of the World* (London, 1638).

A Second Letter to a Member of this Present Parliament, against Comprehension. By the Author of the former Letter for Liberty of Conscience (London, 1668). Wing S 2286.

The Second Part of the Growth of Popery and Arbitrary Government: beginning where the former left, viz. from the year 1677, unto the year 1682. By Philo-Veritas [Robert Ferguson?] ('Cologne' [London], 1682). Not in Wing.

The Second Part of No Protestant Plot. By the Same Hand (London, 1682). LL 2352. Wing F 759.

Selections from the Correspondence of Arthur Capel Earl of Essex 1675–1677, ed. C. E. Pike, Camden Society, 3rd ser., 24 (London, 1913).

SHAFTESBURY, ANTHONY ASHLEY COOPER, THIRD EARL OF, *Anthony Ashley Cooper Earl of Shaftesbury (1671–1713) and 'Le Refuge Français'-Correspondence*, ed. Rex A. Barrell (Lewiston, NY, 1989).

—— *The Life, Unpublished Letters, and Philosophical Regimen of Anthony, Earl of Shaftesbury, Author of the 'Characteristics'*, ed. Benjamin Rand (London, 1900).

SIDNEY, ALGERNON, *Discourses concerning Government* ([London], 1698). *LL* 2666. Wing S 3761.

State Tracts: Being a Collection of Several Treatises Relating to the Government. Privately Printed in the Reign of K. Charles II (London, 1689). *LL* 2759. Wing S 5329.

State Tracts: Being a Collection of Several Treatises Relating to the Government. Privately Printed in the Reign of K. Charles II (London, 1693). Wing S 5330.

Statutes of the Realm, 11 vols. (London, 1810–28).

Strange News from Hicks's Hall (London, 1681). Wing S 5891.

The Third Part of No Protestant Plot, with Observations on the Proceedings upon the Bill of Indictment against the E. of Shaftsbury (London, 1682). *LL* 2353. Wing F 762.

[TOMKINS, THOMAS], *The Inconveniences of Toleration, Or An Answer to a late Book, Intituled, A Proposition Made to the King and Parliament, For the Safety and Happiness of the King and Kingdom* (London, 1667). Wing T 1835, 1835A.

The Triumph of Justice over Unjust Judges (London, 1681). Wing T 2297.

The Tryall of Tho. Pilkington, Samuel Shute…for the Riot at the Guild-hall on Midsommer-day, 1682 (London, 1683). Wing T 2231.

Two Seasonable Discourses Concerning this present Parliament ('Oxford' [London?], 1675). Wing S 2906.

Two Speeches. I. The Earl of Shaftsbury's Speech in the House of Lords the 20th. of October, 1675. II. The D. of Buckinghams Speech in the House of Lords the 16th. of November 1675 ('Amsterdam' [London?], 1675). Wing S 2907.

Two Speeches Made in the House of Peers. The one November 20. 1675. The other in November 1678. By a Protestant peer of the realm of England (The Hague, 1680). Wing S 2908.

Votes &c. of the Honourable House of Commons: Febr. 25 &c. 1662. Upon Reading His Majesties Gracious Declaration and Speech, &c. (n.p. [London], n.d.). Wing E 2760B.

WALSH, PETER, *The History & Vindication of the Loyal Formulary, or Irish Remonstrance* (n.p. [London?], 1674). Wing W 634.

—— *Some Few Questions Concerning the Oath of Allegiance: Propos'd by a Catholick Gentleman In a Letter to a Person of Learning and Honour* (London, 1674). *LL* 2113. Wing W 642.

Bibliography

WOOD, ANTHONY, *Athenae Oxonienses. An Exact History of all the Writers and Bishops who have had their Education in the most ancient and famous University of Oxford*, 2 vols. (London, 1691, 1692). Wing W 3382, 3383A.

―― *The Life and Times of Anthony Wood, Antiquary, of Oxford, 1632–1695, described by Himself*, ed. Andrew Clark, 5 vols. (Oxford Historical Society, 1891–1900).

[WOLSELEY, SIR CHARLES], *Liberty of Conscience Upon its true and proper Grounds, Asserted & Vindicated. Proving That no Prince, nor State, ought by force to compel Men to any part of the Doctrine, Worship, or Discipline of the Gospel* (London, 1668). Wing W 3310.

―― *Liberty of Conscience, the Magistrates Interest: Or, To grant Liberty of Conscience to Persons of different perswasions in matters of Religion, is the great Interest of all Kingdoms and States, and particularly of England; Asserted and Proved* (London, 1668). Wing W 3309.

MODERN PRINTED WORKS (SINCE 1800)

ABERNATHY, GEORGE R., 'Clarendon and the Declaration of Indulgence', *Journal of Ecclesiastical History*, 9 (1960), 55–73.

ADAIR, E. R., and GREIR EVANS, F. M., 'Writs of Assistance, 1558–1700', *English Historical Review*, 36 (1921), 356–72.

ALMAGOR, JOSEPH, *Pierre Des Maizeaux (1673–1745), Journalist and English Correspondent for Franco-Dutch Periodicals 1700–1720* (Amsterdam, 1989).

ARMITAGE, DAVID, 'John Locke, Carolina, and the *Two Treatises of Government*', *Political Theory*, 32 (2004), 602–27.

ASHCRAFT, RICHARD, *Revolutionary Politics & Locke's 'Two Treatises of Government'*, (Princeton, 1986).

ATTIG, JOHN C., *The Works of John Locke: A Comprehensive Bibliography from the Seventeenth Century to the Present* (Westport, Conn., 1985).

AYLMER, G. E., 'Locke no Leveller', in Ian Gentles, John Morrill, and Blair Worden (eds.), *Soldiers, Writers and Statesmen of the English Revolution* (Cambridge, 1998).

BAKER, J. H., *The Order of Serjeants at Law*, Selden Society Supplementary Series, 5 (London, 1984).

BAUMGARTNER, WILHELM, *Naturrecht und Toleranz. Untersuchungen zur Erkenntnistheorie und politischen Philosophie bei John Locke* (Würzburg, 1979).

BEATTIE, J. M., 'London Juries in the 1690s', in J. S. Cockburn and Thomas A. Green (eds.), *Twelve Good Men and True: The Criminal Trial Jury in England, 1200–1800* (Princeton, 1988).

―― *Policing and Punishment in London, 1660–1720* (Oxford, 2000).

BILL, E. G. W., *Education at Christ Church, Oxford, 1660–1680* (Oxford, 1988).

BLACK, JOSEPH, 'The Unrecorded Second Edition of Samuel Parker's *A Discourse of Ecclesiastical Politie* (1670)', *Notes and Queries*, 243 (1997), 187–9.

Bossy, John, *The English Catholic Community, 1570–1850* (London, 1975).

Boxer, C. R., *The Christian Century in Japan* (Cambridge, 1951; repr. Manchester, 1993).

Brown, Louise Fargo, *The First Earl of Shaftesbury* (New York, 1933).

Browning, Andrew, *Thomas Osborne, Earl of Danby and Duke of Leeds, 1632–1712*, 3 vols. (Glasgow, 1944–51).

Buckroyd, Julia, *Church and State in Scotland, 1660–1681* (Edinburgh, 1980).

Burke, John, *A Genealogical and Heraldic History of the Extinct and Dormant Baronetcies of England, Ireland, and Scotland*, 2nd edn. (London, 1844).

Butler, D., *The Life and Letters of Robert Leighton, Restoration Bishop of Dunblane and Archbishop of Glasgow* (London, 1903).

Calamy Revised, ed. A. G. Matthews (Oxford, 1934).

Christie, W. D., *A Life of Anthony Ashley Cooper, First Earl of Shaftesbury 1621–1683*, 2 vols. (London, 1871).

Christophersen, H. O., *A Bibliographical Introduction to the Study of John Locke* (Oslo, 1930).

Clarke, J. S., *The Life of James the Second King of England, &c.*, 2 vols. (London, 1816).

Cobbett's Parliamentary History of England, from the Norman Conquest in 1066, to the Year 1803, 36 vols. (London, 1806–20).

Cockburn, J. S., *A History of English Assizes 1558–1714* (Cambridge, 1972).

—— *Calendar of Assize Records, Home Circuit Indictments, Elizabeth I and James I, Introduction* (London, 1985).

Coffey, John, *Persecution and Toleration in Protestant England, 1558–1689* (Harlow, 2000).

The Complete Peerage, ed. G. E. Cokayne and Vicary Gibbs, 13 vols. (London, 1910–40).

Cowan, Ian B., *The Scottish Covenanters, 1660–1688* (London, 1976).

Cragg, Gerald R., *Puritanism in the Period of the Great Persecution, 1660–1688* (Cambridge, 1957).

Cranston, Maurice, *John Locke: A Biography* (London, 1957).

—— 'John Locke and the Case for Toleration', in John Horton and Susan Mendus (eds.), *John Locke: 'A Letter concerning Toleration' in Focus* (London, 1991).

Crehan, F. J., 'The Bible in the Roman Catholic Church from Trent to the Present Day', in S. L. Greenslade (ed.), *The Cambridge History of the Bible* (Cambridge, 1963).

Creighton, Mandell, *A History of the Papacy from the Great Schism to the Sack of Rome*, 6 vols. (London, 1899–1901).

Cromartie, Alan, *Sir Matthew Hale 1609–76: Law, Religion and Natural Philosophy* (Cambridge, 1995).

Davies, Godfrey, and Hardacre, Paul, 'The Restoration of the Scottish Episcopacy, 1660–1661', *Journal of British Studies*, 1/2 (1962), 32–51.

DAVIS, RICHARD, 'The "Presbyterian" Opposition and the Emergence of Party in the House of Lords in the Reign of Charles II', in Clyve Jones (ed.), *Party and Management in Parliament, 1660–1784* (Leicester, 1984).

Decrees of the Ecumenical Councils, ed. Norman P. Tanner (London, 1990).

DEWHURST, KENNETH, *John Locke (1632–1704), Physician and Philosopher* (London, 1963).

—— *Dr. Thomas Sydenham (1624–1689): His Life and Original Writings* (London, 1966).

Dictionary of National Biography, ed. Sir Leslie Stephen and Sidney Lee, 67 vols. (London, 1885–1903).

DONALDSON, GORDON, *The Scottish Reformation* (Cambridge, 1960).

—— *Scotland: James V to James VII* (Edinburgh, 1965; repr. 1971).

DUNN, JOHN, *The Political Thought of John Locke* (Cambridge, 1969).

—— *Locke* (Oxford, 1984).

FEILING, KEITH, and NEEDHAM, F. R. D., 'The Journals of Edmund Warcup', *English Historical Review*, 40 (1925), 235–60.

FLETCHER, ANTHONY, 'The Enforcement of the Conventicle Acts 1664–1679', in W. J. Sheils (ed.), *Persecution and Toleration*, Studies in Church History, 21 (Oxford, 1984).

FOSTER, W. R., *Bishop and Presbytery: The Church of Scotland 1661–1688* (London, 1958).

FOX BOURNE, H. R. *The Life of John Locke*, 2 vols. (London, 1876).

GOLDIE, MARK, 'John Locke and Anglican Royalism', *Political Studies*, 31 (1983), 61–85.

—— 'Danby, the Bishops and the Whigs', in Tim Harris, Paul Seaward, and Mark Goldie (eds.), *The Politics of Religion in Restoration England* (Oxford, 1990).

—— 'The Theory of Religious Intolerance in Restoration England', in Ole Peter Grell, Jonathan I. Israel, and Nicholas Tyacke (eds.), *From Persecution to Toleration: The Glorious Revolution and Religion in England* (Oxford, 1991).

—— 'Priestcraft and the Birth of Whiggism', in Nicholas Phillipson and Quentin Skinner (eds.), *Political Discourse in Early Modern Britain* (Cambridge, 1993).

GOUGH, J. W., *John Locke's Political Philosophy* (Oxford, 1950).

GREAVES, RICHARD L., *Secrets of the Kingdom* (Stanford, Calif., 1992).

GREEN, I. M., *The Re-establishment of the Church of England 1660–1663* (Oxford, 1978).

HALEY, K. H. D., *The First Earl of Shaftesbury* (Oxford, 1968).

HARRIS, IAN, *The Mind of John Locke* (Cambridge, 1994).

HARRIS, TIM, *London Crowds in the Reign of Charles II: Propaganda and Politics from the Restoration until the Exclusion Crisis* (Cambridge, 1987).

—— *Politics under the Later Stuarts: Party Conflict in a Divided Society, 1660–1715* (London, 1993).

HARRISON, JOHN, and LASLETT, PETER, *The Library of John Locke*, 2nd edn. (Oxford, 1971).

HARTH, PHILLIP, *Pen for a Party: Dryden's Tory Propaganda in its Contexts* (Princeton, 1993).

HARTMANN, CYRIL HUGHES, *Clifford of the Cabal: A Life of Thomas, First Lord Clifford of Chudleigh Lord High Treasurer of England 1630–1673* (London, 1937).

HEAWOOD, EDWARD, *Watermarks Mainly of the 17th and 18th Centuries* (Hilversum, 1950).

HENDERSON, G. D., *Religious Life in Seventeenth-Century Scotland* (Cambridge, 1937).

HOLT, J. C., *Magna Carta*, 2nd edn. (Cambridge, 1992).

HORWITZ, HENRY, 'Protestant Reconciliation in the Exclusion Crisis', *Journal of Ecclesiastical History*, 15 (1964), 201–17.

The House of Commons 1660–1690, ed. Basil Duke Henning, 3 vols. (London, 1983).

HUMPHERY-SMITH, CECIL R., *The Phillimore Atlas and Index of Parish Registers* (Chichester, 1995).

HUNTER, JOHN, *The Diocese and Presbytery of Dunkeld, 1660–1689*, 2 vols. (London, n.d. [*c.*1917]).

HUNTER, MICHAEL, *The Royal Society and its Fellows, 1660–1700* (Chalfont St Giles, 1982).

HUTTON, RONALD, *The Restoration: A Political and Religious History of England and Wales, 1658–1667* (Oxford, 1986).

—— *Charles the Second: King of England, Scotland, and Ireland* (Oxford, 1989).

—— 'The Religion of Charles II', in R. Malcolm Smuts (ed.), *The Stuart Court and Europe: Essays in Politics and Political Culture* (Cambridge, 1996).

JACOB, JAMES R., *Henry Stubbe: Radical Protestantism and the Early Enlightenment* (Cambridge, 1983).

KELLY, J. N. D., *The Oxford Dictionary of Popes* (Oxford, 1986).

KENYON, J. P., *The Stuart Constitution 1603–1688: Documents and Commentary*, 2nd edn. (Cambridge, 1986).

KING, PETER, *The Life of John Locke, with Extracts from his Correspondence, Journals and Common-place Books* (London, 1829; 2nd edn., 2 vols., London, 1830).

LABROUSSE, ELISABETH R., 'Bayle et l'établissement de Desmaizeaux en Angleterre', *Revue de Littérature Comparée*, 29 (1955), 251–7.

LACEY, DOUGLAS R., *Dissent and Parliamentary Politics in England, 1661–1689* (New Brunswick, NJ, 1969).

LEE, MAURICE, Jr., *The Cabal* (Urbana, Ill., 1965).

LONG, P., *A Summary Catalogue of the Lovelace Collection of the Papers of John Locke in the Bodleian Library* (Oxford, 1959).

—— 'The Mellon Donation of Additional Manuscripts of John Locke from the Lovelace Collection', *Bodleian Library Record*, 7 (1964), 185–93.

LYNCH, KATHLEEN M., *Roger Boyle, First Earl of Orrery* (Knoxville, Tenn., 1965).

MACAULAY, T. B., *The History of England from the Accession of James the Second*, ed. C. H. Firth, 6 vols. (London, 1913–15).

MADAN, FALCONER, *Oxford Books: A Bibliography of Printed Works relating to the University and City of Oxford or Printed or Published There*, 3 vols. (Oxford, 1893–1931).

MALPAS, R. M. P., 'An Electronic Text of Locke's *Essay* (and a Complete Wordlist)', *Locke Newsletter*, 21 (1990), 57–110.

MARSHALL, JOHN, *John Locke: Resistance, Religion and Responsibility* (Cambridge, 1994).

MARTYN, B., and KIPPIS, A., *The Life of the First Earl of Shaftesbury*, 2 vols. (London, 1836).

MATAR, NABIL, *Turks, Moors and Englishmen in the Age of Discovery* (New York, 1999).

MATHIESON, WILLIAM LAW, *Politics and Religion: A Study of Scottish History from the Reformation to the Revolution*, 2 vols. (Glasgow, 1902).

MIGNE, J.-P., *Dictionnaire des cardinaux* (Paris, 1857).

MILLER, JOHN, *Popery and Politics in England, 1660–1688* (Cambridge, 1973).

—— *James II: A Study in Kingship* (London, 1978).

—— *Charles II* (London, 1991).

—— *After the Civil Wars: Government in the Reign of Charles II* (Harlow, 2000).

MILLET, BENIGNUS, *The Irish Franciscans, 1651–1665*, Analecta Gregoriana, 129 (Rome, 1964).

MILTON, ANTHONY, *Catholic and Reformed* (Cambridge, 1995).

MILTON, J. R., 'John Locke and the Fundamental Constitutions of Carolina', *Locke Newsletter*, 21 (1990), 111–33.

—— 'John Locke, George Wall and George Walls', *Locke Newsletter*, 22 (1991), 81–91.

—— 'Locke's *Essay on Toleration*: Text and Context', *British Journal for the History of Philosophy*, 1/2 (1993), 45–63.

—— ' "Philanthropy or the Christian Philosophers": A Possible Addition to the Lockean Canon', *British Journal for the History of Philosophy*, 1/2 (1993), 64–6.

—— 'Locke at Oxford', in G. A. J. Rogers (ed.), *Locke's Philosophy: Content and Context* (Oxford, 1994).

—— 'Locke's Pupils', *Locke Newsletter*, 26 (1995), 95–118.

—— 'Locke Manuscripts among the Shaftesbury Papers in the Public Record Office', *Locke Newsletter*, 27 (1996), 109–30.

—— 'Lockean Political Apocrypha', *British Journal for the History of Philosophy*, 4 (1996), 247–66.

—— 'Locke's Medical Notebooks', *Locke Newsletter*, 28 (1997), 135–56.

—— 'The Dating of "Adversaria 1661" ', *Locke Newsletter*, 29 (1998), 105–17.

MILTON J. R., and MILTON, PHILIP, 'Selecting the Grand Jury: A Tract by John Locke', *Historical Journal*, 40 (1997), 185–94.

MILTON, PHILIP, 'John Locke and the Rye House Plot', *Historical Journal*, 43 (2000), 647–68.

NUTTALL, GEOFFREY F., 'The First Nonconformists', in Geoffrey F. Nuttall and Owen Chadwick (eds.), *From Uniformity to Unity, 1662–1962* (London, 1962).

Officials of the Boards of Trade, 1660–1870, comp. J. C. Sainty, Office Holders in Modern Britain, 3 (London, 1974).

OGG, DAVID, *England in the Reign of Charles II*, 2 vols. (Oxford, 1934).

OSLER, SIR WILLIAM, 'John Locke as a Physician', in Jean S. Yolton (ed.), *A Locke Miscellany* (Bristol, 1990).

Oxford Dictionary of National Biography, ed. H. C. G. Matthew and Brian Harrison, 60 vols. (Oxford, 2004).

PATTERSON, ANNABEL, and DZELZAINIS, MARTIN, 'Marvell and the Earl of Anglesey: A Chapter in the History of Reading', *Historical Journal*, 44 (2001), 703–26.

Peerage Creations, 1649–1800, comp. J. C. Sainty (London, 1998).

PLOMER, HENRY R., *A Dictionary of the Booksellers and Printers Who Were at Work in England, Scotland and Ireland from 1641 to 1667* (Oxford, 1907).

—— *A Dictionary of the Printers and Booksellers Who Were at Work in England, Scotland and Ireland from 1668 to 1725* (Oxford, 1922).

POCOCK, J. G. A., 'Machiavelli, Harrington and English Political Ideologies in the Eighteenth Century', in Pocock, *Politics, Language and Time* (London, 1972).

—— *The Machiavellian Moment: Florentine Political Thought and the Atlantic Republican Tradition* (Princeton, 1975).

RAHN, B. J., '*A Ra-ree Show*—A Rare Cartoon: Revolutionary Propaganda in the Treason Trial of Stephen College', in Paul J. Korshin (ed.), *Studies in Change and Revolution* (Evanston, Ill., 1972).

The Register of Admissions to Gray's Inn, 1521–1889, ed. Joseph Foster (London, 1889).

Register of Admissions to the Honourable Society of the Middle Temple, ed. H. A. C. Sturgess, 3 vols. (London, 1949).

RIVERS, ISABEL, 'Grace, Holiness and the Pursuit of Happiness: Bunyan and Restoration Latitudinarianism', in N. H. Keeble (ed.), *John Bunyan: Conventicle and Parnassus* (Oxford, 1988).

—— *Reason, Grace and Sentiment: I, Whichcote to Wesley* (Cambridge, 1991).

ROBBINS, CAROLINE, 'The Oxford Session of the Long Parliament of Charles II, 9–31 October 1665', *Bulletin of the Institute of Historical Research*, 21 (1946–8), 214–24.

ROBERTS, CLAYTON, *Schemes and Undertakings: A Study of English Politics in the Seventeenth Century* (Columbus, Ohio, 1985).

SCHOCHET, GORDON J., 'From Persecution to "Toleration"', in J. R. Jones (ed.), *Liberty Secured? Britain before and after 1688* (Stanford, Calif., 1992).

Bibliography

—— 'Between Lambeth and Leviathan: Samuel Parker on the Church of England and Political Order', in Nicholas Phillipson and Quentin Skinner (eds.), *Political Discourse in Early Modern Britain* (Cambridge, 1993).

—— 'Samuel Parker, Religious Diversity, and the Ideology of Persecution', in Roger D. Lund (ed.), *The Margins of Orthodoxy: Heterodox Writing and Cultural Response, 1660–1750* (Cambridge, 1995).

SCHWOERER, LOIS G., 'The Literature of the Standing Army Controversy, 1697–1699', *Huntington Library Quarterly*, 28 (1965), 187–212.

—— 'Chronology and Authorship of the Standing Army Tracts, 1697–1699', *Notes and Queries*, 211 (1966), 382–90.

—— *'No Standing Armies!' The Antiarmy Ideology in Seventeenth-Century England* (Baltimore, 1974).

SCOTT, JONATHAN, *Algernon Sidney and the Restoration Crisis, 1677–1683* (Cambridge, 1991).

—— *England's Troubles: Seventeenth-Century English Political Instability in European Context* (Cambridge, 2000).

SEAWARD, PAUL, *The Cavalier Parliament and the Reconstruction of the Old Regime, 1661–1667* (Cambridge, 1989).

—— 'Gilbert Sheldon, the London Vestries, and the Defence of the Church', in Tim Harris, Paul Seaward, and Mark Goldie (eds.), *The Politics of Religion in Restoration England* (Oxford, 1990).

Short-Title Catalogue of Books Printed in England, Scotland, Ireland, Wales, and British America and of English Books Printed in Other Countries, comp. Donald Wing, 2nd edn., 4 vols. (New York, 1972–98).

SINA, MARIO, 'Testi teologico-filosofici Lockiani dal Ms Locke c. 27 della Lovelace Collection', *Rivista di filosofia neo-scolastica*, 64 (1972), 54–75, 400–27.

SOMMERVILLE, J. P., 'The Royal Supremacy and Episcopacy "Jure Divino", 1603–1640', *Journal of Ecclesiastical History*, 34 (1985), 548–58.

—— *Politics and Ideology in England, 1603–1640* (London, 1986).

SPURR, JOHN, ' "Latitudinarianism" and the Restoration Church', *Historical Journal*, 31 (1988), 61–82.

—— 'The Church of England, Comprehension and the Toleration Act of 1689', *English Historical Review*, 104 (1989), 927–46.

—— *The Restoration Church of England, 1646–1689* (New Haven, 1991).

—— *England in the 1670s: This Masquerading Age* (Oxford, 2000).

STEELE, ROBERT, *A Bibliography of the Royal Proclamations of the Tudor and Stuart Sovereigns*, 2 vols. (Oxford, 1910).

SWATLAND, ANDREW, *The House of Lords in the Reign of Charles II* (Cambridge, 1996).

SYKES, NORMAN, *Old Priest and New Presbyter* (Cambridge, 1956).

—— *From Sheldon to Secker: Aspects of English Church History, 1660–1768* (Cambridge, 1959).

Bibliography

The Term Catalogues 1668–1709 A.D., ed. Edward Arber, 3 vols. (London, 1903–6).

The Thirty-Third Annual Report of the Deputy Keeper of the Public Records (London, 1872).

THOMAS, ROGER, 'Comprehension and Indulgence', in Geoffrey F. Nuttall and Owen Chadwick (eds.), *From Uniformity to Unity, 1662–1962* (London, 1962).

A Transcript of the Registers of the Worshipful Company of Stationers from 1640–1708 A.D., 3 vols. (London, 1913–14).

TREVOR-ROPER, H. R., 'The Fast Sermons of the Long Parliament', in *Religion, the Reformation and Social Change* (London, 1967).

TULLY, JAMES, 'Locke', in J. H. Burns and Mark Goldie (eds.), *The Cambridge History of Political Thought, 1450–1700* (Cambridge, 1991).

TYACKE, NICHOLAS (ed.), *Seventeenth-Century Oxford*, History of the University of Oxford, iv (Oxford, 1997).

VIANO, C. A., 'L'abbozzo originario e gli stadi di composizione di "An Essay concerning Toleration" e la nascita delle teorie politico-religiose di John Locke', *Rivista di Filosofia*, 52 (1961), 285–311.

VOITLE, ROBERT, *The Third Earl of Shaftesbury, 1671–1713* (Baton Rouge, La., 1984).

WALMSLEY, J. C., and MILTON, J. R., 'Locke's Notebook "Adversaria 4" and his Early Training in Chemistry', *Locke Newsletter*, 30 (1999), 85–101.

WATTS, MICHAEL R., *The Dissenters*, i: *From the Reformation to the French Revolution* (Oxford, 1978).

WHALEY, JOACHIM, 'A Tolerant Society? Religious Toleration in the Holy Roman Empire', in Ole Peter Grell and Roy Porter (eds.), *Toleration in Enlightenment Europe* (Cambridge, 2000).

WITCOMBE, D. T., *Charles II and the Cavalier House of Commons, 1663–1674* (Manchester, 1966).

WORDEN, BLAIR, 'Toleration and the Cromwellian Protectorate', in W. J. Sheils (ed.), *Persecution and Toleration*, Studies in Church History, 21 (Oxford, 1984).

—— *Roundhead Reputations: The English Civil Wars and the Passions of Posterity* (London, 2001).

WROTTESLEY, G., 'A History of the Family of Wrottesley of Wrottesley, Co. Stafford', *Collections for a History of Staffordshire*, NS 6/2 (1903).

YARDLEY, BRUCE, 'George Villiers, Second Duke of Buckingham, and the Politics of Toleration', *Huntington Library Quarterly*, 55 (1992), 317–37.

YOLTON, JEAN S., *A Locke Miscellany* (Bristol, 1990).

—— *John Locke: A Descriptive Bibliography* (Bristol, 1998).

—— *John Locke as Translator: Three of the 'Essais' of Pierre Nicole in French and English* (Oxford, 2000).

YOLTON, JOHN W., *John Locke and the Way of Ideas* (Oxford, 1956).

ZAGORIN, PEREZ, *How the Idea of Religious Toleration Came to the West* (Princeton, 2003).

INDEX OF SUBJECTS

INDEX OF PERSONS

Petre, William, 4th Baron 85, 160, 350, 373
Pilkington, Thomas 122, 127–8
Player, Sir Thomas 128 n
Pocock, J. G. A. 115–16
Powis, William Herbert, 1st Earl of 85
Prideaux, Humphrey 100, 124–5, 136 n, 151
Proast, Jonas 34, 113
Pufendorf, Samuel 116

Ralph, James 110
Rand, Benjamin 101 n
Reresby, Sir John 128
Robartes, John, 2nd Baron 15 n, 161, 373
Roberts, Patricius 95
Rochester, Bishop of, *see* Dolben
Roger, Abraham 157 n, 393 n
Rouse, John 128, 129 n
Rutland, John Manners, 8th Earl of 160, 373

Sagard, Gabriel 388
St George, Sir Oliver 217
Sainsbury, W. Noel 11
Salisbury, James Cecil, 3rd Earl of 159, 351, 352, 360
Sancroft, William, Archbishop of Canterbury 60
Sanderson, Robert, Bishop of Lincoln 93, 375
Sandys, Henry, 7th Baron 160, 373
Sarpi, Paolo 146
Sawbridge, William 96
Sawbridge, Thomas 96, 208
Say & Sele, William Fiennes, 3rd Viscount 160, 350, 352, 373
Schwoerer, Lois G. 213 n
Seymour, Sir Edward 19, 87
Shaftesbury, Anthony Ashley Cooper, 1st Earl of:
 arrested (July 1681) 119
 conversation reported in *A Letter from a Person of Quality* 340, 341–3
 death of, and funeral 10
 defends Declaration of Indulgence 149–50, 342–3
 dislikes Danby and Lauderdale 78 n
 dismissed from Privy Council 7
 escaped to the Netherlands (1682) 10
 Essay concerning Toleration and 48–9, 177
 first meeting with Locke 1

interest in horticulture 8
Letter from a Person of Quality and 89–93, 209–10, 229
letter to Earl of Carlisle (1675) 80, 151, 218
Locke's secretarial services for 5–6, 9
Lord Chancellor 6–7
meeting with Duke of York 89
obtains legal advice 125–6, 127
operation on 4–5, 42
opposes Five Mile Act (1665) 339
opposes Test Bill 86–7, 159, 348–9, 362–3, 368, 369
ordered to stay away from Court 89
payments to Locke 5
praised in *Letter from a Person of Quality* 349
proceedings against (1681) 130–1
protests against Test Bill 350, 351, 352, 354
religious opinions of 27
speeches in House of Lords again Test Bill 86–7, 90–1, 415–16
speeches in House of Lords on *Shirley v Fagg* 92–3, 208–9, 217
Shaftesbury, Anthony Ashley Cooper, 2nd Earl of 1, 3, 106
Shaftesbury, Anthony Ashley Cooper, 3rd Earl of 1 n, 4, 8 n, 53 n, 99, 101, 106–9
 Des Maizeaux and 107–8
 Locke as 'Assistant Pen' 109
Shaftesbury, Margaret Ashley Cooper, Countess of 106
Shaw, William 141
Sheldon, Gilbert, Archbishop of Canterbury 58, 60, 77
Shute, Samuel 122, 128
Sibthorpe, Robert 93
Sidney, Algernon 230 n
Sixtus V 405, 406
Somers, John 115 n
Soto, Domingo de 407
Southampton, Thomas Wriothesley, 4th Earl of 218 n, 339, 366–7, 413
Stafford, William Howard, 1st Viscount 85, 161, 368
Stamford, Thomas Grey, 2nd Earl of 159, 350, 351, 354
Starkey, John 94 n
Stillingfleet, Edward 16 n, 146
Strachey, John 26 n, 174 n
Stringer, Jane 86